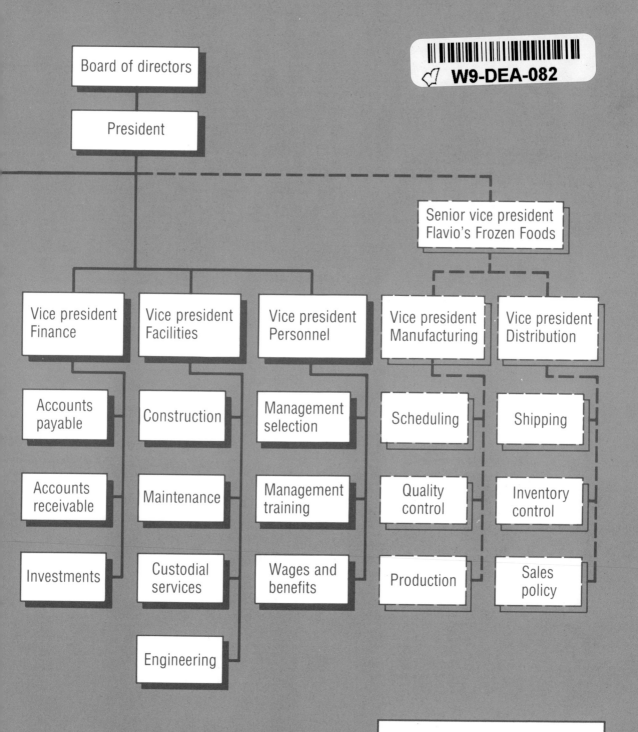

Board of directors

President

Senior vice president
Flavio's Frozen Foods

Vice president
Finance

Vice president
Facilities

Vice president
Personnel

Vice president
Manufacturing

Vice president
Distribution

Accounts
payable

Construction

Management
selection

Scheduling

Shipping

Accounts
receivable

Maintenance

Management
training

Quality
control

Inventory
control

Investments

Custodial
services

Wages and
benefits

Production

Sales
policy

Engineering

Peter's Pan Pizza, Inc.
After the Merger

INDUSTRIAL/ORGANIZATIONAL PSYCHOLOGY

Science and Practice
2nd Edition

INDUSTRIAL/ORGANIZATIONAL PSYCHOLOGY

Science and Practice
2nd Edition

Frank E. Saal
Patrick A. Knight
Kansas State University

Brooks/Cole Publishing Company
Pacific Grove, California

ITP™ The trademark ITP is used under license.

....

Brooks/Cole Publishing Company
A Division of Wadsworth, Inc.

Printed in the United States of America
10   9   8   7   6   5   4   3   2

Library of Congress Cataloging-in-Publication Data
Saal, Frank E., [date]
    Industrial/organizational psychology : science and practice / by
Frank E. Saal and Patrick A. Knight. — 2nd ed.
        p.   cm.
    Includes bibliographical references and index.
    ISBN 0-534-16638-5 :
    1. Psychology, Industrial.   I. Knight, Patrick A., [date]   .
II. Title.
HF5548.8.S225   1995
158.7—dc20   94-88
                                                                             CIP

Sponsoring Editor: *Marianne Taflinger*
Marketing Representative: *Marc Edwards*
Editorial Associate: *Virge Perelli-Minetti*
Production Coordinator: *Fiorella Ljunggren*
Production: *Julie Kranhold, Ex Libris*
Manuscript Editor: *Betty Seaver*
Permissions Editor: *Elaine Jones*
Interior Design: *Nancy Benedict*
Cover Design: *Roy R. Neuhaus*
Cover Photo: *GALA/Superstock, Inc.*
Art Coordinator: Julie Kranhold
Interior Illustration: *Precision Graphics*
Photo Coordinator: *Julie Kranhold*
Typesetting: *Weimer Graphics*
Cover Printing: *Phoenix Color Corporation, Inc.*
Printing and Binding: *Arcata Graphics/Fairfield*

Photo Credits: *Page 484, Richard Bermack, Jeroboam, Inc.;
Page 488, Arnold J. Saxe, Jeroboam, Inc. All other photos by
PhotoDisc.*

To Cathie and Diane, our wives;
and to our children:
Kiersten, Kaele, and Kevin;
Malachi and Mikeile.

BRIEF CONTENTS

CONTENTS

Most college students have held one or more summer jobs, and some have held full-time positions. Almost all will join the workforce in the not-so-distant future. Industrial/organizational (I/O) psychology would, therefore, seem to be a field of study with relevance for all students regardless of their major, their curriculum, or their career plans. We were, therefore, somewhat surprised when many of our students reported that the textbooks we had chosen for them so carefully failed to capture their interest and attention. The reasons most often cited were that the writing style was too dry, abstract, and complex—or too simplistic—and that the coverage of topics was very uneven. The decision to write the first edition of this book evolved from our conviction that these pitfalls are not inevitable, from our fascination with a field that addresses problems experienced by every working woman and man, and from our desire to help students share our enthusiasm.

We were pleased by the reception our first edition received from our professional colleagues and their students. Their comments, encouragement, and suggestions helped us greatly in preparing this second edition. Our primary goals here are similar to those we set for the first edition. Because students who enroll in I/O psychology courses typically bring a diversity of academic backgrounds into their classrooms, we tried *not* to presume any specialized knowledge in psychology or statistics. Our prose is purposefully informal, reflecting our belief that a textbook can be "reader friendly" without trivializing the research and theory it describes. Although the first half of the book contains material that traditionally has been labeled "personnel psychology" and the latter half focuses on "organizational psychology" topics, we emphasize the relationships that exist among various I/O psychology topics by frequently pointing out how material in one chapter ties in with material in other chapters.

Special Features

We remain enthusiastic about our strategy for illustrating the applied nature of I/O psychology. Rather than interrupt each chapter with one or two brief descriptions of I/O psychology in the workplace or append unrelated case studies to the end of each chapter, we rely on a hypothetical organization (Peter's Pan Pizza, Inc.) that employs a fictional I/O psychologist (Dr. Jennilyn A. MacKeven) on its staff. Beginning with Chapter 3, each chapter opens with a memo describing a specific problem or issue that has arisen in our make-believe company. We then examine the subject matter of each chapter in terms of how it might (or might not) facilitate our I/O psychologist's efforts to respond to that problem or issue. For example, the chapter that presents motivation theories and research findings analyzes this material with respect to how it might explain the behavior of a group of employees who don't appear to be expending much effort on their jobs. At the conclusion of each chapter, a memo from Dr. MacKeven describes her thoughts and offers tentative plans for solving the problem or clarifying the issue. Finally, following that memo is a list of review, or "thought," questions and exercises that can stimulate further discussion and analysis of Dr. MacKeven's solution to the problem at hand. Thus, the overall structure of the book is designed to bring I/O psychology to life by showing its relevance to everyday problems and concerns of working men and women.

Users of the first edition asked that Peter's Pan Pizza be made a more integral part of each chapter. We honored that request. As you progress through each chapter, you learn more and more about our hypothetical organization and its staff I/O psychologist. This continuity allows us to present and illustrate new material quickly and efficiently without the necessity of repeatedly acquainting you with unfamiliar organizational contexts and personnel. And, as you become more familiar with Peter's Pan Pizza and Dr. MacKeven, we hope your appreciation of the exciting and relevant nature of her profession will grow.

Changes in the Second Edition

Readers familiar with our first edition will notice several other notable changes throughout this volume. The research and theory that form the foundation of the text have, of course, been updated to reflect the progress our field has seen during the past several years. We eliminated the running glossary, which many readers found distracting, and opted instead to print new terms and concepts in **boldface** letters and then immediately explain or define them in the text itself. We think this imparts a smoother

flow to the exposition. Further, some of the chapter-opening memos have been revised or entirely rewritten to reflect important contemporary concerns and issues. Finally, some chapter-specific changes include the following:

- *Chapter 1* opens with numerous examples (taken from *Time* magazine) of how people's jobs and their work-related behaviors dramatically affect their lives, thereby emphasizing the relevance of I/O psychology.

- *Chapter 2* is now devoted exclusively to methods and procedures. Descriptions of Peter's Pan Pizza and the resident I/O psychologist now appear in a separate insert between Chapters 2 and 3, and the sections devoted to statistical concepts and analyses now appear in an appendix to Chapter 2. The section on ethics has been updated to reflect APA's revised (1992) Ethical Principles and Code of Conduct.

- *Chapter 3* now covers only job analysis, job evaluation, and comparable worth. (Criteria and criterion development are now discussed in Chapter 4.) Job evaluation and comparable worth are discussed in greater detail.

- *Chapter 4* integrates the coverage of criteria and criterion development with explanations of performance appraisal purposes, procedures, and processes.

- *Chapter 5* discusses a "unitarian" (rather than "trinitarian") view of validity, the reemergence of personality tests as valid predictors of job performance, and other contemporary trends in the selection literature.

- *Chapter 6* includes updated analyses of recruiting, validity generalization, and utility literature.

- *Chapter 7* reemphasizes the important roles of needs assessment and program evaluation in a personnel training system.

- *Chapter 8* now includes discussions of emerging topics such as equity sensitivity, self-efficacy, and control theory.

- *Chapter 9* contains expanded and updated coverage of work/nonwork attitudes and organizational commitment and a new discussion of dispositional factors in job attitudes.

- *Chapter 10* includes broader coverage of charismatic and transformational leadership theories, as well as updated coverage of research on women in leadership and management positions.

- *Chapter 11* offers greatly expanded sections on work-related stress, including its causes and consequences as well as strategies for coping with it, and an expanded discussion of organizational culture.

- *Chapter 12* presents recent research on job design, including the revised Job Diagnostic Survey and alternatives to the job characteristics model. Cultural factors in organizational change are also discussed.

- *Chapter 13* focuses on work conditions, safety and accidents, and human factors. Research and statistics have been updated to reflect the most recent knowledge in these areas.

- *Chapter 14.* describes labor unions and the laws governing the unionization process. This chapter is extremely updated to reflect the growing research on the psychological processes associated with union attitudes and behavior.

Acknowledgments

Our gratitude for the professional and personal contributions of our colleagues and friends, which we acknowledged in the first edition, is undiminished. Now five or six years older (and perhaps a week or two wiser), we recognize more clearly than ever the important roles played by reviewers, by competent and energetic editors, and by other publishing professionals. We are particularly grateful to the following reviewers of this edition for their valuable comments and suggestions: Janet L. Barnes-Farrell of the University of Connecticut, T. L. Brink of Crafton Hills College, David M. Carkenord of Longwood College, Caran Colvin of San Francisco State University, R. D. Draper of Montclair State College, Ronald Eggers of Barton College, Ann Fuehrer of Miami University, Karen L. Harris of Western Illinois University, Ira T. Kaplan of Hofstra University, Janet L. Kottke of California State University–San Bernardino, Jean LaCour of California State University–Los Angeles, George Mendoza of the University of Oklahoma, Lawrence R. Murphy of Xavier University, Stephen F. Salinger of Auburn University, William D. Siegfried of the University of North Carolina at Charlotte, and A. A. Witkin, City University of New York Queens College.

We continue to appreciate the opportunity to work with the fine professionals at Brooks/Cole Publishing Company. Special thanks go to Marianne Taflinger, our editor, to Fiorella Ljunggren, who monitored the production process, and to Roy Neuhaus, who designed the cover for our book. We are also grateful to Betty Seaver, who edited our manuscripts, to Nancy Benedict, whose design suggests both professional rigor and reader friendliness, and to Julie Kranhold of Ex Libris, who guided our book through the production process with a firm hand tempered by a much appreciated sense of humor.

Finally, we express our heartfelt thanks and love to our wives, Cathie and Diane, for their constant support and encouragement during the revision of this book, and to our children—Kiersten, Kaele, & Kevin, and Malachi & Mikeile—for the joy and love that only kids can bring to one's heart.

Frank E. Saal
Patrick A. Knight

A WORD TO THE READER

Welcome to the field of industrial/organizational (I/O) psychology! We hope you find our presentation of this material both informative and interesting. As you will see, we have adopted a somewhat different approach to emphasizing the relevance and potential for application that characterize our discipline. The cornerstone of our strategy is a fictional organization, Peter's Pan Pizza, Inc., which provides a background for our discussion and some continuity throughout the chapters that should facilitate your understanding of the material. Please read through the preface for a more detailed description of our approach.

A few more words of advice before you begin:

- Take advantage of the learning points at the beginning and the "thought," or review, questions at the end of each chapter. If you can address them thoroughly and accurately, the chances are excellent that you have gained a satisfactory understanding of the material in the chapters. If you cannot, they will help you to identify gaps in your knowledge that you can eliminate through further study and review.

- As you read the memo at the end of each chapter (beginning with Chapter 3), in which the I/O psychologist at PPP describes her plan for addressing the problem posed in the chapter's opening memo, keep in mind that her approach is only one of

numerous possibilities based on the material presented in the chapter. One way to test your own understanding of that material is to constructively criticize her plan or approach and suggest one or more alternatives for solving the problem at hand.

- Finally, we decided to situate our hypothetical organization within the service-industry sector of the economy because more and more people in our society are gravitating toward this kind of work, whereas fewer and fewer are finding jobs in traditional production and manufacturing organizations. As you proceed through the book, be aware of instances in which our choice of this specific industry (food service) might influence how the subject matter can be applied and how those applications might be different if our I/O psychologist worked in an automobile plant. In most cases, we are confident that our choice of a service industry will *not* undermine your understanding of how I/O psychology can contribute to higher levels of performance and stronger feelings of satisfaction among the women and men whose labor fuels our economy.

Enough "words to the wise." We hope you enjoy the book.

F.E.S
P.A.K

CHAPTER 1

Industrial/Organizational Psychology Today, Yesterday, and Tomorrow

LEARNING POINTS

After studying this chapter you should

- appreciate the importance of the subject matter of industrial/organizational (I/O) psychology in society today;

- be able to describe the content and scope of I/O psychology, how I/O psychologists are trained and where they tend to be employed;

- know the similarities and differences that characterize licensing and certification, as well as the advantages and disadvantages of each of these forms of professional regulation;

- be able to describe how the meaning of work has evolved in various societies;

- understand the roles of World War I and World War II in the development of I/O psychology;

- be able to trace the evolution of I/O psychology before World War I, between the two global conflicts, and after World War II;

- be able to explain the purpose, the results, and the significance of the Hawthorne studies; and

- be prepared to speculate about the future of I/O psychology as a science and as a profession (practice).

"WHAT DO YOU WANT TO BE when you grow up?" Some of us dreaded this question as children because we didn't have the faintest idea what we wanted to "be" when we became adults. Some of us probably still don't. But we knew that our parent or teacher, or whoever was tormenting us with the inquiry, was *not* asking about our plans to be tall, to be a coach for our children's traveling ball teams, or even to be a mother or father. Instead, they were interested in what kind of job or occupation we found appealing, in how we planned to earn a living. Others of us relished this query because it offered an opportunity to be the center of attention while we held forth on our plans to play shortstop for the New York Yankees or right field for the Detroit Tigers, to be a heroic physician who saves lives and cures horrible diseases, to be a brave police officer or firefighter who laughs at danger, or to be a wise teacher whom students love and respect. Regardless of your specific reaction and response, it's a safe bet that you heard this question many times while you were growing up. If you listened "between the lines," you also heard a very important message: the work we do as adults, the job we hold, is a basic component of our lives and, for some of us, actually defines who we are in our own and others' eyes.

Plenty of other evidence speaks to the significance of our jobs and work-related activities. No less a celebrity than Sigmund Freud is reputed to have asserted that the two most important focal points of our lives are love and work (although we know Freud best for his emphasis on the former to the relative exclusion of the latter). Casual perusal of contemporary newspapers and newsmagazines provides more timely support for the thesis that our jobs and behaviors in the workplace continue to affect our lives in dramatic fashion. Consider, for example, the following sample of items that appeared in *Time* magazine over a period of approximately one year:

DISCRIMINATION

- Following 13 years of litigation, an auto and home insurance company agreed to pay $157 million to 814 women in California who had suffered from discriminatory hiring practices during the 1970s ("Costly Policy," 1992).

- Averting a threatened lawsuit, the Federal Bureau of Investigation responded to 300 black agents' complaints of "lingering bias in the way promotions and fast-track assignments are made" by announcing a corrective plan of action ("G-Men of Color," 1992).

SEXUAL HARASSMENT

- The U.S. Navy reported that "at least 14 women officers and 12 female civilians had their breasts, buttocks and other bodily parts grabbed by drunken male pilots" at a convention of naval aviators, but that a common theme of more than 1,500 interviews with officers and civilians was "What's the big deal?" ("What's the Big Deal?" 1992).

- Although suggestive remarks and touching remain common in Japanese workplaces, a judge granted $12,400 to a female office worker who suffered verbal harassment from her boss—the first such award in Japan's history ("Committing *Seku Hara*," 1992).

- Surveys suggest that 90% of Fortune 500 companies have fielded sexual harassment complaints and almost 25% have been sued more than once, that 70% of Japanese women and almost 50% of European women have reported being victimized by sexual harassment, that 15% of male workers have been "hassled" by female and male coworkers, and that harassment costs large companies an average of $282.53/employee/year in the form of lost productivity, absenteeism, and turnover (Castro, 1992a).

- And, of course, much of the world watched and listened as Anita Hill and Clarence Thomas testified before the U.S. Senate's Judiciary Committee. Ms. Hill alleged that Mr. Thomas sexually harassed her from 1981 to 1983 while she worked for the government (including the Equal Employment Opportunity Commission, the agency charged with enforcing federal regulations prohibiting such harassment). Mr. Thomas was subsequently confirmed by the Senate as an associate justice of the U.S. Supreme Court (Carlson, 1991; Ehrenreich, 1991; Gibbs, 1991b, 1991c; Kramer, 1991; Lacayo, 1991; Smolowe, 1991; Toufexis, 1991; White, 1991).

SEXUAL ORIENTATION

- The Superior Court in California ordered a large petroleum company to pay $5.3 million to a 19-year employee who was fired after his supervisor accidentally discovered an invitation to a party for gay men ("Price of Prejudice," 1991).

- The U.S. Defense Department has discharged nearly 1,000 gay and lesbian soldiers from the armed forces since Desert Storm operations in Kuwait and Iraq, despite their fine military performance (Gibbs, 1991a; Henry, 1991).

COMPENSATION

- When bonuses, stock options, retirement packages, and other financial benefits are added to base salary figures, many American chief executive officers (CEOs) were paid well over $1 million during 1991; comparable executives in other industrialized countries do not fare as well. Shareholders, the Security and Exchange Commission, unions, and other interested parties are becoming increasingly vocal about glaring discrepancies between such salaries and those of "average" workers, and the lack of apparent correspondence between executives' pay packages and company profits ("How Sweet It Was," 1992; McCarroll, 1992a, 1992b).

- Responding to such concerns, a large utility and a well-known computer firm slashed the incomes of their CEOs and other top executives by as much as 62% and 40%, respectively ("Getting the Message," 1992).

- Of course, astronomical paychecks can be found in locker rooms as well as boardrooms. In 1991 a New York Mets baseball player signed a five-year contract for $29 million; he will receive 2.5 times as much as Babe Ruth earned during his entire career, 14 times as much as the Mets' manager, 27 times as much as President George Bush, 42 times as much as the mayor of New York City, and (nearer and dearer to our hearts) 200 times as much as the "average" teacher ("Field of Dollars," 1991).

LABOR UNIONS

- The 12,600 striking workers at a large construction-machinery manufacturer were devastated when the company advertised for permanent replacements to fill the $35,000/year positions. Despite the union's $800 million "war chest," which could have provided $60,000 in benefits to each striking worker, the five-month strike collapsed without the union's gaining any con-

cessions on wages or medical-care issues, thereby undermining its future bargaining power ("Bulldozing the U.A.W.," 1992; "Showdown on Labor's Front Line," 1992).

- In a stunning upset, the largest private-sector union in the United States elected a reform-minded president who vows to rid the union of long-standing Mafia influences and who immediately reduced the president's annual salary from $225,000 to $175,000 ("Good Guy Finally Won," 1991).

PERSONNEL SELECTION

- Several employers (including McDonnell Douglas and Macy's) have been charged by the Federal Trade Commission with using applicants' credit reports as an index of "honesty and personal integrity" without informing them or identifying the source of any negative information ("Big Brother Comes Clean," 1991).

- Private security firms have become "dumping grounds" for unstable, dishonest, and violent individuals who are hired without any references and assigned to posts within one day; guards for the leading company have been charged with arson, theft, and physical assault (Behar, 1992).

SAFETY

- Approximately 260,000 coal miners suffer from black-lung disease. Thirteen coal companies and 15 individuals in Virginia who admitted falsifying air samples to underestimate levels of coal dust face fines of up to $500,000 each and $250,000 each, respectively; the individuals also face up to five years in prison. Asphyxiation and cave-ins are among the other threats to coal miners' safety ("Black Marks for the Mines," 1992; Gup, 1991).

- State police in Connecticut banned the use of hand-held radar guns after three officers filed claims that long-term exposure to the speed detectors had resulted in cancer.

Numerous other troopers across the United States have developed rare cancers of suspicious origin (Elmer-DeWitt, 1991).

JOB SECURITY

- In December 1991 industry experts predicted that a major U.S. automobile company would cut as many as 35,000 workers (9% of its work force) from the payroll, that a large defense and credit-reporting firm would cut 10,000 jobs (14% of its work force), and that a large manufacturer of copying machines would lay off 2,500 workers (2.5% of its work force) within the next couple of years ("It's Off the Job We Go," 1991).

- One week later, the automaker announced that it would close 25 plants in North America and reduce its work force by 74,000 people (approximately 19% of its workers) over the next three years. The company had already eliminated 130,000 jobs since 1986 (McWhirter, 1991).

- Between June 1990 and July 1991, the following numbers of layoffs have occurred in the following industries (the numbers in parentheses reflect the percentages of workers who will *not* be able to reclaim their jobs): manufacturing, 804,000 (10%); construction, 495,000 (70%); federal government, 387,000 (100%); retail sales, 356,000 (80%); printing/publishing, 46,000 (50%); finance, 23,000 (100%) (Greenwald, 1991).

ETHICS

- A chief executive officer of a defense contractor resigned after photocopying a confidential report on a rival firm's work costs that had been inadvertently left in his possession, citing an "inappropriate business-ethics decision" and a failure to set a strong moral example ("Unbecoming an Officer," 1991).

WORK HABITS

- The average American worker currently puts in 163 more hours each year than he/she did in 1970; more than 7 million Americans hold two or three jobs at the same time (Castro, 1992b).

LEADERSHIP STYLES

- Tough-guy tactics are out. Management experts and executives are now being encouraged to stress worker participation and teamwork in order to tap into human creativity and ingenuity (Greenwald, 1992).

Despite the fact that the listed items represent an extremely limited and narrow sample (taken from a single newsmagazine and spanning an interval of less than one year), they suggest that many of the topics that constitute the field of industrial/organizational (I/O) psychology are sufficiently important and potentially controversial to warrant national attention. Other, more mundane topics may never receive any ink or airtime (television, radio) in national news media (the proper procedures for analyzing jobs, or the best designs for determining the effectiveness of training programs, for example). Nevertheless, because *all* of the topics that concern I/O psychologists pertain to the workplace, and because almost all of you will have spent 40 to 50 years in the workplace by the time you retire, we believe that the entire field of I/O psychology and the work of I/O psychologists will have (or already has had) profound effects on your lives. It is to that field and those psychologists that we now turn our attention. Who knows? Perhaps some of you will respond to the next person who asks about your career plans by asserting that you want to be an industrial/organizational psychologist "when you grow up."

I/O Psychology and Psychologists

Psychology, derived from the Greek *psychē* (which originally referred to the soul, the spirit, the source of all vitality; Denmark, 1980), is usually defined today as the scientific study of behavior, which includes cognitive and emotional processes as well as observable responses and actions. Industrial/organizational (I/O) psychology is one of more than 40 recognized subdisciplines of the general field of psychology. A brief review of how I/O psychology has been defined during the past six or seven decades supports the contention of singers Simon and Garfunkel that "after changes upon changes, we are more or less the same" (from "The Boxer").

Definition and Description of I/O Psychology

In one of the earliest descriptions of the field, Morris Viteles (1932) defined I/O psychology as the "study of human behavior, with the view of guarding against . . . waste in the form of individual maladjustment and of industrial inefficiency." He added that "the maximum *efficiency* of the individual in industry and his optimum *adjustment* are . . . complementary facets of a single objective" (p. 4). A decade later Tiffin (1942) asserted that I/O psychology transcends the selection (hiring) and placement of new employees, and addresses such issues as the value of merit ratings, causes of accidents in the workplace, work-related visual problems (for example, inspection of product quality), training methods, and employee morale. Following another 10-year interval, Gray's (1952) rather generic description of the field spoke of "the human factor in industry," and the "study of certain factors which affect workers in the procedure of processing materials" (p. 3).

In the mid-1960s, Gilmer (1966) emphasized relationships in his description of I/O psychology. In addition to concerning itself with the "problems of the inner man himself" (p. 11), he indicated that the field focuses on relations between individual people, between individuals and groups, and between individuals and objects. Guion (1965a) sounded a similar note, defining I/O psychology as "the scientific study of the relationship between man and the world at work: the study of the adjustment people make to the places they go, the people they meet, and

the things they do in the process of making a living" (p. 817). About the same time, however, Blum and Naylor (1968) reaffirmed Gray's rather broad perspective, defining the field as "simply the application or extension of psychological facts and principles to the problems concerning human beings operating within the context of business and industry" (p. 4).

During the 1970s I/O psychology experienced some growing pains as it expanded to embrace more abstract organizational issues and concerns, including motivation, job satisfaction, and leadership. Reflecting this growth, Division 14 of the American Psychological Association (APA) amended its name to become the Division of Industrial and Organizational Psychology; and Korman (1971) published the first textbook (to our knowledge) that explicitly recognized the organizational aspects of the field in its title: *Industrial and Organizational Psychology*. Despite this development within the discipline, McCormick and Tiffin (1974)—in the sixth edition of Tiffin's text—reiterated the basic defining theme laid down by their predecessors: the basic justification for the existence of I/O psychology is "the existence of human problems in organizations, and its objective is to somehow provide the basis for resolving these problems or, more realistically, for minimizing them" (p. 4).

Generic definitions similar to Gray's and Blum and Naylor's persisted into the 1980s and 1990s. Schultz (1982), for example, spoke of "the application of the methods, facts, and principles of the science of human behavior to people at work" (p. 7). Aamodt (1991) described "a branch of psychology that applies the principles of psychology to the workplace" (p. 4).

Far more constructive, we believe, is a definition that appeared in the APA's *Specialty Guidelines for the Delivery of Services by Industrial/Organizational Psychologists* (APA, 1981): I/O "psychological services involve the *development and application* [our emphasis] of psychological theory and methodology to problems of organizations and problems of individuals and groups in organizational settings" (p. 666).

Embracing the distinction between the *development* of theory and methodology and the *application* of that knowledge to organizational issues and problems, while at the same time acknowledging the insights of Viteles and his more contemporary colleagues, we offer the following two-part definition of I/O psychology: it is

1. the *study* of the behavior, thoughts, and feelings of women and men as they adjust to the people, objects, and surroundings they encounter in the workplace; and

2. the *use* of that information to maximize the economic and psychological well-being of all employees and constituencies (men and women, minority and majority groups, labor and management, employees and owners, and others).

This two-part definition reflects a dichotomy between the **science** of I/O psychology, which searches for new knowledge about work-related behavior, and the **practice** of I/O psychology, which applies that knowledge for the benefit of organizations and all their members and constituencies. At the same time, it acknowledges the potentially close relationship between these two components of the field.

Although many I/O psychologists operate as both successful scientists and effective practitioners, the relationship between these two domains of the field has not always been characterized by harmony and mutual respect. "Pure" researchers (scientists) have traditionally been accorded positions of highest status in the psychological hierarchy (Meltzer & Stagner, 1980). Bruce Moore (1962), who in 1921 received the first doctoral degree in industrial psychology, offered a relevant quote from a so-called eminent psychologist: "Now that the war is over [this was 1919], psychologists ought to be getting back to the *real* science of psychology." The tension between "pure" and "applied" members of APA led in 1936 to the establishment of the American Association of Applied Psychology. Recent evidence suggests

that academics and scientists have begun to show some flexibility by entertaining and adopting practitioners' points of view, but practitioners seem to be less influenced by their academic colleagues' perspectives (Barley, Meyer, & Gash, 1988).

Such bickering was (and is, to the extent it still exists) misguided. Any schisms between the scientific and applied branches of I/O psychology are counterproductive. Although the prospect didn't exactly excite him, even Wilhelm Wundt (who in 1879 established the first scientific laboratory for the study of psychology in Leipzig, Germany, and is therefore often acknowledged as the "father" of the discipline) was aware of the practical implications of some of his work. There is no question that attempts to apply the results of "pure" scientific research have often yielded valuable insights into the theoretical nature of a research problem; conversely, many procedures and ideas developed entirely in response to theoretical curiosity have turned out to be surprisingly practical. One of several contemporary descriptions of the viability of the **scientist-practitioner model** of I/O psychology appeared in a volume edited by Murphy and Saal (1990). In chapters focusing on such varied topics as evaluation of job performance, drug testing, sexual harassment, and organizational conflict, several I/O psychologists addressed the symbiotic nature of the relationships that have emerged between scientific research and practical applications of data and theory. We believe that the scientist-practitioner model is alive and well among I/O psychologists as we contemplate the workplace challenges of the year 2000 and beyond.

Having settled on an abstract definition of the field, let's turn to a brief look at some of the more specific components of I/O psychology. Just as many other professional disciplines have become more and more specialized in recent years, so too has I/O psychology. A rather common distinction today is that between the "I" ("industrial") and the "O" ("organizational") segments of the field. The former concerns itself with such personnel or human-resources topics as analyzing jobs and determining their dollar values in today's economy, recruiting and hiring new employees and assigning them to jobs, measuring and evaluating the work performance of individuals and work groups or teams, and training both newly hired and veteran employees to perform better the various aspects of their jobs. The latter addresses more theoretical issues, such as social influences on work-related behaviors, job satisfaction, work motivation, communication, leadership, and organizational design and development. Other related subdisciplines include industrial and labor relations (usually involving organized labor unions), vocational and career psychology, engineering psychology (focusing on the interface between human beings and work-related machinery and equipment), and consumer psychology. Most of these, however, have evolved into more or less autonomous fields of study in their own right, and are identified less and less with "mainstream" I/O psychology.

The chapters to follow will therefore concentrate on the subject matter of the two primary segments ("I" and "O") of the field. However, we intend to downplay the separateness of these segments and convince you, for example, that a thorough understanding of such traditional "O" topics as work motivation and job satisfaction demands a similar appreciation of such "I" topics as job analysis, personnel selection, and performance appraisal. In like fashion, we will argue that the effectiveness of any personnel training program (an "I" component) derives in part from the motivation of the women and men who undergo training, and the degree to which the organization's climate or culture supports acquisition of new knowledge or skills (classic "O" topics). Thus, you will not find any artificial separation of these segments in the pages to follow.

Education and Employment of I/O Psychologists

Most I/O psychologists active today have completed one or more graduate programs in their chosen specialties. Master's and doctoral degrees in the field can now be earned at numerous colleges, universities, and professional schools. The Society for Industrial and Organizational Psychology (SIOP) periodically publishes descriptions of these programs in *Graduate Training Programs in Industrial/Organizational Psychology and Organizational Behavior*. As you might expect, programs differ in emphasis and quality. According to 122 members of SIOP who responded to a survey soliciting their opinions of 39 institutions that offered the Ph.D. in I/O psychology, the ten programs with the most favorable ratings had (1) faculty members and graduates who had strong reputations and were widely known among their professional colleagues; (2) curricula that emphasized quantitative methods, an experimental approach, and topics related to selection and training of employees; and (3) ready access to a wide variety of research tools (Greenberg, Thomas, Dossett, Robinson, DeMeuse, & Pendergrass, 1981).

Although I/O psychologists themselves find employment in many kinds of work settings, three prototypical types of jobs tend to predominate. First, many I/O psychologists work full time for individual companies, corporations, or government agencies, where they spend their days doing applied research and using their professional expertise to help their organizations solve problems and create conditions that will facilitate the economic and psychological well-being of those organizations and all their members. A second group finds employment in consulting firms that range in size from two or three partners to literally hundreds of professional I/O psychologists and other behavioral scientists. Organizations that do not employ a full-time I/O psychologist, or that encounter problems that might overwhelm the small number of I/O psychologists who are on staff, will often contact one of these consulting firms, which will in turn assign one or more of its psychologists to work with the organization to overcome the difficulty. Sometimes this can be done in a day or two, and sometimes it requires extended contact (and geographical

I/O psychologists can choose from three main areas of employment: corporations, consulting firms, and academic institutions.

relocation of the consulting I/O psychologists) over a period of several weeks or months. Larger consulting firms often have the luxury of assigning individual I/O psychologists to organizations based on the psychologists' unique areas of experience and expertise. Smaller firms must be content to assign "generalists"—professionals who are comfortable and competent dealing with a wide variety of different organizational problems and issues.

A third distinguishable group of I/O psychologists are primarily affiliated with academic institutions. Employed as professors and/or administrators, they conduct basic and/or applied research and teach classes and seminars in the field to graduate and/or undergraduate students. Many also engage in private consulting activities that resemble those of their colleagues who work for consulting firms, although usually on a somewhat smaller scale. Such efforts to combine multiple professional roles can be intellectually and economically gratifying but can also lead to frustration in the form of role conflicts and ambiguity (Saal, 1992).

Licensing and Certification.   All 50 states in the United States currently regulate the practice of psychology by law. Although such legislation tends to have its most dramatic effects on those who specialize in clinical, counseling, and school psychology, some I/O psychologists choose to become licensed or certified in their home states, especially those who are *not* primarily affiliated with academic institutions. Psychologists, of course, have not been singled out by state governments for special attention or harassment; approximately 800 occupations in the United States are affected by licensing or certification regulations (including those of nurses, physicians, pharmacists, barbers, horseshoers, and lightning rod installers) (Shimberg, 1981).

Licensing is the process whereby a government agency officially grants someone permission to engage in a particular occupation. Such permission is typically granted only after the agency determines that the individual is sufficiently competent that his occupational pursuits will not threaten the health, safety, or welfare of the public. The licensing process usually specifies a legitimate "scope of practice" that specifies what the licensee may do. Thus, it is illegal for unlicensed individuals to engage in activities within that scope of practice. This is a more restrictive form of regulation than is certification.

Certification is basically a form of "title control" that assists employers and the public in identifying practitioners who have met a standard of performance that usually surpasses the minimal level required for licensure. This form of regulation, however, does not prohibit uncertified individuals from engaging in specific occupation-related activities. It merely forbids them to use a particular title, such as "psychologist" (Shimberg, 1981).

Licensing requirements have been soundly criticized (Danish & Smyer, 1981; Locke, 1982b), and licensing seems to be on the wane among I/O psychologists (Howard & Lowman, 1985). Insisting that applicants for licenses earn minimum scores on written multiple-choice examinations does little to ensure the practical competence of helping professionals such as psychologists. Licensing procedures can also lead to several undesirable (albeit unintentional) consequences, such as inflated costs associated with services, uneven public accessibility to services, restricted mobility of professional service providers, and inhibited innovation and autonomy within the graduate programs that produce these professionals. Further, it is less than clear that any governmental agency is capable of setting rational standards for licensing that balance the potential harms and benefits of state regulation in any morally justifiable way. Licensing may constitute a blatant violation of individual rights by prohibiting free trade among consenting adults. It is possible that noncoercive alternatives to licensing such as private certification, competition for professional reputation, public education, and strict enforcement of existing antifraud legislation could promote the benefits while minimizing the dangers of state regulation (Locke, 1982b).

As you might imagine, it is difficult to discuss licensing and its effects in a detached, unemotional manner because several vital interests are involved (Danish & Smyer, 1981). Concern for the future of psychology (both the science and the profession), concern for the consumer and the community, and concern for the livelihoods of individual psychologists are among those that head the list. Although we acknowledge the flaws inherent in current licensing and certification procedures, we suspect that the potential benefits outweigh the costs. Elimination of all legal restrictions would leave the public vulnerable to charlatans and quacks sufficiently glib to pass themselves off as qualified professionals. Individuals and organizations would pay the price, and the reputation of the science and practice of psychology would suffer, too. Of course, our position in no way implies that existing regulations cannot benefit from scrutiny and improvement. Some professional occupations (dentistry, for example) require those who apply for licensure to pass rigorous performance tests in addition to standard paper-and-pencil exams. Others (including psychology in many states) recognize a need for periodic re-examination, peer review, audits of records, and/or continuing education as prerequisites for license renewal. Such procedures improve the effectiveness of licensing and certification laws for protecting the welfare and reputations of the public and the professions involved.

Past, Present, and Future of Work and I/O Psychology

In the chapters that follow we will introduce you to the field of I/O psychology as it exists and is practiced today. You will see that it is a complex, diversified discipline that focuses on many different aspects of human behavior in and related to the workplace. However, because most of us can better understand and appreciate information when it comes to us in a meaningful context, we want to share with you some observations and comments concerning events and accomplishments that have played important roles in the evolution of I/O psychology. An appreciation of our discipline's past will facilitate your understanding of its present status and its prospects for the future.

Views of Human Work

Recall that early definitions of industrial psychology emphasized people's efficiency and adjustment in the workplace (Viteles, 1932). The meanings women and men attach to their labors, their perspectives on their work, can dramatically influence both efficiency and adjustment. Prior to the Industrial Revolution in Europe and North America, we can identify three basic, quite different perspectives on human work (Lofquist & Dawis, 1969; Tilgher, 1930). One of these characterized work as a hard, painful, and burdensome activity, as a more or less necessary evil. The ancient Hebrews saw work as a way of atoning for one's sins, including the "original sin" that resulted in the eviction of Adam and Eve from the Garden of Eden. (The first example of "involuntary turnover"?) Other ancient philosophers conceptualized work as drudgery doled out by the gods (Heneman, 1973). Writings from classical Greece specified that all work in the city-states of Sparta and Athens was done by slaves, serfs, and other noncitizens. It is easy to see, then, how the Greeks came to view work as "inherently servile and degrading" (Neff, 1968, p. 61).

A second perspective depicted work as an instrumental activity, as a means for achieving (often religious) ends. For many of the early Christians, work was a way to express charity toward one's neighbors. Saint Benedict's prescriptions for the behavior of monks described both manual and intellectual labor as a religious duty (Neff, 1968). Others who agreed that work was a duty stressed that one should not labor to acquire goods or property but only to provide sustenance. A variation on this theme emerged during the Protestant Reformation when Martin Luther proclaimed that perfect performance of the work required by one's occupation or profession was the best way to serve God. Calvin went even further, declaring that "work alone sufficed to curb the evil bent of man" (Lofquist & Dawis, 1969, p. 8). As you can see, the Protestant Reformation was a powerful force in promoting the idea that work was an ennobling activity.

According to a third perspective, work is an intrinsically good activity because it involves creative acts of human beings. Renaissance philosophers and artists such as Leonardo da Vinci saw work as a way to master nature, to "move away from the animal and nearer to the divine" (Lofquist & Dawis, 1969, p. 8). Although this statement hints at instrumentality (means to an end), the essence of this view is that work is to be valued for its own sake. Some have suggested that this vision of work, as well as all its religious connotations, evaporated with the Industrial Revolution (Heneman, 1973). The advent of the machine had important implications for workers' personal identities. According to Lofquist and Dawis (1969), the expansion of automation in society improves the odds that work will dehumanize men and women, reducing them to the status of "machine-tenders" and stripping manual labor of much of the value it once enjoyed. Further, industrialization has affected the way we value different *kinds* of work. Although most still agree that it is more virtuous to work than to be idle, certain kinds of work are now judged to be "better" than others according to rather elaborate occupational hierarchies (Neff, 1968).

We hope this brief description of how the meanings attached to human work have evolved convinces you that perspectives on this basic human activity have not been static. It seems a very safe bet that there will be more such changes (Dunnette, 1973).

Browsing Through I/O Psychology's Scrapbook

Because the history of "modern" I/O psychology is surprisingly short, it is impossible to draw parallels between our field and the various perspectives on human work described in the previous section. It is not only possible but imperative, however, that we try to understand our discipline in the context of *today's* perceptions of the meaning of work. As the meaning and importance of work in our lives continue to evolve, so must the science and practice of I/O psychology.

The Early Years. Some contend that the origins of industrial psychology go all the way back to biblical times when Gideon used a rather interesting "performance test" (based on how one drank water) to select soldiers (Stagner, 1982). Others have referred to procedures developed by the Chinese for assessing individual differences in occupational proficiency approximately 4,000 years ago (DuBois, 1970). By the time of the Han dynasty (206 B.C. through A.D. 220), "written examinations had been introduced for civil servants working in such areas as geography, agriculture, civil law, and military affairs" (Minton & Schneider, 1980, p. 5). Ancient Greeks also recognized the importance of individual differences in work performance. Plato, a student of Socrates, emphasized in *The Republic* that the ideal state was one in which individuals were assigned to perform the tasks for which they were best suited, and recommended use of an aptitude test to identify those most qualified to pursue military careers.

Concerns about differences among people waned following the classical Greek and Roman periods. This trend reached its extreme during the Middle Ages, when the individual in European society was deemed *inseparable* from the group to which he belonged (Williams, 1961). "A person was identical with his role in society; he was a peasant, an artisan, [or] a knight, and not an individual who happened to have this or that occupation" (Fromm, 1941, pp. 41–42). This perspective prevailed until the time of the Renaissance. With the emergence of capitalism based on *individual* economic initiative and the flowering of the Protestant Reformation, which displaced the central authority of the church, individual men and women once again emerged as separate entities who merited *individual* treatment.

We typically identify the emergence of "modern" industrial psychology with the be-

ginning of the twentieth century. Among the earliest contributions were a description of how professional telegraphers developed the necessary skills for sending and receiving Morse code (Bryan & Harter, 1897) and a recommendation that APA members conduct research on concrete behaviors that are part of everyday life (Bryan, 1904). Muchinsky (1990) reported an interesting footnote to Bryan's work:

> The term industrial psychology was apparently used for the first time in Bryan's 1904 article. Ironically, it appeared in print only as a typographical error. Bryan was quoting a sentence he had written five years earlier (Bryan & Harter, 1899) in which he spoke of the need for more research in *individual* psychology. Instead, Bryan wrote industrial psychology and did not catch his mistake. (p. 11)

Early landmark contributions to the emerging field of industrial psychology came from Frederick Taylor, Walter Dill Scott, and Hugo Münsterberg. Taylor (1911) addressed such issues as violent strikes, labor turnover, discipline problems in factories, work restrictions and other group influences on people's work behaviors, and lack of motivation among workers (Nord, 1982; Stagner, 1982). Along with other industrial engineers such as the wife-husband team of Lillian and Frank Gilbreth, Taylor redesigned jobs, developed training programs, and used selection methods to increase workers' efficiency. In his well-known *Principles of Scientific Management*, he urged organizations to implement work methods and procedures that had been designed scientifically, to select in a systematic fashion employees who were capable of being trained to use those work methods and procedures, and to facilitate cooperation between workers and managers in assuming responsibility for designing and accomplishing work.

Scott and Münsterberg trained under Wilhelm Wundt in Germany. Scott's professional interests were varied, encompassing the use of suggestion and argument for influencing people, and the promotion of competition, loyalty, concentration, and imitation as means to maximize human efficiency. His work in the area of human motivation led to a distinction between "selfish" and "selfless" motives (Stagner, 1982). Scott is probably best known, however, for his application of psychology to advertising in two volumes entitled *Theory of Advertising* and *Psychology of Advertising,* published in 1903 and 1908, respectively. Münsterberg came to Harvard University at the invitation of William James, a noted American psychologist. Münsterberg also entertained a variety of interests, including the selection of workers, the design of work stations, and the application of psychology to sales. His book *Psychology and Industrial Efficiency,* published in 1913, is acknowledged by some to have laid the foundation for subsequent research in the areas of personnel selection and training (Stagner, 1982). In one of his better-known studies, he analyzed the job of streetcar motorman and developed a relevant selection test for a Boston company. Although his outspoken support of Germany during World War I substantially undermined his professional influence, many consider Münsterberg to be the "father" of industrial psychology.

Thus, we can identify two primary roots that nourished the field of industrial psychology prior to America's entry into World War I. One was the influence of industrial engineers, who often relied on the traditional procedures of experimental psychology to discover and support generalizations about human capabilities and limitations. Based on an assumption that universal laws of behavior awaited discovery, this approach led Taylor and his colleagues to conduct "time and motion" studies in order to discover the *one best way* to design and perform any given job. The second influence came from differential psychologists, who downplay the importance of universal laws of behavior and focus on the differences that exist between and among individuals. Emphasizing the uniqueness of each person, this approach served as the

foundation for Münsterberg's work on the systematic selection of job applicants to fill carefully defined job openings.

Conflict and accommodation between these two approaches has played a major role in the evolution of psychology in general and industrial psychology in particular. For example, Moore (1962) believed that the history of industrial psychology *began* with an argument between Wilhelm Wundt and James McKeen Cattell (who had also studied under Wundt's supervision) on the relative importance of universal laws of the mind versus individual differences in how those laws functioned. These two perspectives led to two approaches to collecting and analyzing psychological data. The methodology of **experimental psychology** is based on presumed relationships between sets of circumstances or stimulus conditions controlled or manipulated by an experimenter and particular behaviors of interest. Given such an assumption, any individual differences that emerge among subjects exposed to the same circumstances or conditions are attributed to carelessness, chance, or other sources of error. The contrasting methodology of **differential psychology** typically eschews manipulation or control of circumstances and conditions. Instead, differential psychologists measure naturally occurring variables or events and use statistical procedures designed to detect relationships among those variables or events. Although debates between these two camps have sometimes been acrimonious, many contemporary psychologists try to accommodate them both by simultaneously acknowledging the roles of individual differences and experimental manipulations in their efforts to understand complex human behaviors (Cronbach, 1957, 1975; Owens, 1968). I/O psychologists are among those who recognize the value of integrating these two approaches.

World War I. Ghoulish as it may be, global armed conflict has proven to be an invaluable stimulus to the field of I/O psychology. Korman

(1971) unabashedly asserted that "it took World War I to start the first great growth of industrial psychology in this country" (pp. 3–4). Dunnette and Borman (1979), having acknowledged that tests had been used for centuries to make decisions about people, declared that the modern era of personnel selection began on April 6, 1917, the day the United States declared war on Germany. Recall that the armed forces were faced with an immense task as the United States entered the war. Decisions had to be made about how to utilize the tremendous pool of manpower that became available through enlistments and the military draft, and they had to be made quickly. Who should be trained for advanced, technically skilled jobs? Who should be handed a rifle and sent to the deadly trenches that scarred European battlefields? Who should be enrolled in officer training schools, and who should be assigned to the enlisted ranks?

Robert Yerkes and other psychologists who became involved in the war effort in order to answer such questions proceeded from the basic assumption that intelligence was *the* major factor that distinguished among those who could perform difficult tasks and those who could not (Korman, 1971). Unfortunately, instruments for assessing human intelligence were not plentiful. There were, of course, procedures that implicitly equated people's mental skills with the speed of their reaction times or their abilities to discriminate among various sensory stimuli. However, Yerkes and his colleagues recognized that these tests, developed by Galton and Cattell, did not capture the essence of the intellectual abilities presumed to be crucial for effective military performance. The only other readily available alternative was a measure of intelligence developed by Alfred Binet in response to the French minister of education's request to identify children who could not be expected to benefit from a recently instituted system of public education because of inadequate mental abilities. Although that test addressed relevant intellectual capabilities, it could be administered by an examiner to only

one person at a time. Given the large number of potential examinees and the shortage of time, such an individual test was hopelessly inappropriate.

The solution to the dilemma came to be known as the Army Alpha test, a paper-and-pencil measure of intelligence that assessed the same basic mental skills as Binet's individual test but could be administered to large numbers of people at the same time by a single examiner or proctor. Because inadequate language skills (rather than low intelligence) might have been responsible for some recruits' low scores on the Alpha test, a second "parallel" test (the Army Beta) was developed that relied less on verbal skills and more on performance of other intellectually demanding tasks. Within two years Yerkes, Walter Bingham, and other members of APA had tested more than 1.5 million men; written job specifications and constructed job-knowledge tests; developed forms for rating officers' performance; and initiated training and psychological counseling programs. Some consider this "the beginning of large-scale use of tests and other systematic methods to aid personnel decisions in the world of work" (Dunnette & Borman, 1979, p. 478).

There can be little doubt that these intelligence tests were *perceived* to be very effective for selecting and placing recruits during World War I. The "Army Alpha was so successful in achieving the goals set for it that this achievement probably stands as the major single reason for the increase in the use of psychology by U.S. industry after World War I" (Korman, 1971, p. 4). More contemporary assessments of personnel testing during the war are less laudatory. Consider that the Adjutant General's Office did not issue the final order that conferred complete authority to the testing program until August 1918, only three months before the Armistice was signed and the "war to end all wars" came to a close (Muchinsky, 1990). Thus, although almost 1.75 million people were ultimately tested, actual use of test results had to be far more modest. Others have concurred that intelligence tests developed and used during this period were not nearly as effective as many reports indicated (Samelson, 1977). Nevertheless, the recognition and legitimacy that accrued to psychologists because of the widespread perceptions that these tests were successful served to invigorate the discipline of psychology in general, and the specialty of industrial psychology in particular. As you have no doubt occasionally observed, perceptions can be far more important than whatever "reality" may be.

Scott also contributed to U.S. participation in World War I, working extensively with the Committee on Classification of Personnel that was attached to the Adjutant General's Office. His contributions to classifying and placing enlisted soldiers in specialized situations, to developing performance ratings for officers that would contribute to promotion decisions, and to preparing descriptions of qualifications and duties for more than 500 jobs were judged sufficiently important that he was later awarded the Distinguished Service Medal (Korman, 1971).

Although it had nothing directly to do with World War I, another event occurred in 1917 that would have a substantial impact on the field of industrial (and later, I/O) psychology in years to come: publication of the first issue of *Journal of Applied Psychology*. Today, approximately three-quarters of a century later, many I/O psychologists acknowledge this periodical as one of the primary, most respected vehicles for disseminating theory and research in their field.

A Peaceful (?) Interlude.   Industrial psychology's testing program emerged from World War I with a reputation as a useful tool for managing human resources. After the war, managers in private (and public) organizations quite reasonably assumed that they could use similar tests to select new employees from among all those who were applying for postwar civilian jobs. Several psychological research bureaus emerged with the expressed goal of harnessing industrial psychology's perceived power to solve practical personnel problems. Among these was Bing-

ham's Bureau of Salesmanship Research at the Carnegie Institute of Technology, which focused on selection, classification, and development of sales personnel, as well as clerical and executive personnel. Cattell's Psychological Corporation, established in 1921 as an information clearinghouse and source of reference checks for people and organizations interested in hiring psychologists, has developed into one of this nation's primary sources of psychological tests.

The field's fame in the civilian workplace was short-lived. As the "Roaring 1920s" came to a close, many managers were becoming discouraged about the potential of industrial psychology to promote organizational efficiency and individual well-being. There were several reasons that the field's image became tarnished: many of the tests used to make selection decisions were simply not effective; employees hired on the basis of test scores were *not* superior to those hired without the use of tests; the ability tests then in vogue ignored other important factors that might predict performance on a variety of jobs, which included motivation and personality, among others; and many managers had gravitated toward industrial psychology as a means to improve workers' well-being, and thereby make them less vulnerable to the appeals of organized labor (trade) unions. Because the relatively affluent 1920s rendered unions less attractive and therefore less powerful, the managers saw less need to cloak their businesses in the protective armor of industrial psychology's theories and principles.

Several other events that occurred between World Wars I and II merit our attention. During the 1930s, the first edition of the *Dictionary of Occupational Titles* (*DOT*) appeared. The *DOT*, a mammoth document commissioned by the U.S. Department of Labor, describes characteristics of jobs as well as the human traits and abilities deemed necessary for performing them. It is currently in its fifth revision (1993), and remains a valuable reference tool for employment counselors, trainers, and other professionals concerned with jobs and workers' performance. Other notable events included the publication of two influential books by Viteles (*Industrial Psychology,* 1932; *The Science of Work,* 1934) and Joseph Tiffin's arrival in 1938 at Purdue University, where he established what was to become a large and important program for training graduate students in industrial psychology. It was also about this time that industrial psychology in the United States benefited from the emigration of numerous eminent social scientists who were escaping the gathering storm of fascism in Adolf Hitler's Nazi Germany. Neither should we overlook the tremendous impact of the Great Depression of the 1930s. It is impossible to understand the evolution of theory and research pertaining to job satisfaction, work motivation, and union-management relations (among other concerns of I/O psychology) without appreciating the role of this unparalleled economic disaster in altering the ways in which men and women viewed employment. Millions of people lost their jobs, and there were no unemployment or welfare programs in place to cushion the blows.

Hawthorne Studies.   If asked to point to a single event between World War I and World War II that had the most powerful impact on the development of I/O psychology, however, we must acknowledge a series of studies that began in the 1920s at the Hawthorne plant of the Western Electric Company located just outside Chicago. In 1924 several researchers from Harvard University, none of whom were industrial psychologists by training, began a collaborative effort with Western Electric to identify relationship(s) between different levels of illumination and optimal work efficiency. To everyone's surprise, no clear-cut relationships emerged. Productivity seemed to increase, or at least remain at satisfactory levels, regardless of any changes in illumination. When it eventually became clear that factors other than lighting were affecting productivity, the researchers designed a subsequent series of studies to clarify matters.

The results of the studies initiated the "human relations" movement in industry (Bass & Barrett, 1981), and eventually led to a change in the name of our field to industrial *and organizational* psychology. Among the relevant findings were the following (Roethlisberger & Dickson, 1939; Sonnenfeld, 1982; Whitehead, 1938):

1. An individual's work behaviors are rarely consequences of simple cause-and-effect relationships but are more often determined by complex sets of multiple factors.

2. Groups of workers develop their own norms or expectations of group members' behaviors that interact with each individual worker's personal needs and the demands of the work setting.

3. Job-related symbols of prestige and power influence the social structures of these work groups.

4. An individual's unique needs and satisfactions can be understood only in the context of her personal life.

5. Workers' almost reflexive resistance to changes can be reduced by acknowledging their feelings and including them in the decision-making process.

6. The workplace is a social system, not merely a system for producing goods or services.

   A particular contribution of the Hawthorne studies that took on a life of its own is the "Hawthorne effect." Recall that workers' productivity during the early illumination studies occasionally increased regardless of the nature of the lighting adjustment. The **Hawthorne effect,** which is similar to a placebo effect in medicine (Bass & Barrett, 1981), attributes these improvements in workers' job performance to nothing more than the novelty of the situation. Factories at that time were usually intimidating and socially oppressive places to work, and it was rather unusual for employees to see any signs that their supervisors cared at all about their working conditions (Locke, 1982a). Unfortunately, behavior often returns to its original level (or lower) after the novelty of a new situation wears off; Hawthorne effects therefore tend not to constitute permanent solutions to productivity problems.

A half century of debate has confirmed that the Hawthorne studies do *not* represent perfect field research (Yorks & Whitsett, 1985). For example, statistical reanalysis of the data suggested that more than 90% of the improvements in the Hawthorne employees' performance could be explained by such extraneous factors as improved raw materials, increased supervisory discipline, and workers' anxieties about being laid off (Franke & Kaul, 1978). We have also witnessed a spirited argument concerning the relevance of Marxism's emphasis on worker-capitalist conflict and its skepticism about how easily workers can be fooled for properly interpreting and understanding the Hawthorne results (Bramel & Friend, 1981, 1982; Feldman, 1982; Locke, 1982a; Parsons, 1982; Sonnenfeld, 1982; Toch, 1982; Vogel, 1982).

Despite these methodological flaws and philosophical and economic debates, there can be little question concerning the benefits that have accrued to workers and to the science and practice of I/O psychology since the Hawthorne studies. In *Man and Work in Society*, which describes the proceedings of a symposium held to commemorate the fiftieth anniversary of the original research, the editors asserted that they had compiled the "views of a varied group of contemporary authorities on some of the topics rooted in the [Hawthorne] Studies—*topics which continue to have wide implications for today and for the future*" (Cass & Zimmer, 1975; our emphasis). In the words of one who interviewed four of the original workers who had participated in the relay-assembly–test-room segment of those studies, "The many rebuttals to the same critical charges, the views of the participants, the decades of supportive research, and the plainly observable results of Japanese management

practices indicate that *the value and validity of the Hawthorne findings is no longer a point of intellectually legitimate contention*" (Sonnenfeld, 1982, p. 1399; our emphasis).

World War II.   Industrial psychologists were better prepared to contribute to U.S. participation in World War II. This time, the armed forces took the initiative to approach the psychologists. Recall that during World War I psychologists focused primarily on selection and placement of personnel. These concerns were not ignored during World War II. For example, a major accomplishment in this domain was the development of the Army General Classification Test (AGCT), a paper-and-pencil test that could be administered to many individuals at the same time. The AGCT was designed to separate new recruits into several basic categories according to their predicted abilities to learn various military duties and responsibilities. In addition to the AGCT, an advisory committee chaired by Bingham contributed tests designed to measure trade proficiencies and other aptitudes, including the potential to complete officer training school successfully.

Industrial psychologists became heavily involved in a variety of other projects, too. The pressing need to train pilots who could operate the complex war planes that were being designed and produced led to major strides in the realm of personnel training. Some of this training took place in actual aircraft; some of it occurred in **simulators,** facsimiles of actual equipment. Simulators were also used by engineering psychologists as they studied and tested technical innovations in flight-deck design. In an effort to make pilots' jobs easier and safer, the psychologists tried to standardize cockpits across types of aircraft and modify instruments to improve the interface between pilots and their planes. Engineering psychologists' opportunities to make important contributions to contemporary space programs are in no small way attributable to the successes of these behavioral scientists during World War II.

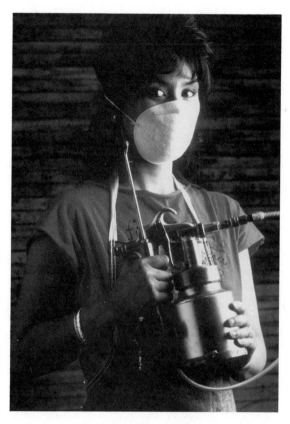

"Rosie" lives and works in the 1990s.

The mission of the U.S. Office of Strategic Services (OSS) led to a major advance of a different sort. Because this agency's responsibilities included espionage, sabotage, and other very demanding and dangerous tasks, the OSS was interested in assessing applicants' abilities to withstand and function effectively under high levels of stress. With this goal in mind, psychologists designed a series of situational stress tests (Murray & MacKinnon, 1946). These tests, which were typically administered over several consecutive days, placed candidates for OSS assignments in extremely stressful, often impossible situations where failure was almost guaranteed. Small teams of observers watched candidates' behaviors and performance closely, paying particular attention to their emotional

stability and ability to tolerate frustration. This general approach evolved into what we know today as **assessment centers.** Pioneered in the civilian sector by American Telephone & Telegraph (Finkle, 1976), assessment centers present standardized sets of experiences that represent simulated job situations to permit evaluation of applicants' behaviors and performance under a variety of job-relevant conditions. (Assessment centers are discussed in more detail in Chapter 5.)

We would be remiss if we dismissed the World War II era without examining a fascinating phenomenon known as "Rosie the Riveter." With millions of men serving overseas or "stateside" in the armed forces, there was insufficient *man*power to keep industries running at the peak capacities necessary to support the Allied war efforts against the Axis nations. Women were therefore encouraged to join the work force and "pick up the slack." They responded by the thousands, and within months women could be found welding in shipyards, packing artillery shells in ammunition plants, and performing many other distinctly "unladylike" tasks such as riveting (hence, the nickname) aluminum skins onto combat aircraft. When the war ended, most of these women relinquished (often under duress) their relatively high-paying and challenging jobs to the men who returned from the European and Pacific theaters of operations. They returned to their homes as full-time homemakers, spouses, and mothers, or accepted more menial jobs (short-order cook, domestic servant, and so on) for far less pay (Gluck, 1987). Nevertheless, their accomplishments in the factories and plants during the war should have debunked the myth that women cannot perform certain kinds of jobs. Unfortunately, this myth is still alive and well in certain sectors of our economy.

Latter Half of the Twentieth Century. Recall that the period immediately following World War I was a time of growth and prosperity for the field of industrial psychology. In like manner, the decade following World War II also saw significant strides in our field's march toward scientific and professional maturity. Korman (1971) highlighted several notable events during those ten years:

1. The number of specialized graduate programs in industrial psychology increased dramatically.

2. The number of interdisciplinary research centers devoted to industrial problems and issues also increased.

3. Reorganization of the American Psychological Association (APA) included a separate Division of Industrial Psychology.

4. More and more industrial psychologists were being employed by private companies and government agencies.

5. A new professional journal, *Personnel Psychology,* was established in 1948, providing another outlet (along with *Journal of Applied Psychology*) for industrial psychologists to publish their empirical data and theoretical ideas.

Interestingly, the postwar similarities did not stop with the "good times." Just as the fine reputation of industrial psychology disappeared 10 or 15 years following the end of World War I, so too did our discipline suffer a reversal of fortunes in the late 1950s and early 1960s, when it came "under as concentrated [a] series of attacks from as wide a variety of sources as have probably been made on any area of professional and/or scientific activity" (Korman, 1971, p. 10). Among the criticisms were the following:

1. Industrial psychology had forfeited its status as a science because it had developed tools and techniques that were specifically designed to aid personnel managers do their jobs, and thereby became nothing more than a technical assistant to "management."

2. Industrial psychology persisted in using tools and techniques that were hopelessly

outdated and based on assumptions about the workplace (for example, that the work force would remain overwhelmingly male and blue-collar) that were no longer valid.

3. Industrial psychologists' activities and recommendations were heavily influenced by fads and other popular (but scientifically indefensible) ideas.

Taking a long-range perspective, we agree with Korman's assessment that these criticisms were fortunate because they were also accurate. They stimulated serious self-examination within the field, and led to modifications that have rendered I/O psychology an established and respected scientific and theoretical discipline.

Industrial psychology has also witnessed a substantial amount of specialization since World War II. Subdisciplines such as engineering psychology, military psychology, and consumer psychology now publish their own professional journals, hold their own national meetings and conventions, and are recognized as autonomous divisions within APA. This "splintering effect" has been sufficiently strong that the work of most contemporary behavioral scientists who identify themselves as I/O psychologists tends to be concentrated in the subdisciplines of industrial psychology (personnel/human resources) and organizational psychology (social, motivation, and leadership topics, among others) described earlier.

Antidiscrimination Legislation.   Our discussion of I/O psychology during the years since World War II would be sadly incomplete if we neglected to mention the dramatic impacts of several pieces of national legislation. For example, the Civil Rights Act (1964) made it expressly illegal to discriminate against certain groups of "protected" individuals (for example, Native Americans, Asian Americans, Hispanic Americans, women, blacks) in such diverse realms as housing, education, and employment. Title VII of that legislation created the Equal Employment Opportunity Commission (EEOC), which is responsible for investigating allegations of employment discrimination and for eliminating and preventing such discrimination. In addition, Title VII led to a set of guidelines that emphasize the importance of *job-relatedness* for techniques used to select or promote workers (for example, paper-and-pencil tests, interviews, application blanks). That is, applicants for jobs (or promotions) should be selected or rejected on the basis of information (for example, test scores or personal histories) that is systematically related to how well or how poorly they would perform the job in question if given an opportunity to do so. Personnel psychologists must now not only develop techniques that are useful for selecting and promoting employees but also limit themselves to procedures that do not discriminate against any of the groups specifically protected by Title VII (or other legislation, such as the Age Discrimination in Employment Act, 1967).

As substantial numbers of individuals belonging to one or more of these groups have filed lawsuits, believing themselves to be victims of illegal discrimination, many I/O psychologists have found themselves in courts of law providing expert testimony regarding the validity of measures based on particular selection or promotion tests and techniques. Given the almost inherent incompatibilities between an *adversarial* system (the courts) and a *scientific* system (I/O psychology), this new role often proves to be especially challenging. Their elder colleagues (prior to 1964) had only to satisfy the manager(s) who engaged their services; today's practicing I/O psychologists must satisfy the U.S. Congress as well.

More recently, Congress passed the Civil Rights Act of 1991, partly in response to several decisions issued by the U.S. Supreme Court perceived by many to alter substantially the balance of power between organizations that wished to use personnel tests in a *responsible* manner and members of protected groups. It is still far too early to comment definitively about the effects of this legislation. It seems safe to

Federal legislation affects personnel policies.

predict, however, that it will continue to make the professional lives of practicing I/O psychologists interesting and challenging.

Another piece of legislation that will certainly have a similar effect is the Americans with Disabilities Act (ADA), which went into effect in July 1992. The basic intent of the ADA is to require employers to make reasonable accommodations for employees with disabilities who are otherwise qualified to perform given jobs. Among the interesting questions to be resolved are the following: (1) What, exactly, qualifies as a "disability"? (2) What, exactly, constitutes a "reasonable" accommodation? (3) Are psychological tests equivalent to medical examinations, and therefore prohibited prior to the organization's making a preliminary job offer? Because none of these questions is "scientific" in nature, each will be answered by the legal and political communities rather than by I/O psychologists or other behavioral scientists. We can only hope that the former groups will consult the latter as they wrestle with these thorny issues.

The Future?   Unfortunately, palmistry and reading tea leaves or goat entrails lie outside our areas of expertise. Nevertheless, rather than resigning ourselves to reacting to events as they happen, we cannot resist a few cautious attempts to anticipate what the future will bring for I/O psychology. Anticipation occasionally enables us to help shape our future. The observations below represent a sample of some I/O psychologists' views of the future. As you will see, some of their predictions already show signs of "coming true."

Stagner (1982) offered a rather detailed view of our discipline's future. Among his predictions were the following:

1. High-technology jobs will demand greater emphasis on cognitive variables (perception, judgment, reasoning, and the like) during the personnel selection process.

2. Personality variables such as tolerance for stress will also become more important predictors of job success.

3. Assessment centers will play larger roles in selecting and evaluating employees.

4. I/O psychologists will be expected to assume counseling roles more frequently than they have in the past.

5. It will become more important for our measuring instruments to "look like" they measure whatever it is they are intended to assess (high "face validity").

6. I/O psychologists will persist in their efforts to satisfy EEOC requirements and guidelines.

7. Unions will play increasingly important roles, especially in the 1990s.

Finally, Stagner speculated about the importance of redesigning jobs with the direct assistance of workers who know the jobs best. The goal is to render those jobs inherently more interesting and "fun," and thereby increase employees' intrinsic motivation to perform them.

Nord (1980) agreed that I/O psychologists will have to pay more attention to labor unions and their impact on employees' work behaviors. However, continuing declines in the strength and size of unions suggest that these prognosticators may have been "off the mark" with this prediction. More on target, Nord (1982) emphasized that we must contemplate our discipline's future in the context of the political and economic processes that might prevail in years to come. More specifically,

- I/O psychologists must not ignore our own political and economic assumptions as we determine exactly whose interests are being served by our work.

- Measures of work quality, efficiency and waste, and the value of human resources will become more important as "bottom-line" financial data become less satisfactory guides for managerial decisions.

- Different forms of organizational control will become necessary as the demographic character of the work force moves beyond white males. For example, organizations that persist in their efforts to reconcile routine work and rigid control with our society's increasingly liberal value system will fall victim to fads and other promising short-term solutions that will serve only to exacerbate the problems rather than solve them.

Tenopyr (1981) focused on the national concern with productivity in her presidential address to the Society for Industrial and Organizational Psychology. If our discipline is to contribute to greater productivity, we must

1. Define productivity in a way that makes individual employees and work groups relevant factors.

2. Accommodate economists and other professionals who analyze the behavior of larger social groups and broad societal phenomena. One step involves "narrowing the gap" between the statistical procedures favored by these professions and those we embrace to analyze the behaviors of individual men and women.

3. Design and conduct long-term research that can complement our short-term investigations, and implement carefully evaluated action plans capable of addressing productivity in a broad, integrated fashion.

4. Open lines of communication between I/O psychologists and policymakers from private industries and governmental agencies.

5. Improve communication between researchers and practitioners in our field, and between I/O psychologists and scholars and professionals in other disciplines as well.

Tenopyr's final recommendation has been echoed by others in our field (Meltzer & Stagner, 1980; Nord, 1980; Ronen, 1980). Among the anticipated advantages associated with better cooperation are improved access to research sites, more and larger monetary grants to support research activities, more frequent and diverse consulting opportunities, and greater responsiveness on the parts of organization members during training and development seminars and workshops (Strasser & Bateman, 1984). Not surprisingly, calls for increased cooperation between researchers and practitioners have also been heard within the field of engineering psychology (Alluisi & Morgan, 1976). On a more cautionary note, however, researchers in I/O psychology must not fall victim to "dustbowl empiricism" in their efforts to cooperate with their practitioner colleagues (Gordon, Kleiman, & Hanie, 1978). Reports of empirical relationships between variables, associations that might be used by practitioners, which ignore the logical or theoretical underpinnings of those relationships, run the risk of providing "guidance" in the field that is based on poor science at best, and on nothing more than measurement errors at worst.

More recent observations concerning I/O psychology's future challenges can be found in *The Industrial-Organizational Psychologist* (*TIP*), a quarterly newsletter published by the Society for Industrial and Organizational Psychology. Among the issues discussed in an interesting forum led by Kurt Kraiger are the following (Kraiger, 1990, 1991a, 1991b, 1992):

1. The workplace will become a far more demographically diverse setting as we move into the 21st century. White employees currently constitute approximately 85% of the work force, but nearly 30% of all *new* workers by the year 2000 will be nonwhites. We can expect up to 600,000 immigrants to the United States each year who will be seeking employment. Managing such diversity will constitute a formidable challenge to supervisors and managers, most of whom are still white males.

2. Workers' average age is also expected to increase substantially during the next two decades. This is attributable to the movement of the (post–World War II) "baby-boom" generation into middle age and its progression toward retirement.

3. Female employees throughout the work force will continue to wrestle with a phenomenon known as the "glass ceiling." Although many women have gained entry into business and industry, partly as a function of the civil rights legislation discussed above, those who pursue managerial careers still encounter resistance as they try to earn promotions from lower-level managerial positions into middle- and upper-level (executive) positions.

4. I/O psychologists will continue to work with organizations as they strive to comply with the Americans with Disabilities Act (1990). Although physical disabilities will

be relatively easy to identify and accommodate, some psychological and mental disabilities will present far greater challenges. Yet to be determined, too, is the status of psychological tests used during the hiring process. If they are judged to be "medical" exams, they will be forbidden by the ADA prior to selection. The consequences of such a decision to organizations (not to mention I/O psychologists!) would be staggering.

5. Existing jobs and those to be created in the near future will demand higher and higher levels of skills from the women and men who perform them. Skills involving language, reasoning, and mathematics will continue to be especially crucial. Cross-training may present at least a partial solution to this dilemma. Undermining the efforts of managers and I/O psychologists in this domain are existing literacy problems in the workplace.

Thus, there can be no doubt that the coming years will present many fascinating and frustrating challenges to those who practice the discipline and/or pursue the science of I/O psychology. Ongoing and projected changes in the makeup of the work force will have serious implications for the ways in which I/O psychologists are trained (Offerman & Gowing, 1990). Many pitfalls and obstacles, both pragmatic and conceptual, loom. Just as surely, however, our potential to advance the original goals of our discipline, to promote the efficiency and adjustment of women and men as they strive to satisfy their diverse needs in the workplace (Viteles, 1932), is sufficient to propel I/O psychologists onward. We are humbled and inspired by the words of a recent editor of *Journal of Applied Psychology*, who reminded us in his "farewell editorial" that we deal with societal issues of fundamental importance (Campbell, 1982).

Plan of Our Book

We present this text in a way that emphasizes the relevance and applicability of I/O psychology to the everyday concerns of women and men who work in organizational environments. Immediately following Chapter 2, we will describe a hypothetical organization (Peter's Pan Pizza, Inc.) and a hypothetical I/O psychologist who is employed on the staff of that fictitious company (Dr. Jennilyn MacKeven). Our goal is to provide our readers with a sufficiently realistic and detailed context to facilitate their understanding and appreciation of I/O psychology. And we hope to inject some "life" into the discussions of theory and research that make up the substance of this book.

As you have probably already noticed, each chapter begins with a list of "learning points" that convey the goals we hope to achieve in the pages that follow. Beginning with Chapter 3, immediately after the list of learning points we present a one-page memo addressed to our hypothetical I/O psychologist from one or more members of the fictitious organization. Each memo delineates a specific issue or problem that the writer believes is undermining the organization's effectiveness. Of course, the contents of each memo also pertain directly to the domain of I/O psychology that is presented and discussed in the chapter that follows. The heart of each chapter then deals with relevant research and theory.

Because our field is dynamic and complex, you will discover (perhaps to your dismay) that research results and related theory do not always present clear, uniform, consistent pictures of what's going on. Instead, they often reflect conflict and blatant contradiction. Rather than insult your intelligence by implying consistency where, in fact, none yet exists, we have chosen to present I/O psychology to you as we perceive it currently *does* exist. We hope you agree that the confusion and occasional frustration that may accompany our admissions that "we just don't know *the answer* to that question yet" are reasonable prices to pay for presenting you with two or more perspectives on a given issue, none of which can be dismissed on the basis of available evidence. This is *not* to say, of course, that we will refrain entirely from burdening you with our opinions. When we do, however, we promise to identify them meticulously as such. Throughout each chapter, we try to highlight ways in which the I/O psychologist might use the information presented (conflicting or otherwise) to address the issue or problem posed in the introductory memo. Each chapter then concludes with a return memo from our I/O psychologist that contains her suggestions and/or specific recommendations for solving (or at least minimizing) the problem raised in the opening memo.

We hope this approach serves to convince you that the science and practice of I/O psychology can be instrumental in addressing problems and concerns that anyone who works for a living can expect to encounter in the workplace. Admittedly, the specific issues and problems described in the introductory memos are only a small sample of the challenges that confront organizations and the men and women they employ. We therefore include a series of questions at the end of each chapter that should stimulate your ideas about how the material in the chapter could be used to remedy other organizational difficulties that predictably arise from time to time.

Chapter Summary

Contemporary definitions of psychology focus on people's observable behaviors and actions, as well as their thoughts, feelings, and other mental processes that cannot be observed directly. Industrial/organizational (I/O) psychology concentrates on women's and men's behaviors and mental processes as they function in and around the workplace, and attempts to maximize the economic well-being of work organizations and the personal well-being of employees. The field of I/O psychology is guided by the scientist-practitioner model, which acknowledges the importance of empirical research and the application of knowledge gained from that research, respectively, in its efforts to improve organizational and individual well-being. Most I/O psychologists have earned one or more graduate degrees, and many are certified or licensed by state regulatory agencies. I/O psychologists are employed as organizational staff members, as members of consulting firms, as independent consultants to business and industry, as instructors or professors in colleges and universities, and in numerous other professional capacities.

I/O psychology emerged as a recognizable subdiscipline of psychology during the early part of the 20th century with Münsterberg's work on personnel selection, Taylor's ideas about scientific management, and Scott's contributions to advertising. World War I and World War II brought dramatic growth in the areas of personnel testing and engineering psychology, respectively, and the Hawthorne studies focused attention on the importance of "human relations" in the workplace. More recently, I/O psychologists' willingness to revise their assumptions and adapt their procedures and techniques to dramatic changes in the workplace and society (for example, increased technological sophistication, greater demographic diversity among workers, important civil rights legislation) has built upon these past events to yield a science and profession more capable of promoting economic and personal well-being than ever before. We are excited and optimistic about what the future will bring.

CHAPTER 2

....

Methods and Procedures
of Industrial/Organizational Psychology

LEARNING POINTS

After studying this chapter (and its statistical appendix) you should

❑ understand the scientific method and be able to explain its advantages and disadvantages for I/O psychologists;

❑ be able to describe four ways to use numbers as measures of psychological variables;

❑ be able to explain the complementary strengths and weaknesses of experimental and observational research strategies, and of laboratory and field research sites;

❑ appreciate the (potential) contributions of meta-analysis to psychological research and theory;

❑ be familiar with some of the cross-cultural work being done by I/O psychologists;

❑ understand the ways in which professional ethical principles both support and challenge I/O psychologists' research and practice;

❑ understand the difference between descriptive and inferential statistics;

❑ be able to explain how descriptive statistics can be used either to describe or to misrepresent empirical data; and

❑ be able to describe what a correlation coefficient means, as well as what it doesn't mean.

IN THE PREVIOUS CHAPTER we alluded to the scientist-practitioner approach to I/O psychology. This perspective acknowledges the many ways that scientific research and theory can be translated into constructive practical applications in organizational settings, as well as the potential of day-to-day problems and issues in the workplace to stimulate informative model building and data collection. It also implicitly acknowledges that the explosion of research and theory in the field has made it virtually impossibile today for anyone to learn all there is to know about I/O psychology during a few years of formal undergraduate and graduate education. Students of the field are therefore encouraged (forced?) to learn how to go about discovering solutions to the many and varied problems they are bound to encounter whether they ultimately seek employment in a manufacturing or service organization, in a consulting firm, or in an academic institution.

By far the most widely accepted empirical approach to answering questions is the **scientific method,** which has been broadly described as "a set of attitudes and some general rules for gathering information . . . all of which are aimed at maximizing the objectivity of reported findings" (Howell & Dipboye, 1986, p. 2). A series of steps summarizes the scientific method. The researcher

1. selects or identifies an area of inquiry and formulates a problem to be studied;

2. advances a tentative solution to the problem (a hypothesis) based either on previous research or anecdotal experience;

3. collects data or information relevant to the hypothesis; and

4. tests the hypothesis by confronting it with the empirical data (often through the use of statistical analyses).

If the data tend to support the hypothesis, the researcher may

5. specify the extent to which the hypothesis can be generalized to other situations;

6. make predictions about solutions to similar problems; and

7. integrate the hypothesis into an existing theory, or develop a theory around the hypothesis that can contribute to further explanation of the problem identified and the solution suggested by the data (McGuigan, 1978).

Of course, if the data do not support the hypothesis, the researcher, using the procedure summarized above, should formulate alternative explanations that lend themselves to confirmation or refutation.

Explanations based on this approach rely upon "empirical fact rather than speculation, [on] objective data rather than opinion, faith, anecdote, or pure logic" (Howell & Dipboye, 1986, p. 2). More specifically, the scientific method has several important characteristics:

1. *Self-correcting.* Checks are built in all along the way to obtain scientific knowledge.

2. *Empirical.* Beliefs, attitudes, and perceptions are carefully verified against objective reality.

3. *Open to public inspection.* Other qualified researchers can replicate scientific procedures and compare their results to the hypothesis under investigation.

4. *Objective and statistically based.* Data are collected in a relatively unbiased fashion, and results are accepted with specified levels of confidence.

5. *Controlled and systematic.* Researchers strive to systematically rule out alternative hypotheses or explanations for the results they obtain.

Further, the scientific method serves several purposes (see Box 2.1).

No one who has benefited from the wonders of modern medicine or witnessed the launching of a space shuttle (two examples

---

BOX 2.1 What the Scientific Method Does

- *Tests hypotheses.* Tentative propositions about the relationships among various phenomena are evaluated in the light of empirical observations.

- *Generates theories.* Conceptual frameworks for organizing and explaining empirical observations can also suggest new hypotheses and guide future research.

- *Facilitates explanation, understanding, prediction, and change.* Only through explanation and understanding can I/O psychologists hope to solve organizational problems efficiently and appropriately.

SOURCE: Adapted from *Organizational Behavior and Personnel Psychology*, by K. N. Wexley and G. A. Yukl. Copyright 1984 by Richard D. Irwin, Inc. Reprinted by permission.

among many) can reasonably doubt the power of scientific methodology and research to unravel nature's secrets or overcome its apparent limitations and restrictions. Nevertheless, I/O psychologists' *applied* research efforts might progress more rapidly if we acknowledge that the traditional scientific method often ignores some of the harsh realities encountered in ongoing organizational settings (Boehm, 1980). Figure 2.1 juxtaposes the scientific method (on the left) and Boehm's suggested alternative model of the research process within organizations (on the right). As you can see, Boehm's alternative model includes several processes not found in the traditional scientific method (such as analyzing organizational contexts and restraints), describes more numerous and complex interactions among the processes, and emphasizes organizations' needs to solve ongoing or anticipated performance or productivity problems.

Boehm (1980) observed that I/O psychologists' allegiance to the traditional scientific method has limited our progress in four specific ways:

1. The scientific community has ignored large amounts of real-world research because of its apparent methodological impurities.

2. Organizations have ignored much academic (traditional) research because it appears to overlook practitioners' real-world concerns and limitations and is therefore deemed impractical.

3. Organizational research has been restricted to the areas of inquiry and problems that *do* conform to the assumptions and requirements of the traditional scientific model, and very important topics (such as the relationship between staffing procedures and workers' productivity and satisfaction) have been avoided because such research is scientifically "messy."

4. Many advantages of conducting real-world research in organizational settings have remained unrecognized.

She concluded that the traditional scientific method and her alternative approach to organizational research are *not* contradictory. Rather, they complement each other with respect to their basic orientations, their appropriate topics of inquiry, their research designs, their use of samples of individuals, and their interpretations of results. Her closing remarks said it best:

> Organizations do not exist primarily as research laboratories for behavioral scientists. If this basic fact of life is recognized and [an alternative model] . . . is accepted as being equally legitimate as the [traditional scientific] model . . . , there are exciting possibilities for the advancement of I/O psychology. . . . If, however, I/O psychologists continue to adhere solely to a model based on the ideal, in which organizational realities are viewed solely as problems to be circumvented, stagnation of the field is a strong possibility, and widening of the communications gap between academic and organizational I/O psychologists a virtual certainty. (pp. 502–503)

We endorse an eclectic methodological orientation that acknowledges the value of the traditional scientific method of doing research but recognizes its limitations and the viability of alternative methodologies (Goodman & Kruger, 1988). We also suggest that psychological research (including that of I/O psychologists) is considerably more biased and value-laden than Wexley and Yukl (1984) indicated. Attempts to understand behavior do *not* occur in a vacuum. Existing cultural and professional values provide contexts for psychologists' research endeavors, and these factors can (and do!) influence both the kinds of questions we set out to answer and the ways in which we collect and analyze information. Thus, the scientific method is best construed as an ideal, a rather demanding standard to be imposed by and on I/O psychologists who hope to purge their work of *avoidable* biases and *un*necessary subjectivity. It should *not*, however, remain an altar upon which we sacrifice any and all research projects that do not (and perhaps *can*not) conform to that exacting standard.

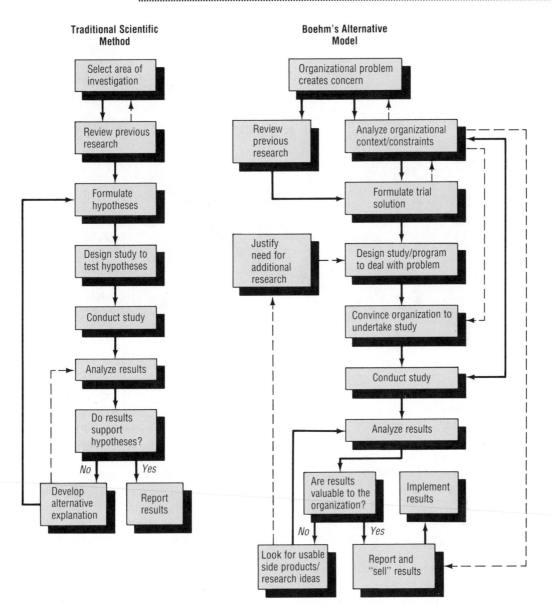

FIGURE 2.1
Alternative Research Models
Source: Adapted from "Research in the 'Real World'—A Conceptual Model," by V. R. Boehm, *Personnel Psychology*, *33*, 495–503. Copyright 1980 by Personnel Psychology. Adapted by permission.

Psychological Measurement

All research in psychology, whether it takes place in laboratories or in organizations, depends upon measurement of the events or phenomena of interest. Measurement is nothing more than the application of rules for assigning numbers to relevant attributes or properties of the things or events we observe (Young, 1984). Sometimes

The meaning of these numbers depends on the measurement scale used.

these attributes or properties are qualitative in nature (differing in *kind,* such as religious affiliations or organizational departments), and sometimes they are quantitative (differing in *amount,* such as years of experience on a job or dollar value of merchandise sold). It is important to recognize, however, that the numbers we assign to attributes of things or events cannot always be interpreted in the same fashion. In fact, psychologists rely upon four kinds of measurement scales that correspond to four ways we can use numbers to convey information about things and events (Stevens, 1946, 1951).

The most basic approach is to use numbers simply to identify or name things (people, events, and the like). Examples of this approach are the numbers that appear on athletes' uniforms, or using the numbers "1," "2," and "3" to code (for subsequent computer analyses) the religious affiliations of Jews, Catholics, and Protestants, respectively. Numbers used in this way convey *none* of the information we typically expect from them. We do not expect the

baseball player with a "4" on his uniform to be either twice as skilled as the one who wears a "2" or only half as valuable to the team as the player who wears an "8." Similarly, we do not assume that Catholics (if coded "2" for purposes of our analysis) are twice as religious as Jews (coded "1") or any less devout than Protestants (coded "3"). After all, these numbers (like the numbers on athletes' uniforms) are assigned more or less arbitrarily. We could just as easily have coded Catholics "1," Protestants "2," and Jews "3" (or, for that matter, Catholics "23," Protestants "−13," and Jews "476"). Numbers used in this way, assigned arbitrarily and serving no other purpose than to *name* or *identify* people or phenomena of interest, constitute what Stevens (1946, 1951) called a **nominal** scale of measurement.

Numbers convey a bit more information when we use them to order or rank a set of people, events, or things along a continuum or dimension. For example, if a supervisor rank orders workers based on her perceptions of the quality of their work by designating Ms. Smith "1," Mr. Jones "2," and Ms. Kelly "3," the numbers go beyond merely naming the subordinates; they reflect the supervisor's opinion that Smith is a better worker than Jones, who in turn is a superior employee to Kelly. Numbers used in this way, to show which persons or events have *more or less* of some attribute or property than other persons or events, reflect an **ordinal** scale of measurement (Stevens, 1946, 1951).

Although the supervisor's rankings in the example given above reveal that Smith is better than Jones, who is better than Kelly, the numbers do not tell us *how much* Smith excels over Jones or how superior Jones is to Kelly. The same set of ranks can describe many possibilities. Smith might be enormously superior to Jones, who is only slightly better than Kelly; alternatively, Smith could be only marginally better than Jones, who is far superior to Kelly; or, the difference between the quality of Smith's and Jones' work might be very similar to the difference between that of Jones and of Kelly. Ordinal measures, then, reveal nothing about the size(s) of the intervals that separate people, events, or things on a continuum or dimension. Now consider the numbers etched on a Fahrenheit or Celsius (centigrade) thermometer designed to measure the amount of heat in the atmosphere. You know that the amount of additional thermal energy necessary to raise the temperature from, say, 10 degrees to 15 degrees is exactly the same as the amount of additional heat required to raise it from 15 degrees to 20 degrees. This is so because successive numbers on these scales are designed to reflect *equal increments* in temperature. Numbers used in this way, when the differences or "distances" between successive numbers are assumed to reflect equal amounts of the property or attribute being measured, constitute an **interval** scale of measurement (Stevens, 1946, 1951).

We trust you will agree that interval-scale measures convey almost all of the information we typically expect from numbers. The only unusual property of interval-scale numbers is that

the number zero (0) cannot be assumed to reflect a complete absence of whatever attribute is being measured. Reconsider the Fahrenheit and Celsius temperature scales. Zero degrees on either of these does *not* mean that the atmosphere is totally devoid of heat. Zero, in these cases, is nothing more than a number that lies precisely halfway between two other numbers, -1 and $+1$. "So what?" you ask. Well, an important implication of this fact is that we cannot declare with any accuracy that Monday, when the temperature reached a high of 20 degrees, was twice as warm as Tuesday, when the thermometer rose to only 10 degrees. That is, the amount of thermal energy in the air on the first day was not two times greater than the amount on the following day.

Assessing thermal energy with a Kelvin temperature scale, however, is entirely different. In this case, zero degrees *does* reflect a total absence of heat. Consequently, an environment that registers 300 degrees Kelvin *is* twice as warm as one that reads 150 degrees Kelvin. A similar situation involves comparing the weights of objects. We can quite properly say that a carton weighing 4 kilograms is twice as heavy as one weighing 2 kilograms. This is so because an "object" that weighs zero (0) kilograms is, in fact, weightless. Numbers used in such a way that the intervals between successive numerals reflect equal increments in whatever is being measured and the number zero (0) reflects a complete absence of whatever is being assessed reflect a **ratio** scale of measurement (Stevens, 1946, 1951). You can see that as we move from nominal measures through ordinal, interval, and finally ratio measures, we introduce additional properties of numbers with each new scale. These incremental pieces of information reflect magnitude, equal intervals, and absolute zero (Kaplan & Saccuzzo, 1982).

I/O psychologists use all four of these measurement scales in the process of conducting their research on work-related behaviors. Nominal scales are used to code not only religious preferences but also sex (for example,

"1" = men, "2" = women), work organization (for example, "1" = Peter's Pan Pizza, Inc.; "2" = IBM; "3" = General Electric) or occupational type (for example, "1" = clerical; "2" = managerial; "3" = unskilled), to name but a few possibilities. In addition to supervisors' rank orderings of subordinates' work performance, we might use ordinal scales to indicate the relative difficulties of several different tasks, or employees' relative preferences for different kinds of benefits (for example, medical insurance, stock options, vacation days). When we use questionnaires to measure workers' levels of job satisfaction or to assess applicants' levels of intelligence or motivation, we usually assume we are dealing with interval measures. (Although an applicant who obtains a score of zero (0) on our intelligence test is unlikely to win any Nobel Prizes in the near future, we *cannot* assume that person is totally lacking in intellectual capacity.) Finally, if we evaluate workers' levels of performance by counting the numbers of units they produce on the factory floor or noting the value in dollars (or yen, or marks) of the sales they generate, we are using a ratio-measurement scale.

Research Strategies

A variety of approaches are available to I/O psychologists who conduct research in an effort to understand women's and men's work-related behaviors. We can conceptually organize these approaches with the help of two dichotomies. First, we can distinguish between *experimental* and *observational* approaches to research; second, we can distinguish between research that is conducted within a *laboratory* and inquiries that are pursued outside the confines of a lab. The latter setting is usually referred to as the *"field."*

Experimental Versus Observational Procedures

The hallmark of experimental research is control. The researcher strives to manipulate certain conditions in a systematic fashion, and then obtains measures to determine whether the manipulations had any influence(s) on a second set of conditions. For example, an I/O psychologist might encourage one group of workers to set their own productivity goals, and then impose those same goals on a second group of workers to determine whether the two groups' subsequent levels of productivity reveal any differences. The set of conditions manipulated by the researcher (self-set versus externally imposed productivity goals, in this example) is known as the **independent variable.** The set of circumstances subsequently examined and measured for the purpose of identifying any changes (the two work groups' levels of productivity, in this example) is the **dependent variable.** If the *only* difference between the two work groups in our example was, in fact, that one group was permitted to set its own performance goals and the other had its goals set for it, any discrepancies in the two groups' subsequent levels of productivity could reasonably be attributed to this difference in goal setting. That is, the researcher could deduce that the discrepancy in the groups' productivity levels *must* have been caused by the different goal-setting conditions because everything else about the two work groups and their situations was identical or strictly controlled. This is the major advantage of doing experimental research.

Unfortunately, it is usually very difficult (and sometimes impossible) to create two or more experimental groups that are identical in every way except for the independent variable manipulated by the researcher. In the example given above, the workers in one of the groups may have been (on the average) more intelligent or more experienced, or may have been assigned to easier tasks than those in the other group. If any of these (or any other) differences coexisted with the manipulated difference (method of setting work goals), the subsequent discrepancy in the two groups' levels of productivity could have been due to one or more of these *un*controlled group differences rather than to the manipulated independent variable. Such bothersome possibilities are usually referred to as **confounding** or **contaminating variables** because they contaminate the purity of the otherwise controlled experiment, and thereby confound researchers who would like to draw cause-and-effect conclusions about the variables under investigation. Not surprisingly, experimental researchers typically take steps to control or eliminate as many contaminating variables as possible.

One way to achieve such control is through a procedure known as **random assignment** of subjects to groups. If every subject who participates in a study has an equal chance of being assigned to any of the experimental groups, whatever differences exist among the subjects should be distributed more or less evenly across all groups. Thus, there would be no reason to expect that the subjects in one group would be (on average) any more intelligent or less experienced than the subjects in another group. On the contrary, there would be every reason to anticipate that the average levels of intelligence and experience (and other potentially confounding variables) within the experimental groups would be essentially the same. If they *are* similar, subsequent discrepancies in dependent variables cannot reasonably be attributed to anything other than the manipulated differences in the independent variable. Random assignment works best when experimental groups are large.

An alternative procedure for controlling potential confounds when the numbers of subjects to be assigned to experimental groups are relatively small is known as **matching.** In this case, the researcher ensures that subjects assigned to one group are "matched" by very similar (ideally, identical) subjects assigned to the other group(s). This process could, for example, result in groups that contain the same ratios of women to men, of more experienced to less experienced workers, of more intelligent to less intelligent workers, of younger to older workers, and so forth. Once again, the resulting experimental

groups will be similar in every way except for their status on the manipulated independent variable. Therefore, any subsequent difference(s) in the dependent variable cannot reasonably be attributed to anything other than this manipulated difference, and the researcher is on relatively solid ground drawing cause-and-effect conclusions about the independent and dependent variables. Of course, this matching procedure is effective only to the extent that the researcher can anticipate most (ideally, all) of the potentially contaminating variables.

Although observational research procedures also confront researchers with certain challenges (Mitchell, 1985), they are generally simpler to implement than experimental procedures because the researcher is under no obligation to manipulate anything, and control of potential confounds can often be accomplished through statistical analyses. We merely observe and record (measure) the events or variables of interest and submit the resulting data to one or more statistical procedures designed to reveal any relationships that might exist among those events or variables. The observational approach is sometimes referred to as **correlational** research because a particular statistic, the correlation coefficient, often plays a central role in the statistical procedures. (A brief introduction to statistical analyses in general, and to the correlation coefficient in particular, is provided in an appendix to this chapter.)

The fact that observational research involves no manipulation has several important implications. The "good news" is that this strategy can be very convenient and inexpensive compared to experimental strategies, especially when large amounts of data must be collected. Observational or correlational research is also useful when it is unethical for a researcher to manipulate a particular variable. For example, suppose we are interested in the relationship between our employees' levels of job performance during a specified time interval and the quality of their marriages or other intimate personal involvements. Obviously, it is unethical to manipulate a worker's relationship with his or her spouse or loved one. It is not unethical, however, to ask employees to respond voluntarily to a questionnaire that yields a numerical index of marital satisfaction. (It may be obnoxious, perhaps, but it isn't unethical.) We can then compare those data with job-performance information to determine whether the two variables are related in any way.

As you might expect, the good news (convenience, cost effectiveness, and avoidance of some ethical problems) that comes with observational research techniques must share its headlines with some "bad news." Because no variables are systematically manipulated or controlled, it is very difficult (some say impossible) to ascertain from correlational research which variable is a "cause" and which an "effect," or even if there is any causal relationship at all. In the example above, suppose we discover that workers with happy marriages tend to receive higher performance ratings from their supervisors than do employees who are less satisfied with their spouses. What's the cause and what's the effect? Perhaps a happy marriage causes workers to perform better on their jobs (because they can concentrate better on their work tasks?), and an unhappy marriage causes workers to perform poorly (because they are distracted or angry?). Or, perhaps employees' happy marriages result from their exemplary job performance (because better performance results in higher pay, which translates into happier marriages?), and poor job performance may lead to less happy marriages (because poor performance leads to anxiety about job security, which, in turn, leads to unpleasant or even abusive behavior at home?). And if these possibilities aren't sufficiently confusing, a third alternative exists. Perhaps both variables— marital satisfaction and job-performance level—are caused by a third variable that we haven't even thought to measure. In this case, perhaps the levels of our employees' interpersonal skills are responsible for both the states of their marriages (better communication skills im-

prove the quality of marriages?) and their levels of work performance (especially if one's job involves communicating with others).

Fortunately, the advantages and disadvantages of experimental and observational research strategies often (but not always) complement each other. For example, we might use an observational approach to collect data from all our employees that can reveal existing relationships between variables of interest, such as workers' levels of satisfaction with their physical work environment and their levels of job performance. If such a relationship emerges, we might then design a controlled experiment to determine which variable (if either) is the cause and which is the effect. (On the other hand, if we use an observational approach to study the relationship between marital satisfaction and job performance, as in our example above, ethical concerns would still inhibit the design of any experiment that manipulated or controlled workers' satisfaction with their spouses.) Conversely, we might discover in the course of an experiment with two groups of employees that openly friendly behavior from a supervisor tends to result in better work performance than does more formal or unfriendly behavior. We might then conduct a larger observational study to determine whether a similar relationship exists in all (or many) of the other work groups that make up our organization. We hope you can appreciate that in both of these cases, a combination of experimental and observational research strategies can provide us with more comprehensive and more satisfying answers to the question at hand than can either approach used by itself.

Laboratory Versus Field Research

The distinction between laboratory and field research refers to the setting where we conduct research. Investigations conducted in settings specifically created for the purpose of doing research are typically referred to as "lab studies." Of course, an I/O psychologist's "laboratory" may consist of nothing more than a room containing a table and a few chairs (or, for that matter, an entirely empty room). Field studies are investigations that take place in settings that have *not* been created for research purposes. The "field" for I/O psychologists is typically an actual workplace or organization where the emphasis is on producing a product or providing a service. Usually, the ultimate goal is to make a profit rather than to provide opportunities for research psychologists to collect data.

Review and Evaluation of Research Strategies

No necessary or explicit relationships exist between the way one designs and conducts research (experimental versus observational studies) and the setting (laboratory versus field) in which one implements the procedure. We can manipulate and control variables in a lab or in the field, just as we can simply observe and record data in a realistic environment (the field) or an artificial one (the lab). However, just as experimental and observational strategies have complementary advantages and disadvantages, so too do laboratory and field settings; and the two sets of complementary strengths and weaknesses are sometimes *implicitly* associated with each other. For example, because a laboratory setting is defined as one that has been created for the specific purpose of conducting scientific investigations, it should come as no surprise that careful experimental control over independent and contaminating variables and precise measurement of independent and dependent variables are more easily accomplished in a lab than in the field. Alternatively, an I/O psychologist who wants to take advantage of the observational strategy's potential to handle large amounts of information about many people or events will be able to gain access to large samples more quickly and conveniently in the field than in a laboratory. Nevertheless, experiments *can* be conducted in the field, and observational studies *can* be conducted in a laboratory setting.

I/O psychologists and other applied social scientists have long debated the premise that field settings, because they are "natural," predictably permit researchers to generalize their findings to a greater extent than do laboratory settings, which are contrived and therefore "artificial." In this context, **generalization** involves making inferences about qualitatively *different* groups of people in different social or organizational settings, based on specific behaviors of a (usually) smaller sample of people in a particular situation. Can we reasonably expect other people in other settings to behave similarly to those we have observed during the course of our research? This debate is far from over.

A survey of several professional journals in which I/O psychologists publish their research led to the conclusion that field research, rather than being more conducive to generalization than laboratory research, tends to deal with rather narrow and limited subsets of organizational settings, subjects (workers), and behaviors, and that the greater generalizability of field research is therefore a myth (Dipboye & Flanagan, 1979). It was found that laboratory studies tended to suffer from the same weaknesses, but data based on lab studies were *not* decidedly less generalizable than data obtained during field research. In a subsequent article, the same authors further polished the somewhat tarnished image of lab research by concluding that (1) laboratory research in I/O psychology is *not* unusual, (2) researchers in applied fields do, in fact, publish lab studies, and (3) field research does *not* tend to be, on the whole, more "applied" than lab research.

Others have disagreed, reminding us not to confuse generalizability (to possibly dissimilar groups of subjects) with *representativeness* (Bass & Firestone, 1980). **Representativeness** refers to the *similarity* of the people, settings, and behaviors we study to the people, settings, and behaviors about which we would like to make inferences. A lack of representativeness does *not* preclude the possibility of generalization any more than the occurrence of representativeness guarantees generalizability. The *meaning* that research subjects attach to their behaviors and their surroundings influences generalizability to a far greater extent than does demographic representativeness (similarity of personal characteristics such as sex, age, and level of formal education, for example) or the apparent lack of realism that characterizes the research setting (Berkowitz & Donnerstein, 1982). No one would suggest that college students, who serve as subjects in much I/O psychological research, are representative of nonstudent populations of (older) women and men who hold full-time jobs. The legitimacy of generalizing results obtained from student samples to nonstudent groups probably depends on numerous factors. In any case, it has yet to be resolved (Gordon, Slade, & Schmitt, 1986, 1987; Greenberg, 1987).

Some of the published critiques of laboratory research reveal a serious misunderstanding of the purposes and limitations of such studies (Berkowitz & Donnerstein, 1982; Mook, 1983). Laboratory research is ideally suited to empirical inquiries about what *can* occur under specified circumstances. Lab studies are *not* appropriate for investigating what actually *does* or *will* occur in a given situation. More specifically, laboratory research allows us to (1) ask whether something *can* happen (rather than whether it *does* happen); (2) determine whether something that *ought* to happen under certain circumstances, based on an existing theory or model of behavior, does in fact happen; and (3) test the power or robustness of a behavior or event by demonstrating that it can happen even in an unnatural, artificial (laboratory) context that might be expected to preclude it (Mook, 1983). In short, field studies are not necessarily preferable to lab studies; it all depends upon what the researcher wants to know.

Examples of Specific Research Strategies

Although a lengthy, comprehensive list of alternative research techniques and strategies is beyond the scope of this text, we think it appropriate at this point to provide you with several examples of specific research strategies available to I/O psychologists who study women's and men's work-related behaviors.

A Laboratory Experiment. In our earlier discussion of experimental and observational research procedures, we alluded to an experiment to investigate possible relationships between work groups' levels of productivity and the manner in which the groups' goals were determined (either by the groups themselves or by a supervisor or the researcher). A typical laboratory experiment would find an I/O psychologist forming work groups through random selection of workers from all departments and divisions throughout an organization. The manner in which each group's work goals were set would be carefully manipulated, and the researcher would obtain relatively precise measures of the groups' levels of productivity. Most likely, this would all take place away from the workers' actual work sites, perhaps within a suite of research rooms assigned to the I/O psychologist or in a work space specifically reserved for research or perhaps training purposes.

A Field Experiment. Our I/O psychologist might try to answer the same research question by collecting data from employees who remain at their work stations and continue to perform their jobs. A typical field experiment would entail assignment of employees to experimental groups so that they were matched with respect to sex, age, experience, and so on. Of course, a reasonable rationale for creating "new" work groups must be provided to participating employees and their supervisors. The I/O psychologist would then (1) manipulate, as carefully as possible, the manner in which each work group's productivity goals were set; (2) obtain, as accurately as possible, measures of each group's subsequent work performance; and (3) accomplish all this while minimally disrupting the work groups' actual tasks and regular work environments. As you can imagine, field experiments confront researchers with formidable challenges as they try to maintain sufficient control over independent and potentially contaminating variables to permit causal inferences based on the results of those experiments. Thus, field experiments are often reserved for situations when it is of prime importance to be able to generalize experimental results to workers' regular work behaviors and environments. When our interest is focused primarily on the *possibility* of a cause-and-effect relationship between two or more work-related variables, laboratory experiments are usually far more convenient than field experiments.

A Field Study. Field studies are similar to field experiments in that they take place in employees' normal work settings. They are not experiments, however, because the researcher exercises little or no control over the variables of interest. **Field studies** are observational procedures. An I/O psychologist might try to answer the research question highlighted in our examples so far by collecting productivity data from two or more *existing* work groups, as well as information concerning the manner(s) in which those groups' work goals had been set or assigned. Possible relationships between these variables could then be examined using correlational analyses. This observational approach is clearly much simpler to implement than either of the experimental strategies described above. Unfortunately, relinquishing control over the variables in question makes it very difficult (impossible, according to some) to draw any causal conclusions from the findings. Any variable or combination of variables, measured or unmeasured, might be causes or effects in any statistical relationships that emerge.

A Survey. Another observational strategy is available to the I/O psychologist interested in the relationship between the dynamics of goal assignment and work groups' subsequent levels of productivity. Typical surveys involve asking people questions about the variables under study. Questions can be asked in a face-to-face format, using the telephone, through traditional paper-and-pencil questionnaires, and (more recently) using electronic (computer) mail technology (Sproull, 1986). In this case we might ask

- How do you prefer to have your work goals determined?
- Do you work harder when you have set your own goals?
- How has your most effective supervisor determined your goals?

Employees' responses could then be statistically analyzed to shed some light on the research question of interest. The simplicity and convenience of this approach are obvious. It should be equally obvious, however, that we cannot infer anything about causes and effects from subjects' responses to these questions. An additional problem, of course, is that the responses may or may not accurately reflect employees' actual behaviors and beliefs.

A Simulation Study. A fifth research technique merits our attention, even though it is usually a special case of one of the four approaches described above. (This approach usually amounts to a "laboratory" experiment, although field experiments could possibly rely upon simulations.) A typical simulation study involves creation of an artificial work environment that is as similar to the actual work environment as our imaginations and our resources allow. The work environment that is approximated can be physical or technological (such as a flight simulator, which recreates the instrumentation found in an airplane cockpit), or it can be social and interpersonal (as when experimental subjects are asked to role-play or pretend that they hold given organizational positions or face particular sets of circumstances). Simulations permit researchers to exercise a great deal of control over independent and potentially contaminating variables, and are conducive to extremely precise measurement of responses. Nevertheless, to the extent that subjects perceive and respond to the *lack* of realism inherent (by definition) in any simulation, confident generalization of results to actual work settings can be undermined. Despite the fact that recent innovations in computer technology have rendered some simulators incredibly realistic (airplane cockpits and supertanker control rooms, for example), research subjects remain aware that "flying" into the side of a mountain or "ramming" a pier will not *really* cause millions of dollars in damages and perhaps result in their untimely demise.

Summing Up.   These specific examples support our earlier contention that the advantages and disadvantages of different research strategies can complement each other. Because this is so, I/O psychologists can combine them in ways that provide useful and appropriate answers to research questions as efficiently and conveniently as possible. For example, we might begin our investigation of possible relationships between work groups' productivity levels and the manner(s) in which their goals were assigned or determined by administering a written survey questionnaire to all (or a representative sample) of our employees. The survey data may reveal several existing work groups with very different perspectives on, and experiences with, setting work goals. A field study of these groups might then reveal that different levels of productivity do, in fact, seem to be associated with different procedures for setting work goals. We could then design a series of laboratory experiments to investigate more specific hypotheses about which aspects of goal assignment are responsible for which aspects of the groups' work performance (quantity, quality, and so forth).

Methodological Trends

Social scientists continue to develop new methodological procedures and approaches to advance understanding of human behavior. I/O psychologists are no exception. Two relatively recent innovations or trends in I/O psychologists' research are meta-analytic studies and cross-cultural investigations.

Meta-analysis.   For many years psychologists have tried to combine or integrate results obtained from multiple empirical studies of similar topics. Considered simultaneously in a systematic way, the wealth of data available in professional psychological journals should allow us to draw more general conclusions about human behavior with greater confidence. In fact, one of the periodicals published by the APA (*Psychological Bulletin*) is largely devoted to "review" articles intended to accomplish this purpose. Until recently, however, authors of these reviews were limited to reading as many relevant studies as they could find and then, through some totally subjective and completely idiosyncratic cognitive process, drawing general conclusions that seemed to make sense.

Although some reviewers still rely upon this basic approach, others have adopted **meta-analysis,** which consists of more systematic, more objective, and more statistically based procedures for combining and comparing results of studies conducted and reported by different researchers (Glass, 1976; Rosenthal, 1978; Walberg & Haertel, 1980). Many of these procedures depend upon descriptive statistics (for example, means, variances) discussed in the appendix to this chapter. I/O psychologists have applied meta-analytic techniques to a wide variety of topics all across their discipline, including leadership (Strube & Garcia, 1981; Vecchio, 1983), job classification (Cornelius, Schmidt, & Carron, 1984), and personnel selection (Hunter & Hunter, 1984; Schmidt & Hunter, 1984; Schmitt, Gooding, Noe, &

Busy organizations don't often lend themselves to the traditional scientific method.

Kirsch, 1984). When we discuss personnel selection issues in Chapter 6, we will examine meta-analysis in more detail under the heading of "validity generalization."

Cross-cultural Research.   A second trend apparent in the work of many social scientists, including I/O psychologists, reflects the obvious fact that human behavior is not confined within the borders of any single country, and that psychological research, theory, and practice must therefore transcend national, ethnic, and cultural boundaries. Once we acknowledge that people's environments can have important effects on their behaviors, it becomes clear that social scientists who ignore the cultures in which women and men live and work might thereby undermine the validity and usefulness of their research and practice. Given the rich cultural diversity to be found on this planet, it should be equally obvious that I/O psychologists who implement the scientist-practitioner

model in the United States or Canada cannot presume that the results of their research and the value of their recommendations will generalize to very different cultures and societies, such as those found in other parts of North America, in South America, in Asia, or in Africa. In fact, vast cultural differences *within* given national boundaries (Anglophones and Francophones in Canada; Asian, Hispanic, and African-Americans in the United States; and so on) should make us cautious even when we are willing to limit our generalizations to a given country. Numerous articles dealing with diverse cultures and societies have begun to appear in the professional literature. Within the pages of *The Industrial-Organizational Psychologist* (*TIP*), the quarterly newsletter published by SIOP, examples include a look at production sharing in Mexico (Dorfman & Howell, 1984), an examination of performance appraisal in Japan (Sekimoto, 1983), and discussions of I/O psychology in Egypt (Summers, 1984), in Germany (Wilpert, 1983) and in Switzerland (Dachler, 1983).

The remainder of this chapter is devoted to a discussion of ethical considerations that affect research and practice among I/O psychologists (and our colleagues in other psychological specialties). Just as we must acknowledge the impact of different social mores and cultural expectations on the meaning and value of our specific research findings and professional recommendations, so too must we accommodate certain ethical standards as we engage in the professional activities that lead to those findings and recommendations.

Professional Ethics

The word *ethics,* derived from the Greek *ēthos,* refers to character, custom, or usage (Reese & Fremouw, 1984). All I/O psychologists who belong to the APA, and many who do not, subscribe to two sets of evolving guidelines that are periodically published in the *American Psychologist.* One of these, entitled "Ethical Principles of Psychologists and Code of Conduct" (1992), lists six principles (A–F) and numerous standards (organized under eight major headings) derived from those principles that are intended to guide psychologists' research and practice in all specialty areas. As you examine these principles (summarized below) and standards (see Box 2.2), you will see that they are highly relevant and directly applicable to I/O psychologists' professional activities.

General Principles

A. Competence. Psychologists stay informed about contemporary scientific and professional developments, and recognize the limits of their competence and their techniques. They provide only those services for which their training and experience qualify them.

I/O psychologists recognize the importance of cross-cultural research.

B. Integrity. Psychologists are honest and fair, and respect others' rights and needs. They refrain from making false or misleading statements. They recognize the effects of their own values and needs on their professional activities. They clarify roles, and avoid harmful or improper dual relationships.

C. Professional and Scientific Responsibility. Psychologists accept responsibility for the consequences of their behaviors. They cooperate with other professionals and institutions in the best interests of their clients. Although they acknowledge the personal nature of their own moral standards and conduct, they are sensitive to their potential impact on the public's trust in

BOX 2.2 Ethical Standards Derived from APA Ethical Principles

1. *General Standards.* These pertain to applicability of the ethics code; the relationship of ethics and law; professional and scientific relationships; boundaries of competence; maintaining expertise; the basis for scientific and professional judgments; describing the nature and results of psychological services; human differences; respecting others; nondiscrimination; sexual and other types of harassment; personal problems and conflicts; avoiding harm; misuse of psychologists' influence and work; multiple and exploitive relationships; barter with clients; consultations and referrals; third-party requests for services; delegation to and supervision of subordinates; documentation of professional and scientific work; records and data; fees and financial arrangements; accuracy in reports to payers and funding sources; and referrals and fees.

2. *Evaluation, Assessment, and Intervention Standards.* These address evaluation, diagnosis, and interventions in professional contexts; competence and appropriate use of assessment and interventions; test construction; use of assessment in general and with special populations; interpreting assessment results; unqualified persons; obsolete tests and outdated test results; test scoring and interpretation services; explaining assessment results; and maintaining test security.

3. *Advertising and Other Public Statements Standards.* These focus on definition of public statements; statements by others; avoidance of false or deceptive statements; media presentations; testimonials; and in-person solicitation.

4. *Therapy Standards.* These concern structuring the (therapeutic) relationship; informed consent to therapy; couple and family relationships; providing mental health services to those served by others; sexual intimacies with current patients or clients; therapy with former sexual partners; sexual intimacies with former therapy patients; interruption of services; and terminating the professional relationship.

5. *Privacy and Confidentiality Standards.* These deal with discussing the limits of confidentiality; maintaining confidentiality; minimizing intrusions on privacy; maintenance of records; disclosures; consultations; confidential information in databases; use of confidential information for didactic or other purposes; preserving records and data; ownership of records and data; and withholding records for nonpayment.

6. *Teaching, Training Supervision, Research, and Publishing Standards.* These speak to the design and description of education and training programs; accuracy and objectivity in teaching; limitation on teaching; assessing student and supervisee performance; planning research; responsibility; compliance with law and standards; institutional approval; informed consent to research; dispensing with informed consent; informed consent in research filming or recording; offering inducements to research participants; deception in research; sharing and utilizing data; minimizing invasiveness; providing participants with information about the study; honoring commitments; care and use of animals in research; reporting of results; plagiarism; publication credit; duplicate publication of data; and professional reviewers.

7. *Forensic Activities Standards.* These concern professionalism; forensic assessments; clarification of role; truthfulness and candor; prior relationships; and compliance with law and rules.

8. *Resolving Ethical Issues Standards.* Of interest here are familiarity with ethics code; confronting ethical issues; conflicts between ethics and organizational demands; informal resolution of ethical violations; reporting ethical violations; cooperating with ethics committees; and improper complaints.

SOURCE: From "Ethical Principles of Psychologists and Code of Conduct," *American Psychologist, 47,* 1597–1611. Copyright 1992 by the American Psychological Association. Adapted by permission.

psychologists and psychology. When necessary, they consult with their colleagues in order to prevent or avoid unethical scientific or professional conduct.

D. Respect for People's Rights and Dignity.

Psychologists respect individuals' rights to privacy, confidentiality, self-determination, and autonomy. They are sensitive to cultural, individual, and role differences (for example, age, gender, race, ethnicity, religion, sexual orientation), and strive to eliminate any biases in their work based on these factors.

E. Concern for Others' Welfare.

Psychologists are sensitive to differences in power between themselves and others, and refrain from exploiting or misleading others in the context of professional relationships. They weigh the welfare of animal research subjects.

F. Social Responsibility.

Psychologists share their knowledge in order to contribute to human welfare, and attempt to prevent misuse of their work. They obey the law, and are encouraged to contribute some professional time for little or no personal compensation.

Specialty Guidelines for I/O Psychologists

A second document, "Specialty Guidelines for the Delivery of Services by Industrial/Organizational Psychologists" (1981), supplements the *Standards for Providers of Psychological Services* adopted by the APA in 1974 (subsequently revised) and directly addresses I/O psychologists' concerns. After rather precise definitions of the background necessary to become a fully qualified I/O psychologist and of the nature of I/O psychological services, the document sets out and elaborates on three guidelines intended to regulate the profession and protect the public interest (see Box 2.3).

A growing body of literature confirms that psychologists are serious about implementing these principles and guidelines. Thoughtful ethi-

cal discussions of testing and assessment (London & Bray, 1980; Messick, 1980) along with empirical investigations of perceived invasions of privacy (Fusilier & Hoyer, 1980; Stone, Gueutal, Gardner, & McClure, 1983; Tolchinsky, McCuddy, Adams, Ganster, Woodman, & Fromkin, 1981) are appearing regularly in professional journals. Psychologists' collaboration with managers' potentially "antiunion" efforts to control the work force has been addressed (Ronan, 1980), and has led to recommendations that I/O psychologists ensure that (1) psychological interventions are not intended as antiunion activities; (2) workers are fully informed about interventions and their implications; (3) economic benefits that ensue from interventions are equitably shared with workers; and (4) workers can opt out of any experiment or research procedure without prejudice or reprisals.

Recent research suggests that ethical standards evolve from a variety of sources, including societal norms and organization-specific factors (Victor & Cullen, 1988). Sometimes the multiple ethical norms that underlie I/O psychologists' activities come into conflict. We should confront such conflicts openly and honestly. A possible solution to this dilemma is to develop specific guidelines with specific clients in the context of specific projects (Mirvis & Seashore, 1979, 1980). There are, of course, dangers inherent in "negotiating" ethical principles with clients. Recognizing these, some writers insist that certain minimum standards must always prevail, such as setting realistic expectations and protecting people's privacy, esteem, and freedom (Walter & Pinder, 1980). Given the complexities of organizational research and practice, we suggest that identification and mutual acceptance of ethical guidelines in the context of a specific professional relationship better accommodates the dilemmas that confront I/O psychologists. The potentially negative consequences of automatically imposing the psychologist's (or anyone's) absolute, inflexible standards of behavior on a client organization probably outweigh the dangers of negotiated

> **BOX 2.3 Specialty Guidelines for I/O Psychologists**
>
> GUIDELINE 1: *Providers.* I/O psychologists keep up to date on scientific and professional developments, limit their practice to demonstrated areas of competence, and strive to develop innovative procedures and theory within their discipline.
>
> GUIDELINE 2: *Professional Considerations.* This guideline speaks to the issue of protecting the user of one's services, and to planning organizational goals. With regard to the former, I/O psychologists support the legal and civil rights of those who use their services, they abide by relevant APA policies, and they keep informed of relevant statutes, regulations, and legal precedents established by federal, state, and local governments. As to the latter, I/O psychologists explicitly state what can and cannot be reasonably expected from their services, they do not try to gain any competitive advantage through the use of privileged information, they carefully coordinate their activities with those of other professionals involved in the same project, and they systematically protect the confidentiality of their records.
>
> GUIDELINE 3: *Accountability.* Guided primarily by the principle of promoting human welfare, I/O psychologists' services should be subjected to periodic, systematic, and effective evaluations.
>
> SOURCE: From "Specialty Guidelines for the Delivery of Services by Industrial/Organizational Psychologists," *American Psychologist, 36,* 664–669. Copyright 1981 by the American Psychological Association. Adapted by permission.

ethical principles. This assumes, of course, that organizational representatives are sufficiently astute and assertive to protect their employees' rights and welfare, and that the I/O psychologist accepts in principle the basic professional guidelines listed above.

I/O psychologists who are employed by a single organization confront somewhat different ethical challenges than do their colleagues who work for consulting firms or engage in independent consulting activities. For example, those who work in a single organization can develop or "negotiate" a fairly stable set of expectations with the employer. This contrasts markedly with consultants who offer services to a variety of clients and are therefore continually challenged to establish ethical professional relationships with diverse organizations. Balancing the scales, I/O psychologists in the former group, because they serve and depend upon only one organization for their livelihoods, run a greater risk of allowing their organizational loyalties to conflict with and perhaps overrule their professional standards. Consultants' professional relationships are usually more transient, so they are less likely to succumb to such temptations. Regardless of the particular circumstances surrounding an I/O psychologist's professional activities, however, the responsibility to integrate generally accepted ethical principles and guidelines with sound research and practice prevails. Ethical considerations do not supplement professional research and practice; they lie at the very heart of these endeavors.

Chapter Summary

While pledging allegiance to the traditional scientific method, I/O psychologists must often be flexible in their pursuit of the scientist-practitioner model. They can adopt either experimental or observational research strategies, and sometimes both, as they generate measures of work-related behavior with nominal, ordinal, interval, or ratio scale properties. Whether they collect data in a laboratory or in "the field," they rely upon descriptive statistics to summarize the data, and inferential statistics to draw conclusions from known samples to larger populations of individuals (see the appendix to this chapter). Contemporary trends in I/O psychologists' methods include meta-analysis and cross-cultural research and practice. Ethical principles and guidelines, intended to protect the dignity and welfare of the women and men whose behavior is the focus of our research and practice, are matters of continued importance and concern.

Review Questions and Exercises

1. When is zero not zero in psychological measurements?

2. Design a research strategy to investigate the relationship between college professors' teaching styles and their effectiveness as instructors. Explain the rationales for each of your choices or decisions.

3. Describe three different ways to "lie with statistics."

4. Is it ethical for an I/O psychologist to collect data on workers' behaviors if the workers are not aware that they are "participating" in a research project?

Statistical Appendix

AFTER USING ONE OR MORE of the specific research techniques described in this chapter to collect empirical data pertaining to a research question, I/O psychologists typically rely upon certain arithmetic procedures to determine how the data answer the question. Those procedures are statistical analyses. Because this is *not* a statistics textbook, we will refrain from torturing you with complex laws of probability or arcane statistical formulas. Instead, we intend only to acquaint (or perhaps reacquaint) you with a few concepts and formulas that can help you become an informed consumer of the psychological research presented throughout this textbook.

A useful distinction to make at the outset is that between descriptive statistics and inferential statistics. As the label implies, **descriptive statistics** serve to describe or summarize sets of empirical data. Some scholars contend that summarization of evidence (as opposed to "establishing facts") is the primary role of statistical analyses (Rosenthal & Rubin, 1985). Descriptive statistics also constitute the "raw materials" for **inferential statistics,** which help us determine whether the data we obtain from a sample of individuals or events can be generalized to draw conclusions about larger populations of people or events.

Descriptive Statistics

After the I/O psychologist collects data pertaining to a given variable from a sample of people or events, the next task is to discern the meaning(s) of the data. Suppose we obtain a single measure of job performance for each of 15 employees. Specifically, suppose we ask each worker's supervisor to evaluate him or her on a 7-point rating scale, where "7" indicates outstanding job performance and "1" reflects totally unsatisfactory work performance. (In Chapter 4 we'll explain why this would *not* be a particularly good measure of job performance.) The hypothetical ratings for the 15 employees are presented in Table 2.1.

Although the table contains data for a relatively small number of people, it is still rather difficult to get an impression of how well or how poorly the employees are performing their jobs simply by scanning the raw numbers. Imagine how hard it would be to examine a much larger column of numbers (job-performance scores for *all* employees in a multinational organization, for example) and make any sense of them! Here is where descriptive statistics are useful. The data in Table 2.1 are presented in a more easily interpretable fashion in Figure 2.1. The bar graph (sometimes called a **histogram**) shows us the numbers of employees

TABLE 2.1 Custodians' Job-Performance Scores

Name	Score
Adams, Kermit	4
Baker, Cindy	5
Cato, Amy	2
Davis, Ken	3
Ellis, Tom	4
Faber, Greg	6
Gray, Kathy	5
Houts, Vicky	3
Innes, Ray	6
Jones, Russ	4
Keck, Ruby	7
Lang, Jill	1
Martin, Debbie	3
Nash, Rick	5
Odle, Steve	4

who received each of the seven possible ratings on our measure of job performance. In other words, it shows how our data are distributed across all possible performance scores.

Two categories of descriptive statistics can also convey a mental picture of how a given set of data is distributed across all possible scores. These are commonly known as (1) indices of **central tendency,** which tell us which score in a distribution of scores is most "typical" for a given sample, and (2) indices of **variability** or dispersion, which describe the extent to which scores are concentrated or spread out around the most typical score.

Indices of Central Tendency

Three indices of central tendency that I/O psychologists use to identify the most typical score in a distribution of data are the arithmetic mean, the median, and the mode. The **arithmetic mean** is simply the average of all the scores, obtained by dividing their sum by the number of scores or data points in the distribution. The mean performance score for the data presented in Table 2.1 and Figure 2.1 is calculated as follows:

$$\overline{X} = \frac{\Sigma X}{N} = \frac{62}{15} = 4.13$$

where Σ indicates summation or addition, X indicates the scores to be added, and N indicates the number of scores to be summed.

The mean is the most frequently used index of central tendency because its meaning (sorry!) is easy to understand, and because it is most useful as "raw material" for subsequent analyses involving inferential statistics. You can see that the mean of 4.13 is a reasonable index of central tendency for our sample of 15 job-

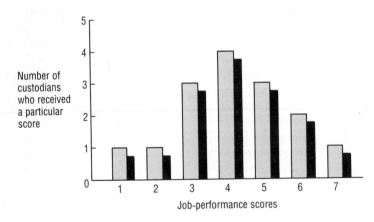

FIGURE 2.1
Histogram of Custodians' Job-Performance Scores

performance scores by referring to the histogram in Figure 2.1. (In fact, the value 4.13 is the "center of gravity" of this distribution of scores.) There are circumstances, however, where the mean is *not* a representative index of central tendency. Suppose that instead of the job-performance scores listed in Table 2.1, eight of the workers had received ratings of "7" and the other seven employees all received ratings of "1." The histogram for this (admittedly unusual) distribution of performance scores appears as Figure 2.2. Simple arithmetic will confirm that the mean of this modified distribution (63/15 = 4.20) is very similar to the mean of the original ratings displayed in Table 2.1 and Figure 2.1. For the modified data displayed in Figure 2.2, however, the mean (4.20) is a rather misleading index of central tendency because it isn't really typical of *any* of the scores in the distribution.

A more useful index of central tendency in unusual situations such as this is the **mode,** defined as the most frequently occurring score in a distribution. Truth be told, it would also be rather misleading to describe the data in Figure 2.2 by reporting a mode of "7," which misrepresents almost half of all the scores in the distribution. In this case, a more appropriate way to describe the central tendency of these scores is to acknowledge that the distribution is bimodal, that it has two modes, one at "7" and the other at "1."

Another set of circumstances where the mean is not the best index of central tendency appears in Figure 2.3. In this distribution of performance scores, 11 employees received ratings of either "1" or "2," and the remaining four workers received ratings of "7." The arithmetic mean in this case (46/15 = 3.07) is, once again, a somewhat misleading index of central tendency. After all, not a single employee actually received a rating of "3." In cases like this, when one or a few scores in a distribution (called "outliers") are notably larger or smaller than the main body of more or less contiguous scores, and these outliers cause the mean to fall

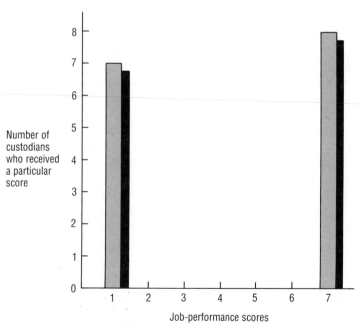

Number of custodians who received a particular score

Job-performance scores

FIGURE 2.2
Modified Histogram of Custodians' Job-Performance Scores

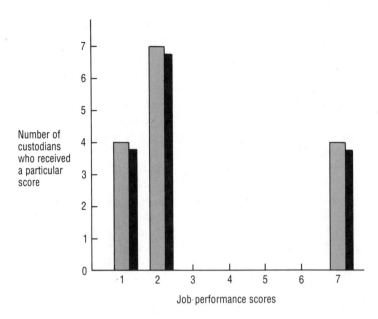

FIGURE 2.3
Another Modified Histogram of Custodians' Job-Performance Scores

above or below most of the scores in that distribution, the median is usually the most informative index of central tendency. The **median** score is defined as the value that, when all scores are listed in increasing or decreasing numerical order, separates the "top half" of the distribution of scores from the "bottom half." The median score for the data presented in Figure 2.3 is "2," which better represents the majority of the workers' performance ratings that fell toward the lower end of the distribution.

Summing Up. The mean, mode, and median are alternative descriptive statistics that can represent the most typical or representative score in a distribution of data points. None is necessarily the "right" or "wrong" index to use in a given situation. As our examples suggest, however, there are circumstances when one of them is perhaps more representative, or at least less misleading, than the others. We should also acknowledge that the type of measurement scale used can dictate the most appropriate index of

central tendency. Because it depends upon the arithmetic process of division, the mean is appropriate for ratio-scale and (except among the purists) interval-scale measures. A mean would be much less informative, however, if we used nominal-scale measures to reflect people's religious preference, for example. How would you interpret the phrase "average religious preference"? In this case the mode would be a more appropriate index of central tendency because it reflects the most common religious preference among a sample of individuals. In the event our distribution of data contains one or more extreme outliers, we might opt for the median as the most representative index of central tendency.

Indices of Dispersion or Variability

No matter how appropriate or representative a given index of central tendency may be, it will not be sufficient by itself to describe a distribution of numerical data unambiguously. Examine

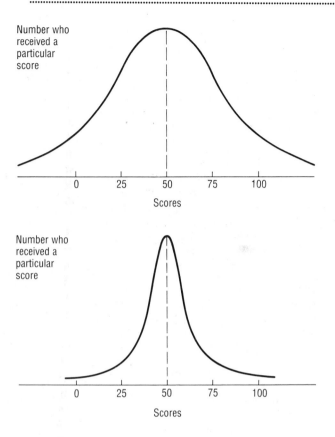

Number who received a particular score

Scores

Number who received a particular score

Scores

FIGURE 2.4
Two Frequency Distributions with Identical Means of 50 but Different Variabilities

the two distributions in Figure 2.4. Although they have identical means, these distributions are very dissimilar in the extent to which the scores or data points are spread out around that mean. A second category of descriptive statistics addresses this property of a distribution of numbers: indices of dispersion or variability. Two such indices are the range and the standard deviation. As we describe the latter, we will also discuss the concept of variance, which will come up again and again in chapters to follow. Understanding variance will also help you to understand the concept of standard deviation.

The **range** of a distribution of numbers is formally defined as the difference or numerical "distance" between the largest and smallest. Look at Table 2.1 again. The highest of these scores is "7" and the lowest is "1"; the difference between them is $7 - 1 = 6$ points on the rating scale. But you can readily see that there are *seven* different scores in this distribution. Thus, when we formally calculate the range of a distribution of numbers, we subtract the smallest number from the largest and then add 1. The range of the scores in Table 2.1, then, is $(7 - 1) + 1 = 7$. (We typically describe the range of a distribution of numbers simply by stating that the largest and smallest range from 1 to 7.)

Just as a mean can be unduly influenced by one or two extremely large or small scores, so too can the range be distorted by an outlier or two. Suppose, for example, that all the employees' ratings in Table 2.1 were "6" or "7" except for one, which was "1." The range would still be 7, but we think you'll agree that this is a somewhat misleading description of the dispersion that characterizes these ratings. After all, 14 of the 15 ratings are within a single point of one another on the scale. Although you won't encounter it very often, an alternative index known as the interquartile range can eliminate this shortcoming. The **interquartile range** is the difference or numerical distance between the score at the 75th percentile of the distribution (that is, the score that separates the highest quarter of the distribution from the lowest three quarters when the scores are arranged in numerically increasing or decreasing order) and the score at the 25th percentile (which separates the lowest quarter of the distribution from the highest three quarters). In other words, the interquartile range represents the numerical distance between the highest and lowest numbers in a distribution after disregarding 50% of that distribution, the highest and lowest quartiles.

An index of dispersion used far more frequently by I/O psychologists is the standard deviation. To understand this index better, however—both computationally and conceptually—we do well to begin by examining a closely related index, variance. A formula for calculating the **variance** of a distribution of numbers, usually symbolized s^2, is as follows:

$$s^2 = \frac{\Sigma(X - \overline{X})^2}{N}$$

where Σ indicates summation or addition, X indicates the individual scores in the distribution, $\overline{X}$ indicates the mean of the scores in the distribution, and N indicates the number of scores in the distribution.

In other words, variance is equal to the average squared difference between each of the scores in a distribution of numbers and the

mean of those scores. If you think about it, this will "make sense" as an index of the extent to which scores are spread out around the mean. When scores are closely clustered around the mean, the (squared) differences between those scores and the mean will be relatively small, as will the variance; scores that are more spread out, so that the (squared) differences between them and the mean are relatively large, will yield a relatively large index of variance. (The differences are squared to eliminate negative algebraic signs generated when the mean is subtracted from scores that are smaller than the mean. Given the nature of the mean, failure to square these differences will *always* lead to a value of zero (0) when the differences between individual scores and the mean are summed. This will, in turn, always lead to a calculated average difference of zero. You can verify this for yourself by generating a group of numbers, calculating the mean, subtracting the mean from each number, and summing those differences *without squaring them*.)

Recall that the mean of the ratings in Table 2.1 is 4.13. The variance of those scores is therefore calculated as follows:

$$s^2 = \frac{[(4 - 4.13)^2 + (5 - 4.13)^2 + \cdots + (4 - 4.13)^2]}{15}$$

$$= \frac{[.017 + .757 + \cdots + .017]}{15}$$

$$= 2.382$$

Now that you understand variance, you are well on your way to understanding the standard deviation. The **standard deviation** of a distribution of scores is nothing more than the square root of the variance of those scores. Thus, the standard deviation of the ratings presented in Table 2.1 is equal to the square root of 2.382, or 1.543.

Standard deviations are very useful indices of dispersion. The distributions of many human characteristics (for example, height, weight, in-

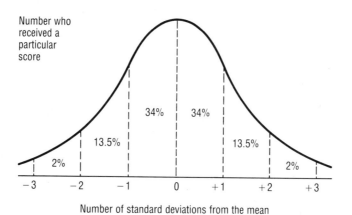

Number who received a particular score

34%   34%

13.5%   13.5%

2%   2%

−3   −2   −1   0   +1   +2   +3

Number of standard deviations from the mean

FIGURE 2.5
Approximate Percentages of Scores Under Various Segments of a Normal Curve

telligence, level of job performance) tend to be shaped something like a bell, as shown in Figure 2.5. These symmetrical, bell-shaped curves are known as **normal** distributions (the mathematical properties of which are precisely defined, and well beyond the scope of this textbook). Of greater relevance to us is the fact that the standard deviation of a normal distribution provides information about the percentages of scores in that distribution that fall within given distances from the mean (see Figure 2.5). Thus, if the mean is 4.13 and the standard deviation is 1.54 (as we calculated earlier), and the scores or ratings are normally distributed (here our example breaks down a bit because normal distributions typically require more than 15 scores), we can conclude that approximately 68% of those scores fall between −1 standard deviation (4.13 − 1.54 = 2.59) and +1 standard deviation (4.13 + 1.54 = 5.67). As it turns out, 10 of the 15 scores presented in Table 2.1 (67%) are greater than 2.59 *and* less than 5.67.

Standard deviations also allow us to compare scores from two or more normal distributions in a meaningful way. For example, Figure 2.6 depicts two normal distributions of scores obtained by the same sample of individuals on

two different tests. As you can see, Mr. Smith earned a score of 30 on Test A and a score of 36 on Test B, and Mr. Jones obtained scores of 36 and 30 on Tests A and B, respectively. The mean score on each test was 30. If both scores are equally important, and we don't know anything about the standard deviations of the two distributions, we have no choice but to judge Smith's and Jones' overall performances (across the two examinations) to be equivalent. After all, each earned a total of 66 points on the two tests, and each obtained a score equal to the mean (30) on one of those tests. However, once we learn that the standard deviations of the scores on Tests A and B are 2.0 and 10.0, respectively, our conclusion about Smith's and Jones' composite performances changes. Now we can see that in addition to his mean score of 30 on Test B, Jones' score of 36 on Test A places him three standard deviations above the mean on that test, or approximately in the 99th percentile. By contrast, in addition to his mean score of 30 on Test A, Smith's score of 36 on Test B places him only between the mean and one standard deviation above the mean on that test, or approximately in the 72d percentile. Now we are in a position to judge Jones' overall

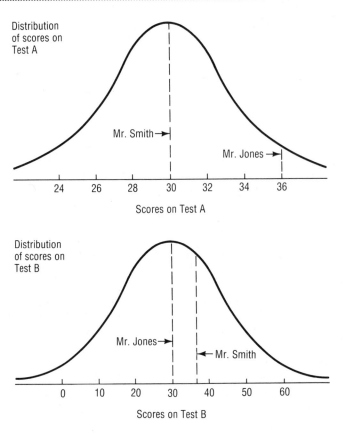

FIGURE 2.6
Use of Standard Deviations to Compare Scores in
Two Different Frequency Distributions

performance across the two tests to be superior to Smith's overall performance.

Of course, not all distributions of data are normal, or bell shaped; sometimes scores are distributed in a manner more similar to one of the patterns presented in Figure 2.7. The distributions in Figure 2.7a and 2.7b, which are characterized by a preponderance of high and low scores, respectively, are said to be **skewed.** When high scores outnumber low scores, the distribution is described as negatively skewed; when low scores outnumber high scores, it is positively skewed. The distri-

butions in Figure 2.7c and 2.7d also depart from normality but in a different way. They demonstrate the property known as **kurtosis,** the extent to which a distribution is flatter or more peaked than the normal bell shape. More peaked distributions are described as **leptokurtic;** flatter distributions are **platykurtic.** Because none of the distributions in Figure 2.7 is normal (bell shaped), the standard deviation is less useful for putting particular scores in proper perspective. You can readily see that the percentages of scores that fall between the mean and plus or minus a given number of

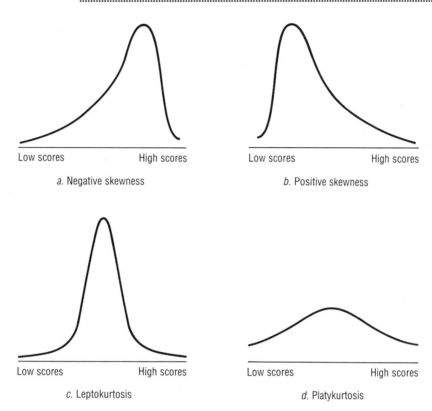

Low scores   High scores

a. Negative skewness

Low scores   High scores

b. Positive skewness

Low scores   High scores

c. Leptokurtosis

Low scores   High scores

d. Platykurtosis

FIGURE 2.7
Distributions Characterized by Skewness and Kurtosis

standard deviations will be quite different from those shown in Figure 2.5.

Inferential Statistics

Recall that regardless of the specific research question we ask or the particular research strategy we adopt, we almost always collect data from a sample of individuals or events that is limited in some way. Inferential statistics help us make decisions about the wisdom of generalizing our empirical results beyond that limited sample to a larger population of people or events. Among the inferential statistics com-

monly used by researchers in I/O psychology are the chi-square test, the *t*-test, and analysis of variance and its associated *F*-test. Because this is not a statistics text, we will refer you to one of the many excellent volumes designed to provide basic instruction in inferential statistics for further enlightenment concerning these procedures (Guilford & Fruchter, 1978; Hays, 1973; McNemar, 1969; Wright, 1976).

Correlation Coefficient

The correlation coefficient, symbolized *r*, which can be used both to describe and to make infer-

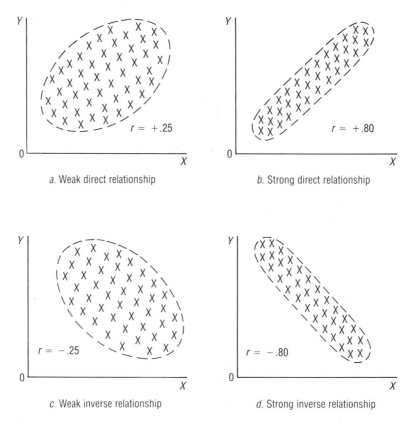

FIGURE 2.8
Scattergrams Showing Direct and Inverse Relationships Between Two Variables (X, Y)

ences about data, is perhaps the most widely used statistic in all of I/O psychology; this status within the realm of personnel or human-resources psychology is beyond debate. Formally known as the Pearson **product-moment correlation coefficient** (Karl Pearson originally derived this statistic), it is used to assess the degree to which two variables are linearly associated with each other. A computational formula for the correlation coefficient is as follows:

$$r = \frac{N\Sigma XY - (\Sigma X)(\Sigma Y)}{\{[N\Sigma X^2 - (\Sigma X)^2][N\Sigma Y^2 - (\Sigma Y)^2]\}^{1/2}}$$

where X and Y are the two variables whose interrelationship is of interest, and N is the number of pairs of observations or measures on X and Y that are available or collected by the researcher.

Calculated values of r can range from −1.00 through zero (0.00) to +1.00. A positive algebraic sign denotes a direct relationship between the two variables: as the numerical value of one of the variables increases, so does the other. Direct relationships and positive correlations are depicted in Figure 2.8a and 2.8b. These graphic plots of observations on two variables using coordinate axes (X, Y) are known as scatter diagrams, or **scattergrams** for short. A negative algebraic sign denotes an inverse relationship between the two variables: as the numerical value of one of the variables increases, the value of the other decreases. The scattergrams

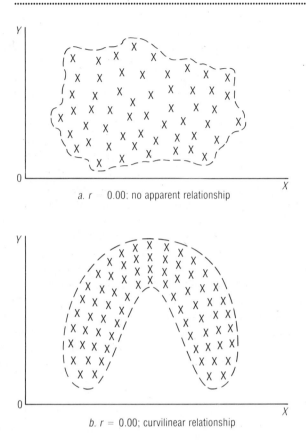

a. r   0.00: no apparent relationship

b. r = 0.00; curvilinear relationship

FIGURE 2.9
Scattergrams Showing r = 0.00

in Figure 2.8c and 2.8d reveal inverse relationships/negative correlations.

A correlation equal to zero (0.00) indicates that there is no *linear* relationship between the two variables of interest; that is, there exists no relationship that can be represented graphically by a straight line. The scattergram in Figure 2.9a depicts a situation where r = 0.00 and there is no apparent relationship *of any kind* between the two variables. The one in Figure 2.9b also reflects a situation where r = 0.00, but in this case it is clear that some kind of relationship *does* exist between the two variables of interest. In this instance X and Y are related in a *curvilinear* fashion: as X increases, so does Y up to a point, beyond which Y decreases as X continues

to increase. The two scattergrams in Figure 2.9 illustrate that the correlation coefficient (*r*) describes only linear relationships between pairs of variables; it tells us nothing about any nonlinear (that is, curvilinear) relationships that might exist. (Other statistics are available for describing nonlinear relationships between variables.)

Another important property of the correlation coefficient (to which we alluded briefly during our discussion of research strategies) is that it says nothing about *cause-and-effect* relationships between two variables. Although two variables may be very strongly correlated (positively or negatively—the algebraic sign refers only to the direction of the relationship, not to its magnitude), we cannot conclude that either is responsible for the other. Variable X might cause changes in Variable Y; Variable Y might effect changes in Variable X; or perhaps a variable that we haven't even measured is responsible for changes in both Variables X and Y. Recall from our earlier discussion that experimental research strategies are best suited to examining and determining causality. This is still true, despite recent innovations (for example, cross-lagged correlations, path analyses, linear structural relations analysis) designed to "tease" causal conclusions out of correlational analyses (Heise, 1975; Pedhazur, 1982; Randolph, 1981; Rogosa, 1980).

I/O psychologists use correlation coefficients in a variety of ways. When we want to estimate the consistency with which we can assess a psychological variable using a given measuring instrument, we often calculate r for two sets of scores obtained by the same sample of people on two different occasions and consider it a "reliability coefficient." When we want to assess the degree to which job applicants' subsequent levels of job performance can be predicted from their scores on tests taken during the hiring process, we can calculate r and refer to it as a "validity coefficient." (See Chapter 5 for detailed discussions of measurement reliability and criterion-related validity, as well as procedures for estimating these psychometric properties of measuring instruments.) Your acquaintance with the Pearson product-moment correlation coefficient has only begun!

So What?

You might be wondering why we have tormented you with even this small dose of statistical information. Although we know that some of our students would offer a second opinion, we are not sadistic. We have devoted time and space to these topics because the more you understand them, the better you will be able to

appreciate the procedures that have generated the research findings discussed throughout the remainder of this book. Evidence also suggests that the methodological and statistical rigor that characterizes research studies can have direct effects on the results of those investigations.

A systematic examination of 52 research studies published in the *Journal of Applied Behavioral Science* between 1965 and 1980 illustrated this latter point very nicely (Terpstra, 1981). Each of these studies described and evaluated the application of some sort of organizational intervention (for example, training, organizational development). The basic finding was an *inverse* relationship between the degree of methodological and statistical rigor used to evaluate the results of each study and the apparent degree to which the intervention procedure was deemed "successful." That is, studies that were *more* rigorous (that is, that had larger and more scientifically selected samples, that used control groups and assigned subjects to those groups randomly, that employed sound measurement strategies and procedures, and that reported a level of statistical significance) were *less* likely to report a positive, beneficial effect of the organizational intervention. A more recent review of 50 studies published between 1978 and 1983 led to a similar conclusion with respect to organizational *process* interventions (Woodman & Wayne, 1985). Although these findings are not without their detractors (Bullock & Svyantek, 1983), and there are other reasonable explanations for such results (Bass, 1983), few I/O psychologists deny the importance of sound methodology and analysis to the science and practice of I/O psychology. A review of 65 organizational-development studies published between 1948 and 1982 revealed an encouraging trend in the direction of more rigorous methods, designs, and statistics (Nicholas & Katz, 1985). As a student of the field, you should appreciate the differences between research studies based on sound procedures and those that are not.

Peter's Pan Pizza, Inc.

LEARNING POINTS

After reading this insert, you should

❑ be able to describe the organizational structure and goals of our hypothetical company; and

❑ be familiar with our hypothetical organization's hypothetical I/O psychologist, and be able to describe her academic background.

PETER'S PAN PIZZA, INC. (PPP) is a hypothetical organization that sprang full blown from between the ears of your two authors. (You are, of course, free to speculate about any deep-seated, psychodynamic pathologies that might account for our choice of a pizza firm instead of a plant that produces computer chips or heavy construction equipment.) As we indicated in Chapter 1, we will rely upon PPP throughout the remainder of our book to provide an organizational context that is sufficiently detailed and realistic to facilitate your understanding and appreciation of the field of I/O psychology. It is our hope that embedding our discussions of theory and research in the context of everyday problems and challenges that confront profit-oriented organizations will emphasize the relevance of our discipline and bring the material to "life."

Peter's Pan Pizza, Inc., encompasses a nationwide chain of restaurants that serve pizza and a variety of other Italian specialties at reasonably competitive prices. Approximately one-third of the organization's 527 retail operations are owned by the parent company (PPP); the other two-thirds are owned and operated under franchising arrangements by more or less independent entrepreneurs. The company's headquarters is located in Suardell Springs, Colorado. In addition to the restaurants and the home office, PPP recently acquired Flavio's Frozen Foods, Inc. (FFF). FFF is a leader in the prepared-food industry. Major products include pizza, lasagna, and assorted other dinners and appetizers. Based in Manhattan Harbor, Massachusetts, FFF has production plants in the Northeast and Southwest; distribution centers are located in Phoenix, Arizona, and Manhattan Harbor.

The president of PPP, who reports to a board of directors, exercises organizational control through a senior vice president in charge of operations, three other vice presidents (responsible for finance, facilities, and personnel), and a second senior vice president in charge of FFF (see organizational chart on next page). The senior vice president in charge of operations directly supervises four (more junior) vice presidents who are responsible for purchasing, marketing, distribution, and retail operations. The senior vice president in charge of FFF directly supervises two (more junior) vice presidents (responsible for manufacturing and distribution). The three FFF executives and their subordinate department managers (scheduling, shipping, and so on) are physically located in Manhattan Harbor. The president and the other vice presidents, along with their subordinate department managers, operate out of PPP's home office in Suardell Springs.

Three additional departments that provide various professional services for PPP personnel are also housed in the home office: the Legal Department, the Data-Processing Department, and the Human-Resources Department. The managers of these departments report to the president; however, their primary functions involve "internal consulting" for all company personnel through their supervisors, managers, and executives.

The Human-Resources Department is run by a doctoral-level I/O psychologist, Dr. Jennilyn A. MacKeven. She supervises another professional psychologist, who holds a master's degree, and two psychological technicians who have earned bachelor's degrees in psychology. At any given time, two or three graduate and undergraduate students are serving internships within the department for periods ranging from three months to one year. Most of the current concerns of the Human-Resources Department and its coordinator revolve around three basic issues. First, and of broadest concern, there is a strong commitment to utilizing behavioral-science theory and research in constructive ways to contribute to the economic viability of PPP and to the professional and personal welfare of all its employees. Second, PPP is profoundly committed to equal employment opportunity. The Human-Resources Department is therefore very serious about ensuring that the company's personnel policies and practices are consistent with Title VII of the 1964 Civil Rights Act (which forbids racial, ethnic, religious, and sex discrimination in the workplace), with the Equal Pay Act of 1963, with the more recent Civil Rights Act of 1991, and with other relevant federal and state legislation. Third, the recent acquisition of Flavio's Frozen Foods has led to some psychological and organizational outcomes with important implications for the company's future. The Human-Resources Department is understandably concerned with easing former FFF employees as well as PPP employees through this potentially disruptive transition. Of course, Dr. MacKeven and her department must deal with the myriad of unforeseen personnel-related emergencies that predictably arise within an organization as large and as diverse as Peter's Pan Pizza. It's safe to conclude that her days are not dull.

Before we move on to the research and theory that constitute the heart of our textbook, let's take just a moment to get better acquainted with PPP's resident I/O psychologist. PPP hired Dr. Jennilyn A. MacKeven to serve as the company's human-resources coordinator almost ten years ago. Her academic credentials include a bachelor of science degree from a small liberal arts college on the East Coast, where she completed requirements for a dual major in psychology and business; and master of science and doctor of philosophy degrees from a large midwestern state university, where she complemented her concentration in I/O

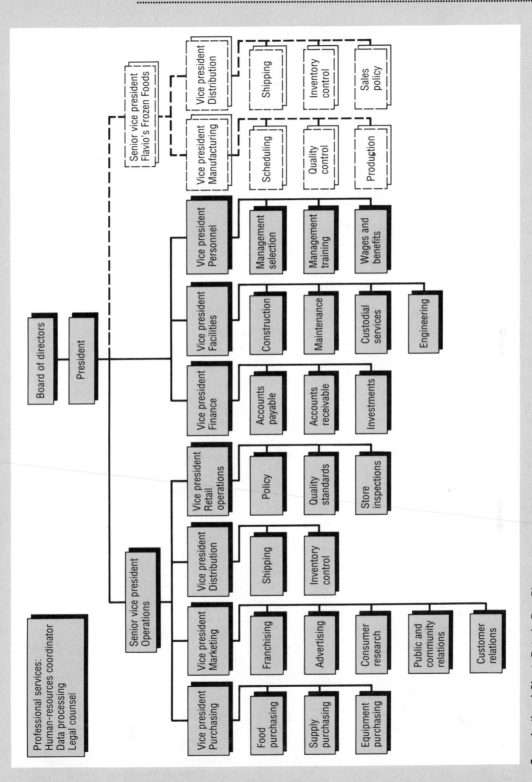

Organizational Chart, Peter's Pan Pizza

psychology with a secondary emphasis in statistics and research design. Prior to completing her doctoral studies, she served a six-month internship in the personnel department of a large public utility on the West Coast. In many ways, her preprofessional preparation was similar to that of many of her colleagues in the discipline of I/O psychology.

Also typical of many doctoral-level I/O psychologists, Dr. MacKeven's graduate course work fell into four basic categories of preparation:

1. I/O psychology,
2. general psychology,
3. supporting disciplines (for example, business and computer science), and
4. statistical analysis and research methodology.

The basic content areas covered in her graduate courses in I/O psychology can be seen by glancing at the Table of Contents in this textbook. Specific courses included "Work Motivation," "Personnel Training," "Leadership," "Personnel Selection," "Performance Appraisal," and "Organizational Psychology." Most of these followed a seminar-like format that emphasized in-depth discussion, debate, and analysis of theory and research.

Among the courses in general psychology that appear on Dr. MacKeven's graduate transcripts are "Theories of Personality," "Social Psychology," "Motivation and Learning," "Physiological Psychology," and "Perception." With an eye toward other fields that support or complement I/O psychology, she also enrolled in formal courses in the departments of computer science, sociology, philosophy, management, and industrial engineering. The remainder of her graduate course work dealt with research procedures and techniques for analyzing empirical data; with only a few exceptions, these courses in research methodology, psychological measurement, and psychological statistics were offered within the Department of Psychology. (Brief overviews of some of the basic research, measurement, and statistical issues that are indispensable to contemporary I/O psychologists appear in Chapter 2 and its appendix.)

In addition to providing her with an opportunity to apply some of the research and theory learned in the classroom to everyday problems encountered by women and men in organizational settings, Dr. MacKeven's off-campus internship offered invaluable lessons in two separate yet related domains. First, she was exposed to organizational politics. She learned that employees often have their own hidden agendas that may or may not be congruent with the organization's goals, and that one cannot naively apply rational theories or empirical relationships to work-related problems without taking these "political" factors into account. Second, she learned the importance of being able to translate obscure psychological jargon into language that can be understood by intelligent men and women who have no experience with academic psychology and its often complex terminology. An I/O psychologist's intelligence, education, and diligence avail an organization little (or nothing) if he is unable to share expertise in terms understandable to clients. Fortunately for Dr. MacKeven (and for PPP), her brief sojourn to a large public utility during her graduate-school years afforded her ample opportunities to complement her academic preparation with off-campus lessons in "politics" and communication.

CHAPTER 3

Job Analysis, Job Evaluation, and Comparable Worth

LEARNING POINTS

After studying this chapter you should

- be familiar with the kinds of information that typically emerge from a job analysis;

- be able to describe three basic orientations to job analysis and three (or more) specific techniques for conducting job analyses;

- be able to respond to questions about "the best" job-analysis technique;

- understand the relationship between job analysis and job evaluation;

- be able to describe four basic job-evaluation procedures, and to comment on the strengths and weaknesses of each; and

- understand the concept of comparable worth and be able to explain why it is so controversial.

COMPARABLE-WORTH ISSUES have generated a great deal of interest and no small amount of debate at national, state, and local levels during the past decade. Dr. MacKeven was therefore not surprised when she received Mr. LeGette's memo (p. 60). Nor should you be surprised to learn that many women and men in the public and private sectors find the idea of comparable worth so appealing. After all, to deny comparable pay to people who hold jobs that, although not identical, make comparable contributions to an organization's goals is akin to critizing parenthood, patriotism, and pecan pie. "Comparable worth" sounds right!

Unfortunately, it's neither as simple nor as straightforward as it sounds. To determine **comparable worth**—whether two or more jobs make equal contributions to organizational objectives—we must know a great deal about those jobs. What are the employees who hold those jobs required to *do*? What must they *know* in order to do those things effectively? What *skills* and *abilities* must they possess? Under what kinds of *conditions*, physical and social, are they expected to do their jobs? I/O psychologists try to answer these questions using procedures that are generally known as *job analysis*. When they turn to assigning specific monetary values to required tasks and jobs, or to the knowledge, skills,

INTEROFFICE MEMO

To: J. A. MacKeven,
    Human Resources Coordinator

From: A. LeGette,
      Director of Wages and Benefits

Subject: Comparable Worth Concerns

During the past few months, several directors and managers from various units throughout PPP have made a point of informally asking me about the degree to which our organization attended to comparable-worth issues as we developed and administer our overall compensation package (salaries and wages, benefits, and so on). Most of these organizational leaders were surprised to learn that we did *not* specifically address this issue, which has generated so much discussion and controversy across the United States and Canada.

I was quick to remind them, of course, that PPP determines wages and salaries using a set of systematic procedures that attach "dollar values" to various components or aspects of jobs (that is, job evaluation), and that these procedures are compatible with the spirit of comparable worth. That is, our procedures should result in comparable pay for different jobs throughout the organization that make comparable contributions to PPP's goals and objectives. Nevertheless, I think several of my colleagues were disappointed, and even a bit frustrated, that they could not assure their subordinates of our commitment to confronting the challenges of comparable worth head-on.

Why has PPP not made this commitment? What are the expected costs and benefits of adopting a comparable-worth approach to paying PPP employees? In what ways and to what extent would such a commitment require us to modify our current job-analysis and job-evaluation procedures? I am convinced that comparable-worth concerns will only increase in the foreseeable future, so I (personally) would like to see PPP address them directly. I will appreciate any information and guidance you can provide.

and abilities that enable employees to perform those tasks and jobs, they often rely on *job-evaluation* procedures. Job evaluation, in turn, is one way to address the question of whether organization members who hold different jobs are compensated fairly, and whether employees who hold comparable jobs are compensated comparably.

In this chapter we introduce concepts and procedures that will help you better understand the issues Mr. LeGette raised in his memo. We begin with a close look at job analysis, especially general approaches to analyzing jobs and several specific job-analytic techniques. We then describe how results of job analyses can contribute to job evaluation. Finally, we focus on comparable worth, and describe some alternatives to job evaluation for developing and administering pay plans that compensate employees equitably. We will refer to Mr. LeGette's memo throughout the chapter as we highlight the relevance of the material to his and his colleagues' concerns.

Job Analysis

Job analysis refers to the process of collecting information about jobs, including:

1. work activities, including desired job outcomes and employee behaviors necessary to accomplish those outcomes;
2. machines, tools, equipment, and work aids;
3. materials processed;
4. knowledge applied;
5. standards of work performance;
6. job context (physical and social); and
7. personnel requirements (for example, education, experience, aptitudes) (McCormick, 1976; McCormick & Ilgen, 1985).

The distinction between work outcomes and employee behaviors necessary to effect the outcomes reflects an important distinction between two types of information about jobs. First, every job in an organization should make a meaningful contribution to organizational goals, whether the goals include producing a product (for example, pizza), providing a service (for example, selling it in a restaurant environment), or both. Job-analysis procedures designed to assess intended job outcomes or results and the conditions under which employees generate the results are known as *job-oriented* procedures. As important as such information is, we must go beyond the goals or purposes of a job. We must also discover the behaviors and activities required of the job incumbents who accomplish the results. Procedures designed to assess workers' behaviors and activities on their jobs are known as *worker-oriented* approaches to job analysis. Both kinds of job-analysis information are important. An I/O psychologist who is aware of specific behaviors demanded by a job but knows nothing about the purposes of the behaviors (not to mention the physical, social, and psychological conditions under which the behaviors typically occur) is in a poor position to assess the appropriateness or efficiency of the behaviors. Similarly, the I/O psychologist cannot be satisfied with only the rationale for a job's existence. She must also identify specific behaviors demanded by a job so that job-analysis information can be used to develop behavior-based personnel procedures (for example, training programs, performance-appraisal systems).

Although much less is known about it, a third approach to job analysis that can complement job- and worker-oriented strategies is *trait-oriented* job analysis. This approach focuses on whether specific psychological traits contribute to job performance. If they do, the extent to which such traits are present among successful employees can be assessed (Lopez, Kesselman, & Lopez, 1981). By emphasizing psychological traits, I/O psychologists may eventually discover systematic relationships between performance on a job and human characteristics that underlie successful performance. We should not expect such relationships to be simple, however. A single trait might contribute to performance of several different job behaviors or tasks, and there is every reason to expect performance of a discrete task to require several different psychological traits (Hughes & Prien, 1989). We must also be sensitive to the unpleasant possibility that an emphasis on human characteristics can degenerate into destructive and illegal group stereotypes based on race, sex, age, and other demographic variables. These cautions notwithstanding, trait analysis is an interesting third perspective on job analysis.

Used in combination, the three approaches to job analysis can provide I/O psychologists with the information they need to carry out a variety of personnel functions (for example, selection, training, appraisal). Job-oriented procedures reveal the reason(s) a job exists and the conditions under which its purpose is accomplished. Worker-oriented procedures describe the actual behaviors required of workers as they accomplish a job's purposes. Trait-oriented procedures suggest human characteristics needed to engage in those behaviors or activities. If Dr. MacKeven chooses to address Mr. LeGette's memo by basing comparable-worth judgments on the results of job analyses, she should consider a combination of procedures that can generate all three kinds of information.

Overview of Job-Analysis Methods

Whether she seeks job-, worker-, or trait-oriented information, Dr. MacKeven can choose from among several traditional strategies for collecting job-analysis data:

1. questionnaires—workers respond to written questions about their jobs;

2. checklists—workers indicate the tasks (from among a list of possible tasks) that are part of their jobs;

3. individual interviews—workers respond to oral questions about their jobs;

4. group interviews—small groups of workers respond to oral questions about their jobs;

5. diaries—workers record their daily work activities in written form;

6. technical conferences—"experts" (usually people who supervise the job in question) identify the components of a job;

7. critical incidents—workers and/or "experts" describe components of the job in question that are important determinants of success or failure;

8. observation interviews—workers are interviewed at their work stations by a job analyst, who also observes employees as they go about their daily activities; and

9. work participation—the job analyst performs the job in question.
(From Blum & Naylor, 1968; Morsh, 1964.)

The list is by no means exhaustive; many other possible strategies exist. Nevertheless, each of the strategies (and any others you might be able to imagine) can be categorized under one of three general headings: (1) "asking," (2) "observing," or (3) "doing." As a rule, more sources of information yield more complete and accurate job analyses. In most cases, however, job analysts restrict themselves to "asking" or "observing," or a combination of these. It is often impractical, illegal, or downright dangerous for a job analyst to actually perform tasks required by a given job.

When she uses one or both of the first two methods, Dr. MacKeven must consider some of the problems inherent in conducting job analyses by asking workers questions about their jobs or observing them at their work stations. Asking questions presumes that the employee has the necessary verbal skills to understand and respond to the questions. This is not always the case. Even when it is, workers' responses may not be accurate or truthful. Some employees who sincerely want to answer the job analyst's questions accurately may provide erroneous information unintentionally because of ignorance or simple oversight. Others are threatened by job analysts; they view analysts as "efficiency experts" committed to making them work harder and longer for the same (or possibly less) pay. In this case, employees supply incorrect information that intentionally portrays them in unrealistically favorable lights. Observation has its drawbacks, too. Many of us behave differently when we know that someone is "looking over our shoulder." To make matters worse, job analysts don't always know exactly what to look for, so a quick movement that is rarely or never repeated during a single work shift may go unnoticed even though it is crucial to job success. Finally, many important work behaviors such as thinking, making decisions, and planning do not lend themselves to observation.

A reasonable question may have occurred to you by now: When a job analyst obtains information by observing or asking workers about their jobs, do the workers' characteristics influence the nature of the information obtained? Several studies have addressed this issue, and the results are quite consistent. Very similar information about job tasks and necessary knowledge, skills, and abilities is obtained from those who perform their jobs well and those who don't perform so well, from individuals at different levels of the organizational hierarchy who perform the same generic job (for example, a range of middle-management positions), and from workers with different levels of formal education (Conley & Sackett, 1987; Landy & Vasey, 1991; Schmitt & Cohen, 1989). When female and male workers, or workers from different racial or ethnic groups do provide inconsistent information, the inconsistencies are usually attributable to systematic differences in job experience or in the work tasks typically assigned to members of these groups. For example, in one study women were less likely to report being involved in budgetary or financial tasks, or tasks that involve public speaking and representing the organization to outside groups; in another, ethnic-minority workers typically reported that they were responsible for fewer tasks than their white colleagues (Landy & Vasey, 1991; Schmitt & Cohen, 1989).

The effects of employees' job experience are less consistent. Middle managers with at least one year of experience in state civil-service occupations did not differ with respect to "difficulty" or "time spent" responses on a task inventory (Schmitt & Cohen, 1989). However, a study of police patrol officers who also had at least one year of job experience revealed that less-experienced officers spent more time on traffic-related tasks but less time on "general social work" tasks than their more-experienced fellow officers. Officers with moderate levels of experience (6–10 years) devoted more time to criminal-intervention activities than their more- or less-experienced colleagues (Landy & Vasey, 1991). Similarly, a study of mental-health workers revealed that different procedures for selecting employees who will complete job-analysis questionnaires can generate qualitatively different groups of workers, and that these groups may not be equally accurate (Green & Stutzman, 1986). Data from 140 managers in a large gold- and silver-mining organization also revealed individual differences in their ratings of how important various skills are (Waldman, Yammarino, & Avolio, 1990). Finally, training can improve the reliability and accuracy of employees' job-analysis ratings (Hahn & Dipboye, 1988). Thus, job analysts who observe workers or ask them questions about their jobs do well to focus on a sample of employees that includes workers with a wide range of job experience.

The job analyst's primary concern when questioning or observing employees is to select a sample of workers whose job duties represent all the tasks that constitute a given job, as well as all the knowledge, skills, and abilities demanded by that job. Respondents' proficiency at the job doesn't seem to be important. Demographic characteristics (for example, sex, racial or ethnic group membership, education, experience) are important only when they covary with different job responsibilities. There is no evidence that workers' social skills (for example, friendliness) or their perceptions of a job as "interesting" or "dull" influence job-analysis results (Arvey, Davis, McGowen, & Dipboye, 1982). However, when the job in question is an especially dynamic one or is not particularly well defined, incumbents are more likely to have unique perspectives on their work, so selection of representative job-analysis respondents can be very important (Green & Stutzman, 1986).

Examples of Specific Job-Analysis Techniques

Job analysts can choose from among a variety of techniques. Those discussed here do not make up an exhaustive list. Instead, we have chosen to focus on specific techniques because they are used often in organizational settings, because they have stimulated a great deal of empirical research, or because they represent new and interesting approaches to job analysis.

Functional Job Analysis (FJA). The United States Employment Service adopted functional job analysis (FJA) to generate the job information

and descriptions published in the *Dictionary of Occupational Titles* (*DOT*) (U.S. Department of Labor, 1991). **Functional job analysis**

> begins by examining the purpose and goals of the work . . . [and then] determine[s], step by step, what must be done to accomplish it. Two types of information are derived . . . (*a*) what gets done (. . . procedures/methods and processes with which the worker is engaged as he/she performs a task), and (*b*) how the worker does it (. . . the physical, mental, and interpersonal involvement of the worker as he/she carries out procedures and processes). . . . It provides explicit terminology for getting at and understanding what workers do to accomplish the objectives of an organization. (Olson, Fine, Myers, & Jennings, 1981, p. 352)

As you can see, FJA yields both job-oriented (*what* gets done) and worker-oriented (*how* it gets done) information. The job analyst typically relies on one or more of the "asking" (for example, interviews, questionnaires) or "observing" techniques listed earlier to obtain the necessary information.

The specific focus of FJA is the extent to which a job requires a worker to deal with three

TABLE 3.1   Hierarchies of Worker Functions

Data	People	Things
0 Synthesizing	0 Mentoring	0 Setting up
1 Coordinating	1 Negotiating	1 Precision working
2 Analyzing	2 Instructing	2 Operating-controlling
3 Compiling	3 Supervising	3 Driving-operating
4 Computing	4 Diverting	4 Manipulating
5 Copying	5 Persuading	5 Tending
6 Comparing	6 Speaking-signaling	6 Feeding-offbearing
	7 Serving	7 Handling
	8 Taking instructions-helping	

Note: Smaller numbers (toward the top of each column) indicate more complex functions, which are generally assumed to include all functions in that column of lesser complexity (larger numbers). McCormick and Ilgen (1985), however, asserted that "there are instances in which the implied hierarchical relationships are limited, imprecise, reversed, nonexistent" (pp. 45–46); they advised caution in interpreting these levels too rigidly.

SOURCE: U.S. Department of Labor, Employment and Training Administration (1991). *Dictionary of Occupational Titles* (5th ed.). Washington, DC: U.S. Government Printing Office.

domains: data (information); people (for example, coworkers, supervisors, subordinates, customers); and things (objects). Every job can be described according to the level of complexity it demands in each domain. Complexity levels are arranged in hierarchies. It is assumed that a job that demands more complex levels of interaction with data, people, or things will automatically require a worker to confront all of the less-complex interactions in a given domain. The hierarchies of worker functions in each domain appear in Table 3.1.

Some examples of specific levels of complexity from each of the three hierarchies appear in Box 3.1.

The paragraph that follows was taken from the *DOT*. It describes the position of "Manager, Fast Food Services," which bears a striking re-

---

BOX 3.1 Examples of Levels of Complexity in Functional Job-Analysis Hierarchies

DATA

0 = "Synthesizing": integrating analyses of data to discover facts and/or develop knowledge concepts or interpretations.

1 = "Coordinating": determining time, place, and sequence of operations or actions to be taken on the basis of analysis of data; executing determination and/or reporting on events.

6 = "Comparing": judging the readily observable functional, structural, or compositional characteristics (whether similar to or divergent from obvious standards) of data, people, or things.

PEOPLE

0 = "Mentoring": dealing with individuals in terms of their total personality in order to advise, counsel, and/or guide them with regard to problems that may be resolved by legal, scientific, clinical, spiritual, and/or other professional principles.

3 = "Supervising": determining or interpreting work procedures for a group of workers, assigning specific duties to them, maintaining harmonious relations among them, and promoting efficiency. A variety of responsibilities is involved in this function.

8 = "Taking Instructions—Helping": helping applies to "nonlearning" helpers. No variety of responsibility is involved in this function.

THINGS

0 = "Setting Up": adjusting machines or equipment by replacing or altering tools, jigs, fixtures, and attachments to prepare them to perform their functions, change their performance, or restore their proper functioning if they break down. Workers who set up one or a number of machines for other workers or who set up and personally operate a variety of machines are included here.

7 = "Handling": using body members, hand tools, and/or special devices to work, move, or carry objects or materials. Involves little or no latitude for judgment with regard to attainment of standards or in selecting appropriate tool, object, or material.

SOURCE: U.S. Department of Labor, Employment and Training Administration (1991). *Dictionary of Occupational Titles* (5th ed.). Washington, DC: U.S. Government Printing Office.

Some jobs demand high levels of "people" skills, whereas others require high levels of interaction with data. (Courtesy of Pat Knight and McCall Pattern Co.)

semblance to the position of restaurant manager in PPP's retail outlets.

185.137-010 MANAGER, FAST FOOD SERVICES

Manages franchised or independent fast food or wholesale prepared food establishment: Directs, coordinates, and participates in preparation of, and cooking, wrapping, or packing types of food served or prepared by establishment, collecting of monies from in-house or take-out customers or assembling food orders for wholesale customers. Coordinates activities of workers engaged in keeping business records, collecting and paying accounts, ordering or purchasing supplies, and delivery of foodstuffs to wholesale or retail customers. Interviews, hires, and trains personnel. May contact prospective wholesale customers, such as mobile food vendors, vending machine operators, bar and tavern owners, and institutional personnel, to promote sale of prepared foods, such as doughnuts, sandwiches, and specialty food items. May establish delivery routes and schedules for supplying wholesale customers. Workers may be known according to type or name of franchised establishment or type of prepared foodstuff retailed or wholesaled. (U.S. Department of Labor, Employment and Training Administration, 1991)

As you can see in this sample job description, a nine-digit code number is attached to each job. The first three digits identify a particular group of jobs; here, 185 indicates a job that belongs to the group "Wholesale and Retail Trade Managers and Officials." (See *DOT* for lists of other job groups.) The middle three digits describe a job's levels of complexity with respect to data, people, and things, respectively. The numbers 1, 3, and 7 (137) in our example indicate that this job involves "coordinating" data (1), "supervising" people (3), and "handling" things (7). The final three digits reflect the alphabetical order of specific job titles within job groups identified by the first six digits. If a six-digit code applies to only one job title, the numbers 010 are always assigned as the final three digits (as is the case with our

sample *DOT* job description for fast-food manager).

FJA is an intuitively appealing technique because it generates both job- and worker-oriented information. Nevertheless, job analysts should be cautious when using FJA or consulting FJA ratings in the *DOT*. Cain and Green (1983) investigated the extent to which job analysts agreed with one another when independently rating the complexity levels (that is, relative to data, people, and things) inherent in a variety of jobs. Agreement among 42 analysts was high with respect to data and people, but agreement about the complexity of things was less impressive. The authors urged analysts to use *DOT* ratings only in an informed and selective way.

Position Analysis Questionnaire (PAQ). The Position Analysis Questionnaire (PAQ) is another widely used job-analysis technique (McCormick, Jeanneret, & Mecham, 1972). Basically a worker-oriented approach, the PAQ includes 194 statements (job elements) describing human behaviors that any given job might demand. The job elements are organized into six categories or dimensions: (1) information input, (2) mental processes, (3) work output, (4) relationships with other persons, (5) job context, and (6) other job characteristics. Box 3.2 presents the central question that underlies each category and the major subheadings within each.

The PAQ should be used to guide a highly structured oral interview. The job analyst reads each of the 194 items to the job incumbent, listens carefully to each response, and asks any necessary clarifying questions. The analyst then mentally integrates the information obtained from the worker and chooses the appropriate response on a rating scale applicable to that item or job element. Depending on the item, the rating scale addresses (a) *extent of use*: response alternatives range from "nominal" or "very infrequently" to "very substantial"; (b) *importance to the job*: response alternatives range from "very minor" to "ex-

BOX 3.2 Position Analysis Questionnaire Job-Element Categories

1. *Information Input:* (Where and how does a worker get the information to be used in performing the job?)

    1.1. Sources of Job Information

        1.1.1. Visual Sources of Job Information

        1.1.2. Nonvisual Sources of Job Information

    1.2. Sensory and Perceptual Processes

    1.3. Estimation Activities

2. *Mental Processes:* (What reasoning, decision-making, planning, and information-processing activities does the job involve?)

    2.1. Decision Making, Reasoning, and Planning/Scheduling

    2.2. Information-Processing Activities

    2.3. Use of Learned Information

3. *Work Output:* (What physical activity does the worker perform, and what tools or other devices are used?)

    3.1. Use of Devices and Equipment

        3.1.1. Hand-held Tools or Instruments

        3.1.2. Other Hand-held Devices

        3.1.3. Stationary Devices

        3.1.4. Control Devices (on Equipment)

        3.1.5. Transportation and Mobile Equipment

    3.2. Manual Activities

    3.3. Activities of the Entire Body

    3.4. Level of Physical Exertion

    3.5. Body Positions/Postures

    3.6. Manipulation/Coordination Activities

4. *Relationships with Other Persons:* (What relationships with other people are required to perform the job?)

    4.1. Communications

        4.1.1. Oral (Speaking)

        4.1.2. Written

        4.1.3. Other Communications

treme"; (c) *amount of time*: response alternatives range from "less than one-tenth of the time" to "almost continually"; or (d) *possibility of occurrence*: response alternatives range from "no possibility" to "high." The PAQ also includes some statements or items that require special rating scales and response alternatives. A sample page from the PAQ containing the

BOX 3.2 *Continued*

4.2. Miscellaneous Interpersonal Relationships

4.3. Amount of Job-Required Personal Contact

4.4. Types of Job-Required Personal Contact

4.5. Supervision and Coordination

    4.5.1. Supervision/Direction Given

    4.5.2. Other Organizational Activities

    4.5.3. Supervision Received

5. *Job Context:* (What are the physical and social contexts in which the work is performed?)

    5.1. Physical Working Conditions

        5.1.1. Outdoor Environment

        5.1.2. Indoor Temperatures

        5.1.3. Other Physical Working Conditions

    5.2. Physical Hazards

    5.3. Personal and Social Aspects

6. *Other Job Characteristics:* (What activities, conditions, or characteristics other than those already described are relevant to the job?)

    6.1. Apparel Worn

    6.2. Licensing

    6.3. Work Schedule

        6.3.1. Continuity of Work

        6.3.2. Regularity of Working Hours

        6.3.3. Day-Night Schedule

    6.4. Job Demands

    6.5. Responsibility

    6.6. Job Structure

    6.7. Criticality of Position

    6.8. Pay/Income

SOURCE: *Position Analysis Questionnaire*, by E. J. McCormick, P. R. Jeanneret, and R. C. Mecham, pp. 347–368. Copyright © 1969 by Purdue Research Foundation. Reprinted with permission.

final item from the Mental-Processes section (49), which requires a special rating scale, and the first five items from the Work-Output section (50–54), each of which is answered using the *"Importance to this Job"* rating scale, is reproduced as Figure 3.1.

Several studies have examined the meanings that underlie several of the PAQ's rating

Mental Processes and Work Output

49 |S___   Using mathematics (indicate, using the code below, the highest level of mathematics required by the job)

Code   *Level of Mathematics*

N   Does not apply
1   Simple basic (counting, addition and subtraction of 2-digit numbers or less)
2   Basic (addition and subtraction of numbers of 3 digits or more, multiplication, division, etc.)
3   Intermediate (calculations and concepts involving fractions, decimals, percentages, etc.)
4   Advanced (algebraic, geometric, trigonometric, and statistical concepts, techniques, and procedures, usually applied in standard practical situations)
5   Very advanced (advanced mathematical and statistical theory, concepts, and techniques, for example, calculus, topology, vector analysis, factor analysis, probability theory, etc.)

3 WORK OUTPUT

3.1 Use of Devices and Equipment

3.1.1 Hand-held Tools or Instruments

Consider in this category those devices which are used to move or modify workpieces, materials, products, or objects. Do *not* consider measuring devices here.

Code	*Importance to this Job (I)*
N	Does not apply
1	Very minor
2	Low
3	Average
4	High
5	Extreme

Manually powered

50 |I___   Precision tools/instruments (that is, tools or instruments powered by the *user* to perform *very accurate* or *precise* operations, for example, the use of engraver's tools, watchmaker's tools, surgical instruments, etc.)

51 |I___   Nonprecision tools/instruments (tools or instruments powered by the *user* to perform operations *not* requiring *great* accuracy or precision, for example, hammers, wrenches, trowels, knives, scissors, chisels, putty knives, strainers, hand grease guns, etc.; do *not* include long-handle tools here)

52 |I___   Long-handle tools (hoes, rakes, shovels, picks, axes, brooms, mops, etc.)

53 |I___   Handling devices/tools (tongs, ladles, dippers, forceps, etc., used for moving or handling objects and materials; do *not* include here protective gear such as asbestos gloves, etc.)

Powered (manually controlled or directed devices using an energy source such as electricity, compressed air, fuel, hydraulic fluid, etc., in which the component part which accomplishes the modification is hand-held, such as dentist drills, welding equipment, etc., as well as devices small enough to be entirely hand-held)

54 |I___   Precision tools/instruments (hand-held powered tools or instruments used to perform operations requiring *great* accuracy or precision, such as dentist drills, soldering irons, welding equipment, saws, etc., used for *especially accurate* or *fine* work)

FIGURE 3.1
Sample Page from the PAQ

SOURCE: *Position Analysis Questionnaire*, by E. J. McCormick, P. R. Jeanneret, and R. C. Mecham, pp. 347–368.
Copyright © 1969 by Purdue Research Foundation. Reprinted with permission.

scales. One investigation concluded that judgments of task *importance* depend heavily on two perceptions: (1) how critical the task is to the overall accomplishment of the job, and (2) how difficult it is to learn to perform the task (Sanchez & Levine, 1989). Earlier results had suggested that the difficulty inherent in learning an occupation could be measured by assessing workers' perceptions of the time required to learn relevant tasks (Mumford, Weeks, Harding, & Fleishman, 1987). A more recent study examined the extent to which ratings of *time spent* on a task, task *importance*, and *frequency* with which a task is performed tend to overlap. The results suggest that *time spent* ratings and *importance* ratings are somewhat redundant (Friedman, 1990). Armed with results such as these, Dr. MacKeven and other job analysts may be able to construct more efficient job-analysis questionnaires and interview protocols capable of soliciting more precise responses from job experts (for example, workers, supervisors).

The PAQ may be less appropriate for jobs that would be located further down on the FJA's "Things" hierarchy, because such jobs would prompt greater numbers of "Does Not Apply" responses to PAQ items (Cornelius, DeNisi, & Blencoe, 1984; DeNisi, Cornelius, & Blencoe, 1987). Nevertheless, one of the PAQ's greatest strengths is its applicability to many kinds of jobs. This is particularly important when job-analysis information is used for job evaluations and comparable-worth analyses (discussed later in this chapter) because these procedures are based on meaningful comparisons across a wide range of jobs. Of course, the price one pays for such broad applicability is less specificity in the descriptions of individual jobs (Schneider & Mitchel, 1980). (For the sake of comparison, recall the highly job-specific language that FJA encourages.)

The PAQ has also been used by researchers whose interests go well beyond the boundaries of job analysis. For example, profiles of PAQ dimensions can differentiate among some of the types of vocations identified by Holland (for example, "realistic" versus "investigative" jobs) (Hyland & Muchinsky, 1991). PAQ data have also proven useful for predicting types of stress associated with particular jobs. For example, jobs that demand more from workers in certain domains (say, "Information Input," "Mental Processes," or "Relationships with Others")

tend to be more stressful than jobs that demand less in these areas (Shaw & Riskind, 1983).

Psychometric studies of PAQ ratings have yielded mixed results. When pairs of individuals use the PAQ to analyze the same set of jobs, average interrater reliability coefficients range between .74 and .89 (McCormick et al., 1972). Although these coefficients reflect encouraging levels of agreement, several researchers have suggested that they are artificially inflated. When two analysts agree that certain PAQ items do not apply (DNA) to a particular job ("does not apply" is one of the available, albeit less informative responses to PAQ items), this relatively uninformative agreement tends to inflate statistical indices of agreement or reliability (DeNisi et al., 1987). In fact, one study suggests that reliability coefficients as large as .50 can result when pairs of job analysts rule out as few as 15–20% of the PAQ items through DNA responses, even though they respond *randomly* to the rest of the items (Harvey & Hayes, 1986)! As we might expect, given the known positive relationship between the number of items in a "test" and the magnitude of reliability estimates (see Chapter 5), interrater agreement with respect to individual PAQ items tends to be relatively low. Agreement improves dramatically, however, when responses are analyzed at the level of job dimensions or major PAQ categories (for example, "Information Input," "Mental Processes") (Jones, Main, Butler, & Johnson, 1982). This is consistent with results obtained with other (non-PAQ) job-analysis scales. Broader, more abstract ratings are more reliable than ratings focused on highly specific job characteristics (Geyer, Hice, Hawk, Boese, & Brannon, 1989).

Another issue that has generated research and controversy in recent years is the experience and expertise required of job analysts who use the PAQ. Some writers have suggested that individuals who are naive about the PAQ and unfamiliar with the jobs to be analyzed can still provide PAQ ratings that are comparable to those obtained from professionals who are more familiar with the jobs in question. If so, this would suggest that either (a) the PAQ is such a "user-friendly" job-analysis tool that it eliminates the need for expert, experienced analysts, or (b) the PAQ is not an effective measuring instrument because it reflects only analysts' preconceptions or stereotypes about particular jobs. One of the studies that launched this debate reported that workers, their supervisors, trained job analysts, and students all provided similar information about job content when they used the PAQ (Smith & Hakel, 1979). More recently, however, most of the evidence has contradicted these findings. At this point, the soundest conclusions seem to be that (1) students and other job-naive individuals cannot generate PAQ ratings that are equivalent or even comparable to those obtained from expert analysts who are familiar with the jobs in question (especially when the frequency of "Does Not Apply" responses is low); and (2) small pieces of job-relevant information (for example, job titles) are not sufficient by themselves to trigger common job stereotypes or preconceptions (Cornelius et al., 1984; DeNisi et al., 1987; Friedman & Harvey, 1986; Harvey & Lozada-Larsen, 1988).

Other researchers have criticized the PAQ as an unwieldy (lengthy) measuring instrument that is difficult to use (read) (Dunnette & Borman, 1979). In its present form, the PAQ requires reading skills typical of advanced high-school or college-level students (Ash & Edgell, 1975). (Look again at Figure 3.1. Do you agree?) This means that job analysts who interview workers with less advanced verbal skills may have to "translate" some PAQ items into language that is more readily understood by these workers. Such translations can only undermine the PAQ's reliability. The large number of items included in the PAQ (194) make its use very time-consuming and tiring for the respondent and especially for the job analyst, who must often wade through all those items on multiple occasions with different respondents.

The literature contains several suggestions for overcoming these troublesome aspects. One is to reduce the difficulty of the reading level by making the PAQ's response scales more concrete and standardized through developing and attaching verbal anchors that are more specific than those described earlier (Tenopyr & Oeltjen, 1982). A second is to allow the job analyst to generate PAQ ratings directly from narrative job descriptions rather than lengthy face-to-face interviews (Jones et al., 1982). Unfortunately, recent evidence suggests that PAQ ratings based on lesser amounts of job-relevant information are characterized by lower levels of interrater reliability and are simply not comparable to ratings based on more comprehensive information (Friedman & Harvey, 1986; Harvey & Hayes, 1986; Harvey & Lozada-Larsen, 1988). A third suggestion is simply to "bypass" the many items that make up the PAQ by asking analysts to provide only overall ratings of major job dimensions. Unfortunately, empirical data do not support this approach either. Job-dimension scores based on overall ratings do not converge with job-dimension profiles based on ratings of individual PAQ items generated by professional job analysts (Butler & Harvey, 1988). A fourth strategy for rendering the PAQ less time-consuming and more labor-efficient is to rely on only a subset of the 194 items to collect information about jobs (Friedman & Harvey, 1986). Recent evidence indicates that subsets of lengthy task inventories can yield acceptably reliable scores (that is, reliability coefficients between .70 and .80) over short time intervals (Wilson, Harvey, & Macy, 1990).

Critical Incidents. The critical-incidents technique focuses on specific behaviors that are crucial for successful (or unsuccessful) job performance (Flanagan, 1954). "Job experts" (usually jobholders or their supervisors) are asked, either individually or in groups, to provide anecdotes or examples of behaviors they have performed (or witnessed, in the case of supervisors) or neglected to perform that had profound effects on work quality. That is, they are asked to supply "critical" work-related incidents. After collecting as many of these incidents as possible, the job analyst eliminates redundancies and, often with assistance from the job experts, organizes the surviving incidents into job categories or dimensions. These categories and critical incidents, both good and bad, constitute composites of the essential elements of the jobs under investigation.

A very similar approach focuses on job objectives and goals in order to generate task statements that are neither extremely general (for example, "Supervises restaurant operations") nor extremely specific (for example, "Inserts key into lock when opening doors for business"). The job analyst proceeds as follows:

1. Convenes a panel of experts;

2. Asks the panel to identify the broad, all-encompassing objectives that an ideal job incumbent should meet;

3. Asks the panel to list all of the specific behaviors required to meet each of those broad objectives;

4. Asks the panel to identify "critical" tasks from among those behaviors that are vital to effective job performance due to their frequency, their importance, or the costs associated with making mistakes; and

5. Determines the extent to which the experts agree on the relative importance of the major dimensions of the job. (Robinson, 1981)

Because most of the empirical work on critical incidents has been done by researchers interested in performance appraisal, we'll reserve our detailed comments on this procedure for Chapter 4. It is worth noting here, however, that investigators concerned with the critical-incidents approach to job analysis have addressed the same basic question raised earlier during our discussion of the PAQ: Do qualitatively different groups of workers generate systematically different job-analysis information? There is, in fact, evidence that groups of job experts (for example, workers, supervisors) characterized by different levels of job performance

and leadership skills may provide different job-analysis outcomes. However, those outcomes do not appear to be affected by such variables as seniority or amount of formal education (Aamodt, Kimbrough, Keller, & Crawford, 1982; Conley & Sackett, 1987; Mullins & Kimbrough, 1988). These findings suggest that job analysts who wish to obtain representative samples of job experts must determine which group characteristics tend to be reliably associated with different job-analysis outcomes and choose their samples accordingly. When critical incidents are obtained from a representative sample, this job-analysis technique can be very useful, especially if there are relatively few individuals performing each job (Robinson, 1981).

Miscellaneous Techniques. Although FJA, the PAQ, and critical incidents are the most heavily researched job-analysis techniques, several other interesting approaches deserve at least brief mention. The **Job Components Inventory (JCI)** highlights five kinds of job requirements—tools and equipment, perceptual and physical demands, mathematical demands, communication, and decision making and responsibility—and may be useful for analyzing low-skill jobs (Banks, Jackson, Stafford, & Warr, 1983). Supervisors and jobholders who used the JCI showed significant agreement, and the JCI seems to facilitate differentiation among various low-skill jobs.

The **Occupational Analysis Inventory (OAI)** is a structured job-analysis questionnaire containing 617 "work elements" (descriptions of work activities and conditions) to be used when rating jobs and occupations. The work elements are organized into five major divisions: information received, mental activities, work behaviors, work goals, and work context. The OAI is similar to the PAQ in its emphasis on information processing and its assumption that the task performer is "an agent who transforms information and materials into prescribed outcomes" (Cunningham, Boese, Neeb, & Pass, 1983, p. 234). According to Cunningham and colleagues, who described the OAI as more job-oriented than the PAQ, each of the 617 work elements is rated by a job analyst on one of four scales: significance, extent, applicability, or a special scale designed for a particular item or element. (Again, note the similarity to the PAQ.) Based on their study of OAI ratings from 12 job analysts and 21 graduate students in psychology, these investigators concluded that OAI job-related factors are appropriate for describing the less abstract, more specific activities demanded by jobs, as well as the concrete working conditions under which those activities typically take place.

Another structured job-analysis questionnaire specifically modeled after the PAQ is the **Job Element Inventory (JEI)**. The JEI is characterized by a much lower reading level than the PAQ, however. Data based on 85 municipal government positions and from more than 2,000 members of the U.S. Coast Guard demonstrated that the job factors or components that emerge from the JEI closely parallel those from the PAQ (Harvey, Friedman, Hakel, & Cornelius, 1988).

Although these studies of the JCI, the OAI, and the JEI represent interesting empirical excursions into new territory, a review of the literature concluded that "a plethora of new job analytical procedures has not recently emerged" (Zedeck & Cascio, 1984). The reviewers were encouraged by this observation, however, "since many of the previously developed methodologies [had been] accepted uncritically" (p. 466). They called for comparative research aimed at the validity, the accuracy, and the usefulness of some of the better-known and more widely used job-analysis techniques. We turn now to brief summaries of some evaluative research that responds to these reviewers' recommendations.

Comparisons of Job-Analysis Techniques

Some of the most comprehensive comparison studies have come from Levine and his colleagues (Levine, Ash, & Bennett, 1980; Levine,

Ash, Hall, & Sistrunk, 1983). Focusing attention on the relative usefulness of each job-analysis technique for purposes of personnel selection, one of these investigations asked 64 specialists to compare four procedures: critical incidents, the PAQ, task analysis (part of FJA), and job elements. The job-elements procedure requires job analysts to judge the importance of 55 qualities that a given job might demand, such as keenness of vision, contact with the public, and rapid work pace (Primoff, 1975). The critical-incidents technique was perceived to be more costly than either the PAQ or the job-elements procedure; it was also seen as generating job analyses of higher quality. These personnel-selection specialists also favored the critical-incidents method "for providing adequate information to develop performance measures" (Levine et al., 1980, p. 529). The PAQ, on the other hand, was viewed as less effective than other techniques for establishing the job relevance of personnel-selection instruments (for example, tests, interviews), for "highlighting general job areas as well as specific job components, [and] for providing adequate information to develop performance measures" (p. 529). The researchers were surprised to find that these preferences did not translate into many *important* differences among the outputs of the job-analysis procedures, however.

In the more recent study, 93 experienced job analysts evaluated the quality and practicality of seven job-analysis techniques: critical incidents, the PAQ, job elements, ability requirements (Fleishman, 1975), FJA, a task-inventory procedure (Christal, 1974), and threshold traits analysis (Lopez et al., 1981). For organizational purposes such as writing job descriptions, classifying jobs, and designing or evaluating jobs (see following section), FJA and the task-inventory approach were consistently rated as most effective. The PAQ also received high marks for purposes of job evaluation and job classification. The PAQ and the task-inventory approach received consistently high ratings for their practicality; critical incidents and job elements were seen as less practical. These job analysts generally preferred various combinations of techniques over single methods used alone. Frequently favored combinations included (a) the PAQ and task inventories, (b) FJA and critical incidents, (c) the PAQ and critical incidents, and (d) FJA, critical incidents, and task inventories (Levine et al., 1983). It comes as no surprise that these combinations of job-analysis techniques tend to complement one another's strengths and weaknesses in terms of cost, job specificity, and other important criteria.

A different approach to comparing job-analysis procedures examined global (overall) judgments of job requirements, more specific judgments of job components combined statistically, and specific judgments of components that subjects subsequently combined "in their heads" (that is, nonstatistically). The last procedure (nonstatistical combinations of job-component judgments) generated job-analysis information of lower quality than either of the other two (Cornelius & Lyness, 1980). It probably overloaded subjects (96 workers from four organizations) with more information than they could reasonably be expected to process "mentally." These subjects also viewed global judgments as quicker and less expensive for classifying jobs and assessing similarities among jobs (Sackett, Cornelius, & Carron, 1981). Sackett, Cornelius, and Carron acknowledged, however, that it is "not clear that the global judgement approach could stand alone from a legal perspective" (p. 802). In another study, college students who were asked to estimate the physical effort required to perform a number of tasks provided additional data that support the usefulness of more general ratings of job requirements. The students' ratings corresponded well to the actual physical effort expended when performing those tasks (Hogan, Ogden, Gebhardt, & Fleishman, 1980).

It appears, then, that there is no "one best way" to conduct job analyses. The technique or combination of techniques deemed "most effec-tive" depends on the specific purpose of the job analysis. Recall that Mr. LeGette's memo at the beginning of this chapter expressed concern about comparable worth, which usually depends on some form of job evaluation. As we mentioned earlier, job evaluation requires meaningful comparisons across many different jobs. This demand puts a premium on job-analysis techniques that rely on a relatively small number of general job dimensions or components to describe a variety of jobs (for example, the PAQ). Other techniques that yield highly specific information peculiar to small numbers of jobs, or even to a single job (for example, critical incidents), are less appropriate in the context of Mr. LeGette's questions about comparable worth.

Now that you understand the basics of job analysis, let's turn to job evaluation. After describing some job-evaluation procedures, we'll conclude this chapter with a discussion of comparable worth. We'll examine how comparable worth relates to job evaluation and summarize the controversy that surrounds this issue (and that prompted Mr. LeGette's memo).

Job Evaluation

Job evaluation is the process of determining the value of one or more jobs to an organization; it usually takes the form of assigning monetary values to jobs, or to job components or job factors identified during job analysis. Although many specific techniques are available, they are all based on one or a combination of four basic procedures: (1) ranking, (2) classification, (3) factor comparison, or (4) point systems (Snelgar, 1983). Ranking is the simplest of these procedures. The job evaluator is required only to rank order jobs according to some global criterion or concept of each job's relative value to the organization. Classification involves placing all jobs into a taxonomy (that is, a classification system) of grades or classes. This basically amounts to rank ordering *groups* of jobs according to the mean of each group's relative value to the organization. The "GS system" for evaluating U.S. federal civil-service jobs is perhaps the best-known example of such a taxonomy. Although you might wonder whether evaluators are capable of making global assessments of the relative values of jobs, a recent study suggests that such judgments are quite consistent with more objective measures of job worth based on other organizational documents (Bobko & Donnelly, 1988).

The factor-comparison method is an extremely complex procedure that depends upon identifying "key" or "landmark" jobs within an organization—jobs that are well known and generally acknowledged as being compensated at appropriate rates (Benge, Burk, & Hay, 1941). The key jobs are examined to determine the extent to which they incorporate particular job factors (for example, mental requirements, physical requirements, responsibility). The current pay for each job is then apportioned or "assigned" to those job factors according to their

---

BOX 3.3 Compensable Factors for Jobs in the Banking Industry

I. Skills:

    A. Basic Knowledge and Experience

    B. Judgment

    C. Developing and Maintaining Customer and Public Relationships

    D. Relationships inside the Bank

    E. Accuracy

    F. Manual Dexterity

II. Responsibilities:

    G. Supervisory and Advisory or Line Control

    H. Management Advisory or Staff Capacity

    I. Policy Formulation and Interpretation

    J. Investment of Funds

    K. Care of Bank Assets

III. Effort:

    L. Physical Demands

    M. Concentration Demands:

        1. Visual Effort Required

        2. Mental Effort Required

IV. Working Conditions:

    N. Physical Surroundings

    O. Personal Hazards

SOURCE: *Bank Personnel Administration: A Basic Plan*, by C. M. McCurry, from the Bank Administration Institute, 1979. In T. H. Patten, Jr. *Fair Pay: The Managerial Challenge of Comparable Job Worth and Job Evaluation.* Copyright © 1988 by Jossey-Bass.

relative importance to each job. Other jobs in the organization can then be examined to assess the importance of the same job factors, and those jobs can be "fit" into a job-comparison scale that uses the key jobs (and their known and accepted rates of pay) as reference points. Selection of "key jobs" to be used for comparison purposes is obviously a very important component of the factor-comparison method. As you might suspect, this procedure is so complex that it is very difficult to explain to ordinary employees, especially those who believe themselves to be underpaid (Nash & Carroll, 1975).

Point systems involve assigning points to various levels of compensable job factors or dimensions such as responsibility, working conditions, and required knowledge or skill (to name only a few possibilities) and then summing the assigned points to obtain a total for each job. This approach is widely used and has been carefully researched (Doverspike & Barrett, 1984; Doverspike, Carlisi, Barrett, & Alexander, 1983; Gomez-Mejia, Page, & Tornow, 1982; Sigelman, Milward, & Shepard, 1982; Taber, Beehr, & Walsh, 1985). An example of a point system developed for the banking industry addresses the compensable job factors listed in Box 3.3. Instructions, rating options, and numbers of points associated with various levels of one compensable job factor ("Judgment") are presented in Figure 3.2.

One of the major challenges for the user of point systems is determining the relative importance of the different compensable factors. For example, is "Basic Knowledge and Experience" more important than "Judgment," less important, or of equal importance? If it is more or less important, *how much* more or less important? A

Relative Importance of Decisions

Difficulty in Reaching Independent Decisions	A Small consequence; decisions subject to close follow-up	B Some significance; subject to review by supervision before serious consequence	C Important to bank; adverse effects accrue before ordinarily reviewed by supervision	D Major importance to bank; serious economic benefits or losses only proved by experience
Degree	**Point Value**			
1. No independent decisions required, or of negligible importance.	0	0	5	10
2. Most facts available; one course indicated or rely on specific precedents.	10	20	35	55
3. Most facts available, alternate courses open.	30	50	85	105
4. Limited facts obtainable; alternate courses open.	50	75	105	155
5. Base decisions principally on broad policy interpretation.	80	110	155	220

FIGURE 3.2
Skill Requirements—Judgment

Source: *Bank Personnel Administration: A Basic Plan*, by C. M. McCurry, from the Bank Administration Institute, 1979. In T. H. Patten, Jr. *Fair Pay: The Managerial Challenge of Comparable Job Worth and Job Evaluation.* Copyright © 1988 by Jossey-Bass.

recent study addressed this issue by comparing five schemes for weighting the points assigned to different job factors that made up 71 managerial and service jobs in a metropolitan university (Davis & Sauser, 1991). When the compensable factors were relatively independent (that is, when there was little or no conceptual overlap among them), some weighting schemes did a better job of re-creating existing salary classifications than did other schemes. Under these conditions, "unit" factor weights (all weights are set equal to "1") were superior to "rational" weights (developed "logically" by a job-evaluation committee). When there was more overlap among job factors (that is, they were more closely related), no significant differences emerged among the various weighting schemes.

Given the obvious differences that characterize these four job-evaluation techniques (ranking, classification, factor comparison, and point systems), the choice of which one to use is *not* an organizationally trivial decision. In two separate studies, job-classification decisions and gender-based discrimination that resulted from those decisions (about which we will say more later) differed according to method of job evaluation used (Madigan, 1985; Madigan & Hoover, 1986).

Most of the recent job-evaluation research has been concerned with variables that might influence the process. For example, there is compelling evidence that the level at which a job is *currently* paid has a predictable effect on the results of a job evaluation. Jobs that are paid at higher rates tend to be identified during job evaluation as jobs that are worth more than jobs currently paid at lower rates (Grams & Schwab, 1985; Mount & Ellis, 1987; Rynes, Weber, & Milkovich, 1989; Schwab & Heneman, 1986). Whether the job evaluator is a man or a woman appears to have no effect on job-evaluation results, however (Huber, 1991; Schwab & Grams, 1985). There is some evidence that workers tend to evaluate their own jobs higher than do their supervisors when job

dimensions are relatively abstract (for example, responsibility, judgment). Workers and supervisors are in closer agreement when evaluating more specific job factors (for example, physical surroundings) (Huber, 1991). Another recent study looked at cognitive factors that might affect job evaluations. Results indicated that job evaluations based on *written* job descriptions tended to be influenced by a **primacy effect,** where relevant information that appeared toward the beginning of the written descriptions had more impact than did identical information presented toward the middle or end of the document (Smith, Benson, & Hornsby, 1990). These data also supported the hypothesis that job evaluators incorporate "new" information about a job *not* by simply adding that new material to already available information but, rather, by "averaging" the value of the new information with the value of information already on hand.

Most job-evaluation research has relied exclusively on written job descriptions. Job evaluators are typically asked to read the descriptions and *independently* assess the worth of job factors. An alternative approach is to provide groups of evaluators with multiple sources of information about jobs (for example, obervations of and interviews with workers, in addition to written job descriptions) and ask the *groups* to arrive at consensus regarding the relative standings of jobs on various job factors. An empirical test of this approach that used two independent groups of job evaluators generated data that were reasonably reliable and valid (Schwab & Heneman, 1986).

We have, until now, said nothing about a variable that may profoundly affect the results of job evaluations: the gender composition of the job in question. If a job is numerically dominated by men or by women, does the imbalanced sex ratio influence the assessed "worth" of that job? This is the central question that underlies the controversial issue of comparable worth, to which we now turn.

Comparable Worth

The Equal Pay Act (1963), which amended the Fair Labor Standards Act (1938), stipulates that women and men who are employed by the same company must receive the same pay if their working conditions are the same and their jobs demand equal levels of effort, responsibility, and skill. (Pay differentials based on seniority or merit and performance are permissible.) Administered by the Equal Employment Opportunity Commission (EEOC), this legislation prohibits sex discrimination with respect to pay (except in certain unusual circumstances). We hope you agree that job analysis is the only rational, defensible way to demonstrate that two or more jobs demand equal skill, effort, responsibility, and working conditions.

Pay rates for men and women who hold qualitatively different jobs in an organization (or, on a broader scale, in society) are not affected by the Equal Pay Act (1963). If different jobs make equal or "comparable" contributions to attainment of an organization's or society's goals, should those jobs be compensated at similar or comparable rates? This is the crux of the debate surrounding comparable worth, a debate that has stimulated numerous lawsuits. For example, in *Lemons v. City of Denver* (1980), female nurses contended that their jobs' contributions were no less important than the contributions of higher-paid male plumbers. In *Christensen v. State of Iowa* (1977), female clerical workers compared the worth of their jobs to that of (male) physical-plant employees. The U.S. Supreme Court's ruling in *Gunther v. County of Washington* (1981) that compensation-related claims of sex discrimination are *not* limited to equal-work situations left the door open for further litigation in this area.

How difficult is it to determine the relative contributions or worths of different jobs in organizations or society? Can we not meet this challenge through careful application of job analyses and job evaluations? We believe the answer to this second question is yes. Nevertheless, we acknowledge that the dilemma is more complex than it might appear. Those job analyses and job evaluations must be free of sex biases that can be extremely subtle (Arvey, 1986). We will conclude this chapter with a brief discussion of how such biases can contaminate the results of job analyses and evaluations.

A rather obvious possibility that lies at the heart of many comparable-worth concerns is that unequal ratios of female and male jobholders might influence the results of job analyses and evaluations. That is, jobs of otherwise equal or comparable worth might be evaluated differently because the job-analysis and/or the job-evaluation scheme minimizes or ignores job factors that are more characteristic of jobs dominated by women than jobs dominated by men. For example, suppose our job-evaluation point system either ignores or awards only relatively few points to jobs that emphasize nurturing or care-giving behaviors and, on the other hand, rewards jobs characterized by mechanical job factors or adverse working conditions. Because the former group of jobs is numerically dominated by women in our society, and the latter group tends to be dominated by men, our otherwise "objective" point system for doing job evaluations is inherently biased against female-dominated jobs (for example, nurse, clerical worker) in favor of male-dominated jobs (for example, plumber, construction worker).

Interestingly, recent research suggests that this kind of hypothesized bias cannot explain the pay discrimination women still suffer in our society (Grams & Schwab, 1985; Rynes, Weber, & Milkovich, 1989; Schwab & Grams, 1985). (Specific survey results vary by a few pennies in either direction, but women still earn approximately 70 cents for every dollar earned by men.) In fact, one study reported statistically marginal evidence of bias in job evaluations *in favor* of jobs numerically dominated by women (Mount & Ellis, 1987). Other studies have fo-

Can job evaluation determine the comparable worth of these hospital employees?

cused on the possibility that redundancies among job dimensions or components might lead to gender discrimination. Still others have explored statistical procedures that might be appropriate for assessing differences between female- and male-dominated jobs when the job-evaluation data are not particularly reliable (Arvey, Maxwell, & Abraham, 1985; Madigan, 1985). Although the research continues and the "final word" has yet to be spoken, at this point there is every reason to include careful job analyses and job evaluations in our investigations of comparable worth.

A very different approach is to rely upon "market wages" when assigning monetary worth to jobs. Market wages reflect the willingness of organizations to pay certain wage levels in order to fill particular jobs. In this case, the wages assigned to jobs are influenced by economic considerations such as supply and demand, not by job analyses and job evaluations. If, for example, the "supply" of women who apply for jobs that are already numerically dominated by women exceeds the "demand" for employees, we cannot expect "the market"

to correct any existing wage inequities. Given this approach, such an adjustment will occur only when the supply begins to lag behind the demand. Those who advocate more proactive comparable-worth policies are reluctant to await such economic shifts (which usually occur at glacial speed).

Economic forces are not dismissed lightly in our capitalist society. When 406 compensation administrators were asked to assign new pay rates to nine jobs, all of which were numerically dominated by either men or women, the current market rates (assessed by surveys) were far better predictors of assigned pay than were points generated during job evaluations (Rynes, Weber, & Milkovich, 1989). Similarly, a review of recent judicial decisions revealed that market wages seem to be more compelling indicators of job worth inside the courtroom than are ranked lists of job-evaluation points (Rynes & Milkovich, 1986). Rynes & Milkovich reminded us, however, that the validity of market-wage surveys has not been scrutinized as carefully as the reliability and validity of job-analysis and job-evaluation techniques. We must also acknowledge that the laws of supply and demand do not always function in the labor market with the same precision attributed to them in the pages of economics texts. For example, rather than increasing wages in response to a decrease in the supply of labor, an organization might simply redefine (that is, lower) the qualifications deemed necessary among applicants and employees, thereby increasing the supply of eligible, "qualified" applicants.

Although we are aware that comparable-worth legislation has been implemented in both the public and private sectors of the Canadian economy with some success (Kovach & Millspaugh, 1990), we remain skeptical that the debate surrounding comparable worth will ever be resolved to everyone's satisfaction. Whether we rely on job experts' judgments in the context of job analyses and/or job evaluations, or we accept job-market values (which are influenced by highly subjective social, political, and economic factors), the definition and measurement of job worth will always be a subjective, judgmental undertaking. However, if we pursue the goals of comparable worth through the accepted process of job analysis and job evaluation, we can at least make that subjectivity public. That is, we can put the job factors or components and our guidelines for making judgments about them "out on the table" for all to see. In this way, we can increase the likelihood that all parties to the debate are discussing the same information. These are some of the complications and challenges that confronted Dr. MacKeven as she formulated her response to Mr. LeGette's memo.

Chapter Summary

Job analyses are procedures designed to collect descriptive information about jobs. Because this information forms the "building blocks" for other organizational personnel procedures such as selection, training, and performance ap-praisal, we cannot overstate its importance. Regardless of whether functional job analysis (FJA), the Position Analysis Questionnaire (PAQ), critical incidents, or a combination of these and perhaps other specific techniques is used, most job-analysis procedures require the job analyst to ask workers (and perhaps their supervisors) about their jobs, and sometimes to watch them while they go about accomplishing their work-related tasks. No single technique is consistently superior to the others in all situations. Instead, they are characterized by (often complementary) strengths and weaknesses that make them more or less useful, given specific organizational needs and conditions.

Job evaluation is the process of determining the value of jobs to a given organization, usually by assigning monetary values to jobs or to specific components or elements of jobs. Some procedures are relatively straightforward (for example, ranking, classification), but others are extremely complex (for example, factor comparison). The most widely used and intensively researched approach to job evaluation is the point system. Appealing to market wages is an alternative to job evaluation for determining the monetary value of jobs. This approach depends on the willingness of organizations in a given market to pay wages at given levels in order to attract employees who can accomplish specific tasks and jobs.

Those who advocate comparable worth assert that jobs making comparable (although not necessarily identical or equal) contributions to the achievement of organizational goals deserve to be comparably (similarly) compensated. Many believe this approach to setting wages will help to eliminate persistent pay discrepancies between women and men. Although we enthusiastically endorse this goal, it must be acknowledged that procedures for establishing the worth (comparable or otherwise) of two or more jobs necessarily depend on subjective judgments such as those inherent in job analysis and job evaluation. We therefore remain skeptical that a commitment to comparable worth will be sufficient

INTEROFFICE MEMO

To: Andy LeGette,
        Director of Wages and Benefits

From: Jennilyn MacKeven,
        Human Resources Coordinator

Subject: Comparable Worth Concerns

Your colleagues' surprise, disappointment, and frustration that PPP has not made a specific commitment to comparable worth are understandable, especially considering the tremendous amounts of publicity that have surrounded recent efforts by private and public agencies to implement such policies. I'm glad you assured them that our wages are set according to a professionally developed and implemented system of job evaluation, and that this (point) system generates wage recommendations that should stand up to any comparable-worth inquiries. Given this fact, the senior executives and I determined that the "costs" of making a public commitment to comparable-worth principles and issues would far outweigh the "benefits."

Because it would be unnecessary for us to modify the point system that currently underlies PPP's job evaluations, the "costs" to which I refer would not be incurred here. In fact, the immediate "costs" of addressing comparable worth head-on would not be monetary at all. Rather, the president and a select group of vice presidents believe (and I concur) that those "costs" would show up in the form of dissatisfaction and lower morale on the part of our employees. *Comparable worth* is a term that is neither politically nor emotionally neutral. Making a public commitment to comparable worth will serve only to "rattle the cages" of many employees who are otherwise perfectly content with their paychecks and PPP's compensation system. Because that system does not systematically discriminate against any subset of jobs, we believe that the goals of comparable worth are already being met at PPP without making a "big deal" about it.

Thank you for calling my attention to this issue. Let me know if I can provide you with any additional information or assistance.

to eliminate sex (and other) biases in organizations' compensation plans.

Review Questions
and Exercises

1. What is your reaction to Dr. MacKeven's response to Mr. LeGette's memo (p. 82)? Are the concerns expressed by PPP's senior executives legitimate ones?

2. Based on the little you know about PPP's job-evaluation system, do you share Dr. MacKeven's conviction that it is free of bias?

3. Do you think PPP should set wages based on the results of job evaluations, or should the organization rely upon "market" forces to determine its pay scales? How would you defend your answer to someone with the opposite view?

4. Is comparable worth a reasonable organizational goal, or does the necessity to "compare apples and oranges" render it impractical (or even impossible) to attain?

5. Do you think the average wage gap that separates men's and women's pay rates (approximately 30 cents on the dollar) is a social and economic (and perhaps political) evil that should be eliminated with all due haste? How would you justify your answer to someone who disagrees with you?

6. Based on your admittedly limited knowledge of the kinds of jobs within Peter's Pan Pizza, which approach(es) to job analysis would you recommend to Dr. MacKeven? Which approaches should she avoid?

CHAPTER 4

Performance Appraisal: Criteria, Data, Systems

LEARNING POINTS

After studying this chapter you should

- be able to describe the important role of criteria in I/O psychology;
- understand the potential relationships between an "ultimate criterion" of job performance and criteria actually used to evaluate job performance;
- be able to distinguish among single, multiple, and composite criteria, between proximal and distal criteria, and between "hard" and "soft" criteria;
- understand how job-analysis information is transformed into job-performance criteria, which are in turn converted into performance-appraisal instruments;
- be able to describe three reasons for appraising job performance, and the kinds of performance data most suitable for each purpose;
- understand how "objective" performance data are really not very objective, and why personnel data are deemed superficial;
- understand why most organizations rely on judgmental performance data;
- be able to describe three procedures for comparing two or more workers' job performance;
- appreciate the strengths and weaknesses of supervisory ratings, peer ratings, and self-ratings;
- be able to explain how different rating-scale formats affect the ambiguity of performance ratings;
- be able to define leniency and severity, central tendency, and halo, and describe how each of these undermines the three purposes of performance appraisal;
- appreciate the "process" approach to understanding performance ratings; and
- be familiar with some of the issues that affect implementation of performance-appraisal systems.

MS. DIECKMAN'S MEMO addresses a common source of anxiety for employees at all levels of organizations: performance appraisal. **Performance appraisal** involves comparing a worker's job performance with established standards or criteria of performance. Very few of us enjoy performance appraisal. When it is our work that is being evaluated, we face the possibility of failing to measure up, which can lead to such unpleasant outcomes as lower self-esteem, smaller (or withheld) pay raises, or even dismissal. Some employees who are dismissed on the basis of subjective performance

INTEROFFICE MEMO

To: J. A. MacKeven,
           Human Resources Coordinator

From: E. Dieckman,
           Director of Advertising

Subject: Rating-Scale Woes

Last Friday, literally minutes before the 5:00 P.M. deadline, I submitted performance ratings for each of the employees in the Advertising Department to your office. Each time we are asked to complete these performance appraisals, I experience the same set of misgivings. Consequently, I procrastinate until the very last minute. Informal discussions with other directors, managers, and supervisors have convinced me that my concerns are shared by others. It seems appropriate, then, to share them with you and your staff.

Our system requires us to use 5-point rating scales (1 = unsatisfactory; 3 = average; 5 = excellent) to evaluate each employee on several job dimensions. Here in Advertising, these dimensions include Job Knowledge, Judgment, Initiative, and Productivity, among others. Although I am satisfied with the appropriateness of evaluating these aspects of employees' work performance (because they came directly from the job analyses you conducted for us), I am *not* satisfied with our current procedures. Specifically, the rating scales seem to be too subjective in some ways and too restrictive in others. That is, I'm concerned that my ratings may be biased, either consciously or unconsciously, or simply unfair. At the same time, I'm frustrated by the expectation that I must capture the breadth and depth of each employee's performance in a given area (dimension) by making a single mark on a rating scale. Unfavorable comments about our evaluation system during individual performance-review sessions with employees only add to my discomfort.

What can we do?

appraisals seek redress in court (Barrett & Kernan, 1987). On the other side of the desk, many managers dislike the idea of "playing God" by judging other human beings, especially when their judgments can have serious consequences. These concerns exist throughout manufacturing and service organizations, from steel mills and automobile assembly plants to hospitals and food-service industries.

This chapter focuses on issues that confront I/O psychologists when they develop and install performance-appraisal systems in organizations. We begin by describing the purposes of performance appraisal. Why, after all, do we subject employees to the process? We turn next to a discussion of how performance criteria are developed and to some of the challenges and issues that confront I/O psychologists during the criterion-development process. We then describe various kinds of information that can help us evaluate job performance, paying particular attention to the role of human judgment in the performance-appraisal process. Finally, we address some of the challenges of integrating a useful performance-evaluation system into an organization's personnel procedures. Who should evaluate whom? How often? How can appraisals be used to maximize benefits to the organization and its employees? Throughout the chapter we will allude to Ms. Dieckman's memo, and direct our discussion to her concerns.

Please note the relationship between this chapter and the information in Chapter 3, where we described processes for analyzing jobs. The focus there was on *jobs*. The women and men who perform the jobs were of little or no concern. Except for a brief look at performance criteria, this chapter concentrates on *workers*—on evaluating their skills, abilities, and most important their job performance. Of course, this distinction in no way denies the logical and intimate relationship between these two chapters. Evaluating workers' performance presumes knowledge of what they are supposed to be doing and accomplishing. Perfor-

mance appraisal therefore depends upon criteria developed during job analyses, criteria that reflect workers' contributions to organizational goals.

Purposes of Performance Appraisal

Performance appraisal can contribute to three basic procedures: (1) making administrative decisions (for example, regarding pay raises, promotions, demotions, transfers, dismissals); (2) providing employees with feedback concerning their individual strengths and weaknesses on the job; and (3) conducting applied research that benefits the organization and demonstrates compliance with federal and state regulations (Landy & Farr, 1983). Let's briefly examine each of these.

Administrative Decisions

Every organization needs to recognize and reward employees who perform their jobs well. Behavior that is reinforced is more likely to be repeated than behavior that is ignored or punished (Skinner, 1953). Organizations benefit when more competent employees are assigned more difficult or demanding tasks, when less competent workers are given less crucial tasks to perform or are trained to accomplish more difficult tasks, and when incompetent workers are dismissed. In each case we must be able to distinguish between satisfactory and even exemplary employees and those who are marginal or unsatisfactory workers. "Merit-based" decisions presume knowledge of merit, which is assessed through performance appraisal.

Employee Feedback

It is unrealistic to expect employees to improve weak job performance, or to maintain (or improve) satisfactory performance in the absence of diagnostic information about their strengths and weaknesses. Imagine trying to become a better archer if you are not permitted to observe your arrows hit or miss the target. Quite literally, you would be shooting blind. Although the value of accurate and detailed performance information to workers at Peter's Pan Pizza (PPP) may not be quite so obvious, the same principle applies. Advertising specialists in Ms. Dieckman's department cannot know whether their publicity campaigns are effective unless they receive feedback concerning changes in sales volume or shifts in public perceptions and opinions of their products and services.

Personnel Research

Since passage of the 1964 Civil Rights Act and adoption of the EEOC *Guidelines* in 1978, job-performance information has become more important to organizations striving to comply with federal and local statutes concerning hiring procedures. Identification of techniques for hiring (or promoting) employees who will perform their work well presumes a capacity to distinguish between good and poor performance. Of course, many organizations conduct research just to improve their human-resources systems. Selecting applicants who can perform successfully and rejecting those who cannot maximizes the organization's overall performance and profits (and complies with relevant laws).

Summary

Performance appraisals can help organizations accomplish their goals in several ways. Unfortunately, different kinds of performance measures are optimally suited to the three different uses of appraisal data. Basing administrative decisions on job performance ultimately requires a *single* or (preferably) *composite* index for each employee. Promotions, differential salary adjustments, transfers, and selective training assignments all require us to compare eligible employees. Ordinal-scale properties are suffi-

cient for these single or composite measures that will be used to rank order eligible workers. Constructive performance feedback, however, requires *multiple* indices that should be characterized by interval- or ratio-scale properties. Informing a worker that her overall performance is unsatisfactory does little to help the worker improve upon weaknesses. Nor is it particularly helpful to learn that one is the "second-best" worker in the department unless one is also informed about the specific level of performance that rank reflects. Depending upon the specific question(s) under investigation, personnel research might require single (preferably composite) or multiple measures of job performance, or both.

Two properties that must characterize appraisal data become obvious when we understand the potential reasons for collecting that information. First, the data must distinguish among employees according to level of job performance. Merit-based decisions cannot be made when performance data suggest no differences in employees' levels of job performance. If everyone is "average," or even if everyone is "outstanding," who should receive a promotion? Second, performance data should be free of systematic bias. Feedback that consistently misrepresents workers' performance levels will not help those who wish to eliminate their deficiencies. As we describe various kinds of job-performance information later in this chapter, we'll indicate the extent to which each type satisfies these two important requirements. A "between-the-lines" reading of Ms. Dieckman's opening memo suggests that PPP's current performance-appraisal system generates data that satisfies neither requirement.

Job-Performance Criteria

It's no exaggeration to say that all of personnel psychology depends upon sound criteria for assessing workers' job performance. In the context of this chapter, how can we select specific measures of job performance unless we know precisely what we want to measure? Thinking ahead to future chapters, how can we choose or design procedures for hiring employees unless we know precisely what they must do on their jobs? How can we determine the success of a training program, or even whether a training program is necessary, unless we can describe effective job performance? Finally, how can we pay workers according to their "merit" unless we can recognize "good" job performance? Each of the phrases in these questions (what we want to measure; what employees are expected to do; [the nature of] effective job performance; "good" job performance) reflects the pivotal role of job-performance criteria in personnel psychology.

The dictionary informs us that a **criterion** (this is the singular form of the word; the plural is *criteria*) is a rule or standard that enables us to make judgments. I/O psychologists refer to criteria as measures "for judging the effectiveness of persons, organizations, treatments, or predictors of behavior" (Smith, 1976, p. 745). Just as we use a yardstick (or meter stick) as a criterion for judging a person's height, I/O psychologists need "yardsticks" to measure the adequacy of workers' performance or the effectiveness of organizational training programs. Because inappropriate measurement of performance can have very serious consequences (for example, unwarranted dismissal or promotion, erroneous continuation of expensive but ineffective training programs), choosing an appropriate yardstick is not trivial.

The Ultimate Criterion

A useful tool when making these choices is the concept of an **ultimate criterion,** which comprehensively describes the desirable outcomes of a particular job. Unfortunately, ultimate criteria are not easily measured. Typically a complex combination of multiple job components, such a criterion "is ultimate in the sense that we

cannot look beyond it for any higher or further standard in terms of which to judge the outcome of a particular personnel program" (Thorndike, 1949, p. 121). You can think of it as the most complete, error-free yardstick imaginable for assessing a worker's job performance—a standard that ignores nothing of importance and includes nothing irrelevant.

Given that an ultimate criterion is an abstraction that is difficult or impossible to measure, how can it be useful? Its utility lies in its capacity to provide us with a context or frame of reference for evaluating criteria of job performance that we might develop and actually use. An ultimate criterion is, in effect, an ideal standard against which to compare admittedly less-than-ideal but more easily measured *actual* criteria. Figure 4.1 clarifies this point. Assume that the top circle represents Dr. MacKeven's idea of the ultimate criterion (an inclusive but errorless standard) for assessing the performance of PPP employees who hold a specific job (for example, restaurant managers). The bottom circle represents whatever actual criterion measures she contemplates using, such as performance ratings or monthly profit-to-loss ratios. Ideally, the two circles will overlap perfectly. Unfortunately, this never happens. Her goal, then, is to develop the best description of the ultimate criterion that she can imagine, and then identify criterion measures that she can actually use that come as close as possible to duplicating this ultimate criterion.

The extent to which she succeeds is reflected by the area in which the two circles overlap. This is known as **criterion relevance**, the degree to which an actual criterion captures part of the ultimate criterion. The portion of the ultimate criterion that is *not* addressed (overlapped) by an actual criterion is known as **criterion deficiency**. Finally, the portion of the actual criterion that does not overlap any part of the ultimate criterion is known as **criterion contamination**. In attempting to maximize criterion relevance, Dr. MacKeven will strive to minimize criterion deficiency and contamination. Con-

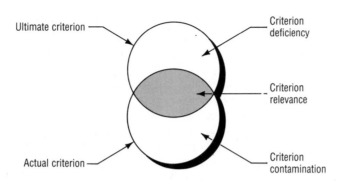

FIGURE 4.1
Comparison of Ultimate and Actual Criteria
SOURCE: From *Industrial Psychology: Its Theoretical and Social Foundations*, by Milton L. Blum and James C.
Naylor. Copyright © 1968 by Milton L. Blum and James C. Naylor. Reprinted by permission of HarperCollins.

sider the following example. Components of the ultimate criterion for a restaurant manager's performance might include (a) highly satisfied customers who return again and again, and who recommend PPP to their friends and relatives; (b) compliance with legislation that governs food preparation and employment conditions; and (c) employees who derive satisfaction and fulfillment from their jobs—to name but a few. Imagine how difficult it would be actually to measure these components. Nevertheless, Dr. MacKeven can use them to assess the adequacy of any actual job-performance criteria that she contemplates using.

Among the many actual performance criteria potentially available to Dr. MacKeven are ratings—in this case, ratings of restaurant managers provided by subordinate employees (cooks, waiters). Can she conclude that a restaurant manager who receives positive ratings from subordinates is more effective than another who is evaluated less favorably by subordinates? Let's see how this actual criterion compares to the components of the ultimate criterion listed earlier. Positive ratings of a manager from restaurant employees tell us nothing about satisfied customers who return again and again, or who recommend PPP to their friends and relatives. Similarly, positive subordinate

ratings do not necessarily speak to compliance with governmental laws and statutes. Do favorable ratings reflect employees whose jobs are sources of satisfaction and fulfillment? Again, not necessarily. These comparisons suggest criterion deficiency in that the actual criterion (subordinate ratings) ignores portions of the ultimate criterion.

What about criterion contamination? The actual criterion (ratings) is contaminated if it reflects factors that are not part of the ultimate criterion. For example, a restaurant manager might receive favorable ratings from subordinates simply because they like him—and they like him because he lets them go home early every other day. Of course, this necessitates closing early on those days, which increases the likelihood that potential customers will be greeted by a locked door. Such folks are not apt to have very flattering things to say to their friends about this manager's restaurant. If being popular among one's subordinates is not part of the ultimate criterion, this represents criterion contamination. Do these subordinates' ratings contain any criterion relevance? Perhaps. If a manager receives poor ratings from employees because of rudeness to customers, who then do not return again and again or recommend the establishment to their relatives, those ratings *would* be relevant to the ultimate criterion. Similarly, favorable ratings prompted by strict adherence to legal and safety codes would also reflect relevance.

Now that you understand the concepts of criterion relevance, deficiency, and contamination, you can appreciate some of the decisions I/O psychologists must make as they choose or develop actual criteria to evaluate workers' job performance. Some of these dilemmas involve the number of actual criteria to use, when the criteria should be used, and how subjective the criteria may be.

Single, Multiple, and Composite Criteria

It's always very tempting to search for a single measure that can serve as *the* actual criterion of job performance. Such an index would minimize the time and expense associated with criterion assessment. Unfortunately, the search for a single criterion that is acceptable—a measure that is highly relevant but neither deficient nor contaminated—will almost always fail. It is difficult to imagine a job in today's workplace that is so lacking in complexity that a worker's performance can be described adequately using a single measure. At the very least, everyone's work can be described in terms of both quantity and quality, which may or may not be related. Certainly, the job of restaurant manager at PPP, which involves making a profit and obeying applicable laws (among numerous other components), is sufficiently complex to preclude capturing performance with a single index. Dr. MacKeven should therefore waste no time searching for a single performance criterion.

What she cannot escape, however, is the need *to be able* to describe each worker's job performance with a single index or number. As we stated earlier, one of the reasons we conduct performance appraisals is to generate information that can facilitate merit-based personnel decisions. Consider a promotion decision. Several employees are usually eligible and qualified

for any given opportunity. Regardless of any statistical or mental gymnastics that might precede the decision, all eligible candidates must eventually by placed in some sort of rank order according to overall merit, so that the "most-qualified" person can be identified and promoted. Fortunately, we can *derive* the necessary single index of merit without relying on a hopelessly deficient (and, most likely, contaminated) single criterion of job performance.

The solution is to acknowledge the complexity of jobs by collecting several measures that, when considered in combination, approximate the ultimate criterion as closely as possible. You might visualize these multiple criteria "filling in" the ultimate criterion like pieces of a jigsaw puzzle. Possible multiple criteria for the job of PPP restaurant manager include (1) customers' ratings of the quality of the food and service received; (2) number of customers who patronize the restaurant on the recommendations of friends and relatives; (3) number of recorded violations of federal and local codes; (4) net profit; and (5) nearby homeowners' perceptions (ratings?) of the restaurant's demonstrated level of social responsibility (trash-disposal procedures, sponsorships of local children's athletic teams, and so on). Multiple measures are essential for providing specific, job-performance feedback, which facilitates improvement in weak areas and maintenance or improvement of already satisfactory or even exemplary performance. A single criterion of job performance is almost useless for providing such feedback. When the situation demands a single index of each worker's performance (for example, promotion decisions), multiple criterion measures can be combined to form a composite criterion. For example, composite criteria can be created simply by adding up all the multiple criteria. An alternative approach is to weight multiple criteria in ways that reflect their relative importance or contributions to the ultimate criterion, and then sum them. Unfortunately, the "correct" weights for given multiple criteria are not always obvious.

Not all I/O psychologists agree that it is always appropriate to combine multiple criteria to form composite measures. Some maintain that multiple measures should be combined only if the individual criteria are highly related (correlated) and will therefore form a "meaningful" composite (Dunnette, 1963). Others argue that all multiple criteria are conceptually related in one way or another to an organization's economic well-being, so criteria can always be combined into a meaningful composite regardless of their empirical correlations (Brodgen & Taylor, 1950). We believe that the decision to use multiple or composite criteria should be guided by the intended use of those criteria (Schmidt & Kaplan, 1971). Recall that personnel decisions (for example, selection, promotion, transfer, demotion, dismissal) typically require that each worker's status relative to all other employees must be summarized by a single number. Because a single criterion is almost always overly simplistic, these decisions demand composite criteria. On the other hand, multiple criteria are necessary when we need feedback information that can facilitate workers' efforts to remedy poor performance and maintain satisfactory or outstanding performance. After all, learning that one is a "3" on a 7-point scale of overall performance effectiveness provides few or no clues to a conscientious employee about how to improve.

Several recent studies have examined the basic construct of work performance, and some have searched for small numbers of "core concepts" that might underlie this broader, more abstract construct. Measures of such core components could be very appropriate multiple criteria of job performance. An examination of more than 9,000 workers in nine entry-level jobs in the U.S. Army suggested that five basic factors may underlie workers' performance in these positions: (1) core technical proficiency, (2) general soldiering proficiency, (3) effort and leadership, (4) personal discipline, and (5) physical fitness and military bearing (Campbell, McHenry, & Wise, 1990). Further, it might be useful to group the five dimensions into two even more basic categories: job-specific and organization-wide factors (Campbell, Ford, Rumsey, Pulakos, Borman, Felker, de Vera, & Riegelhaupt, 1990). Others have suggested that we view the construct of work performance from a broader perspective that includes such components as making changes in one's assigned tasks under appropriate circumstances (Staw & Boettger, 1990).

Reaching consensus about the presence or absence of certain "core" job-performance dimensions within an organization may be only the first step toward using the dimensions as multiple criteria. Although large numbers of superiors, subordinates, and peers of 344 managers in a Fortune 100 company agreed on both the role behaviors and the personal traits of managers that should serve as criteria of managerial effectiveness, there was marked disagreement about the relative weights that should be assigned to the behaviors and traits (Tsui & Ohlott, 1988). Similarly, a sample of U.S. Army officers all relied on a core set of concepts when making work-performance judgments, but different officers tended to emphasize different combinations of those core concepts (Borman, 1987). Such different weights and combination strategies may or may not be a problem. Certainly, each supervisor should be allowed some latitude to define the relative importance of subordinates' job-performance dimensions when providing them with feedback. Less latitude seems appropriate, however, when we compare employees with different supervisors in order to make pay or promotion decisions. In this case, a supervisor's idiosyncratic weights might result in misguided decisions at best and discriminatory and illegal personnel practices at worst (if, for example, those weights systematically devalued the performance of women or protected minority-group members). Thus, in addition to knowing *which* job-performance concepts or dimensions are being measured and used as multiple criteria, Dr. MacKeven must also en-sure that various PPP supervisors are not weighting and combining the concepts in differ-ent ways when creating composite criteria to make administrative decisions.

Proximal and Distal Criteria

Dr. MacKeven must also consider *timing* when she develops job-performance criteria for PPP employees. "When should one obtain . . . crite-rion data? At what moment in time is our crite-rion 'ripe'?" (Blum & Naylor, 1968, p. 182). Once again, answers to such questions should depend, at least in part, on the ways in which the criterion data are to be used. PPP's Director of Management Development might want to evaluate a new training program *as soon as pos-sible* in order to avoid wasting time and money on an ineffective program. She would be inter-ested in more **proximal** criteria. Alternatively, the Director of Management Selection might prefer to *defer* performance assessment until re-cently hired managers have *had adequate time* and opportunity to demonstrate (in)effective job performance. She would therefore be interested in more **distal** criteria. Of course, each director could have different priorities that might affect preferences for proximal or distal criterion mea-sures. Thus, the decision to assess criteria rela-tively soon (proximally) or following the passage of some time (distally) should be made on the basis of the intended use(s) of those data.

When we consider the impact of time on criterion measurement, we confront a related is-sue that has stimulated debate among I/O psy-chologists: the idea of dynamic criteria. If performance criteria for a job change with the passage of time, Dr. MacKeven and her col-leagues must accommodate this instability as they implement performance-appraisal proce-dures in their organizations year after year (Bass, 1962; Fleishman & Fruchter, 1960; Ghiselli & Haire, 1960). Criteria can be de-scribed as "dynamic" when one or more of three kinds of changes occur: (1) changes over

time in the average *level* of group performance; (2) changes over time in *validity coefficients* (cor-relations between specific selection tests and specific criterion measures); and (3) changes over time in the *relationships among multiple cri-teria* (Barrett, Caldwell, & Alexander, 1985).

A review of all issues of *Journal of Applied Psychology* published between 1917 and 1984 and all issues of *Personnel Psychology* published between 1948 and 1984 led to the conclusion that dynamic criteria are rare; that validity coefficients are generally stable over time; that apparent criterion changes recorded in the liter-ature can be attributed to specific methodolo-gies or procedures; and that we might better spend our time trying to eliminate sources of criterion unreliability than continuing to search for dynamic criteria (Barrett & Alexander, 1989; Barrett et al., 1985). Others have urged us to abandon the search for procedural artifacts that might "explain away" apparent criterion insta-bility and focus instead on understanding job-performance criteria in and of themselves (Aus-tin, Humphreys, & Hulin, 1989). A recent study revealed that the weekly performance of 509 sewing-machine operators became consistently less stable (more erratic) over longer and longer time intervals. The decline in stability was not affected by employees' prior job experience, cognitive ability, or psychomotor ability. The study also reported changes over time in valid-ity coefficients associated with both objective and subjective performance criteria (Deadrick & Madigan, 1990). However, another recent study of students' ratings of faculty teaching perfor-mance over more than a six-year interval indi-cated that those criteria were quite stable, and that the stability became apparent rather quickly (Hanges, Schneider, & Niles, 1990).

This debate is far from resolution. Dr. MacKeven should therefore at least acknowl-edge the possibility that performance criteria for PPP employees may eventually reflect one or more of the three kinds of time-related changes described above. For example, a successful retail restaurant operation two or five or ten years in the future might be very different from a successful operation today. If so, PPP's performance-appraisal instruments and procedures will have to be modified to reflect that difference. Although some things will probably never change (for example, customers' preference for friendly and attentive service), other factors almost certainly will (for example, relevant governmental regulations).

"Hard" and "Soft" Criteria

A final distinction that Dr. MacKeven must consider as she develops job-performance criteria is that between objective and subjective standards of performance. **Objective, or "hard," criteria** can be directly counted and usually depend on some form of record keeping. **Subjective, or "soft," criteria** are based on human judgments (Smith, 1976). Examples of "hard" criteria include number of units produced during a specified time interval, number or monetary value of items sold, salary, promotion frequency, length of time an employee remains with the company, number of accidents, and recorded instances of tardiness or absenteeism. "Soft" criteria typically take the form of one person's ratings or rankings of others' job performance. A worker's immediate supervisor is usually asked to provide these judgments, but other potential raters or rankers include a worker's peers (that is, colleagues at the same level of the organizational hierarchy), subordinates, or even the worker herself. In Dr. MacKeven's situation, she might also solicit judgments from some of PPP's customers.

Developing Job-Performance Criteria

As we stated earlier, development of performance criteria should begin with a careful job analysis (see Chapter 3). Regardless of whether Dr. MacKeven develops multiple criteria that are more proximal than distal or more "soft" than "hard" (or vice versa), her goal is to maximize criterion relevance while minimizing criterion deficiency and contamination. Job analysis and criterion development can be tedious and time consuming, and it is tempting to take shortcuts. See Box 4.1 for a "tongue-in-cheek" description of an I/O psychologist who succumbs to such temptation. In the unlikely event that Dr. MacKeven follows this psychologist's poor example, she can expect to make little or no progress toward resolving Ms. Dieckman's concerns about PPP's performance-appraisal procedures.

Following job analysis, Dr. MacKeven must transform that information into useful job-performance criteria. This involves *operationally* defining various levels of work effectiveness. Simply stated, an **operational definition** is a measurement procedure that we accept as a working definition of whatever it is we are trying to measure. For example, if job analysis reveals that interpersonal skills are important components of a particular job, Dr. MacKeven might develop a questionnaire to collect customers' opinions of PPP employees' interpersonal skills. Responses to the questionnaire would be an operational definition of the interpersonal skills. Although this particular operational definition may or may not conform to your *conceptual* definition of what constitutes interpersonal skills, at least everyone can agree on the meaning of this job component as it is used to assess the effectiveness of PPP employees. This is why all scientists rely on operational definitions of the variables they study. They help to reduce ambiguity and promote understanding—major goals of any scientific undertaking.

Regardless of the exact nature of the performance criteria that evolve from job analyses, the criteria must have three important properties. They must be reliable; they must be valid; and they must be practical. **Reliability** is the consistency with which something is measured. If we want to measure a variable that can be expected to remain fairly constant over a given interval of time, it is important that our measurement of that variable also remain fairly

BOX 4.1 From the "Ultimate" to the "Best Available" Criterion

1. The psychologist has a hunch (or insight!) that a problem exists and that he can help solve it.

2. He reads a vague, ambiguous description of the job.

3. From these faint stimuli, he formulates a fuzzy concept of the ultimate criterion.

4. Being a practical psychologist, he may then formulate a combination of several variables which will give him—as nearly as he can guess—a single, composite measure of "satisfactoriness."

5. He judges the relevance of his measure: the extent to which it is neither deficient nor contaminated.

6. He may judge the relative importance of each of the elements in his composite and assign some varying amount of weight to each.

7. He then finds that the ideas required for his carefully built composite are not available in the company files, nor is there any immediate prospect of having such records reliably kept.

8. Therefore, he will select "the best available criterion." Typically, this will be a rating, and the criterion problem, if not resolved, can at least be overlooked for the rest of the research.

SOURCE: Adapted by permission from "Criterion Measurement and Personnel Judgment," by R. M. Guion, 1961, *Personnel Psychology, 14,* 141–149.

constant. Consider the following "weighty" example. For most of us, weight remains fairly stable over short periods of time. Imagine hopping on your bathroom scales first thing in the morning and watching the dial climb to 165 pounds. You know you didn't gobble that much pizza the night before, so you step down, take a deep breath, and warily step back on the scales. Now it reads 115 pounds. At this point you shake your head, brush your teeth, wash your face, and then jump back on the scales for the third time in five minutes. To your astonishment, the dial now registers 142 pounds. How much do you really weigh?

This rather silly example demonstrates a major problem associated with unreliable measurement. In this case, of course, you would probably have some idea of what your "true

weight" actually is, so you wouldn't be completely baffled (and you'd suspect that it was time to invest in new bathroom scales). I/O psychologists who attempt to measure employees' levels of work performance, however, are not in a similarly advantageous position. Dr. MacKeven probably has little or no idea about the "true" levels of workers' effectiveness. To make matters worse, performance measures are usually administered only once during each evaluation period. Dr. MacKeven must therefore trust that the measure she obtains the first (and only) time would be obtained again if she took the trouble to reassess people's performance. Such trust can be placed only in reliable measures.

Important as reliability is, it isn't enough. Job-performance criterion measures must also be valid. **Validity** is the extent to which an instrument measures whatever it is intended to measure. Your bathroom scales are designed to assess your weight, not some other personal characteristic such as your intelligence, charm, or sense of humor. If your scales do, in fact, provide data that reflect your weight but none of these other variables, they are a valid measuring instrument. Similarly, job-performance criteria must provide an index of work effectiveness, not some other variables (for example, satisfaction with the job, extent to which a worker and supervisor socialize outside the workplace). Sometimes accuracy is a component of validity. For example, your bathroom scales might be very reliable but hopelessly inaccurate. If your "true weight" is 123 pounds but your scales *consistently* read 134 pounds, those scales would be providing measures that are reliable but not valid. Similarly, a supervisor might *consistently* rate an employee's performance as "outstanding" (perhaps because they are social friends) when, in fact, that worker's effectiveness is only average. This is another example of a measure that is reliable but not valid. Thus, reliability is *necessary* for valid measurement but not *sufficient* by itself to guarantee valid measurement.

Beyond the psychometric properties of reliability and validity, job-performance criteria must also be *practical*. I/O psychology is, after all, an applied discipline. Although workers' performance must be assessed reliably and validly, the measurement process cannot seriously disrupt ongoing work activities. Dr. MacKeven would not be very popular if she developed reliable and valid measures of work performance that required unreasonable amounts of supervisors' time to complete, or measures that were outrageously expensive. Performance criteria must also be *acceptable* to those who use and are affected by them. It isn't practical to waste people's time with measuring instruments they neither like nor trust. They will predictably resist and possibly subvert such measures, and

thereby undermine the value of any data obtained.

Types of Job-Performance Data

Although the number of actual performance criteria that might be identified for any given job is unlimited, they all fall into one of three categories: (1) productivity, or "objective," data, (2) personnel data, and (3) judgmental data. Let's examine these kinds of performance data in some detail.

Objective Performance Data

Job-performance information is objective if it includes measures of work performance that can be counted. Examples include number of units or items produced during a specified time interval, amount of time required to complete a specified set of tasks, and the dollar value of goods produced or services rendered. Table 4.1 presents some objective performance measures (Landy & Farr, 1983). The major advantage associated with these criteria is that they can be directly counted. Regardless of the personal likes and dislikes of those who do the counting, careful tallies of workers' outputs should yield the same results. In this sense, then, these data are unbiased. A meta-analysis of 53 samples of objective data confirmed that race bias, for example, was negligible (Ford, Kraiger, & Schechtman, 1986).

Unfortunately, objective performance data can be biased or contaminated by other irrelevant factors. First, the decision to use one objective index instead of another is *not* objective. For example, Ms. Dieckman could count the number of ads each of her employees places in the mass media (for example, radio, television) during a specified time interval. Alternatively, she could count the number of formal advertising

TABLE 4.1 Examples of Objective Job-Performance Measures

Job title	Measure
Typist	Lines per week
Forester	Cords (of wood) cut
Keypuncher	Number of characters; number of errors
Service representative	Errors in processing customer orders
Toll collector	Dollar accuracy/axle accuracy
Clerk	Errors per 100 documents checked; number of documents processed
Wood harvester	Number of cords delivered
Tree planter	Bags of tree seedlings planted
Skateboard maker	Number produced; number rejected
Sewing-machine operator	Minutes per operation
Logger	Weight of wood legally hauled
Dentist	Errors in reading radiographs
Open-hearth foreman	Time between "taps"
Inspector	Errors detected in finished product
Tool/die maker	Dies produced
Helicopter pilot	Deviations from proper instrument readings
Bank teller	Number of shortages; number of overages
Air-traffic controller	Speed of movement of aircraft through the system; correction of pilot error; errors in positioning aircraft for final approach; errors in aircraft separation

SOURCE: From *The Measurement of Work Performance: Methods, Theory, and Applications,* by F. J. Landy and J. L. Farr. Copyright © 1983 by Academic Press. Adapted by permission.

campaign proposals each subordinate submits to upper management. These are only two of the possibilities. In all likelihood, employees' relative levels of performance will not be the same across two or more "objective" indices. Second, many countable measures of job performance are influenced by factors beyond workers' control. Compared with their colleagues who prepare ads for radio broadcasts, those in Ms. Dieckman's department who work with television stations will be limited in the number of ads they can run at a given overall cost. If the focus is on the number of potential customers reached, however, those working with national television networks will have a marked advantage. As you may have anticipated, these two objective indices of performance might be combined into a single measure that is relatively free of extraneous influences: number of potential customers reached for ev-

ery dollar spent. Once again, however, the decision to use such a combination of measures can hardly be considered objective.

A third vulnerability of objective performance measures is their lack of reliability (consistency) over time. What can we conclude about a particular employee's effectiveness on the basis of a single ad, or even on the basis of a single advertising campaign? What can we say about a worker's performance based on a single day's or a single week's output? After all, people have "good" days or weeks and "bad" days or weeks. This problem can be partially solved by obtaining objective performance measures over longer time intervals, thereby allowing good days to compensate for bad days. A study of sewing-machine operators, folders, and packers in a large textile company found that average hourly output rates over a span of three and one-half years were about as consistent as

Pallets of patterns counted, sealed, and ready to be shipped. (Courtesy of Pat Knight and McCall Pattern Co.)

scores typically obtained on standard psychological tests (Rambo, Chomiak, & Price, 1983). This suggests that the time intervals necessary to achieve acceptable levels of reliability may be quite long. A more recent study looked at the reliability of foundry chippers' and grinders' output over a six-year period and reported somewhat more encouraging results. Median week-to-week correlations ranged from 0.79 to 0.85, suggesting reasonable levels of short-term consistency in objective performance measures. As longer and longer time intervals were examined (from 1 to 219 weeks), reliabilities initially *declined* a bit but recovered as the intervals became longer (Vinchur, Schippmann, Smalley, & Rothe, 1991). Thus, some objective performance measures may be more consistent than others. Those who use them must attend to the reliability of their specific measures.

Two additional weaknesses of objective performance measures deserve some attention. First, such measures are unavailable or inappropriate for many jobs. How, for example, should Ms. Dieckman go about objectively measuring

her subordinate managers' job performance? What should she count? This is a serious problem whenever employees' organizational contributions do not translate into "things" that are easily or appropriately counted. Second, objective indices of performance are sometimes criticized precisely because they are too restricting. They do not allow appraisers to insert sufficient detail or qualitative information into their evaluations. How adequately, after all, can one or two numbers represent the intricacies and subtleties associated with many jobs? (See Ms. Dieckman's memo.) This is a particularly vexing problem because we typically search for objective performance data precisely because they are relatively invulnerable to subjective, qualitative influences.

Personnel Performance Data

Personnel performance data include information that is often available in employees' personnel folders. Instances of tardiness or absenteeism, accidents, grievances, letters of reprimand or commendation, and turnover (when one's job performance simply stops) are examples of this kind of performance information. Like objective data, personnel data can be counted. Once again, this property is the major advantage associated with using these data. Regardless of the counter's biases, prejudices, or predispositions, two or more careful tallies should yield the same accurate results. Unlike objective data, however, personnel data are *indirect* measures of job performance; they require a certain amount of inference. For example, we infer that a worker who is absent from the workplace is less effective than one who is present. We assume that an employee who quits makes less of a contribution to the organization than one who remains. We often accept a supervisor's negative characterization of workers who file grievances as "troublemakers."

Because such inferences are not always warranted, personnel performance data can be misleading. For example, absenteeism is known to be affected by local and national levels of unemployment (Markham, 1985). Further, some jobs don't require a worker's physical presence at the workplace. Artists, copywriters, and those in PPP's advertising department who devise creative ad campaigns (not to mention certain textbook authors) often do their best work at home, away from distractions and annoyances common to many office environments. Accidents that are attributable to unavoidably dangerous working conditions should not *automatically* translate into poor job performance. A worker who files grievances might not be a troublemaker or an ineffective employee (Klaas & DeNisi, 1989) but may, in fact, be more conscientious and a better organizational citizen than those who do nothing to improve unsatisfactory situations.

Credible evidence indicates that good performers are less likely to quit their jobs than poor performers (Mathieu & Baratta, 1989; McEvoy & Cascio, 1987). However, those who terminate their own employment may not always harm the organization. A study of 731 managers of convenience stores reported a significant *negative* correlation ($r = -.20$, $p < .001$) be-

tween job performance and turnover—poorer performers were more likely to quit their jobs (O'Connor, Peters, Pooyan, Weekly, Frank, & Erenkrantz, 1984). A review of 18 studies revealed similar negative relationships between job performance and turnover in eight of the studies; a positive relationship (better performers were more likely to quit) in five studies; and no significant relationship in five studies (Jackofsky, 1984). No doubt these inconsistent findings are at least partially attributable to such external factors as the state of the job market and the economy (Bhagat, McQuaid, Lindholm, & Segovis, 1985; McEvoy & Cascio, 1987; Steel, Shane, & Griffeth, 1990; Wells & Muchinsky, 1985). People were probably less willing to quit their jobs when they saw fewer alternative opportunities. (See Chapter 9 for further discussion of this issue.) When a highly paid employee quits and is replaced by an equally (or more) competent worker who does not demand such a high salary, we speak of **functional turnover** (Boudreau, 1983a; Boudreau & Berger, 1985). This concept also applies when a marginally competent (or incompetent) worker quits and is replaced by a better performer, or whenever an employee's resignation improves the organization in any way. Finally, it is useful to distinguish between turnover that can be prevented and turnover that cannot be controlled by either the organization or the employee (Mathieu & Baratta, 1989). Examples of the latter include students who leave their jobs following graduation, and spouses of military personnel who are subject to frequent transfer.

Choice of operational definitions constitutes a second problem associated with personnel performance data. When, for instance, should a worker be classified as "late"? (Five minutes after the starting whistle? Ten minutes? Half an hour?) Of course, one is technically "late" within seconds after work is scheduled to begin, but the important question is "When does it really matter?" Gaudet (1963) identified 41 indices of absence. Is an employee who is absent a total of 26 days over a one-year period because of two extended absences (of 8 and 18 days, for example) as effective as another worker who is absent on 26 Mondays during that year? Under what conditions is an absence to be considered "excused"? Is the distinction between excused and unexcused absences important? (After all, workers whose presence is required at the workplace cannot contribute to the organization when they are absent, regardless of whether they are in a hospital bed or on a golf course.) Empirical relationships suggest that the distinction is meaningful. Unexcused absences were more frequent when workers were dissatisfied with pay, promotion, or their coworkers, but such absences were not related to perceived alternative job opportunities. Excused absences were associated with lower levels of job involvement and career commitment, with perceptions that alternative job opportunities were relatively plentiful, and with dissatisfaction with the actual work one does (Blau, 1985; Larson & Fukami, 1985).

Other difficulties with personnel data include unavailability and unreliability. Most workers never have work-related accidents, never file grievances, and never receive letters of reprimand or commendation. Such skewed ("lopsided") distributions of data make it very difficult to discriminate among workers in terms of their job performance. What are the appropriate time intervals for accumulating these measures (McEvoy & Cascio, 1987)? The consistency (reliability) with which individuals file grievances is probably low (Gordon & Miller, 1984), and a study of three measures of absenteeism revealed that all three suffered from a lack of reliability (Hackett & Guion, 1985). As with objective data, the reliability of personnel data can be improved by taking measures over longer time intervals.

Finally, personnel data are sometimes characterized as "sterile" because they fail to capture the richness and totality of workers' job performance. This perception is based on the idea that these measures (that is, number of days a worker is tardy or absent; number of accidents recorded or grievances filed; whether a worker quits) are shallow, uninformative reflec-

tions of performance. They do not capture the rich, qualitative details that underlie the numbers, so they overlook much of what is traditionally considered job performance.

As we did during our discussion of objective performance data, we seem to be talking out of both sides of our mouths at the same time. We applaud personnel data because they are countable and relatively free of personal biases, but we criticize them for being too simplistic and psychologically sterile. It is these perceived inadequacies of countable performance measures that prompt most organizations to turn to the third category of job-performance data. Typically referred to as "judgmental" measures, these indices permit (and often demand) the rich, qualitative subjectivity that is unavailable in objective and personnel measures. We now turn to these overtly *non*objective measures of job performance.

Judgmental Performance Data

Unlike objective and personnel data, judgmental data are usually *not* obtained by counting things. Instead, they represent one person's judgment or opinion about the work performance of another person. Because no one except the "judge" (and sometimes not even her or him!) has direct access to the cognitive processes that produce these judgments, they are (by definition) subjective. Thus, there is no such thing as an "objective judgment." To be sure, some judgments are more free of biases and prejudices than others; but even those that are not contaminated by obvious racial or sex biases, or other systematic rating errors, are still undeniably subjective. This is, after all, the primary rationale for the popularity of judgmental performance measures. They afford opportunity, and sometimes *require* the appraiser to clarify and elaborate on less informative ("objective") indices of work performance.

Most judgmental performance measures result from one of two basic procedures: rating or direct comparison of employees. Ratings typically require one person (a rater) to record judgments about the performance of another person (a ratee) using an instrument (a rating scale) that describes various criteria or standards of excellence. The rater compares the ratee's job performance with the various standards, and indicates which of the standards most accurately describes the performance. The standards may reflect absolute, externally defined levels of performance or accomplishment, with no reference to other individuals, or they may use other employees' levels of job performance as reference points. The two types of scales are known as **criterion-referenced** and **norm-referenced** measures, respectively. A meta-analysis of 23 studies that examined relationships between supervisors' ratings and more objective, results-oriented measures of job performance revealed stronger relationships between these criteria when relative (norm-referenced) rather than absolute (criterion-referenced) judgments were solicited (Heneman, 1986). By their very nature, employee-comparison procedures are norm referenced. Because judgmental data are so widely used in organizations, we devote the next two major sections to these subjective performance measures.

Employee Comparisons

Employee comparisons generate judgmental performance data with ordinal-scale properties. They tell us which employees are more or less effective than others, but they reveal nothing about *how much* better or worse than any others a given employee performs. We'll examine three comparison procedures: paired comparisons, rankings, and forced distributions.

Paired Comparisons

The simplest paired-comparison procedure requires the evaluator to consider every possible pair of workers to be assessed and to indicate, for each pair, which worker's performance is better. Indices of individuals' relative standings are then obtained by counting the number of times each employee was judged to be superior. Although this procedure is intuitively appealing, its use is inhibited by two factors. First, as the number of workers to be evaluated increases, the number of possible pairs becomes dramatically larger. Given N employees to be evaluated, the number of possible pairs is determined according to the following formula:

$$\frac{N(N-1)}{2}$$

As few as ten employees necessitate 45 comparisons; 20 necessitate more than four times as many, 190! Fortunately, there is some evidence that comparable results can be obtained when the appraiser judges only a selected half of all possible comparisons (McCormick & Bachus, 1952; McCormick & Roberts, 1952).

The second potential problem with paired comparisons is a violation of logic known as **intransitivity**. For example, if Ms. Jones is judged superior to Mr. Smith, and Smith is deemed superior to Ms. Adams, then logic dictates that Jones should be judged superior to Adams. Unfortunately, this doesn't always occur, especially when comparisons are based on overall job performance and the perceived differences between employees' levels of performance are small (Tversky, 1969). (Recall that ordinal measures reveal nothing about the size of the differences between measures.) Modified paired-comparison procedures that focus on specific aspects of job performance, and that permit "ties" when two workers are thought to be equally effective with respect to any of the aspects, may eliminate some of these problems.

Rankings

A second approach is to ask appraisers to list *all* their employees in order of relative merit without going through the paired-comparison procedure. Because each worker is evaluated only once on each aspect of job performance, the danger of intransitivity is eliminated. Yet, rankings have their own problems. As with paired comparisons, ranking becomes an unwieldy task when many workers must be evaluated. Reliability often suffers under these conditions. Think of the last time you tried to rank order ten or more things (for example, songs, foods). You probably had no trouble identifying your two or three "most-favorite" and your two or three "least-favorite" items, but we suspect it was very difficult to assign specific ranks to items that fell somewhere in the middle of your list. In fact, you may have assigned ranks "4" through "7" to items in an almost arbitrary way. If asked to reproduce those ranks several days later, whatever you ranked "4" might just as easily have been ranked "6" or "7" the second time around. If Ms. Dieckman ranked her subordinate managers and only the "top four" would receive salary increases, you can see how this lack of reliability could be a very serious problem. Permitting ties, where two or more workers are assigned the same rank, may partially solve this problem, but the power of rankings to distinguish among employees on the basis of their performance is also reduced. A modified procedure known as **alternation ranking**, where the appraiser alternates between identifying the "best" and "worst" performers from an ever-shrinking list, may also provide some relief. Nevertheless, most appraisers will still experience some uneasiness as they work their way further and further into the "middle of the pack."

A second drawback that rankings share with other employee-comparison procedures is an unavoidable consequence of using norm-referenced measures. The fact that Ms. Jones may emerge as the top-ranked employee in a given section of the Advertising Department conveys no specific information about her level of performance with respect to an absolute standard of excellence. Stated another way, Ms. Jones may be the "best of a bad lot." Similarly, someone who is ranked last among a group of employees is not necessarily an unsatisfactory performer. All the workers in that group might be outstanding performers; some may be just "more outstanding" than others. A third difficulty with rankings (and any other evaluation procedure that explicitly or implicitly compares workers to one another) is their potential to have a negative effect on workers' attitudes toward the organization in general, and toward the performance-appraisal system in particular. A study of federal civil-service employees revealed that workers whose performance was assessed somewhere in the "satisfactory" range experienced reduced levels of commitment to their organization, and were more likely to express negative attitudes toward the appraisal system than were workers who fell in the "outstanding" range of the performance continuum (Pearce & Porter, 1986). The message that one is "not as good as" someone else apparently overrides the message that one is performing at an acceptable level.

Forced Distributions

The forced-distribution comparison procedure is a form of modified ranking, where ties are not only permitted but required. The evaluator is typically asked to assign employees to groups or categories that represent different levels of performance. The percentages of workers to be placed in given categories are fixed, thereby forcing the appraiser to "distribute" employees among the various levels of performance in a specified manner. For example, the appraiser might be asked to place workers in categories so that 10 percent end up in the top ("best") category, 20 percent in the second-highest category, 40 percent in the middle category, 20 percent in the next-to-lowest category, and 10 percent in the lowest ("worst") category. This would approximate a normal distribution (see the appendix to Chapter 2). Alternatively, the evaluator could be instructed to place 20 percent of the workers in each of the five categories, thereby producing a uniform or "rectangular" distribution.

Although forced distributions relieve some of the anxiety associated with making more or less arbitrary distinctions among people in the "middle of the pack," they do not completely eliminate this problem. Assigning a person to the middle or to the second-highest of five categories can still boil down to flipping a coin, but the consequences of that decision might be very serious. Forcing an appraiser to place specified proportions of workers in the "lowest" (or "highest") category may also create frustration if she is very pleased (or displeased) with most or all of the subordinates' job performance.

Summing Up

There is both "good news" and "bad news" about the ways in which employee-comparison procedures contribute to the goals of performance appraisal. The good news is that these procedures discriminate among employees, especially the paired-comparison and ranking procedures. Meta-analyses of the correlations between tests of clerical abilities and five types of performance criteria revealed that rankings were strongly related to the measures of clerical skills. In fact, the relationships involving rankings tended to be stronger than those involving other kinds of criteria such as ratings (Nathan & Alexander, 1988). Similarly, compared with supervisors' ratings of job performance, measures of promotion rates were more highly correlated with scores on ability tests in two separate studies of technical employees (Meyer, 1987). Promotions, of course, are always based on implicit (and sometimes on explicit) rankings of eligible employees. Thus, employee-comparison procedures may be particularly useful when job-performance data are to be used in making administrative decisions (for example, promotions, raises). In fact, as we suggested earlier, such decisions ultimately require us to transform performance data into ordinal measures.

The bad news is that these procedures do not facilitate comparisons between workers who have been evaluated by different supervisors, and they generate very little useful information that can be passed on to employees as feedback. Learning that one is first, last, or somewhere in the middle of a group of workers doesn't provide much information about how to remain at the top or improve one's performance. Constructive feedback requires criterion-referenced information such as objective or personnel data, or job-performance ratings (which we examine in detail in the next section). Because they are undeniably subjective and perhaps too restrictive ("forced" distributions?), it is unlikely that employee-comparison procedures can allay the two basic concerns Ms. Dieckman expressed in her memo. Although they are no less subjective, some of the rating procedures described below impose fewer restrictions on those who must evaluate others' job performance.

Performance Ratings

Ratings are produced when one person compares his perceptions of another person's job performance with various criteria or standards of excellence. The standards are usually displayed on a scale, which the rater uses to record judgments. Because workers' performance is compared to external standards rather than to other workers' performance, ratings are usually classified as criterion-referenced measures. Of all the available procedures for appraising job performance, ratings are most widely used (Guion, 1965b; Landy & Rastegary, 1988). Our discussion of ratings is divided into four sections. First, we address who should rate whose performance. Second, we describe a variety of rating-scale formats and point out the relative advantages and disadvantages associated with each. Next, we examine the standards or criteria used to assess the quality and usefulness of rating data, and summarize the research evidence concerning the relative superiority of different scale formats. Finally, we present a theoretical

Peers can provide unique performance information.

model of rating behavior, and explain how this model reflects changes in the ways we study job-performance ratings.

Who Should Rate Whom?

We can obtain ratings (as well as employee-comparison procedures) from a variety of sources, including workers' immediate supervisors, their peers or coworkers, the workers themselves, and their clients or customers. The most common situation is that found in Ms. Dieckman's Advertising Department, where immediate supervisors provide the ratings (Landy & Farr, 1983). Nevertheless, coworkers' ratings and self-ratings can also provide very useful information.

Peer Ratings. A review of the peer-assessment literature concluded that coworkers are capable of providing reliable and valid job-performance information (Kane & Lawler, 1978). Peer *ratings*, however, tend to be less reliable and less valid than peer *nominations*, which require employees only to identify and categorize their "best" and/or their "worst" group(s) of coworkers (an employee-comparison procedure). Nevertheless, empirical evidence and common sense suggest that coworkers have access to unique information about one another's job performance. Peer appraisals are especially useful when performance is assessed for the purpose of providing detailed and accurate feedback to workers (Kane & Lawler, 1978; McEvoy & Buller, 1987). Peer appraisals are less useful when performance data will be used to make administrative personnel decisions. Lack of trust and suspicions that peer evaluations are nothing more than "popularity contests," along with a competitive environment (that is, many employees compete for limited numbers of promotions or raises), render peer assessments less appropriate and less acceptable (Brief, 1980).

Self-ratings. As you might suspect, self-ratings aren't very appropriate for making administrative decisions either (Levine, 1980; Meyer, 1980; Thornton, 1980). The basic problem is that workers tend to evaluate their own performance too leniently. This tendency is particularly pronounced when self-ratings are solicited specifically for the purpose of making personnel decisions (rather than for "research" purposes), and when workers see little danger that their self-ratings will be verified in some way (Eder & Fedor, 1989; Farh & Werbel, 1986). Evidence also suggests that workers are more likely to have inflated views of their own performance when their self-esteem is high, when the performance dimensions to be rated are relatively ambiguous, and when they do *not* have access to comparative performance information about their coworkers (Farh & Dobbins, 1989a; Farh & Dobbins, 1989b). Upward biases in self-ratings are also more likely among nonmanagerial employees (Pearce & Porter, 1986). There are, however, individual differences among employees with respect to this self-serving bias (Waldman, Yammarino, & Avolio, 1990). **Verbal protocol analysis**, a procedure where raters "think aloud" as they go through the evaluation process, is a promising technique that may help us better understand differences in the ways raters process information about their own (and others') job performance (Martin & Klimoski, 1990).

Self-ratings can be very useful for helping employees to improve their own job performance. They can complement ratings obtained from supervisors, and can serve as useful reference points during one-on-one feedback sessions (Bassett & Meyer, 1968; Campbell & Lee, 1988; Meyer, Kay, & French, 1965; Vance, MacCallum, Coovert, & Hedge, 1988). Workers who conscientiously evaluate their own performance are better able to discuss that performance in a rational way, and to request specific kinds of feedback and perhaps assistance from their supervisors. "**Feedback-based self-appraisal**," a technique that encourages workers to base their self-appraisals *exclusively* on formal or informal feedback they have already received from their supervisors, may render the self-rating situation less ambiguous and thereby minimize inappropriate responses (Steel & Ovalle, 1984). Of course, supervisor-dependent self-ratings will complement supervisors' ratings less effectively than will independent self-ratings.

Comparisons of Ratings from Different Sources. Several studies have compared ratings obtained from immediate supervisors with those obtained from peers or coworkers. Some suggest that supervisors' ratings tend to be generally less favorable than peers' ratings (Rothaus, Morton, & Hanson, 1965; Springer, 1953; Zedeck, Imparato, Krausz, & Oleno, 1974). Others report substantial agreement between supervisors' and peers' appraisals of the same employees (Booker & Miller, 1966; Pulakos,

White, Oppler, & Borman, 1989). Recent data indicate that this agreement may be stronger for more global (as opposed to more specific) ratings and for ratings of personality traits (as opposed to behaviors) (Harris & Schaubroeck, 1988). There is also some dispute concerning levels of agreement *within* these two groups of raters. Some researchers have reported greater agreement among supervisory raters (Klieger & Mosel, 1953; Springer, 1953); others have found more consistency among peer raters (Gordon & Medlund, 1965).

Considered together, these data are consistent with a rather commonsense hypothesis that there will be reasonably strong convergence between supervisors' and peers' ratings of workers' job performance but not perfect agreement. After all, these two groups of raters have greater or lesser access to different aspects of workers' performance, and they may be more or less concerned with individual aspects of performance. We can therefore expect them to evaluate performance on different tasks with different degrees of precision (Borman, 1974; Landy, Farr, Saal, & Freytag, 1976; Vance et al., 1988; Zedeck et al., 1974).

When ratings from peers are compared with self-ratings, lower levels of agreement are typically reported, but the convergence may be higher for blue-collar and service workers than for managerial and professional employees (Harris & Schaubroeck, 1988). A recent study that examined ratings of emotional traits (rather than job performance) suggests that agreement between these two groups may become stronger as the peer raters and self-raters become better acquainted and as the number of peers who provide ratings increases (Watson & Clark, 1991). Once again, the sensible conclusion is that there is both agreement and disagreement when peers' ratings are compared to workers' self-ratings (although the agreement may not match that between supervisors' and peers' ratings) (Vance et al., 1988).

When supervisors' ratings are compared to workers' self-ratings, a typical finding is that self-ratings tend to be more favorable (Hauenstein & Foti, 1989; Kirchner, 1965; Parker, Taylor, Barrett, & Martens, 1959; Steel & Ovalle, 1984). Although there is no indication that the favorable bias inherent in self-ratings is different for men and women (Shore & Thornton, 1986), ratees' ages may be important. Supervisors rated older subordinates lower than younger subordinates who were doing the same job, but older workers tended to rate their own performance higher than did the younger workers (Ferris, Yates, Gilmore, & Rowland, 1985). Even here, however, results are not consistent. Both Parker and colleagues and Kirchner reported moderate levels of agreement between supervisors' and self-ratings. Several more recent studies have also reported moderate to high levels of correspondence between these two sets of raters (Farh, Werbel, & Bedeian, 1988; Pearce & Porter, 1986; Steel & Mento, 1986; Vance et al., 1988). Agreement may be greater when self-raters have access to the same comparative information about other workers' performance that is normally available to supervisors (Farh & Dobbins, 1989a). Agreement may also be stronger for ratings of blue-collar or service workers compared to ratings of managers or professional employees (Harris & Schaubroeck, 1988). Additional inconsistency comes from a small number of studies that have reported self-ratings as *less* favorable than supervisors' ratings. For example, Chinese workers rated their own performance less favorably than did their supervisors; and this "modesty bias" was relatively constant across genders, levels of formal education, and ages (Farh, Dobbins, & Cheng, 1991). Recall that earlier data had suggested that age *was* a relevant consideration—younger registered nurses evaluated their own performance less favorably than did their supervisors (Ferris et al., 1985).

Finally, a recent study compared managers' self-ratings with ratings obtained from their subordinates (London & Wohlers, 1991). The two groups showed higher levels of agreement when the manager being rated was a woman and when she was a "line" manager (in the organization's chain of command) rather than a "staff" manager (in an advisory capacity to a line manager). Agreement grew stronger over a one-year interval.

Considered together with numerous other relevant studies (Klimoski & London, 1974; Lawler, 1967; Mount, 1984; Tsui, 1984), these investigations suggest that any search for the *best* source of judgmental performance data is a waste of time. Instead, they direct our attention to the *relative* characteristics of ratings obtained from different sources under a variety of conditions. In this context, Dr. MacKeven would be wise to recall an old expression: "The more, the merrier." Judgmental data obtained from many sources are more likely to provide information that can be used effectively and appropriately in a variety of situations to accomplish a variety of purposes (for example, making fair and profitable personnel decisions; providing accurate and timely performance feedback during constructive one-on-one sessions).

Rating-Scale Formats

Rating scales have been around for many years. Although Sir Francis Galton is commonly credited with introducing rating scales as psychological measuring devices (Garrett & Schneck, 1933), it seems that Robert Owen, founder of an experimental community in 1825 in New Harmony, Indiana, was using "highly developed" psychological rating scales to assess children's capabilities "when Galton was a child" (Ellson & Ellson, 1953). Donald Paterson introduced "graphic" rating scales to psychologists in 1922 (Landy & Farr, 1983).

Graphic Rating Scales. The sample of graphic rating scales reproduced in Figure 4.2 (Guion, 1965b) highlights three characteristics that can affect the quality of the scales: (1) clarity or ambiguity of the *dimensions* of job performance to be rated; (2) clarity or ambiguity of the meaning of various "points" on the scale (*scale **anchors***);

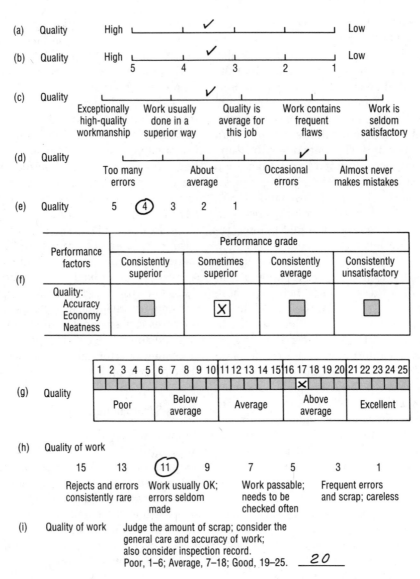

FIGURE 4.2
Examples of Graphic Rating Scales
Source: From *Personnel Testing*, by R. M. Guion. Copyright © 1965 by McGraw-Hill, Inc. Reprinted by permission of the author.

and (3) clarity or ambiguity of the rater's *intended response*. Look at examples (f) and especially (i) where the performance dimension to be rated ("Quality") is relatively well defined. Compare these to examples (a), (b), (e), and (g), which lack any explanatory information about the meaning of "quality of work." Now look at examples (c) and especially (h), which include anchors or benchmarks at various points along the scales that convey the meanings associated with those parts of the scales. Compare these to examples (a), (b), and especially (e), which offer few or no clues to the meanings of specific locations on the scales. Finally, look at examples (g) and especially (f), which permit the rater to respond in a way that is relatively (or completely) unambiguous; there can be little or no doubt about where the rater intends to mark these scales. Compare these to examples (a), (b), (c), and (d). What does the rater's check mark in example (b) really mean? A rating of "3"? or "4"? or "3.5"? We can use the three dimensions of rating-scale quality to evaluate each of the scale formats discussed in this section. Formats that provide specific definitions of the job-performance dimensions to be rated, that provide descriptive and informative anchors or benchmarks at various points along the scales, and that reduce the likelihood that the rater's intended response will be misinterpreted tend to be more acceptable to raters and to yield performance data that are more accurate and useful (Barrett, Taylor, Parker, & Martens, 1958; Bendig, 1952a, 1952b, 1953; Maas, 1965; Peters & McCormick, 1966).

Other desirable properties of graphic rating scales include an optimal number of response options and an emphasis on job behaviors rather than abstract personality traits. A series of studies by Bendig and others suggests that the optimal number of rating options lies somewhere between five and nine (Bendig, 1952a, 1952b, 1953, 1954a, 1954b; Finn, 1972; Jenkins & Taber, 1977; Lissitz & Green, 1975). Fewer than five options prevents raters from making judgments with as much precision as they like; more than nine reduces the reliability of ratings. Of course, any anchors that are attached to rating scales should reflect meaningful distinctions among levels of performance (Barnes & Landy, 1979; Landy & Guion, 1970; Rotter & Tinkleman, 1970; Wells & Smith, 1960). Those who develop rating scales might do well to assume the role of a "test developer," who must pay close attention to selecting, analyzing, scoring, and interpreting alternative responses and rat-

ings (Banks & Roberson, 1985). ("Tests" are discussed in detail in Chapter 5.)

The question of *what* should be rated has yet to be resolved. Some see no reason to eliminate personality traits as potential rating targets (Harris & Schaubroeck, 1988; Heneman, 1988; Kavanagh, 1971). Others contend that performance appraisal should avoid personality traits (for example, honesty, emotional stability), and that raters should focus instead on observable job behaviors (for example, documented theft, "shouting matches") (Brumback, 1972; Kane & Lawler, 1979). Kane and Lawler declared that personality traits serve only to facilitate or impair job performance, that they are not separate aspects of job performance. Recognizing that many raters rely on traits to predict people's behaviors in given situations, Landy and Farr (1983) proposed a compromise that permits "dimension labels [to] be trait names whereas the dimension definitions and scale anchors may be task and behavior oriented" (p. 87).

Researchers have developed numerous alternative scale formats to improve upon traditional graphic rating scales. Let's look at some of them.

Forced-Choice Rating Scales. The U.S. Army developed forced-choice rating scales in the late 1940s in response to dissatisfaction with unrealistically high or flattering ratings obtained from the graphic rating scales then in use (Travers, 1951). A widely used version of this format presents a rater with four examples of behaviors that employees might reasonably be expected to demonstrate; all four are either positive and desirable, or negative and undesirable examples of job performance. The rater must select two examples of positive (or negative) behaviors that, in the rater's opinion, most accurately describe the ratee's job performance. Thus, the rater is *forced* to choose among alternatives that seem to be equally positive (or negative). The key is that, based on prior background research, only two alternatives within each group of four actually discriminate between satisfactory and unsatisfactory workers. The other two alternatives "sound good" (or "bad") but are *not* empirically related to job performance. Each ratee's overall evaluation is derived by summing the number of *discriminating* alternatives selected by the rater.

Because raters are not informed about which alternatives actually discriminate between satisfactory and unsatisfactory job performance and which do not, their overall evaluations of ratees remain unknown to them (Zavala, 1965). Many raters resent being "kept in the dark" this way, and therefore resist using forced-choice rating scales (Berkshire & Highland, 1953). In addition, the rather general, nonspecific nature of these overall evaluations does not contribute to providing employees with useful performance feedback. Finally, a recent study warns that it is very easy to overestimate the reliability of responses on forced-choice scales (Tenopyr, 1988).

Checklists.   In its simplest form, a checklist presents a rater with a list of items that describe a variety of possible work behaviors and/or personality traits. The rater indicates ("checks") the items that are applicable to the worker being evaluated. Overall evaluations can be derived by summing the number of positive items checked. The total number of negative or undesirable items checked can then be subtracted from the number of positive items. **Summated checklists** are a variation of this format. The rater is typically instructed to use a 5-item scale to indicate his or her level of (dis)agreement concerning the extent to which *each* of a series of items accurately describes the job performance of the worker being rated. Unlike simple checklists, these require raters to respond to every item. Overall evaluations are then determined by summing the ratings.

Behavior-Observation Scales (BOS).   A relatively recent variation of summated checklists, behavior-observation scales (BOS) present raters with a list of behaviors related to job performance and ask them to indicate *how fre-*

quently they have observed the ratee engaging in those behaviors (Latham & Wexley, 1977). Raters typically choose from among several "percentage-of-the-time" options, such as 0–19, 20–39, 40–59, 60–79, or 80–100% of the time. BOS evaluations are not necessarily limited to general, overall assessments (Latham, Fay, & Saari, 1979).

Some researchers have suggested that BOS present a rating task that is simpler than that demanded by other scale formats (Latham & Wexley, 1981), but others have disputed this assertion (Murphy, Martin, & Garcia, 1982). A recent study suggests that interrater agreement and rating accuracy are higher when raters are asked to make judgments that are simpler still than those inherent in estimating frequencies of observed behaviors (that is, BOS ratings) (Jako & Murphy, 1990). On the other hand, asking raters to estimate frequencies of behaviors has the advantage of implicitly asking them to describe ratees' *typical* levels of job performance. Typical performance, which is not highly correlated with workers' *maximum* performance levels (Sackett, Zedeck, & Fogli, 1988), is a better indicator of employees' contributions to an organization's objectives. Compared with graphic ratings, BOS ratings provide feedback information that leads to higher levels of goal clarity, goal acceptance, and goal commitment among ratees (Tziner & Kopelman, 1988).

Raters seem to prefer BOS to some other scale formats. Managers and subordinates reported that BOS did a better job of differentiating good from poor performers, generating feedback information, and suggesting training needs, and that BOS were more objective and easier to use than trait scales or behavioral *expectation* scales (described later). Attorneys believed that BOS ratings would be easier to defend in court (Wiersma & Latham, 1986). Like the two scale formats discussed below, BOS are based on **critical incidents** (Flanagan, 1954). As we stated in Chapter 3, these are behaviors or events that are crucial to workers' successes and failures.

TABLE 4.2   Procedures for Developing BARS

Identification and definition of performance dimensions	Group A of job experts identifies all important dimensions of performance for job in question. They also define conceptually each performance dimension and define high, average, and low performance on each dimension.
Generation of behavior examples	Group B of job experts gives examples of good, average, and poor job behaviors for each performance dimension. (Examples are edited by personnel researchers to reduce redundancy and to place each example in the expectation format.)
Retranslation and allocation	Group C of job experts is presented with a randomized list of behavioral examples and a list of the performance dimensions. They each independently allocate or classify each behavioral example to the performance dimension that it best represents. (A behavioral example is eliminated by the personnel researcher unless a large majority [e.g., 70 percent] of the group assigns it to the same performance dimension.)
Scaling	Group D of job experts evaluates the behavioral examples meeting the allocation criterion in the previous step in terms of the effectiveness of the performance described.
Scale-anchor selection	Personnel researcher computes the mean and standard deviation of the ratings given to each behavioral example in the scaling step. Examples are selected as anchors for each performance dimension such that items have mean values that provide anchors for the entire performance scale (from low to high) and that items have relatively small standard deviations.

SOURCE: From *The Measurement of Work Performance: Methods, Theory, and Applications,* by F. J. Landy and J. L. Farr. Copyright © 1983 by Academic Press. Adapted by permission.

Behaviorally Anchored Rating Scales (BARS). Originally developed by Smith and Kendall (1963), behaviorally anchored rating scales (BARS) have generated more empirical research than any other scale format or component of the performance-appraisal process. BARS were designed to reduce or eliminate some of the ambiguities in rating scales described by Guion (1965b) and illustrated in Figure 4.2. A summary of procedures for developing BARS is presented in Table 4.2 (Landy & Farr, 1983).

BARS present raters with examples of actual job behaviors that "are intended as anchors to define levels of the characteristic [being rated], and the operational definitions of the dimension[s] being rated" (Smith & Kendall,

1963, p. 150). Misinterpretations of raters' responses are minimized by asking them to elaborate on each of their ratings by writing descriptive notes about observed behaviors right on the rating scales. One of Smith and Kendall's original BARS is reproduced in Figure 4.3. BARS have been developed for many different jobs (for example, teachers, police officers, nurses, engineers). Although typically designed to be used by ratees' supervisors, BARS have also been used for peer ratings (Landy et al., 1976).

Several researchers have modified Smith and Kendall's (1963) original procedures for developing BARS (Campbell, Dunnette, Arvey, & Hellervik, 1973; Carroll & Schneier, 1982) or

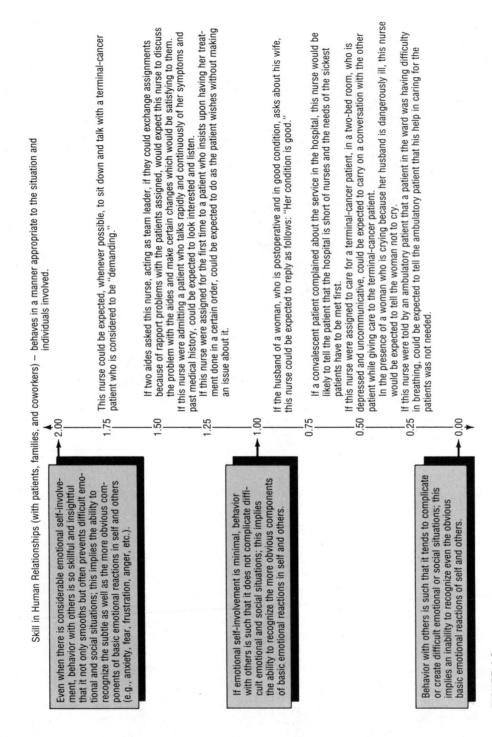

FIGURE 4.3
A Behaviorally Anchored Rating Scale

SOURCE: From *A Method for Rating the Proficiency of the Hospital General Staff Nurse: Manual of Directions.* Copyright 1964 by the National League for Nursing. Research and Studies Service, New York. Reprinted by permission.

changed the actual format of the scales (Landy & Farr, 1975). Because it is unlikely that specific behavioral anchors on any given BARS will correspond exactly to a rater's unique observations of a ratee's behavior, and because BARS ratings may be biased in the direction of conspicuous behavioral anchors that may *not* be representative of a ratee's behaviors (Murphy & Constans, 1987; Piotrowski, Barnes-Farrell, & Esrig, 1989), some scales ask for raters' *expectations* concerning ratees' job performance rather than reports of behaviors actually observed. The anchors attached to this variation of BARS usually begin with the phrase "Could be expected to . . . ," and these scales are known as behavior-expectation scales (BES). Unfortunately, BES have their own unique weaknesses, not the least of which is the questionable legal status of administrative decisions based on supervisors' expectations of subordinates' behaviors instead of work behaviors they have actually witnessed. Such flaws, combined with recent data indicating that the "conspicuous-but-unrepresentative" bias described above does *not* tend to spread across dimensions (Murphy & Pardaffy, 1989), convince us that BES are not an improvement over BARS.

Numerous studies have used indices of rating quality (which we discuss in the next section) to compare BARS with other rating-scale formats. The consensus is that BARS are *not* superior to other formats (Dickinson & Glebocki, 1990; Jacobs, Kafry, & Zedeck, 1980; Kingstrom & Bass, 1981; Murphy & Constans, 1987; Schwab, Heneman, & DeCotiis, 1975). One explanation for this finding (which has surprised some of us) is that raters may share common, implicit theories of job performance and personality, and they may therefore engage in the same cognitive processes when they evaluate others' performance regardless of which specific rating-scale format they use (Krzystofiak, Cardy, & Newman, 1988; Nathan & Alexander, 1985). (We will discuss cognitive processes later in this chapter.) Nevertheless, we share others' belief that it would be unwise to abandon BARS

at this point, primarily because of several desirable "spin-offs" of the procedures used to develop these rating scales (Blood, 1974).

Reexamination of Table 4.2 will suggest some of the positive "spin-offs" Blood (1974) described. The most important is the intensive participation of those who will use the scales (raters) and those whose job performance will be evaluated (ratees), which often renders BARS more relevant and therefore more acceptable to all parties. You can also see in the table that the first three steps in developing BARS constitute a legitimate job analysis using Flanagan's (1954) critical-incidents methodology (see Chapter 3). Beyond these specific side benefits, BARS generate judgmental performance data that are sufficiently quantitative to facilitate personnel decision making and sufficiently specific to contribute to constructive performance feedback. For all these reasons, neither Jacobs and associates (1980) nor Kingstrom and Bass (1981) were willing to conclude that the time, money, and effort that go into the development of BARS are wasted. Neither are we.

Mixed-Standard Rating Scales (MSS). Developed by Blanz in his doctoral dissertation and subsequently refined by Blanz and Ghiselli (1972), mixed-standard rating scales (MSS) also rely on critical behaviors and bear a resemblance to summated checklists. The developmental process is similar to that for BARS, up to the point where behavioral anchors are "attached" to the BARS. Job experts (supervisors, workers, and others) generate an exhaustive list of work dimensions and specific examples of job behaviors that reflect the dimensions. Using scaling techniques similar to those described for BARS (see Table 4.2), three specific examples of work behaviors are identified for each dimension: one that describes excellent job performance; one, average performance; and one, poor performance. At this point, rather than attaching these examples as anchors to performance-dimension scales and then asking raters to check the appropriate value on each scale, the examples of work behavior (excellent, average, poor) for all dimensions are listed in a random order. Job dimensions are neither identified (labeled) nor defined for raters; in fact, they do not appear on the scales at all. For example, if the scale-development procedure yielded nine job dimensions, the MSS would be a randomized list of 27 work behaviors (three for each dimension) with no dimension labels or definitions. The rater's task is to indicate, for each example of work behavior, whether the ratee's job performance is better than, worse than, or about the same level as the example. Raters provide no numerical ratings.

Several scoring schemes are available for transforming raters' "better than," "worse than," and "same as" judgments into numerical ratings. Blanz and Ghiselli's (1972) original scoring system contains some omissions and logical inconsistencies (Saal & Landy, 1977). Saal (1979) offered a complete scoring system that eliminates most of those inconsistencies. Both scoring systems are presented in Table 4.3. A comparison of Saal's system with two other schemes for scoring MSS responses revealed no differences in interrater reliability or validity (Hughes & Prien, 1986). Thus, the usefulness of MSS ratings may not depend on the specifics of the scoring system.

Although MSS have received only a fraction of the research attention that has been lavished on BARS, several studies have compared MSS to other scale formats (Arvey & Hoyle, 1974; Dickinson & Glebocki, 1990; Dickinson & Zellinger, 1980; Saal & Landy, 1977). The results are mixed (sorry!), reflecting neither clear superiority nor inferiority with respect to common criteria of rating quality. The procedures used to generate examples of excellent, average, and poor work performance that constitute MSS were examined in an attempt to understand **logical-inconsistency errors** (Barnes-Farrell & Weiss, 1984). An example of such an error would be a rater's statement that a ratee is "better than" the example of excellent job performance but "worse than" the example of average

or poor performance within the same job dimension. Their data suggest that these errors cannot be "primarily attributed to individual differences in raters or ratees [as Blanz and Ghiselli (1972) originally proposed], but [are] more likely associated with the instrument and the way raters respond to a mixed standard scale format" (p. 313). A more recent comparison between ratings based on the original format and three modified MSS formats revealed no differences in the numbers of illogical response combinations (Dickinson & Glebocki, 1990). This study supports the notion that these logical inconsistencies (which are another example of the intransitivity problem discussed earlier) reflect a flaw in the scale format that undermines the utility of MSS. On the other hand, if this format can tell us something useful about raters, ratees, or job dimensions, this would be more encouraging (Prien & Hughes, 1987).

Overall, the evidence that supports MSS is far from overwhelming. The usefulness of the format for diagnosing problematic raters, ratees, or job dimensions is questionable, and empirical comparisons have not revealed any consistent psychometric advantages (such as higher levels of reliability or validity) associated with MSS ratings. In addition, as was the case with forced-choice ratings, MSS have been known to generate hostility among raters who are kept uninformed about the ultimate numerical ratings assigned to ratees on the basis of their judgments. Like BARS, however, MSS may be useful because of the job analyses and the employee participation inherent in their development.

Summing Up.   Ms. Dieckman's memo to Dr. MacKeven described her dissatisfaction with the subjectivity and restrictiveness of the rating scales that are currently part of PPP's performance-appraisal system. We hope it is clear that *none* of the rating-scale formats discussed here (or anywhere else!) can eliminate the so-called problem of subjectivity. Dr. MacKeven will have to educate the advertising director (and

TABLE 4.3   Original and Revised Systems for Scoring Mixed-Standard Scale Response Combinations

No.	Superior behavior	Average behavior	Inferior behavior	Original	Revised[b]
	Response combination[a]			Numerical ratings	
1	+	+	+	7	7
2	+	+	0	7	6
3	+	+	−	7	5
4	+	0	+	4	6
5	+	0	0	3	5
6	+	0	−	4	4
7	+	−	+	3	5
8	+	−	0	2	4
9	+	−	−	1	3
10	0	+	+	6	6
11	0	+	0	6	5
12	0	+	−	6	4
13	0	0	+	omitted	5
14	0	0	0	4	4
15	0	0	−	4	3
16	0	−	+	5	4
17	0	−	0	2	3
18	0	−	−	1	2
19	−	+	+	5	5
20	−	+	0	5	4
21	−	+	−	5	3
22	−	0	+	4	4
23	−	0	0	omitted	3
24	−	0	−	3	2
25	−	−	+	3	3
26	−	−	0	2	2
27	−	−	−	1	1

[a] + indicates "ratee is better than this behavior"; 0 indicates "ratee is the same as this behavior"; − indicates "ratee is worse than this behavior."

[b] Revised numerical ratings were derived as follows: numerical equivalent of response to superior behavior (+ = 8, 0 = 7, − = 6) + numerical equivalent of response to average behavior (+ = 5, 0 = 4, − = 3) + numerical equivalent of response to inferior behavior (+ = 2, 0 = 1, − = 0) − 8.

SOURCE: From "Mixed Standard Rating Scale: A Consistent System for Numerically Coding Inconsistent Response Combinations," by F. E. Saal, *Journal of Applied Psychology, 64,* 422–428. Copyright © 1979 by the American Psychological Association. Reprinted by permission of the author.

probably many other managers, too) about the advantages associated with subjective rating scales and the reasons we use them instead of (or along with) other, more objective indices of job performance. Choice of format may reduce or eliminate some of the concerns about restrictiveness, however. When used as originally intended, BARS encourage raters to elaborate on their ratings by describing (right on the rating scales) specific instances of relevant work behaviors. Of course, even the plainest graphic rating scale could be improved in a similar fashion. What is important is that the 5-point scales with ambiguous anchors ("unsatisfactory," "below average," and so on) that PPP currently uses *can* be improved by making the anchors more descriptive of actual work behaviors and by allowing or encouraging raters to supplement their ratings with specific observations. This will make the ratings more informative and therefore more useful for feedback purposes. Any of the behaviorally based rating-scale formats (BOS, BARS, MSS) can contribute to such improvements.

Psychometric Indices of Rating Quality

As we mentioned during our discussion of forced-choice ratings and MSS, rating scales must be acceptable to those who use and are affected by them. Acceptability can be influenced by cost, time required to develop and use the scales, the problem of a "hidden scoring system," and many other factors. In addition to acceptability, however, ratings must also possess certain psychometric properties if they are to be useful in distinguishing among workers on the basis of job performance or contributing to constructive and specific performance feedback. This section deals with several properties of ratings that can undermine their quality and usefulness. These undesirable properties do not result from random rating errors (for example, marking the wrong place on a scale by mistake) or from overt prejudices (for example, age-, race-, or sex-related bias). Instead, the focus here is on biases that influence either the variability of ratings or the relationships among ratings on different dimensions.

Leniency and Severity.   Some raters consistently evaluate ratees more positively or more negatively than is warranted by ratees' actual job performance. These tendencies are known as "leniency" and "severity," respectively (Saal, Downey, & Lahey, 1980). Although raters are not always aware of these biases, it is easy to understand how they can emerge. A rater might exaggerate the quality of ratees' performance because of (a) a desire to be liked; (b) a desire to avoid hostility on the part of ratees, particularly during subsequent performance-feedback ses-

sions (Benedict & Levine, 1988; Napier & Latham, 1986); (c) a concern that other raters will exaggerate the performance of their ratees, who will then have an unfair advantage when ratings are used to determine promotions or pay raises; (d) a perception that it will reflect positively on the rater's own capabilities; or (e) abnormally low standards of excellence. On the other hand, a rater may consistently underestimate the quality of others' work performance for a variety of reasons, including (a) a perception that employees who receive very positive ratings may eventually compete for the rater's job; (b) a wish to motivate employees by giving them "room for improvement"; and (c) unusually high and perhaps unreasonable standards of excellence.

A series of recent empirical studies has identified other factors that can affect leniency or severity in ratings. When raters who have participated in and concur with a decision to hire or promote an employee are later required to evaluate that worker's performance, the ratings tend to be lenient. On the other hand, when raters have participated in but disagree with the decision to hire or promote an employee, their subsequent ratings tend to be severe (Schoorman, 1988). More extreme (lenient or severe) evaluations can also be expected from novice raters who express confidence in their ratings (Zalesny, 1990). Ratings have also been more lenient when (a) raters were female; (b) ratees tended to be moderately low (as opposed to moderately high) performers (Benedict & Levine, 1988); (c) raters were in a good mood (Sinclair, 1988; Tsui & Barry, 1986); and (d) ratees tended to meet raters' expectations concerning job performance (as opposed to ratees whose performance diverged from raters' expectations) (Hogan, 1987; Mount & Thompson, 1987). However, neither leniency nor severity was apparent in ratings obtained from raters who had recently experienced stress (Srinivas & Motowidlo, 1987).

Whatever dynamics might underlie leniency or severity, the implications for accomplishing the purposes of performance appraisal are unfortunate. If all or most ratees are rated high (or low), the restriction in the range of the ratings makes it difficult to discriminate among employees in the context of promotion or pay-raise decisions. And because lenient (or severe) ratings are, by definition, higher (lower) than they should be, subsequent performance feedback based on those ratings will be inaccurate. Overly lenient feedback can lead to complacent ratees, and feedback that is too severe can be extremely discouraging.

Central Tendency.   Another example of restriction in the range of ratings is known as central tendency. Instead of consistently rating people too high or too low, the rater in this case rates all or most ratees somewhere in the middle of the rating scale, or "about average." Again, this is not always done consciously, and it is easy to understand how it can happen. Sometimes raters are unwilling to "stick their necks out" and commit themselves to very high or very low ratings because they haven't observed ratees' job performance very carefully. This may be attributable either to a rater's own inadequacy (for example, poor observation skills or laziness) or to the nature of the ratees' job(s). Some jobs, such as store inspector in PPP's Retail-Operations Division or truck driver in the Shipping Department, take employees away from their supervisors, which can make observation extremely impractical or even impossible. In any event, when raters don't want to focus others' attention on their (uninformed) ratings, they may give average ratings that will be "safe," or "unlikely to raise any eyebrows." Some rating scales actually *encourage* central tendency by requiring raters to justify either very high or very low ratings with written descriptions of the specific work behaviors that merited such extreme ratings. Although Ms. Dieckman and her colleagues might jump at such an opportunity, many raters are either too apathetic, too lazy, too short of time, or too uninformed to provide such specific docu-

mentation. Regardless of the cause(s), central tendency undermines performance appraisal in the same ways that leniency and severity do. Discrimination on the basis of performance is impaired because most or all employees receive "about average" ratings, and feedback is inaccurate to the extent that ratees' performance exceeds or falls short of those average ratings.

Halo.   Halo is "a rater's failure to discriminate among conceptually distinct and potentially independent aspects of a ratee's behavior" (Saal et al., 1980, p. 415). Unlike leniency, severity, and central tendency, however, all of which reflect a rater's tendency consistently to assign inappropriate ratings to several ratees, halo reflects exaggerated relationships among dimensions of job performance. A rater's inability to distinguish between dimensions of a ratee's job performance can result from a number of influences operating singly or in combination. You have probably experienced some of these yourself. For example, if an employee makes a notably good (or bad) first impression on a rater, subsequent ratings on different dimensions (that may or may not have anything to do with the first impression) can be unduly influenced by that first, *overall* impression (or aura—this is how "halo" was named). If the first impression is a good one, the halo hovering above a ratee's head can prevent a rater from seeing anything other than outstanding job performance. If the general impression is negative, the rater may subsequently see (and record) only inadequate performance, regardless of the quality of the ratee's actual performance on different job dimensions (Latham, Wexley, & Pursell, 1975).

A second explanation for halo reflects the possibility that *one aspect* of a worker's performance can be so remarkable that it overrides other areas where the employee's performance is closer to "average." It's common for a rater to infer that an employee whose behavior is so extreme (good or bad) in a particular domain of job performance must be similarly remarkable in other dimensions of performance. Consequently, the rater assigns uniformly high (or low) ratings to that ratee on *all* job dimensions. Each of these explanations for halo becomes even more reasonable when raters lack the necessary information to provide accurate ratings on all job dimensions.

A third possibility is a rater who does not understand the difference between two or more job dimensions, and therefore assigns similar ratings on those aspects of employees' work performance. Recent investigations of the "systematic distortion hypothesis" have examined the possibility that raters' perceptions of similarities across performance dimensions might explain observed halo. Most of these studies tend to support this hypothesis (Kozlowski & Kirsch, 1987; Kozlowski, Kirsch, & Chao, 1986; Murphy & Jako, 1989), although others have questioned the viability of illusory associations among distinct stimuli as a reasonable explanation for observed halo in performance ratings (Feldman, Camburn, & Gatti, 1986).

Still other studies have identified additional factors that might be associated with halo. For example, raters who were under stress generated ratings with increased halo across performance dimensions. In the absence of stress, raters with stronger Type A behavior patterns (that is, always in a hurry, very competitive) generated less halo (Srinivas & Motowidlo, 1987). Halo was also less pronounced when raters were depressed (Sinclair, 1988). Other factors or situations associated with greater levels of halo in ratings include (a) ratees whose performance is congruent with raters' expectations (Mount & Thompson, 1987); (b) raters who have greater opportunity to observe ratees' behaviors (Jacobs & Kozlowski, 1985); (c) raters with positive or negative affect (Tsui & Barry, 1986); and (d) raters who experience longer delays between observing ratees' behaviors and marking ratings on a scale (Murphy & Balzer, 1986). We do not yet know the extent to which observed halo is affected by actual relationships between job performance on two or more

dimensions (Murphy & Jako, 1989; Murphy & Reynolds, 1988; Weekley & Gier, 1989).

Because halo can be limited to specific rater-ratee dyads, it need not restrict the range of ratings assigned to multiple ratees (as do leniency, severity, and central tendency). Some ratees might receive uniformly high ratings while others receive uniformly low or consistently "average" ratings from the same rater. Thus, halo does not necessarily inhibit discrimination among workers in the context of making administrative (for example, pay or promotion) decisions. Of course, if distinctions among employees are based on erroneous global impressions, the ensuing decisions will not be in the best interests of the organization (or the employees). The damage halo inflicts when ratings are used for feedback purposes is more predictable. Few of us are uniformly excellent or inadequate across all aspects of our jobs, so consistently high or low ratings will usually be inaccurate.

Reliability.   Lack of reliability can undermine the quality and usefulness of rating data. Recall (from Chapter 2) that **reliability** refers to the consistency with which something is measured. If Ms. Dieckman rates one of her subordinates today, Dr. MacKeven would like to assume that identical or at least similar ratings would be forthcoming if Ms. Dieckman rated the same subordinate tomorrow. We cannot assess the reliability of ratings in this way, of course, because it is impractical to do so (that is, completing even one set of ratings can be very time-consuming) and because Ms. Dieckman would certainly remember the ratings she assigned the day before and simply reproduce them from memory. In this latter case, we would not have two *independent* measures of performance that are necessary to estimate interrater reliability. For these reasons, reliability of ratings is typically assessed by asking two or more individuals to provide independent ratings of ratees' job performance.

Although it is usually desirable for raters to evaluate a group of ratees, several researchers have suggested procedures for computing inter-rater agreement when only a single worker has been rated (James, Demaree, & Wolf, 1984; Schmidt & Hunter, 1989). To the extent that raters tend to agree with one another we can have more confidence in the reliability of their ratings. This is usually referred to as *interrater reliability*. If the raters' assessments do not agree, we often conclude that the ratings lack reliability. Agreement between two or more raters who evaluate the same ratee(s) tends to be greater when (a) raters share the same affect, either positive or negative (Tsui & Barry, 1986); (b) raters are asked to make simple performance judgments (that is, when complex performance dimensions are broken down into more basic job components) (Jako & Murphy, 1990); and (c) raters are permitted longer exposure to ratees' behaviors (although most of the benefits accrue during the first 12 months of observation) (Rothstein, 1990). Lower interrater agreement occurs when ratings are contaminated by leniency or halo, or when raters disagree about

the relative importance of different dimensions (Tsui & Ohlott, 1988).

Operational Definitions of Rating Quality. I/O psychologists cannot be satisfied with *conceptual* definitions of reliability and rating biases such as leniency or halo. We must also *operationally* define rating-quality measures if we are to help raters generate judgments that contribute to the purposes of performance appraisal. Unfortunately, a bewildering array of operational definitions has appeared in the literature, and they do *not* all lead to the same conclusions. For example, a review of relevant studies published in the *Journal of Applied Psychology, Personnel Psychology*, and *Organizational Behavior and Human Performance* (now *Organizational Behavior and Human Decision Processes*) identified three operational definitions of leniency and severity, four of central tendency, four of halo, and five of interrater reliability (Saal et al., 1980) (see Table 4.4). Saal and colleagues also asked police sergeants to evaluate their subordi-

TABLE 4.4   Operational Definitions of Rating-Quality Criteria

Rating-quality criterion	Operational definitions
Leniency or severity	Mean dimension ratings
	Rater main effect (in an ANOVA)
	Skewness
Central tendency	Mean dimension ratings
	Ratee main effect (in an ANOVA)
	Standard deviations
	Kurtosis
Halo	Rater × ratee interaction (ANOVA)
	Standard deviations
	Dimension intercorrelations
	Principal components analysis (a complex, multivariate statistical procedure)
Interrater reliability	Ratee main effect (ANOVA)
	Rater × ratee interaction (ANOVA)
	Standard deviations
	Pearson product-moment correlations
	Intraclass correlations (basically an ANOVA procedure)

Source: From "Rating the Ratings: Assessing the Psychometric Quality of Rating Data," by F. E. Saal, R. G. Downey, and M. A. Lahey, *Psychological Bulletin, 88,* 413–428. Copyright © 1980 by the American Psychological Association. Reprinted by permission of the authors.

nate patrol officers' performance, using both graphic rating scales and MSS. They reported that "reliance on one operational definition [sometimes] produced results diametrically opposed to those that . . . emerged with a different quantification strategy" (p. 421). More recent studies that focused on correlational or variance and standard-deviation approaches to measuring halo reported that these two types of operational definitions are appropriate only when a rater's average ratings on each performance dimension are approximately equal (Pulakos, Schmitt, & Ostroff, 1986). These results are rather unsettling because they suggest that much of the research literature comparing measures of rating quality for different rating-scale formats should be "taken with a grain of salt." The fact that different researchers used different operational definitions of these rating-quality indicators may at least partially explain the inconsistent results that have appeared in the journals. Recall that no rating-scale format has consistently emerged as superior to any of the others.

The operational definitions of the quality of rating data in Table 4.4 suffer from one additional, very serious shortcoming: none directly addresses rating *accuracy*. For example, we discover that a rater gives all of her subordinates very high ratings and describe her as too lenient. We find a particular ratee who receives uniformly high or low ratings and infer that halo is responsible. We observe that two raters disagree about the performance level of an employee and conclude that their ratings are unreliable. Such inferences might not be warranted.

Consider leniency. Might we not expect that employees who have been carefully selected and well trained will perform their jobs in an exceptional manner? Consistently high ratings would then be accurate, not a symptom of leniency. Alternatively, might we not expect some workers to be uniformly good at all or most aspects of their jobs? What appears to be halo could actually be accurate judgments. Critiques of proposed statistical procedures for

eliminating halo from ratings have emphasized this possibility (Feldman, 1986; Henik & Tzelgov, 1985; Lance & Woehr, 1986). Finally, why should we insist that two or more raters must agree about the performance of every employee? Some discrepancies are entirely predictable because different raters typically observe ratees under different sets of circumstances. Furthermore, different raters are likely to have different opinions about which aspects of job performance are more important and which are more peripheral; and the different viewpoints are likely to influence their respective ratings (Freeberg, 1969). Thus, two raters who disagree can still both be "right." Of course, when we find two or more raters who agree, should we not at least consider the possibility that their congruent ratings might be a function of shared biases (error) rather than job-relevant considerations (Schmitt, Noe, & Gottschalk, 1986)? That is, might they not be consistently *in*accurate?

Rating Accuracy.　I/O psychologists have become more concerned with accuracy in recent years. No longer do we operate under the implicit assumptions that ratings characterized by less leniency or severity, less halo, or greater interrater reliability are necessarily more accurate. Although several studies have provided empirical support for this commonsense hypothesis (Athey & McIntyre, 1987; Becker & Cardy, 1986; Fisicaro, 1988; Jako & Murphy, 1990; Sinclair, 1988), others have suggested that accuracy and the traditional psychometric indices of rating quality can be independent (Becker & Cardy, 1986; Borman, 1975, 1979; Murphy & Balzer, 1989; Pulakos, 1984). Still other studies have concluded that more accurate ratings are characterized by *more* halo and leniency (Becker & Cardy, 1986; Bernardin & Pence, 1980; Hedge & Kavanagh, 1988; Mount & Thompson, 1987; Nathan & Tippins, 1990). So you see, this issue is far from resolved.

Quite a few researchers have examined various conditions that affect the accuracy of performance ratings. Ratings tend to be more accurate when (a) potentially complex judgments are broken down into a series of simpler judgments (Jako & Murphy, 1990); (b) ratees' performance is relatively consistent over time (Padgett & Ilgen, 1989); (c) ratees' performance matches raters' expectations (Foti & Lord, 1987; Mount & Thompson, 1987); (d) raters have more opportunities to observe ratees, and distribute their observation time approximately equally across ratees (Kamouri & Balzer, 1990); (e) traits are evaluated instead of behaviors (Heneman, 1988); (f) raters show more signs of being depressed (Sinclair, 1988); (g) performance evaluation is not the rater's primary task and a time delay separates observations from evaluations (Murphy, Philbin, & Adams, 1989); (h) raters have a more articulated (complex) cognitive style (Lee, 1988); (i) true correlations among performance dimensions are high and raters are more intelligent (Smither & Reilly, 1987); and (j) raters organize performance information according to ratees instead of according to tasks (DeNisi, Robbins, & Cafferty, 1989). Accuracy is lower, however, when a rater's liking for a ratee is inconsistent with the ratee's level of performance (for example, when a well-liked ratee performs poorly) (Cardy & Dobbins, 1986).

The effect of training on raters' accuracy remains unclear. Some research has reported no effects of training on rating accuracy (Heneman, 1988); other investigators have suggested that training can actually *decrease* raters' accuracy (Hedge & Kavanagh, 1988). A more reasonable assessment at this point is that training programs that are consistent with the judgmental tasks that raters will actually perform are more likely to improve the accuracy of subsequent performance evaluations (Lee, 1985; Pulakos, 1986; Smith, 1986). Further, because we now recognize the relevance of raters' cognitive processes (for example, inferences, implicit theories), training programs that ignore these processes will probably have few beneficial effects on the accuracy of subsequent ratings (Nathan & Alexander, 1985).

Just as some of the inconsistent research findings pertaining to halo and leniency might be due to the different ways these concepts have been operationally defined, some of the inconsistencies in the rating-accuracy research might be explained in the same way. Implicit in the concept of accuracy is an external standard or criterion that is "absolutely correct." That is, we cannot assess rating accuracy without knowing the "true" performance of the ratees. Several standards have been used as benchmarks in the research discussed in this section. Among the better known are (a) consensus or average ratings provided by so-called job experts (Borman, 1975, 1979; Smither, Barry, & Reilly, 1989); (b) objective measures of workers' output (Smither et al., 1989); (c) tallies of "hits" and "misses" (false alarms and so on) based on signal-detection procedures (Borman & Hallam, 1991; Lord, 1985); and (d) several rather complex accuracy component scores (Cronbach, 1955). Unfortunately, these operational definitions of accuracy don't always tell us the same thing when two or more are applied to the same set of ratings (Sulsky & Balzer, 1988).

Summing Up. All of the foregoing suggests a rather discouraging conclusion. Much of the research comparing rating-scale formats and rater-training programs has relied on criteria that do not consistently reflect our primary concern: rating accuracy. Furthermore, researchers who have examined accuracy offer no consensus on operational definitions of this important construct. Until we develop relevant and acceptable criteria for assessing the quality of rating data, neither researchers nor practitioners will make much progress toward improving the quality and usefulness of job-performance ratings.

Rather than concentrating on the end product (that is, the ratings), an alternative approach to studying ratings focuses on the *processes* involved when one person uses a rating scale to record judgments about another's behavior. In

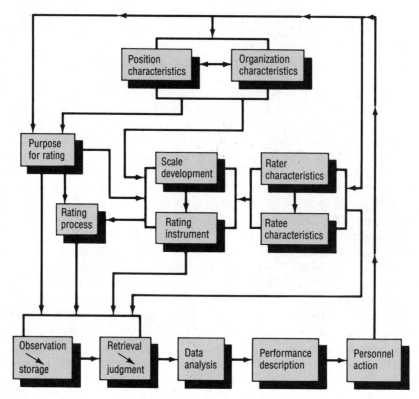

FIGURE 4.4
Landy and Farr's Process Model of Performance Rating
SOURCE: From "Performance Rating," by F. J. Landy and J. L. Farr, *Psychological Bulletin, 87*, 72–107. Copyright
© 1980 by the American Psychological Association. Reprinted by permission of the authors.

the irreverent words of Landy and Farr (1983): "It appears likely that greater progress in understanding performance judgments will come from research on the rating process than from a continued search for the 'Holy Format' " (p. 90). A model that reflects this approach is described below, along with some examples of relevant empirical research.

A Model of Performance-Rating Processes

Following an extensive review of performance-rating literature published since 1950 (see Wherry, 1950, for a review of earlier studies), Landy and Farr (1980) offered a comprehensive model of performance-rating processes. Their model, which is presented in Figure 4.4, comprises several kinds of processes. First and foremost are the rater's *cognitive* processes. These include observation of ratees' job performance as well as storage, retrieval, and judgment (evaluation) of that information. Many studies of raters' cognitive styles (Cardy & Kehoe, 1984; Lahey & Saal, 1981; Lord, 1985; Nathan & Lord, 1983), memory processes (Larson, Lingle, & Scerbo, 1984; Murphy, Balzer, Lockhart, & Eisenman, 1985; Phillips, 1984), and judgmental inferences (Nathan & Alexander, 1985) attest to the centrality of raters' cognitive processes in a performance-rating system.

Recent investigations have continued to examine how ratings are influenced by the order in which raters obtain information and the nature of previous ratings (Williams, DeNisi, Meglino, & Cafferty, 1986). When a single instance of poor or good performance was presented to raters *last* (that is, in closest proximity to when ratings were made), overall performance ratings were heavily influenced by that performance event—a **recency effect**. The same study found some support for an **assimilation effect**, where performance that is inconsistent with an established stable impression of an employee is cognitively biased in the direction of that stable impression (Steiner & Rain, 1989). When raters were asked to recall ratees' behaviors, they showed a bias in favor of behaviors that were consistent with their general impression of a ratee, further supporting an assimilation effect (Murphy, Gannett, Herr, & Chen, 1986).

In another study, when raters learned about a ratee's prior performance from having seen his performance ratings, an assimilation effect emerged. However, when prior knowledge was obtained through direct observation of a ratee's behavior, a **contrast effect**—where ratings of "discrepant" behaviors are even more extreme when they are appraised in a context of otherwise "average" or "expected" behaviors—was reported (Smither, Reilly, & Buda, 1988). When observations and ratings were separated by a three-week interval, however, the contrast effect disappeared. Other studies have also reported contrast effects that tend to decay or disappear over time (Balzer, 1986; Hogan, 1987; Murphy, Balzer, Lockhart, & Eisenman, 1985). Recent evidence suggests that contrast effects may be attributable to special encoding of unexpected information, or perhaps heavy reliance upon such information. Contrast effects are probably *not* due to short-term shifts in raters' standards or criteria for evaluating performance (Maurer & Alexander, 1991).

A second set of processes includes the organization's *administrative* procedures that influence performance ratings. These include procedures used to develop rating scales, actual rating instruments or scale formats used, determination of who should rate whom, and training of raters. Because much of the early research on training programs for improving the quality of raters' judgments relied on halo, leniency, and interrater reliability as criteria, it is difficult to interpret the results (Bernardin, 1978; Bernardin & Walter, 1977; Brown, 1968; Ivancevich, 1979; Latham, Wexley, & Pursell, 1975). Following a review of 24 rater-training studies, Smith (1986) concluded that **rater-error training**, which focuses on reducing halo and leniency, is inappropriate for improving rater accuracy. Others have agreed (Hedge & Kavanagh, 1988).

Other investigators have acknowledged the importance of accuracy as *the* crucial criterion of rater-training success (Bernardin & Pence, 1980; McIntyre, Smith, & Hassett, 1984; Pulakos, 1984). Although not all of the findings are encouraging (for example, Heneman, 1988), much of the evidence suggests that accuracy can be improved when the training is consistent with the tasks required of raters (for example, observation and/or evaluation of behavior) (Pulakos, 1986). **Frame-of-reference training**, which teaches raters to adopt a common perspective from which to evaluate employees' performance, thereby "standardizing" their perceptions and subsequent ratings, has shown some potential for making ratings more accurate (Athey & McIntyre, 1987; Hauenstein & Foti, 1989).

Characteristics of raters and ratees can also play important roles in a rating system. For example, a meta-analysis of race effects in performance ratings indicated that "both black and white raters gave significantly higher ratings to members of their own race" (Kraiger & Ford, 1985, p. 60). These same-race biases were more noticeable in field studies than in laboratory settings, and in samples where blacks constituted relatively small minorities. However, a more recent study of 486 heterogeneous work groups from a variety of jobs and organizations failed to detect any influence of the groups' racial composition on performance ratings (Sackett, DuBois, & Noe, 1991).

Although reports of blacks receiving lower ratings than their white colleagues have appeared in the literature (Greenhaus, Parasuraman, & Wormley, 1990), most studies of race effects on performance ratings report either no differences or differences that explain only very small proportions of the variability in ratings (Ford, Kraiger, & Schechtman, 1986; Pulakos, White, Oppler, & Borman, 1989; Thompson & Thompson, 1985). Furthermore, the data suggest that effects of race on subjective measures of job performance are no greater than its effects on more objective performance measures (Ford et al., 1986). However, it also appears that supervisors' ratings of black employees bear a closer relationship to more objective measures of work performance than do their ratings of white employees (Kraiger & Ford, 1990). These studies suggest that the effects of raters' and ratees' race(s) on performance ratings are complex. We are encouraged, however, that these effects are probably not very powerful.

Effects of raters' and ratees' sex on performance ratings are certainly no less complex. Although numerous studies have concluded that the influence of sex on ratings is either nonexistent or negligible (Barnes-Farrell, L'Heureux-Barrett, & Conway, 1991; Farh, Dobbins, & Cheng, 1991; Izraeli & Izraeli, 1985; Pulakos et al., 1989; Shore & Thornton, 1986; Swim, Borgida, Maruyama, & Myers, 1989; Thompson & Thompson, 1985), other data lead to more troubling conclusions. Reports of rating biases among both male and female raters that favor male over female ratees are quite common (Mobley, 1982; Pazy, 1986; Peters, O'Conner, Weekley, Pooyan, Frank, & Erenkrantz, 1984; Wexley & Pulakos, 1982).

This promale bias seems to be more prevalent under specific circumstances, suggesting that other characteristics of ratees, raters, jobs, and work groups may be important. For example, although evaluations of male ratees were *not* affected by their physical attractiveness, the situation is probably more complicated for women. Women who held *non*managerial positions were evaluated more favorably if they were physically attractive; but attractive female managers received less favorable performance evaluations (Heilman & Stopeck, 1985b). Women were also rated less favorably when they constituted a smaller proportion of the employee group (Sackett, DuBois, & Noe, 1991). Although there was no indication that assertive women were evaluated less favorably than assertive men, male raters reserved their highest ratings for male employees who took a "tactical" (calculating) approach to influencing others, and they assigned similarly favorable ratings to female subordinates whose approaches were more "ingratiating" or "noninterventionist" (Kipnis & Schmidt, 1988).

Finally, rater characteristics can be important. Women who were evaluated by lower-level raters received less favorable ratings than their female colleagues who were rated by more senior organizational personnel (Izraeli & Izraeli, 1985). Women whose raters held traditional stereotypes about women received less accurate and less favorable ratings than their female colleagues whose supervisors held nontraditional stereotypes. Men's evaluations were not affected by their raters' stereotypes concerning appropriate sex-role behaviors (Dobbins, Cardy, & Truxillo, 1988). Recent evidence also suggests that female raters may be more willing than their male counterparts to assign extremely high or extremely low ratings (Northcraft, Huber, & Neale, 1988). As you have no doubt surmised by now, the influences of gender on performance ratings are probably far more complex and less easily dismissed than the effects of race.

Age effects on performance ratings have also been examined. Although some supervisors may be less positively disposed toward older workers than younger (regardless of the supervisor age), older workers seem to be more positive about themselves and their own performance than are younger workers (Bird & Fisher, 1986; Cleveland & Landy, 1981; Ferris et al., 1985). Relationships between age and performance ratings can be better understood in a context of cultural and societal norms pertaining to age (Farh, Dobbins, & Cheng, 1991; Lawrence, 1988). It is also important to recall that age, in and of itself, may be less important than other factors typically associated with age. For example, a recent study found that experience was a better predictor than age of performance on nonmanagerial jobs (Avolio, Waldman, & McDaniel, 1990). Although age bias in performance evaluation is specifically forbidden by federal regulations, a review of 53 federal court cases based on the Age Discrimination in Employment Act (1967) suggests that "formal performance evaluation procedures have not been required for an employer-defendant to mount a successful defense" (Miller, Kaspin, & Schuster, 1990, p. 575). We are not yet in a position to draw any firm conclusions regarding the effects of age on performance evaluations.

Although the literature is far less voluminous than that dealing with demographic variables (that is, race, sex, age), potential effects on performance ratings of other rater and ratee characteristics have been investigated. Examples of recent findings include the following: (a) novice raters with greater levels of confidence in their ratings were willing to provide more extreme (both high and low) evaluations (Zalesny, 1990); (b) ratees who were perceived to be satisfied with their jobs received more favorable evaluations than did ratees who were thought to be dissatisfied (Smither, Collins, & Buda, 1989); (c) raters' values have implications for their evaluations of others' performance (Jolly, Reynolds, & Slocum, 1988); (d) ratings of job performance are positively related to raters' perceptions of ratees' levels of job knowledge (Schmidt, Hunter, & Outerbridge, 1986); (e) raters' positive or negative affect toward ratees is related to performance ratings (Cardy & Dobbins, 1986; Tsui & Barry, 1986); (f) ratees' interpersonal styles for influencing their supervisors, as well as ratees' abilities to manage supervisors' impressions, stimulated different performance evaluations (Kipnis & Schmidt, 1988; Wayne & Kacmar, 1991); (g) ratees with emo-

tional instabilities were evaluated more favorably in the absence of clear performance standards (Czajka & DeNisi, 1988); and (h) ratings were more favorable when actual and perceived similarities between raters and ratees were greater (Tsui & O'Reilly, 1989; Turban & Jones, 1988). Thus, there is strong empirical evidence that rater and ratee characteristics have important effects on performance ratings (Landy & Farr, 1980).

Landy and Farr's (1980) process model also acknowledges the importance of the *context* in which ratings are generated. Organizational size, characteristics of the ratee's position (for example, level in the hierarchy, blue- versus white-collar), and the purpose for which the ratings are generated help to define this context. A recent study of more than 8,000 enlisted personnel in the U.S. Army reported that performance ratings were significantly affected by job type, although the effect was not very large (Pulakos et al., 1989). In another relevant investigation, occupational type influenced the size of the relationship between workers' ages and their performance in nonmanagerial jobs (Avolio, Waldman, & McDaniel, 1990). Ratings generated strictly for research purposes tended to be more severe than ratings generated to make administrative decisions (McIntyre et al., 1984). This finding is typically explained by appealing to raters' compassion and their reluctance to deprive subordinates of organizational rewards such as pay increases. However, "the purpose of an appraisal decision may [also] serve a cognitive function in addition to the motivational function usually proposed" (Williams, DeNisi, Blencoe, & Cafferty, 1985, p. 334). That is, raters who know that their ratings will be used for administrative purposes may actually observe, categorize, and remember subordinates' work behaviors differently than raters who have been assured that their ratings will be used exclusively for research (or feedback) purposes. Recent evidence indicates that raters who endorse traditional stereotypes concerning appropriate behavior for women tend to rate female workers less accurately, but only when appraisals are made expressly for administrative (rather than research) purposes (Dobbins, Cardy, & Truxillo, 1988). Dickinson (1987) suggested a research design that is capable of isolating the influences of raters, ratees, and context factors on performance ratings.

Summing Up. Whether future research ultimately confirms and expands upon Landy and Farr's (1980) process model or refutes it, this model and others like it (see, for example, DeNisi, Cafferty, & Meglino, 1984) have stimulated important contributions to our understanding of subjective performance appraisals. They are rich sources of hypotheses, and they offer guidance to Dr. MacKeven, Ms. Dieckman, and others who wrestle with the challenges of developing and implementing performance-appraisal systems that can accomplish their desired purposes fairly and efficiently. Dr. MacKeven will be wise to consult these models as she revises PPP's performance-appraisal system, and explains their respective roles in that system to Ms. Dieckman and other raters. Acknowledging the importance of observation and other cognitive skills (for example, storage, retrieval) demanded by the system, and providing systematic training to help employees develop those skills (see Chapter 7), can alleviate managers' fears about bias. Modifying the rating-scale format and allowing raters to elaborate on the meanings of their ratings should reduce their feelings of constraint and restriction. These suggestions anticipate the final section of this chapter, where we discuss some of the obstacles that litter the paths of those who would implement performance-appraisal systems.

Putting a Performance-Appraisal System to Work

Among Dr. MacKeven's challenges as she attempts to integrate a performance-appraisal system into PPP's personnel procedures are the following: (1) clarifying managers' and workers' respective roles; (2) determining how often employees' performance should be formally appraised; (3) actually using performance data to make administrative decisions and provide feedback, effectively and efficiently; and (4) obeying federal and state laws.

Employees' Roles

Any performance-appraisal system will generate data that are more reliable and more accurate if the system is accepted and used willingly, if not enthusiastically, by those who are affected by it, from hourly workers to the chief executive officer. Upper-level managers' support is crucial to the system's credibility. They must provide adequate time to complete appraisals, and they must reward raters for providing accurate assessments of workers' performance. Rank-and-file workers will not take feedback seriously nor will they believe that personnel decisions are being made fairly unless they respect the system. As we suggested earlier, asking employees from all levels of the organizational hierarchy to participate in developing and implementing a performance-appraisal system can stimulate this kind of support and respect. We cannot ignore raters' willingness or motivation to provide accurate ratings as we develop models based largely on cognitive processes (Banks & Murphy, 1985; Dipboye, 1985).

Frequency of Formal Appraisals

Although there are no hard-and-fast rules, formal performance appraisals should be conducted at least once each year. Less frequent appraisals place excessive demands on raters' cognitive abilities (especially memory) and force employees to go too long without any formal indication of where they stand. Asking supervisors to provide formal evaluations more frequently is probably "too much of a good thing." Demands on raters' time may generate resistance, which can translate into unreliable and/or inaccurate performance measures. More is not always better (Chhokar & Wallin, 1984).

Informal appraisals are another matter. Supervisors should provide their workers with feedback as soon as possible after observing their job performance. Corrections can then be timely, and workers realize that their supervisors are paying attention to their behaviors in the workplace. Informal feedback is inherently dynamic (Larson, 1984). Any worker whose formal performance appraisal comes as a surprise, pleasant or unpleasant, works for a supervisor whose own performance with respect to providing informal appraisals is unsatisfactory.

Use of Performance Data

We have emphasized that performance measures must be reliable and accurate in order to facilitate effective and profitable personnel decisions. Providing workers with constructive performance feedback also depends upon reliable and accurate information. But something else is

required: a one-on-one feedback interview that doesn't sabotage the entire appraisal system. Such a session can render performance appraisal either a very useful management tool or an unmitigated disaster.

Job-Performance Feedback.   Research and theory pertaining to feedback abounds in the literature. Consistent with the recent emphasis on process, we present a process model of feedback in Figure 4.5. The model focuses on workers' responses to feedback (Ilgen, Fisher, & Taylor, 1979). A great deal of research reflects the influence of the model.

Recipient (*ratee*) characteristics that have been studied include sex and feedback-seeking strategies. Women tend to be more responsive than men to evaluative feedback. Perhaps men adopt a competitive, self-confident stance toward evaluation, and women view feedback situations as opportunities to acquire information about their abilities (Roberts, 1991). Women's generally lower levels of self-confidence (even when men and women receive equivalent feed-

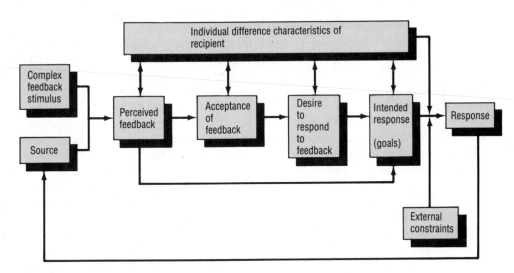

FIGURE 4.5
A Process Model of Performance Feedback
SOURCE: From "Consequences of Individual Feedback on Behavior in Organizations," by D. R. Ilgen, C. D. Fisher, and M. S. Taylor, *Journal of Applied Psychology, 64*, 349–371. Copyright © 1979 by the American Psychological Association. Reprinted by permission of the authors.

Giving and receiving performance feedback isn't always a pleasant task.

fear of failing to reach performance goals (Ashford, 1986). Workers who suspect that they are performing poorly often adopt feedback-seeking strategies designed to minimize the amount of negative information. This tendency is probably a function of workers' levels of self-esteem (Larson, 1989). However, employees who seek negative feedback may enhance their perceived overall effectiveness, and those who seek positive feedback may appear less effective to others (Ashford & Tsui, 1991). A theoretical framework that addresses the role of impression-management behavior during the feedback-seeking process is now available (Morrison & Bies, 1991). This model specifically acknowledges that impression-management behavior can either facilitate or inhibit feedback by influencing when, how, and from whom employees seek feedback.

Performance feedback can come from at least five sources: supervisors, coworkers, tasks, the formal organization, and the worker's own ideas and feelings (Herold, Liden, & Leatherwood, 1987). Several investigations have focused on these sources. The primary concern is perceived credibility. A recent study reported that feedback from women was more delayed and more lenient, especially for relatively weak performers, than feedback from men (Benedict & Levine, 1988). Data from an earlier study suggested that raters' expertise was positively associated with the perceived accuracy of the feedback they provided (Stone, Gueutal, & McIntosh, 1984). Other evidence suggests additional factors that can undermine feedback credibility. Raters who know they will be required to provide face-to-face feedback to their subordinates tend to distort their ratings in a positive (lenient) way. Alternatively, raters who are aware of a subordinate's unfavorable self-assessment tend to distort their ratings in a negative (severe) direction (Klimoski & Inks, 1990). Also, "later" feedback is more credible if it follows "earlier" feedback that was favorable, and if there is consistency in the feedback over time (Stone & Stone, 1985). Finally, two separate

back) may also explain their greater responsiveness to performance feedback (McCarty, 1986).

Workers differ in the extent to which they actively seek feedback about their performance, and the strategies they use to obtain that information (Ashford & Cummings, 1983). Among the variables known to affect the frequency with which employees seek feedback are (a) their expectations about whether the feedback will be positive or negative, and the degree to which the feedback will be public (Northcraft & Ashford, 1990); (b) the amount of credibility they ascribe to the source of the feedback (Fedor, Eder, & Buckley, 1989); (c) their self-esteem (Knight & Nadel, 1986; Northcraft & Ashford, 1990); and (d) their seniority and their studies indicate that specific, self-generated feedback about one's job performance is more credible than feedback from a supervisor (Earley, 1988; Northcraft & Earley, 1989).

The nature of the feedback itself (that is, whether it is positive or negative) has implications for other components of a feedback system. Recall that women's feedback to relatively low-performing workers tended to be delayed and lenient (Benedict & Levine, 1988). In an earlier study, women and men tended to give feedback less often to subordinates who had performed poorly; when it was provided, however, feedback about poor work performance tended to be more specific than feedback about good performance (Larson, 1986). The effects of positive feedback seem to be less dependent on its credibility than are the effects of negative feedback (Podsakoff & Farh, 1989).

Not surprisingly, most recent research concerning job-performance feedback has focused on its effects. After all, the purpose of providing feedback is to help employees improve in areas where their performance is weak and maintain (or improve upon) current levels of performance in stronger areas. There is no doubt that feedback can affect work performance (along with other variables such as satisfaction and motivation) in a constructive way (Balzer, Doherty, & O'Connor, 1989; Chalykoff & Kochan, 1989; Ilgen & Moore, 1987; Rodgers & Hunter, 1991). Because feedback is a form of communication (see Chapter 12), we have borrowed a taxonomy from that discipline to organize our discussion of feedback's effects. We shall concentrate here on characteristics of the source of the message and the nature of the message itself. (We have already discussed the third element of the taxonomy, the target or recipient of the message.)

Turning first to source-related variables, it isn't clear whether self-generated feedback or feedback from one's superior has stronger effects on subsequent job performance. A study that used the Job Feedback Survey (Herold & Parsons, 1985) and multiple sources of perfor-mance data found that feedback from supervisors was related to later job performance, but self-feedback and feedback from peers was not (Becker & Klimoski, 1989). On the other hand, results of two other investigations suggest that self-generated feedback *is* associated with improved performance, and feedback from supervisors is *not* (Earley, 1988; Northcraft & Earley, 1989). If feedback comes from a supervisor (the most common scenario), the importance of the supervisor's relationship with the recipient of the feedback has been well established (Nathan, Mohrman, & Milliman, 1991). Supervisors who express support for a subordinate can increase his level of motivation (Dorfman, Stephan, & Loveland, 1986). Supervisors whose intentions are perceived as constructive when providing feedback generate more positive reactions in recipients (Fedor, Eder, & Buckley, 1989), but destructive criticism results in anger, tension, and other negative reactions (Russell & Goode, 1988). Finally, a supervisor's credibility influences recipients' responses to feedback from that supervisor, especially negative feedback (Bannister, 1986; Podsakoff & Farh, 1989).

Several properties of the feedback message itself also influence employees' responses to it. Contrary to earlier beliefs (Meyer, Kay, & French, 1965), recent studies suggest that workers are *more* satisfied with feedback sessions that include discussion of career advancement and especially pay (Dorfman et al., 1986; Giles & Mossholder, 1990; Prince & Lawler, 1986). Combined with goal setting, feedback about work processes and outcomes has been shown to improve performance (Earley, Northcraft, Lee, & Lituchy, 1990). Similarly, both procedures and outcomes influence recipients' perceptions of appraisal fairness (Greenberg, 1986). As you might expect, whether feedback is positive or negative also affects recipients' responses (Baron, 1988). Positive feedback tends to increase workers' performance expectancies; negative feedback tends to reduce their self-confidence (McCarty, 1986). Women may be more responsive than men to the direction of the feedback they receive (Roberts, 1991). Finally, more specific feedback (based on BOS rather than graphic rating scales) led to increased goal clarity, as well as acceptance of and commitment to those goals (Tziner & Kopelman, 1988).

Attributions.   Our discussion of feedback's effects would be incomplete if we ignored the ways in which performance information influences supervisors' behaviors toward subordinates. Those behaviors, and the beliefs that prompt them, are often a function of supervisors' attributions for their subordinates' performance. That is, a supervisor typically responds to the observed level of a subordinate's performance, and the response is influenced by the supervisor's beliefs concerning the underlying causes of that performance.

A useful taxonomy for understanding supervisors' attributions and responses is based on two orthogonal (independent) dimensions. Underlying causes of performance can be stable or unstable, and they can be internal or external to the worker (DeNisi et al., 1984). Examples of internal attributions for performance that are stable and unstable, respectively, are ability and effort. Examples of external attributions that are stable and unstable, respectively, are task difficulty and luck. As you might suspect, a supervisor's actions based on a subordinate's performance may be very different, depending on which of these four attributions she uses to explain the subordinate's actions. For example, exemplary performance that is attributed to ability might lead to a promotion; equally fine behavior that is attributed to an easy task probably will not. Similarly, poor performance that is attributed to lack of effort will probably stimulate different supervisory responses than will equally dismal performance that is attributed to bad luck.

Many researchers have explored conditions that lead to internal or external attributions for performance. For example, supervisors of blackjack dealers in a casino were more likely to attribute poor performance to lack of effort or to poor supervision by others; the dealers themselves were more apt to attribute poor performance to task difficulty. Further, supervisors without any experience were more likely to attribute poor performance to poor working conditions as well as task difficulty (both external causes) (Smither, Skov, & Adler, 1986). External attributions also seem to be more likely when the number of poor performers is large, and when tasks are highly interdependent (Brown & Mitchell, 1986).

Because of their implications for subsequent personnel actions (for example, promotions, merit pay raises), ability attributions and their predictors are particularly important. Two studies identified possible complications involving age and sex. In one, lower performance among older workers (compared to younger workers) was more likely to be attributed to lack of abil-

PEANUTS, 1979. Reprinted by permission of United Feature Syndicate, Inc.

ity, and older workers' higher performance was less likely to be attributed to ability (Ferris et al., 1985). A second study revealed that attractive men who were successful were more likely to have their success attributed to ability; attractive women's success was less likely to be attributed to their ability (Heilman & Stopeck, 1985a).

Several studies have focused on the relationships between specific attributions for individuals' job performance and other work outcomes. Whether a supervisor attributes a subordinate's performance (especially poor performance) to ability or to effort can influence the nature of subsequent supervisor-subordinate interactions (Dugan, 1989; Heneman, Greenberger, & Anonyuo, 1989). Although a worker's "likeableness" did not influence his or her supervisor's attributions for poor performance, disliked subordinates who performed poorly were more likely to be punished (Dobbins & Russell, 1986). As for sex effects, physically attractive women in *non*managerial positions were more likely to receive promotions and pay raises based on their performance; similarly attractive female managers were less likely to receive such organizational rewards. Physical attractiveness did not affect the organizational consequences of men's work performance (Heilman & Stopeck, 1985b). Worse yet, there is evidence that promale biases in organizational treatments persist even when attributions for performance are experimentally controlled (L'Heureaux-Barrett & Barnes-Farrell, 1991; Pazy, 1986).

Utility of Performance Appraisal.

Given the need to justify each expenditure, managers can be expected to ask about the utility of personnel procedures. Utility reflects a comparison of the economic benefits and costs associated with a procedure. Because I/O psychologists' initial concerns with utility emerged in the context of personnel selection (hiring), we'll reserve a detailed discussion of this concept for Chapter 6.

More recently, however, these economic concerns have been extended to performance appraisal (Landy, Farr, & Jacobs, 1982). Landy and Farr (1983) predicted that "utility calculation will become a standard tool . . . in the years to come [and] this will help strengthen the bond between research and practice" (p. 274). Because establishing and fortifying that bond is crucial to the continued growth of I/O psychology (Banks & Murphy, 1985), we hope they're right.

There can be little doubt that a convincing analysis of the cost-benefit ratio for PPP's performance-appraisal system will be of great interest to Ms. Dieckman (among other managers and executives). Dr. MacKeven's assurances regarding the inherent subjectivity of performance ratings, as well as any changes she makes in the performance-appraisal system, will surely be better received if they are accompanied by a dollars-and-cents analysis of the system's value to the organization.

Legal Concerns.

Recall that Title VII of the Civil Rights Act (1964) mandated that personnel decisions must be based on job-related factors, and that discrimination based on such personal characteristics as race, sex, or ethnic background was forbidden. The EEOC, charged with enforcing Title VII, devoted most of its early attention and efforts to personnel selection, where the most blatant examples of illegal discrimination seemed to be taking place. Nevertheless, if performance data are used to make personnel decisions (for example, promotion, demotion, transfer, dismissal), those data are also subject to Title VII regulations (Bernardin & Beatty, 1984) and other legislation designed to protect employees from discrimination based on age or disabilities. After all, promotion is nothing more than a form of selection where the pool of applicants is located within (rather than outside) the organization. Seen in this light, the need for performance measures to be based on careful job analyses is obvious. How better can

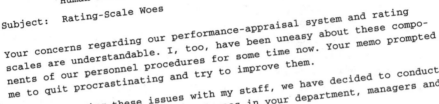

INTEROFFICE MEMO

To: E. Dieckman,
         Director of Advertising

From: J. A. MacKeven,
         Human Resources Coordinator

Subject: Rating-Scale Woes

Your concerns regarding our performance-appraisal system and rating scales are understandable. I, too, have been uneasy about these components of our personnel procedures for some time now. Your memo prompted me to quit procrastinating and try to improve them.

After discussing these issues with my staff, we have decided to conduct a series of workshops with *all* employees in your department, managers and workers. These sessions will

1. Inform employees regarding the basic rationales for conducting performance appraisals at PPP;
2. Acquaint them with the different kinds of performance information that we might collect, and explain why we put so much weight on judgmental (that is, rating) data;
3. Describe alternative judgmental procedures for collecting judgmental performance information, as well as the different rating-scale formats that are available to us; and
4. Distribute job analyses and descriptions to employees (their own— the same ones we completed for you about a year ago), and ask for their ideas and preferences concerning the "best" kind(s) of performance data for assessing the criteria that emerged from those job analyses.

Armed with information from the workshops, we will design some tentative performance-appraisal instruments and procedures. We will then conduct a second series of workshops to allow your employees to help us identify and "fine tune" preferred instruments and procedures. We will also use the second set of workshops to train employees (especially supervisors and managers) in the use of our new performance-appraisal tools.

Finally, my staff and I will analyze the performance data generated through these new instruments and procedures over a one-year period. By then we should be able to detect employees' levels of satisfaction with the system, as well as any psychometric problems (for example, lack of reliability or accuracy). If the results of our analyses are encouraging, we'll begin to schedule similar series of workshops in other departments and divisions of PPP.

What do you think?

we demonstrate the job-relatedness of performance-appraisal data?

Chapter Summary

Job-performance criteria are standards for evaluating the quality of employees' work behaviors. Most jobs require multiple criteria that can be combined to form a composite criterion. Criterion measures must be reliable and practical. They must also be valid, reflecting all the important aspects of a job but no irrelevant factors. Valid criteria should therefore be based on careful job analyses.

Criteria form the basis for performance appraisal, which is done to make merit-based personnel decisions, to provide employees with constructive feedback concerning their job performance, and to generate data that can be used for human-resources research. To contribute to these goals, performance data must distinguish between superior and inferior workers, and must convey unbiased and accurate information about multiple aspects of workers' job performance.

Objective and personnel performance data can be counted, but each is vulnerable to contaminating factors beyond workers' control. Because these kinds of data are often unavailable or inappropriate, most organizations rely on judgmental data. Employee comparisons are reasonably useful for discriminating between "better" and "poorer" performers, at least at the extremes, but they are less suitable for providing feedback. Ratings—which can come from supervisors, peers, or the workers themselves and can be based on a variety of scale formats—are more useful for feedback purposes, assuming they are not contaminated by leniency or severity, central tendency, or halo. Contemporary performance-appraisal research emphasizes the accuracy of ratings, and the cognitive factors that influence the rating process. Models are available that focus our attention on observation, memory, information integration, and judgment. These models should facilitate productive research and may also lead to better procedures for designing performance-appraisal systems and putting them to work in organizations.

Review Questions and Exercises

1. What do you think of Dr. MacKeven's plan?

2. What are the advantages and disadvantages associated with the degree of employee participation inherent in her plan?

3. Should supervisors and managers and their subordinates attend the same workshops? Why (not)?

4. What kind(s) of performance data do you think should be included in the Advertising Department's performance-appraisal system? Explain your answer.

5. What kind(s) of performance data would you specifically recommend *excluding* from that department's system? Why?

6. What should Dr. MacKeven look for when she analyzes the performance data collected during the one-year interval?

7. How might Dr. MacKeven take advantage of process models of performance appraisal as she carries out the steps described in her return memo to Ms. Dieckman? Do you see any problems with relying on such a model?

8. What recommendations would you offer to Dr. MacKeven if she decides to extend the process described in her memo to other departments and divisions throughout Peter's Pan Pizza, Inc.?

CHAPTER 5

Personnel Selection: Measurement Issues and Hiring Procedures

LEARNING POINTS

After studying this chapter you should

- understand the classical definition of reliability based on the concept of true score;
- be able to explain why we must estimate the reliability of measuring instruments, and to describe three methods for deriving such estimates;
- understand how test characteristics, characteristics of people taking a test, and the testing environment or surroundings can influence estimates of test reliability;
- understand the concept of validity, and be able to describe three approaches to assessing validity of test scores;
- be able to describe the validities of scores on paper-and-pencil tests of intelligence, motivation, and personality for predicting job performance; and
- be able to describe the validities of biographical data and data obtained from personal interviews, work samples and situational exercises, letters of recommendation, and assessment centers for predicting job performance.

RECALL FROM CHAPTER 1 that concerns about personnel selection have been around for a long time. Ancient Chinese and Classical Greek societies developed procedures for selecting civil servants and soldiers, respectively, thousands of years ago. More recently, Boston was the site of Hugo Münsterberg's efforts during the early 1900s to design a system for selecting streetcar motormen. Since that time, personnel selection has become far more complex due to rapidly changing technologies and the dramatically altered social, political, and legal contexts in which organizations operate.

Because personnel selection is so complicated today, we will devote two chapters to the relevant issues. In this first chapter we concentrate on psychometric concepts and specific selection instruments. Following a discussion of reliability and validity, crucial measurement concepts that underlie the effectiveness of any selection device, we will describe a variety of instruments and procedures that are currently being used during the personnel-selection process to predict future job performance. We will then continue our examination of selection issues in Chapter 6, where we will place the selection techniques discussed here in the context of effective personnel-selection *systems*. Such systems include recruiting (that is, identifying pools of job ap-

INTEROFFICE MEMO

To: J. A. MacKeven,
            Human Resources Coordinator

From: J. Schiftner,
            Director of Management Selection

Subject: "Home Grown" versus External Managerial Talent

Most of the current managers at Peter's Pan Pizza began their employment with us at lower, nonsupervisory levels of the organization, and have "come up through the ranks." My attention and efforts as Director of Management Selection have therefore been focused on identifying potential managerial talent among our current employees. Although we have experienced our share of problems with this promotion-from-within policy (for example, putting managers in the sometimes awkward position of exercising authority over former colleagues, friends, and coworkers), overall results have been generally satisfactory.

Given this "track record," I think it would be foolish to abandon this policy and strategy for staffing PPP's managerial ranks. Nevertheless, I am also convinced that relying almost exclusively on a promotion-from-within policy is a self-defeating approach to management selection that will ultimately lead to complacency and stagnation. In today's rapidly changing and increasingly multicultural business environment, this will eventually hurt us.

I therefore intend to develop a set of procedures for identifying and selecting managerial talent that can be effective when applied either to our current employees or to women and men outside the PPP family (for example, recent MBAs or managers in other organizations). I will appreciate any help you can provide in the areas of (a) recruiting strategies, (b) specific selection tests or procedures, (c) overall management-selection strategies, and (d) relevant legal considerations.

plicants from among whom new employees can be selected), combining and integrating selection information obtained from several specific instruments or procedures, utility considerations (that is, the relative costs and benefits of selection systems), and legal issues pertaining to personnel selection. As always, we will continue to lace our discussions with specific references to the memos that introduce each of the chapters.

Psychological Measurement Issues

As you learned in Chapter 2, measurement involves assigning numbers to objects or events according to certain rules. Recall that nominal, ordinal, interval, and ratio measurement scales reflect four sets of such rules (Stevens, 1946). The basic assumption that underlies personnel selection is that job applicants will differ with respect to the skills and abilities they bring to an organization, and that some of the differences will be associated with different levels of job performance. The first step in developing any selection system, then (assuming suitable job-performance criteria have been identified through appropriate job analyses), is to devise measuring instruments (selection "tests") that can highlight individual differences and thereby help us to discriminate among potentially more and less successful employees. As we explained in Chapter 3, useful measures are both reliable and valid. We now turn our attention to these important psychometric concepts.

Reliability

Reliability is consistency of measurement. If measures are to be useful, the numbers we generate must be as stable as the underlying variable(s) (for example, skills or abilities) we are trying to describe. Put another way, reliable measures are relatively free of errors that are

random, or at least without discernible pattern.[1] This leads us to a formal definition of reliability (Ghiselli, 1964; Nunnally, 1978): A measure is **reliable** to the extent that the variance in a set of observed scores reflects variance in the true scores of the people, objects, or events being measured, and does not reflect random error variance. More precisely, reliability is equal to the ratio of true-score variance to observed-score variance (Aiken, 1979; Allen & Yen, 1979; Lemke & Wiersma, 1976). To understand this formal definition and how it relates to consistency of measurement, we must understand the concepts of true score, random error score, and observed score. Let's examine these now.

Whenever we measure something, the number we obtain and record is the **observed score**. If I measure your height with a yardstick and obtain a reading of 5'8", or we measure your algebra skills with an examination and you receive a score of 86 (out of a possible 100) points, those numbers (that is, 68 inches and 86 points) are your observed scores. We sometimes refer to them as "total scores" because they represent the sum of two subscores: your true score on each variable and random error scores. For the sake of simplicity, we will continue to call them "observed" scores.

A **true score** is the number we would obtain and record if our measuring instrument and the person who uses it are completely free of error. Few of us will disagree that we each have an actual, precise height, and that if we could measure carefully enough, we could determine exactly what those heights are. However, if ten of your friends independently measure your height with the same yardstick, you'll discover that not everyone will record the same observed score. Instead, one or two might record 5'8" (which we'll assume is your true height) and the others will obtain and record scores as low as

[1] Systematic errors that show a pattern also undermine useful measurement, but the problem is not one of reliability. By definition, systematic errors are in some way consistent, and therefore reliable. The problem in these cases is one of validity (or accuracy), which we will discuss in the next section.

5'7" or as high as 5'9". That is, there will be variance in the observed scores that results from repeated measurement of the same variable. If each of your ten friends measures your height within a five-minute interval, we can be fairly certain that your actual height (that is, your true score) did not vary during that short time period. Because your true score remained constant while the observed scores varied, we can attribute the variance to random errors. Most of your friends made small mistakes when assessing your height, some of which resulted in overestimates while others yielded underestimates of your true height. This reflects a lack of reliability in these measures. If all ten of your friends had recorded your height as exactly 5'8", there wouldn't be any variance in those observed scores. Because your true score *should have been exactly the same* each time it was measured within a five-minute interval, those measures would have been perfectly reliable.

The same ideas apply when we obtain measures for many different individuals (or events). Suppose we measure the heights of all the students in your class. The observed score for each student is the sum of her true height and a greater or lesser amount of random error. The variance in the observed scores is equal to the variance in their true scores plus the variance in the error scores that contaminate their observed scores (Horst, 1968). If each student's height had been measured without any random error, the variance in the observed scores would equal the variance in the true scores, and the measure would be perfectly reliable. The same can be said about students' scores on an algebra test or applicants' scores on selection tests encountered during the hiring process. If those test scores are to be useful, they must represent students' or applicants' true scores on whatever variables are of interest (for example, algebra skills, intelligence, communication skills), and be relatively free of random error. That is, they must be reliable.

With some notable exceptions (for example, Lumsden, 1976), the classical definition of reliability is still widely accepted today. Unfortunately, defining reliability in terms of a ratio of true-score variance to observed-score variance does not readily lead to an operational definition of this psychometric concept. True scores are abstractions that cannot be directly measured or calculated. This makes it impossible to calculate reliability directly. Because it is essential to know how reliable measures are before they are used to select or reject individual job applicants, I/O psychologists must *estimate* the reliability of their measures. There are several ways to do this, but most of them depend upon correlation coefficients (r). As we describe three of these strategies for estimating reliability, you will see that each approaches the task from a different perspective.

Test-Retest Estimates. Perhaps the easiest approach to understand, the test-retest method estimates reliability by administering the *same "test"*[2] to the *same sample* of individuals on two *different occasions* separated by a time interval. The correlation coefficient that describes the linear relationship between people's scores on the same test taken at two different times is one estimate of reliability, and is referred to as a **reliability coefficient**. As this index approaches its upper limit of +1.00, it indicates that individuals who scored high (or low) the first time the test was administered were more and more likely to score high (or low) the second time. That is, there is more and more consistency in people's scores. In this case, the reliability coefficient reflects consistency *over time*—the interval between the two administrations of the test.

Consistency over time is an especially important property of test scores used to predict job applicants' levels of job performance months (or even years) after they were hired. The major problem associated with this ex-

[2] In the interest of convenience, we will refer to measuring instruments in general as "tests," even though many selection devices (for example, interviews, application blanks) bear little or no resemblance to traditional tests or examinations.

SHOE, reprinted by permission: Tribune Media Services.

tremely relevant approach to estimating reliability is determining the proper time interval that should separate the two administrations of the test. If the interval is too short, people will remember how they responded the first time, and simply reproduce those responses the second time. A desire to appear consistent or perhaps plain old laziness will prompt folks to rely on their memories instead of taking the test again as if they had never seen it before. To the extent this occurs, the correlation between the two sets of scores will reflect memory instead of the consistency with which the test can assess the variable of interest (for example, intelligence or communication skills). If, on the other hand, the interval between the two test administrations is too long, individuals' true scores on whatever variable is being measured might change. Although we would not expect dramatic changes in adults' levels of intelligence during a six-month interval, we might expect rather drastic changes in communication skills during that time. In the latter case (that is, communication skills), a small reliability coefficient could reflect changes in true scores rather than an unreliable measuring instrument.

As you can see, choosing the proper time interval can be a challenge. Those who use the test-retest method to estimate selection-test reliability must be able to describe the nature of the variable they want to measure, and then identify time intervals that are not so lengthy that true scores can be expected to change but not so brief that individuals can recall exactly how they responded the first time and simply reproduce those responses from memory the second time.

Equivalent-Forms Estimates. A second method for estimating reliability requires two *different tests* that measure the same variable. Both tests are consecutively administered to the *same sample* of individuals. The correlation coefficient that describes the linear relationship between people's scores on the two tests is the estimate of reliability. As this reliability coefficient approaches +1.00, it indicates that people who score high on one of the tests also tend to score high on the other, and that those who obtain low scores on the first test also score low on the other. As before, we assume that individuals' more or less constant true scores constitute most of their observed scores on both tests. Smaller reliability coefficients suggest less consistency in people's scores on the two tests. In this case, reliability refers to consistency *across separate measuring instruments* designed to measure the same variable.

This method for estimating reliability is used less frequently than the test-retest approach. (An exception is interrater reliability estimates discussed in Chapter 4, where two or more raters are treated as if they were equivalent measuring devices.) Equivalent forms (sometimes referred to as "parallel" forms) of tests must meet rigorous statistical criteria (for example, equal means, equal standard deviations, equal correlations with other measures), and it is very difficult to create two or more tests that actually do so. The basic challenge in developing equivalent forms is to devise two or more tests that actually measure the same variable in the same way. To the extent that we fall short of this goal, correlations between scores will underestimate the reliability with which a given variable might be measured because the observed scores used to calculate the reliability coefficient reflect true scores on *non*identical variables. Given these difficulties, you can see why this is not a particularly popular method for estimating reliability, despite the fact that "classical psychometric theory is based on the conception of exactly parallel [equivalent] measures" (Guion & Ironson, 1983).

Internal-Consistency Estimates. The third method for estimating reliability of test scores requires only that a *single test* be administered to a *single sample* of people on a *single occasion*. The test items are subsequently partitioned to form two or more subtests, and correlations are computed between individuals' scores on the subtests. Correlations that approach +1.00 indicate that people who do well on one portion of the overall test also do well on the other portion(s) of the test, and that those who perform poorly on one subgroup of items also do relatively poorly on the other subgroup(s) of items. Once again, this is evidence of consistency, but this time it is consistency *within a given measuring instrument* (that is, "internal" consistency). Because this is the most convenient method for estimating reliability, in that it requires only one test, one sample of people, and one administration of the test, it isn't surprising that this method is reported most frequently in the empirical research literature.

There are several ways to estimate the internal consistency of a test. The simplest is a split-half estimate, where test items are divided into two groups to form two subtests, and individuals' subscores on half of the items are correlated with their subscores on the other half. If we have a 100-item test, the most obvious strategy is to correlate people's subscores on items 1 through 50 with their subscores on items 51 through 100. This is *not* a defensible strategy, however, for at least two reasons. First, some people may perform less effectively on the second 50 items because of fatigue. Because everyone in the sample will not grow tired in the same way at the same time, this will lower the split-half correlation coefficient and thereby (perhaps erroneously) suggest a lack of internal consistency among the test items. Second, some tests are designed so that earlier items are relatively easy to answer correctly and later items become progressively more difficult. Because these tests do not measure the same thing in the same way throughout, correlating people's scores on the first 50 items with their scores on the second 50 items yields low estimates of internal consistency. Other tests known as "speed tests" contain relatively simple items throughout, but persons taking the test are allowed only a limited amount of time to complete all the items. If everyone manages to respond to the first 50 items, but individuals vary in terms of how many of the second group of 50 items they are able to complete, we can again expect low correlations between scores on these two subtests.

A rather obvious solution to both these dilemmas is to create the subtests in a different way. The most common practice is to obtain subscores based on all of the even-numbered items and correlate them with subscores based on all of the odd-numbered items. Any effects of fatigue or boredom will be controlled because they will be evenly distributed across both sets of subscores. The resulting internal-consistency reliability coefficient will then reflect only internal consistency. This is known as an "odd-even, split-half" estimate of reliability.

There are, of course, many ways to divide a test in half for the purpose of estimating internal consistency. Any particular division is arbitrary. One could theoretically avoid this arbitrariness by averaging the reliability coefficients obtained from *all* of the possible ways that a test might be divided in half. Unfortunately, this would be very time-consuming even with the aid of a computer. A test of only 50 items would require us to calculate and average 1,225 split-half reliability coefficients (Aiken, 1979). Several psychometricians have developed shortcuts for obtaining estimates of these average split-half correlations (Cronbach, 1951; Hoyt, 1941; Kuder & Richardson, 1937). Kuder and Richardson developed more than 20 formulas for obtaining such estimates under a variety of conditions. Their most popular formula (KR-20), which is appropriate when some of the test items are more difficult to answer correctly than other items, is known as *coefficient alpha* (Cronbach, 1951). Even a cursory review of the empirical literature reveals that coefficient alpha is the most frequently reported estimate of internal-consistency reliability.

Two additional considerations are important when we use internal-consistency methods to estimate reliability. First, because reliability estimates are influenced by the number of items in a test, any correlation based on split-half subscores will underestimate a test's reliability. Split-half estimates for a 100-item test actually reflect the reliability of 50-item subtests. Because the entire 100-item test will actually be used during personnel selection, the estimate based on 50-item subtests must be corrected. The Spearman-Brown prophecy formula is often used for this purpose:

$$r' = \frac{Kr}{1 + (K - 1)r}$$

where *r'* is the corrected split-half reliability coefficient;

 r is the uncorrected split-half reliability coefficient; and

 K is the factor by which the subtests must be increased in order to equal

the length of the actual test that will be used (that is, $K = 2$ for split-half estimates because the uncorrected correlation is based on subtests that are half the length of the test that is to be used).

We can also use this formula to estimate the increase in internal-consistency reliability that we can expect if we increase the number of test items by a factor of K. Further, an algebraic manipulation of this formula can be used to determine the factor (K) by which the number of test items must be increased in order to obtain a desired internal-consistency reliability (r'). Suppose, for example, that Dr. MacKeven has a 35-item test with reliability = .52. Algebraic manipulation of the Spearman-Brown formula to "solve for" K yields the following equation:

$$K = \frac{(r' - rr')}{(r - rr')}$$

If she wants her test to have a reliability coefficient = .80, she can solve this equation to learn that $K = 3.7$. Thus, Dr. MacKeven would have to increase her 35-item test by a factor of 3.7 (to almost 130 items) in order to have an internal-consistency reliability = .80. Of course, she would need to determine the feasibility of developing 95 additional items to add to her test.

This leads to the second important consideration when using internal-consistency estimates of reliability: the content of the test items. Remember that this method of estimating reliability focuses on consistency *within a single measuring instrument* rather than consistency over time or across different tests. It is an appropriate measure of reliability, then, only when a test measures a single variable or construct. If, instead, a test is multidimensional in that it assesses two or more components of people's abilities, personality, or motivation, and if those components are not perfectly (or at least very highly) correlated, the internal consistency of that test will be lower than it would be if the test measured only a single construct. In the hypothetical example described above, Dr. Mac-Keven would have to develop 95 additional items that measured the same construct. This could be a very challenging task. In the event she chooses to try, it will be important for her actually to reassess the internal consistency of her expanded test.

At this point, we expect that you appreciate the importance of test reliability as well as the advantages and disadvantages associated with different methods of estimating this psychometric property. Before we move on to a discussion of validity, however, we want to acquaint you with several factors known to influence the size of reliability coefficients. These factors can mislead us as we try to develop reliable personnel-selection instruments.

Factors That Influence Reliability Estimates

Among the factors that can affect the magnitude of reliability estimates are the estimation method used, the characteristics of the items that make up the test, the characteristics of the sample of individuals whose test scores are used to estimate reliability, and the environment or context in which the test is administered.

Estimation Method. We just described three correlation-based methods of estimating test reliability. Coefficient alpha and corrected split-half internal-consistency estimates are best interpreted as upper boundaries or reliability ceilings (Nunnally, 1978). Equivalent-forms estimates, on the other hand, tend to be too low if the two forms do not actually measure the same construct (Ghiselli, 1964). Such estimates are therefore best interpreted as lower limits of reliability. Test-retest estimates tend to fall somewhere in between these extremes, depending on the appropriateness of the time interval that separates the two administrations of the test. Because it is so difficult to determine the proper interval for a specific test-retest estimate, Nunnally (1978) advised against using this method to estimate reliability. He contended that "co-

efficient alpha provides a good estimate of reliability in most situations" (p. 230). As we indicated earlier, the empirical literature suggests that many researchers agree with Nunnally.

As we describe the other kinds of factors that influence reliability estimates, remember that more reliable measurement is relatively free of random error and therefore reflects individuals' true scores on whatever construct or variable is being assessed. Thus, a useful way to understand and appreciate these factors is in terms of how they promote or inhibit random measurement error.

Characteristics of Tests. First, you already know that increasing the *number of test items* will increase the reliability of the scores, assuming that all of the items assess the same construct. If, for example, Mr. Schiftner were interested in measuring a managerial candidate's spelling ability, he wouldn't ask her to spell only one or two words. After all, the candidate might be a good speller, but Mr. Schiftner might happen to choose a word or two that she doesn't know. He could be far more confident that the candidate was a poor speller (that is, has a low true score on spelling ability) if she misspelled a relatively large number of words from a longer list of "test words." Because a longer list of test items affords the candidate a better opportunity to display her true spelling ability, a low observed score is less likely to be attributable to random error due to selection of particular (and perhaps peculiar) words, loss of concentration, or other extraneous factors.

Two additional factors influence the relationship between number of test items and reliability. One is based on the "law of diminishing returns." As more and more items are added to a test, the increments in reliability become smaller and smaller (Lemke & Wiersma, 1976). The second is really an extension of the first. If a test becomes so lengthy that those who take it grow bored or fatigued (or fall asleep!), the ad-

A test must reliably measure the applicant's qualifications that it is intended to assess.

ditional items certainly will *not* add to the reliability of the observed scores.

Other test-related factors include the order in which relatively easy and difficult items are presented, the appropriateness of the test's overall difficulty level, the diversity of the items' content, and the extent to which the items' format inhibits or facilitates correct guessing in the absence of any relevant knowledge or skill. We will briefly discuss each of these factors.

Tests often begin with relatively easy items and then progress to more demanding items. This sequence allows people taking the test to build up their confidence before they encounter difficult items, which increases the likelihood

that their performance on the test will reflect their actual abilities (that is, their true scores). If, on the other hand, examinees encounter difficult items at the very beginning of the test, they may become discouraged or anxious. Either emotional reaction can result in incorrect answers to subsequent, easier test items that would have been answered correctly had the examinee been in a less negative frame of mind. In this way, the *serial order of easy and difficult test items* can introduce random error into observed scores.

Entire *tests that are either much too easy or too difficult* for those being examined will also generate observed scores that can be relatively unreliable. In each case, the distribution of observed scores will be highly skewed and the variance will be restricted because everyone's scores are either very high or very low. Remember that reliability estimates depend on correlations, which in turn depend on related variance in the measures being compared. Restrictions in the ranges of observed scores therefore deflate the magnitude of calculated reliability coefficients. In addition, tests that are uniformly too easy or too difficult don't provide people with an opportunity to demonstrate their true scores on the variables or constructs being measured.

Diversity of item content operates in a similar fashion. It matters little if a test consists of many items if they all address the same skill or piece of knowledge. Imagine a ten-item arithmetic test that includes the following four items:

$$1. \quad 7 + 4 = ?$$
$$4. \quad 4 + 7 = ?$$
$$8. \quad \begin{array}{r} 7 \\ + 4 \\ \hline ? \end{array}$$
$$9. \quad \begin{array}{r} 4 \\ + 7 \\ \hline ? \end{array}$$

Would this really be a ten-item test or would it actually be a seven-item test? After all, four items measure the same piece of knowledge; anyone who answers one of these four items (in)correctly will probably answer the other three items (in)correctly, too. Thus, lack of item diversity affects observed scores in a way that reduces the size of reliability estimates. Of course, such an array of items also reduces individuals' opportunities to demonstrate their true arithmetic-ability scores.

Finally, test items that make it *easier for people to guess the correct answers* in the absence of any relevant knowledge or skill will generate less reliable observed scores. Correct guesses are nothing more or less than random error that inflates observed score relative to true score. True-false questions are most vulnerable to correct guessing because the probability of answering any item correctly by chance alone is equal to .5. Multiple-choice tests with four or five alternative answers reduce the probability of correct guesses to .25 or .20, respectively (although "test-wise" examinees can often increase these probabilities, as we will explain momentarily). Questions that ask individuals to "fill in the blanks" reduce the likelihood of correct guessing even more, thereby contributing to more reliable observed test scores. (Of course, the subjectivity of the scheme used to score such open-ended responses can undermine the reliability of the observed test scores.)

Characteristics of Examinees. We just alluded to one of these factors, the *test-wiseness* (often a function of test-taking experience) of those who take the test. This is perhaps most applicable to multiple-choice items. It is "common knowledge" among many test-wise students that the correct answer to a multiple-choice question is more likely to be

- alternative *b* or *c* rather than *a* or *d*
- the alternative that contains the largest number of words
- alternatives such as "all (none) of the above"

In addition, correct answers to some questions sometimes appear in the stems of other ques-

tions. Regardless of which of these operates, the effect (if it "works") is to reduce the reliability of observed test scores by introducing random error.

People's *attitudes* toward taking a test can also influence the reliability of their observed scores. Individuals who are highly motivated to perform well will obtain scores that better reflect their true scores than will individuals who don't care whether they do well or not (assuming, of course, that motivation is not so high that they become distracted or overly anxious and cannot concentrate). As a rule, observed scores are less reliable when examinees are ill than when they are feeling well. Those who voluntarily take a test often demonstrate their true scores more reliably than those who are forced or coerced into taking a test (perhaps by a supervisor or manager).

A final factor in this category is the *variance in true scores* among those who take the test. As you might have predicted by now, a very homogeneous sample of test takers will generate observed scores characterized by relatively little variance, which in turn will inhibit the magnitude of calculated reliability coefficients. By definition, heterogeneous samples will generate observed scores with greater variance, which can translate into larger reliability coefficients.

Characteristics of the Testing Environment. The context or physical surroundings in which people take a test can introduce random error into their observed scores. A testing environment that promotes concentration tends to increase the reliability of observed test scores. Relative quiet, comfortable temperature and humidity, sufficient illumination, and absence of pollutants are relevant considerations here. Those who administer and/or score tests can also contribute to reliability by creating proper atmosphere, morale, and motivation among the test takers; by providing instructions that are consistent and understandable; and by scoring the test according to a relatively objective set of criteria.

Validity

As we stated earlier, reliability is a necessary psychometric property of test scores, but it isn't sufficient by itself to guarantee useful measurement. It's not enough for a selection test to measure some aspect of applicants' qualifications consistently. A test must also measure the qualifications (that is, variables or constructs) it is designed and intended to assess. This property is known as **validity**. Consistent measures of an irrelevant quality or characteristic of job applicants are of no use to anyone.

Just as there are several ways to estimate reliability of test scores, so too are there multiple approaches to analyzing the validity of measurements. Before describing them, however, we want to reemphasize a point that was discussed in the *Standards for Educational and Psychological Testing* (American Educational Research Association, 1985) and *Principles for the Validation and Use of Personnel Selection Procedures* (SIOP, 1987), and summarized very well by Lawshe (1985): "It is not tests which are valid or invalid, but, rather, inferences [drawn] from test scores" that are valid or invalid. Suppose, for example, that Dr. MacKeven administers a test of managerial motivation to a group of prospective managers. Lawshe's point is that it would be inappropriate to refer to the validity or invalidity of those applicants' *test scores*. Rather, it is the inferences or conclusions about future job performance that one draws, on the basis of those test scores, that are valid or invalid. The distinction is important because a validity-analysis strategy should be adopted on the basis of the kinds of inferences about job applicants one wants to make. Let's now take a look at the inferences that Dr. MacKeven might want to draw on the basis of managerial applicants' test scores, and the different validity-analysis strategies available to her.

Content-Validity Analysis. Content-validity analysis has been recommended when we want to make inferences about applicants' future job performance on the basis of their *current abilities to perform relatively simple* components of a job, or their *current levels of relevant knowledge*. The emphasis is on candidates' competence at the moment rather than on their potential to achieve given levels of competence sometime in the future. **Content-validity analysis** addresses the extent to which successful test performance requires behavior or knowledge that is similar or identical to that demanded by the job in question (Lawshe, 1985). For example, drawing inferences about a typist's future job performance from scores obtained on a typing test today can be supported through content-validity analysis. In this case, the behavior required to do well on the test is extremely similar, if not identical, to the behavior required to perform well on the job. Unfortunately, the job of manager at Peter's Pan Pizza or any other organization entails behaviors that are far more abstract (for example, planning, decision making) than typing or other concrete, observable tasks. As a result, content-validity analysis is less likely to satisfy Dr. MacKeven's and Mr. Schiftner's needs than one or more of the other approaches to validity analysis (Sackett & Dreher, 1982, 1984).

Content-validity analysis is usually a judgmental rather than a statistical procedure. The questions of whether knowledge in a given domain is tapped by a particular test or whether such knowledge is important for successful job performance lend themselves very nicely to judgmental answers. Nevertheless, several quantitative approaches to answering such questions are available (Distephano, Pryer, & Erffmeyer, 1983; Faley & Sundstrom, 1985; Lawshe, 1975). The best known example of these is Lawshe's Content Validity Ratio (CVR) for a single test item:

$$CVR = \frac{(n_e - N/2)}{(N/2)}$$

where n_e = the number of judges (usually job experts) who say that the knowledge or skill tested by an item is "essential" to job performance; and

N = the total number of judges whose opinions are solicited.

A Content Validity Index (CVI) for an entire test can be calculated by averaging the CVR values for all items included in the test. As you can see from the formula shown above, a CVR will have a negative algebraic sign when fewer than half of the judges indicate that the knowledge or skill tapped by a test item is essential to job performance. If more than half of the judges say it is essential, the CVR will have a positive sign. CVRs can range from −1.00 to 0.00 to +1.00 when none, exactly half, or all of the judges, respectively, indicate that the knowledge or skill measured by a test item is essential to job performance. Although it is less sophisticated than many of the statistics I/O psychologists typically use, and although large positive values tell us nothing about the extent to which test items represent the entire range of skills or abilities essential to job performance, the CVR does introduce some level of quantification into content-validity analysis.

An important distinction can be made between content validation and other forms of validity analyses. Tenopyr (1977) asserted that content-validity analysis is more appropriate for making inferences about the *construction of tests* than the meaning of applicants' scores on those tests. The idea is that a test should be constructed in such a way that it includes all, or a representative sample, of the behaviors one is interested in assessing. In the context of personnel selection, those behaviors include the tasks that make up the job for which applicants apply. Recent evidence suggests that a content-validity approach to constructing selection tests may be more appropriate when job applicants have some relevant job experience (rather than when they have no prior, relevant experience) (Carrier, Dalessio, & Brown, 1990). Other researchers, however, have described modified content-oriented procedures for developing se-

lection tests that can be administered to inexperienced applicants (Schmitt & Ostroff, 1986).

Thus, the role of content-validity analysis in assessing the psychometric quality of personnel-selection tests is a matter of some debate. Those who would apply the strategy only to assess how well the content of a test samples the kinds of situations or behaviors of interest (for example, Tenopyr, 1977) are opposed by those who think that content-validity analysis can address the validity of inferences about subsequent job behaviors based on test scores. What *does* seem clear is that those who use content-validity analysis to support predictions about applicants' subsequent job-performance levels should limit themselves to situations where the behaviors required by the test and those demanded on the job are *relatively simple* and *directly observable*.

Because Dr. MacKeven must identify personnel-selection tests that can discriminate among applicants who possess the requisite knowledge, skills, and abilities (KSAs) to become competent managers and those who do not, and because such KSAs (for example, planning, deciding, organizing) are very abstract and *not* directly observable, she will probably restrict her use of content-validity analysis to making inferences about test construction. The quality of her inferences about applicants' future levels of job performance, based on their test scores, will be better assessed using one or more of the alternative approaches to validity analysis, criterion-related or construct-validity analyses.

Criterion-Related Validity Analysis.   Criterion-related validity analysis has been recommended when we want to make inferences about how well job applicants will perform on the job (if hired) on the basis of statistical relationships between selection-test scores and numerical measures of job performance. The emphasis here is squarely on quantitative prediction. Statistical relationships between test scores and job-performance measures are often expressed in the form of correlation coefficients (*r*), which are referred to in this context as validity coefficients (Lawshe, 1985). Thus, criterion-related validity analysis requires at least two measures for each applicant, a selection-test score and a job-performance score. Although there are numerous procedures for obtaining these scores (Sussman & Robertson, 1986), I/O psychologists typically rely on two basic strategies. The first of these, known as **predictive validity analysis**, involves the following steps:

1. Obtain selection-test scores from *actual job applicants*;

2. Select some of the applicants for available jobs using a strategy that has nothing to do with those test scores;[3]

3. After a reasonable amount of time has elapsed, obtain quantitative measures of job performance for applicants who were hired; and

4. Calculate a validity coefficient that describes the linear relationship between the employees' selection-test scores and their subsequent job-performance scores.

The second strategy, known as **concurrent validity analysis**, is far more convenient. In this case the selection test under consideration is administered to *current employees* rather than to applicants. Job-performance scores for the employees are concurrently obtained from their personnel files or from their supervisors, and a validity coefficient is calculated. Unfortunately, the convenience of the second strategy does not come without a price. However, the two approaches to criterion-related validity have strengths and weaknesses that tend to complement each other.

The major advantage associated with predictive validity analysis is that it examines validity of inferences under conditions that are very similar to those typical of actual selection-test use. That is, test scores are obtained from actual job applicants who are genuinely interested in securing employment, and the scores are then examined at a later time to determine how well they predicted hired applicants' job performance. If applicants were indeed selected in a manner that was unrelated to their selection-test scores, those scores will usually reflect some variance. That is, there should be little or no restriction in the range of the selection-test scores used to calculate the validity coefficient. If present, such restrictions impose an upper limit on the size of any validity coefficients that might be computed (just as range restriction in true scores limits the size of reliability coefficients). Unfortunately, predictive validity analysis suffers from two basic flaws. First, few employers are willing to go to the trouble of administering a selection test to applicants and then *ignore* the test scores when making hiring decisions. Second, this approach to assessing criterion-related validity takes time. After some of the applicants are hired, an interval sufficiently long to allow them to learn their jobs and demonstrate their abilities must elapse (that is, the criterion should be a relatively distal one). Given these two drawbacks, many managers and I/O psychologists rely on the second approach to criterion-related validity analysis: concurrent analysis.

Unlike the predictive approach, concurrent validity analysis involves no lengthy time interval. The selection test under consideration is administered to current employees at the same time that job-performance measures are obtained from their records. A second factor that renders the concurrent approach more acceptable to managers and executives is that they are not obliged to ignore selection-test scores during the hiring process. There are costs associated with this convenience and acceptability, however. The primary drawback is that the people who generate scores on the selection test under investigation and whose job performance is concurrently assessed may not represent the

---

[3] Usually organizations continue to rely on whatever selection instruments or procedures are currently in use while the criterion-related validity of a new selection device is being studied.

population of folks who will subsequently apply for jobs. The employees have already been selected in one way or another and have already gained certain levels of experience with their jobs. Because they already have jobs, they may not be as highly motivated to obtain high scores (true scores?) on the selection test (Arvey, Strickland, Drauden, & Martin, 1990). If the strategy used to select them *was* in any way related to their scores on the selection test under investigation, the range of their scores on the "new" selection test would be restricted, as we indicated above. People who would have obtained low scores on the test under consideration would not have been hired, and would therefore be unavailable to participate in the concurrent validity analysis. Further, employees' job experiences can influence their scores on the selection test under consideration. Because actual job applicants will not have the benefit of such experience, the results of concurrent analyses might not generalize to the applicant population.

Not surprisingly, the relative merits of predictive and concurrent validity analyses have generated some debate among I/O psychologists. Some assert that the conceptual distinction between the two approaches has been exaggerated, that any differences have minimal (and probably conservative) effects on the magnitude of validity coefficients, and that sound concurrent studies can provide acceptable estimates of predictive validity (Alexander, 1988; Barrett, Phillips, & Alexander, 1981; Kleiman & Faley, 1985). Others emphasize conceptual and practical considerations when asserting that the two approaches are neither equivalent nor interchangeable (Guion & Cranny, 1982). We should point out that the potential problem of range restriction inherent in the concurrent approach is not insurmountable. Many researchers have described statistical corrections for the effects of range restriction on validity coefficients (Lee, Miller, & Graham, 1982; Linn, Harnisch, & Dunbar, 1981; Olson & Becker, 1983; Sackett & Wade, 1983). Others have iden-

tified parameters (for example, sample size) that render range restriction more or less serious (Alexander, Carson, Alliger, & Barrett, 1985; Raju, Edwards, & LoVerde, 1985). A general model that goes beyond traditional formulas that correct for range restriction is now available. It permits researchers to estimate validities when criterion scores are not available for all employees, even if they had been selected on the basis of variables related to the criterion (Gross & McGanney, 1987).

A review of criterion-related validity studies published in the *Journal of Applied Psychology* and *Personnel Psychology* between 1960 and 1979 revealed that I/O psychologists used predictive designs as often as they used concurrent designs (Boehm, 1982). The review also identified the following trends:

1. A significant decrease in the number of articles that even report the results of validity studies;

2. Published articles tend to focus on individuals and jobs at higher occupational and organizational levels, such as managerial and professional positions; and

3. The magnitudes of reported validity coefficients are not very impressive (the mean of 176 studies was only $r = .219$), and this has not changed much over the years.

A meta-analytic review of 99 criterion-related validity studies published in the same two journals between 1962 and 1982 reported an average overall validity coefficient of .28, corroborating Boehm's findings (Schmitt, Gooding, Noe, & Kirsch, 1984). These relatively small validity coefficients, which indicate that selection-test scores explain only 4% to 6% of the variance in workers' job-performance scores, have prompted several researchers to investigate alternative strategies for assessing criterion-related validity. These include validity generalization, synthetic validity analysis, and moderator and suppressor variables, all of which are discussed in the next chapter. Others have questioned whether alternative statistics (for example, confidence intervals, *J*-coefficients) might describe criterion-related validities better than simple correlation coefficients (Fowler, 1986; Hamilton & Dickinson, 1987; Humphreys & Swets, 1991).

Two issues have recently attracted the attention of those who are concerned with the relative strengths and weaknesses of criterion-related validity analysis: the stability of validity coefficients over time and their stability across the entire range of selection-test scores. The first of these is a question of dynamic criteria, which we discussed in the previous chapter. If performance criteria do, in fact, change over time, should we not expect criterion-related validity coefficients to change as well. Researchers who warn of time-related declines in validity coefficients (Henry & Hulin, 1987, 1989) are opposed by researchers who see no evidence of such decrements (Ackerman, 1989; Barrett, Caldwell, & Alexander, 1989). The jury is still out on this one, but the question is important not only to those who use criterion-related validity analyses but also to those concerned about validity generalization and utility issues (see Chapter 6). The second issue is also yet to be resolved. A study of almost 70,000 U.S. Navy recruits who took the Armed Forces Qualification Test (AFQT) indicated that validity coefficients were generally larger for those whose AFQT scores were in the higher ranges than for those who obtained lower scores on this predictor (Lee & Foley, 1986). This suggests that the test might be an appropriate predictor of subsequent performance in the Navy for recruits characterized by higher levels of the constructs assessed by the AFQT, but might *not* be an appropriate predictor for those with lower levels of those skills and abilities. On the other hand, a more recent study based on measures of cognitive, numerical, and verbal abilities failed to generate validity coefficients that were meaningfully different at higher and lower points along the entire range of test scores (Waldman & Avolio, 1989). Although the research literature does not allow

us to provide you with conclusive answers to either of these issues, it's clear that I/O psychologists who use criterion-related validity analyses cannot blithely dismiss the possibility that their validity coefficients might not be stable over time or across the entire range of selection-test scores.

Most likely, Dr. MacKeven will have to rely on criterion-related validity analysis as she responds to Mr. Schiftner's request for help in selecting men and women who can succeed as managers. Fortunately, she may not find herself in a position of having to choose between predictive and concurrent approaches. She might be able to use both. Specifically, she could administer whatever selection tests or devices she considers appropriate to all (or a representative sample of) nonmanagerial employees, wait until a sufficient number of them have been promoted "from within the ranks," and then assess their subsequent performance as managers. Of course, this will take some time. In the interim, she could administer the selection test(s) under consideration to women and men who hold managerial positions in PPP's hierarchy, and concurrently obtain their job-performance scores. In any case, there is little doubt that Dr. MacKeven will use criterion-related validity analyses to investigate the predictive power of inferences about managerial success based on one or more selection-test scores.

Construct-Validity Analysis.   A third approach to validity analysis has been recommended when one wants to make inferences about relatively abstract and complex traits or characteristics thought to be critical to effective job performance. **Construct-validity analysis** is designed to demonstrate that the job in question demands a given trait or attribute (typically referred to as a **construct**), and that the selection test under consideration actually measures that trait or attribute (Lawshe, 1985). The similarities between construct- and content-validity analyses have led to some confusion (Tenopyr, 1977). The key to understanding the distinction lies in the nature of the variable(s) we are trying to measure. Construct-validity analysis is more appropriate when we wish to assess psychological constructs (that is, hypothetical or abstract traits) believed to underlie more concrete, observable behaviors. Intelligence and motivation are two examples of constructs that can help us explain a wide variety of work-related behaviors. Content-validity analysis, on the other hand, is more appropriate if we wish to assess relatively simple skills or factual knowledge necessary for satisfactory job performance. Typing skills and knowledge of word-processing procedures are examples of skill and knowledge that are amenable to direct observation and understanding without appealing to abstract, hypothetical, and unobservable constructs or traits.

We do not mean to imply, of course, that psychological constructs are irrelevant to typing skills. *All* inferences about test scores or any other behaviors are ultimately based on one or more underlying constructs (Tenopyr, 1977). Typing skill and performance are influenced by manual dexterity, visual acuity, intelligence, and motivation, all of which are constructs. The point is that we do not *need* to appeal to these abstractions to understand how performance on a typing test is related to subsequent job performance as a typist, so content-validity analysis is sufficient. Making inferences about the relevance of performance on intelligence or motivation tests for understanding performance as a manager requires a much greater "logical leap," however. Construct-validity analysis helps us make that leap, and in the process enhances our understanding of selection-test and job-performance measures and the conceptual links that join them (Pulakos, Borman, & Hough, 1988).

There are several ways to approach construct-validity analysis. Our review of recent literature turned up four strategies: (1) nomological networks (Friedman, 1983; Kopelman, Greenhaus, & Connelly, 1983); (2) multitrait-multimethod matrices (Campbell & Fiske, 1959; Neidig & Neidig, 1984); (3) complex statistical procedures (known as factor analyses) for identifying patterns among numerous correlation coefficients (Neidig & Neidig, 1984; Sackett & Dreher, 1982); and (4) latent trait theories (Maxwell & Delaney, 1985). A combined approach, "construct modeling," incorporates nomological networks and theoretical mechanisms (that is, information-processing strategies) that underlie a person's responses to test items (Embretson (Whitely), 1983). Nomological networks and multitrait-multimethod matrices are among the more common approaches to construct-validity analysis, so we'll describe them in a bit more detail. We will also say a few words about latent trait theory because it is currently generating some interest among researchers.

A **nomological network** is a pattern of empirical, statistical relationships between individuals' scores on the test of interest and their scores and status on other variables. Based on a conceptual definition of the variable we are trying to measure (for example, intelligence), we predict how people who score relatively high or low on our "intelligence test" *should* perform on other specific tests or tasks. For example, we might reasonably expect that those who score high on our (so-called) intelligence test should also (a) earn higher grades in school; (b) read more books during a specified time interval; (c) score higher on other tests *known* to measure intelligence (for example, Wechsler or Stanford-Binet tests); and (d) be "only" or first-born children. Each of these predictions is based on common sense or empirical data.

To use a nomological-network approach to construct-validity analysis, we must obtain scores on the test being considered (our "intelligence test," for example) from a sample of people, along with their scores and status on the other variables involved in the relationships predicted above. If the correlations between scores on our "intelligence test" and measures of the other variables are in the predicted direction(s), that nomological network would support the construct validity of the test under investigation. That is, if people who score

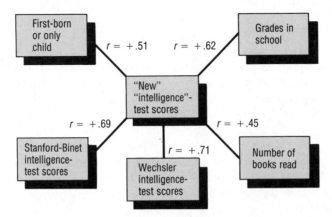

a. Evidence that supports the construct validity of
scores obtained on a "new" "intelligence" test

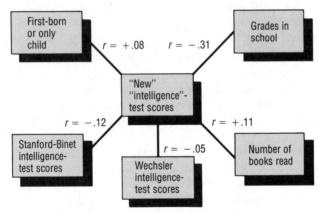

b. Evidence that fails to support the construct validity
of scores obtained on a "new" "intelligence" test

FIGURE 5.1
Nomological Networks

higher on our "intelligence test" *do* earn higher grades, *do* read more books, *do* score higher on other well-known intelligence tests, and *do* tend to be "only" or first-born children, we would have reason to believe that all these measures are tapping the same underlying construct (that is, intelligence). Alternatively, if one or more of these correlations has an algebraic sign opposite to that predicted, or is not significantly different from zero (0), we must question whether our

test actually measures the construct we intended to measure. A major strength of this approach is its appeal to our common sense. Examples of two nomological networks, one that supports the construct validity of scores obtained on our "intelligence test" and one that fails to provide such support, are depicted in Figure 5.1.

You can think of the **multitrait-multimethod matrices** approach to construct validity

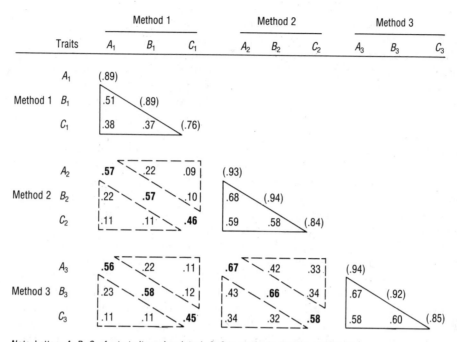

Traits	Method 1			Method 2			Method 3		
	A_1	B_1	C_1	A_2	B_2	C_2	A_3	B_3	C_3
Method 1 A_1	(.89)								
B_1	.51	(.89)							
C_1	.38	.37	(.76)						
Method 2 A_2	**.57**	.22	.09	(.93)					
B_2	.22	**.57**	.10	.68	(.94)				
C_2	.11	.11	**.46**	.59	.58	(.84)			
Method 3 A_3	**.56**	.22	.11	**.67**	.42	.33	(.94)		
B_3	.23	**.58**	.12	.43	**.66**	.34	.67	(.92)	
C_3	.11	.11	**.45**	.34	.32	**.58**	.58	.60	(.85)

Note. Letters *A, B, C* refer to traits, subscripts 1, 2, 3 to methods. Validity coefficients (monotrait–heteromethod) are the three diagonal sets of boldface numbers; reliability coefficients (monotrait–monomethod) are the numbers in parentheses along principal diagonals. Solid triangles enclose heterotrait–monomethod correlations; broken triangles enclose heterotrait–heteromethod correlations.

FIGURE 5.2
Hypothetical Multitrait–Multimethod Matrix
SOURCE: From "Convergent and Discriminant Validation by the Multitrait–Multimethod Matrix," by D. T. Campbell and D. W. Fiske, *Psychological Bulletin, 56*, 81–105. Copyright © 1959 by the American Psychological Association. Reprinted by permission of the authors.

as an extension of nomological networks; it is an attempt to demonstrate not only that test scores correlate highly with other variables to which they *should* be related but also that they do *not* correlate significantly with other variables from which they should differ. The first of these conditions is known as **convergent validity;** the second is **discriminant validity** (Campbell & Fiske, 1959).

An example of a multitrait-multimethod matrix appears in Figure 5.2. This matrix contains correlations between scores obtained on three ostensibly different variables, traits, or constructs (let's say A is intelligence, B is motivation, and C is manual dexterity), each of

which has been measured in three ways (for example, Method 1 might be supervisory ratings; Method 2 might be peer ratings; and Method 3 might be self-ratings) (Lawler, 1967). The three diagonals of boldface numbers are correlations between different measures of the same traits or constructs (that is, monotrait-heteromethod correlations)—convergent validity. The correlations in the solid triangles reflect relationships between different traits or constructs measured using the same method (that is, heterotrait-monomethod correlations). Correlations in the "broken" triangles reflect relationships between different traits or constructs measured using different methods (that is, heterotrait-heteromethod correlations). The second and third groups of correlations reflect discriminant validity. The correlations in parentheses on the main diagonal of the matrix are reliability coefficients (that is, monotrait-monomethod correlations).

Evidence of satisfactory construct validity consists of convergent-validity coefficients that are larger than the correlations (in the triangles) that reflect discriminant validity. That is, we can be more confident that we are measuring a given construct when the correlation between two different measures of that construct exceeds the correlations between two different constructs measured either in the same way (that is, using the same method) or in different ways. As you can see, the evidence in Figure 5.2 is somewhat mixed. Although the (boldfaced) convergent validity coefficients are uniformly larger than the correlations (in broken triangles) between different traits measured using different methods, they are *not* consistently or notably larger than the correlations (in solid triangles) between different traits measured using the same method. These data, then, provide some indication of construct validity, but they also reflect a troublesome level of "common-method variance." **Method variance,** which occurs when a given method of measurement (such as supervisors' ratings) fails to distinguish between ostensibly different constructs or traits (review our discussion of halo error in Chapter 4), has been the focus of several recent studies (Bagozzi & Yi, 1990; Millsap, 1990).

Latent trait theory is also known as **Item Response Theory** (IRT) because it addresses whatever is measured by *individual test items*, as well as what is measured by tests in their entirety (Maxwell & Delaney, 1985). Although there are a number of such theories, they all assume that the probability of a given response to a test item is related to an individual's standing on an underlying, latent characteristic or construct (Hulin, Drasgow, & Parsons, 1983). Latent trait theory addresses some of the problems that plague classical psychometric mea-

surement theory (Guion & Ironson, 1983). These include dependence on specific samples of subjects, difficulties associated with obtaining equivalent or parallel test forms, and lack of concern with patterns of item responses on a given test—the same observed test score can be obtained in a variety of different ways. Basic theoretical concepts, computer programs, and other analytic procedures available to I/O psychologists who wish to use latent trait theory to understand what is being measured by particular tests and test items have been described in the literature (Oltman, Stricker, & Barrows, 1990).

Although some of the problems associated with latent trait analysis are widely recognized (for example, importance of larger samples, increased cost, and complexity; inappropriate in a number of specific situations), many researchers believe that this approach "has enough advantages over classic psychometric theory to make it worth considering . . . as a promising addition to the repertoire of measurement methods in [I/O] psychology" (Guion & Ironson, 1983, p. 84). Given the importance of construct validity to the measurement process, we agree that latent trait theory (IRT) merits careful empirical and theoretical evaluation. Time will tell whether these more complex, item-specific approaches to construct validity will replace or supplement strategies based on classical psychometric assumptions or whether they represent nothing more than a procedural fad or "gizmo" (McIntyre, 1990a) that will ultimately be confined to the pages of esoteric journals and specialized psychometric textbooks.

Dr. MacKeven's need to conduct a construct-validity analysis will depend on the nature of the selection test(s) she examines in response to Mr. Schiftner's memo. If well-known and widely used tests (the construct validity of which is already well established) are available for measuring constructs important to effective job performance, it will probably be unnecessary for her to "reinvent the wheel" and repeat those analyses. On the other hand, if she decides to develop new tests, there will be greater need for construct-validity analyses. Criterion-related validity analysis in the absence of construct-validity analysis will leave her vulnerable to charges of **dustbowl empiricism,** the act of documenting statistical relationships between variables without understanding the nature (that is, the how and why) of the relationships.

Summing Up. If a personnel-selection test or device is to be useful, it must generate reliable scores from which valid inferences can be drawn. Just as there are several ways to assess reliability, so too are there alternative approaches to validity. If we want to make inferences about the items that make up a test, or about relatively simple and directly observable skills or behaviors that are obviously important to successful job performance, then content-validity analysis may be appropriate. If we want to make statistical predictions about applicants' future work behaviors, then criterion-related validity analysis is appropriate. Finally, if we want to make inferences about relatively complex, abstract psychological constructs (or latent traits) that are critical to job performance, then construct-validity analysis is necessary.

Although all three of these approaches share an obvious concern with predicting applicants' future job behaviors, a disturbing tendency to view them as three qualitatively different kinds of validity has evolved over the years (Cronbach & Meehl, 1955). The process of determining which of the three approaches is appropriate in a given set of circumstances has been likened to the process of collecting stamps, where the philatelist examines a stamp, compares it to the depictions in the stamp album, and attaches it to the "correct" spot (Landy, 1986). Several experts have recently advocated a more parsimonious and understandable perspective. According to their view, *every* validation process is nothing more or less than an exercise in hypothesis testing. The applied researcher's task becomes one of designing stud-

ies that can generate empirical evidence to support (or undermine) a conceptual framework that includes abstract psychological constructs (for example, intelligence, job performance) and operational definitions (that is, measures) of those constructs (for example, paper-and-pencil test scores, supervisory ratings) (Binning & Barrett, 1989; Landy, 1986). This "unitarian" view of validation, as opposed to the older, "trinitarian" view rejected by Landy (1986), has the salutary effect of reducing the sanctity of single correlation coefficients, and making the validation process more cumulative and comprehensive (Guion, 1987).

Now that you know about the important psychometric properties of personnel-selection instruments, we can turn our attention to the variety of measures and procedures that have been used to facilitate hiring decisions. Up to this point, we have referred to selection "tests" in a rather generic fashion. Some of the selection instruments available to Dr. MacKeven, however, bear little or no resemblance to traditional paper-and-pencil tests. The psychometric properties of those instruments are no less important, however. During our discussion of specific selection instruments in the latter half of this chapter, we will present evidence of their reliability and validity (or lack thereof), and assess the usefulness of each to Dr. MacKeven as she devises a system for selecting managers at Peter's Pan Pizza.

Personnel-Selection Procedures

Dr. MacKeven can choose from among a wide variety of personnel-selection procedures and instruments. These include traditional paper-and-pencil tests, performance tests (for example, work samples and situational exercises), application blanks, interviews, letters of recommendation, performance appraisals (especially peer assessments), and formal assessment centers. You've probably had some firsthand experience with one or more of these.

Paper-and-Pencil Tests

Literally hundreds of paper-and-pencil tests have been used to generate information for selecting job applicants. One scheme for categorizing the tests focuses on whether a test can be administered to a group of people all at the same time (that is, *group tests*), or whether it must be administered to a single individual at a time (that is *individual tests*) (Kaplan & Saccuzzo, 1982). A second distinction is that between "speed" tests and "power" tests. We discussed these test characteristics earlier. If we look instead at the variables or constructs that different paper-and-pencil tests are designed to measure (that is, test content), the diversity of available tests becomes apparent. We'll use the following taxonomy as we describe some of these measures: (a) measures of general and specific intellectual abilities; (b) measures of motivational variables; and (c) measures of personality variables (Guion, 1965b).

Intelligence Tests. Examples of intelligence measures include the Wechsler Adult Intelligence Scale—Revised, the Wonderlic Personnel Test, and the Miller Analogies Test (which is required for admission to some graduate programs), as well as numerous nonverbal tests. Early evidence indicated that these *general intelligence* tests are better predictors of performance in training programs than performance on the job (Ghiselli & Brown, 1955). The data also suggested that such tests are especially appropriate for selecting managerial and sales personnel (average validity coefficient for predicting managerial proficiency was +.37). A discussion of validity generalization (which we will consider in Chapter 6) suggested that $r = .37$ is an underestimate of the *true* average validity coefficient for such tests (Schmidt & Hunter, 1977). A more recent meta-analysis led to the conclusion that if "general cognitive ability alone is used as

a predictor, the average validity *across all jobs* [our emphasis] is .54 for a training-success criterion and .45 for a job-proficiency criterion" (Hunter & Hunter, 1984, p. 81). Although the precise magnitudes of validity coefficients based on measures of general intellectual ability remain open to debate, published studies continue to confirm that these measures are potentially useful selection tools, especially in situations (like Dr. MacKeven's) where the concern is prediction of managerial job performance (Hattrup & Schmitt, 1990; Pulakos et al., 1988; Pynes & Bernardin, 1989).

Measures of *specific* intellectual abilities include tests of clerical aptitude, spatial relations, creativity, and judgment. Multiattribute test batteries yield measures of a variety of specific cognitive skills. Examples of such batteries are the Differential Aptitude Test (DAT), which assesses verbal reasoning, numerical ability, abstract reasoning, space relations, mechanical reasoning, and clerical speed and accuracy; and the General Aptitude Test Battery (GATB) developed by the U.S. Employment Service. If the specific intellectual abilities assessed are congruent with the requirements of the job(s) in question, the encouraging conclusions about tests of general cognitive ability can be extended to these more specific measures (Gordon & Leighty, 1988; McHenry, Hough, Toquam, Hanson, & Ashworth, 1990; Silver & Bennett, 1987). It should therefore come as no surprise to you that a survey of psychologists and educational specialists revealed that these experts tend to have positive attitudes concerning the validity and usefulness of cognitive ability tests (Snyderman & Rothman, 1987).

Although useful empirical relationships between cognitive ability tests and job-performance criteria are widely acknowledged, the *consistency* of the relationships across a variety of conditions is still being actively investigated. Available evidence suggests that these empirical relationships tend to be linear (rather than curvilinear), and that they tend to be stable at both the low and high ends of the continuum of test scores (Coward & Sackett, 1990; Waldman & Avolio, 1989). Less clear-cut, however, is the effect of experience. Although a recent study concluded that the relationship between general mental-ability test scores and job performance remained essentially constant throughout five years of job experience (Schmidt, Hunter, Outerbridge, & Goff, 1988), other research suggests that the relationship between abilities and performance may vary at different stages of job experience and learning (Murphy, 1989). Although its focus is not limited to cognitive or intellectual abilities, a recently proposed causal model of the relationship(s) between ability and performance at different stages of job experience and learning can help to guide future researchers' efforts to determine the effects of experience and learning on ability-performance relationships (Fleishman & Mumford, 1989).

A more long-standing and controversial debate concerns the consistency of cognitive ability–job performance relationships across different racial and ethnic groups. Many experts continue to believe that intelligence tests are racially and/or socioeconomically biased against certain demographic groups (Snyderman & Rothman, 1987). A **biased** test, in this context, is one that makes systematic errors in measurement or prediction for one or more demographic group(s) (Murphy & Davidshofer, 1991). Nevertheless, recent evidence is consistent with a large body of earlier research suggesting that the predictive and construct validity of aptitude-test scores does *not* differ as a function of ethnic-group membership (Zeidner, 1987). Other authors have emphasized that even when test items *do* generate group differences, such items are *not* necessarily biased (that is, erroneous) (Humphreys, 1986; Roznowski, 1987). We suspect that this debate will continue for some time to come.

Motivation Tests. Motivational measures designed to assess people's desires to manage others' activities might be particularly useful to Dr.

MacKeven. Miner and colleagues have demonstrated the validity of the Miner Sentence Completion Scale for identifying individuals who eventually attain higher levels of responsibility and authority in organizational hierarchies (Berman & Miner, 1985). He has also used his approach to examine managerial potential among minorities (especially blacks) and women (Miner, 1977a). Similarly, a Managerial Potential Scale for the California Psychological Inventory (CPI) significantly predicted performance ratings for 143 military officers ($r = .20$) (Gough, 1984).

McClelland and others addressed manager-selection issues by extending the original work on achievement, affiliation, and power motivation (Atkinson, 1958; McClelland, Atkinson, Clark, & Lowell, 1953). A study of 237 managers revealed that those (in *non*technical managerial positions) who displayed a **leadership motive pattern (LMP)** obtained more promotions after 8 and 16 years than did those with different patterns of motives (McClelland & Boyatzis, 1982). The LMP did *not* predict performance for technical managers with engineering responsibilities, however. A study of people who managed second-language-instruction centers generated similar results (Cornelius & Lane, 1984). Although LMP predicted managerial success for those with broad supervisory responsibilities, it was not a valid predictor for managers with more specific administrative and public-relations responsibilities. Interestingly, the LMP in both studies involved moderate-to-high need for power and low need for affiliation, but it did not depend upon need for achievement (see Chapter 8). Stahl (1983) reported somewhat different results. He "operationalized" high managerial motivation as high scores on both need for power and need for achievement, and found that "those who scored high in managerial motivation had higher managerial performance . . . [and] a higher managerial promotion rate than others, [and] . . . were more likely to be managers than blue collar workers" (p. 775). Although the exact composition(s) of motive patterns that predict successful managerial performance are still open to question, it seems clear that motivation scores obtained from certain paper-and-pencil procedures hold promise as valid predictors of managerial performance.

Other "motivation-like" measures include interest inventories such as the Strong-Campbell Interest Inventory and the Kuder Occupational Interest Survey. Although these measures may have some value for predicting the kinds of occupations people eventually pursue and the amount of satisfaction they derive from those occupations, the measures were not designed to predict levels of job performance or success. Because their primary usefulness lies in the area of career counseling, we will not discuss them any further here.

Personality Tests.   Personality tests include the Minnesota Multiphasic Personality Inventory (MMPI), which was designed to assess certain psychopathologies (and has recently been revised); the CPI, which focuses on "normal" behavior, and which Gough (1984) used to develop his Managerial Potential Scale; and various instruments designed to measure temperament, values, and other assorted personality factors. Although Guion's (1965b) summary of the validity of these measures was not very enthusiastic, recent research has been somewhat more optimistic.

The thrust of contemporary findings in this area is that *specific* personality variables can be important predictors of *specific* job-performance criteria in the context of *specific* occupations and organizations (Pulakos et al., 1988). Even after the effects of cognitive ability had been controlled, scores on three personality scales (orientation toward work, interpersonal orientation, and ascendancy—dominance or lack of self-criticism) predicted important aspects of accountants' performance (Day & Silverman, 1989). A recent meta-analysis of relationships

between five basic dimensions of personality (extraversion, emotional stability, agreeableness, conscientiousness, and openness to experience) and three job-performance criteria (job proficiency, training proficiency, and personnel data) revealed that most of these aspects of personality were *selectively* predictive of performance criteria. Only conscientiousness was consistently associated with all three criteria across all five occupational groups included in the study (Barrick & Mount, 1991). Composites of several specific personality measures predicted U.S. Army enlisted troops' performance on three job components: giving extra effort, supporting peers, and exhibiting personal discipline (McHenry et al., 1990). In another study of enlisted military personnel, six personality constructs emerged as significant predictors of specific criterion constructs (Hough, Eaton, Dunnette, Kamp, & McCloy, 1990).

Researchers continue to investigate the predictive power of specific aspects of personality. The efforts have led to (a) the Work Opinion Questionnaire for predicting job performance among low-income workers (Johnson, Messe, & Crano, 1984); (b) the Work Orientation Scale for the CPI, which assesses self-discipline, dedication to obligations, and adherence to rules (Gough, 1985); (c) a measure of service orientation, or the tendency to be helpful, thoughtful, considerate, and cooperative (Hogan, Hogan, & Busch, 1984); (d) a measure of truck drivers' proneness to become bored (Drory, 1982); (e) a behavior-based measure of work maturity—time consciousness and sociability (Love & O'Hara, 1987); (f) an index of social extraversion (Harrell & Alpert, 1989); and (g) indices of social maladjustment and organizational delinquency: theft, insubordination, temper tantrums, and so on (Hansen, 1989; Hogan & Hogan, 1989). Although it is premature to be unguardedly optimistic, given the unimpressive history of personality measures as predictors of job performance (Guion, 1965b), it would be similarly unwise to dismiss this progress toward identifying useful predictors of important performance criteria. Among other avenues of potentially fruitful inquiry, we might find that the predictive power of some of these measures increases over time intervals that exceed those typically incorporated in most research (Helmreich, Sawin, & Carsrud, 1986).

An aspect of personality that has received a great deal of recent research attention in the context of personnel selection is the **Type A behavior pattern** (Matthews, 1982). Typically conceptualized as a composite of two subdimensions—achievement striving, and impatience or irritability—Type A behavior was originally investigated as a potential predictor of coronary disease (Friedman & Rosenman, 1974). More recently, however, data have suggested that individuals who display higher levels of Type A behavior perform their jobs better than those with lower levels of this behavior pattern, especially when they perceive themselves in control of their work situations (Lee, Ashford, & Bobko, 1990). Other findings suggest that only one of the two Type A subdimensions is a valid predictor of work performance: achievement striving. A study of insurance-policy salespersons revealed that achievement striving predicted numbers of policies sold (as well as employees' satisfaction with their work); impatience or irritability predicted emotional depression but no specific job-performance criteria (Bluen, Barling, & Burns, 1990). This finding replicated earlier conclusions that achievement striving is related to performance, and impatience or irritability predicts frequency of physical complaints (Spence, Helmreich, & Pred, 1987; Spence, Pred, & Helmreich, 1989). Other research has supported the notion that components of Type A are more powerful predictors than global measures of this behavior pattern, and that the impatience or irritability (hostility?) subdimension predicts mental and physical symptoms rather than job performance

(Edwards & Baglioni, 1991; Ganster, Schaubroeck, Sime, & Mayes, 1991). Thus, a number of studies suggest that the achievement-striving component of the Type A behavior pattern may be a valid predictor of certain job-performance criteria. Nevertheless, there is still some concern about the construct validity of the data obtained through different procedures (for example, interviews, questionnaires) used to assess this aspect of personality (Edwards, Baglioni, & Cooper, 1990).

Other efforts to identify aspects of personality that can predict job performance have yet to meet with much success. A review of research on paper-and-pencil measures of honesty, operationally defined as the absence of theft in the workplace, found no compelling evidence of validity in the context of employee selection (Sackett & Harris, 1984). Although a more recent review of integrity tests was cautiously more optimistic, compelling data that support their use are still unavailable (Sackett, Burris, & Calahan, 1989). Graphologists' attempts to assess job-relevant traits through analyses of employees' handwriting have been similarly discouraging (Ben-Shakhar, Bar-Hillel, Bilu, Ben-Abba, & Flug, 1986; Murphy, 1993; Rafaeli & Klimoski, 1983). Thus, some recent evidence supports the earlier pessimistic views of personality measures' small or nonexistent contributions to personnel selection (Guion, 1965b; Keinan, Friedland, Yitzhaky, & Moran, 1981).

Summing Up. Considering available research evidence, Dr. MacKeven will be wise to limit her use of paper-and-pencil tests for predicting managerial success to measures of intellectual abilities, to instruments specifically designed to assess individuals' motivation to manage, and to measures of specific personality constructs designed to predict specific criteria of managerial performance. Dr. MacKeven might also use test batteries made up of several paper-and-pencil instruments (Campbell, 1990; Peterson,

Hough, Dunnette, Rosse, Houston, Toquam, & Wing, 1990; Vale, Keller, & Bentz, 1986). Fortunately, she has several other personnel-selection procedures at her disposal.

Biographical Information

Biographical information (biodata) includes demographic data as well as information about a person's past life and work experiences. Demographic data include age, sex, race, formal education, and marital status. Experiential data include information about the number and variety of jobs an individual has held, how the individual spends leisure time, military service, and so forth. Most organizations collect biodata by asking each job applicant to complete an application blank and/or to submit a résumé describing background and relevant work experience. Biographical information that is particularly sensitive in the context of EEOC guidelines (for example, race, religious preference, number of children) is sometimes solicited only after individuals have been hired. If such information is collected prior to the hiring decision, the organization must not use it to make personnel decisions. In fact, the organization should take reasonable and prudent action to avoid giving even the appearance of using such information to select some applicants and reject others.

Most of the reviews and discussions of biodata in the literature have been encouraging about their reliability and validity for predicting job performance (Hakel, 1986; Owens, 1976; Tenopyr & Oeltjen, 1982; Zedeck & Cascio, 1984). Hunter and Hunter's (1984) review of various predictors of job performance referred to prior reviews by Dunnette (1972) and Reilly and Chao (1982), which indicated that only biodata yield validity coefficients that are comparable to those associated with cognitive ability tests (that is, in the .34 to .39 range). A review of military studies also endorsed biodata as valid predictors of job performance, although validity coefficients were somewhat smaller (in the .20 to .29 range) (Vineberg & Joyner, 1982).

The literature continues to abound with encouraging reports of relatively impressive validity coefficients associated with biodata. Specific biodata predictors examined in these studies include (a) prior job experience and job seniority (Gordon, Cofer, & McCullough, 1986; Hansen, 1989; Jacobs, Hofmann, & Kriska, 1990; Lance, Hedge, & Alley, 1989; McDaniel, Schmidt, & Hunter, 1988; McEnrue, 1988; Rodgers, Helburn, & Hunter, 1986; Vance, Coovert, MacCallum, & Hedge, 1989); (b) educational achievement (Childs & Klimoski, 1986; Howard, 1986; Meritt-Haston & Wexley, 1983); (c) extracurricular activities (Howard, 1986); (d) marital status (Wells & Muchinsky, 1985); and (e) prior absenteeism (Ivancevich, 1985).

Prior drug use has also received serious attention as a predictor of job performance. A longitudinal study of more than 5,000 applicants for U.S. Postal Service jobs revealed that those who tested positive for use of illicit drugs had higher rates of absenteeism and involuntary turnover for a period exceeding one year than did those who tested negative, but there were no differences with respect to injuries or accidents (Normand, Salyards, & Mahoney, 1990). Similarly, studies of young adults and background investigations have supported the criterion-related validity of preemployment drug use (McDaniel, 1988, 1989). Because organizational drug testing is a potentially controversial procedure, several researchers have examined the effects of applicants' attitudes toward such screening. As you might guess, frequency of drug use was negatively related to acceptability of drug testing among college students, although these subjects acknowledged that drug testing is appropriate and necessary in some situations (Murphy, Thornton, & Reynolds, 1990). Similarly, undergraduate students expressed more positive attitudes toward organizations that did *not* have drug-testing programs, as well as firms that were perceived not to *need* such programs (Crant & Bateman, 1990). Finally, a study of blue-collar workers revealed that their attitudes toward drug testing were more positive when the organization provided advance notice of the testing, and when positive results led to enrollment in an employee assistance program rather than dismissal or rejection during the hiring process (Stone & Kotch, 1989). Thus, we are beginning to understand the potential of information about prior drug use to contribute to personnel-selection decisions, and to appreciate the effects of drug testing on applicants' opinions about organizations.

When biodata are actually used to predict performance in organizations, validity coefficients may be smaller than those reported in research journals. Scoring keys for transforming information from application blanks into biodata often do not generalize from one organization to another, or from one specific criterion measure to another. Second, biodata scoring keys tend to become less valid over time (Davis, 1984; Eberhardt & Muchinsky, 1984). The empirical process of developing scoring keys is also vulnerable to capitalization on chance or random error because of the relatively small sample sizes typically used in such research (Hunter & Hunter, 1984). After removing the influences of chance or random error, the validity of biodata based on an **empirical scoring** system was substantially reduced, although validity coefficients remained significantly greater than similar indices based on a more **rational scoring** key[4] (Mitchell & Klimoski, 1982). Rational scoring systems may produce validity coefficients that are more generalizable, however (Mitchell & Klimoski, 1986).

The principle of behavioral consistency, which asserts that the best predictor of future behavior is relevant past behavior, has been applied to soliciting and scoring experiential data (Hough, 1984; Hough, Keys, & Dunnette, 1983; Pannone, 1984). Hough's **accomplishment-record method** yields self-reports of accom-

plishments that pertain to relevant behavioral job dimensions. These reports can be rated reliably ($r = .82$). Although they appear to be unrelated to such traditional psychological measures as aptitude tests, grades, or honors, they do correlate with measures of job performance ($r = .25$). A study of 329 attorneys suggested that the accomplishment-record method predicts performance equally well for minorities and nonminorities, and for men and women (Hough, 1984). Further, it "capture[s], in an objectively scorable way, the types of information usually gathered and interpreted via more subjective personnel procedures such as application blanks (background information), interviews (interests, opinions, and previous accomplishments), and reference checks (accomplishments)" (Hough et al., 1983, p. 274). Hough and colleagues acknowledged that applicants' accomplishment records can be scored and meaningfully interpreted only in the context of accurate and complete job analyses (see Chapter 3). When properly scored and interpreted, however, this method provides "a means of systematically and objectively evaluating the professional accomplishments of employment candidates who have worked in other organizations since obtaining their professional training" (p. 275).

We are aware of only one drawback to the behavioral-consistency approach to soliciting and scoring biodata. In a comparison of four methods for evaluating and scoring relevant training and experience, a "behavioral consistency" method required almost twice the time required by two other scoring methods (Ash & Levine, 1985). However, this may be time well spent. A growing body of evidence suggests that highly relevant educational or job information, such as that obtainable through the accomplishment-record method of collecting biodata, can weaken some effects of negative stereotypes that commonly plague female job applicants (Dunbar & Novick, 1988; Heilman, 1984; Heilman & Martell, 1986; Heilman, Martell, & Simon, 1988). Thus, this approach may

[4] In a "rational" scoring key, specific pieces of biographical information are used to predict performance criteria based on logic, theory, or "common sense." An empirically based scoring key assigns predictive value to specific pieces of information solely on the basis of demonstrated ability to predict performance criteria for a specific sample of individuals.

help to reduce sex discrimination (and perhaps other forms of discrimination) during personnel selection. Because available data clearly indicate that being older, female, or nonwhite is often a disadvantage in the context of personnel decisions, we should not dismiss this property of accomplishment records (Hitt & Barr, 1989; Lee & Clemons, 1985; Olian, Schwab, & Haberfeld, 1988; Waldman & Avolio, 1986; Wells & Muchinsky, 1985).

Certain circumstances can render the accomplishment-record approach to collecting biodata less appropriate, however. Sometimes applicants are too young or inexperienced to have had the kinds of experiences normally tapped by this approach. Sometimes the job in question is so unusual that *no one* could reasonably be expected to have any directly relevant experience. An interesting alternative approach in such cases is to extract biodata from "retrospective life-history essays." Focusing on four generic life experiences that most of us have in common (for example, individual accomplishments, disappointing situations, stressful situations, and group accomplishments), U.S. Naval Academy students wrote essays that yielded biodata items predictive of academic and military performance, as well as peer leadership ratings (Russell, Mattson, Devlin, & Atwater, 1990).

Summing Up. Admittedly, biodata present scoring challenges and can be influenced by "inflation bias" when applicants fraudulently claim to have observed or performed actual or even bogus job-related tasks (Anderson, Warner, & Spencer, 1984). Further, some studies have either failed to confirm the validity of biodata or demonstrated only weak relationships between biodata and job-performance criteria (Turnage & Muchinsky, 1984; Wakabayashi & Graen, 1984). Nevertheless, most reviewers have emphasized the relative superiority of biodata for predicting subsequent job performance. Recent work with the accomplishment-record method for assessing and evaluating biodata has tended to support these reviewers' conclu-

sions. Other data suggest that even unverifiable responses to biodata questions are usually accurate (Shaffer, Saunders, & Owens, 1986), and that biodata can be stable predictors of performance over time and across geographical and organizational boundary lines (Lautenschlager & Shaffer, 1987; Rothstein, Schmidt, Erwin, Owens, & Sparks, 1990). It therefore seems highly appropriate for Dr. MacKeven to consider supplementing applicants' scores on cognitive-ability, motivation, and personality tests with scores derived from biodata, especially scores based on the accomplishment-record method.

Interviews

Interviews can take a variety of forms but they all share one thing in common, an opportunity for job applicants and organizational representatives to interact face to face. You have probably already participated in one or more interviews. If so, you know that these personal encounters may or may not be informative, comfortable, or useful, depending on how the interview is conducted and the goals that the organization has for this personnel-selection procedure.

The most basic distinction among types of interviews is between structured and unstructured procedures. In a **structured interview,** the interviewer asks applicants a preplanned series of questions. Because all applicants are asked the same basic set of questions, the interviewer (and the organization) can directly compare applicants' responses, and thereby make more informed hiring decisions. Unstructured interviews, which you are more likely to have experienced, are more freewheeling affairs where the interviewer asks whatever questions come to mind. Because there is no guarantee that all applicants will be asked the same questions, the interviewer is usually in the uncomfortable position of "comparing apples and oranges" when it is time to make selection decisions.

Some interviews are more stressful than others.

Structured interviews are much easier to incorporate in a validation process. Given a known, preplanned content, structured interviews more closely resemble paper-and-pencil tests—all applicants respond to the same set of questions in the same order. The validity of interviewers' inferences, based on applicants' responses to particular questions (items), can be determined by any of the three validity analyses discussed earlier in this chapter. Unstructured interviews are much less amenable to the validation process. There is no set content, so content-validity analysis is out of the question. Because different applicants respond to different questions in more or less random, unpredictable order, unstructured interviews typically do not yield the kind of data necessary for reliability analyses, or for criterion-related or construct-validity analyses. The only information that can be quantitatively analyzed is the interviewer's overall predictions about the ultimate job success of each applicant. Although there is no question that some interviewers are able to make valid predictions more consistently than others (Landy, 1976; Zedeck, Tziner, & Middlestadt, 1983), even those relatively valid predictions have a "hollow ring" to them because the underlying content and substance on which they are based are variable, undocumented, and often unknown.

Recent comparisons of unstructured interviews and a specific kind of structured interview, the **patterned behavior-description interview,** illustrate the superiority of a structured approach. Based on critical incidents that "suggest specific occasions in the applicant's experiences that are predictive of future job behavior" (Orpen, 1985, p. 774), patterned behavior-description interviews generated valid predictions of both the dollar value of sales and supervisor's ratings of life-insurance salesmen. An earlier study reported similar findings for teaching assistants (Janz, 1982). The validity of patterned interviews for predicting students' ratings of teaching performance was .54; the corresponding coefficient for unstructured inter-

views was .17. Interestingly, Orpen's data revealed no differences in test-retest reliability between structured and unstructured interviews ($r = .70$ for both), and Janz's structured interview data were *less* reliable than the unstructured data ($r = .46$ and .71, respectively). A more recent investigation of structured interviews revealed a more encouraging reliability coefficient ($r = .88$) along with satisfactory validity (Campion, Pursell, & Brown, 1988). A second kind of structured interview asks applicants what they would do in specific situations. Based on the assumption that stated intentions predict actual subsequent behaviors, **situational interviews** have demonstrated acceptable reliability and validity in a series of studies (Latham & Saari, 1984; Latham, Saari, Pursell, & Campion, 1980; Maurer & Fay, 1988; Motowidlo, Dunnette, & Carter, 1990; Weekley & Gier, 1987).

Other interview taxonomies focus on the number of interviewers or the amount of stress that is intentionally created during the interview session. Some organizations have two or more interviewers present for each session (for example, Landy, 1976). Sometimes interviews are purposely designed to make applicants anxious by creating stressful environments. Such "stress interviews" can be justified through content-validity analysis when high levels of interpersonal stress are inherent in the job (for example, police officer).

Literature Reviews. Published reviews of empirical research on selection interviews appear in the professional literature from time to time. Most have *not* been encouraging with respect to reliability or validity. The first comprehensive review of this literature reported a mean reliability coefficient of .27 (Wagner, 1949). Wagner encouraged us to use patterned or structured interviews, and recommended that we combine information collected during interviews statistically rather than "clinically" or subjectively. Mayfield (1964) reviewed the literature published after Wagner's commentary, and re-

BOX 5.1 Interviewers' Decision-Making Processes

- Interviewers make final decisions about applicants relatively quickly, often during the first few minutes of the interview session.

- Interviewers are influenced more by negative information about an applicant than by positive or flattering information.

- Interviewers often compare applicants to stereotypes of the "ideal," successful job applicant.

- Interviewers make more reliable decisions when they are better informed about the nature of the job(s) to be filled.

- Interviewers differ in how they interpret pieces of information, and in their use of that information to make final decisions about applicants.

- Interviewers rely on applicants' nonverbal cues as well as their verbal and oral behavior when making decisions.

- Race and gender of both interviewers and applicants can affect interviewers' decisions.

- Less experienced interviewers are vulnerable to "contrast effects," where an average applicant is evaluated inordinately high or low when the prior interviewee was unusually unqualified or highly qualified, respectively.

- Structured interviews are superior to unstructured interviews.

SOURCE: From "The Employment Interview: A Summary and Review of Recent Research," by R. D. Arvey and J. E. Campion, *Personnel Psychology, 35,* 281–322. Copyright © 1982 by Personnel Psychology, Inc. Adapted by permission.

ported that interview research was still generating relatively low reliability and validity coefficients. He also concurred with his predecessor by advocating structured interview formats. A third review published only six months later reinforced Mayfield's conclusions (Ulrich & Trumbo, 1965). In addition, Ulrich and Trumbo advised that interviewers should concentrate on assessing applicants' interpersonal skills and levels of work motivation, and that assessment of other traits and skills should be left to more appropriate selection instruments. Wright (1969) and Schmitt (1976) reviewed research that investigated the decision-making processes inherent in selection interviews. Their conclusions are summarized in Box 5.1. Based on their review of more recent research, Arvey

and Campion (1982) offered the generalizations that appear in Box 5.2.

Arvey's (1979) earlier review focused on the role of various biases during employment interviews. These include prejudices based on race, sex, age, and physical handicap. The conclusions were as follows:

- Women are usually evaluated less favorably than equally qualified men, especially if the job in question is traditionally "masculine" (for example, manager);

- There is little evidence that race affects interviewers' decisions;

- An applicant's age plays an important role in the interviewer's decisions; younger applicants are generally favored; and

BOX 5.2 Generalizations Based on Empirical Research on Selection Interviews

- Panel interviews (two or more interviewers) may improve the reliability and validity of interview data.
- Interview questions should be derived directly from job analyses or from other appropriate job-related information.
- Studies have become more methodologically sophisticated in trying to reproduce more realistic stimulus and response conditions.
- Interviewers are still influenced by contrast effects as well as primacy and recency effects, where information that emerges very early or very late in the interview session, respectively, makes a greater impression than information that emerges in midsession; first impressions and personal biases also affect interviewers' decisions.
- Applicants' nonverbal behaviors (for example, gestures, eye contact) influence interviewers' decisions.

SOURCE: From "The Employment Interview: A Summary and Review of Recent Research," by R. D. Arvey and J. E. Campion, *Personnel Psychology, 35*, 281–322. Copyright © 1982 by Personnel Psychology, Inc. Reprinted by permission.

- Handicapped applicants receive less enthusiastic hiring recommendations than able-bodied applicants; however, stronger work motivation is typically attributed to handicapped job seekers.

Finally a summary of research findings published since Arvey and Campion's (1982) review is considerably more encouraging about the reliability and validity of interviews (Harris, 1989). In his summary of findings, Harris offered the following set of recommendations for future research:

1. More sophisticated analytic techniques, including causal modeling and meta-analysis, and more innovative research designs should be used to develop new theoretical models of interview processes and outcomes.

2. Studies should focus on actual interviewers during actual interviews (instead of college-student subjects with little or no actual interviewing experience).

3. Practical issues such as adverse impact, acceptability (to both managers and applicants), and cost effectiveness must *not* be ignored.

Examples of Recent Research. Many empirical investigations of selection interviews have addressed and elaborated on the conclusions from the reviews described above. Some of the evidence supports their conclusions; other data refute them. For example, several studies have examined the hypothesis that interviewers tend to make up their minds during the first few minutes of an interview, and then spend the remaining time trying to generate information from the applicant that confirms the earlier impression. Although there is reason to believe that interviewers' preinterview impressions of applicants are positively related to their impressions following an interview (Macan &

Dipboye, 1990; Phillips & Dipboye, 1989), most of this research failed to provide strong support for "confirmatory-information-seeking" questioning strategies, especially among more experienced interviewers (Macan & Dipboye, 1988; McDonald & Hakel, 1985; Sackett, 1982). However, one study suggested that the situation might be a bit more complicated (Binning, Goldstein, Garcia, & Scattaregia, 1988). Its authors reported that both female and male interviewers planned to ask more negatively biased questions of "weaker" applicants (on the basis of résumés and other information) than of "stronger" applicants, regardless of the applicant's sex. Furthermore, both female and male interviewers planned to ask more positively biased questions to weaker applicants of the same sex, thereby demonstrating a *disconfirmatory* questioning strategy. Thus, an applicant's sex and qualifications may interact with the interviewer's sex to generate confirmatory or disconfirmatory questioning strategies during an interview (Binning et al., 1988).

Several studies have continued to document the relevance of interviewers' and applicants' sex to the outcome of selection interviews. Three experienced police officers who interviewed 150 male and 129 female applicants during a six-month interval displayed systematically different policies for evaluating the two sexes (James, Campbell, & Lovegrove, 1984). Interviews of 517 applicants for seasonal jobs at a large amusement park resulted in female applicants receiving higher ratings than male applicants on nonverbal behaviors and on overall qualifications (Parsons & Liden, 1984). Women who interviewed for positions as seasonal retail salesclerks received higher average interview evaluations than did male applicants (Arvey, Miller, Gould, & Burch, 1987). Other data suggest that female applicants for managerial positions who wear more "masculine" (that is, less "feminine") clothing receive more favorable hiring recommendations. Only when women wore extremely masculine clothes did they receive less favorable hiring recommenda-

tions (Forsythe, Drake, & Cox, 1985). Finally, Baron (1983) reported that female interviewers gave higher ratings to male or female applicants who wore a popular brand of cologne or perfume, respectively; male interviewers gave lower ratings to more fragrant applicants, however. (Apparently, this line of research "nose" no bounds!)

Other studies have focused on other demographic characteristics. Although the aforementioned study of applicants for retail salesclerk positions reported that older applicants received higher average interview evaluations than younger applicants (Arvey et al., 1987), the role of age in the interview process is probably more complex, involving variables such as interviewers' accountability for their recommendations and job status. Preliminary findings suggest that when interviewers are held accountable (by their organization) for their selection decisions, younger applicants may be evaluated more positively than older applicants (Gordon, Rozelle, & Baxter, 1988). An earlier study showed that judges who were held more accountable for the results of their decisions generated descriptions of applicants that more reliably reflected applicants' actual characteristics (Rozelle & Baxter, 1981). Under "neutral information" conditions, managers preferred hiring younger applicants for low-status jobs. When provided with "age-relevant" information, however, managers shifted their preference to older applicants for low-status jobs (Singer & Sewell, 1989).[5] Effects of still other demographic variables are probably also complex. For example, interviewers tend *not* to view all disabled applicants in the same way. Those who appeared on crutches received higher evaluations than applicants with other disabilities (for example, hearing loss, wheelchair) (Cesare, Tannenbaum, & Dalessio, 1990). These findings have important implica-

[5] Students who assumed the role of managers expressed different preferences. These and earlier findings suggest that student subjects do *not* behave the same as experienced managers or professional interviewers do. Therefore, these populations should not be used interchangeably in interview research (Barr & Hitt, 1986).

tions as we begin the challenging task of assuring equal employment opportunities to applicants (and employees) protected by the Americans with Disabilities Act (1991).

Although this body of research suggests that effects of sex, age, and disabilities are complex, other findings are more reassuring. When a model designed to explain the role of demographic and other variables was tested using actual employment interviews, the data indicated that interview decisions are influenced more by job-relevant variables, such as applicants' skills, than by demographic variables (Raza & Carpenter, 1987). Of course, we cannot allow these data to distract us from attending to the *possible* influences of irrelevant interviewee characteristics on interview outcomes.

Applicants' nonverbal behaviors and social skills displayed during interviews have been examined in some detail. As we indicated earlier, female applicants for seasonal jobs in an amusement park were rated more favorably with respect to their nonverbal behaviors (for example, facial expressions, gestures) than were their male counterparts (Parsons & Liden, 1984). Effects of nonverbal behaviors on interview outcomes can be especially important when applicants' job-relevant credentials (and other behaviors) are very similar. Under such circumstances, more exaggerated nonverbal behaviors tend to make strong applicants look even better and weak applicants even worse (Rasmussen, 1984). However, because some studies report no effects of "body language" or attire on interview data, it is still premature to draw firm conclusions in this area (Sterrett, 1978).

There is reason to believe that interviews are better suited to assessing applicants' social skills than other personal characteristics or abilities (for example, motivation to work). Data suggest that interviewers assess social skills by looking at three specific forms of nonverbal behavior: (1) amount of time an applicant spends talking; (2) formality of an applicant's clothing; and (3) rate at which an applicant makes hand movements and other physical gestures (Gif-

ford, Ng, & Wilkinson, 1985). Other data suggest that interviews are useful for assessing self-efficacy, the belief that one can perform a task successfully (Gist, 1987).

The criterion-related validity of interview data is still relatively weak compared to the validity of cognitive ability measures, biodata, and some personality measures (Hunter & Hunter, 1984; Inwald, 1988; Latham & Saari, 1984). Further, predictive validities based on interviews may not measure up to validities based on statistical procedures (Dougherty, Ebert, & Callender, 1986). Nevertheless, more encouraging results are beginning to appear in the research literature:

1. Structured interviews for selecting entry-level production employees generated data that were reliable ($r = .88$) and valid (rs between .34 and .56) (Campion et al., 1988).

2. Interviewers' judgments for selecting seasonal retail sales clerks yielded strong validities (rs between .34 and .61) (Arvey et al., 1987).

Finally, some other recent findings have enhanced our understanding of selection interviews:

1. Interviewers' judgments based on specific, job-relevant dimensions are superior to judgments based on more general, all-inclusive judgments (Osburn, Timmreck, & Bigby, 1981).

2. Because individual interviewers base hiring decisions on different interview impressions, and are likely to differ in their abilities to generate valid data, it is inappropriate to combine data from several interviewers in a single validation study (Dreher, Ash, & Hancock, 1988; Kinicki, Lockwood, Hom, & Griffeth, 1990).

3. Although a stereotype of a "good worker" might be useful to interviewers (assuming it is based strictly on job-related factors and is *not* related to demographic variables such

as race, sex, or age), we should expect assessments of "general employability" to differ from assessments of "fit" between an individual applicant and a specific organization (Rynes & Gerhart, 1990). Such congruence with respect to personality characteristics is especially important when applicants' levels of competence are very similar (Paunonen, Jackson, & Oberman, 1987). Further, there is some indication that organizations actually foster the development of particular worker stereotypes (Dickey-Bryant, Lautenschlager, Mendoza, & Abrahams, 1986).

4. It is common knowledge that applicants attempt to "put their best foot forward" during interviews, but their attempts at impression management vary with such interviewer characteristics as status and familiarity (Gardner & Martinko, 1988). Whether the use of computers to administer interviews will inhibit applicants' tendencies to behave and respond in socially desirable ways remains unclear (Lautenschlager & Flaherty, 1990; Martin & Nagao, 1989).

Summing Up. Despite the fact that interview data have been traditionally less reliable and less valid than data obtained in other ways (for example, biodata, scores on paper-and-pencil tests of cognitive ability), and despite some preliminary evidence that information generated by group-administered questionnaires may predict certain aspects of performance just as well as interview data (Tubiana & Ben-Shakhar, 1982), Arvey and Campion (1982) confessed that they knew of only one organization that hired applicants "sight unseen," without any form of personal interview. They suggested four possible explanations for the persistence of this selection technique:

1. The interview *is really valid* for making inferences about applicants' sociability and verbal skills, and perhaps work motivation, but our psychometric models and statistical procedures are not sufficiently sensitive to detect this validity. (Some of the recent, more encouraging validity reports [Harris, 1989] may be at least partially attributable to improved models and procedures.)

2. The interview *may not be valid*, but it retains its popularity because of one or more of the following considerations: (a) there are too few applicants to warrant more expensive and elaborate selection procedures; (b) an erroneous assumption is made that EEOC *Guidelines* do not apply to "unscored" interviews; and (c) it furnishes an opportunity to answer applicants' questions and provide them with realistic sets of expectations about available jobs.

3. The interview *is not valid*, but interviewers remain confident about their judgments, partially because they usually receive little or no feedback about the quality of their hiring decisions.

4. The interview *is not valid*, but it accomplishes other purposes very well, such as "selling" the applicant on the job and creating good public relations in the surrounding community.

SOURCE: Adapted from "The Employment Interview: A Summary and Review of Recent Research," by R. D. Arvey and J. E. Campion, *Personnel Psychology, 35,* 281–322. Copyright © 1982 by Personnel Psychology, Inc. Reprinted by permission.

Regardless of which of these explanations is closest to the truth, Mr. Schiftner will, no doubt, question Dr. MacKeven's sanity if she suggests a set of procedures for identifying and selecting managers that does not include some kind of personal interview. It will therefore be necessary for her to review the relevant research literature, and to supplement paper-and-pencil tests and biodata forms with selection interviews that generate maximally reliable and valid data. Those interviews should have limited and realistic goals, such as evaluating *only* applicants' interpersonal and communication skills. They should be structured or patterned, and based on job-analysis data for managerial positions. They should minimize or eliminate harmful effects of personal biases based on sex, age, race, or ethnic group membership, as well as contrast, primacy, and recency effects. Finally, they should be analyzed by focusing on data generated by individual interviewers as the appropriate "units of analysis."

Work Samples, Situational Exercises, and Other Miscellaneous Predictors

Other selection procedures available to Dr. MacKeven include work samples, situational exercises, letters of recommendation, and peer assessments.

Work samples can provide useful information about applicants' job skills.

Work Samples.   So far we have described selection tests and procedures that bear little or no resemblance to the work tasks that successful applicants will actually have to perform on the job. **Work samples** are different because they present applicants with opportunities to perform small, manageable segments of job tasks or duties. Prediction of job performance is more straightforward, so content-validity analysis should be useful. In a criterion-related validity analysis, a work sample designed for mechanics yielded a validity coefficient of .46 with an overall mechanical-ability criterion (Campion, 1972). Validity coefficients of this magnitude are typical for work-sample predictors (Hunter & Hunter, 1984). A disadvantage of using work samples to predict job performance is that these samples can be time-consuming and expensive to administer. Because they are usually "individual" tests, they typically require one examiner per applicant. Necessary equipment can be costly, and often requires substantial amounts of time to "set up" or prepare. A second problem with work samples is their focus on applicants' capabilities at the time they are being considered for jobs. Their *potential* to acquire important job skills during formal training or to benefit from on-the-job experience is ignored.

Miniature job training represents a partial solution to the second of these problems (Siegel, 1983). During this procedure, "the job seeker is trained to perform a sample of tasks involved in the job for which he is an applicant and, immediately following the training, his ability to perform these tasks is measured." It is assumed that "a person who can demonstrate the ability to learn and perform on a job sample will be able to learn and perform on the total job" (Siegel, 1983, p. 42). A recent meta-analysis of validities associated with seven "minicourses" used to predict performance criteria on the job and in more formal training contexts indicated that those validities were comparable with validities typically associated with ability or work-sample tests (Reilly & Israelski, 1988). Other evidence suggests, however, that "trainability tests" may predict short-term success in more formal training programs better than more distal training performance (Robertson & Downs, 1989).

Situational Exercises. Unlike work samples, which are more or less exact replicas of job segments, **situational exercises** approximate components of jobs. For professional and especially managerial jobs, leaderless group discussions (Bass, 1954) and in-basket tests (Frederiksen, 1968) are still popular situational exercises. For jobs that require manual labor or other physical activities, tests of strength or other physical capabilities are potentially appropriate situational exercises.

Leaderless group discussions bring together small groups of applicants who are asked to talk about a topic that is usually job related. No other structure or directions are provided, no rules or procedures are imposed, and no leader is appointed. The objective is to see who emerges as a group leader, who addresses group members' social and emotional needs, who structures or organizes the group's discussion and activities, and the means by which these individuals accomplish these ends. Typical validity coefficients based on observers' ratings of these discussions and subsequent criteria of managerial performance (for example, salary progress) seldom exceed .40.

In-basket tests require applicants to work their way through an "in-basket" filled with memos, telephone messages, short reports, and other documents that often demand managers' attention. Observers record applicants' priorities as they undertake the various tasks, and their approaches to those tasks (for example, placing telephone calls, writing letters or memos, convening meetings). Although in-basket tests can require several hours to complete, their apparent content validity (sometimes referred to as **face validity** because the procedure "looks like" it measures what it's intended to measure) has discouraged many organizations from abandoning them. Unfortunately, recent empir-

ical evidence is not very encouraging. An investigation of two alternate in-basket exercises revealed little convergent validity and troublesome method bias (that is, scores were influenced by the measurement method rather than by the construct or variable under study). This study also questioned the wisdom of making inferences about individual differences in managerial abilities from in-basket scores (Brannick, Michaels, & Baker, 1989). A review of the psychometric properties of in-basket measures reported "marginal" evidence of validity (even though they *can* be scored reliably) and offered only modest support for their usefulness as a selection instrument (Schippmann, Prien, & Katz, 1990). These reviewers did suggest, however, that validity tends to improve when organizations specifically design in-basket exercises for particular target jobs rather than purchasing predesigned, generic, "off-the-shelf" procedures.

Validity analyses of strength tests and tests of other physical abilities and characteristics have also produced inconsistent results. Tests of body density, balance, and static strength have yielded valid scores for predicting safe job performance for telephone line workers (Reilly, Zedeck, & Tenopyr, 1979). A single measure of static arm strength (an arm dynamometer) significantly predicted performance on a variety of tasks accomplished by both male and female steelworkers (Arnold, Rauschenberger, Soubel, & Guion, 1982). A minimum level of cardiovascular fitness for firefighters has been established and validated (Sothmann, Saupe, Janesof, Blaney, Fuhrman, Woulfe, Raven, Pawelczyk, Dotson, Landy, Smith, & Davis, 1990). And personnel specialists seem to be capable of providing reliable and valid judgments of the physical efforts demanded by a variety of occupational tasks, suggesting that actual physical measures may not be necessary (Hogan & Fleishman, 1979).

Unfortunately, Hogan's (1985) more recent data are less encouraging. Her evaluation of the validity of five well-known physical-fitness batteries for predicting attrition among U.S. Navy divers during fitness training revealed that these batteries were "less effective predictors of performance in a physical conditioning training program than originally expected" (p. 223). An earlier review of this literature concluded with the following cautionary statement: "although the relationship between maximum performance physical ability measures and maximum performance job samples seems to be strong, the relationship between physical ability measures and typical on-the-job performance has not been established" (Campion, 1983, pp. 545–546). A more recent review summarized court cases prompted by applicants' concerns about physical tests or standards used to select employees. Precedents and lines of argument necessary to demonstrate or rebut claims of unlawful discrimination were also discussed, with particular attention paid to cases involving lifting or physical-stature requirements (Hogan & Quigley, 1986). Such requirements may be especially vulnerable to charges of sex discrimination. In this same vein, a recent study of apparent sex differences in manual dexterity revealed that women's typically superior performance on tasks and tests requiring this ability is entirely attributable to systematically different finger and thumb sizes (Peters, Servos, & Day, 1990).

Several researchers have gone beyond traditional tests of physical strength and abilities to assess the validity of more unusual situational measures for predicting job performance. A study of individuals' sensitivity to glare reported sufficient individual differences to justify further research that could lead to minimum night-driving standards for truck and bus drivers (Sturgis, Pulling, & Vaillancourt, 1981). Another investigation used a computer-based simulation to establish the validity of petroleum-product transport drivers' selective attention for predicting an accident criterion (Arthur, Barrett, & Doverspike, 1990). Even the possibility of using genetic factors to screen applicants for employment in work sites where some individuals may be susceptible to negative effects of chemical and other pollutants has been discussed (Olian, 1984). (Genetic factors have also been linked to job satisfaction by Arvey, Bouchard, Segal, and Abraham, 1989.) Perhaps we have only begun to explore the potential of situational tests to predict job performance.

Letters of Recommendation. Other people's opinions of applicants' qualifications, job-related abilities, and experience constitute another category of measures that Dr. MacKeven might use to help Mr. Schiftner select successful managers for Peter's Pan Pizza. Although they can be solicited over the telephone, such recommendations are usually conveyed in writing. You may already have been in a position where you had to ask a teacher, professor, or former boss to write a letter recommending you for admission to an academic institution or for a new job.

Although many organizations continue to use letters of recommendation as they select some candidates and reject others, available research evidence does *not* support the popularity of this approach. Bias is almost built into the procedure. Who in her right mind would ask a person to write such a letter without being quite certain that the writer would convey favorable information and impressions? It will come as no surprise, then, that an examination of letters of recommendation for 40 graduate-school applicants revealed "a pattern of nondiscriminative, nonconsensual, and nondifferentiating descriptions" (Baxter, Brock, Hill, & Rozelle, 1981, p. 296). In other words, letter writers failed to discriminate among several applicants, and they failed to agree on the important characteristics possessed by individual applicants. This pattern does not bode well for the validity of these measures. Meta-analyses revealed average validities ranging between .16 and .27 (Hunter & Hunter, 1984).

The Buckley Amendment to the Family Educational Rights and Privacy Act (1974) permits postsecondary students to request either "open" letters of recommendation (from individuals who know that their comments will be accessible to the student) or "confidential" letters (from individuals assured that their comments will not be shared with the student). An unintended by-product of the amendment is that those who make selection decisions tend to favor applicants who request confidential letters from their sponsors (Shaffer & Tomarelli, 1981); they probably conclude that "open" letters will be even more biased in a positive direction than is typically the case.

Knouse (1983) examined the effects of three specific factors on the perceived favorability of letters of recommendation. Letters that described specific examples of applicants' qualifications were reviewed more favorably and made the writer appear more credible. Although a single negative statement in a letter tended to undermine several perceptions of an applicant's ability, such a statement also rendered that applicant "most hireable" when it was combined with specific examples of his strong points. Nevertheless, "the influence of unfavorable statements is still unclear . . . whether unfavorable statements add realism to the letter or condemn the recommendee with a 'kiss of death' remains [a topic] for future research" (Knouse, 1983, p. 340).

Self-, Peer, and Subordinates' Ratings.
The validities of self-, peer, and subordinates' ratings of characteristics and job-related skills for predicting various performance criteria have also been examined. Reilly and Chao's (1982) review reported "some" validity for self-assessments. Although the danger of inflation bias in self-ratings is well documented (Anderson et al., 1984), one cannot ignore the possibility that socially desirable responses in the interest of impression management (as opposed to responses based on self-deception) may, for some jobs, reflect important job-related variance rather than a contaminant (Zerbe & Paulhus, 1987). A review of 55 studies that compared self-evaluations of abilities with more objective measures of performance revealed a "low" mean validity coefficient of .29 (Mabe & West, 1982). This general conclusion received recent support from a study of men's self-assessments as they were being screened for a prestigious military course. Although some of the validity coefficients linking their self-ratings to eventual training-success criteria were statistically significant, none exceeded .24 (Fox & Dinur, 1988).

Evidence concerning the validity of peer ratings is more encouraging. Validity coefficients of .49, .49, and .36 for criteria based on promotions, supervisors' ratings, and training success, respectively, have been reported (Hunter & Hunter, 1984; Kane & Lawler, 1978). Peer ratings seem to be particularly useful predictors of future job performance in military settings. Although validity coefficients based on subordinates' ratings are considerably scarcer, one recent study of managers in law-enforcement agencies found that such ratings showed some promise for predicting relatively proximal criteria, and that subordinates' ratings outperformed assessment-center ratings over two- and four-year time spans (McEvoy & Beatty, 1989).

Summing Up.
Based on available evidence, Dr. MacKeven might consider several situational exercises as she responds to Mr. Schiftner's memo, especially those that assess problem-solving abilities (for example, leaderless group discussions). She might also consider soliciting recommendations from former peers. Work samples, tests of physical strength or other physical capacities, and self-assessments will probably be far less useful for selecting PPP managers.

We have reserved the final section of this chapter for a brief discussion of a personnel-selection procedure that will allow Dr. MacKeven and Mr. Schiftner to collect a variety of potentially valid data from applicants under controlled sets of conditions in reasonable amounts of time. This procedure, known as an assessment center, has evolved into a very promising approach to identifying potentially successful managers.

Assessment Centers

Assessment centers are "group-oriented, standardized series of activities which provide a basis for judgments or predictions of human behaviors believed or known to be relevant to work performed in an organizational setting" (Finkle, 1976, p. 861). This approach to personnel selection has four central, defining characteristics. Applicants are (1) assessed or evaluated in groups (2) by groups of assessors (3) using a variety of measurement techniques (4) to determine the applicants' suitability for managerial positions. Originally used by the Office of Strategic Services (the forerunner of today's Central Intelligence Agency) during World War II to identify people who were suitable for espionage activities, assessment centers were subsequently developed by American Telegraph & Telephone (AT&T), Standard Oil of Ohio, IBM, Sears, General Electric, and J.C. Penney, among many other organizations, to assist in identifying men and women who were likely to succeed as managers.

Included among the multiple measurement techniques typically found in assessment centers are

1. Objective paper-and-pencil tests;
2. Projective tests such as sentence-completion tests and the Thematic Apperception Test (TAT) (McClelland, Atkinson, Clark, & Lowell, 1953; Murray, 1938);
3. Interviews;
4. Peers' and other candidates' ratings; and
5. Situational exercises such as leaderless group discussions and in-baskets (Borman, 1982; Finkle, 1976; Turnage & Muchinsky, 1982; Tziner & Dolan, 1982).

Groups of assessors observe the candidates as they perform these exercises, and then typically arrive at some consensus of opinion concerning each candidate's managerial potential. A simple statistical decision rule can often substitute for the more laborious and time-consuming process of achieving consensus (Sackett & Wilson, 1982).

Although the occasional discouraging word can be found in the research literature (McEvoy & Beatty, 1989; Pynes & Bernardin, 1989; Sackett & Dreher, 1982; Turnage & Muchinsky, 1982, 1984), most published studies attest to the validity of assessors' judgments. Validity coefficients of approximately .50 were obtained for assessors' predictions of training performance among military recruiters and female military officers (Borman, 1982; Tziner & Dolan, 1982). This is only slightly more impressive than the validities reported in reviews and meta-analyses (for example, $r = .40$) (Cohen, Moses, & Byham, 1974; Gaugler, Rosenthal, Thornton, & Bentson, 1987; Hunter & Hunter, 1984). Ritchie and Moses (1983) reported that assessment-center ratings were significantly related to female managers' career progress seven years following assessment, and that the skills required for success were no different from those required by successful male managers. A recent study suggests that validity coefficients for a generic assessment center that is "taken on the road" (that is, a predesigned set of exercises implemented in multiple physical and geographic locations) can vary a great deal, depending on the conditions that prevail (for example, type of assessor used, administrative arrangements) (Schmitt, Schneider, & Cohen, 1990). Sackett (1987) agreed that the ways in which stimulus materials are presented to assessees and how their responses are evaluated can affect the validity of assessment centers. Other evidence suggests an encouraging level of consistency in the validities associated with different assessors' judgments and predictions (Borman, Eaton, Bryan, & Rosse, 1983).

Several researchers have suggested that the positive results summarized above can be attributed to the fact that many validity studies relied upon candidates' subsequent rates of promotion as the criterion (London & Stumpf, 1983; Turnage & Muchinsky, 1984). The implication is that assessment-center ratings are less predictive when the criterion is some other measure of job performance (Hunter & Hunter, 1984; Klimoski & Strickland, 1977). Although the reservations are reasonable, an interesting study found that assessment-center ratings of school administrators *did* predict subsequent performance ratings from supervisors, teachers, and support staff (Schmitt, Noe, Meritt, & Fitzgerald, 1984). These data suggest that assessment-center ratings may do more than merely capture an organization's promotion policy. Although it's reassuring to believe that assessment centers "work" because they tap important job-related constructs, we cannot discount other possible explanations, including the following:

1. Assessees conform to both the assessors' and subsequent supervisors' role expectations for a manager (Russell, 1987);

2. Assessees' subsequent promotions or performance ratings are at least partially *based on* assessors' judgments;

3. Assessees who are selected to participate in assessment centers experience increased feelings of self-efficacy, which lead to subsequent performance improvements (a self-fulfilling prophecy); and

4. Assessors base their ratings *not* on assessment-center performance but, rather, on assessees' previous job performance, which tends to be consistent with their subsequent performance (Klimoski & Brickner, 1987)

We look to future research to refute or confirm these (and other) alternative explanations for the encouraging validities typically associated with assessment centers.

A substantial amount of assessment-center research has focused on the role of the assessors. How do they arrive at consensus? Is it actually necessary that they do so? Evidence indicates that effective assessors need *not* be trained as behavioral scientists (Borman, 1982).

In fact, managers who serve as assessors may improve their own skills in the domain of acquiring, evaluating, and communicating information about people (Lorenzo, 1984). Recent findings that speak to assessors' information-processing activities include the following:

1. Male and female assessors use similar formal and informal methods to arrive at "overall" assessment ratings and to differentiate among performance dimensions (Russell, 1987).

2. Two or three weeks of training did *not* enhance assessors' abilities to use greater amounts of information in arriving at "overall" ratings or to differentiate among performance dimensions (Dugan, 1988).

3. Assessors' ratings tend to reflect situation-specific factors peculiar to individual *exercises* rather than cross-situational managerial abilities (Bycio, Alvares, & Hahn, 1987). However, assessors do seem to be able to differentiate between two broad categories of assessment dimensions: "performance style" and "interpersonal style" (Shore, Thornton, & Shore, 1990). Further, the validities of assessors' ratings can differ depending on whether they are organized according to exercises or dimensions (Silverman, Dalessio, Woods, & Johnson, 1986).

4. Behavior checklists may reduce the cognitive demands placed on assessors and thereby increase the validity of their ratings (Reilly, Henry, & Smither, 1990). Similarly, reducing the number of assessment dimensions can improve the accuracy of assessors' classifications and ratings of assessees' behaviors (Gaugler & Thornton, 1989).

Summing Up. Given the definite managerial orientation of assessment centers, and considering their comprehensive utilization of several personnel-selection procedures, not to mention the procedures' apparent validity, there is no

INTEROFFICE MEMO

To: J. Schiftner,
          Director of Management Selection

From: J. A. MacKeven,
          Human Resources Coordinator

Subject: Identifying Managerial Talent

I've given your recent memo a lot of thought, and I believe you are wise not to limit yourself to the organizational boundaries of PPP in your search for effective managers. The following comments pertain to specific selection tests and procedures. (I'll reserve my gems of wisdom about recruiting, overall selection strategies, and legal considerations for another time.)

I understand that your current selection procedures rely upon a combination of personal recommendations, interviews, and a "quick-and-dirty" test of intelligence to identify potentially successful managers among PPP's nonmanagerial employees. You alluded to a good "track record" using these procedures, and I don't doubt your perceptions. However, I know of only one or two small research studies conducted to determine the validity of your selection process. Based upon a far more extensive set of more rigorous research findings (not to mention our evolving legal environment), I recommend that we take a very close look at your current selection instruments. This might entail a full-blown, comprehensive study to determine the validity of the inferences you (we!) have been drawing from candidates' scores on those devices. At the same time, I think we should discuss several ways we might revise those instruments (for example, structuring the interviews a bit more), as well as several possible innovative procedures that might enable us to identify promising managers more accurately and efficiently.

Let me know when you have a few minutes to toss around some ideas.

question that Dr. MacKeven will consider this approach as she responds to Mr. Schiftner's request for help in selecting new managers.

Chapter Summary

Any useful selection test must be both reliable and valid. Reliability, which decreases as test scores are influenced by random error, can be estimated using test-retest, equivalent-forms, or internal-consistency methods. Each approach has its own strengths and weaknesses. Test-score reliability can be affected by anything that admits random error: characteristics of the test (for example, number and diversity of items, format and serial order of items); characteristics of the sample of test takers (for example, "test-wiseness," attitudes and motivation); and characteristics of the testing environment (for example, the administrator or proctor, temperature, illumination, noise). Validity of test scores can also be analyzed in different ways, depending on the nature of the inference one wants to draw on the basis of the scores. These include content-validity analysis, criterion-related validity analysis, and construct-validity analysis.

Personnel-selection tests that have been widely used and researched include various paper-and-pencil tests of intelligence, motivation, and personality (for example, creativity, honesty, psychopathology). Tests of cognitive abilities and motivation to manage other people have the highest validities for predicting job performance. Biographical information, especially relevant work experience, also seems to be predictive. Evidence concerning interviews is less encouraging unless the interview is structured, and the interviewer concentrates on assessing a limited number of applicant characteristics (for example, interpersonal communication skills). Work samples and situational exercises can yield valid predictions if they are designed to reflect appropriate job-analysis data. Letters of recommendation tend to be far less useful than their popularity suggests. A particularly useful approach for selecting managers is the assessment center, where applicants take a variety of tests and participate in numerous exercises under the close scrutiny of observers, who then typically arrive at consensus predictions of each applicant's subsequent job performance.

Review Questions and Exercises

1. What do you think of Dr. MacKeven's response to Mr. Schiftner? How would your response differ from hers?

2. What will Dr. MacKeven suggest regarding Mr. Schiftner's reliance on personal recommendations? Why?

3. Based upon your knowledge of the relevant research, prepare a set of specific recommendations for Mr. Schiftner concerning his continued use of personal interviews.

4. Given what you know (so far) about Peter's Pan Pizza, what kinds of validity analyses will be appropriate in the context of Dr. MacKeven's proposed "comprehensive, full-blown" validity study? Which approach(es) to validity will be less appropriate? What would you recommend? Why?

5. Which specific selection instruments do you anticipate Dr. MacKeven will suggest for possible inclusion in Mr. Schiftner's selection procedures? Are any of these more (or less) appropriate for internal (or external) candidates for managerial positions? Which ones will she *not* recommend? (Explain your answers.)

6. How should Dr. MacKeven and Mr. Schiftner estimate the reliabilities of whatever selection "tests" they decide to consider? Describe some of the factors that will influence the magnitudes of their reliability estimates.

CHAPTER 6

Personnel Selection: Recruiting, Selection Strategies, and Utility

LEARNING POINTS

After studying this chapter, you should

❑ appreciate the variety of recruiting options available to organizations, and be able to explain how the Civil Rights Acts (1964, 1991) apply to recruitment;

❑ be able to describe the pros and cons of realistic job previews (RJPs);

❑ be able to construct individual and organizational expectancy charts (assuming, of course, you have the necessary data), and to interpret them for someone who has never heard of I/O psychology;

❑ be able to describe the strengths and weaknesses of regression approaches and multiple-cutoff approaches to personnel selection;

❑ understand how moderator and suppressor variables, synthetic validity, and validity generalization can contribute to effective personnel selection; and

❑ be able to explain the concept of utility and describe how it is related to validity.

MS. CREIGHTON'S MEMO REFLECTS a basic fact of organizational life. Human-resources (personnel) procedures such as recruiting, selecting, and training employees, as well as evaluating their work performance, are often viewed as necessary organizational expenses—things a company must do to survive but that do not translate into tangible returns. For this reason, corporate officers who want to spend money on new equipment, for example, which will have demonstrable effects on work productivity, are usually more successful in obtaining permission to make such expenditures than are personnel officers who want to develop and install new selection or training programs. Until relatively recently, human-resources specialists have been stymied in their efforts to demonstrate the cost effectiveness of their techniques and procedures in informative, credible ways.

In this chapter we continue our discussion of personnel selection by examining recruitment and some other procedures and strategies available to Dr. MacKeven and Ms. Creighton as they try to combine and integrate information obtained from applicants using selection instruments (that is, predictors) like those described in the previous chapter. We also examine the concept of utility, for assessing the costs and especially the benefits associ-

INTEROFFICE MEMO

To: J. A. MacKeven,
         Human Resources Coordinator

From: A. Creighton,
         Vice President for Personnel

Subject: Human Resources Procedures and the "Bottom Line"

As you know, on June 1 every year all PPP vice presidents submit proposed budgets for anticipated activities and purchases in their divisions during the upcoming fiscal year (July 1–June 30). Following a preliminary review by the president, each vice president then meets with him individually and, later, in a group setting to discuss and often defend proposed expenditures and anticipated profits.

During the past few years, I have found myself at more and more of a disadvantage during these discussions. Although all my fellow vice presidents incur expenses, most of them can demonstrate the cost effectiveness of those expenditures. That is, they can credibly predict tangible financial returns on the funds they are allocated and authorized to spend. For example, Ed Clark in Retail Operations and Dick Roe in Flavio's Frozen Foods can supply profit and loss statements; Katie Tuck in Marketing can point to increased sales volume attributable to specific franchising policies and advertising campaigns. Because they can specify expected returns on their "investments," the president has been more inclined to allocate PPP's increasingly scarce financial resources to them and their divisions, and less willing to look favorably on budget requests from those of us who are not in a position to project such returns. In my case, human-resources procedures have always been viewed as "maintenance expenses"—things PPP must do in order to stay in business that have little or no potential to increase the company's profitability or corporate worth.

I want to change this common but fallacious belief. I want the president and other vice presidents to understand that our human-resources procedures are more than mere expenses, that everything we do actually contributes to the positive side of PPP's ledger.

Can you help?

ated with particular selection (and other personnel) procedures. As you will see, utility estimates constitute at least a partial solution to Ms. Creighton's dilemma.

Recruiting

Recruiting procedures are designed to identify potentially suitable job applicants and entice them to apply for available jobs. It is impossible to overestimate the importance of successful recruiting because, no matter how valid a given selection procedure or strategy may be, its effectiveness will always be limited by the quality of the applicants who serve as "input" to the personnel-selection system. Recruiting procedures are part of the personnel-selection process, hence subject to the Civil Rights Acts of 1964 and 1991 and other legislation that prohibit discrimination in employment on the basis of demographic variables, such as sex and race, that are unrelated to effective job performance.

Organizations can use many strategies and vehicles to inform potential applicants about job opportunities, including personal communications from organization members (for example, recruiter visits to university and college campuses to speak with potential job candidates); written notices posted in and around the organization; employment agencies; announcements in the mass media (usually newspapers but also radio and television); and through friends or relatives who are familiar with the organization. When organizations use enough of these recruiting strategies to reach all or at least a representative sample of those who are qualified to apply for given jobs, the possibility of illegal discrimination is reduced. The size and geographic limits of potential applicant populations are determined by such factors as the amount of prior training required to perform a job effectively, and the willingness of applicants to relocate in order to accept specific jobs in the company. If, however, an organization selec-

tively uses only certain recruiting strategies that systematically preclude individuals from one or more protected demographic groups from learning about available jobs, it is in legal jeopardy. Examples of exclusionary recruiting strategies include newspaper classified ads that specify "man wanted" or "woman wanted," and radio announcements broadcast only by certain stations or only at certain times of the day such that certain identifiable groups of potential applicants are selectively reached and others are bypassed. Although the research literature on recruiting is not abundant, several studies have investigated the relative effectiveness of some of the recruiting strategies listed above, the effects of various recruiter behaviors and characteristics, the effects of informing applicants about specific aspects or characteristics of available jobs, and other factors that might affect recruiting effectiveness.

Results pertaining to the effectiveness of various recruiting strategies are mixed. One study of technical salespersons reported that different strategies did *not* systematically lead to different levels of worker productivity or job longevity (Swaroff, Barclay, & Bass, 1985). An earlier study of store clerks, however, found that informal recruiting strategies such as employee referrals led to longer job tenure among *white* clerks, but more formal procedures such as use of employment agencies led to greater tenure among *black* clerks (Caldwell & Spivey, 1983). A more recent investigation of life-insurance agents failed to clarify this picture. Although informal strategies generated significantly larger selection ratios (that is, numbers of applicants per job opening) and attracted applicants with stronger backgrounds who remained on the job for longer periods of time, an alternative index of job performance (number of new commissions) revealed no differences attributable to the formality of the recruiting strategy (Kirnan, Farley, & Geisinger, 1989). This study provided some indirect support for Caldwell and Spivey's results, however. Female and black applicants tended to use formal recruiting

College graduates are a ready source for recruiters.

vehicles more frequently than did male, nonminority, and Hispanic applicants. There is some consensus that different recruiting strategies can be differentially effective because they reach potential applicants from populations whose attendance, time on the job, and performance are likely to be systematically different (Schwab, 1982; Taylor & Schmidt, 1983). Because such applicant populations might include one or more groups specifically protected by Title VII of the Civil Rights Act (1964), it is wise to use as many recruiting strategies as possible.

Regarding the effects of recruiter behaviors and characteristics (for example, answering applicants' questions, showing interest in applicants, being familiar with applicants' backgrounds), earlier data suggested that such behaviors did *not* affect the likelihood that college graduates would accept a given job offer (Powell, 1984). Other findings suggested that job applicants might interpret recruiters' behaviors as signals regarding their chances of receiving job offers (Rynes & Miller, 1983). It is reasonable

to assume that encouragement from a recruiter might lead to more confident applicant behaviors, which in turn could lead to additional encouragement from the recruiter and ultimately a job offer. An opposite "downward spiral" could also occur. Recent evidence is more definitive with respect to the influence of recruiters' behaviors and characteristics. Two well-designed studies of college students' reactions to on-campus interviews revealed that certain recruiter characteristics (for example, personableness, informativeness, competence) *can* affect students' perceptions of available jobs (for example, nature of job, work and company environments, compensation, job security), their regard for the job and the company, and the extent to which they expect to receive and accept job offers (Harris & Fink, 1987; Powell, 1991). Additional evidence suggests that female interviewers may be perceived as more personable and more informative (Liden & Parsons, 1986).

Substantial amounts of data confirm that job characteristics *do* influence the perceived desirability of jobs, as well as the likelihood that applicants say they would accept given jobs if they were offered. Such job attributes as variety of work activities, opportunity to use abilities, compensation and security factors (for example, salaries, career paths), and work environment (for example, company reputation and location) affect the probability that applicants will accept job offers (Powell, 1984; Taylor & Bergmann, 1987). Although Posner (1981) identified some notable differences among the perceptions of students, faculty members, and corporate recruiters concerning the desirability of various job factors (and the relative importance of various applicant characteristics as well), his study was based on the assumption that the job factors are, in fact, important determinants of recruiting outcomes. Of course, perceived alternative job opportunities can moderate the impact of job attributes (Liden & Parsons, 1986).

A survey of Fortune 1000 companies revealed that most college recruiting programs provide recruiters with little or no formal training, collect only limited amounts of data, and include very little or no empirical evaluation of recruiting effectiveness (Rynes & Boudreau, 1986). The survey respondents tended to *believe* that the use of relevant criteria to select recruiters and recording information about new hires would increase the effectiveness of their recruiting programs. However, many also indicated that such ostensibly helpful practices as providing recruiters with broad training and developing extensive human-resources information systems are *negatively* related to the effectiveness of recruiting programs. Although this perception may reflect a belief that companies with serious personnel problems are more likely to invest in such systems or that employers resort to training only when recruitment is seen as ineffective, it may also reflect confusion among corporate officers who are responsible for recruiting activities.

A wider view of how applicants are attracted to organizations may help to dissipate some of this confusion (Rynes & Barber, 1990).

The perspective suggests that organizations can attract applicants by using any or all of three approaches, only one of which emphasizes recruitment. (The others focus on inducements and the nature of applicant pools.) Better yet, the authors describe several contingencies that can (1) influence the effectiveness of each approach (for example, labor-market conditions, legal considerations) and the likely interrelationships among attraction strategies, (2) integrate attraction strategies into networks of other human-resources practices (for example, selection, job design), and (3) specify dimensions of attraction outcomes (for example, quantity, quality). Our understanding of the recruiting process will surely benefit from broader views of the applicant-attraction process such as this one.

Realistic Job Previews (RJPs)

Early in our discussion of recruiting, we acknowledged that one of the purposes of this process is to "sell" the organization and its available jobs to promising applicants. In trying to accomplish this goal, organizations are sometimes guilty of painting an overly rosy picture of a particular job and its physical and social environments. Subsequent high rates of voluntary turnover have been attributed to the unrealistic expectations created earlier. **Realistic job previews** (RJPs) are direct organizational efforts to ensure that applicants accept job offers on the basis of specific and accurate information.

Quite a bit of empirical research has investigated RJPs' capacity to avoid giving applicants unrealistic ideas about what given jobs entail and to negate unreasonable expectations based on fictional literature, television programs, or other sources of inaccurate information. Some of the results have *not* been encouraging. For example, whether RJPs were presented on film or through actual visits to the job site, they had no effect on telephone-service representatives' rates of job acceptance or levels of commitment; nor did RJPs affect the extent to which these employees reported that their job expectations had been met (Reilly, Brown, Blood, & Malatesta, 1981). Most important, rates of voluntary turnover were *not* affected. In a similar vein, neither written nor videotaped RJPs produced significant change in the turnover rate among basic-care staff in a residential facility for retarded individuals (Zaharia & Baumeister, 1981). A meta-analysis of 98 studies led to the same conclusion: the average impact of job previews on workers' productivity was *not* statistically significant (Guzzo, Jette, & Katzell, 1985). A second meta-analysis revealed that job-enrichment interventions, which grant employees more autonomy and responsibility in their duties, were twice as effective as RJPs for reducing organizational turnover (McEvoy & Cascio, 1985).

On the brighter side, a study of business-school alumni concluded that those who had received accurate information about jobs were less likely to leave their organizations than those who had been given inaccurate information (Caldwell & O'Reilly, 1985). A field experiment with bank tellers compared the effectiveness of two kinds of RJPs (one very specific, one a bit more general) with a control condition where subjects received no RJP (Dean & Wanous, 1984). Although no differences in tellers' initial attitudes, levels of performance, or overall survival rates on the job emerged, the researchers reported that both forms of the RJP influenced the *rate* at which new employees quit their jobs. Specifically, tellers who had received either a specific or general RJP were more likely to quit *sooner* (that is, during an initial three-week training program), which limited the time and organizational resources that were "wasted" on these extremely short-term employees. Another study of bank tellers reported that RJPs provided by current tellers reduced turnover among new hires more substantially than did written brochures or no RJP at all (Colarelli, 1984). However, these data did *not* support the hypothesis that self-selection and increased commitment explained the effec-

tiveness of the personal RJPs. U.S. Army trainees who were exposed to both "enhancement" RJPs (designed to improve overly pessimistic expectations) and "reduction" RJPs (designed to reduce overly optimistic expectations) had lower subsequent rates of turnover and (after five weeks) saw the army as more caring and trustworthy, were more committed to the army and satisfied with their jobs, and experienced less role ambiguity (Meglino, DeNisi, Youngblood, & Williams, 1988). Although turnover was greater among those exposed only to reduction RJPs, all previews were more effective in reducing turnover among trainees who were more intelligent and initially more committed to the army. A meta-analysis of 21 experiments led to the conclusion that RJPs *do* tend to increase self-selection during the hiring process, along with employees' levels of organizational commitment, job satisfaction, and job performance, and their rates of job survival (Premack & Wanous, 1985). This review also indicated that audiovisual RJPs might be superior to those presented in written formats.

Although Premack and Wanous' (1985) review uncovered little or no evidence that personal or situational variables had any effect on the influence of RJPs, McEvoy and Cascio's (1985) meta-analysis of 20 relevant experiments tended to support an earlier suggestion that RJPs may be more effective in reducing turnover among people who are hired for more complex jobs (Reilly et al., 1981). Recall that Meglino and associates (1988) pointed to individual-differences variables that might influence the effectiveness of RJPs (that is, new workers' levels of intelligence and initial commitment to the organization).

Thus, empirical research has *not* consistently supported the effectiveness of RJPs for reducing turnover or effecting other desirable organizational outcomes. Nevertheless, evidence that RJPs can be useful under certain circumstances is sufficiently strong to encourage continued theory and research (Premack & Wanous, 1985; Vandenberg & Scarpello, 1990).

A realistic job preview would reveal that this activity occupies very little of a police officer's work time.

3. Should RJP content be strictly descriptive (and relatively objective) or should it be *judgmental (and admittedly subjective)*?

4. Should the RJP be extensive, including all pertinent information, or should it be *intensive, emphasizing only a few issues as forcefully as possible*?

5. Should the RJP include negative information that is extremely negative or should negative information be *only moderately so*?

6. Should the RJP be written or *audiovisual*?

7. Should the RJP's message come from "actors" or from *actual employees*?

8. Should the RJP be provided relatively *early* or relatively late in the organizational-entry process?

9. Should the RJP be implemented on a trial basis or *as a matter of organizational policy*?

10. Should an organization keep the results of an RJP secret from its competitors, or should it *disseminate the results to others*?

Although RJPs seem to be logical, intuitively appealing procedures for negating new employees' unrealistic job expectations, and thereby reducing their voluntary turnover, they have received mixed support in the empirical research literature. Although it is much too soon to abandon the concept that underlies RJPs, Dr. MacKeven and other organizational researchers and practitioners have to be "realistic" about the potential of this procedure to reduce turnover or improve workers' performance.

Those who consider using RJPs still face some tough choices when it comes to actually implementing them in organizations, however. Wanous (1989) identified the following decisions that must be made when developing and implementing RJPs (his recommendations appear in italics):

1. Do we initiate RJPs in reaction to a current problem, or do we *initiate them to avoid a future problem*?

2. When an RJP is prompted by apparent organizational problems, should the diagnosis of the problems be highly structured to produce quantifiable results, or *relatively unstructured to allow for qualitative data*?

Summing Up

Because Mr. Schiftner's memo at the beginning of Chapter 5 specifically referred to tapping sources outside as well as within the organizational boundaries of Peter's Pan Pizza, the topic of recruiting must occupy an important place in Dr. MacKeven's response. Her recruiting procedures must be sufficiently broad to bring managerial job openings to the attention of all (or a representative sample of) potential job candidates, thereby increasing the likelihood of finding the best women and men for the jobs, and minimizing the possibility that PPP will violate EEOC guidelines on nondiscrimination. This can be accomplished by using as many recruiting strategies as possible. Because managerial jobs tend to be relatively complex, and most applicants will be relatively intelligent, Dr. MacKeven might consider including some form of RJP in the recruitment process. Personal communications from current managers and audiovisual materials will probably be more effective than printed brochures. She will also consider Wanous' (1989) specific recommendations as she makes the tough choices associated with RJPs.

Following recruitment and after some of the predictors (that is, selection instruments) described in the previous chapter have been administered, Dr. MacKeven must identify a strategy or set of procedures for integrating all the information generated by each applicant in a way that facilitates decisions to hire or reject. Let's look at some of the decision-making strategies that are available to her now.

Decision-Making Strategies

After generating the necessary information to conduct one or more of the validity analyses described in the previous chapter, Dr. MacKeven can use the data in a variety of ways to make hiring (or other personnel) decisions. The alternatives include the use of relatively simple expectancy charts or tables, considerably more complex multiple-regression equations, moderator or suppressor variables, and a more analytic approach that focuses on prediction of performance on separate job components rather than overall job performance. Following descriptions of each of these, we will examine a relatively new approach known as validity generalization. We will also discuss utility analyses, procedures that directly address the concern Ms. Creighton expressed in the memo that opened this chapter.

Expectancy Charts

An expectancy chart usually takes the form of a bar graph that depicts the probabilities of successful job performance given certain scores on one or more predictors or selection instruments (tests, interviews, and so on). There are two different yet related kinds of expectancy charts. An example of the first, an **individual expectancy chart,** appears in Figure 6.1. For a given sample of applicants or employees (depending on whether a predictive or concurrent criterion-related validity analysis is done), the chart depicts the probabilities that *individuals* whose selection-test scores fall into specified ranges will perform successfully on the job. Figure 6.1 reflects a positive validity coefficient because those who score higher on the predictor are more likely to be successful employees.

The same empirical predictor and criterion data can be summarized another way; an **organizational** or **institutional expectancy chart** shows the percentages of successful employees that an organization can anticipate when everyone who is selected has certain minimum scores on the selection test(s) (see Figure 6.2). If an organization is in the favorable position of having many more applicants than jobs to be filled, it can be "choosey" and hire only the applicants with the greatest probabilities of job success. This maximizes the overall percentage of new hires who will succeed. Alternatively, when the numbers of applicants for available jobs are small, the organization may have to hire people with lower individual probabilities of job success. This reduces the overall percentage of new hires who will succeed. The ratio of job applicants to job openings is known as the hiring rate, a concept we will discuss in more detail when we consider the usefulness of personnel-selection systems.

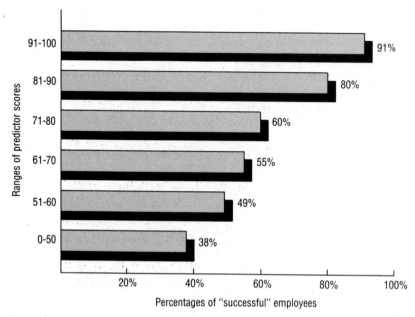

FIGURE 6.1
Individual Expectancy Chart

Expectancy charts are probably the simplest, most straightforward way to describe relationships between individuals' scores on one or more predictors and their levels of job performance. The charts do *not* depend on technical psychological terminology or complex statistical procedures (beyond calculation of percentages or proportions), and they are very useful for describing an important outcome of a selection procedure: the anticipated percentage of successful employees. Unfortunately, expectancy charts reveal nothing about the magnitude of job-performance improvements or the cost effectiveness associated with given personnel-selection systems. More complex procedures are required to generate such information.

Regression Analysis and Equations

Regression analysis is a statistical procedure that is based on the correlation coefficient (*r*). Recall from Chapter 5 that a criterion-related validity coefficient describes the size and direction (positive or negative) of the linear relationship between scores on a predictor and scores on a criterion of job performance. More precisely, the square of the validity coefficient (r^2) represents the percentage of variance in criterion scores that is predictable from scores on the selection instrument. The validity coefficient (or its square) itself, however, tells us very little about *how to use* selection-test scores to make predictions about job performance. To make such predictions, we must transform correlation or validity coefficients into **regression equations,** the simplest of which is the generic equation for a straight line:

$$\hat{Y} = a + bX \qquad (1)$$

where $\hat{Y}$ = predicted criterion (job-performance) scores;

a = a constant numerical value that describes the point at which the regression line intercepts the ordinate (vertical axis) on a set of coordinate axes;

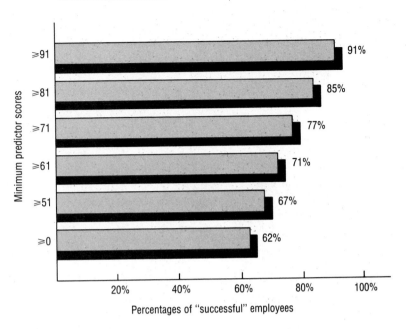

FIGURE 6.2
Organizational (Institutional) Expectancy Chart

X = observed or measured scores on the predictor (selection test); and

b = a constant numerical value that describes the slope of the regression line (that is, the number of units of change in the criterion score associated with one unit of change in the predictor score).

Although the mathematical procedures for deriving the constants (a and b) for a given set of predictor and criterion scores are beyond the scope of this book, they are calculated to minimize the distance between the derived straight line described by the regression equation and the data points that make up the scattergram for the predictor and criterion scores.[1] Figure 6.3 depicts an example of a scattergram for a set of predictor and criterion scores, the regression line that describes (best "fits") the joint scores, and the equation that describes that straight line.

[1] Pedhazur (1982), among other statistical textbooks, describes the procedures for deriving regression equations.

Equation (1) is a "simple" regression equation because it is based on scores from a single predictor. If we generate two or more sets of scores based on two or more selection tests, we can derive a multiple regression equation that simultaneously uses information from all the predictors to forecast job-performance scores. An example of a multiple regression equation looks like this:

$$\hat{Y} = a + b_1X_1 + b_2X_2 + b_3X_3 \qquad (2)$$

where $\hat{Y}$ = predicted criterion or job-performance scores;

a = the constant Y-intercept; and

b_1, b_2, b_3 = constant regression coefficients that reflect relationships between scores on the three predictors (X_1, X_2, and X_3) and scores on the job-performance criterion.

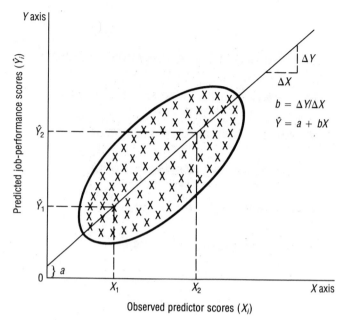

FIGURE 6.3
Scattergram with Best-Fitting Regression Line and Associated Equation
Note: Job applicant 1, who obtained a lower score on the predictor/selection test (X_1) than applicant 2 (X_2), is predicted to obtain a lower job-performance score than applicant 2 ($\hat{Y}_1 < \hat{Y}_2$), too (since this regression line/ equation reflects a positive validity coefficient, r_{XY}).

When two or more predictors are used to derive a multiple regression equation, the overall relationship between the multiple predictors and the criterion is described by the multiple correlation coefficient (R). R is interpreted just like its simple counterpart (r), except the algebraic sign is always positive. The percentage of variance in the criterion that can be explained or predicted by the multiple selection-test scores is given by R^2.

Although predictions about individuals' job performance based on regression equations are mathematically precise and tend to be far more accurate in the long run than more subjective (that is, "clinical") predictions that are *not* based on statistical or mechanical combinations of data (Meehl, 1954, 1957, 1965), the mathematical procedures that underlie that precision and accuracy can be complex. As a result, it is more challenging for Dr. MacKeven to explain regres-

sion equations to Mr. Schiftner (or any other manager who isn't familiar with such statistical procedures) than it is to explain expectancy charts. Like expectancy charts, however, regression equations can be derived only from more or less complete sets of predictor and criterion scores *from a given sample* of job applicants or workers (that is, during a predictive or concurrent validity study). Remember that scores from any specific sample will *not* be perfectly reliable. The mathematical procedures for deriving regression equations do *not* distinguish between true-score and error-score components of observed predictor and criterion scores, however. (A quick review of our discussion of true, random-error, and observed scores in Chapter 5 might be helpful at this point.) Thus, the value of R^2 associated with a regression derived from any single sample almost always *over*estimates the size of the true relationships between the criterion and the predictors. Adding insult to injury, the size of R^2 is also artificially inflated when the number of predictors (selection tests) in an equation is large relative to the number of individuals who make up the sample used to generate the equation.

Fortunately, there are two ways to correct for these inflationary biases in sample-specific regression equations. One approach is to apply what is known as a "shrinkage" formula to the obtained value of R^2:

$$R_s^2 = 1 - (1 - R^2)\left[\frac{N - 1}{(N - k - 1)}\right] \quad (3)$$

where R_s^2 = the "corrected" estimate of the percentage of criterion variance explained by the predictors;[2] and

R^2 = the uncorrected squared multiple correlation coefficient calculated for a given sample of N job applicants or employees using k different predictors (selection tests).

As we said, inflationary bias (and therefore shrinkage) is greater when the size of the sample used to derive an equation is small relative to the number of predictors in the equation. In the extreme case where $N = k$, the uncorrected value of R^2 will be equal to 1.00. A typical guideline for minimizing shrinkage is to obtain at least ten observations (that is, subjects, cases) for each predictor in the equation. Thus, if a regression equation is based on four selection tests, there should be at least 40 applicants or employees in the sample used to derive that equation.

A second method for eliminating sample-specific inflationary bias involves a set of procedures known collectively as **cross-validation.** A common cross-validation strategy includes the following steps:

[2] Lautenschlager (1990) suggested that inappropriate assumptions and erroneous terms in such "correction" formulas can lead to overestimates of corrected squared multiple correlation coefficients.

1. Divide the sample of job applicants or employees into two subsamples: a "primary" sample that consists of a randomly selected two-thirds of the entire sample, and a "hold-out" sample that consists of the remaining one-third of the original sample.

2. Derive a regression equation using only the data obtained from the primary sample. (The original sample should be sufficiently large so that the necessary $N:k$ ratio described above is at least 10:1 in the primary sample.)

3. Use the regression equation derived from the primary sample to calculate predicted criterion scores for members of the holdout sample by entering the holdout individuals' predictor scores into the equation derived from the primary sample's data.

4. Compute the correlation coefficient (r) that describes the linear relationship between the holdout sample's actual criterion scores and the criterion scores predicted for its numbers by using the primary sample's regression equation.

A large, positive correlation indicates that the regression coefficients (b_x) and the constant (a) derived from the primary sample's data did a good job of predicting the holdout sample's criterion scores. This suggests that the regression equation is *not* contaminated by large amounts of random error. A small or negative correlation indicates that the equation derived from the primary sample is contaminated with error, and is therefore *not* representative and should *not* be used to predict criterion scores of other samples of applicants or current employees.

Murphy (1983, 1984) argued that the more costly and time-consuming cross-validation procedures offer no clear-cut advantages over the simpler, quicker, and less expensive shrinkage-formula estimates, unless the primary and holdout samples are *independently* drawn from the population of job applicants or employees (rather than created by partitioning a single sample of individuals). On the other hand, if the two subsamples are knowingly drawn from two *different* populations (for example, from different geographic regions or different jobs), the differences can have unpredictable effects on cross-validation results (McIntyre, 1990b). Thus, Dr. MacKeven must attend carefully to the selection of subsamples if she decides to pursue a cross-validation strategy.

Another characteristic of multiple-regression equations can be an advantage or a disadvantage, depending on the specific predictors and criterion under consideration. Multiple-regression equations are **compensatory** tools for making selection and other personnel decisions. This means that individual applicants can be judged acceptable even though one or more of their predictor scores is very low, as long as the remainder of their predictor scores are sufficiently high to compensate for the low score(s). An example will help to explain this property of multiple-regression equations.

Suppose that Dr. MacKeven uses applicants' scores on an intelligence test, a motivation-to-manage test, and a structured interview to predict job performance as a PPP manager. Suppose further that the combined scores on the three tests obtained from two applicants yield identical predictions of their success as managers. Although their predicted criterion scores are the same, their individual predictor scores can be very different. Applicant 1 might have slightly above average scores on all three predictors, which lead to a prediction of "satisfactory" managerial performance. Applicant 2, on the other hand, might have an average interview score, a very low motivation-to-manage score, and an exceptionally high intelligence score. The second applicant's predicted level of managerial performance is the same as the first applicant's because the multiple-regression approach to personnel selection allows the second applicant's extremely high intelligence score to compensate for a lackluster motivation-to-manage score. The compensatory property of multiple-regression equations can be a "plus" if

Mr. Shiftner believes that high intelligence *can* indeed compensate for lower levels of motivation. Alternatively, if he thinks that no amount of intelligence can compensate for low levels of motivation, this property of multiple-regression equations represents a weakness or flaw in the procedure.

Imagine a different scenario. Suppose Dr. MacKeven had been asked to hire a pilot for PPP's corporate jet, and that two of her predictors were intelligence scores and corrected visual acuity (eyesight) scores. Would you be willing to fly with a pilot who is legally blind if you knew that pilot was also a "genius"? You can understand, then, that Dr. MacKeven's and Mr. Shiftner's perspectives on the compensatory property of multiple-regression selection strategies will depend heavily on the specific predictors included in the equations, and the nature of the jobs to be performed. If they deem it inappropriate for high scores on some predictors to compensate for low scores on others, they will choose an alternative decision-making strategy. The most common alternative is the multiple-cutoff approach.

Multiple-Cutoff Selection Strategies

Multiple-cutoff strategies are designed for situations when it is *not* appropriate, acceptable, or safe to permit applicants' extremely high scores on some predictors to compensate for very low scores on other predictors. In such cases, a personnel-selection specialist identifies minimum "cutoff" scores for each predictor. To be hired, applicants must obtain *at least* the minimum scores. Applicants whose scores fall below the minimum cutoff on any predictor are automatically eliminated from further consideration, regardless of how high they score on other selection instruments.

The biggest challenge associated with multiple-cutoff selection strategies is setting minimum cutoff scores that facilitate valid prediction of job performance but do not discriminate against applicants who could perform the

> **BOX 6.1 Setting Cutoff Scores**
>
> - There is no single, "best" method for setting cutoff scores in all situations.
> - Cutoff scores should be based on job analyses that identify necessary levels of proficiency on critical skills or abilities.
> - Assessment procedures must be valid and job related.
> - The meanings (and appropriate levels) of cutoff scores depend on whether criterion- or norm-referenced tests are used.
> - The nature of the relationship between test scores and criterion scores should not be ignored.
> - Cutoff scores should be sufficiently high to ensure that minimum job-performance requirements are satisfied.
> - Cutoff scores should reflect normal expectations concerning acceptable performance within the work force.
>
> SOURCE: From "Setting Cutoff Scores: Legal, Psychometric, and Profession Issues and Guidelines," by W. F. Cascio, R. A. Alexander, and G. V. Barrett, *Personnel Psychology, 41*, 1–24. Copyright © 1988 by Personnel Psychology, Inc. Adapted by permission.

job satisfactorily if given an opportunity to do so. That is, there must be logical or empirical evidence to support the use of any particular cutoff score for a given selection test. Cutoff scores cannot be set arbitrarily. Sometimes an expectancy chart can supply the empirical evidence to support a particular cutoff score. A review and analysis of several literatures (for example, legal, psychometric, professional) that have addressed the use and misuse of cutoff scores led to several conclusions and guidelines summarized in Box 6.1 (Cascio, Alexander, & Barrett, 1988).

Multiple-Hurdle Strategies. When an organization uses two or more predictors in its personnel-selection system, those multiple measures usually involve different investments of money and time to purchase, administer, and score. If the hiring rate is favorable from the organization's perspective (that is, if there are many applicants for each available position), a variation of the multiple-cutoff strategy can take advantage of the different costs. Known as **multiple-hurdle strategies,** these approaches order multiple selection tests as successive "hurdles" that applicants must "jump" if they are to receive a job offer. Of course, the order in which particular hurdles are laid out for a track meet is irrelevant because all the hurdles are identical; the situation can be very different for multiple predictors of job performance.

The purpose of multiple-hurdle selection strategies is to identify potentially successful job applicants in the *most efficient* and *least expensive* way. The basic idea is to administer the least expensive and/or time-consuming selection test to the entire sample of job applicants, and to eliminate those whose scores fall below the minimum cutoff for that predictor. The next-more-expensive and/or next-more-time-consuming predictor is then administered to the applicants who survived the first hurdle. Those who score below the minimum cutoff for the second predictor are then eliminated from further consideration. The "weeding out" continues as relatively more expensive and more time-consuming selection tests are administered to smaller and smaller groups of applicants until very few remain for each available job. Only those "survivors" are afforded an opportunity to take the most costly and/or time-consuming selection tests. Final hiring decisions are made on the basis of applicants' scores on the final hurdles.

Suppose, for example, that Dr. MacKeven and Mr. Shiftner agree on a useful multiple-hurdle strategy, arranging these selection instruments in the following serial order: (1) an application blank to collect biographical data; (2) paper-and-pencil tests to measure motivation-to-manage and intelligence; (3) a structured personal interview to assess interpersonal (communication) skills; and (4) a two-day set of assessment-center exercises as predictors of performance as a PPP manager. This is the sequence that would be least expensive and most efficient.

We want to point out here that the compensatory multiple-regression approach and the noncompensatory multiple-cutoff (and multiple-hurdle) approach are *not* necessarily antagonistic or mutually exclusive strategies for making personnel decisions. That is, they can be combined to take advantage of each procedure's relative strength. Dr. MacKeven could identify minimum cutoff points for any or all of the selection tests that she includes in her selection system, in order to eliminate applicants who are clearly unacceptable. She could then use the remaining applicants to derive a multiple-regression equation to be used with subsequent samples of applicants (assuming successful cross-validation or application of a shrinkage formula), or she could "plug" the surviving applicants' predictor scores into an existing regression equation. The best answer to questions that take the form "Which is the best . . . ?" is often Neither! None is best; they are best used in combination.

Efforts to Improve Prediction of Job Performance

Although I/O psychologists have persisted in trying to improve the predictive validity of var-

ious selection instruments since early in the twentieth century, success has been rather limited. Several critical reviews of the validity literature confirmed the discouraging conclusion that predictive validity coefficients rarely exceed .50, and more typically fall at or below .35 (Ghiselli, 1956, 1966, 1973; Hull, 1928; Hunter & Hunter, 1984). Such modest coefficients can be very useful under certain circumstances (for example, see our discussion of utility at the end of this chapter). The implications of these numbers, however, are that we rarely explain more than 25% of the variance in job performance with our predictor scores, and that we often explain less than 10%. In response to these unimpressive findings, researchers and theoreticians devised several approaches to improve the validity and accuracy of job-performance predictions. In the following sections we will acquaint you with several of these efforts, which include searching for moderator or suppressor variables and a more analytic approach to validation that focuses on specific job components rather than trying to predict overall job performance.

Moderator Variables.   Searches for moderator variables are based on an assumption that some individuals are more predictable than others in specific circumstances. Given a certain set of predictors (that is, selection-test scores) and an associated set of job-performance criterion scores for a specific group of people, Dr. MacKeven might be able to identify other variables that will enable her to distinguish between the individuals whose predictor scores actually predict job-performance levels and those whose levels of performance are less predictable from that set of predictors. Such variables are known as **moderator variables.** An example will help to illustrate this concept.

The scattergram in Figure 6.4 enclosed within the *solid* line presents joint predictor and criterion scores for a sample of job applicants. As you can probably deduce from its shape, the validity coefficient associated with this scattergram would be quite small (for example, $r =$

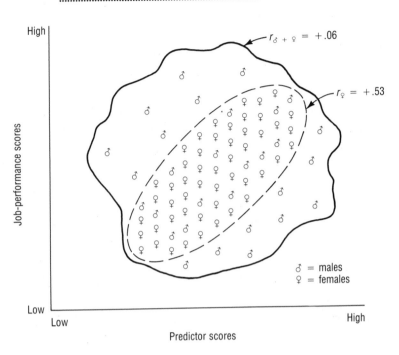

FIGURE 6.4
Example of a Moderator Variable: Sex

.06). Suppose, however, that the portion of the scattergram enclosed within the *broken* line represents joint predictor and criterion scores for a known subsample of all the applicants, women. The elongated shape of the subsample's scattergram reflects a more substantial relationship between predictor and criterion scores ($r = .53$). In this example, where criterion-related validity coefficients are different for women and men, applicants' sex is operating as a moderator variable.

Moderator variables can take forms other than the one depicted in Figure 6.4; some examples are shown in Figure 6.5a, b, and c. Bartlett and O'Leary (1969) provided several such examples. In each case, the I/O psychologist who focuses exclusively on the scattergram or correlation coefficient based on data from the entire sample will come away with an inaccurate (and possibly illegal) interpretation of those data. (Figure 6.5d depicts an entirely different situation.)

According to James and Brett (1984), moderator variables should display the following characteristics:

1. They are uncorrelated (or show, at most, minimum covariation) with the predictor and criterion variables. In the example shown in Figure 6.4, neither women nor men outscored each other as a group on either the predictor or the job-performance criterion.

2. They reflect a significant interaction with a predictor variable. Referring again to Figure 6.4, knowledge of an applicant's score on the predictor, *or* whether the applicant is a man or a woman, by itself tells us nothing about the person's job performance. However, knowing *both* these things enables us to predict job performance for the "predictable" group (women, in this case) and to refrain from making predictions for the "unpredictable" group, men. In Figure 6.5b,

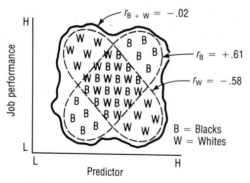

a. Moderator: Race

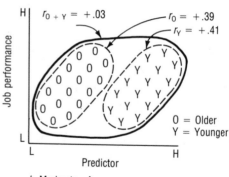

b. Moderator: Age

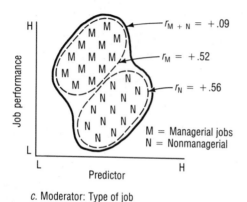

c. Moderator: Type of job

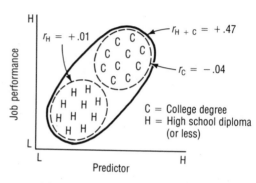

d. Moderator: None
(Education is another predictor!)

FIGURE 6.5
Additional Moderated Predictor–Criterion Relationships

knowing both an applicant's age and score on the predictor suggests we might use the selection test in one way for "older" applicants (a lower cutoff score?) and another way for "younger" applicants (a higher cutoff score?). The fact that the 1991 Civil Rights Act expressly forbids the use of different cutoff scores for different groups highlights one of the challenges that confront human-resources specialists who simultaneously strive to select and place those applicants most likely to succeed on their jobs, to be fair to members of recognizable (especially protected) demographic groups, and to operate within the boundaries of current employment legislation.

3. They do *not* imply any causal relationships. Figure 6.4 does not suggest that being a woman "causes" one to be more predictable in these circumstances, or that being a man "causes" one to be less predictable. The groups just *are* more and less predictable, respectively.[3]

Several procedures for identifying moderator variables exist. First, a researcher may simply have a "hunch" or hypothesis, based either on past experience or common sense, that job-performance scores for one group of applicants

[3] Among the suggested "mechanisms" by which moderator variables might operate are neutralization, enhancement, substitution, supplementation, and mediation (Howell, Dorfman, & Kerr, 1986).

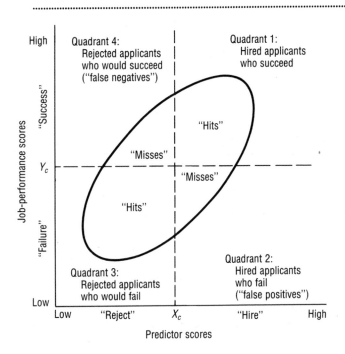

FIGURE 6.6
Quadrant Analysis

might be more or less predictable than another group's scores. Second, the investigator might have a theory or model that hints at one or more potential moderator variables for a given combination of predictor and criterion scores. Third, one can engage in a "fishing expedition" by subjecting a scattergram to a process known as **quadrant analysis** (Hobert & Dunnette, 1967).

If you examine the scattergram in Figure 6.6, you will notice that the cutoff points that separate hired from rejected applicants (on the X-axis) and successful from unsuccessful job performers (on the Y-axis) serve to partition all the joint data points into four subgroups or quadrants. People whose data points fall in the upper-right or lower-left quadrants are designated "hits." On the basis of their selection-test scores, we predict success or failure, respectively, on the job. If given an opportunity to perform the job, these folks confirm our expectations. Individuals in the upper-left or lower-right quadrants are "misses." Those in the upper-left are "false negatives" because their low

predictor scores lead us to predict *erroneously* that they will *not* succeed on the job if given an opportunity to perform. These people are potentially valuable human resources that the organization mistakenly rejects. Those in the lower-right are "false positives" because their high predictor scores lead us to predict *erroneously* that they will succeed on the job. These are folks the organization should have "let get away" but didn't. Thus, in its simplest form, quadrant analysis involves separating "hits" from "misses," and then examining other variables (demographic, biographical, situational, and so on) to discover any systematic differences between the more and less predictable groups. Of course, if quadrant analysis reveals a possible moderator variable, a process similar to cross-validation is necessary to determine whether the moderated predictor-criterion relationship is likely to generalize to other samples of applicants or employees.

Ghiselli (1956) suggested a similar but simpler strategy for identifying moderator variables. You will notice in Figure 6.3 that some of the joint data points lie extremely close to the "best-fitting" straight line and that other data points lie at greater distances from the line. If we draw two lines that are parallel to the best-fitting regression line, one above and one below, we separate individuals who are more predictable (that is, whose data points lie closer to the line) from those who are less predictable (that is, whose data points lie further away from the regression line). We can then examine other variables to determine whether the two subgroups differ in any systematic way(s).

Although the specifics of the arguments are too complex to discuss here, you should be aware of a controversy in the literature concerning appropriate statistical analyses for identifying moderator variables. One camp advocates various forms of "moderated" regression analysis that incorporate interaction terms (between predictors and potential moderators) among the predictor variables (Cronbach 1987; Stone & Hollenbeck, 1984). In recent years, this group asserts that it has demonstrated that its approach can detect differences of *degree* as well as *form* in empirical relationships, and that the regression procedure in its basic (or a modified) form is *not* seriously biased as long as the predictors are measured reliably and are *not* highly correlated with one another (Dunlap & Kemery, 1987, 1988; Lubinski & Humphreys, 1990; Paunonen & Jackson, 1988; Shepperd, 1991; Stone & Hollenbeck, 1989). Others are less enthralled with regression procedures (Arnold, 1982; Blood & Mullet, 1977; Morris, Sherman, & Mansfield, 1986). Regardless of how the debate is ultimately resolved, we concur that researchers should *not* depend exclusively on any single statistical technique. Analytical procedures should be chosen on the basis of their capacity to provide appropriate answers to the questions we ask of our data (Arnold, 1984).

Empirical evidence suggests that moderator variables *can* contribute to more accurate and more valid predictions of job performance. For example, the extent to which a job is characterized by decision-making or information-processing dimensions has been shown to moderate the validities of general-intelligence, verbal-ability, and numerical-ability test scores (from the GATB). Further, validities of finger- and manual-dexterity test scores for predicting performance on 111 diverse jobs were moderated by the presence or absence of manual job dimensions (Gutenberg, Arvey, Osburn, & Jeanneret, 1983). Interpersonal stress among cadets at the U.S. Coast Guard Academy moderated the validity of intellectual-ability test scores (from the Scholastic Aptitude Test) for predicting performance in an academic setting. Validity coefficients for freshmen and sophomores were .66 under low-stress conditions but dropped to .37 under high-stress conditions (Barnes, Potter, & Fiedler, 1983). The relationship between performance on a clerical task and certain individual-difference variables (for example, relevant experiences and abilities) was moderated by the extent to which the experimental situation *permitted* more or less variability in task performance. Not surprisingly, when performance was situationally restricted, validity coefficients were smaller (Peters, Fisher, & O'Connor, 1982).

You may have noticed that each of these examples involves *situational* rather than *individual* or demographic moderator variables. In a study that addresses current concerns with fairness and discrimination in employment, Heilman and Herlihy (1984) documented the role of an individual moderator variable. Their data suggest that a woman's perceptions about whether other women have been hired because of their job-related skills or because the company needed more women on its payroll to avoid the appearance of discrimination moderates the relationship between the proportion of women who hold a particular job and the level of the woman's interest in obtaining that job. That is, women were more interested in obtaining jobs held predominantly by other women only when they perceived that the female employees had been hired on the basis of merit, *not* just because they were women.

Although identification of moderator variables will not solve all our validity problems, available evidence suggests that partitioning large samples of people into subgroups that are more or less predictable, on the basis of either personal or situational variables, *can* result in larger validity coefficients. Hence, it seems unwise for Dr. MacKeven to dismiss the possibility of finding moderator variables as she develops procedures for selecting PPP managers.

Suppressor Variables. Suppressor variables can also improve prediction of criterion scores, even though they are completely unrelated to the criterion. Because it is *not* correlated with the criterion variable, a suppressor variable does *not* add to the absolute amount of criterion variance explained by the predictor(s). Instead, a **suppressor** improves the efficiency or accuracy of predictions by identifying variance in the *predictor scores* that is uncorrelated with the criterion. This irrelevant variance can then be ignored through statistical analyses.

Figure 6.7 helps to explain how a suppressor variable works. The diagram at the top of the figure (Figure 6.7a) depicts predictor- and criterion-score variance, as well as the overlap between them (validity). As you can see, a substantial portion of the predictor-score variance is completely unrelated to the variance in the criterion. This can lead to erroneous prediction. In the middle of the figure (Figure 6.7b), we add a suppressor variable that shares an appreciable amount of variance with the predictor but is totally unrelated to the criterion. By subtracting or "partialing out" the portion of predictor variance that is unrelated to criterion variance (usually through multiple-regression procedures), we are left with less variance in the predictor that can result in erroneous predictions of criterion scores (see Figure 6.7c). Although the absolute amount of criterion variance that is explained remains the same, the *proportion* of remaining predictor variance that is shared with

criterion variance is larger. Increasing this proportion serves to increase the value of R^2 associated with the multiple-regression equation that includes the predictors and the suppressor variable.

Unfortunately, we have not enjoyed the level of success identifying suppressor variables that has characterized our search for moderator variables. In fact, suppressors are quite rare. Sorenson's (1966) study of mechanics is a notable exception to this generalization. In this study, scores on a very practical, "nuts-and-bolts" test of mechanical knowledge predicted industrial mechanics' job performance with a reasonable degree of validity ($r = .22$). A second, academically oriented test of mechanical insight was completely unrelated to the measure of job performance but was very highly correlated with the nuts-and-bolts test of mechanical skills ($r = .71$). When the second, more academic test was included in the regression equation, Sorenson was able to make predictions about mechanics' job performance that were less contaminated by verbal skills and abstract "book learning" that was unrelated to performance.

Although it would be shortsighted to rule out the possibility of finding suppressor variables to improve prediction of managerial performance at PPP, there isn't much cause for optimism. Dr. MacKeven might use her time more wisely by exploring an approach to empirical validation known as "synthetic" validity.

Synthetic Validity. The basic idea that underlies synthetic validity is that it is easier to find valid predictors for specific components of job performance than it is to predict overall performance. **Synthetic validation** (also known as job-component validation) involves identifying measures that can predict performance on job components, and then building or "synthesizing" valid predictions of overall job performance by combining component predictors in a systematic way.

To use this approach, Dr. MacKeven must be able to describe a number of jobs in the orga-

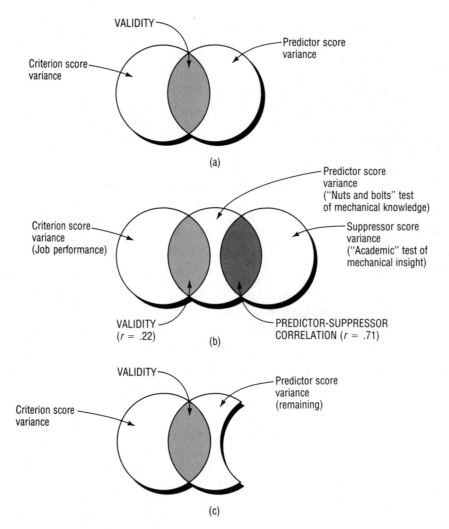

FIGURE 6.7
A Suppressor Variable
SOURCE: From *Industrial Psychology: Its Theoretical and Social Foundations,* by M. L. Blum and J. C. Naylor. Copyright © 1968 by the authors. Adapted by permission of HarperCollins Publishers, Inc.

nization using the same set of job dimensions or components. Functional job analysis (which describes jobs in terms of their focus on people, data, and things) or the Position Analysis Questionnaire (which uses a small number of information-processing dimensions to describe jobs) can be particularly useful in this context. Using either of these job-analysis procedures (see

Chapter 3), she can develop a matrix like the one that appears in Figure 6.8, where an X at the intersection of a particular job and a specific job dimension identifies the dimension as an important component of the job. Given the information conveyed in Figure 6.8, and one or more selection devices for making valid predictions about performance on each of the 11 dimen-

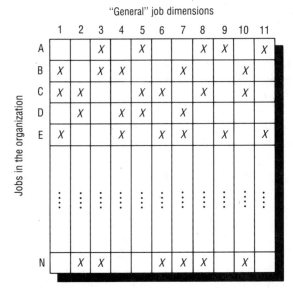

"General" job dimensions

FIGURE 6.8
Synthetic Validity Matrix

sions, Dr. MacKeven can combine the predictors for Dimensions 3, 5, 8, 9, and 11 to predict overall performance on Job A. A combination of predictors for Dimensions 1, 3, 4, 7, and 10 will predict overall performance on Job B, and so forth. The combinations can be created either by *assimilating several job-component validity coefficients*, each of which describes a linear relationship between a unique set of predictors and performance on a unique combination of job components, or by integrating multiple combinations of predictors and performance criteria before computing a *single, overall validity coefficient* (Hollenbeck & Whitener, 1988).

Beyond the logical expectation that it should be easier to predict more specific kinds of performance, an important advantage of synthetic validity is that empirical validity analyses are possible with much smaller total samples of job applicants or employees than are deemed necessary for traditional criterion-related validity analyses. Whether she chooses predictive or concurrent validation, Dr. MacKeven will *not* have to wait until sufficient numbers of people

become available in each unique job in order to proceed. Because her primary concern is finding valid predictors for separate job components, she can collect data from individuals in every job that depends upon a given component or dimension. For example, referring again to Figure 6.8, a validity analysis for a predictor of Dimension 1 can include individuals who hold Jobs B, C, and E; the analysis for a predictor of Dimension 2 can use people in Jobs C, D, and N; and so forth. This logistical advantage can be especially important to smaller organizations and companies with low turnover rates, where it takes a long time to amass sufficient numbers of applicants or workers to conduct traditional criterion-related validity analyses. Of course, the vulnerability of small-N validation studies to inflated sampling error (see our discussion of validity generalization in the next section) is *not* eliminated through synthetic-validation procedures.

After tracing its origins and historical development (for example, Balma, 1959; Lawshe, 1952), Mossholder and Arvey (1984) described the two dominant approaches to synthetic validation. The first relies on the *J*-coefficient, which in turn depends upon *subjective estimates* of the relationships among certain job dimensions, performance on selection tests, and performance on the job. The second approach, known as the Job Component Model, focuses on the centrality of certain PAQ dimensions and their relationships either to selection-test scores or to criterion-related validity coefficients. Both approaches are quite complex, and there is some disagreement concerning which comes closer to satisfying the validation requirements specified in the EEOC's guidelines (1978). Some argue that the Job Component Model is superior because it identifies selection tests that actually distinguish between successful and unsuccessful jobholders (Mecham, Jeanneret, & McCormick, 1983). Others advocate the *J*-coefficient because it breaks jobs down into specific knowledge, skill, and ability components (Trattner, 1982).

Although synthetic validity may eventually contribute to improved personnel selection, the available research evidence available speaks only to the concept's feasibility (Mossholder & Arvey, 1984). Much remains to be done before we can assess the actual usefulness of synthetic validation for making personnel-selection decisions. Because Dr. MacKeven has access to fairly large samples of managerial applicants and employees, there is little reason for her to adopt synthetic-validity analysis on logistical grounds. This does not rule out the possibility, however, that she may opt to predict specific components of managers' jobs at PPP instead of trying to predict overall managerial performance.

A very different approach to dealing with the small and inconsistent validity coefficients typically generated during traditional criterion-related validity analyses is known as "validity generalization" (Schmidt & Hunter, 1980). On the cutting edge of personnel-selection research, validity generalization has also spawned some controversy.

Validity Generalization. The goal of **validity generalization,** which is a form of meta-analysis (see Chapter 2), is to apply the results of validity analyses conducted in specific organizational settings to other, similar settings and sets of circumstances. The current EEOC guidelines (1978) do not rule out the possibility that an organization can justify use of a specific selection instrument by appealing to validity studies conducted elsewhere. Any company that does so, however, must be prepared to demonstrate (on the basis of appropriate job analyses) that the selection instrument is being used for similar jobs, and that the test is fair for each race, sex, and ethnic group represented in the applicant population. This admonition is sufficiently strong to conclude that the EEOC implicitly endorses the **situational-specificity hypothesis,** which assumes that one or more individual or situational variables typically moderate validity coefficients that describe relationships between scores on given selection instruments and performance on particular jobs. Employers who appeal to validity generalization must demonstrate that no such moderator variables are operating.

Even a superficial review of the literature will appear to confirm the existence of such moderator variables. That is, the validity coefficients reported for specific selection tests and specific job-performance measures have *not* been very consistent across studies and analyses. In fact, it is quite common to learn that a specific selection test predicts performance well in some studies but very poorly or not at all in others. Advocates of validity generalization contend that most, if not all, of this variability in validity coefficients is attributable *not* to individual or situational moderator variables but, rather, to inadequate measurement and other procedural artifacts that have no actual bearing on the "true" magnitude of a given predictor-criterion validity coefficient (Hirsh, Northrop, & Schmidt, 1986; McDaniel, Hirsh, Schmidt, Raju, & Hunter, 1986; Schmidt & Hunter, 1980; Schmidt, Hunter, & Raju, 1988; Schmidt, Ocasio, Hillery, & Hunter, 1985). The measurement and procedural artifacts include the following:

1. differences across studies in criterion reliability;

2. differences across studies in selection-test reliability;

3. differences across studies in range restriction associated with relevant variables;

4. sampling error attributable to small sample sizes;

5. differences across studies in amounts and kinds of criterion contamination and deficiency;

6. computational and typographical errors in written or published reports and articles; and

7. differences in factor structures (based on factor analyses) across ostensibly similar tests.

The general approach for supporting validity generalization (and thereby refuting the situational-specificity hypothesis) utilizes a variety of statistical procedures designed to explain and eliminate inconsistencies (variance) across a set of validity coefficients that are attributable to the artifacts listed above. A guideline that has evolved is to reject the situational-specificity hypothesis when 75% or more of the variance in validity coefficients can be explained by the first four of the artifacts. It is then assumed that the other three, which are extremely difficult and sometimes impossible to assess accurately, account for most or all of the remaining variance in reported validity coefficients. The average of all validity coefficients reported for a given predictor-criterion pair is then accepted as the estimate of the "true" validity coefficient.

The concept of validity generalization has generated vast amounts of computer-simulated (Callender & Osburn, 1981; Millsap, 1988, 1989) and empirical (Schmidt, Hunter, & Pearlman, 1981) research, and plenty of controversy. Empirical studies have focused on jobs in petroleum (Schmidt, Hunter, & Caplan, 1981) and life-insurance (Brown, 1981) industries, on stenographers (Schmidt & Hunter, 1984), and on law-enforcement occupations (Hirsh et al., 1986). The studies examined validity generalization for a number of selection instruments, including biographical inventories (Brown, 1981) and paper-and-pencil tests of various cognitive and intellectual abilities (Hirsh et al., 1986; Schmidt et al., 1985). At its most basic level, the controversy pits those who use and advocate validity generalization (Callender & Osburn, 1988) against those who question the conceptual foundation and/or some of the specific procedures and statistical manipulations that underlie validity generalization. Some of the reservations expressed by the latter group focus on

1. a logical fallacy known as "affirming the consequent," which refers to the practice of ignoring equally plausible alternative explanations or models (for example, some form of situational specificity?) when a set of empirical data is consistent with a specific, hypothesized explanation (for example, validity generalization) (James, Demaree, & Mulaik, 1986; James, Demaree, Mulaik, & Mumford, 1988);

2. the inappropriateness of the 75% rule for rejecting the situational-specificity hypothesis (Rasmussen & Loher, 1988; Schmitt & Noe, 1986; Spector & Levine, 1987);

3. overestimates (and occasionally underestimates) of the proportions of variance in distributions of validity coefficients that can be attributed to methodological and psychometric artifacts (Kemery, Mossholder, & Roth, 1987; Paese & Switzer, 1988);

4. confusion concerning criteria for determining the "transportability" of validity-generalization results from one organizational setting to another (Kemery, Mossholder, & Dunlap, 1989; Whitener, 1990); and

5. inadequacies in the individual studies that underlie investigations of validity generalization, including unavailable (or a very small number of) studies, inadequate documentation of data-coding procedures, and lack of precision in defining content domains (Bullock & Svyantek, 1985; Burke, 1984; Orwin & Cordray, 1985).

Even those who accept the basic premises that underlie validity generalization disagree about appropriate specific procedures and statistical manipulations. One of the longest-running debates has focused on the equations used to estimate an important parameter in validity-generalization research, the variance of "true" predictor-criterion relationships (that is, validities). Schmidt, Hunter, and colleagues (Hunter, Schmidt, & Pearlman, 1982; Schmidt,

Hunter, & Pearlman, 1982) have been opposed by Callender, Osburn, and their allies (Callender & Osburn, 1981; Osburn, Callender, Greener, & Ashworth, 1983). Others have joined the fray by suggesting additional revisions in procedures used to study and evaluate the merits of validity generalization (Raju & Burke, 1983; Thomas, 1988, 1990). Interestingly, these different procedures often result in very similar conclusions (Alexander, Carson, Alliger, & Cronshaw, 1989; Burke & Doran, 1989; Burke, Raju, & Pearlman, 1986; Hedges, 1989; Osburn & Callender, 1990; Raju, Pappas, & Williams, 1989). Not long ago *Personnel Psychology* published a lengthy report summarizing many of the key criticisms that have been leveled against validity generalization, along with advocates' responses to the concerns and related questions (Sackett, Schmitt, Tenopyr, Kehoe, & Zedeck, 1985; Schmidt, Hunter, Pearlman, & Hirsh, 1985). Unfortunately, the papers neglected to provide practitioners with some important, specific recommendations for implementing validity-generalization results in their organizations. Thus, there is a shortage of answers to some questions that Dr. MacKeven might have about the potential of validity generalization to address the human-resources problems and challenges confronting PPP. Along with the rest of us, she will have to "stay tuned" as more and more is learned and published.

Utility equations can provide estimates of the dollar value of a personnel system.

Utility of Personnel Decision-Making Systems

Although the concept of utility is not new (Brogden, 1949; Cronbach & Gleser, 1965), it is only in recent years that the professional literature has begun to reflect the realization that statistical significance does *not* guarantee that predictors will make *useful* contributions to organizations' personnel-selection systems. In our capitalist economy, "making a useful contribution" usually means increasing productivity and/or profits and decreasing costs. In its most

basic sense, then, the **utility** of a personnel or human-resources system can be expressed as the difference between what the system contributes to an organization and what it costs (Cronshaw & Alexander, 1985). Utility concepts have been applied to a number of personnel systems, including training and other "intervention" programs (Schmidt, Hunter, & Pearlman, 1982), recruiting (Boudreau & Rynes, 1985), and performance appraisal and feedback (Florin-Thuma & Boudreau, 1987; Landy, Farr, & Jacobs, 1982). However, the primary focus of utility analyses has been (and remains) personnel selection. Before we describe some of the earlier efforts to capture this very important property of selection systems, and show you an

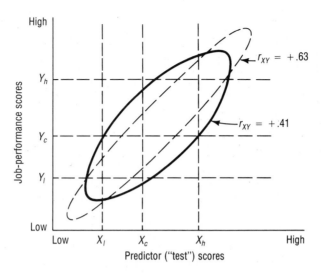

FIGURE 6.9
Factors Influencing the Utility of a Personnel-Selection System

example of a basic utility formula, a picture might be worth the proverbial thousand words.

Figure 6.9, which depicts traditional scattergrams that show two positive correlations between a predictor and a criterion, highlights some of the factors that determine just how useful a predictor-criterion relationship can be. First, utility increases as the *reliability* and the *quality of the criterion* measure increase. Predicting an unreliable criterion is impossible; predicting a contaminated or deficient criterion is futile. Second, utility of predictor-criterion relationships increases as the *reliability of the predictor* increases. No measure can predict another measure better than it "predicts" itself. Third, because the utility of a selection system is directly related to the ratio of "hits" to "misses" that it generates (see Figure 6.6), utility increases as the *size of the validity coefficient* increases. Given any combination of cutoff scores on the predictor and criterion (e.g., X_c and Y_c in Figure 6.9), the ratio of "hits" to "misses" is greater when r is larger (for example, .63) than when it is smaller (for example, .41).

Fourth, the utility of any "new" selection system (designed to replace a preexisting sys-

tem) is influenced by the proportion of employees previously selected using the "old" system who perform satisfactorily on their jobs. If Y_l in Figure 6.9 represents the dividing line between "successful" and "unsuccessful" job performance, it is obvious that the job performance of almost all the people whose data make up this scattergram falls into the "successful" category. In this case, the benefit to be gained from a new selection system (its utility) is minimal or perhaps nonexistent. On the other hand, if Y_c or Y_h represents the difference between success and failure on the job, there is a sufficient number of unsuccessful employees to render a new selection system at least potentially useful. This parameter of a selection system is its **base rate of success**.

Fifth, the utility of a selection system is a function of the *selection ratio* and the *hiring rate*. The **selection ratio** is the proportion of individuals in the *population* from which an organization attracts applicants whose scores on a predictor exceed a given cutoff score. This is to be distinguished from the **hiring rate,** "which refers to the percentage of total applicants hired" in a specific sample of applicants (Alexander, Barrett, & Doverspike, 1983, p. 342). These two indices are equivalent only when the sample of applicants has been drawn randomly from the larger population, a condition that is probably more the exception than the rule. The important point is that the utility of a selection system increases as the cutoff score on the predictor is set increasingly higher (until, of course, it is set so high that none of the applicants' scores exceeds it). Higher cutoff scores on a predictor enable an organization to choose the "cream of the crop." Predictor cutoff scores can be set at such high levels, however, only when there are many applicants for each job to be filled (hiring rate), and when a sufficient proportion of individuals in the applicant population have predictor scores that exceed that cutoff point (selection ratio).

You can see, then, that a statistically significant validity coefficient is only the first step down the path toward a useful personnel-selection system. The ultimate goal is a system with demonstrable utility. As we said before, utility is *not* a completely new and different idea.

Early Expressions of Utility: Taylor-Russell and Naylor-Shine Tables

Taylor and Russell (1939) generated a set of tables designed to illustrate the percentages of newly hired employees who can be expected to achieve levels of "successful" job performance given specific predictor validities, selection ratios, and preselection base rates of successful job performance. Although the tables were very useful tools for personnel psychologists who were interested in the practical implications of a selection test or system, they suffer from some important flaws. First, they presume that an organization can identify a single cutoff score on the criterion that separates "success" from "failure" on the job. This is often an arbitrary exercise, at best. A second, related problem is that the tables do not recognize different *degrees* of success or failure on the job. Performance on many jobs does not lend itself to neat, dichoto-

mous categorization as "success" or "failure," with nothing in between.

Naylor and Shine (1965) responded to these weaknesses with a set of tables that treat job proficiency as a continuous variable. These tables identify differences in average job-performance scores that can be expected for groups of employees who are selected using "new" and "old" systems. Although the Naylor-Shine tables were an improvement over those of Taylor and Russell (1939), they do *not* allow human-resources specialists to describe the impact of their procedures in monetary units. Utility equations do.

Utility Equations

A typical formula for calculating the utility of a selection test or system is shown below (Boudreau, 1983b):

$$U = (N)(T)(r_{xy})(SD_y)(Z_x) - C \qquad (4)$$

where U = increase in average dollar-value payoff that results from selecting N employees by using a test or procedure (x) instead of random selection;

N = number of employees selected;

T = expected average tenure of the selected group;

r_{xy} = correlation between predictor scores (x) and dollar-value payoff (y);

SD_y = standard deviation of dollar-value payoff for the selected group of applicants;

Z_x = average standardized predictor score for the selected group; and

C = total selection costs for all applicants.

Each of these parameters is relatively easy to estimate, with the notable exception of SD_y, the standard deviation of selected applicants' job-performance scores expressed in dollar-value terms. Not surprisingly, much of the utility literature has addressed the challenge of estimating this term in the equation. Several strategies have emerged.

Based on the assumption that job performance in dollar-value terms is distributed normally (see the appendix to Chapter 2 for a description of normal distributions), one approach asks supervisors of the workers in question to estimate the dollar value of those whose job performance (in the opinion of the supervisors) places them at the 15th, 50th, and 85th percentiles of the normal distribution (Schmidt, Hunter, McKenzie, & Muldrow, 1979). The 15th and 85th percentiles represent points within the normal distribution that lie approximately -1.00 and $+1.00$ standard deviations, respectively, away from the mean of the distribution (the 50th percentile; see Figure 2.6). A final estimate of SD_y is obtained from this **global-estimation method** by averaging several supervisors' estimates of the *discrepancies* in dollar-value between 50th percentile workers and either 15th or 85th percentile workers. Data collected in a large insurance company provided empirical support for both the initial assumption of normally distributed performance and the use of the 15th, 50th, and 85th percentiles for estimating SD_y in utility equations (Bobko, Karren, & Parkington, 1983).

A second approach for estimating SD_y equates this parameter with certain **percentages of employees' salaries,** or the dollar values of their average work outputs. A review of empirical data from the research literature offered support for these estimates (Schmidt & Hunter, 1983). A third approach, known as the **CREPID method** (Cascio-Ramos Estimate of Performance in Dollars; Cascio, 1982), "is based on the economic premise that the value of an individual's labor is equivalent to what an organization is willing to pay in order to obtain that labor" (Reilly & Smither, 1985, p. 652). Other methods for estimating this crucial parameter of utility equations have been suggested by Burke

and Frederick (1984), Eaton, Wing, and Mitchell (1985), Cascio and Ramos (1986), and Orr, Sackett, and Mercer (1989).

Several studies have used simulated or actual data to compare some of these estimation procedures in order to determine their relative properties and, perhaps, the superiority of one or more of them. Although there is some convergence in utility values obtained from different procedures, there are also some notable discrepancies. For example, estimates of SD_y derived from a policy-capturing procedure (based on multiple-regression analysis) were positively correlated with estimates based on Schmidt's global-estimation method ($r = .45$; Orr et al., 1989). Similarly, a comparison of the 40%- and 70%-of-salary rules and Schmidt's global procedure led to the conclusion that "the different . . . estimation procedures produced somewhat similar utility estimates" (Burke & Frederick, 1986, p. 334). However, other research has indicated that utility estimates based on Schmidt's global procedure tend to be substantially larger (higher) than estimates based on percentage-of-salary rules or the CREPID method (Edwards, Frederick, & Burke, 1988; Greer & Cascio, 1987; Reilly & Smither, 1985; Weekley, Frank, O'Connor, & Peters, 1985). Hence, Dr. Mac-Keven should not rely exclusively on Schmidt's global-estimation procedure until we learn more about the psychometric issues and cognitive processes that underlie supervisors' judgments of employees' overall worth to their organization (Bobko, Karren, & Kerkar, 1987).

Assuming, for a moment, that appropriate procedures for estimating SD_y can be identified, there is ample evidence that utility analysis can reveal dramatic monetary gains associated with effective human-resources procedures, especially personnel selection. This goes right to the heart of Ms. Creighton's wish to portray personnel procedures as "investments" rather than operating or maintenance costs. For example, Schmidt, Mack, and Hunter (1984) examined the utility of using a valid test instead of a structured interview for selecting U.S. Park Service rangers. A portion of one of their tables, which shows the estimated increases in productivity (expressed in thousands of dollars) to be expected when using a general mental-ability test rather than an interview for a period of one year, is presented as Table 6.1. You can see from this table that

> if 80 park rangers are hired in a given year (the 1978–81 average was 83 . . .) using a reliable test of general mental ability instead of the interview, the resulting increase in the dollar value of their output over their tenure will be approximately $1.16 million if they average 5 years on the job and approximately $2.3 million if they stay on the job an average of 10 years. (p. 495)

Even more impressive monetary gains in productivity were predicted if computer programmers were selected on the basis of their scores on a programming-aptitude test (Schmidt et al., 1979). Tables 6.2 and 6.3 show the estimated increases in productivity (expressed in *millions* of dollars) that would result if the Programmer Aptitude Test (Hughes & McNamara, 1959) were used for a period of one year to select computer programmers in the federal government and in the U.S. economy as a whole. Recent evidence suggests that productivity gains may grow even larger as the complexity of the job(s) in question increases (Hunter, Schmidt, & Judiesch, 1990).

Despite these encouraging predictions, or perhaps because they are *so* encouraging, utility analysis has a number of detractors, who tend to fall into two groups. The first supports the use of utility analysis, *if* the equations are modified to reflect important economic "facts of life" that will, in most cases, substantially reduce the size of derived utility estimates. The second group questions the basic value of utility analysis, and advocates replacing it with other approaches based on theories of economics and finance. A leader among the first group, Boudreau suggested that standard utility equations (for example, Equation 4) are too simplistic because they ignore the fact that employees are

TABLE 6.1   Estimates of Productivity Increases Obtainable from One Year's Substitution of a General Mental Ability Test for an Interview in Selecting U.S. Park Rangers (in Thousands of Dollars)

Number selected	Number of years on the job	
	5	10
30	434	868
40	579	1158
50	724	1447
60	868	1737
70	1013	2026
80	1158	2316
90	1303	2606
100	1448	2895
110	1592	3184
120	1737	3474
130	1882	3764

SOURCE: From "Selection Utility in the Occupation of U.S. Park Ranger for Three Modes of Test Use," by F. L. Schmidt, M. J. Mack, and J. E. Hunter, *Journal of Applied Psychology, 69,* 490–497. Copyright © 1984 by the American Psychological Association. Adapted by permission.

continually moving in and out of the work force (Boudreau, 1983b; Boudreau & Berger, 1985; Boudreau & Rynes, 1985). Further, the equations ignore key economic concepts, such as variable costs (for example, bonuses and commissions), taxes, and "discounting," which refers to changes in the value of money over time (Boudreau, 1983a). The first omission (worker mobility) leads to underestimates of utility; the second batch of oversights (economic concepts) results in overestimates. Other oversights that have resulted in overestimates of utility include changes in external labor-market conditions (for example, unemployment rates) and the related fact that applicants who receive job offers from organizations often decline them in favor of other (better) offers from other companies (Becker, 1989; Murphy, 1986).

Another contingent of the first group of critics asserts that validity coefficients do *not* remain constant over time, especially over

TABLE 6.2   Estimates of Productivity Increases Obtainable from One Year's Use of the Programmer Aptitude Test to Select Computer Programmers in the Federal Government (in Millions of Dollars)

| Hiring rate* | True validity of previous procedure | | | | |
	.00	.20	.30	.40	.50
.05	97.2	71.7	58.9	46.1	33.3
.10	82.8	60.1	50.1	39.2	28.3
.20	66.0	48.6	40.0	31.3	22.6
.30	54.7	40.3	33.1	25.9	18.7
.40	45.6	34.6	27.6	21.6	15.6
.50	37.6	27.7	22.8	17.8	12.9
.60	30.4	22.4	18.4	14.4	10.4
.70	23.4	17.2	14.1	11.1	8.0
.80	16.5	12.2	10.0	7.8	5.6

*Number of jobs to be filled divided by the number of applicants for those jobs.

SOURCE: From "Impact of Valid Selection Procedures on Workforce Productivity," by F. L. Schmidt, J. E. Hunter, R. C. McKenzie, and T. W. Muldrow, *Journal of Applied Psychology, 64,* 609–626. Copyright © 1979 by the American Psychological Association. Reprinted by permission.

TABLE 6.3   Estimates of Productivity Increases Obtainable from One Year's Use of the Programmer Aptitude Test to Select Computer Programmers throughout the U.S. Economy

| Hiring rate* | True validity of previous procedure | | | | |
	.00	.20	.30	.40	.50
.05	1605	1184	973	761	550
.10	1367	1008	828	648	468
.20	1091	804	661	517	373
.30	903	666	547	428	309
.40	753	555	455	356	257
.50	622	459	376	295	213
.60	501	370	304	238	172
.70	387	285	234	183	132
.80	273	201	165	129	93

*Number of jobs to be filled divided by the number of applicants for those jobs.

SOURCE: From "Impact of Valid Selection Procedures on Workforce Productivity," by F. L. Schmidt, J. E. Hunter, R. C. McKenzie, and T. W. Muldrow, *Journal of Applied Psychology, 64,* 609–626. Copyright © 1979 by the American Psychological Association. Reprinted by permission.

lengthy intervals. Because the size of the coefficients directly affects the magnitude of utility estimates (see Equation 4), the estimates will shrink as validity coefficients deflate with the passage of time (Henry & Hulin, 1987; Hulin, Henry, & Noon, 1990). These concerns emphasize the need for procedures that can help us to understand the lack of precision that characterizes typical estimates of utility (Alexander & Barrick, 1987).

Finally, although they did not reject the basic idea of utility estimation, several researchers have suggested that we should abandon "dollar value of performance" as the foundation of such analyses (Sadacca, Campbell, Difazio, Schultz, & White, 1990; Vance & Colella, 1990). Admittedly, this would solve some difficult problems, including the challenges inherent in estimating SD_y in dollars and coping with situations where the dollar value of performance is not an appropriate concept (for example, the military). However, it is precisely this aspect of utility analysis, the potential to attach dollar values to human-resources procedures, that makes it so attractive to I/O psychologists (like Dr. MacKeven) who must convince corporate decision makers (like Ms. Creighton) of the value of their techniques and procedures.

The second group of detractors includes those who propose more radical solutions to the problems associated with utility analysis. Most of the solutions involve replacing, or at least supplementing, utility analysis with one or more risk-assessment procedures based on finance, accounting, or economic concepts.[4] This group, in turn, is opposed by those who contend that many of these techniques are conceptually, logically, and numerically inappropriate substitutes for utility analysis of human-resources programs (Cascio & Morris, 1990; Greer & Cascio, 1987; Hunter, Schmidt, & Coggin, 1988; Rich & Boudreau, 1987; Schmidt, Hunter, Outerbridge, & Trattner, 1986). Still others suggest the possibility of compromise, pointing out that some of the traditional methods for estimating SD_y (for example, CREPID and percentage-of-salary approaches), and thus for estimating utility, are special cases of procedures that can potentially link utility analysis with economic and accounting concepts (Raju, Burke, & Normand, 1990).

---

[4] The specifics of these procedures are beyond the scope of this text, but interested readers are invited to consult discussions of techniques for capital budgeting, risk simulation, sensitivity analysis, break-even analysis, and human-resources accounting (Cronshaw & Alexander, 1985; Cronshaw, Alexander, Wiesner, & Barrick, 1987; Rich & Boudreau, 1987; Steffy & Maurer, 1988).

It is obviously too soon to expect consensus in the literature concerning the specifics of utility analysis or the appropriateness of other finance-based techniques for assessing the cost effectiveness of human-resource procedures. This does *not* mean, however, that we can afford to "sit on the sidelines" until these issues are resolved. As Ms. Creighton's memo demonstrates, Dr. MacKeven and her colleagues in the field of I/O psychology will continue to experience pressure to defend the cost effectiveness of their personnel procedures. At this point, you should understand the science and some of the economic factors that underlie one of our responses to that pressure, utility analysis, and appreciate the debate that currently surrounds that response.

Chapter Summary

Organizations recruit new employees through personal contacts, posted notices, professional employment agencies, and the mass media. Because recruiting is part of the overall personnel-selection process, we must strive to reach qualified women and men of all racial and ethnic groups, encouraging them to apply for vacant organizational positions. Realistic job previews that provide job applicants with relatively unbiased descriptions of available jobs may help to improve the efficiency and effectiveness of the recruiting process.

After administering one or more selection tests to job applicants, we can organize and present the forthcoming information in several ways in order to facilitate the decision-making process. Expectancy charts are easy to understand, but they convey only a broad picture of a selection system's impact on workers' performance. Regression equations are more mathematically sophisticated and precise, and they can reveal the size of the relationship between selection-test scores and job-performance cri-

INTEROFFICE MEMO

To: A. Creighton,
           Vice President for Personnel

From: J. A. MacKeven,
           Human Resources Coordinator

Subject: Utility of PPP's Human Resources Procedures

Yes, I think we can help you convince the president that PPP's personnel procedures do, in fact, represent investments of the company's financial assets that can lead to tangible monetary returns.

The key to our argument is known as "utility analysis," which can help us to estimate the dollar-value payoff (over and above the costs incurred) of implementing various human-resources procedures (for example, selection). In the case of selection, this approach requires us to make credible estimates of such things as the numbers of people placed in particular positions during a specified interval, the average length of time they can be expected to remain in their jobs, the size (and stability) of the validity coefficients that describe the empirical relationships between our selection instruments and our criteria of job performance, and several other statistical and economic parameters. Perhaps the most challenging of these is the variability of selected applicants' job performance expressed in terms of "dollars and cents." We can discuss the variety of ways in which this variability can be estimated during our meeting scheduled for next week.

teria. They are compensatory, however, in that they allow an applicant's high score(s) on some selection procedure(s) to make up for low score(s) on others. Multiple-cutoff and multiple-hurdle decision strategies can be used in place of, or in combination with, regression equations when a completely compensatory approach is inappropriate. Efforts to improve the effectiveness of these traditional personnel-selection strategies have focused on moderator and suppressor variables, and pursued the possibilities of synthetic validation and validity generalization.

Beyond the validity of hiring decisions, personnel-selection specialists have become concerned with the utility, or cost effectiveness, of the systems used to make those decisions. The utility of a new selection system is influenced by the reliability and validity of the selection-test scores and the job-performance measures, as well as by the base rate of current employees' success on the job and the current selection ratio and hiring rate. It is becoming more and more necessary for human-resources specialists to be able to demonstrate the economic value of their techniques and procedures in order to compete with colleagues in production, marketing, and other organizational sectors for increasingly scarce financial resources.

Review Questions and Exercises

1. What do you see as the major challenges or obstacles that stand in the way of Dr. Mac-Keven and Ms. Creighton if they decide to implement utility analyses at PPP (see memo, p. 205)?

2. If you were the president of PPP, and you heard a description of utility analyses that conveyed the information contained in this chapter, would you "buy it"? Why (not)?

3. In addition to personnel selection, utility equations have been developed to estimate the cost effectiveness of training programs and performance-appraisal systems. Based on your understanding of the parameters in utility equations for selection, what parameters do you think will require estimation for training? for performance appraisal? (That is, what will we have to know in order to assess the cost effectiveness of training or performance appraisal?)

4. What should Dr. MacKeven look for as she examines PPP's recruiting strategies in the context of utility issues? How does recruiting affect the utility of selection tests?

5. How might moderator variables, suppressor variables, or synthetic validity be incorporated into utility analyses?

6. What is the appropriate role for validity generalization in utility estimation?

7. Do you agree or disagree that human-resources procedures lend themselves to "dollars-and-cents" utility assessments? Why?

CHAPTER 7

....

Personnel Training

UPON RECEIVING MR. HAMMOND'S MEMO (p. 208), Dr. MacKeven informally surveyed PPP's vice presidents to determine the extent to which other divisions within the organization shared the problem. She was chagrined (but not surprised) to learn that Mr. Hammond's division had plenty of company. Vice presidents in Marketing, Retail Operations, Personnel, and their colleagues in Purchasing, Distribution, and Finance all complained about the lack of programs for initiating technicians, specialists, and other lower-ranking personnel into the mysteries of supervision. Apparently supervisors throughout Peter's Pan Pizza are simply expected to "pick up" necessary skills and abilities as their careers progress.

Although Mr. Hammond has identified a serious gap in PPP's personnel procedures, Dr. MacKeven can derive some comfort from the fact that she is not alone. The assumption that almost anyone with adequate intelligence and motivation can effectively supervise others is alive and well in many organizations. In fact, it is this misconception that underlies the so-called Peter Principle (no relation to PPP), according to which inappropriate criteria for promotion allow people in hierarchical organizations to rise through the ranks until they reach their respective levels of *in*competence. Only then do the promotions cease (Peter &

....

INTEROFFICE MEMO

To: J. A. MacKeven,
             Human Resources Coordinator

From: R. Hammond,
             Director, Engineering

Subject: Supervisory Training

Last month marked my 30th year with Peter's Pan Pizza. I was hired fresh out of college with the ink on my bachelor of science degree in engineering barely dry. Through a lot of hard work and, quite frankly, a bit of good luck, I have been promoted through the ranks of the organization until, several years ago, I became director of engineering. As one promotion followed another, I found myself doing less and less actual engineering, and more and more supervisory work. Although I think I have become a competent supervisor and manager, my only credential in that domain is an imaginary diploma from the "School of Hard Knocks." That is, I *never* received any formal training in supervisory or managerial skills. I was promoted to first-level supervision because my own supervisor (and her managers) thought I was a good engineer; I became a manager because I apparently excelled at first-level supervision; and so forth.

Since becoming director, I have been carefully observing the managers and first-level supervisors in Engineering. It is clear to me that most of these folks are guiding others' work with no more formal training than I have. They have been promoted out of engineering specialties into supervisory positions *not* because they apparently know anything about supervising others but because they are excellent engineers. What can we do to break this illogical chain of events? Is it possible to develop some sort of training program for professional engineers who are asked to assume formal supervisory and managerial responsibilities? My own experience tells me that competent supervision is based on more than just high levels of motivation and reasonable portions of common sense.

Do you agree? More important, can you help?

Hull, 1969). For a variety of reasons (including a healthy dose of good luck), Mr. Hammond has either managed to circumvent the Peter Principle, or he just hasn't reached his level of incompetence—*yet*.

Dr. MacKeven cannot afford to depend upon good fortune, so Mr. Hammond's memo will prompt her to investigate the need for a more or less formal program that can train employees to meet the demands and challenges of supervising other workers. Although she will probably focus initially on Engineering, any training program she develops should be useful in Construction, Maintenance, Custodial Services, and throughout much of PPP. Job analyses and relevant research suggest that first-level supervision in most departments of an organization involves a common core of tasks and requires similar sets of behaviors (for example, observing, planning, communicating) (Dowell & Wexley, 1978).

This chapter examines personnel training in organizations. **Training** is "a planned effort by an organization to facilitate the learning of job-related behavior on the part of its employees" (Wexley & Latham, 1991, p. 3). It focuses on "the systematic acquisition of skills, rules, concepts, or attitudes that result in improved performance in [the work] environment" (Goldstein, 1993, p. 3). Common to these two definitions is the idea that personnel training involves a systematic set of procedures and experiences that are planned and implemented by an organization to bring about some change among employees that will lead to improved job performance. In this chapter we describe background work that must precede development of effective training programs, and then examine the crucial (yet often overlooked) subject of how to evaluate the effectiveness of training programs. Finally, we describe some of the diverse training techniques and methods in use within organizations, paying particular attention to how diligently they recognize and incorporate widely recognized principles of learning. As always, we try to clarify the material by re-

ferring to the situation at Peter's Pan Pizza, and especially to Mr. Hammond's request for supervisory training in the engineering department.

Once again, we encourage you to appreciate how all the topics discussed in this (and previous) chapter(s) are interrelated in one way or another. Although we divided the personnel functions into separate chapters in the interest of clarity and convenience, remember that an effective personnel system integrates these functions (for example, job analysis, performance appraisal, and personnel selection and training) into a system that maximizes the potential of the organization's human resources.

Training-Needs Assessment

Regardless of which specific training techniques or procedures one ultimately chooses, it's a safe bet that implementation and evaluation will involve expenditures of time and money. It therefore makes sense that organizations should determine whether the expected changes in employees' behaviors or attitudes are *really* necessary and, if they are, whether a training program is the *best* way to effect the changes (as opposed to a more rigorous selection program, for example). This process, known as **needs assessment**, also provides insight into the *kinds* of change that are likely to contribute to improved organizational performance. Not surprisingly, different kinds of change (changes in attitudes versus improved motor skills, or changes in the performance of work teams versus changes in individual workers' performance, for example) are best accomplished through different training techniques and procedures. Thus, for both logical and financial reasons, careful needs assessment should *always* precede development of any training program.

Unfortunately, conscientious needs assessment seems to be the exception among many organizations rather than the rule. A recent survey of 611 companies in a variety of industrial categories, each of which employed at least 1,000 workers, revealed that only 27% had regular practices or procedures for determining the training needs of their managers. Larger companies were more likely to have needs-assessment procedures in place, and the needs of lower-level managers and first-level supervisors were more likely to be regularly assessed than those of top-level managers (Saari, Johnson, McLaughlin, & Zimmerle, 1988). Nevertheless, these data suggest that large numbers of training dollars and substantial amounts of time are being spent without careful assessment of the need for such expenditures.

Proper needs assessment consists of three phases that proceed in a logical order: (1) organizational analysis, (2) task or job analysis, and (3) person analysis (McGehee & Thayer, 1961). As we discuss each of these in turn, the logic of the sequence will become clear to you.

Organizational Analysis

Organizational analysis is the study of "the systemwide components of an organization that may affect a training program [including] . . . an examination of organizational goals, resources of the organization, transfer climate for training, and internal and external constraints present in the environment" (Goldstein, 1993, p. 36). Simply stated, it is illogical to be unhappy with an organization's performance without clearly understanding the organization's purpose(s) and goal(s). Organizational analysis serves to identify the purposes and goals as unambiguously as possible, which is not always as easy as it might seem.

Except for charitable and nonprofit organizations, of course, companies in capitalist economies exist for the purpose of providing their owners with monetary returns on their financial investments. This is, after all, the "bottom line," and Peter's Pan Pizza is no exception. Specifying exactly which intermediate objectives will lead to the "bottom line" is often a tricky prop-

osition. For example, should PPP strive to maximize its profits by offering its customers products made only with the highest-quality ingredients, or can the company make more money by "skimping" and "taking short cuts" whenever possible? Should PPP concern itself with the morale and psychological welfare of its employees, or should it focus on profits and let the workers fend for themselves? Should PPP try to be a responsible community citizen (for example, by sponsoring youth softball teams and discounts for senior citizens, or by rewarding delivery people for driving courteously) or should it restrict expenditures to things that have obvious and immediate impacts on productivity and costs? These are just a few of the questions that a careful organizational analysis should address. Failure to deal openly with these issues can create a breeding ground for idiosyncratic assumptions and many misunderstandings and conflicts, some of which will certainly affect the content and evaluation of training programs. (For some specific "horror stories," see Goodman, 1969; Lynton & Pareek, 1967; and Miller & Zeller, 1967.)

Challenging as it might be, it isn't enough merely to identify organizational goals. Organizational analysis must also determine the resources that are available as well as the limitations and constraints, both inside and outside the organization, that will facilitate or frustrate goal attainment. Resources include money, people, physical facilities, reputation, and anything else at the company's disposal that can help it reach its goals. Constraints are the "flip side" of resources. Internal factors include shortages of money, personnel, or equipment, or an organizational climate that is characterized by fear or suspicion. Examples of external constraints are local, state, or federal regulations that restrict certain activities or practices (for example, the EEOC's guidelines), a limited applicant pool from which to attract new employees, and stiff competition from other retail food outlets.

In short, organizational analysis involves careful specification of what the company

Lectures are important components of many training programs.

wants to accomplish, as well as the internal and external conditions under which it must conduct its business. Without this kind of information, the second and third phases of needs assessment are meaningless. How can we ascertain whether jobs are properly designed or whether employees are performing the jobs effectively unless we understand how the jobs and employees are supposed to contribute to the organization's goals?

When we consider the important role organizational analysis plays in setting the stage for every other aspect of personnel training, it is surprising that relevant empirical research has been relatively scarce. Although Goldstein's (1980) review of this literature included a small number of (hard-to-find) studies that dealt with the negative impact of employees' resistance to organizational training programs (Anastasio & Morgan, 1972; Salinger, 1973), a subsequent review uncovered "no additional empirical research studies" (Wexley, 1984, p. 521). Four years later, Latham (1988) declared that re-

search in this area was guided by two themes: (1) training needs should evolve from corporate strategy; and (2) organizations are ethically bound to develop training programs that protect their workers from technical obsolescence (Kozlowski & Hults, 1987). However, the number of empirical studies cited to support these themes was not large, and even some of those failed to support a relationship between organizational support and successful training outcomes (Russell, Terborg, & Powers, 1985). (Other data had suggested that a favorable organizational climate *is* conducive to effective training [Baumgartel & Jeanpierre, 1972].) The most recent review of the training literature reaffirmed the importance of strategic considerations for training (that is, linking training to organizational strategy), which has continued to dominate literature written by and for practitioners (Tannenbaum & Yukl, 1992). The authors also pointed out that cross-cultural training (addressing different societal norms and values, for example) has become more important as many organizations adopt global business strategies (see Black & Mendenhall, 1990; Early, 1987).

Where does all this leave Dr. MacKeven? Obviously, an absence of unanimous research findings does not negate the importance of careful organizational analysis. To train Mr. Hammond's first-level supervisors successfully, she will have to understand the goals of the Engineering Department, which in turn will depend on the goals of the Facilities Division and, ultimately, on the goals of Peter's Pan Pizza. Of course, Dr. MacKeven must also identify the resources at her disposal, as well as the constraints that can limit PPP's progress toward its goals. She can only hope that subsequent reviews of the training literature will *not* be able to conclude that "training researchers have either intentionally or unintentionally [continued] to ignore the influence of organizational variables on the training function" (Wexley, 1984, p. 521).

Task and Job Analysis

The second phase of needs assessment consists of identifying the tasks that must be performed if an organization is to reach its goals under existing circumstances (that is, resources and constraints). Multiple tasks that require similar behaviors or that lead to the same or at least similar outcomes are often grouped together to form jobs. **Task analysis**, then, "results in a statement of the activities or work operations performed on the job and the conditions under which the job is performed" (Goldstein, 1993, p. 54). It is appropriate here to refer you to our earlier discussion of job analysis (in Chapter 3). Recall that job-oriented job analyses identify the outcomes or "end products" of jobs. The first step in task and job analysis in the context of training-needs assessment is to ensure that the jobs in question generate outcomes that contribute to an organization's overall goals. If significant "gaps" emerge, existing jobs may have to be redesigned or new jobs designed, the outcomes of which will fill in those gaps.

After job outcomes have been specified, the second step in this phase of needs assessment

involves worker-oriented job analyses, which identify actual behaviors required of incumbents in order to accomplish the specified outcomes. This is the first component of needs assessment that has *direct* implications for personnel training. It makes no sense to speak of "training" organizational goals or job outcomes, but we *can* train employees to perform specific behaviors that will lead to desirable job outcomes (which, in turn, contribute to organizational goals). Any of the job-analysis techniques discussed in Chapter 3 (for example, critical incidents, functional job analysis, the PAQ) might be used to complete the second phase of needs assessment.

Two recent reviews of the literature have concluded that today's jobs, and those to be found in future workplaces, put a premium on cognitive or conceptual abilities and are less dependent on physical skills and rote memorization of facts or procedures (Latham, 1988; Tannenbaum & Yukl, 1992). Both reviews also emphasized the growing importance of cross-job training, retraining, and updating (Goldstein & Gilliam, 1990; Kozlowski & Farr, 1988; Lance, Mayfield, Gould, & Lynskey, 1991). Despite these trends, proceeding from task and job analysis to the design of particular training programs based on specific techniques remains one of the most challenging aspects of personnel training (Goldstein, 1980). A popular strategy for making this transition identifies the knowledge, skills, and abilities (KSAs) that individual workers must possess in order to perform the necessary job-related behaviors identified during task and job analysis. This is typically accomplished with the help of "job experts" (job incumbents, supervisors, I/O psychologists, and others). Training procedures and techniques can then be identified or designed that will facilitate learning the KSAs.

Person Analysis

The third phase of needs assessment focuses on the women and men who must perform the tasks that are necessary if the organization is to reach its goals. The first two phases, organizational and task and job analyses, yield descriptions of what workers must be able to do; the final phase results in descriptions of what workers are actually capable of doing at the present time. Person analyses have traditionally relied on one or both of two kinds of information: (1) performance-appraisal data for employees who are already on the job; and (2) data obtained during the selection process from interviews, tests, and application blanks for those about to be hired. These topics were discussed in Chapters 4, 5, and 6. Recent research concerning person analysis has focused on a third source of information, self-assessed training needs (Ford & Noe, 1987; Tannenbaum & Yukl, 1992).

Summing Up

Organizational, job and task, and person analyses enable Dr. MacKeven to answer two questions that lie at the heart of needs assessment: (1) Is a training program necessary for these particular employees at this particular time? If so, (2) What specific objectives should the training address? By comparing the results of organizational and task analyses, which reveal what is required of PPP employees, with the results of person analyses, which describe the capabilities and deficiencies of employees or applicants, Dr. MacKeven can make intelligent, well-informed decisions about the development and implementation of training programs. If there are no discrepancies between people's capabilities and the demands of their jobs, there is no reason to devote time and money to training. Unfortunately, Mr. Hammond's memo suggests that this is not the case. (And sobering predictions about the low levels of education and lack of basic skills that will characterize many job applicants in the coming decades suggest that this situation cannot be expected to change in the near future.) It is just as important to recognize, however, that finding such a discrepancy does *not* automatically indicate that training is the optimal solution. That discrepancy might better be eliminated through improved selection procedures or more attractive incentive conditions (Thayer & McGehee, 1977) (although the predictions alluded to above suggest that such alternatives will become less viable as we move into the twenty-first century). Training programs should be designed only after careful consideration and analysis of the relative costs and benefits associated with alternative solutions.

If a training program does seem to be necessary, needs assessment can suggest *specific* training objectives to be accomplished on the road to eliminating the identified discrepancies. Specific objectives are extremely important. Dr. MacKeven and Mr. Hammond might state that the percentage of first-level supervisors within the Engineering Department who are dismissed due to unsatisfactory performance should not exceed 5% of those who complete the training program. Given such a specific objective, it is easy to evaluate the program's effectiveness. Compare that objective with a much less specific objective, such as "improving supervisors' appreciation of the complexity of supervisor-subordinate relationships." How can Dr. MacKeven unambiguously determine whether this objective has been met? At the individual level, useful training objectives clearly describe what employees should be able to do or accomplish following a training program, along with the conditions under which they will be expected to perform. An example of a good behavioral training objective is that first-level supervisors in the Engineering Department should be able to provide subordinates with timely and accurate performance feedback so that "spot checks" by upper-level managers *never* find employees who "just don't know where they stand" with their supervisor. Compare that with a less specific objective such as "developing better communication skills." Evaluating the former is simple and straightforward; assessing the latter is far more challenging (if not impossible).

You can see, then, the two basic benefits of needs assessment. First, it provides information about whether a training program is necessary at all. If training is indicated, it identifies specific objectives for the training program to accomplish. Second, by identifying specific objectives, needs assessment also suggests criteria that can be used to evaluate the effectiveness of the training program. Obviously, a successful training program is one that meets its objectives. Let's turn now to the process of evaluating training programs.

Evaluation of Training Programs

You might think we are "putting the cart before the horse" by discussing evaluation before describing any specific training techniques or methods. Our rationale is quite simple: we examine evaluation now because this is exactly what Dr. MacKeven would (or, at least, *should*) do. Just as we should assess the need for training prior to designing and implementing a program, we should determine how to evaluate the program before training is actually begun. Planning reduces the likelihood that the training program will not be evaluated at all, and makes it more likely that training will be designed and conducted in ways that facilitate competent evaluation.

The importance of these concerns was highlighted in the survey of 611 companies described earlier (Saari et al., 1988). The researchers concluded that "for the most part, it appears that companies do not conduct extensive management training evaluation activities" (p. 739), even in light of the expenses associated with the programs. For example, 42% of the companies that relied on off-site executive MBA (master of business administration) programs reported that they did nothing to evaluate effectiveness, despite the average cost per participant of $14,000. Although only 8% of the companies reported *no* evaluation of company-specific management training programs, much of the evaluation that took place was neither systematic nor necessarily valid.

We'll divide our discussion of evaluation into three parts. First, we'll list the three basic questions that any useful training-evaluation procedure must address, and describe some of the factors and conditions that can result in misleading or even blatantly inaccurate answers to the questions. Second, we'll describe a variety of research designs that can be used to evaluate training programs. Third, we'll examine some additional considerations that can affect evaluation of training programs. As always, we'll keep Mr. Hammond's memo (and problem) in mind as we proceed.

Asking the Right Questions

Competent evaluation of a training program depends on answering the following questions:

1. Did employees change in any way (that is, in behavior, attitude)? If not, the training program was almost certainly not effective. If they did, we then want to know

2. Was the training program responsible for the change? If not, the training program cannot be judged effective. If it was, we then want to know

3. Will the training program be similarly effective for a different group of employees in the same, or perhaps in a different, organization?

Affirmative answers to the first two questions reflect a training program's **internal validity**, which means that the training "worked" for a specific sample of trainees in a specific setting at a particular time. If, in addition, the answer to the third question is also yes, the training program has **external validity**, which means that it will probably also "work" for other groups of trainees at other times and in other locations.

Whether we are discussing internal or external validity, our concern with training effectiveness requires criterion measures that can be used to gauge our success (or lack thereof). At this point you might want to review our discussion of criteria in Chapter 4. In this context, let's examine some of the kinds of criteria that are available for assessing training effectiveness, as well as some of the factors and conditions that can mislead us about the internal and external validity of training programs.

Training Criteria. I/O psychologists traditionally speak of four kinds or levels of criteria for evaluating the effectiveness of training programs: reaction, learning, behavior, and results criteria (Kirkpatrick, 1967). In the order listed they provide information that is increasingly useful for determining whether the deficiencies identified during needs assessment have been eliminated.

Reaction criteria are nothing more than opinions concerning the perceived effectiveness of a training program. More specifically, such criteria are the "reactions" of the trainees (and sometimes the trainers) to such questions as "What did you think of the training program you just completed? Was it any good?" This kind of information is very easy to obtain, but its value is extremely limited. Admittedly, it's interesting to know whether those who participated in a program enjoyed or hated the experience because a despised program can create more problems than it might solve. And sometimes employees' reactions or emotional responses are important outcome variables themselves, or important sources of diagnostic information that might guide subsequent program (re)design. However, employees' reactions tell us little or nothing at all about whether training is addressing the organization's other important needs. For example, trainees might react favorably to a program for any number of reasons. Perhaps it was fun or entertaining, or it allowed them to escape from their normally boring jobs for a while, or they believe it will lead to greater pay raises or more frequent promotions. None of these explanations for positive reactions constitutes evidence that organizational needs are being met. A study of team development in the Israeli army confirmed

that reactions to training can be very favorable even when every other piece of information indicates that a program produced *no* useful changes in employees' behaviors or the organization's operations (Eden, 1985). Adding insult to injury, reaction criteria do not lend themselves to "before and after" comparisons, without which we cannot answer the first of the three questions posed earlier. (Did a *change* occur?) No doubt the relative ease with which reaction criteria can be obtained accounts for their popularity (Saari et al., 1988).

Learning criteria are typically collected immediately following the completion of training and are intended to reflect whatever trainees learned. The most common learning criteria are final examinations (written or performance). Instead of asking Mr. Hammond's first-level supervisors how much they (dis)liked a training program or whether they think they benefited from it (that is, reaction criteria), Dr. MacKeven can administer a paper-and-pencil examination immediately following training that tests trainees' understanding of supervisory duties and responsibilities, company policies, and whatever else had indicated the need for a training program.

Learning criteria *do* lend themselves to "before and after" comparisons, which allow us to answer the first of the three questions listed above. If Dr. MacKeven administered some sort of pretest before beginning the training program, she could compare each trainee's score on the final exam with her pretest score to ascertain whether a change had occurred in knowledge or skill (or whatever the pre- and posttests were designed to measure). Such comparisons are impossible if no pretraining data are available. Unfortunately, systematic differences between trainees' pre- and posttest scores might have absolutely nothing to do with the training program. We will examine conditions or factors that can produce such changes during our discussion of "threats" to internal validity. In addition, the discovery of systematic changes that *are* attributable to training offers no guarantee that what was learned will be transferred and used back in the employees' work settings. Training programs cannot meet an organization's needs without such transfer. (Conditions that facilitate transfer of training back to the work setting are discussed later in this chapter.)

Behavior criteria specifically address our concern with how workers perform in the job setting after they have completed training. The most common examples of behavior criteria of training effectiveness are job-performance measures (that is, objective, personnel, and especially judgmental data). Behavior criteria are much more useful than reaction or learning criteria for determining whether an organization's needs are being met. Of course, to use behavior criteria to answer the three questions posed at the beginning of this section, we must have some pretraining data for comparison purposes. As you probably anticipated, however, systematic change in trainees' "before" and "after" behavior measures does not guarantee the internal validity of the training program. Once again, any of the threats to internal validity discussed below can operate to effect misleading or erroneous conclusions.

Results criteria directly address the organizational needs identified during the first stage of the needs assessment. This criterion level transcends measures of job performance to address the question of whether changes in work behaviors actually lead to the broad organizational changes identified as necessary or desirable during needs assessment. Examples of results criteria that might be relevant in the context of Mr. Hammond's memo include changes in organizational climate that promote more conscientious, more effective first-level supervision, lower personnel costs attributable to lower rates of turnover among disgruntled subordinates, or better representation of women and minority-group members in supervisory and management positions. Results criteria imply *change* at the level of the organization, so they depend upon comparisons of conditions before and after training. Once again, however, any of

the threats to internal validity described below can produce erroneous conclusions concerning the role of training in producing any measured changes.

Many of those who rely on Kirkpatrick's (1967) taxonomy of training criteria implicitly (and sometimes explicitly) assume that the four levels are positively intercorrelated and, further, that they are causally linked (that is, positive reactions *lead to* high learning scores, which in turn *cause* better job performance, which in turn *is responsible for* improved organizational performance). However, a recent review of 12 published studies that reported a total of 26 correlations between various levels of training criteria failed to support these assumptions, especially as they pertain to reaction criteria (Alliger & Janak, 1989). Specifically, the reviewers suggest that "attitudinal reactions to training should be considered in a category independent from such constructs as learning or behavior [or results]" (p. 337). Of course, the smaller correlations associated with reaction criteria may be attributable to a relative lack of reliability inherent in the measures of trainees' reactions. Other empirical and theoretical work supports the notion that those who evaluate training programs are wise to examine a variety of criteria because they do *not* all assess the same (much less causally related!) performance constructs (Burke & Day, 1986; Campion & Campion, 1987; Mumford, Weeks, Harding, & Fleishman, 1988).

We can summarize our discussion of training criteria as follows:

1. Results criteria are ultimately the most important category of measures from the organization's perspective, but behavior criteria are more informative and more useful to I/O psychologists who, after all, are primarily concerned with the behavior of individuals. Learning and reaction criteria are less useful because they tell us nothing about trainees' subsequent job performance.

2. Unfortunately, results criteria are also most difficult to assess, and behavior criteria can

present measurement challenges, too (see Chapter 4). Learning and reaction criteria are easier to assess.

3. Although one can measure results, behavior, and learning criteria in the absence of pretraining measures of the same constructs, we cannot determine whether any changes have occurred unless we have a baseline measure taken prior to training. Reaction criteria neither require nor lend themselves to pretraining measures.

4. Reaction criteria are logically and empirically independent of learning, behavior, and results criteria. The statistical relationships among the last three criteria are modest at best, and there is no convincing evidence that they are interrelated in a causal fashion.

5. All four categories of training criteria are vulnerable to internal validity threats (which we discuss next); none of them addresses the issue of external validity.

Internal Validity Threats. By **internal validity threats** we refer to factors or conditions that can prompt one who evaluates a training program to conclude *erroneously* that the program was responsible for changes in learning, behavior, or results criteria. They include such things as history, maturation, testing, instrumentation change, statistical regression toward the mean, nonrandom selection of trainees, and experimental "mortality." We will describe each of these potentially contaminating influences and offer examples that are relevant in the context of Mr. Hammond's needs.

History in this context refers to the passage of time or, more specifically, to events extraneous to the training that occur while the training program is in progress. These events, rather than the training itself, can be responsible for changes in training criterion measures. Suppose, for example, that a newspaper article describing the brutal murder of an office supervisor by a subordinate is published while Dr.

MacKeven is training Mr. Hammond's first-level supervisors in the domain of superior-subordinate communication and relationships. She may discover that those trainees treat their subordinates with a great deal more consideration and respect (and, quite possibly, more fearfully) after training than they did prior to it (a behavior criterion). Their altered behavior, however, might be attributable to their realization that poor interpersonal relations with subordinates can have dire personal consequences. The training itself might have had no effect on the supervisors' behaviors at all. In this case, a training evaluator who is unaware of the newspaper article in question might erroneously conclude that the training program was responsible for the observed change.

Maturation is similar to history in this context because it also refers to changes that occur as a function of time. It differs from history in that maturation refers to natural and normal biological and/or psychological changes that are not tied to any specific, external, environmental event. People grow older or more experienced with a particular task simply through normal biological or psychological processes, respectively. Mr. Hammond's relatively inexperienced supervisors might demonstrate greater awareness of the importance and role of authority in an organization (on a paper-and-pencil test of such knowledge, perhaps—a learning criterion) following a rather lengthy training program, simply because they came to appreciate that authority can be constructive and need *not* threaten anyone's freedom. That experience could have been totally *un*related to the training intervention.

Testing threatens internal validity when trainees' higher scores on a test following training (a posttest) are attributable to their experience with a similar or identical test prior to training (a pretest). Suppose Dr. MacKeven administers a test designed to measure supervisors' communication skills before she initiates a training program that, among other things, is intended to improve such skills. (Recall that the purpose of such a pretest is to generate a base-line measure of performance to which trainees' scores following training can be compared, so that any *changes* in knowledge or skills can be recognized.) It is quite possible that Mr. Hammond's supervisors might actually learn something about communication skills while reading and responding to questions on the pretest. If their scores on a test of communication skills following training (another learning criterion) are higher because of what they learned on the pretest rather than what they learned during the training proper, Dr. MacKeven might mistakenly conclude that her training program was responsible for their improved performance.

Instrumentation changes are alterations in the ways criteria are measured. Imagine the following scenario. Prior to beginning training, Mr. Hammond asks upper-level managers to use some graphic rating scales to assess first-level supervisors' abilities to organize the work of others and delegate responsibility. While Dr. MacKeven is in the process of training those supervisors to improve their organization and delegation skills, PPP discards those graphic rating scales in favor of a new performance-appraisal technique that is (unexpectedly!) more vulnerable to leniency error than were the graphic scales. Trainees then receive higher ratings on their abilities to organize and delegate following training simply because of the increased leniency error in managers' ratings of those skills, *not* because they learned how to perform these supervisory functions better during Dr. MacKeven's training program.

Statistical regression toward the mean is a bit more subtle because it depends upon an appreciation of classical psychometric theory (Campbell, 1976; Nunnally, 1978). Recall from prior chapters (especially Chapter 5) that unreliable measurement is attributable to random error. Sometimes this random error artificially inflates people's scores on a test, and sometimes diminishes the scores (with respect to their "true" scores on whatever construct is being measured). Although we can never be sure, it's

a good bet that people with extremely high (extremely low) scores on a measure have probably had their true scores inflated (diminished) by random error. Because the error is random and normally distributed (across many people, or across multiple assessments of a single person), we can expect that individuals who obtain extremely high scores on the first administration of a test or measure will probably score somewhat lower (that is, closer to the population mean score—hence the label "regression toward the mean") on the second administration of that test (or an equivalent form of that test), despite the fact that their true scores do not actually change. That is, the random error during the second administration does not inflate their test scores as much as it did during the first administration, or perhaps that error actually deflates their scores the second time around. Conversely, people who obtain extremely low scores on the first administration (partly because random error deflates those scores) can be expected to obtain somewhat higher scores (again, closer to the population mean score) on a second administration of the test or measure even though their true scores do not change. In this case, the random error on the second test does not diminish their scores as severely as it did on the first test, or perhaps actually inflates their scores the second time around.

If those who take the pretest, experience the training, and take the posttest include people with a wide range of scores on the pretest (some very high, some very low, and some in between), statistical regression toward the mean should not threaten the internal validity of a training program. For each person who obtains a higher score on the posttest due to regression, someone else should obtain a comparably lower score to "balance it out." This is the nature of random-error variance. If, on the other hand, Dr. MacKeven decides to train only first-level supervisors who obtain very low scores on a pretest of their supervisory skills (an apparently reasonable strategy, especially if it is impractical or impossible to train all of Mr. Hammond's supervisors at the same time), then regression toward the mean will constitute a threat. We can expect those initially low-scoring supervisors to score somewhat better on the posttest simply because of error-score variation (rather than any increase in their true scores on the test of supervisory skills). Their scores will improve because of this statistical artifact known as regression toward the mean.

As you can see, the influence of regression toward the mean depends on how we select trainees for a training program. If we choose them to participate on a more or less random basis, the threat to internal validity is reduced. **Nonrandom selection** introduces such threats, however. And unfortunately, selecting trainees on the basis of extremely high or low pretest scores is only one of several ways employees can be selected nonrandomly to participate in training. Another possibility is that Mr. Hammond might ask for volunteers among his first-level supervisors to undergo Dr. MacKeven's experimental training program. Alternatively, he might choose only more experienced supervisors for the "trial run" of the training program. If subordinates of the volunteer trainees file fewer grievances during the six-month period following training (a results criterion) because of the volunteers' high levels of enthusiasm and commitment, and *not* because of anything they learned during training, that is a clear threat to internal validity. If subordinates of the more experienced trainees file fewer grievances, that desirable outcome might be attributable to those trainees' more extensive experience on the job, and *not* to anything they learned during training. We suspect that you can imagine other ways in which differential selection of trainees can threaten the internal validity of a training program.

Experimental mortality does *not* refer exclusively to trainees who "shuffle off [their] mortal coil" (Shakespeare's *Hamlet*, act 3, scene 1) while training is in progress; it refers to situations where trainees drop out of training for any reason. Similar to statistical regression toward

the mean, if trainees withdraw on a more or less random basis, there is little or no threat to internal validity. If there is a pattern to their departures, however, we may have a problem. For example, if the "bottom" (poorest performing) 20 percent of Mr. Hammond's first-level supervisors quit the training program (and perhaps their jobs) while it is in progress, Dr. MacKeven might be led to conclude that her training program was effective when, in fact, it was not. The mean score of the "surviving" trainees on a posttest of their knowledge of supervisory responsibilities will be higher than the average of *all* the pretest scores because the lowest one-fifth of the pretest distribution is not represented in the posttest mean.

As you can see, there are many factors that individually can threaten the internal validity of a training program. Making matters worse, two or more can interact to undermine further our ability to assess accurately the effectiveness of training (Campbell & Stanley, 1963; Cook & Campbell, 1979). For example, maturation and differential selection can interact such that maturation occurs at different rates for younger and older trainees (Goldstein, 1993). In the context of Mr. Hammond's problem, Dr. MacKeven might see more improvement following a lengthy training program among younger trainees than among older trainees. Alternatively, differential selection of trainees might interact with the effect of testing such that younger, less experienced, and perhaps more enthusiastic supervisor-trainees might be more highly sensitized by (and thereby learn more from) a pretest than older, less enthusiastic trainees.

The value of the research designs for evaluating the effectiveness of training programs—discussed in the next section—depends on how successfully they reduce, control, or eliminate the threats to internal validity. At the risk of "getting just a bit ahead of ourselves," we'll tell you now that evaluation designs that include a *control group* as well as an *experimental group*, and designs that randomly assign trainees to these groups, do a better job minimizing these threats than do other types of designs. However, Dr. MacKeven must also contend with some threats to internal validity that cannot be controlled directly through rigorous experimental design, threats that arise primarily *because* the training program is undergoing evaluation (Cook & Campbell, 1979; Goldstein, 1993).

One threat emerges because employees who are assigned (randomly or otherwise) to a control group are often acquainted with other workers who are assigned to the group that receives the experimental training. Control-group subjects may benefit from the training indirectly by "learning through the grapevine," more formally known as **diffusion of treatments**. If a control group does receive "secondhand" training from friends in the experimental group, differences that might have characterized the two groups' performance following training could be reduced.

A second threat that cannot be controlled directly through experimental (evaluation) design is **compensatory equalization of treatments**. In this case, based on their (premature) faith in the value of the experimental training program, managers of employees assigned to the control group "go the extra mile" to provide these "deprived" employees with other benefits in order to make up for their exclusion from the group that actually receives the training. The additional benefits and considerations can also reduce any differences that might have emerged between the experimental and control groups as a result of training.

A third threat that defies direct experimental control is known as **compensatory rivalry**. This occurs when the behavior of control-group members varies from the norm in systematically different ways, based on their perceptions that they have been purposefully (and perhaps maliciously) excluded from the (favored) experimental group that receives training. They may band together to prove that they can perform as well as, or even better than, the group receiving training. This extra effort can reduce or eliminate any differences in learning, behavior, or re-

sults criteria that might otherwise have resulted from the training. Alternatively, members of the control group may become depressed and demoralized because they were not included in the group that receives training. This **resentful demoralization** can result in the control group obtaining lower scores on criterion measures, thereby artificially increasing otherwise moderate (or even nonexistent) differences between the control and training groups. As we stated earlier, none of this group of threats to internal validity can be controlled directly through experimental design procedures. Instead, "it will take other approaches—for example, working with the participants as part of the evaluation model so that they do not feel threatened by events such as being assigned to a control group" (Goldstein, 1993, p. 193).

External Validity Threats. Internal validity (that is, Does the training "work"?) is a prerequisite for **external validity**, where the concern is generalizing the internal validity of a training program across time, settings, and people. When organizations design, implement, and evaluate training programs, they are usually interested in using the programs over and over again. The concern is not only whether the training was effective for the trainees who participated in the experimental evaluation of the program but also whether the same training program will be effective for subsequent groups of trainees. The third of the three questions we posed at the beginning of this section addresses this concern. If Dr. MacKeven asks the control group to participate in the design of a training-evaluation "experiment," as Goldstein (1993) suggested, she must be confident that any training program that proves to be effective for the experimental group will also be effective for the control group when its turn comes. In addition to the program's internal validity, that confidence will depend upon the program's external validity.

Because external validity is basically a question of the generalizability of research (that is, evaluation) results (see Chapter 2), threats to external validity are factors or influences that undermine that generalizability (Cook & Campbell, 1979). Such threats emerge when the group of "experimental" trainees and the training they experience differ in one or more systematic ways from subsequent groups of trainees who experience the training program as a routine part of their employment. For example, just as a pretest (taken prior to training) can undermine a program's internal validity, it can also undermine external validity. If the pretest generates an unusually high level of interest in and sensitivity to the material being taught, subsequent groups of trainees who do not take the pretest (because the training program is no longer "on trial") may benefit less or not at all from the program. Fortunately, Dr. MacKeven can solve this problem relatively easily by administering the pretest to *all* subsequent groups of trainees, as if the pretest were a regular component of the training program.

Other threats to external validity are not so easily banished. Many are a function of the manner in which experimental trainees (that is, those who experience training during its evaluation phase) are chosen to participate in the program under investigation. Unless they are selected randomly from the entire population of employees who will eventually be trained, the danger exists that they will differ systematically from segments of that population in ways that will render the training more or less effective for either group. Suppose, for example, that Mr. Hammond picks one subsection of his Engineering Department to serve as "experimental" trainees, and the folks in that subsection just happen to be more (or less) intelligent or experienced, older or younger, or systematically different in any way from their colleagues in other Engineering subsections. It's quite possible that a training program that proves to be effective for this particular group of experimental trainees may not be similarly effective for their peers in other groups. Unfortunately, as we said in Chapter 2, *non*random selection tends to be the rule rather than the exception in organizational

field studies (such as training-evaluation studies) because managers often (correctly!) perceive random selection as too disruptive of ongoing organizational projects and activities.

Another process that we described earlier (Chapter 1) can also threaten a training program's external validity. Recall that the **Hawthorne effect** is a change in people's behavior that is attributable to their perceptions that they are being observed, that they are the focus of an unusual amount of special attention. Employees who participate in an experimental training program are vulnerable to this influence. If their scores on subsequent posttest criterion measures are affected by this attention, the data will probably not generalize to subsequent groups of trainees who participate in the program after the research "spotlight" has been turned off.

The **Pygmalion effect** represents another threat to external validity. Originally studied in classrooms (Rosenthal & Jacobson, 1968), it occurs when "experimental" trainees' performance on various criteria is inflated because of the trainer's strong expectations that the training will be effective (Eden & Shani, 1982). Trainers convey these expectations to trainees in a variety of ways (encouragment, increased individual attention, and so on) that can affect their scores on subsequent criterion measures in the manner of a self-fulfilling prophecy (Eden, 1990). If the trainer's enthusiasm is not maintained for later groups of trainees, their performance on the criteria might not measure up to that of their more highly encouraged predecessors.

Once again, we must acknowledge that two or more of the threats to external validity can combine or interact in ways that further undermine our efforts to generate accurate answers to the last of the three important questions listed above. For example, trainees who are selected nonrandomly when a training program is being evaluated might be affected by both Hawthorne and Pygmalion effects in highly complex ways.

Finally, we should point out that threats to external validity can vary as a function of the specific population of employees to which one wants to generalize training-evaluation results. Sometimes we might be interested in generalizing our findings only to other employees within the same organization. Other times we might be concerned with a training program's effectiveness in other organizations, or at least in other branches or offices of a large, parent organization. As you might suspect, generalization is riskier in the latter situations because of the greater likelihood of dissimilarities between "experimental" trainees and those to whom we wish to generalize our experimental results.

Now that you are aware of the many challenges that confront Dr. MacKeven as she sets out to develop an effective training program for Mr. Hammond's first-level supervisors, let's take a look at some of the research designs that are available for assessing a training program's effectiveness. In examining the designs, we'll pay particular attention to their capabilities for reducing or eliminating the threats to internal and external validity.

Research Designs for Evaluating Training

As we begin the process of evaluating a training program, it makes sense to think of it as a social science experiment. Although there are many ways to design such a training experiment, they all fall into one of three categories: (1) preexperimental designs, (2) experimental designs, and (3) quasi-experimental designs (Campbell & Stanley, 1963). We will present two examples from each of these categories, and describe the capabilities of each example to address the various threats to internal and external validity. Except where otherwise noted, we'll use the following symbols throughout our discussion of research/evaluation designs:

e = experimental training group

c = control group (receives no training)

T_1 = pretest (administered prior to training)

T_2 = posttest (administered after training)

X = the training program

R = random assignment of individuals to control and experimental groups

Preexperimental designs. The simplest of all designs is the **one-group posttest only** design:

$$X \longrightarrow T_2$$

As you can deduce, this design controls *none* of the threats to internal or external validity discussed above. In the absence of a pretest, it is impossible to interpret trainees' posttest scores in any meaningful way. Did they go up, down, or remain unchanged? Even if there is some change in the criterion construct (unknown to us) that occurs concurrently with training, this design reveals nothing about the source of that change. Is it attributable to history, to maturation, or to any of the other threats to internal validity? We cannot tell. And because this approach fails even to address the process by which trainees are selected, it offers no insight into the generalizability (that is, external validity) of the results. Perhaps the only value associated with data collected in this manner is their potential to provide useful descriptive information that might stimulate future hypotheses (or "hunches") concerning training effectiveness. As a self-contained source of evaluative information, however, the "one-group posttest only" design is virtually worthless.

A second preexperimental design that represents a slight improvement over the first is the **one-group pretest/posttest** design:

$$T_1 \longrightarrow X \longrightarrow T_2$$

Because trainees' pretest scores are now available, it becomes possible to compare them with trainees' scores on the posttest to determine whether any change has occurred. Further, by comparing the pretest scores of those who complete the training with the scores of those who drop out, we can learn something about the role of experimental mortality in explaining any difference between mean pretest and mean post-

Assessing the success of a training program is a challenging but crucial task.

test scores. In the absence of a control group, however, we cannot make any inferences about the influences of any other threats to internal validity. The manner in which trainees are selected is not addressed, so we are not in a position to say anything about external validity either. Unfortunately, when training programs are actually evaluated in applied settings, the process usually depends upon a preexperimental design that focuses exclusively on reaction or learning criteria (Goldstein, 1980; Saari et al., 1988; Tannenbaum & Yukl, 1992; Wexley, 1984; Wexley & Latham, 1981).

Experimental Designs. Experimental evaluation designs are characterized by the use of at least one control group (along with the experimental training group) as well as random assignment of employees to the two (or more) groups. These designs are "most strongly recommended" because they can control for many of the threats to internal and external validity (Campbell & Stanley, 1963, p. 13). When experimental de-

signs are used, the most popular is the **pretest/posttest control-group** design:

$$R_e \longrightarrow T_1 \longrightarrow X \longrightarrow T_2$$
$$R_c \longrightarrow T_1 \longrightarrow T_2$$

Both the experimental group (e) and the control group (c) take the pretest at the same time; later, after the experimental group has completed training and the control group has passed the same amount of time engaged in irrelevant activities, both groups take the posttest at the same time.

If we compare the two groups' changes in criterion scores from the pretest to the posttest (i.e., $T_2 - T_1$ for each group), we can infer whether any observed changes can be attributed to the training program or whether one or more of the following threats to internal validity is responsible: history, maturation, pretesting, instrumentation changes, or statistical regression toward the mean. Because trainees are randomly selected and assigned to either the training or the control group, these influences should affect both groups to the same extent (if they operate at all). Thus, if the *difference* between the training group's pre- and posttest scores exceeds the *difference* for the control group, we are in a reasonably safe position to conclude that the training program is responsible (and therefore effective).[1] Unfortunately, this design does *not* control any of the threats to internal validity associated with the act of intervention (for example, diffusion of training "through the grapevine," supervisors' efforts to compensate the "deprived" group, or a competitive or demoralized response on the part of control-group participants). As we stated earlier, these can be addressed only informally by the experimenter or evaluator.

Random selection can serve to minimize one of the threats to external validity: representativeness of the training-group sample. Because employees are sampled and assigned randomly to one of the two groups, there is no reason to anticipate any systematic differences between the groups, or between the groups and the larger population of workers from which the employees were chosen. However, pretesting and Hawthorne and Pygmalion effects can still undermine the external validity of the "pretest/posttest control-group" design. Nevertheless, taking all relevant factors into consideration (that is, financial and human-resources requirements), we concur with Campbell and Stanley's (1963) strong endorsement of this experimental design.

An even more powerful experimental design is the **Solomon four-group** design:

$$R_e \longrightarrow T_1 \longrightarrow X \longrightarrow T_2$$
$$R_c \longrightarrow T_1 \longrightarrow T_2$$
$$R_c \longrightarrow X \longrightarrow T_2$$
$$R_c \longrightarrow T_2$$

The four groups include one experimental group that is exposed to both the pretest and the training program, and *three* different control groups. The first control group takes the pretest but does *not* experience the training; the second control group is *not* exposed to the pretest but does participate in the training program; the third control group experiences neither the pretest nor the training but takes the posttest at the same time as the other three groups.

The Solomon four-group design controls the same threats to internal validity as the previous experimental design. In addition, the Solomon design allows us to determine the impact of any *interaction* effect based on taking the pretest *and* experiencing the training program. In fact, we can calculate the proportions of the overall pretest-to-posttest change in the experimental group's criterion scores that are attributable exclusively to the training program, exclusively to the pretest, exclusively to the pretest $\times$ training interaction, and to factors such as history, maturity, and other temporally related threats to internal validity.[2] Similar to the pretest/posttest control-group design, this design does *not* control any of the intervention-based threats to external validity except for sample representativeness, which is addressed through random selection and assignment of subjects to groups.

Despite its power, the Solomon four-group design has not been used very widely in organizational settings for at least two reasons. First, it makes demands on a company's human resources that are frequently excessive. Many organizations just do not have access to a sufficient number of potential trainees to create four groups of sufficient size to permit standard statistical analyses. Second, all of the details per-

---

[1] Although the details are beyond the scope of this book, we now know something about necessary sample sizes (numbers of participants in each group) for drawing conclusions about the effects of training on the basis of pretest/posttest difference scores or posttest scores by themselves (Arvey, Cole, Hazucha, & Hartanto, 1985).

[2] This requires systematic comparisons of the four groups' (pre- to posttest) difference scores on the criterion measure. The mean of the first two groups' pretest scores is used as an estimate of the mean pretest score that would have been obtained by the third and fourth (control) groups if they had taken the pretest. Because employees are assigned randomly to the four groups, there is no reason to assume any pretraining differences among them.

taining to these statistical analyses may not have been completely presented until recently (Braver & Braver, 1988). If these statistical questions have now been answered satisfactorily, and if organizations have access to the necessary sample sizes, there is little doubt that the Solomon four-group design represents the "cream of the crop" for evaluating the effects of personnel training programs.

Quasi-experimental Designs. Quasi-experimental research designs represent something of a compromise between preexperimental and experimental designs. As we stated earlier, preexperimental designs are almost never justifiable. On the other hand, experimental designs are often impractical in active, "real-life" organizations. Sometimes there are not enough people to assemble a control group in addition to the experimental training group; and sometimes it would be prohibitively disruptive to break up regular work groups and interrupt the organization's routine operations in order to assign workers to control and experimental groups in a random fashion. **Time-series** designs represent one such compromise:

$$T_1 \longrightarrow T_2 \longrightarrow T_3 \longrightarrow X \longrightarrow T_4 \longrightarrow T_5 \longrightarrow T_6$$

Rather than taking a single pretest and a single posttest, time-series designs ask trainees to take a series of pretests and a series of posttests. Each sequential pair of tests is separated by a more or less equal time interval. In this way, a single group of trainees acts as its own control group. In the time-series design shown above, any changes in mean criterion scores between pretests 1 and 2, between pretests 2 and 3, or between posttests 4 and 5, or posttests 5 and 6, are attributable to history, maturation, or some other time-dependent threat to internal validity. However, any change in criterion scores between the last pretest (T_3 in the example above) and the first posttest (T_4) is attributable to the training program (X) as well as these other temporal factors. If this latter difference ($T_4 - T_3$) is larger than all of the others,

we can conclude that the training program is responsible for at least a portion of that difference. Of course, time-series designs do not control for striking or profound historical events that might occur coincidentally during the interval that includes the training. Because there is no control group, however, time-series designs are less vulnerable to intervention threats to internal validity (for example, resentful demoralization). Threats to external validity are *not* controlled.

A second quasi-experimental design (from an almost infinitely large pool of creative, quasi-experimental approaches to training evaluation) is the **nonequivalent control-group** design:

$$T_1 \longrightarrow X \longrightarrow T_2$$
$$T_1 \longrightarrow T_2$$

In this situation we have a control group that is not exposed to the training program, but employees are *not* assigned to the two groups on a random basis. Instead, preexisting and intact groups within an organization serve as the experimental or training and the control groups. (Of course, this does not prevent us from determining which group receives training and which does not in a random fashion.) The major advantage of this design is its practicality. Use of intact groups is usually much less disruptive to ongoing organizational activities than is the creation of new groups for experimental and evaluative purposes. This often translates into less serious intervention-related threats to internal validity, and can inhibit contaminating Hawthorne effects on external validity. Further, the greater the similarities between the two intact groups (with respect to demographic and psychological variables), the greater the control for history, maturation, and instrumentation changes. As the groups become less similar, this design becomes more vulnerable to these threats to internal validity, and especially vulnerable to interactions between these factors and nonrandom selection of group members.

Summing Up. You can be confident that Dr. MacKeven will choose from among the true experimental designs or the quasi-experimental designs as she plans her strategy for evaluating a training program for Mr. Hammond's first-level supervisors. Even if the Director of Engineering permits *all* of his supervisors to participate in the training research, this amounts to only 11 or 12 trainees. Unless she can enlist cooperation and participation from other first-level supervisors in other departments or divisions of PPP, this small number of trainees will almost certainly preclude the use of any design that includes a separate control group. Under these circumstances, Dr. MacKeven might have to be satisfied with a time-series design in which a single group of trainees can serve as its own control group. On the other hand, if she *can* include additional supervisors in the research design, she might want to use either the true experimental pretest/posttest control-group design or the quasi-experimental nonequivalent control-group design, depending upon how much disruption in existing work groups is deemed tolerable. Unfortunately, the human-resources demands associated with the Solomon four-group experimental design will probably still exceed the pool of available first-level supervisors who might serve as trainees.

Additional Evaluation Considerations

Four other considerations merit Dr. MacKeven's attention as she devises a strategy to evaluate her training program for PPP's first-level supervisors. The first is a perspective that does *not* focus on changes in criterion scores. The second pertains to the legal context that has surrounded all personnel-related activities since passage of the Civil Rights Act in 1964. The third focuses on the ever-important "bottom line" of organizational activities, the dollars and cents of training. And the fourth, which we will mention only in passing here because it is treated in greater detail in Chapter 12, addresses three explanations or attributions for changes in criterion scores.

Content Evaluation. Rather than examining changes in criterion scores associated with training, several researchers have approached training evaluation by empirically comparing the actual content of a training program with the content of the job(s) held by prospective trainees (Bownas, Bosshardt, & Donnelly, 1985; Faley & Sundstrom, 1985; Ford & Wroten, 1984). Training programs that emphasize knowledge, skills, abilities, and other personal characteristics (KSAOs) that are thought to be important to successful job performance, and that employees are *un*likely to learn on the job, are more useful and defensible than programs that ignore those job-relevant KSAOs or programs that stress KSAOs that are *not* crucial for effective job performance. Dr. MacKeven can choose from among several numerical indices of the "overlap" between training content and the content of jobs, including Lawshe's (1975) Content Validity Ratio. Nevertheless, just as content-validation strategies in the context of personnel selection have been accorded "second-class status" relative to criterion-related validation strategies (EEOC, 1978), content-oriented approaches to training evaluation have suffered a similar fate relative to empirical studies of criterion-score changes. The reluctance of many I/O psychologists to embrace these content-oriented approaches stems from the undeniable fact that inclusion of appropriate training content does *not* guarantee that the job-relevant material will be effectively taught or learned. Thus, job-relevant content is necessary but not sufficient for successful training. Furthermore, we would expect the overlap between KSAOs demanded on the job and KSAOs addressed in training to be substantial if the training program were developed on the basis of careful needs assessment—organizational, person, and especially task and job analyses.

Legal Issues. A second alternative perspective on training-program evaluation addresses Title VII of the Civil Rights Act (1964) and the resultant EEOC guidelines, as well as the most recent Civil Rights Act of 1991, and speaks to the acceptability of organizational training in the context of this federal (as well as related state and local) legislation. A review of fair-employment cases in the training domain led to three conclusions concerning program evaluation in today's legal context (Russell, 1984).

1. If training performance is used as a criterion for validating scores on personnel-selection tests (paper-and-pencil tests, interviews, application blanks, and so on), the organization must be prepared to demonstrate the validity of training-performance scores as a *predictor* of subsequent performance on the job. U.S. circuit court rulings indicate that a wide variety of training criteria can be acceptable, including subjective ratings, if they are properly developed and administered.

2. It *can* be acceptable for training-program content to lead to disparate treatment of groups of employees, even if the groups are specifically protected by Title VII (for example, women, African Americans, Hispanics), if the treatment is based on superior abilities and progress during training demonstrated by members of nonprotected groups. This is especially so if the company has made constructive efforts to accommodate the needs of protected group members and if the trainer and training program enjoy a strong reputation. Following descriptions of how charges of differential treatment are typically examined in court and the outcomes of relevant cases, Russell (1984) concluded that "the courts give employers considerable latitude in [implementing] training programs . . . [and that the] courts appear [especially] reluctant to critically examine the content of on-the-job training" (pp. 269–270).

3. Courts have been specific about the conditions under which pay differences between women and men can be justified on the basis of training. Sex differences are *less* likely to be struck down by the courts when

- people are hired with the understanding that they will undergo training;
- the training program is described in written form;
- trainees are rotated through different departments or segments of a training program, and subsequently placed in jobs, on a *predetermined* schedule, and not on the basis of "organizational expediency";
- there is some "formal" component of the training (although this *may* include "self-study");
- there has been no obvious history of excluding women from the training program; and
- advancement following training follows a more or less predictable schedule and progresses toward relatively specific positions.

SOURCE: From "A Review of Fair Employment Cases in the Field of Training," by J. S. Russell, 1984, *Personnel Psychology*, 37, 261–276. Adapted by permission.

Utility. Just as the dollars-and-cents concept of utility has been applied to personnel selection and performance appraisal, so too has utility analysis been used to demonstrate the effectiveness of training. In a study that almost seems to have been designed for Dr. MacKeven and Mr. Hammond and their current challenge, Mathieu and Leonard (1987) modified the traditional utility formula so that it applies to training:

$$U = (T)(N)(d_t)(SD_y) - (N)(C)$$

where U = the dollar value of a training program,

T = the duration (in years) of a training program's effect on job performance,

N = the number of individuals trained,

d_t = the true mean difference in job performance between trained and untrained employees (expressed in standard deviation units),

SD_y = the standard deviation of job performance (in dollars) of the untrained group, and

C = the cost of training per individual.

They reported that a program for training supervisory skills demonstrated considerable dollar benefits. Even their most conservative estimates suggested that the net benefits of training 65 employees were approximately $34,000 at the end of just one year, $99,000 after five years, and $106,000 after 20 years. This kind of evaluative information is certain to capture the attention of organizational authorities who must defend expenditures devoted to training.

Alpha, Beta, and Gamma Changes. Our earlier discussion of pretest-to-posttest changes in criterion scores directly addressed only what Golembiewski, Billingsley, and Yeager (1976) referred to as **alpha changes**: changes in criterion scores that reflect numerical changes in the construct(s) of interest and nothing more (unless, of course, one or more of the threats to internal validity were operating). These researchers suggested that assessed changes in criterion scores might reflect one or two very different kinds of change, which they labeled "beta" and "gamma" changes.

Beta change refers to alterations in criterion scores that are attributable to *calibration* changes in the measuring instrument rather than to simple numerical changes in the construct we are trying to measure. For example, if Dr. MacKeven relied upon upper-level managers' ratings of Mr. Hammond's first-level supervisors' performance as a criterion for her training program and, as the training program was in progress, the managers changed their standards such that a rating of "average" now conveyed a higher level of performance than "average" did before the training program began, that would constitute beta change. Mean performance ratings following training might differ from mean ratings of the same individuals prior to training, but *not* because those workers actually altered their performance as a result of training. Instead, the change is attributable to raters who shifted their standards of what constitutes "good," "average," and "poor" performance. Although beta change may accompany instrumentation change, one of the threats to internal validity that we discussed earlier, instrumentation change is not a prerequisite to beta change. Standards can change even though (in our example) the rating scale does not.

An interesting innovation capable of illuminating beta change is known as "retrospective pretest ratings." In our example of upper-level managers rating the performance of first-level supervisors, this would take the form of asking the managers to rate the performance of the supervisors from three perspectives:

1. pretest ratings obtained before the supervisors began training;

2. posttest ratings obtained after the supervisors completed training; and

3. pretest ratings obtained *after* the supervisors completed training (that is, after the supervisors complete the training, managers are asked to rate the supervisors' performance *as it had been before the training*).

Discrepancies between the ratings from the same managers for the same supervisors obtained during steps 1 and 3 above suggest that beta change (that is, a change in standards or calibration of the measuring instrument) has occurred (Sprangers & Hoogstraten, 1989). Another method for estimating the relative magnitudes of alpha and beta changes focuses on correlations between criterion shifts and a focal (or "benchmark") variable (Van de Vliert, Huismans, & Stok, 1985).

Gamma change is even more fundamental. Either coincident with or because of the training program, a construct that constitutes a criterion of training performance can be reconceptualized. In our example, this might take the form of upper-level managers who basically redefine "effective first-level supervisor performance." Ideas might be added to or deleted from a prior definition, or the basic core of that prior definition might be altered. In either case, pretest-to-posttest changes in criterion scores reflect these altered constructs rather than any change in the construct as it was defined prior to training. Sociopolitical dynamics and technical innovations, among other forces, are capable of stimulating changes in the ways we define (and therefore measure) criterion constructs (for example, performance) (Golembiewski, 1986). A recent innovation for assessing gamma change (as well as alpha and beta changes) when a nonequivalent control-group design has been used is based on structural equation modeling, which we mentioned briefly in the appendix to Chapter 2 (Millsap & Hartog, 1988). We will refer to gamma and beta changes again in our discussion of organizational development (OD) research in Chapter 12. For now, we want you only to realize that observed changes in criterion scores might be far more complex than they appear to be.

Summing Up

We hope it is clear to you that evaluating the effectiveness of training programs is a very complex undertaking. It requires knowledge of criterion-development procedures and experimental research designs, as well as sensitivity to potential contaminating variables (threats to internal and external validity). Familiarity with content-based evaluation strategies and appreciation of the legal context in which training programs operate are also important. The complexity of the process is often enough to discourage trainers from evaluating the effectiveness of their programs. Others shun evaluation because they are already convinced of the effectiveness of their procedures: "If I'm spending so much time and money doing this, it *must* be effective!" Still others avoid evaluation because

they don't want to risk highlighting their own *in*effectiveness, thereby injuring their pride and perhaps jeopardizing their jobs. Although she might occasionally experience such qualms, Dr. MacKeven knows that the difficulties and risks inherent in training evaluation *never* justify reluctance or refusal to evaluate. Regardless of which training methods or procedures she adopts for Mr. Hammond's first-level supervisors, she will not fail to assess their effectiveness.

Training Methods and Procedures

Once training needs have been assessed and an evaluation plan developed, Dr. MacKeven must identify one or more training methods or procedures that can address those needs in ways that permit careful evaluation. The decision to include (or exclude) any particular procedure or technique should be guided by several factors: (1) the extent to which the technique relies on recognized principles and theories derived from the thousands of studies that have examined learning processes; (2) the suitability of the technique for helping trainees acquire the specific knowledge, skills, abilities, and other characteristics (KSAOs) identified during needs assessment; and (3) the practicality (that is, necessary expenditures of time or money) of the technique.

Research and theory pertaining to animal and human learning is extremely vast (Hilgard & Bower, 1966; Schwartz, 1984). We know that several basic principles can facilitate learning, especially in organizational settings. These include motivation and feedback (knowledge of results). Transfer of learning from the training environment to actual work settings is also very important. **Motivation** refers to the purposes or goals toward which behavior is directed, as well as to the intensity and persistence of that behavior (Steers & Porter, 1983). You will learn in Chapter 8 that "instrumentality" or "expectancy" theories are currently very popular among psychologists who study human motivation. A common assumption underlying the theories is that our behavior in any given situation is heavily influenced by our answer to the old, familiar question "What's in it for me?" Women and men engage in and repeat behaviors that lead to favorable outcomes and avoid behaviors that result in negative outcomes. Trainees who perceive that training will lead to positive work or career outcomes, and who therefore have more positive and constructive attitudes toward a training program, tend to learn more during training and are more likely to transform that learning into behavior change than trainees who see no such connection between training and desirable outcomes (Noe, 1986; Noe & Schmitt, 1986). Recent research suggests that trainees who are afforded some choice concerning training participation (and whose choices are honored) are more receptive to, and learn more during, training than do trainees who are denied such choice (Baldwin, Magjuka, & Loher, 1991; Hicks & Klimoski, 1987).

Feedback, or **knowledge of results**, is self-explanatory. As we stated during our discussion of performance appraisal in Chapter 4, it is usually *not* realistic to expect people to improve their behavior systematically unless they are informed about how they are (or are not) progressing toward a specific goal. We tend to prefer feedback that is specific (Liden & Mitchell, 1985), and recent evidence suggests that feedback provided on a more or less random schedule leads to greater learning and retention on certain kinds of tasks than does feedback that is provided on a more predictable schedule (Lee & Carnahan, 1990). Training procedures that generate such feedback for trainees will usually be more effective than methods that do not (McCullagh & Little, 1989). Adams (1987) offered an interesting review of how knowledge of results (as well as transfer of training, distribution of practice, and several other learning principles) affects human motor-skill learning.

Transfer of what one learns during training to the actual job setting is crucial. It will be no consolation to Mr. Hammond to know that his first-level supervisors performed magnificently during training if they are unable to transfer that success back to the engineering department. Specifically, **transfer of training** refers to generalization of material learned during training to job situations and settings, and maintenance of trained skills and knowledge over periods of time (Baldwin & Ford, 1988). Two aspects of training known to promote such transfer are identical elements and transfer through principles (Goldstein, 1993). **Identical elements** refers to the extent to which performance during training and performance back on the job both depend upon the same stimuli (visual displays, interpersonal situations, and so on) and require the same responses or behaviors. **Transfer through principles** occurs when trainees are able to apply general ideas or concepts learned during training to actual job situations; in this case, identical stimuli and responses are not necessary. Training programs that facilitate transfer through either or both of these dynamics are usually more effective than programs that ignore (or even inhibit!) such transfer.

Many training methods and procedures are available to us, and training experts have categorized them in a variety of ways. Does a given technique emphasize content (information), process (behavior), or both? Does the training occur at the workplace, or must trainees go off-site to receive training? Does training emphasize psychomotor skills, cognitive skills, social skills, or some combination of these? Because we see no particular superiority in any of these schemes, and because many training methods straddle the boundaries of these taxonomies, we will not use any of these classification schemes to structure the remainder of our discussion. Instead, we'll describe some of the most widely used and heavily researched training methods with an eye toward assessing each method's capacity to satisfy certain organizational requirements. We will also examine the methods in the context of Mr. Hammond's specific need to transform competent engineers into effective first-level supervisors.

Lectures, Films, and Videotapes

You are probably more familiar with lectures, films, and videotapes (especially lectures!) than any of the other training techniques, so we'll begin our discussion with them. After following our analysis in an area you know well, you will be in a better position to appreciate our assessments of methods and techniques with which you have little or no firsthand experience.

In their simplest forms, lectures, films, and videotapes rely on a one-way flow of information from trainer to trainee(s). Thus, these methods do a singularly poor job of incorporating the important learning principles we described earlier. Trainees' motivation is typically (and often erroneously) taken for granted; and individual differences among trainees' needs and abilities, which can have important effects on individual differences in learning (Ackerman, 1987), are often ignored. Further, these methods offer few or no rewards to trainees, and are sometimes even aversive (for example, lectures are sometimes terminally boring; some films are poorly produced or have poor soundtracks). Feedback is usually nonexistent. With the exceptions of lecturers who are willing and able to respond to listeners' questions, and some of the new interactive electronic technologies, these methods demand passivity from trainees and offer them no opportunities to assess how well they are learning the information being presented. Because very few people have jobs that entail listening to lectures or viewing films and tapes (Messrs. Siskel and Ebert notwithstanding), transfer of training through identical elements is extremely rare. Transfer through general principles remains possible, however.

On the positive side, these methods are usually very efficient. They permit transmission of vast amounts of information to large numbers of trainees in minimum amounts of time at minimal costs. Although some authors (Bass & Vaughan, 1966; Korman, 1971, 1977; McGehee & Thayer, 1961) and training directors (Carroll, Paine, & Ivancevich, 1972) have impugned the effectiveness of lectures, "there appears to be little empirical reason for the bias against the procedure" (Goldstein, 1993, p. 232). Some time ago, Zelko (1967) concluded that the "lecture remains a most important method of training, and it probably always will be" (p. 151). Given recent advances in audiovisual and cinematic technologies and skills, we think Zelko's prophecy extends to films and videotapes, too.

Dr. MacKeven might use lectures to orient Mr. Hammond's supervisors to the training program, and to present some basic information about the duties, responsibilities, and challenges inherent in first-level supervisory positions. Further, she might use films or videotapes as components of other training methodologies, such as computer-assisted instruction or behavioral role modeling (discussed below). It is very unlikely, however, that she will rely exclusively on any of these one-way forms of communication in her efforts to transform engineers into competent first-level supervisors.

Programmed and Computer-Assisted Instruction

Although some contend that teaching machines predate the nineteenth century (and may even go back to the first century A.D., when the "quintain" was developed in Imperial Rome to help gladiators learn to thrust rather than slash with their swords), the "testing machine" Pressey developed in the 1920s is often acknowledged as the first teaching machine (Benjamin, 1988; Buck, 1990; Pressey, 1950). The device presented a series of questions to students and informed them right away whether their answers were correct or incorrect (Lysaught & Williams, 1963). **Programmed instruction** (PI) today is characterized by

1. information that is presented in small units or "frames," each of which can vary in

size from a single sentence to several paragraphs;

2. trainees who respond actively to each frame;

3. trainees who are informed immediately concerning the correctness of their responses;

4. trainees who make relatively few errors because each frame contains only a limited amount of information;

5. programs that maximize learning through careful consideration of learning objectives, the nature of the material to be learned, and prospective trainees' characteristics and abilities; and

6. trainees who work through the program independently, each at his or her own speed

SOURCE: From Bass & Vaughan, 1966; Fry, 1963; Goldstein, 1993.

An example of a program that Goldstein (1993) adapted from a U.S. Civil Service Commission document is reproduced in Table 7.1. Because trainees progress through these items in a rigid, step-by-step fashion, this is known as a *linear* program. *Branching* programs are more

TABLE 7.1   Sample of a Linear Program

	1. You are now beginning a lesson on programmed instruction. The principle of *self-pacing* as used in programmed instruction allows each trainee to work as slowly or as fast as he chooses. Since you can control the amount of time you spend on this lesson, this program is using the principle of self-_____ .
Pacing	2. People naturally learn at different rates. A program that allows each trainee to control his own rate of learning is using the principle of _____ .
Self-pacing	3. If a self-pacing program is to be successful, the information step size must be small. A program that is self-pacing would also apply the principle of small _____ .
Steps	4. The average trainee will usually make correct responses if the correct-size step of information is given. This is utilizing the principle of small _____ .
Steps	5. A program that provides information in a step size that allows the trainee to be successful is applying the principle of _____ .
Small steps	6. A trainee knows the material being taught but has to wait for the remainder of the class. What programming principle is being violated? _____ .
Self-pacing	7. Two principles of programmed learning are: (1) _____ . (2) _____ .

1. *Self-pacing*
2. *Small steps*

Note: For practical reasons, the frames are arranged on one page rather than on succeeding pages. The answers should be covered until the preceding frame has been answered.

SOURCE: Adapted from U.S. Civil Service Commission (1970). *Programmed Instruction: A Brief Evaluation of Its Development and Current Status.* Washington, DC: U.S. Government Printing Office.

complex because they can either usher trainees directly through from start to finish, or move them ahead (to more difficult material) or behind (to simpler material) depending upon the correctness of their responses and the nature of any mistakes they make.

Computer-assisted instruction (CAI) takes the basic characteristics of PI and adds the power and flexibility inherent in our rapidly expanding computer technology. The increasing popularity of personal computers and office work stations has rendered this technique even more accessible in homes and offices. Trainees can use a computer terminal as an infinitely patient tutor for drill-and-practice sessions on a given topic, or they can utilize the immense potential of this technology by interacting with it in dialogue form. A brief excerpt of a geography lesson in the form of such a dialogue appears in Table 7.2 (Collins & Adams, 1977).

PI and especially CAI make excellent use of several learning principles discussed earlier. First, trainees' motivation levels are often high because they find the procedure to be interesting or even fun. Second, they receive immediate feedback (which is usually positive) concerning the accuracy of their responses. Third, they are permitted to progress through the material at their own pace. Unfortunately, transfer of training is not guaranteed, except in cases where CAI is used to train people to use computer terminals, or when a computer is used to increase

TABLE 7.2   An Annotated Excerpt of the Dialogue Between Tutorial Mode of SCHOLAR and a Student

Dialogue	Annotated Comments
WHAT IS CHILE? *COUNTRY IN SOUTH AMERICA* VERY GOOD	This is the most important property of Chile. (A tutor would suppress it on the assumption that the student knows the answer.) In evaluating the answer, it looks for "country," ignores the rest.
CORRECT OR INCORRECT? CHILE IS IN NORTHERN SOUTH AMERICA. *INCORRECT*	Location is the next most important attribute under Chile.
YOU ARE CORRECT. CHILE IS IN SOUTHWESTERN SOUTH AMERICA.	The student answers correctly, so SCHOLAR will go deeper into Location.
THE EASTERN BORDERING COUNTRY OF CHILE IS— *I DON'T KNOW* THE ANSWER IS: ARGENTINA.	This is the most important Bordering-Country of Chile.
THE BOUNDARY OF THE EASTERN BORDERING COUNTRIES OF CHILE IS THE ANDES. THE NORTHERN BORDERING COUNTRY OF CHILE IS PERU. THE NORTHEASTERN BORDERING COUNTRY IS BOLIVIA.	Since the student has missed the question, SCHOLAR presents some related Bordering-Countries.

Note: The student's inputs are between asterisks.

SOURCE: From "Comparison of Two Teaching Strategies in Computer-Assisted Instruction," by A. Collins and M. J. Adams, *Contemporary Educational Psychology, 2,* 133–148. Copyright © 1977 by Academic Press, Inc. Reprinted by permission of the authors.

Computer-assisted instruction is more accessible than ever before. (Courtesy of Pat Knight)

the realism of simulator training (which we discuss below).

Although research results have not always been consistent (Leib, Cusack, Hughes, Pilette, Werther, & Kintz, 1967), there is some consensus today that these autoinstructional techniques can present a given amount of material in ways that are more time-efficient (for trainees and trainers, at least during actual training sessions) than can other training methods (for example, lectures). However, there seem to be no meaningful differences in the achievement scores (learning criteria) of trainees who are exposed to autoinstructional rather than more conventional training methods (Goldstein, 1993; Wexley, 1984). Preparation of PI and

(again, especially) CAI packages can be extremely time-consuming and very expensive, however.

Given these drawbacks, and because other training methods show far more promise for training first-level supervisors, Dr. MacKeven will probably eschew both autoinstructional techniques. Of course, she might subsequently change her mind if her training procedures for Mr. Hammond's engineers turn out to be very successful and she is inundated with requests from other managers throughout PPP to train their supervisors, too. In that event, based on the finding that "there are few differences in the jobs of first-line supervisors regardless of technology or function" (Dowell & Wexley, 1978, p. 563), as well as data suggesting that CAI training is no less effective when trainees work in pairs (Dossett & Hulvershorn, 1983), she might save time in the long run by developing autoinstructional packages.

Conferences, Case Studies, and Sensitivity Training

Conferences, case studies, and sensitivity training are similar training methods in that each relies heavily on verbal communication between trainers and trainees, and among trainees. A **conference** is a "carefully planned meeting with a specific purpose and goals" (McGehee & Thayer, 1961). It is particularly useful when trainees must learn and understand conceptual material, or when specific attitudes are to be developed or modified. Thus, conferences are especially well suited for providing supervisory training (Busch, 1949).

Case studies typically present trainees with written descriptions of specific organizational problems. Each trainee is usually asked to analyze each problem individually, and to prepare one or more solutions based on the material to be learned as well as certain assumptions about available resources (human, financial, physical) and existing organizational, economic, and legal conditions. Trainees then meet as a group to present and discuss their solutions and, with the assistance of the "trainer," to identify the basic principles that underlie the cases. Because many cases are amenable to more than one solution, the trainer must often resist the urge to present a *preferred* solution as the *only* viable option.

Sensitivity training (also known as laboratory training, T-group training, encounter-group training, and so on) consists of face-to-face interactions among individuals under the following conditions and expectations:

1. the "here and now" is the primary concern;
2. feelings and emotions are not only appropriate topics for conversation and analysis, but the primary focus of the training;
3. feedback and analysis concerning individuals' self-disclosing statements occur frequently; and
4. each individual trainee is free to decide when and how to respond to that feedback (Blumberg & Golembiewski, 1976; Goldstein, 1993).

Sensitivity training is designed to promote self-awareness and sensitivity to others' needs and styles of communication, to teach listening skills and the basic principles that guide group dynamics, and to provide a "psychologically safe" environment in which people can experiment with different styles of social interaction (Campbell, Dunnette, Lawler, & Weick, 1970). A recent meta-analysis of 126 studies revealed that laboratory training combined with team training was effective for altering attitudes and promoting satisfaction (Neuman, Edwards, & Raju, 1989).

The role of the trainer or "leader" is crucial to the success of each of these methods. Incompetence here can lead to (1) poorly organized conferences that fail to convey necessary information in ways that facilitate learning and retention; (2) case studies that lead trainees to believe either that there is *no* solution to the organizational dilemma presented, or that the trainer's solution is the *only* acceptable solution

to the problem; or (3) sensitivity groups that not only fail to promote constructive self-awareness but create or exacerbate emotional difficulties for trainees. Of course, the trainer's skills can also affect trainees' motivation levels and the extent to which constructive feedback is made available to them.

Perhaps the most consistent criticism leveled against conferences, case studies, and sensitivity training concerns transfer of training back to the work site. Information gleaned during a conference or skills derived from a sensitivity group can prove to be irrelevant or even damaging if trainees return to organizational environments that do *not* support the use of that knowledge or the practice of those skills. The principles derived from case studies do not always generalize well to trainees' "real-life" organizational situations. Here again, the trainer occupies a central role (Goldstein, 1993; Hinrichs, 1976; McGehee & Thayer, 1961).

Given the inherent dangers and ambiguous goals, it is unlikely that Dr. MacKeven will create sensitivity groups among Mr. Hammond's first-level supervisors. However, she might decide to plan some case studies and conferences to help the engineers learn some of the basic principles that underlie effective supervision and grow more comfortable in their new role. If her objectives are sufficiently specific and she is competent in her own role as "leader" or discussion facilitator, such structured face-to-face exercises can make important contributions to the training of inexperienced first-level supervisors.

Simulations

Simulations are approximations of real-life situations and events. Training simulations can take one of two basic forms: (1) those that rely on a piece of equipment, a machine, or a set of physical tools; and (2) those that replicate a social or interpersonal situation. The purpose of simulation is to reproduce an actual work setting or situation in a way that places it under the control of a trainer or researcher (Thornton

Flight simulators are becoming increasingly complex and realistic.

& Cleveland, 1990). Such control facilitates timely and constructive feedback concerning trainees' performance, and permits the trainer to control the stimuli that confront trainees, which in turn can affect trainees' levels of motivation. Transfer of training can be expected to increase as the physical and/or psychological realism of the simulator increases. In addition, simulation is usually less expensive and less dangerous than training employees in actual work settings.

Among the better known machine simulators are flight simulators for training airplane pilots. The trainer can create all sorts of routine and hazardous situations that afford trainees the luxury of learning proper responses under controlled conditions that do not actually threaten life and limb or jeopardize extremely expensive equipment. The addition of sophisticated computer technology has rendered such simulators extremely realistic (visually, kinesthetically, and so on). However, many equipment simulators are relatively simplistic. For

example, factories often expose new employees to **vestibule training**, where they learn to operate a basic piece of industrial machinery away from the confusion and noise of an actual assembly line or factory floor. Regardless of how technologically simple or complex a machine simulator might be, the key issues are the trainer's control of the situation and stimuli that confront the trainee, and the fidelity (realism) of the approximation to real life. Despite the technological advances made possible through computer and other technologies, we can never be absolutely certain about how seriously trainees take these contrived reproductions of reality. Even in a multimillion-dollar flight simulator, trainees still know that the situation is "make believe" and that even if they "crash" into the side of a mountain, they'll still be able to go home to dinner and a nice warm bed later on.

Social or interpersonal simulations come in a variety of forms. The most widely known is probably **role-playing**, where trainees "act out" various job-related situations and encounters. This method can be very effective when trainees are willing and able to assume their assigned roles, and to suspend disbelief and behave as if they were *really* in their regular work settings (Campbell et al., 1970; Goldstein, 1993). It is relatively easy for trainers to provide timely and useful feedback to trainees. The fidelity of the role-play situation and the accuracy of the feedback will influence the extent to which such training will transfer back to trainees' actual job sites. Some interesting variations of standard role-play situations include (1) reverse role-playing, where trainees whose jobs place them in situations involving personal conflicts (for example, with supervisors, peers, or subordinates; with the public) assume the other person's role in order to appreciate a different perspective; and (2) multiple role-playing, where a large number of trainees are divided into teams, each of which acts out a specific situation and then compares and discusses the outcomes with members of the other teams.

Other popular forms of nonmachine simulation include business games and case studies (discussed earlier in this section). **Business games** typically require trainees to make decisions in contrived situations that approximate normal business environments. Trainees receive almost immediate feedback on the effect(s) of their decisions, and then proceed to make subsequent decisions on the basis of that feedback. Once again, advances in computer technology have rendered business games more realistic and more fun.

Behavioral Role Modeling. By far the most popular social simulation among practitioners and researchers is a set of procedures based on Bandura's (1969, 1977) social learning theory; they are collectively known as **behavioral role modeling**. Social learning theory suggests that observation, modeling, and reinforcement (that is, rewards, both direct and vicarious) play important roles in modifying human behavior. Behavioral role modeling is a set of training procedures based on these concepts. This approach

is extremely well suited for training supervisors to improve their interpersonal skills (Goldstein & Sorcher, 1974). Most behavior-modeling procedures include the following components:

1. *modeling*, during which trainees observe one or more other people engaging in desired behaviors, and experience vicarious reinforcement by watching the model receive rewards for his or her behaviors;

2. *retention* processes, during which trainees encode those observations for later recall;

3. *rehearsal*, when trainees actually practice the observed desired behaviors themselves;

4. *social reinforcement*, where the trainer and other trainees reward individuals for accurately imitating the previously observed model; and

5. *transfer of training*, when trainees experiment with the recently learned behaviors in their actual work settings, and then report their successes and failures back to the training group at a later date (Mann & Decker, 1984).

Thus, behavioral role modeling specifically attends to trainees' motivation, to feedback or knowledge of results, and to transfer of training back to the job site. It goes beyond traditional "behavior modification" techniques (see, for example, Haynes, Pine, & Fitch, 1982; Luthans & Kreitner, 1985) by stressing the important contributions of observation and vicarious reinforcement (over and above actual practice and direct reinforcement) to learning.

Available research evidence indicates that Goldstein and Sorcher's (1974) behavioral role-modeling procedures can improve first-level supervisors' performance in a variety of circumstances (Decker, 1979; Kraut, 1976; Latham & Saari, 1979; Porras & Anderson, 1981; Wexley, 1984). A particularly intriguing application was the inclusion of behavioral role modeling in the InterFace Project, an effort to improve interpersonal relations among black employees and their "mostly white" supervisors in a South African pharmaceutical company (Nossel, 1982; Sorcher & Spence, 1982). Of course, behavioral role modeling is not limited to supervisory training. It has been used effectively to improve the acquisition of computer software skills and feelings of self-efficacy (Gist, Rosen, & Schwoerer, 1988; Gist, Schwoerer, & Rosen, 1989), to raise levels of intrinsic motivation (Cellar & Wade, 1988), and to affect job performance in numerous other contexts and situations. Recent research has focused on *cognitive* (as opposed to overt behavior) modeling, which directly acknowledges employees' cognitive schemata or scripts (which can be assessed by asking participants to "think out loud") that describe specific sets of procedures for accomplishing specific work tasks (Gioia & Manz, 1985; Gist, 1989; Manz & Sims, 1986). Other empirical efforts have been devoted to "fine tuning" some of the basic components of behavioral role modeling. For example, it seems that coding procedures (see 2 above) generated by the trainees themselves might be superior to coding schemes developed by trainers for generating improved job performance after short intervals of time (Hogan, Hakel, & Decker, 1986).

Thus, there is little debate today about the potential usefulness of behavioral role modeling in a variety of training contexts. Given the encouraging empirical evidence, and because behavioral role modeling directly addresses important issues pertaining to trainees' motivation, feedback, and transfer of training, this method will certainly occupy a central position in Dr. MacKeven's plans for responding to Mr. Hammond's and the Engineering Department's needs. In fact, behavioral role modeling might be the cornerstone of PPP's training program for first-level supervisors (and, perhaps, higher-level managers and executives, too).

On-the-Job Methods

A final category of training procedures that merit our attention are those that take place at the work site while trainees are performing their work tasks. These **on-the-job training (OJT)** techniques include orientation sessions, coaching, apprenticeships, mentoring, job rotation, and performance appraisal. **Orientations** are common during the first few days of employment. Human-resources representatives and/or supervisors typically inform new employees about company policies, benefits, and standard operating procedures, as well as how their jobs fit into the organization's overall mission. The sessions usually take the form of a "lecture," but written and audiovisual materials are often used to supplement oral presentations. As long as trainees are not inundated with too much information too rapidly, most new hires report such sessions to be useful.

Coaching consists of periodically providing employees with feedback and advice concerning their job performance. Immediate supervisors and coworkers are the most common sources of coaching (Kram & Isabella, 1985). **Apprenticeships**, which can "last anywhere from two to five years, . . . combine on-the-job instruction together with [many hours] of classroom and shop instruction" (Wexley & Latham, 1991). They are used to help women and men in skilled trades (for example, bricklayers, carpenters, electricians, painters, plumbers) develop into competent "journeymen" through lengthy and intense relationships with other, more experienced workers who can teach them the skills they will need to succeed at their chosen trades (Latack, Josephs, Roach, & Levine, 1987).

In management and professional circles, senior men and women who take newcomers "under their wings" are known as **mentors**. A substantial amount of evidence suggests that having a mentor can facilitate successful psychosocial outcomes and lead to more frequent promotions, higher incomes, and greater satisfaction with pay and benefits (Dreher & Ash, 1990; Hennig and Jardim, 1977; Kanter, 1977; Stumpf & London, 1981; Whiteley, Dougherty, & Dreher, 1991). Although there are those who downplay the importance of gender differences during the formation of mentoring relationships and the effects of such differences on mentor-protégé relationships (Dreher & Ash, 1990; Schuckman, 1987), others emphasize the difficulties that confront women at each stage of their professional development and factors that specifically inhibit women's success in developing mentoring relationships (Noe, 1988a; Noe, 1988b; Primack & O'Leary, 1989). Models of mentor-protégé relationships, based on available empirical literature, that will facilitate future investigations are now becoming available (Hunt & Michael, 1983).

Job rotation consists of "giving trainees a series of job assignments in various parts of the organization for a specific period of time" (Wexley & Latham, 1991) or assigning trainees to different work stations or pieces of equipment on rotating schedules. This method not only serves to "cross-train" employees for a number of different jobs but offers them an overview of how their shop, department, or the organization as a whole operates. We'll have more to say about job rotation in Chapter 12. Finally, as you learned in Chapter 4, one of the purposes of **performance appraisal** is to provide employees with both formal and informal feedback concerning their relative strengths and weaknesses on their jobs. From that perspective, the performance-appraisal process can be construed as an institutionalized form of coaching and, as such, a form of OJT.

The obvious advantage that accrues to OJT methods pertains to transfer of training. With the exception of the classroom component of apprenticeships, these techniques require no transfer at all. Training occurs precisely where it must be applied. OJT methods also incorporate strong feedback components, especially coaching, mentoring, and performance appraisal. Unfortunately, many OJT methods pay little or no attention to trainees' (or trainers') motivation. In the absence of formal, off-site training experiences, trainees sometimes draw the demoralizing conclusion that the organization is unwilling

to devote time or resources to developing their job-related skills and knowledge. Trainers are often expected to provide OJT to new employees in the absence of any incentives or reinforcement. Sometimes coaching and other OJT techniques actually lead to lower levels of productivity and fewer rewards for those designated as "trainers" who may have no ambition or experience in that role, and who must take time and energy away from their own productive behaviors to help their less experienced colleagues. When OJT is used, the role of "trainer" should be included in the job descriptions of those who are asked to assume those responsibilities, and they should be rewarded accordingly.

As you saw in Chapter 4, Peter's Pan Pizza is committed to improving its performance-appraisal procedures, so some OJT is already in progress. Dr. MacKeven will probably also find that coaching and (especially) developing constructive mentor-protégé relationships can make important contributions to a training program that can transform Mr. Hammond's engineers into first-rate, first-level supervisors.

Chapter Summary

Training consists of systematic procedures that are designed and implemented by organizations to effect changes in employees that will lead to improved job performance. Comprehensive needs analysis is a crucial prerequisite to training. Only by explicitly acknowledging or discovering an organization's overall goals and constraints (that is, organization analysis), by defining how specific jobs and associated tasks contribute to those goals (that is, job or task analysis), and by assessing the capabilities of current employees or applicants to perform those tasks (that is, person analysis) can we discover whether training is necessary and what it must accomplish. Careful needs assessment also points to the kinds of criteria that will be appro-

INTEROFFICE MEMO

To: R. Hammond,
          Director, Engineering

From: J. A. MacKeven,
          Human Resources Coordinator

Subject: Supervisory Training

I share your concerns about training supervisors within PPP. My assistant, Sandy Roberts, will soon prepare an overall plan for determining your exact training needs. Once we know what they are, we will be able to design and implement specific training methods and procedures that can address those needs, and devise an evaluation strategy that can tell us whether our training is bringing about the changes we desire. I asked Sandy to concentrate her initial efforts in Engineering but because your situation is not unique, she will investigate the possibility of including supervisors from other PPP departments in her plans.

Although I don't want to forecast the exact outcomes of Sandy's inquiries, I strongly suspect that a set of procedures known as "behavioral role modeling" will play a vital role in any program we might develop to train first-level supervisors. This approach will necessitate a great deal of cooperation from not only "target" supervisors but also their managers and, perhaps, their subordinates, too. It is therefore very important to enlist support from Mr. Nathanson, Vice President for Facilities, at the very beginning of our project.

You'll hear from Sandy very soon, as she initiates the needs-assessment phase of the project. Feel free to contact me with your concerns or questions at any time.

priate for evaluating the effectiveness of training. Although reaction and learning criteria are frequently used, only behavior and results criteria can reveal the extent to which trainees actually use their training in the work setting. To evaluate a training program is to answer three questions: (1) Did a change occur? (2) If so, was the training program responsible? (3) If so, will that change occur again with a new group of trainees?

Answers to the first two questions, which reflect a program's internal validity, can be contaminated by history, maturation, pretesting, instrumentation changes, trainee selection and mortality, and statistical regression toward the mean. Answers to the third question, which reflects a program's external validity, can be confounded by pretesting, trainee selection, and Hawthorne and Pygmalion effects. True experimental designs, which incorporate control groups and random selection and assignment of individuals to those groups, can minimize and even eliminate many of these threats to valid program evaluation. Quasi-experimental designs can also be informative, but preexperimental designs tell us very little about a training program's effectiveness.

A variety of methods and procedures are currently available to organizational trainers. These include techniques based on "one-way" communication (for example, lectures, films, videotapes), autoinstructional techniques (for example, programmed and computer-assisted instruction), discussion-based techniques (for example, case studies, conferences, sensitivity groups), simulations (both machine-based and interpersonal), and on-the-job procedures (for example, coaching, mentoring, performance appraisal). Particular methods should be used because they can address identified needs, and because they can motivate trainees, provide them with feedback, and facilitate transfer of

training. Behavioral role modeling does an especially good job of incorporating all of these basic learning principles into a training regimen.

Review Questions and Exercises

1. What do you expect Sandy Roberts to learn during her organizational, job and task, and person analyses in PPP's Engineering Department (see p. 240)? How are the three kinds of information logically interrelated?

2. Based on your response to Question 1, what type(s) of criteria should be used to evaluate training? Explain your answers.

3. Given your responses to Questions 1 and 2, describe the research design(s) that can promote sound evaluation of training effectiveness in this situation. Explain your answers.

4. Which threats to internal and/or external validity will be eliminated or controlled by your choice of design(s)? Which threats will remain? For each threat you mention, explain how your choice of evaluation design specifically addresses that potentially contaminating factor.

5. Describe the rationale that underlies "content" approaches to training-program evaluation. What are the weaknesses inherent in these approaches?

6. Discuss each of the specific training methods or procedures presented in this chapter with respect to how well or poorly it addresses each of the "person" needs you identified in your response to Question 1 above. How practical is each method in the context of PPP's current situation?

CHAPTER 8

Work Motivation

LEARNING POINTS

After studying this chapter, you should

- ❑ know the three functions of motivation, and be able to evaluate motivation theories in terms of how they address these functions;

- ❑ be able to explain the factors that limit the usefulness of the motivation construct;

- ❑ be able to define the concept of need and explain how it has been used in various theories to explain work motivation;

- ❑ be able to define the components of expectancy theory and explain how, according to the theory, they combine to predict motivational force;

- ❑ be able to describe the concept of equity and explain how it might influence work behavior;

- ❑ be able to list the factors that are necessary for effective goal setting;

- ❑ understand how operant conditioning is used in work organizations;

- ❑ be able to define self-efficacy and explain how it can affect workers' motivation; and

- ❑ be able to evaluate the research results that pertain to each of the motivation theories discussed in this chapter.

MARGARET RUSSELL HAS PRESENTED Dr. MacKeven with an apparent problem in employee motivation. Ms. Russell believes that the interns in her department can perform the work given to them, but most have not lived up to their potential. All organizations face this type of problem from time to time. In some cases, employees with good work records have unexplained lapses in performance; in other situations, cooperative workers develop "bad attitudes" and appear to become lazy. Of course, workers who were once "problem employees" sometimes begin to work harder, produce more, and cooperate with their coworkers. To explain why workers behave in the ways they do, and to help organizations improve their employees' performance, I/O psychologists have spent a great deal of time studying work motivation. In this chapter we examine work motivation, some of the theories developed to explain motivation, and some of the procedures designed to improve motivation.

A Definition of Motivation

Motivation has traditionally referred to the processes by which people are moved to engage in particular behaviors. In a work setting—such as Peter's Pan Pizza—motivation is often used as

INTEROFFICE MEMO

To: J. A. MacKeven,
        Human Resources Coordinator

From: Margaret Russell,
        Director of Consumer Research

For about eight years now Consumer Research, as well as several other units in the Marketing Division, has sponsored a number of interns each summer. These people are generally advanced undergraduates or graduate students in business or the social sciences from colleges and universities in the Rocky Mountain area. I usually have students with some training and experience in either research design or data analysis. The stated purpose of the program, according to Bill Ryan, the vice president of marketing, is to provide support to students interested in the marketing field, while providing Peter's Pan Pizza with qualified, short-term help in technical fields.

Although the program sounds good on paper, I have consistently had problems with the interns in our department. Occasionally we get a dedicated, hard-working student, but most simply don't seem very interested in their jobs. We do all that we can to make sure that we select the best candidates, and in fact we had Personnel develop a biodata-based selection program for interns two years ago. I am convinced that these students are, for the most part, capable of performing the tasks we give them, but they just aren't putting in the effort. I would like to discuss this matter with you further, and see if there is anything that can be done to salvage this interm program.

an explanation for workers' productivity, effort, and attendance. We often hear that some people are "highly motivated" and that others "lack motivation." However, this common use of the term does not suggest *why* some people work harder or are more conscientious about their attendance. To study work motivation scientifically and develop theories that will enable us to understand and improve it, we need a more precise definition.

Although several definitions of work motivation have emerged over the years, most share three components that collectively represent commonly accepted aspects of motivation: **Motivation** is that which *energizes, directs,* and *sustains* behavior (Steers & Porter, 1991). Let's examine each component of this definition.

The *energizing* function of motivation is its most basic element. Motivation is a state that causes people to act, that drives them to engage in particular behaviors. Motivated people are compelled to do something; unmotivated (or less-motivated) people do not feel such a compulsion. According to motivation theories, people would start few tasks, and complete even fewer of them, without this energization.

The *directing* function of motivation implies that motivated behavior has a purpose: achieving specific goals. Motivated people know what they want to accomplish and engage in behavior to help themselves achieve their goals. Less motivated people may be unsure of exactly what they want to accomplish, which certainly lowers their chances of getting anything done.

The *sustaining* function of motivation explains why we persist in our efforts to achieve our goals. It also explains why people sometimes abandon a particular approach to a problem or abandon the problem altogether if they don't succeed immediately. Motivation theories suggest that highly motivated people will sustain their goal-directed behavior longer than those who are less motivated. This does not mean, however, that highly motivated people will hesitate to drop a course of action that is not working. Rather, under conditions of high motivation, a person is likely to try a new, potentially more successful approach to the problem. However, under low motivation the goal may be abandoned after initial failure.

A general model of the motivation process that is consistent with this definition was presented years ago (see Figure 8.1). The source of motivation is a "state of disequilibrium," or a sense of imbalance. This can be a person's need, desire, expectation, or some combination of these things. For example, a person may feel a need for greater control over her work life or a desire to move to a better climate, or she may expect that being late for work just one more time will result in being fired. As you can see, the feeling of disequilibrium is an uncomfortable experience, and thus provides the energizing component of motivation.

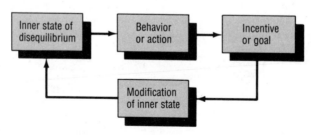

FIGURE 8.1
A General Model of Motivation
Source: From M. D. Dunnette and W. K. Kirchner, *Psychology Applied to Industry*, Copyright © 1965, p. 125. Adapted by permission of Prentice-Hall, Inc., Englewood Cliffs, NJ.

The feeling of disequilibrium is accompanied by an anticipation that certain behaviors will satisfy the needs and desires or fulfill the expectations. The anticipation provides the directive, or goal-oriented, function of motivation. Behavior is sustained, according to this model, by a *feedback* process. A worker engages in certain behaviors to achieve the goal of reducing the inner state of disequilibrium. By seeing the results of these behaviors, the worker can judge whether or not he or she is closer to achieving the goal. Based on this judgment, the person can continue the current behavior, change the behavior, or, if the activation is weak or the goal unclear, give up.

Limitations to Motivation as an Explanation for Behavior

Although motivation is meant to be a general explanation for behavior, it is not sufficient to explain *all* behavior. There are several variables that do not easily fit within the motivation framework. In certain cases, these variables can affect the relevance of motivation for understanding work behavior and performance.

Motivation and Ability. If you have taken a few psychology courses, you have probably heard that performance is a function of both motivation and ability. This means that to perform a task successfully, a person must be motivated to perform the task *and* have the skills, knowledge, and experience to perform. If either factor is missing, successful performance is unlikely. As an example, consider the situation in PPP's Consumer Research Department described by Ms. Russell. Ms. Russell believes that the student interns are uninterested in their work and are not putting much effort into their jobs, which may seem to be a clear-cut case of poor motivation. Let's assume, however, that the interns' poor performance is due to an inability to perform the tasks required in their jobs. They might, for example, be expected to analyze data

from marketing research, but their college programs have not prepared them for this assignment. Therefore, once the interns find out that they lack the skills to perform the task, they see no point in trying further. In this case, the solution would involve improving selection or training procedures, thereby ensuring that interns have the necessary skills, rather than trying to increase motivation.

Individual Differences in Motives. One important way in which people differ is in the goals they pursue. If everyone were motivated to achieve the same goals, managers would have a much easier time getting workers to perform well. The fact that workers have different goals means that efforts to increase the motivation of one worker may have no effect, or even a negative effect, on another worker's motivation. Further, if management makes incorrect assumptions about the workers' goals, efforts to increase motivation may be useless. For example, in PPP's Consumer Research Department, some of the students may have sought their internships because they believe that simply having the experience greatly increases the chance of receiving a job offer. Consequently, they may feel that what is learned or done *during* the internship is unimportant. Other students may have sought the internship to learn particular skills. Efforts by PPP to deal exclusively with either set of motives would have little positive effect on those interns motivated by the other set.

Motivation as an Inferred State. Many of the behaviors that I/O psychologists study are more or less objective; they can be measured in fairly (although not absolutely) unambiguous ways. Productivity, turnover, and absenteeism are some examples. Other variables are not so clear-cut. Motivation is a psychological state of the individual worker, and although it may influence people's observable behaviors, it is not the same as those behaviors. Because we cannot observe motivation directly, we must *infer* it from our observations of the behavior that we can see. Unless everyone with the same level of motivation behaves in the same way (and they do not), this presents a problem for studying and understanding motivation.

The interns at PPP, for example, may all be equally motivated, yet their observable behaviors may differ greatly. Some interns may respond to motivation by engaging in bursts of activity, implementing the first plan of action that occurs to them. Others may respond to the same motives by stepping back to judge the situation and carefully plan their next move. Dr. MacKeven might see the apparent energy level of the first group and conclude that they are more highly motivated; another psychologist might note the careful thought of the second group and conclude that *they* are more highly motivated. Because psychologists and others must infer the state of workers' motivation, such disagreement and ambiguity are both common and problematic.

The Dynamic Nature of Motives. It would be convenient for both organizations and I/O psychologists if people's motives did not change over time. Managers want to know what motivates their workers, and they would like to be able to count on the same factors motivating them tomorrow that motivate them today. Unfortunately, the factors that motivate workers *do* change. When this happens, managers can find themselves out of touch with their workers' needs, and unable to motivate them with the techniques that worked in the past.

Consider again the intern situation in PPP's Consumer Research Department. The internship program was developed on the assumption that the interns would be highly motivated to learn all they can while at PPP. Indeed, motivation may have been high early in the life of the program, when the students appeared to be "dedicated and hard-working." Today, however, it is possible that the interns are not motivated to learn or develop new skills but, rather, by other factors, such as the opportunity to live

in Suardell Springs during the ski season. Such a change might occur if the job market for these students had so improved that they no longer needed to worry about polishing their skills during an internship in order to get a job.

Stereotypes. Understanding worker motivation is also difficult because everyone has stereotypes about what motivates people. These stereotypes fall on a continuum (McCormick & Ilgen, 1980). At one extreme is the "trait" stereotype, the belief that motivation is a characteristic of individual workers. That is, some people have more motivation than others. People who hold this stereotype are likely to believe that the only way to improve work motivation is to replace the workers you have with more highly motivated people. Motivation thus becomes a selection problem. If Dr. MacKeven held this view, she might conclude that the selection process for interns is not sensitive to differences in motivation and change the procedure to include predictors of motivation.

The other extreme is an "external-state" view of motivation. This approach stresses the working conditions and the nature of the supervision, pay, and other aspects of the job that can affect worker motivation. If she held this viewpoint, Dr. MacKeven might look to the work environment to explain the interns' low motivation. For example, the expectations of the supervisors in the Consumer Research Department may not be sufficiently clear so that the students can be sure what is expected of them.

Theories of Motivation

In the following sections we discuss several theories of work motivation. The theories are grouped into general categories, based on similarities in the underlying processes they use to explain motivation. Some of the approaches presented are primarily of historical interest; they played important roles in the development and understanding of work motivation but are no longer considered to be adequate explanations for employees' behaviors. Other theories are currently very popular. Together, this collection of viewpoints should give you a good picture of how psychologists have addressed the issue of motivation.

Need Theories

Some of the earliest theories of motivation were based on the concept of **need.** In general, these theories suggest that people have needs for certain outcomes or events. When these needs are unsatisfied, people experience a **drive** to engage in behaviors that will lead to need satisfaction. The goal of motivated behavior, according to need theories, is to eliminate or satisfy needs, which restores equilibrium. Some theories address basic physiological needs such as those we all have for food and water. In these cases the nature of the drives, hunger and thirst, are clear and familiar to everyone. Most need theories of work motivation, however, rely more heavily on psychological needs. The nature of these needs is not so clear, and defining and measuring them has been one of the biggest challenges for need theorists.

Need-Hierarchy Theory. One of the first need theories of human motivation was proposed by Abraham Maslow (1943, 1970). He suggested that people are motivated to satisfy a number of specific needs. Like all need theorists, Maslow believed that an unsatisfied need leads to behavior designed to satisfy that need, after which that particular need is no longer motivating. What makes Maslow's theory different from other need theories is his belief that human needs are arranged in a **hierarchy**. That is, some needs are more basic, or "prepotent," than others and therefore have greater potential for motivation. Further, when a basic need is unsatisfied or "deprived," it dominates a person's behavior and she will seek to gratify it. Once that need is largely gratified, the next need is acti-

vated and becomes motivating, and so on up the hierarchy. This *satisfaction-progression* principle explains how motives can change over time.

Maslow's hierarchy of needs is presented in Figure 8.2. The most basic needs in this model are **physiological needs**, such as needs for food, water, and sex. Because they are the most basic, when one is not satisfied, other potential motives are ignored until the physiological need is fulfilled. Once all physiological needs are mostly satisfied, **safety needs** begin to motivate the individual. These include needs to maintain a safe environment and a healthy existence that is free from threats. Once an adequate level of safety is assured, **belongingness needs**, or needs to be accepted and liked by others, become the primary motivators. Next are **esteem needs**, which include the need for a positive self-image, as well as needs for recognition from others for personal accomplishments.

Finally, once the first four levels of needs are relatively well satisfied, **self-actualization needs** become the major motivating force in a person's life. Self-actualization refers to a process by which an individual reaches full potential, achieving all that he is capable of achieving. Unlike other needs, the gratification of self-actualization needs results in a strengthening rather than a weakening of the need. This explains the sustained motivation of people who are approaching self-actualization, who have no higher needs to activate (Maslow, 1965). The U.S. Army captured the spirit of self-actualization in its recruiting slogan "Be all you can be!"

Possible need-hierarchy explanations for the problems in PPP's Consumer Research Department are straightforward: either all of the interns' needs are satisfied (which is unlikely) or performance of their jobs does not satisfy their active needs. The latter could happen if job performance satisfies needs that are either too low or too high in the hierarchy. For example, the interns may have a great deal of responsibility, which would normally satisfy esteem needs. Because they still have financial concerns typi-

Physiological needs

1980; Wahba & Bridwell, 1976). Similarly, data from 23 studies did not support the prediction that satisfaction of one need activates needs at the next higher level (Wahba & Bridwell, 1976).

The limited research on need-hierarchy theory thus offers little underpinning for Maslow's ideas. One reason for this lack of support may be that most of the research has been "cross-sectional"—comparing the needs of different people at one point in time—but the theory was designed to predict *changes* in *individuals'* needs over time. It is therefore possible that longitudinal designs to measure changes in the needs of the same people over time would yield greater support for this need hierarchy. Of greater importance is the difficulty psychologists have had in defining basic constructs such as "need" and "self-actualization." Although these concepts are the cornerstones of Maslow's theory, he did not describe how they should be operationally defined for research purposes (Maslow, 1943).

ERG Theory. To deal with some of the criticisms of Maslow's theory, Alderfer (1969, 1972) proposed an alternative motivation theory

cal of college students, however, they are likely to be motivated by lower-order needs and not find the responsibility particularly attractive.

Maslow's theory has been popular with managers and practitioners, even though there is little evidence to support it. Reviews of the research literature on need-hierarchy theory have not found much support for the existence of the five types of needs Maslow proposed, although there is some evidence that higher-order needs and lower-order needs form separate clusters, as shown in Figure 8.2 (Lawler & Suttle, 1972; Wahba & Bridwell, 1976). Also contrary to the theory, there is little evidence that deprived needs dominate motivation (Alderfer, 1972; Hall & Nougaim, 1968; Lawler & Suttle, 1972; Rauschenberger, Schmitt, & Hunter,

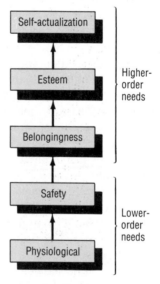

FIGURE 8.2
Maslow's Hierarchy of Needs

based on the hierarchy-of-needs concept. However, this theory introduced substantial changes in both the number of needs and how the needs motivate people. Rather than five needs, Alderfer suggested only three. The name of the theory, ERG, is an acronym for these needs, defined as follows:

> *Existence needs* include all the various forms of material and physiological desires. Hunger and thirst represent deficiencies in existence needs. Pay, fringe benefits, and physical working conditions are other types of existence needs. . . .
> *Relatedness needs* include all the needs [that] involve relationships with significant other people. Family members are usually significant others, as are superiors, coworkers, subordinates, friends, and enemies. . . .
> *Growth needs* include all the needs [that] involve a person making creative or productive effects on himself and the environment. Satisfaction of growth needs comes from a person engaging problems [that] call him to utilize his capacities fully and may include requiring him to develop additional capacities. . . . (Alderfer, 1969, pp. 145–147)

One similarity between need-hierarchy and ERG theories is that the needs are arranged in a particular order. In ERG theory, however, the hierarchy is based on *concreteness* rather than prepotence, with existence needs being the most concrete or tangible, and growth needs the least concrete. As with need-hierarchy theory, however, the satisfaction-progression principle states that the gratification of needs at one level activates the motivating potential of needs at the next level, as shown in Figure 8.3.

Unlike Maslow's need hierarchy, the ERG hierarchy is not absolute; ERG theory provides a means for people to go *down* the hierarchy through a process called *frustration/regression*. After repeatedly failing to satisfy needs at one level, people abandon those needs and become more concerned with satisfying needs at the next lowest level. Thus, rather than the relatively steady progression up the hierarchy described by Maslow, ERG theory suggests that people may

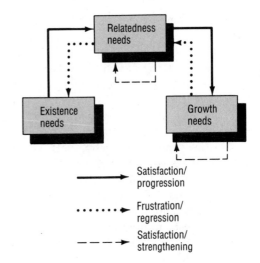

FIGURE 8.3
Existence, Relatedness, Growth Theory

move up or down, depending on their success in gratifying needs at each level. The frustration/regression process is also illustrated in Figure 8.3. ERG theory suggests, too, that satisfaction of relatedness and growth needs results in the strengthening of those needs. This is represented by the arrows at the bottom of the "relatedness" and "growth" boxes in Figure 8.3. As in need-hierarchy theory, this process allows for continued motivation once a person reaches the higher need levels.

ERG is more sophisticated than Maslow's need hierarchy. By allowing for regression toward more basic needs, ERG is more compatible with most people's actual work experiences. PPP's interns, for example, may have been motivated by unsatisfied existence needs when they started working. After the first few paychecks, however, they began to be concerned with relatedness needs, which they found more difficult to satisfy in a temporary job. According to ERG, continued frustration of relatedness needs would cause the interns to return to existence needs as the primary motivator. By this time, however, the interns probably learned that pay and performance are not directly related, which would explain why they are not putting in the effort they had originally shown.

Unfortunately, research testing ERG theory is sparse and has provided little consistent support for the theory (Rauschenberger, Schmitt, & Hunter, 1980; Wanous & Zwany, 1977). The lack of interest in ERG theory is probably due in part to some of the problems that ERG shares with Maslow's need hierarchy. Both theories rely upon the concept of need, which has never been operationally defined to the satisfaction of many researchers. This leads to problems in both testing and applying the theory. Each theory also suggests an ultimate goal of motivated behavior: self-actualization in Maslow's case, growth in Alderfer's. The exact meaning of these terms is not clear, however. Because of questions such as these, ERG, much like Maslow's need hierarchy, has contributed little to our understanding of work motivation.

Manifest-Needs Theory. Another need-based motivation theory is manifest-needs theory, originally developed by Murray (1938). According to Murray, human motivation is determined by a number of needs that regulate both the activation and direction of behavior. In this way, manifest-needs theory is similar to need-hierarchy and ERG theories. However, manifest-needs theory is unique in several important ways. All of these theories, though, have helped to make managers aware of the potential for differences in motives between workers.

The most obvious difference between manifest-needs and need-hierarchy theories is that rather than three or five basic needs, Murray identified more than three dozen. Second, he believed that these needs are not the same for everyone but are learned as people go about their day-to-day lives. Because each person's life and what is learned are unique, not all people experience the same needs. Third, rather than being activated through either the deprivation or satisfaction of a lower-order need, Murray's needs are activated by events or cues in the person's environment. When the appropri-

ate cues for a given need are present, that need becomes active or *manifest*. When the environmental cues are absent, the need is inactive or *latent*. (Of course, if a person does not possess the need in the first place, the cues will have no effect.) Fourth, Murray did not believe that needs were arranged in any type of hierarchy. This means that any need can be activated at any time, regardless of the state of other needs. Finally, Murray did not limit motivation to the effects of a single need at any one time. Instead, motivation can be influenced by a variety of needs working together to determine the ultimate strength and direction of behavior.

Although Murray suggested that there are a relatively large number of human needs, applications of his theory to work motivation have tended to focus on only a few (Steers, 1983). The need most often studied in organizational settings is **need for achievement** or, as it is commonly abbreviated, *n* Ach. People with high need for achievement are competitive, take responsibility for solving problems, have a strong desire for feedback, and are concerned with successfully accomplishing their tasks. People high in *n* Ach prefer tasks of moderate difficulty because easy tasks provide little sense of accomplishment, and very difficult tasks are likely to lead to failure (Atkinson & Feather, 1966; McClelland & Winter, 1969).

Another dimension of achievement-oriented behavior is the tendency for some people to avoid tasks because they are afraid of failing. This has been called the **need to avoid failure** or *n* AF (Atkinson & Feather, 1966). Compared with people who are high in *n* Ach, those high in *n* AF tend to *avoid* tasks with moderate difficulty. Instead, they are more attracted to either very easy tasks, where success is assured, or very difficult tasks, where failure can be blamed on the nature of the task rather than on their own lack of ability.

Another need with implications for work motivation is **need for power**, or *n* Pow. People high in *n* Pow are motivated to control their environment, including other people in that environment. They attempt to influence others by offering opinions, making suggestions, and attempting to persuade. Two different forms of *n* Pow have been identified (McClelland, 1976). The first of these, **need for personal power**, involves the control and domination of other people as an end in itself. People with needs for this type of power are not typically concerned with the goals or accomplishments of the organization. The second, **need for institutionalized power**, also involves controlling other people, but with the goals of the organization rather than personal gain in mind. People with needs for institutionalized power are more likely to seek help with problems and are willing to put aside their personal gain for the benefit of the organization.

Most theory and research on manifest needs in organizations have focused on how they relate to managerial motivation and performance. The most important need for managers appears to be the need for power, specifically the need for institutionalized power (McClelland, 1976). Recognizing that politics plays an important role in business organizations and that obtaining and using power is crucial to political behavior, the manager high in *n* Pow should have the best chances for success. High *n* Ach managers, by comparison, are too concerned with their own personal success to be sufficiently motivated by the needs of the organization.

Indeed, research supports the advantages of *n* Pow among managers. High *n* Pow predicted success over periods of 8 and 16 years among nontechnical managers at AT&T, although not among managers in fields such as engineering, where specific technical skills are more important to performance (McClelland & Boyatzis, 1982). High *n* Ach also predicted success but only among managers at the lower levels of the organization. The fact that high *n* Ach predicted the performance in lower management but not in upper management may be due to differences in managerial jobs at these levels. That is, individual achievement (completing specific job tasks) is more important in determining perfor-

mance at lower levels of organizations, and influencing others (exercising power) is more important at higher levels (McClelland & Boyatzis, 1982). There has been considerable research on *n* Pow and management, and most of it is consistent with McClelland's theory. Because of its importance for managerial behavior and performance, we will discuss this aspect of motivation further in the chapter on leadership.

Although *n* Pow may be the most critical need for managers, there is also substantial evidence of positive effects associated with high *n* Ach. Particularly in settings where individual effort can have a substantial impact, such as entrepreneurial situations or in developing countries, *n* Ach has been shown to be related to individual success (Brockhaus, 1980; McClelland, 1961, 1965, 1975, 1976).

Evaluation of Need Theories. Need theories of motivation have been popular for a long time, probably because they make a great deal of sense. Few would argue with the logic that people who feel deprived of something they need will try to get that "something." But the problem with need theories has involved difficulties in developing adequate definitions of the needs that motivate people, as well as clear descriptions of how they should be measured. The hierarchical theories of Maslow and Alderfer in particular have been criticized on these grounds (Campbell & Pritchard, 1976; Mitchell, 1979; Staw, 1984).

Manifest-needs theory, on the other hand, remains somewhat more promising. Particularly in the context of managerial motivation and behavior, several of the needs initially identified by Murray, and further studied by McClelland and Atkinson, are related to successful performance. It may be that manifest needs have had greater success because they address relatively specific behaviors, and that Maslow's and Alderfer's needs are too broad to apply well to any particular situation. Unfortunately, manifest-needs theory seems to be more appropriate for predicting managerial performance than as a general model of motivation.

Expectancy Theory

Due in part to the problems of need theories, a number of *cognitive* theories of motivation have emerged over the years. Unlike need theories, which suggest that motivation results from basic and often irrational urges or drives, cognitive theories emphasize the role of thoughts, expectations, and judgments in the motivation process. One of the best-known cognitive motivation theories is expectancy theory.

Vroom's Expectancy Models. Modern expectancy theory had its origins in path-goal theory, which is concerned with the role of motivation in worker productivity (Georgopoulos, Mahoney, & Jones, 1957). Vroom (1964) later developed the first formal description of expectancy theory. The theory's basic premise is simple: the tendency for people to engage in a particular behavior is a function of (1) the strength of their expectation that the behavior will be followed by a given outcome, and (2) the anticipated value of that outcome.

Expectancy theory, as described by Vroom, consists of two related models. The first of these is the valence model, which is used to predict the *valences* that workers place on various *outcomes*.[1] In the terminology of expectancy theory, an **outcome** is any event that might follow a worker's behavior, such as praise, punishment, or increased productivity. The **valence** of an outcome is the satisfaction that the worker expects to experience should he or she receive the outcome.

According to the valence model, an outcome will have a positive valence for a worker if he or she believes that it has positive *instrumentality* for obtaining other valued outcomes. **In-**

strumentality is the extent to which a person believes that attaining one outcome is associated with attaining other outcomes, and can range from +1.00 to −1.00. In other words, an instrumentality is the perceived correlation between two outcomes (Vroom, 1964).

Figure 8.4 illustrates how the valence model predicts the valence of performing well on an internship for one of PPP's Consumer Research interns. Four possible outcomes of performing well, along with their valences, are listed on the left side of the figure. The particular intern, Keil Hardy, places positive values on earning higher pay in later jobs, developing new skills, and having greater flexibility in choosing jobs in the future. However, he places little value on making "business contacts" during the internship. In the center of the figure are Mr. Hardy's estimates of the instrumentalities of having a PPP internship for attaining each of the four outcomes. He perceives positive associations between the internship and greater pay in future jobs, learning new skills, and making business contacts. The perceived instrumentality of the internship for achieving flexibility in job choice, however, is negative.

Combining this information, the valence model predicts that the potential for higher pay and improved skills will increase the valence of the internship for Mr. Hardy because (a) he values these outcomes, and (b) the internship is seen by him as a way to attain them. The opportunity to develop business contacts will have no effect on the valence in this case because even though Mr. Hardy believes that contacts can be made through the internship (positive instrumentality), he does not value this particular outcome. Finally, although he would like to have flexibility in his job choices (positive valence), he believes that having a PPP internship will *decrease* the chances of this happening (negative instrumentality), which lowers the valence of the internship.

The second model in Vroom's expectancy theory predicts the motivational force to per-

---

[1] Formally, the valence model is expressed as

$$V_j = f \sum_{k=1}^{n} (V_k I_{jk})$$

where V_j = the valence of outcome j; I_{jk} = the instrumentality of outcome j for attaining outcome k; V_k = the valence of outcome k; n = the number of outcomes.

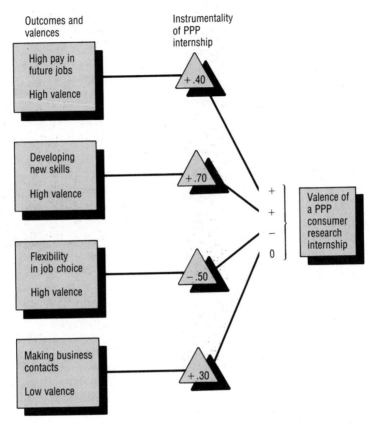

FIGURE 8.4
The Valence Model of Expectancy Theory

form a particular behavior.[2] This model states that the force, or strength of motivation, to engage in any behavior depends upon the *expectancy* that various outcomes will result from performance of the behavior, *and* the valence of those outcomes as defined in the valence model. Vroom (1964) defined **expectancy** as the per-

[2] Formally, the force model is expressed as

$$F_i = \sum_{j=1}^{n} (E_{ij}V_j)$$

where F_i = the force on the individual to perform behavior i; E_{ij} = the strength of the expectancy that act i will be followed by outcome j; V_j = the valence of outcome j; n = the number of outcomes.

ceived probability that an outcome would follow a behavior, so it can range from zero to +1.00.

Figure 8.5 illustrates how the force model predicts Mr. Hardy's motivation to "work hard" on his internship duties. Positive expectancies are associated with three of the four outcomes in the figure. That is, he believes that hard work will help him perform well, lead to good evaluations from his supervisor, and limit his social life. He believes, however, that hard work will have no effect on his chances of receiving a job offer from PPP (due to a policy of the company not to hire its own interns for permanent jobs). Of the four outcomes, all except a limited social

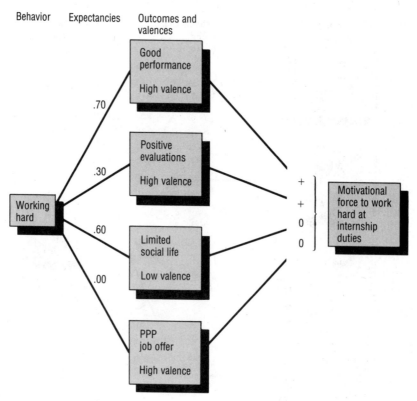

FIGURE 8.5
The Force Model of Expectancy Theory

life have high valences. According to the force model, the limited social life and the possibility of a job offer from PPP will not contribute to Mr. Hardy's work effort because both high valence *and* positive instrumentality are necessary for an outcome to increase motivational force. The belief that hard work will lead to the valued outcomes of good performance and positive evaluations, however, will increase the motivational force on Mr. Hardy to work hard.

Research on Expectancy Theory.   Early research on expectancy theory examined the ability of the valence and force models to predict various criteria. Research on the valence model fell into three categories: predictions of occupational preference, predictions of job satisfaction, and predictions of the valence of effective job performance. Consistently positive support for the model emerged in each category (Mitchell, 1974). Research on the force model, which typically tested predictions of work effort, also supported the theory but not as strongly.

Although early research on expectancy theory provided fairly broad support, a number of methodological, empirical, and theoretical issues concerning that research were raised (Mitchell, 1974). One of the criticisms was that virtually all of the research had used *between-subjects designs*. That is, the research typically presented different groups of subjects with different information about instrumentality, valence, and expectancy. Then the average preferences or effort levels of the various groups were compared. For example, one group of workers might be led to believe that good attendance is instrumental for receiving a large pay raise, while another group is not given this information, and differences in attendance between the two groups are attributed to the instrumentality manipulation. This practice is clearly contrary to Vroom's (1964) description of expectancy theory; he said that the theory was meant to predict *individual* choice—specifically which of a number of options a person would select. The proper research design for testing expectancy theory is a *within-subjects design*. In this type of research, levels of effort under different conditions for the *same* person can be compared, and the ability of the model to predict individual choices can be properly tested.

Following these criticisms, researchers began to use within-subjects designs more often. Consistent with the original theory, a number of researchers found that within-subjects tests of the theory predicted performance better than between-subjects designs (Kopelman, 1976; Mitchell, 1979; Muchinsky, 1977a; Oldham, 1976). Similar conclusions were drawn in a review of 16 studies that used within-subjects designs to predict either organizational attractiveness or actual job choices (Wanous, Keon, & Latack, 1983).

One area in which expectancy theory is particularly effective is the prediction of choices from among several distinct options, such as between different jobs or schools. For example, one version of the expectancy model successfully predicted the attractiveness of graduate business schools among a sample of business-school applicants (Wanous, Keon, & Latack, 1983). Likewise, measures of motivational force (see Figure 8.5) obtained from workers who were about to be permanently laid off predicted the workers' intentions to look for new jobs, their effort to find new jobs, and their actual choice to seek work or remain unemployed (Kinicki, 1989).

Another important issue concerns the cognitive processes implied by expectancy theory.

Expectancy theory assumes that people make decisions in a very careful, rational manner. For example, the theory specifies that even if an outcome has a very positive valence, there will be *no* effort to obtain that outcome if there is not an expectancy that the effort will be effective. A less rational model might predict efforts to obtain highly valued outcomes, even if the probability of doing so was virtually zero. It has, in fact, been suggested that expectancy theory is too complex to be an accurate model of how most people make decisions, and that most of our decisions are made in a less rational, more haphazard manner (for example, Slovic, Fischhoff, & Lichtenstein, 1977).

To determine whether the cognitive processes described by expectancy theory reflect how people really make decisions about work effort, studies of how people combine valences and expectancies were conducted (Stahl & Harrell, 1981). The aim of this research was to see whether each subject was using the rational decision-making process defined by the theory or a simpler, less rational process. The results showed that overall only 37 percent of the 157 subjects made decisions consistent with expectancy theory. The remaining subjects were less rational, indicating, for example, that they would work hard to obtain a desired outcome even if the probability of obtaining it was very low or that they would choose to pursue an outcome that has little or no value if it was sure to be obtained. The presence of positive motivation in the face of low expectancy of success was demonstrated again by Harrell and Stahl (1986), who also found that although raising expectancy increased motivation, it did not increase as much as predicted by the theory.

If people make decisions in different ways, it might be useful to modify expectancy theory to include two force models: one for people who use careful, rational decision-making strategies, and one for people who are not as systematic (Stahl & Harrell, 1981). For example, although some people are indeed influenced by their personal expectancies, other people are more affected by social norms and the expectations of others (Fishbein & Ajzen, 1975). For people who are more aware of their personal expectancies, expectancy and behavior are related as predicted by expectancy theory; for those who are more conscious of social norms, personal expectancies and behavior are more independent (Miller & Grush, 1988).

Other experts attribute the failure of expectancy theory to describe the way all people make decisions to the fact that many problems can be adequately solved using much simpler decision-making processes (Beach & Mitchell, 1990; Lord & Maher, 1990; Mitchell & Beach, 1990). In this view, expectancy theory remains a useful model of decision making under certain conditions (for example, when several acceptable, well-defined alternatives are available), but its failure to address other situations (for example, when decision makers have a great deal of expertise and experience, or when information on available solutions is limited) is acknowledged, as is the need to develop alternative explanations for these situations.

Evaluation of Expectancy Theory. Part of the popularity of expectancy theory stems from the fact that the theory implies that people are logical and that it makes logical predictions of their behavior. Not only does the logical nature of the theory make it easy to understand, but it also makes it easy to use in organizations (Lord & Maher, 1990). If Margaret Russell finds that the interns in her department are not working hard because they do not value the outcomes associated with good work performance, she can try to provide outcomes that they do value and thereby strengthen instrumentalities. If the lack of effort is due to a low expectancy that effort will improve performance, she can assign tasks with relatively high probabilities of success in order to strengthen these expectancies. Because of the rational nature of the theory, such solutions to problems are easily defined.

Expectancy theory is also popular because, as you have seen, it is relatively valid for predicting certain types of behavior, specifically ef-

fort levels and decisions such as occupational choices and job preferences. As you have also seen, however, expectancy-based predictions are hardly perfect. Many decisions in organizations are made in ways that are very different from the highly logical, cognitively intense procedures described by Vroom (1964). These alternative decision-making processes are just beginning to be described and studied (for example, Mitchell & Beach, 1990), but they promise to broaden our understanding of organizational decision making and motivation, and to clarify the legitimate role of expectancy theory in these areas.

Equity Theory

Another cognitive approach to motivation is represented by balance theories. In general, **balance theories** state that a person's behavior is influenced by comparisons between her or his current status and some standard. When the person's status is reasonably close to the standard, a state of balance results and the person is not motivated to change behavior. If, however, the person's status is substantially different from the standard, the lack of balance causes an uncomfortable sense of tension and the person is motivated to restore balance.

The best-known balance theory of work motivation is Adams' equity theory (Adams, 1965). **Equity theory** is based on workers' perceived **inputs**, or what they believe they contribute to their job or organization, and their perceived **outcomes**, or what they acknowledge the organization provides them in return. Because of the notion of trading inputs for outcomes, equity theory is often referred to as an *exchange* theory.

Inputs can take a variety of forms, such as labor, time, skill, and years of education or experience that workers have accumulated. Outcomes can also vary, ranging from pay and fringe benefits to praise and recognition from a superior, to opportunities for social interaction with coworkers. According to the theory, each worker forms a ratio of her or his outcomes to inputs. This ratio is compared to what the worker perceives as the outcome-to-input ratio of a comparison person, or what Adams called a "significant other." The two ratios are equal when the worker and the comparison person are seen as receiving the same level of outcomes for each unit of input. Under these conditions the worker will experience feelings of equity, and there will be no motivation to change behavior. If, on the other hand, the ratios are not equal, the worker will experience inequity, and tension will result (Adams, 1965). To eliminate the tension, the worker will be motivated to restore equity. The following list (summarized from Adams, 1965) suggests some of the ways to do so.

1. Alter inputs to bring O/I ratio into balance with the comparison person's ratio.

2. Alter outcomes to bring O/I ratio into balance with the comparison person's ratio. (Adams believed that people will generally try to increase their outcomes and avoid increasing inputs in their efforts to restore equity.)

3. Cognitively distort or change perceptions of either the worker's own or the comparison person's inputs and outcomes to bring the two ratios into balance. (Adams said that people are likely to find it easier to distort perceptions of the inputs and outcomes of the other person than to distort their own.)

4. "Leave the field," or quit the job. (Adams said that this would usually happen only if the inequity was extreme.)

5. Engage in behaviors designed to change the inputs and/or outcomes of the comparison person.

6. Select a new comparison person for the purpose of judging equity. (Adams implied that this course of action is unlikely.)

The amount of tension and the strength of motivation are proportional to the degree of perceived inequity. Equitable and inequitable comparisons are illustrated in Figure 8.6. As in-

Equity conditions	Examples
$\dfrac{O_P}{I_P} = \dfrac{O_0}{I_0}$	$O_P = O_0$ and $I_P = I_0$ $O_P = K(O_0)$ and $I_P = K(I_0)$, where K is any constant value

Inequity conditions	Examples
$\dfrac{O_P}{I_P} < \dfrac{O_0}{I_0}$	$O_P = O_0$ and $I_P > I_0$ $O_P < O_0$ and $I_P = I_0$ $O_P < O_0$ and $I_P > I_0$
$\dfrac{O_P}{I_P} > \dfrac{O_0}{I_0}$	$O_P = O_0$ and $I_P < I_0$ $O_P > O_0$ and $I_P = I_0$ $O_P > O_0$ and $I_P < I_0$

P = person (worker)
o = significant other (comparison person)

FIGURE 8.6
Conditions of Equity and Inequity

dicated in this figure, feelings of inequity, and therefore motivation, result if the worker's ratio is *either* smaller or larger than the ratio for the comparison person.

To illustrate equity theory further, let's consider how it might explain the poor performance of the interns at PPP. Margaret Russell said that the interns are not putting forth enough effort. In equity terms, they have reduced the level of their inputs. This would happen, according to equity theory, if the interns believed that other workers were receiving *greater* outcomes for the *same* amount of input, or if others were receiving the *same* outcomes in return for *lower* inputs. Before Dr. MacKeven can suggest any solution, she would have to discover whom the interns are comparing themselves to, and what inputs and outcomes the interns consider important. One possible explanation is that the interns believe that they are contributing the same inputs as higher-paid, permanent employees.

Research on Equity Theory. Most of the early research on equity theory examined the effects of inequity due to overpayment or underpayment, under either piece-rate or hourly wage systems.

TABLE 8.1   Predicted Responses to Pay Inequity Based upon Equity Theory

	Underpayment	Overpayment
Hourly wages	Production will decrease or be of lower quality.	Production will increase or be of higher quality.
Piece rate	Production will increase, but quality will be lower.	Production will decrease, but quality will be higher.

The predictions made for these conditions are presented in Table 8.1. Notice that workers can alter their inputs by changing either the quantity or quality of their work, and that the type of inequity and the type of pay system affect the nature of the predicted response.

Although laboratory studies of equity theory provide fairly strong support for the underpayment predictions, studies of overpayment yield results that are less consistent and more open to alternative explanations (Mowday, 1983). One method for making subjects feel overpaid is to tell them that they are not qualified for the "job" they are performing in the study. This technique is designed to make the subjects believe that they deserve neither the job nor the pay. Although this type of manipulation may result in feelings of overpayment, it may also threaten subjects' self-esteem. Rather than working harder to increase inputs and reduce inequity, the subjects may be working harder to prove that they are qualified to perform the task (Andrews & Valenzi, 1970; Wiener, 1970). Studies using other manipulations of overpayment, such as giving higher-than-normal wages or unearned raises, have generally found less support for equity theory than those challenging subjects' qualifications (for example, Pritchard, Dunnette, & Jorgenson, 1972; Valenzi & Andrews, 1971). In fact, the en-

tire notion of overpayment in work organizations has been questioned (Locke, 1976). Rather than feeling inequity, overpaid workers may be more likely to adjust their perceptions of their inputs, based on the assumption that the organization would not pay them more than they are actually worth.

Because of the mixed results of equity research, psychologists have tried to improve the predictive power of the theory. One issue that has received some attention is the selection of comparison persons. For example, workers can compare their outcome:input ratios to several standards, each of which has been found to be related to pay satisfaction (Goodman, 1974):

1. the ratios of other people in the same or in other organizations;

2. any of the ratios that the workers themselves have experienced in the past, either in the same organization or in other organizations; and

3. formal or informal understandings or agreements with the organization concerning outcomes and inputs, such as collective-bargaining agreements.

Another aspect of equity theory that has been examined is the possibility that one outcome might compensate for the lack of another outcome. For example, giving subjects an impressive-sounding but unearned job title led to increased productivity during an unpaid work period (Greenberg & Ornstein, 1983). This production boost was apparently an effort to restore equity by increasing inputs after unexpectedly receiving the new title (an outcome). By comparison, subjects who were asked to perform the unpaid work but were *not* given the job title dramatically reduced their productivity, thereby restoring equity by *reducing* inputs. However, the production increase among subjects with the unearned title was short-lived. After a while, the additional work apparently became too demanding to be balanced by a job title alone and production began to fall.

In another study of nonpay outcomes, the reactions of workers experiencing a temporary salary reduction were examined (Greenberg, 1989). The workers saw nonmonetary outcomes as being more important in determining equity during the period of reduced pay than they had before the pay reduction. In other words, when pay went down, the workers began to place more value in their nonpay outcomes such as amount of floor and desk space, number of windows, and ability to decorate the work space, in order to maintain feelings of equity.

Similar results were found when insurance-company employees experienced temporary changes in office space (Greenberg, 1988). While their offices were being remodeled, employees were temporarily reassigned to offices that were of higher, equal, or lower status than their regular offices. Workers assigned to higher-status offices increased their performance; those assigned to lower-status offices decreased their performance. These effects are consistent with equity-theory predictions for conditions of increased and decreased outcomes, respectively, and highlight the importance of symbolic outcomes in the workplace.

Another equity-theory issue is the possibility that individual differences may affect the relationship between perceived equity and behavior. An interesting example is a study by Vecchio (1981), who examined the role of moral maturity in predicting reactions to piece-rate overpayment. He reasoned that people whose moral standards are determined by concern for rights or responsibilities (high in moral maturity) would be sensitive to the unfairness of being overpaid, and would therefore behave in a manner consistent with equity theory. People whose ideas of right and wrong are based on satisfying their own needs, or adherence to rules and authority (lower in moral maturity), would behave in a more "hedonistic" manner. That is, they would do more work of lower quality in order to *maximize* (not equalize) the input-to-outcome ratio, similar to the behavior predicted by expectancy theory. (See Kohlberg,

1968, for more information on the notion of moral maturity.)

In his research, Vecchio (1981) found that students classified as high in moral maturity responded to overpayment in the manner predicted by equity theory: They produced less than equitably paid subjects, but their work was higher in quality. Subjects low in moral maturity performed in the opposite pattern, as predicted by expectancy theory (see Figure 8.7). Vecchio's study is interesting and important not only because it helps clarify the nature of responses to overpayment but also because it represents an effort to reconcile conflicting predictions from two theories (equity theory and expectancy theory), thereby increasing the usefulness of both theories.

Another individual factor that might explain differences in responses to inequity is **equity sensitivity** (Huseman, Hatfield, & Miles, 1987). The basic idea here is that different people have preferences for different levels and types of equity. Some people have strong preferences for equitable outcome-to-input ratios (these people are called "equity sensitives") and are motivated to maintain that balance, as suggested by Adams (1965). Other individuals (called "benevolents") prefer situations in which their comparison person receives more than they receive themselves, and are therefore motivated to increase the outcomes of others. Finally, some people (called "entitleds") prefer to receive more than their comparison person, and are motivated to maximize their own outcomes. According to this theory, underpayment will cause the entitleds to experience distress, and overpayment will make the benevolents feel guilty, but only the equity sensitives will experience both of these reactions as suggested by traditional equity theory.

Moral maturity and equity sensitivity are personality variables, but there may be other individual characteristics that predict reactions to inequity. For example, some studies have found that men are likely to distribute rewards on the basis of equity and women are more likely to

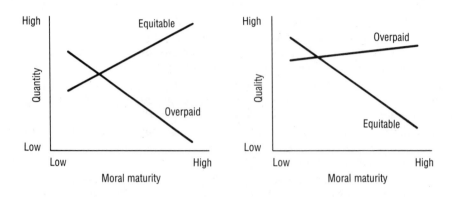

FIGURE 8.7
Relationships between Moral Maturity, Equity, and Performance
Source: From "An Individual Differences Interpretation of the Conflicting Predictions Generated by Equity Theory and Expectancy Theory," by R. P. Vecchio, *Journal of Applied Psychology, 66,* 478. Copyright © 1981 by the American Psychological Association. Adapted by permission of the author.

demonstrate *equality*, where all parties receive the same rewards. Because men are more likely to use equity principles in distributing rewards, it is not surprising that the relationship between equity and satisfaction is stronger for men than for women (for example, Brockner & Adsit, 1986). That is, women's satisfaction with their jobs does not seem to be closely associated with the perceived equity of their rewards, and men's satisfaction *is* related to these perceptions.

Cultural differences in equity and equality norms have also been studied and seem to be very small. For example, both U.S. and Korean students saw equity as the most fair way to allocate rewards when productivity was emphasized, and equality as the most fair when "harmony" was emphasized (Leung & Park, 1986). In a comparison of U.S., Japanese, and Korean students, a strong equity norm was found for all three nationalities, although the preference for equity was slightly lower among the Korean subjects. The researchers suggested that the weaker equity norm in the Korean sample was due to a less individualistic culture than that in the United States or Japan (Kim, Park, & Suzuki, 1990).

Finally, there is evidence that interpersonal or social factors have an impact on perceptions of equity and reactions to inequity. For example, the similarity between workers and the people with whom they compare themselves can have an effect on how the workers attempt to restore equity. Specifically, when subjects are *overpaid*, the presence of an attractive (that is, similar to the subject) comparison person has been shown to increase feelings of overpayment inequity relative to the presence of an unattractive (dissimilar) comparison person. This heightened inequity led to greater efforts to restore equity through better performance. In *underpayment* situations, an attractive comparison person seems to make the underpayment easier to endure and reduces feelings of underpayment inequity relative to the presence of an unattractive comparison person (Griffeth, Vecchio, & Logan, 1989). In another study, subjects who observed a coworker's being laid off worked harder than subjects who had not witnessed the layoff, apparently to reduce feelings of guilt over not being laid off themselves (Brockner et al., 1985). The effect of this "survivor guilt" on feelings of equity was more pronounced when the layoff was random. When the coworker was laid off because of poor performance, there was no guilt and little effect on performance (Brockner, Greenberg, Brockner, Bortz, Davy, & Carter, 1986).

Evaluation of Equity Theory. Equity theory has made a useful contribution to the motivation literature. Admittedly, it works best in underpayment conditions where the predictions may seem obvious or even trivial. However, it has been valuable in pointing out the potential effects of *relative* rewards and outcomes on behavior. Rather than considering only the absolute levels of rewards and compensation, managers must be aware of how workers evaluate rewards. Recent research on the effects of personality and compensating outcomes promises to clarify the rather inconsistent literature on overpayment. There is, of course, no theoretical reason to limit equity theory to conditions of overpayment and underpayment. As our discussion illustrates, nonpay outcomes can have important effects on perceptions of equity and levels of effort. As additional outcomes are considered along with pay, the ability to predict the level of worker inputs will be enhanced.

Goal Setting

A third cognitive approach to motivation is goal setting. Some authors view goal setting not as a theory but, rather, as a general approach to motivation that is consistent with a variety of theoretical viewpoints (McCormick & Ilgen, 1985). Indeed, goals are explicit or implied components in many motivation models (consider the outcomes in expectancy theory; Locke, 1978). However, the goal-setting process has attracted a great deal of attention and has become one of the major approaches to work motivation in its own right.

The basic idea behind goal setting is that people's behaviors are guided most directly by their intentions, and that intentions in organizations are revealed through personal perfor-

mance goals (Locke, 1968; Locke, Shaw, Saari, & Latham, 1981). Goals serve a number of functions important to worker motivation. The first of these is the *direction* provided. That is, goals clarify what needs to be accomplished and set standards for judging workers' progress. The more specific the goals, the more effective they will be in directing behavior toward particular aspects of performance.

Goals also provide for the energization or *mobilization* of behavior, allowing workers to judge the effort requirements of tasks. All else being equal, the more difficult the goal, the greater workers' efforts. Further, when combined with performance feedback, goals also provide for the *sustaining* of task behavior. That is, workers adjust their effort levels, based on feedback, in order to assure goal attainment. Also important for effective goal setting, according to Locke, is *goal commitment*. Goal commitment refers to a determination to reach a specific goal. Without such commitment, goals will be irrelevant to worker performance.

The predictions derived from goal setting have direct implications for improving worker performance. If workers are committed to the goals, have the necessary skills to perform at goal levels, and receive adequate performance feedback, then specific and difficult goals will result in better performance than less specific or easier goals. An important task for management, then, is to facilitate development of specific, difficult goals that are both within the range of workers' abilities and acceptable to the workers. For example, the Consumer Research Department interns at PPP might be given specific goals for their projects. These goals would specify deadlines, quality standards, and other relevant performance criteria based on job-analysis results and past performance data, so that they would be challenging but not impossible.

Research on Goal Setting. Goal-setting theory specifies several variables that should affect worker performance, such as goal difficulty, goal specificity, and goal commitment. In this section we summarize some research results concerning these variables. As you will see, goal setting can be described in a fairly straightforward fashion, but the psychological processes involved are a bit more sophisticated.

Early in the history of goal-setting research, Locke and his associates conducted a series of laboratory studies that found strong and consistent evidence of a positive relationship between goal difficulty and productivity (Locke, 1968). (Recent analyses, however, have found that the size of the goal effect is related to how goal difficulty is measured; Wright, 1990.) Similar positive results have been obtained by other laboratory researchers, although at least one meta-analysis of the goal-setting literature found that in *field* studies the effects of difficult goals were significantly smaller than in lab studies (Tubbs, 1986; cf. Mento, Steel & Karren, 1987). This may be because field studies often use more difficult and more complex tasks than lab studies. As tasks become more difficult, it is harder to increase productivity; this limits the effects of difficult goals. Also, in easy-goal conditions, laboratory subjects are often instructed to stop once the goal is reached (for example, Locke, 1982; Locke, Cartledge, & Knerr, 1970). Thus, the goal-difficulty effect may be at least partly due to the *suppression* of productivity in easy-goal conditions rather than, or in addition to, the positive effects of difficult goals (Locke, 1982).

Another way in which difficult goals might affect performance is through the high standards or achievement norms that they convey to workers. That is, the level of goal difficulty implies that certain standards of performance are expected or acceptable. Given easy goals, workers are likely to assume that a relatively low level of performance is adequate, and they will be unlikely to work harder. Given difficult goals, however, higher performance norms will be inferred and higher personal goals and greater effort are likely to result (Meyer & Gellatly, 1988).

In addition to goal-difficulty research, many studies have compared the effects of specific, difficult goals to instructions to "do your best." Again, as predicted by the model, specific, difficult goals almost always result in better performance than either "do-your-best" instructions or no goals at all (for example, Latham, Mitchell, & Dossett, 1978; Latham & Steele, 1983; Locke, 1968; Umstot, Bell, & Mitchell, 1976). Higher performance with specific goals is probably due to the ambiguity of the instruction "do your best," which provides little guidance for defining what is expected from the worker. No matter how subjects interpret "do your best," the results are obviously *not* their best because similar subjects with specific goals do better. The clear advantage of specific, clear performance goals over pleas for best efforts is one of the most important lessons to emerge from goal setting.

Another issue is whether feedback is an important component of successful goal setting, as Locke proposed. Goal-setting theory states that feedback, by itself, should have little effect on performance, but that the absence of feedback should greatly reduce goal-setting effects (Locke et al., 1981). However, meta-analyses of the goal-setting literature are generally inconclusive about the effects of feedback on goal setting. In one case, feedback was found to have a positive effect only when subjects had been given difficult, specific goals (Mento et al., 1987); another reviewer concluded that not enough research has been conducted to draw reasonable conclusions about the effects of feedback (Tubbs, 1986).

Research has also been conducted on the relative effectiveness of goals assigned by management versus goals that are set with workers' participation. Based on their review, Locke and his associates concluded that although there are theoretical reasons to expect better performance when workers participate in goal setting, there is little consistent evidence of such an effect (Locke et al., 1981). Meta-analyses support these conclusions, finding only small, inconclusive effects for participation (Mento et al., 1987; Tubbs, 1986). It seems that *how* goals are set is less important than *whether* they are set.

As we mentioned earlier, goal commitment is an essential aspect of goal setting. Without commitment, goals are unlikely to affect workers' effort and performance. Until recently, however, little has been done to understand *why* or *how* workers become (or don't become) committed to difficult performance goals (Hollenbeck & Klein, 1987; Locke, Latham, & Erez, 1988). One model of goal commitment is shown in Figure 8.8 (Hollenbeck & Klein, 1987).

In this model, situational (*work*-related) and personal (*worker*-related) factors are responsible for the attractiveness of difficult goals and the expectancies workers have of achieving those goals. These, in turn, determine goal commitment. Indeed, research has shown that public commitment to a difficult goal (a situational factor) and high need for achievement and internal locus of control (both personal factors) are related to higher goal commitment (Hollenbeck, Williams, & Klein, 1989).

Finally, research has examined whether task characteristics influence the effectiveness of

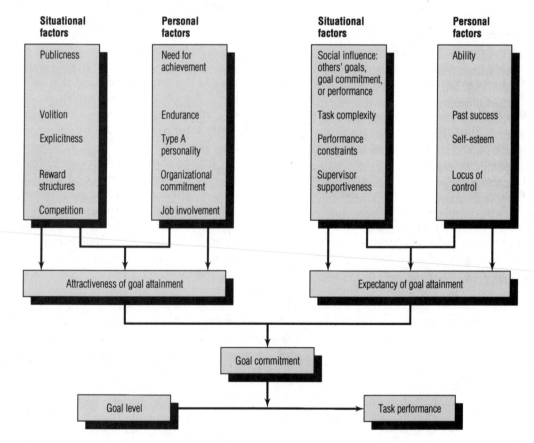

FIGURE 8.8
Expectancy-Theory Model of the Antecedents and Consequences of Goal Commitment
SOURCE: From "Goal Commitment and the Goal-setting Process: Problems, Prospects, and Proposals for Future Research," by J. R. Hollenbeck and H. J. Klein, 1987, *Journal of Applied Psychology, 72,* 215. By permission of the authors.

difficult goals. Recall that goal effects are stronger in lab studies than in field studies, in part because motivation can have a greater effect on performance when tasks are easier. Consistent with this, another meta-analysis of goal-setting studies found that goals had greater effects with simple tasks involving reaction time or simple arithmetic than with more complex tasks, such as college courses or scientific work (Wood, Mento, & Locke, 1987). Also, people who are given specific, difficult goals spend more time developing and evaluating task strategies (Campbell, 1988). Thus, specific, difficult goals may *impair* performance on tasks where strategies are difficult or time-consuming to evaluate. This is because the goal may misdirect the workers' effort from the task itself to the evaluation of strategies, thereby lowering task performance (Earley, Connolly, & Ekegren, 1989; Huber, 1985).

Evaluation of Goal Setting.   The positive effects of specific, difficult goals on productivity are well documented. It is clear that goal setting is a useful technique in a wide variety of settings where productivity is low or where workers are directing their efforts inappropriately. A goal-setting analysis of the situation in PPP's Consumer Research Department might find that the interns are not sure which tasks are more or less important to successful performance. If Margaret Russell were to set specific performance goals for each intern, the efforts of each should, according to Locke, be channeled into the desired activities. Alternatively, the interns may be mistaken about the overall quantity of work that is expected. Again, goal setting should alleviate this problem. Finally, it may be that although the interns have realistic expectations about what is important and how much work is expected, they have neither accepted nor developed commitment to the goals that have been imposed. Based on the model presented earlier (Figure 8.8), Ms. Russell might consider making the goals public or encouraging supervisor supportiveness in order to increase goal commitment (Hollenbeck & Klein, 1987).

In sum, goal setting seems to be a useful technique for increasing worker productivity. However, the research on commitment, task characteristics, and other variables suggests that the relationship between goals and performance is not as simple as we once thought. We can expect additional research on the processes by which goals affect behavior to clarify further the relationship and raise new issues concerning the use of performance goals.

Reinforcement

One of the best-known schools of thought in psychology is **behaviorism**, which deals with the learning of behaviors through conditioning processes. Of particular interest in I/O psychology is the approach known as **operant conditioning**, which was popularized by B. F. Skinner (1959). Skinner believed that behavior is controlled by its *consequences*. When a person (or other organism) engages in a behavior, that behavior is followed by an event or consequence. The consequence might be obvious, such as being "chewed out" by the boss, or it might be subtle, such as a nod of approval from a coworker. The nature of the consequence affects the probability that the person will repeat the behavior. This viewpoint has a simple yet powerful implication for behavior in organizations: control the consequences of workers' behavior and you will have a great deal of influence over that behavior.

Skinner described two types of consequences that affect learning. The first of these is **reinforcement**, any consequence that increases the probability that the behavior that preceded it will be repeated. In organizations we usually consider such things as pay, praise, recognition, promotions, and other rewards when we think of reinforcement. The second type of consequence discussed by Skinner is **punishment**, which occurs when the consequence of a behavior makes it *less* likely that the behavior will be repeated. Examples of punishment in organizations might include docking a worker's pay, denying a manager a promotion, or simply scolding a worker. Notice that no reference is made to needs, expectancies, equity, or any other emotional state or cognitive process. Instead, the emphasis is strictly on the effects of reinforcing and punishing events on the overt, observable behavior of workers (Luthans & Kreitner, 1985).

Behaviorists have strongly emphasized the superiority of reinforcement over punishment for controlling behavior (Luthans & Kreitner, 1985; Skinner, 1969; Wiard, 1972). Perhaps the most compelling reason for this is that although punishment may keep undesirable behaviors in check, it does not help workers learn desirable alternative behaviors. Reinforcement, on the other hand, teaches workers what they *should* be doing and by making certain that rewards do not follow undesired behaviors, that those behaviors will eventually stop.

To use reinforcement effectively, any rewards given by an organization must be *contingent* upon the desired behaviors. If rewards are distributed in a manner that does *not* emphasize the connection between the rewards and the desired behavior, the rewards will be *ineffective*. For example, if Dr. MacKeven were to start *monthly* pay bonuses for the consumer research interns whose work met certain standards, it would not be a proper use of reinforcement because such a bonus is a noncontingent reward. Skinner said that workers do not work on Monday for pay they will receive on Friday because there is no clear relationship between any specific behavior and the paycheck (Jordan, 1972). A more promising approach to reinforcement would begin by identifying specific behaviors that are related to high performance among PPP's interns, such as completing reports within a specified period of time. Supervisors could then be trained to provide immediate reinforcement, such as praise or recognition, when these behaviors occur.

The above example raises some interesting points about how most people are paid for their work. Hourly wages and salaries are both noncontingent forms of pay. That is, as long as workers show up for work they will be paid,

and the manner in which they behave and how well they perform make relatively little difference. Consequently, these types of pay should not be useful as reinforcers. Some psychologists have suggested that piece-rate pay systems are better examples of contingent reinforcement because the amount of money a worker gets depends directly upon productivity (Landy, 1989). There are problems associated with using piece-rate pay as a reinforcer, however. First, there is the issue of the timing of the reinforcement. Piece-rate workers are paid once every week or two, just the same as other workers, and Skinner's statements about the timing of pay should apply here as well as to other forms of pay. Second, rewards are effective when they are used to reinforce specific behaviors, but piece-rate systems reward productivity. How much a worker produces is not a behavior; productivity is a result of behavior *and* a number of other factors, such as skill, health, the behavior of co-workers, the weather, and so on. Unless workers' jobs are so simple that it is obvious how to improve performance, there is no assurance that piece-rate pay will reinforce the behaviors that lead to higher productivity.

Of course, to deliver contingent reinforcement, managers must pay attention to their subordinates' behavior. Unless they know how their workers are performing, it is not possible for managers to reward performance appropriately. Managers who are effective at motivating their workers have been found to spend more time gathering information about performance than do less effective managers. Specifically, they spend more time *monitoring* subordinates' work, which involves watching the workers as they perform their tasks and sampling work outcomes (Komaki, 1986; Komaki, Desselles, & Bowman, 1989). These findings show that it is safe to assume neither that managers always know how their workers are performing nor that they know the most effective way to gather performance information.

In laboratory research with animals, behaviorists have studied the effects of different *reinforcement schedules* on behavior. A **rein-**

forcement schedule refers to the timing and frequency of reinforcement. For example, a *continuous* schedule involves reinforcing the desired behavior each time it is performed. Other schedules are referred to as *intermittent* schedules because they involve reinforcement on a less-than-continuous basis; a summary of intermittent-reinforcement schedules is provided below:

1. *Fixed-ratio schedule.* A specific number of responses, or occurrences of the behavior, must take place before reinforcement is given. For example, PPP's interns could be given praise after turning in every third report.

2. *Variable-ratio schedule.* Reinforcement occurs after the behavior is performed a certain number of times *on average*, although the actual number varies from one reinforcement to another. For example, PPP's interns could be praised after turning in two reports, then after turning in five, then after three and so on, with the average equaling reinforcement after every three reports.

3. *Fixed-interval schedule.* Reinforcement occurs only after a specific interval of time has elapsed since the last reinforcement. Using this schedule, PPP's interns could be reinforced weekly by being praised following the first report filed after the start of work each Thursday.

4. *Variable-interval schedule.* Reinforcement occurs after a specific interval of time has elapsed since the last reinforcement *on average*, although the actual amount of time varies from one reinforcement to the next. Here, PPP's interns might be reinforced after five days, then after eight, then after three and so on, with the average interval equaling one week.

Differences in reinforcement schedules have been shown to have substantial and predictable effects on rate of learning and persistence of behavior. Intermittent schedules, particularly variable schedules, maximize persistence; continuous schedules minimize learning time (Skinner, 1959).

Research on reinforcement schedules in organizations has been less consistent. For example, in one study a continuous-reinforcement schedule was compared to a variable-ratio schedule; workers on the latter performed better than those reinforced continuously (Saari & Latham, 1982). In other field studies continuous and variable schedules showed no differences in effectiveness (Yukl & Latham, 1975; Yukl, Latham, & Pursell, 1976). Pritchard and his associates found that although comparisons of contingent-reinforcement schedules revealed no differences in effectiveness, *all* contingent schedules resulted in better performance than noncontingent reinforcement (Pritchard, Hollenback, & DeLeo, 1980; Pritchard, Leonard, VonBergen, & Kirk, 1976).

One problem in the use of reinforcement is the amount of time and effort that it entails. Careful records of employee behavior must be maintained in order to administer rewards effectively. Although evidence of a behavior is sometimes easy to obtain, in other cases employees must be directly observed. Further, it seems that once a contingent-reinforcement policy is established, it must be maintained if it is to remain effective. For example, a program based on operant principles was effective in reducing accident rates of bus drivers while the program was in operation, but the improvements did not carry over into the following months (Haynes, Pine, & Fitch, 1982). Another study showed that when a reward program was discontinued, employee perceptions of management's use of punishment increased, and their perceptions of managers' use of rewards, legitimate influence, and interpersonal power decreased (Greene & Podsakoff, 1981).

Evaluation of Reinforcement. The weight of the evidence strongly indicates that contingent reinforcement is a reliable way to improve performance. Unfortunately, it isn't clear *why* reinforcement works. Of course, radical behaviorists would argue that the issue of why reinforcement works is unimportant. In fact, the entire issue of motivation is irrelevant to these psychologists. In their opinions, all that is needed to understand performance is knowledge of workers' behaviors and the events in the environment that reinforce or punish those behaviors; motivation, reasoning, needs, and other abstract constructs are unnecessary baggage. Cognitive psychologists are not satisfied with simply knowing that reinforcement works, however; they are interested in discovering the underlying processes that make events reinforcing. Let's examine a well-known case of reinforcement and show how two cognitive theories, expectancy theory and goal setting, might explain the results.

Emery Worldwide is a large air-freight forwarder. An important key to its success is the use of air-freight containers, large shipping crates that hold many smaller packages. By putting packages into the freight containers, Emery saves handling time and expense and can earn greater profits. Because the company had spent a lot of money instructing employees on how to use the freight containers, management was surprised to learn that they were being used only 45% of the times possible (Where Skinner's theories work, 1972). To remedy this problem, Emery executives implemented a program of positive reinforcement and self-feedback. Workers recorded their performance on a checklist, which kept them informed of how closely they were meeting management's goals for container usage. In addition, supervisors were trained to provide positive reinforcement (praise) to workers who were meeting their goals or showing improvement (At Emery Air Freight, 1973). The results of this program were dramatic: Performance approached the goal on the first day, and during the first three years Emery attributed savings of $2 million to the program.

Behaviorists often cite the Emery case as an example of the power of reinforcement (Jordan,

1972; Luthans & Kreitner, 1985). However, this type of program might work because of the performance goals that are established; attributing the effects exclusively to reinforcement and self-feedback may be an oversimplification (Locke, 1980). Similarly, expectancy theorists could argue that supervisors' praise establishes strong instrumentalities between performance and outcomes or that the setting of goals might increase the valence of goal achievement; either of these could increase motivation. Of course, the question of *why* reinforcement works is unimportant to most people in organizations. Psychologists, however, cannot be satisfied with predicting and controlling behavior. They also want to understand and explain behavior, and in this regard reinforcement has fallen short. We agree with Landy (1989) that reinforcement is more a technology than a theory, and that although it is a useful tool, it has not promoted our understanding of work behavior.

Self-Efficacy

I/O psychologists have borrowed many theories and concepts in order to understand work behavior better. One of the most recent and most interesting of the concepts is *self-efficacy* (Bandura, 1977, 1982; Gist, 1987). **Self-efficacy** is the extent to which a person believes that she has the skills, knowledge, and abilities to accomplish a particular task. The beliefs develop slowly over time as a result of an individual's experiences.

Self-efficacy has implications for several of the theories we have already discussed. For example, if a person has high self-efficacy, he or she will set high goals that promote high productivity. Self-efficacy is not the same as expectancy or instrumentality, but workers who believe that they are *capable* of performing behaviors that lead to valued outcomes should be more likely to attempt those behaviors than would those with lower self-efficacy. Finally, receiving rewards and punishments will raise or lower self-efficacy, respectively, and affect performance through the setting of goals or changes in expectancies.

Although its proposed effects are consistent with a variety of motivation theories, self-efficacy is much more than a means to reconcile alternative explanations for behavior. Bandura believes that *all* efforts to improve motivation operate through self-efficacy (Bandura, 1986). That is, reinforcement and punishment work through their positive and negative effects on self-efficacy, and personal goals reflect levels of self-efficacy and the results of accumulated feedback on the success of achieving past goals.

Research has supported the role of self-efficacy in motivated behavior. For example, self-efficacy was found to predict performance on a physical-exercise task across a variety of goal and feedback conditions. The higher the subjects' self-efficacy, the better they performed on the task (Bandura & Cervone, 1986). In a very different realm, computer trainees who were high in "computer self-efficacy" reached higher levels of mastery in a software training program than did trainees who were lower in self-efficacy (Gist, Schwoerer, & Rosen, 1989; see Figure 8.9).

Self-efficacy has positive effects not only on physical effort and learning but on more abstract and complex processes as well. In a study of managerial decision making in a simulated organization, subjects higher in self-efficacy were more likely to use effective, systematic strategies to arrive at solutions to problems (Wood, Bandura, & Bailey, 1990). Similarly, university faculty who were high in self-efficacy published more articles and books, had higher performance goals, and were more likely to be involved in multiple research projects (Taylor, Locke, Lee, & Gist, 1984).

Evaluation of Self-Efficacy. Although self-efficacy has only recently been applied to work motivation, it shows a great deal of promise as a predictor of, and explanation for, work performance. This may be partially due to the fact that feelings of self-efficacy are associated with

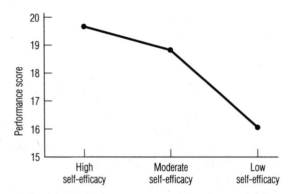

FIGURE 8.9
Performance and Self-Efficacy
SOURCE: From "Effects of Alternative Training Methods on Self-Efficacy and Performance in Computer Software Training," by M. E. Gist, C. Schwoerer, and B. Rosen, 1989, *Journal of Applied Psychology, 74,* 877. Adapted by permission.

every task that people perform. Thus, self-efficacy is more universal than many of the motivation constructs that I/O psychologists have traditionally studied. As we learn more about the operation of efficacy beliefs in the workplace, our understanding of many motivational processes will improve.

Other Motivation Issues

In addition to general theories of motivation such as those just presented, psychologists have studied a number of more specific motivation issues. Most of these concern the application or use of motivational techniques. We shall briefly present two such issues. The first addresses whether motivation comes from within a person or is controlled by external events. The second deals with the effects of worker participation in decision making.

Intrinsic Motivation

Although it was present in earlier theories (Herzberg, 1966), recent research on intrinsic

Intrinsic motivation

motivation is based on ideas developed by Deci (1975, 1976). According to Deci, work behavior can be motivated by both *intrinsic* and *extrinsic* factors. **Intrinsic motivation** occurs when people achieve feelings of competence and control from their work. **Extrinsic motivation** occurs when people receive external rewards, such as pay from their employer. Deci also asserts that workers who receive extrinsic rewards for otherwise intrinsically motivating work will experience reduced feelings of control, which will in turn reduce the overall level of motivation.

Deci and others have found support for his predictions (for example, Deci, 1972, 1975; Lepper & Greene, 1975; Jordan, 1986). Other researchers, however, have been unable to replicate these results (for example, Arnold, 1976; Scott & Erskine, 1980; Scott, Farh, & Podsakoff, 1988). Several studies have found that the effects of extrinsic and intrinsic rewards depend upon the nature of the job. For example, it seems that for uninteresting or boring tasks, extrinsic rewards *increase* intrinsic motivation

(Calder & Staw, 1975; Mossholder, 1980). On interesting tasks, however, extrinsic rewards have been shown to *decrease* intrinsic motivation (Daniel & Esser, 1980; Mossholder, 1980).

Beyond extrinsic rewards, other factors can affect the level of intrinsic motivation. Setting specific, difficult goals has been found to have a negative effect on intrinsic motivation for interesting tasks, but a positive effect when the tasks are less interesting (Hirst, 1988). Goals may undermine intrinsic motivation in the former case by drawing attention to the goal itself rather than the interesting task as the reason for performing the task. On the other hand, with less interesting tasks goals can't reduce intrinsic motivation much because it is already low. In this case, the positive aspects of goals such as performance feedback and increased challenge can increase the level of interest in the task and thereby boost intrinsic motivation.

In another study, subjects performed a task on a computer. Those who were told that the task was a game had higher intrinsic motivation than those who were told that the task was a work simulation (Cellar & Barrett, 1987). Labeling the task a "game" apparently triggered the subjects' standard reactions to game situations, or their "game scripts." (Scripts are well-learned, virtually automatic series of behaviors that are activated in specific, familiar situations.) As you might expect, the game scripts included greater intrinsic interest and task persistence than the subjects' standard reactions to work situations (or "work scripts").

People's reactions to tasks and their intrinsic motivation to perform the tasks can also be triggered by social cues. That is, people can develop intrinsic motivation on a task simply by watching an intrinsically motivated person performing the task (Cellar & Wade, 1988). It could be, therefore, that the PPP interns have simply observed other PPP employees who appear to be unmotivated, and have thereby acquired a *lack* of intrinsic motivation.

Participative Decision Making.   One of the most widely advocated motivational techniques is **participative decision making,** or PDM, which is based on the premise that worker motivation, as well as satisfaction, morale, creativity, and other desirable characteristics, can be enhanced by allowing workers to participate in making job-related decisions.

A large number of research programs have studied the issue of participation, and some have reported impressive support for the effectiveness of PDM. Most reviews of the participation research show, however, that support for PDM is mixed at best (Dachler & Wilpert, 1978; Locke & Schweiger, 1979). The reviews have, in turn, been criticized for ignoring or downplaying the possibility that the effects of PDM might depend upon the type of participation used (Cotton, Vollrath, Froggatt, Lengnick-Hall, & Jennings, 1988), or upon contextual or situational factors (Miller & Monge, 1986). It appears that the effectiveness of PDM depends, in part, upon our definition of *participation*. Until researchers can agree on what PDM is, disagree-

ment on its effectiveness will continue (Cotton, Vollrath, Lengnick-Hall, & Froggatt, 1990; Leana, Locke, & Schweiger, 1990).

Although Locke and Schweiger (1979) seem to have taken an unusual amount of pleasure in criticizing it, we think that their conclusions about participation are fair. They said that the research provided only equivocal support for the effects of PDM, although the effects on satisfaction seemed to be stronger than those on productivity. Subsequent reviews agree on this point (Miller & Monge, 1986; cf. Wagner & Gooding, 1987). One thing is certain: The once widespread acceptance of PDM is giving way to more cautious consideration of its potential benefits.

Combining Motivation Theories

We have presented three theories of motivation based on needs, three cognitive approaches to motivation, the behaviorist viewpoint on work behavior, and self-efficacy theory. Most of these theories have been supported by research to some extent. None has provided a comprehensive explanation for work motivation. One way to improve our understanding of motivation is to combine the processes specified in several theories into a more extensive model, thereby playing the strengths of each approach against the weaknesses of the others.

A number of theories have combined different approaches to motivation. We offer two examples: a classic model by Porter and Lawler (1968), and a more recent effort based upon control theory (Klein, 1989). Both models illustrate how components of several motivation theories can be combined to provide a broader perspective than any single theory can provide.

The Porter-Lawler model was developed as an expanded version of expectancy theory, as you can see by examining the first three cells in Figure 8.10. Here valences (Cell 1) and expectancies (Cell 2) combine to produce effort (Cell 3). Consistent with Vroom's (1964) description of expectancy processes, effort does

FIGURE 8.10
The Porter-Lawler Model of Motivation
SOURCE: From *Managerial Attitudes and Performance,* by L. W. Porter and E. E. Lawler, III. Copyright © 1968 by Richard D. Irwin, Inc. Reprinted by permission.

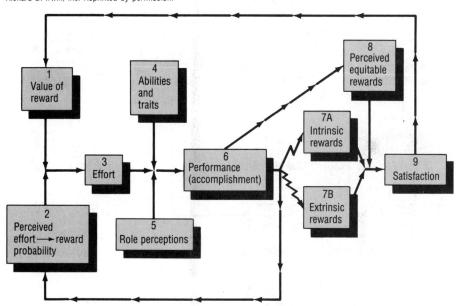

not determine performance directly but, rather, combines with ability and other worker characteristics (Cell 4) and the worker's perceptions of what is expected on the job (Cell 5) to produce performance (Cell 6). As Deci (1975) later emphasized, performance can result in intrinsic and/or extrinsic rewards (Cells 7a and 7b). The levels of these rewards may have implications for future expectancies. Consistent with equity theory, the rewards received are compared to a standard representing what the worker believes is fair (Cell 8). This comparison can have positive or negative effects on job satisfaction (Cell 9), which in turn has implications for the valence of rewards available in the future.

Several models based upon control theory have appeared recently in the organizational literature (for example, Hollenbeck, 1989; Lord & Hanges, 1987; Taylor, 1983). We focus here on a version of control theory described by Klein (1989). **Control theory** is based on a simple

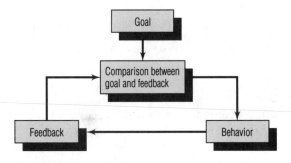

FIGURE 8.11
The Control-Theory Feedback Loop

feedback loop where behavior is triggered by unmet goals, and the results of the behavior are evaluated against the goal through a feedback process (see Figure 8.11).

The full control-theory model of work motivation is illustrated in Figure 8.12 (Klein, 1989). In this model, the immediate causes of

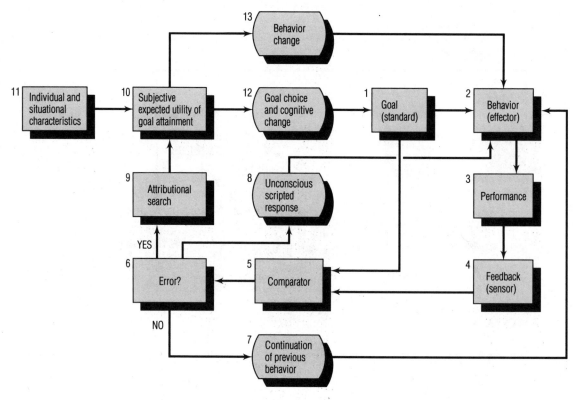

FIGURE 8.12
An Integrated Control Theory Model of Work Motivation
Source: From "An Integrated Control Theory Model of Work Motivation," by H. J. Klein, 1989, *Academy of Management Review, 14*, 153. Reprinted by permission.

behavior are goals (Cell 1). Behavior (Cell 2), in turn, determines performance (Cell 3), about which the worker receives feedback (Cell 4). A comparison is made between the performance feedback and the goal (Cells 5 and 6), and if the goal is being met (that is, no "error" is detected), the behavior is continued (Cell 7). If the goal is not being met (that is, an "error" is detected), two processes may occur. First, there may be what Klein calls an "unconscious scripted response" (Cell 8). That is, if the perceived performance "error" has occurred often in the past, the worker may unconsciously engage in a series of behaviors (a script) that has been found to be effective in correcting the error.

If an unconscious scripted response is not available, a series of conscious problem-solving behaviors is initiated. The first of these is an attributional search (Cell 9). That is, workers will develop attributions, or explanations, for why the goal has not been met, which in turn influence their expectancies that the goal can be attained (Cell 10). For example, if PPP's interns attribute their failure to complete assignments on time to temporary conditions, such as a computer malfunction, their expectations for goal attainment should not change. However, if they attribute their failure to their own lack of ability, the expectancies should drop.

Subjective expected utility (SEU; Cell 10) is a multiplicative function of goal attractiveness

THE WIZARD OF ID, by permission of Johnny Hart and News America Syndicate.

and the expectancy of attaining the goal, so it is very similar to the force model of Vroom's (1964) expectancy theory. In addition to attributions, SEU is influenced by individual and situational characteristics (Cell 11), such as past experience and environmental barriers to performance. If the SEU of goal attainment is low, the worker will withdraw, either physically or mentally—essentially abandoning the goal. If the SEU is high, the goal is pursued through one of two processes. First, cognitive changes may occur (Cell 12), such as changes in goal commitment or goal level, or the goal itself (Cell 1) may be adjusted. Second, behavioral change may occur (Cell 13), such as changes in effort level or in strategy, which in turn affect behavior (Cell 2).

Neither the Porter-Lawler model nor control theory represents the "final word" on motivation. Nevertheless, we believe they are good examples of the direction that will be most productive in future motivation research and theory. Rather than relying on any one process, these theories combine the basics of several viable models in frameworks that allow for dynamic changes in workers' motives. Given the flexibility and change that permeate our society and our workplaces, it is unlikely that the "final word" on motivation will ever be uttered. Dynamic, multifaceted theories such as these are therefore the best chance we have for understanding the activation, direction, and persistence of work behavior.

Conclusion

In this chapter we presented a number of theories designed to explain work motivation. The theories reflect a wide range of perspectives on human behavior. With the exception of the earliest need approaches, all of the theories have received at least modest support from research. We know more about what motivates workers than did previous generations.

Even though psychologists have been able to identify many factors related to work motivation, problems such as the one involving PPP's interns have not become less frequent or less important. This is true in part because managers often fail to take advantage of what we have learned from motivation research. There are many reasons for this, including lack of awareness of the theories, difficulties associated with applying motivation theories in dynamic and complex organizations, and, in some cases, managers' fears that following a psychologist's advice will limit their freedom to supervise subordinates as they see fit. These considerations illustrate some of the problems facing Dr. MacKeven as she develops a plan to deal

INTEROFFICE MEMO

To: M. Russell,
        Director of Consumer Research

From: J. A. MacKeven,
        Human Resources Coordinator

I have just completed a meeting with my staff, at which we discussed the situation involving the summer interns in your division. Let me briefly summarize what we have done regarding this situation and outline our recommendations.

After receiving your memo describing the motivation problems that you have been experiencing, we interviewed a number of the interns in the program--both good and poor performers, as identified by your staff. Our major goal in doing this was to determine what the interns perceived to be the major responsibilities of their jobs, as well as what they believed were management's expectations of them. I personally interviewed the immediate supervisors of these interns, to determine their perceptions of the same issues. Upon comparing notes from the intern and supervisor interviews, it was clear that there were two totally different perspectives on what the intern program is all about.

A detailed report on our research will be forthcoming in the next two weeks, in which we will explain the differences between interns' and supervisors' views. Also in that report will be detailed recommendations for policy changes to help avoid this sort of misunderstanding in the future. Briefly, these recommendations will propose that detailed performance standards be established for each intern, and that each intern be required to submit weekly reports describing his or her status relative to those standards. After you have had time to study the report, we should meet to work out specific details of the program.

with the situation in the Consumer Research Department.

Chapter Summary

Work motivation is concerned with people's goal-directed behavior in the workplace. Specifically, motivation theories attempt to explain the energizing, directing, and sustaining of behavior that leads to the achievement of individual or organizational objectives. Although motivation is a potentially powerful concept, its effects can be limited by such factors as individual ability level, changes in motives, and the operation of stereotypes about workers.

Theories developed to explain work motivation specify a variety of processes by which behavior may be directed. Some of the better-known theories based on need satisfaction, such as Maslow's need hierarchy and Alderfer's ERG, have not received much empirical support, although models based on Murray's manifest-needs system show more promise. One of the most widely researched cognitive theories of motivation is Vroom's expectancy model, which states that motivation is a function of workers' expectations that behavior will result in the attainment of desired outcomes. Other motivation theories propose that behavior is controlled by perceptions of equity, setting of performance goals, use of reinforcement and punishment, and workers' self-evaluations of their ability to perform job tasks. Each of these approaches has received some research support, but none has proved to be a good general explanation for worker motivation.

In addition to general theories of work motivation, I/O psychologists have studied such issues as the effects of extrinsic rewards on intrinsic motivation and the value of participative decision making. Research on these more specific issues has been useful for defining the limits of motivation, and in efforts to integrate motivation theories, such as the Porter-Lawler model and control theory.

Review Questions and Exercises

1. Dr. MacKeven's recommendation could be justified by several theories presented in this chapter. Which theories, and how would each explain the potential success of the proposed program?

2. Dr. MacKeven's suggestion, as we have described it, is somewhat incomplete. What additional recommendations would you make to help assure the program's success?

3. Although Dr. MacKeven's recommendation is consistent with several theories, a number of alternative programs could have been proposed. Given what you have learned about motivation, describe one such alternative, and contrast its strengths and weaknesses with those of Dr. MacKeven's proposal.

4. Early in the chapter we presented a list of factors that limit the practical usefulness of the motivation concept. Discuss how each factor might cause the proposed program to fail (or appear to fail).

CHAPTER 9

....

Work Attitudes

LEARNING POINTS

After studying this chapter, you should

- be able to define *attitude*, and explain how job satisfaction is an attitude;

- be able to describe the basic ideas of scientific management, and explain how the Hawthorne and Hoppock studies changed the way I/O psychologists thought about work behavior;

- be able to describe two-factor theory, differentiating between the role of motivators and the role of satisfiers;

- understand the basic principles of comparison theories of job satisfaction, and be able to explain how the principles were used by Maslow, Murray, Locke, and Lawler;

- be able to explain the roles of social learning and attributions in the development of job attitudes;

- be able to discuss the potential role of dispositions in determining work attitudes, and describe the reasons why we are still uncertain about dispositional causes of attitudes;

- be able to define organizational commitment, and distinguish between attitudinal and calculated commitment;

- be able to define withdrawal, and describe the relationship between withdrawal and job attitudes;

- be able to describe the relationship between job performance and job satisfaction, and explain why this relationship is not what many people believe it should be;

- be able to define work and nonwork, and describe how they seem to be related; and

- be able to discuss various measures of job satisfaction and organizational commitment, and recommend different measures for different uses.

The Nature of Work Attitudes

....

In this chapter we will discuss attitudes that workers have regarding their jobs. It is clear, from examining our own experiences in schools, families, businesses, or other organizations, that people have a variety of attitudes toward the groups to which they belong. I/O psychologists have studied both how such attitudes develop and the effects of these attitudes on work behavior. The turnover and absenteeism problems described by Joanna Richmond are typical of those that psychologists have found to be re-

INTEROFFICE MEMO

To: J. A. MacKeven,
           Human Resources Coordinator

From: Joanna Richmond,
          Director of Inspections

I am writing to see if you might be able to help me with a puzzling, and in fact embarrassing, problem that I recently became aware of. Last month I called a meeting of my staff to discuss the latest federal regulations that apply to our store operations, and how they might have implications for the enforcement of certain common state regulations. Quite unexpectedly, Ed Clark, Vice President of Retail Operations, attended the meeting. Normally this would not be threatening to me, and it wasn't in this case until Mr. Clark mentioned that he didn't seem to recognize many of the people at the meeting, and asked me to introduce everyone. It was clear to me that he was making a point when he mentioned the "importance of keeping good people" after the meeting. While I was aware that there had been a number of people leaving my division in recent months, I was surprised to find, upon checking, that the annual turnover rate has been running at approximately 50%. I did some more checking with the directors of the Policy and Quality Standards Divisions, and found that both turnover and absenteeism are problems throughout Retail Operations. Although I cannot judge the extent of the problem elsewhere in the company, it is a very real problem here, especially given the large number of inspectors and the high costs of training. I would like to arrange a meeting with you to discuss this situation in detail.

lated to job attitudes. If these attitudes have an effect on work behavior, then an understanding of how work attitudes develop would be invaluable. Before examining the research on these issues, we will first consider the nature of attitudes in general.

Psychologists, particularly social psychologists, have been studying attitudes for many years. **Attitudes** can be defined as *relatively stable affective, or evaluative, dispositions toward a specific person, situation, or other entity*. The thing about which we have an attitude, such as a job, is commonly referred to as an "attitude object." Attitudes are typically described as consisting of three basic components. The first is a *belief* about the attitude object, sometimes referred to as the *cognitive* component of attitudes. For example, the store inspectors at Peter's Pan Pizza may believe that their work is dull and boring. That belief, however, does not necessarily mean that they have a negative attitude toward their jobs—it may be that they *enjoy* dull and boring work!

The second component of an attitude is *evaluative* or *emotional*. If you have an attitude toward something, you either like it or dislike it to some degree. It is the evaluative component that distinguishes attitudes from simple beliefs. For example, a store inspector from Peter's Pan Pizza might be overheard to say, "I am paid $5.10 an hour." In this case the inspector has simply reported what she believes to be true. A second inspector might be overheard to say, "I am paid $5.10 per hour, and I'm worth a lot more." In this case, the inspector has expressed a degree of dislike or dissatisfaction with his pay, thereby revealing a negative attitude. Finally, another inspector, paid the same $5.10 per hour, might be overheard to say, "I can't believe they pay me so much money to do this work!" This also indicates an attitude, but positive in nature rather than negative. It is important to note that there are no "neutral" attitudes. If you find yourself in a situation for which you have no evaluative response, positive or negative, then although you may have

beliefs about the situation, you do not have an attitude toward it.

The third component of attitudes is a *tendency or disposition to act* in a certain way toward the attitude object. Returning to our store inspectors, the person who feels he is underpaid might look for a new job, whereas the person who feels she is overpaid is less likely to engage in job hunting. Thus, work attitudes should have implications for work motivation.

Workers have attitudes toward many aspects of their work and psychologists have studied many of these attitudes. In this chapter we will focus on two specific work attitudes: job satisfaction and organizational commitment. This is not to downplay the importance of other work attitudes, such as job involvement, career commitment, and job security. However, job satisfaction and organizational commitment are two of the most widely studied work attitudes, and illustrate the potential role of attitudes in work settings.

Multidimensionality of Work Attitudes

As we stated, work attitudes refer to a worker's emotional, affective, or evaluative response toward his job, supervisor, organization, or other aspect of work. It should be clear, however, that work is complex and has many characteristics or facets. Consequently, it is possible for a person to have very different attitudes toward the different aspects of his or her work. For example, Dr. MacKeven suspects that the employees in PPP's Retail Operations Division have low job satisfaction, and that this results in the high rates of turnover and absenteeism in this unit. Based on these suspicions, she may administer an attitude survey, and find that the workers are indeed unhappy with their jobs. Dr. MacKeven would then want to know precisely *what* it is about their jobs that the workers dislike. It is possible that the inspectors are all reasonably happy with their pay, benefits, and the work that they do, but are very unhappy about the amount of travel that their jobs require and the amount of time that they must spend away from their families.

Psychologists describe the complex nature of work attitudes by saying that they are *multidimensional*, meaning that they have a number of distinct, relatively independent components. The multidimensionality has at least two important implications. The first is that it is misleading to speak of work attitudes without specifying the precise aspect of the job to which the attitude refers. Using job satisfaction as an example, there are times when Dr. MacKeven is interested in general or global job satisfaction. This would reflect some combination of a workers' satisfaction with all aspects of the job and indicate whether the workers are generally happy. In other cases, such as when Dr. MacKeven must recommend what to do to improve workers' satisfaction, it might be more useful to know exactly what it is about the job that is causing the problem.

The second implication of the multidimensionality of work attitudes concerns the *measurement* of attitudes. Clearly, if you are interested in workers' global satisfaction, you need to use a very different measure than if you are interested in satisfaction with only a single facet of the job, such as pay or the quality of supervision. Consequently, psychologists have developed a variety of measures of work attitudes, ranging from very general measures of overall feelings toward a job to very specific readings of attitudes toward individual aspects of work. We will discuss some of the issues involved in the measurement of work attitudes later in this chapter. For now, just keep the complex, multidimensional nature of work attitudes in mind as we examine some of the attitude theories that have been developed.

Job Satisfaction

While preparing to write and then revise this book, we reviewed all of the articles published in numerous journals over a number of years. We found that more articles addressed some aspect of job satisfaction than any other single topic. I/O psychologists have certainly shown a great interest in worker attitudes. This was not always the case, as evidenced by the perspective taken in one of the earliest systematic approaches to dealing with worker behavior: Frederick Taylor's "scientific management."

Scientific Management

Frederick W. Taylor was an engineer who, in the early part of the 20th century, became interested in increasing workers' efficiency. As might be expected, given his engineering background, Taylor's efforts focused on ways to change or redesign jobs in order to allow workers to be more efficient. In *Principles of Scientific Management* (1911), Taylor described what he saw as the necessary steps to increased efficiency. Although critics do not always realize this, he advocated the development of cooperation and shared responsibility between management and labor. The major aspects of scientific management, however, concerned the systematic study and design of jobs in order to eliminate inefficient behaviors and techniques. To this end, Taylor introduced **time-and-motion studies**, which analyzed the individual movements made by workers and identified the most efficient set of behaviors to perform the tasks required by a job. One result of performing time-and-motion studies was that the jobs were greatly simplified; workers performed only a few very simple tasks.

Taylor's view of the role of workers was based on a simple, and much disputed, assumption about motivation. He believed that *all* workers desired *only* economic rewards, and that they would increase their levels of effort to obtain these rewards. Consequently, it was assumed that once pay was linked with productivity, workers would accept whatever job changes were introduced in order to get higher pay. As a result, workers were seen as interchangeable components of jobs. Because motivation was guaranteed by the link between productivity and economic rewards, and because time-and-motion studies could be used to simplify jobs so that ability made little difference, research on worker behavior focused on working conditions that might improve productivity. Topics such as temperature and illumination levels were commonly studied by psychologists, and a great emphasis was placed on the identification of efficient behaviors that all workers could be trained to perform. Workers' attitudes toward their jobs were simply not considered to be important.

The Hawthorne and Hoppock Studies

In 1924 a series of long-term research projects was begun at the Hawthorne plant of the Western Electric Company (Landsberger, 1958; Roethlisberger & Dickson, 1939; see Chapter 1 for additional details). Consistent with the then-prevalent view of worker behavior and the emphasis on efficiency, the original purpose of the Hawthorne studies was to determine the level of illumination at which workers' productivity and efficiency were highest. One early study showed that the performance of both experimental and control groups, rather than that of the experimental group alone, increased during the course of the research. Other studies showed that productivity increased even when the level of illumination was dramatically lowered, or when the researchers tricked the workers into *believing* that the lights had been changed when in fact the illumination levels were the *same* as before.

These results left the Hawthorne researchers "in the dark," and prompted them to conduct a number of additional studies in the hope of identifying factors that could explain the workers' bizarre behavior. In some studies the workers kept diaries, and their comments clearly indicated that the experimental manipulations were accompanied by changes in attitudes toward coworkers and company management.

Further, these attitudes provided a better explanation for the changes in workers' productivity than did the manipulations themselves.

The Hawthorne studies have been criticized for poor experimental design, inaccurate reporting of results, and a variety of other shortcomings (see Chapter 1). They remain, however, one of the most important research projects in the history of I/O psychology because of two influential conclusions that were drawn from the studies. The first is that work attitudes and perceptions of job characteristics determine (at least in part) the effects of such things as pay, hours of work, working conditions, and the physical work environment. Managers no longer assume that all workers respond in the same way to similar jobs nor that their reactions are easily predictable. The second conclusion is that workers respond not only to the rules, goals, and expectations of the formal organization but also to the pressures and norms established by informal work groups, over which management has little or no control.

These conclusions led researchers to ask new questions about workers' attitudes, emotions, and perceptions, and the differences between workers on these types of variables. Some of the earliest influential research on job satisfaction to follow the Hawthorne studies was conducted by Robert Hoppock (1935). In the best known of his projects, he surveyed all adult residents of New Hope, Pennsylvania, in 1933. New Hope was described by Hoppock as a "typical" American town of about 1,100 residents, of whom 351 were employed adults. One notable aspect of Hoppock's results is their similarity to those of more recent surveys (Weaver, 1980). For example, he found that New Hope residents were generally quite satisfied with their jobs, with 77 percent reporting that they "liked," were "enthusiastic about," or "loved" their jobs. Also, virtually no differences were found between the satisfaction levels of men and women. There were, however, more substantial differences between the satisfaction levels for different occupational and socioeconomic groups, with professional, managerial, and executive workers having the highest satisfaction, and unskilled manual workers having the lowest.

The Hawthorne studies focused attention on the importance of workers' needs and perceptions; Hoppock's (1935) work addressed many of the practical issues involved in conducting job-satisfaction research. Together, these pioneering efforts shaped much of the theory and research on job attitudes that was to follow. Over the years there have been a number of such theories designed to explain the causes and effects of job satisfaction. Many of the theories are more than simply theories of satisfaction, however; they are also concerned with worker motivation, work-group interaction, and leader-follower relationships. Consequently, as we examine these theories you will recognize many of the concepts from previous chapters, and you will also be getting a preview of some of the things to come in later chapters.

Frederick Herzberg's Two-Factor Theory

In 1957 Herzberg, Mausner, Peterson, and Capwell published a review of the early satisfaction research literature. Contrary to other reviews that had found no relationships between job satisfaction and work performance (for example, Brayfield & Crockett, 1955), Herzberg concluded that there *were* systematic relationships between workers' attitudes and their behavior. However, Herzberg believed that these relationships had gone unnoticed because researchers had confused job satisfaction and job dissatisfaction. According to Herzberg, job satisfaction depends upon a certain set of conditions, whereas job *dis*satisfaction is the result of an entirely different set of conditions. Thus, although it is possible to think of satisfaction and dissatisfaction as two extremes of a single continuum, they are determined by different factors. Failure to recognize this, said Herzberg, had resulted in the mistaken conclusion that

work attitudes were unrelated to work behaviors.

Motivators and Hygiene Factors. Herzberg, Mausner, and Snyderman (1959) conducted new research to test the relationship between satisfaction and performance, and formalized a theory based on their results. According to the theory, people have two major types of needs. The first of these Herzberg called *hygiene* needs, which are influenced by the physical and psychological conditions in which people work. Herzberg called the second set of needs *motivator* needs, and described them as being very similar to the higher-order needs in Maslow's (1943) need-hierarchy theory (see Chapter 8).

Herzberg asserted that the two types of needs were satisfied by different types of outcomes or rewards (Herzberg et al., 1959). Hygiene needs were fulfilled by certain conditions called **hygiene factors**, or **dissatisfiers**:

1. Supervision
2. Interpersonal relations
3. Physical working conditions
4. Salary
5. Company policies and administrative practices
6. Benefits
7. Job security

These factors are all concerned with the context or environment in which the job exists. When these factors are unfavorable, job dissatisfaction is the result. This might be the case in the Retail Operations Division at Peter's Pan Pizza if the workers believe they are being paid too little, or if the travel involved in their jobs is a hardship. When hygiene factors are positive, such as when workers feel that their pay is fair and their working conditions are good, then barriers to job satisfaction are removed. The fulfillment of hygiene needs, however, cannot by itself result in job satisfaction but only in the reduction or elimination of dissatisfaction. Herzberg compared hygiene factors to modern water- and air-pollution controls: although they do not cure any diseases, they serve to prevent the outbreak of disease. In the same way, he believed that hygiene factors did not cause satisfaction but that they could *prevent* dissatisfaction.

Unlike hygiene needs, motivator needs are fulfilled by what Herzberg called **motivator factors** or **satisfiers** (Herzberg et al., 1959). He identified the following:

1. Achievement
2. Recognition
3. Work itself
4. Responsibility
5. Advancement

Whereas hygiene factors are related to the context of work, motivator factors are concerned with the nature of the work itself and the consequences of work. According to the theory, the factors that lead to job satisfaction are those that satisfy one's need for self-actualization in one's work, and it is "only from the performance of a task that the individual can get the rewards that will reinforce his aspirations" (Herzberg et al., 1959, p. 114).

Compared to hygiene factors, which result in a "neutral state" when present, motivator factors result in job satisfaction. When recognition, responsibility, and other motivators are absent from a job, however, the result will not be dissatisfaction, as with the absence of hygiene factors, but the same neutral state associated with the presence of hygiene factors. Figure 9.1 illustrates the nature of the relationships between hygiene factors, motivator factors, job satisfaction, and job dissatisfaction.

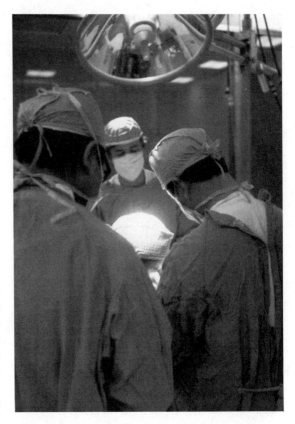

Motivator factors are concerned with the nature and consequences of work.

Evaluation of Two-Factor Theory. It is easy to imagine how two-factor theory might work in a particular situation. For instance, Dr. MacKeven might suspect that the turnover problem in Retail Operations stems from employee dissatisfaction. If she were to base her recommendations on two-factor theory, she might try to eliminate dissatisfaction by suggesting that a

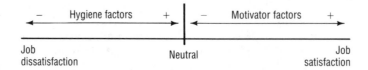

FIGURE 9.1
Two-Factor Theory

higher mileage rate be paid to inspectors who must travel or, perhaps, by adjusting pay or other fringe benefits. By improving these deficient hygiene factors, Dr. MacKeven would be removing the source of worker dissatisfaction. If she wished to make the workers *satisfied*, however, she would have to bolster their feelings of esteem or self-actualization. This would require job changes that would enable workers to receive recognition for their achievements and to have responsibility for what they do and how it is done. These changes should also affect the actual work they perform, so that it has personal meaning and significance.

Unfortunately, two-factor theory just doesn't work out in practice. One problem with the theory is that it is based on face-to-face interviews of workers conducted by Herzberg and his colleagues. This is a problem because unhappy workers are likely to assert that their dissatisfaction is due to circumstances beyond their control, such as the boss, working conditions, or company policy. When something happens that *satisfies* a worker, such as receiving recognition or a promotion, it is more likely to be attributed to the worker's own skills or effort. Thus, the theory may reflect the way in which the data were gathered more than the actual causes of satisfaction and dissatisfaction. Indeed, efforts to replicate Herzberg's results using noninterview techniques have generally not been successful (for example, Ewen, Smith, Hulin, & Locke, 1966; Hulin & Smith, 1965). Another factor that has probably contributed to the lack of support for two-factor theory is that Herzberg and associates (1959) based the theory solely on samples of accountants and engineers. It is hardly surprising that efforts to replicate their results with more representative samples of workers have failed—the same could be expected with any theory based on a restricted sample of workers from highly technical occupations.

Another, more theoretical problem is that Herzberg was not consistent in his description of two-factor theory, nor in the roles played by motivation and hygiene factors (King, 1970). At least five versions of two-factor theory have been found in Herzberg's writings (for example, Herzberg, 1964, 1966), ranging from the statement that, collectively, motivators have a stronger effect on satisfaction than on dissatisfaction whereas hygiene factors have a stronger effect on dissatisfaction than on satisfaction to the relatively strict statement that only motivators influence satisfaction and only hygiene factors influence dissatisfaction. This inconsistency, however, seems to make little practical difference because little support for *any* version of two-factor theory has been found (King, 1970).

The problems associated with two-factor theory, particularly the difficulty researchers have had replicating Herzberg's results, virtually halted research on this approach during the late 1970s and early 1980s. Although there have been rare articles reporting results consistent with Herzberg's model (for example, Machungwa & Schmitt, 1983), it is now clear that two-factor theory is not an adequate explanation for work attitudes. However, two-factor theory served an important function in the study of job satisfaction, as it went beyond consideration of external rewards and emphasized the satisfying effects of intrinsic factors. It has also proven valuable for its ability to describe what people find satisfying or dissatisfying (Landy, 1989).

Comparison Theories of Job Satisfaction

Two-factor theory states that certain aspects of work are related to job satisfaction, whereas other aspects are related to dissatisfaction. Workers who have, on balance, more satisfiers in their jobs will tend to be more satisfied; those with more dissatisfiers will be more dissatisfied. If you change the level or amount of either factor, the theory would predict a change in satisfaction. Further, because two-factor theory focuses on work and job characteristics as the causes of satisfaction (and dissatisfaction), the same changes would be predicted for *all* workers. Most satisfaction theories, however, specify more complex processes involving a comparison between a worker's current status and some standard or expectation. These *comparison theories* differ on what the standard of comparison is, but they share the notion that meeting the standard leads to satisfaction, whereas failure to meet the standard leads to dissatisfaction.

Need Theories.   Perhaps the earliest application of the comparison approach to job satisfaction involved the concept of *needs*. Need theories were developed primarily to explain motivation, and were discussed in detail in Chapter 8. Briefly, need theories state that we have certain physiological and psychological requirements or needs that may be fulfilled through our work. We continually compare the current status of our needs to the level of need fulfillment that we obtain or desire from our jobs. When our needs are unfulfilled, an unpleasant state of tension results and we are not likely to experience job satisfaction. Fulfillment of our needs removes the tension, thereby allowing us to feel satisfied.

Need theories have been researched extensively, and a number of problems with this approach to studying behavior have been identified. The most troublesome is the inability of psychologists to define adequately the concept of needs, and to identify a set of needs that is adequate to explain behavior over a variety of situations (see Chapter 8). Based on the research evidence so far, it appears that although some need approaches may have value in explaining and predicting managerial behavior, including satisfaction, more general satisfaction theories must rely on other processes.

Locke's Value Theory.   A second comparison theory of job satisfaction is the value theory developed by Locke (1976). Rather than focusing on needs, Locke suggested that job satisfaction may be more closely related to whether or not our work provides us with what we *want, desire,* or *value.* We examine what our jobs provide us in terms of, for example, pay, working conditions, and promotion opportunities. We then compare those perceptions to what we value or find important in a job. To the extent that the two match, job satisfaction results.

To illustrate Locke's theory, consider the absenteeism and turnover in PPP's Retail Operations Division. Assuming that these problems are indeed related to poor job satisfaction, value theory would lead Dr. MacKeven to identify the outcomes that the workers value from their jobs and, if possible, adjust the level of those outcomes to match their desires. It should be noted that because different workers have different values, this would not be an easy task.

There is a subtle difference between Locke's (1976) viewpoint and that of need theories such as Maslow's (1943). The difference can be illustrated by considering the effects of a potential pay raise for PPP's workers. Let's assume that PPP pays its employees very well compared to other companies in the food industry. Despite this, few of us would be surprised to learn that PPP workers *want* a pay raise. It would be unlikely that money could be identified as a *need* for these workers, in the way that either Maslow or Murray (1938) define needs. It is easy, however, to believe that most workers would *value* more money than they are currently receiving.

An interesting implication of Locke's (1976) theory is that although knowing the importance or value that a worker attaches to a particular outcome does not by itself predict how satisfied the worker will be, importance should predict the *range* of potential worker attitudes. Consider, for example, the possible effects of pay on the satisfaction of workers at PPP. Some workers attach a high value to the level of their pay; to them money is one, if not *the*, major outcome associated with working. Consequently, differences in pay will be strongly related to their satisfaction, as illustrated in Figure 9.2. (We show only positive effects for pay on satisfaction, although some equity approaches suggest a nega-

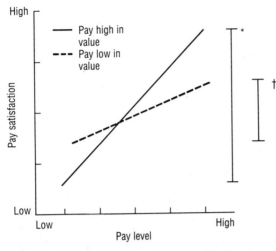

* Range of satisfaction for workers who place high value on pay

† Range of satisfaction for workers who place low value on pay

FIGURE 9.2
An Illustration of the Potential Effects of Value on the Range of Worker Satisfaction
SOURCE: From "The Nature and Causes of Job Satisfaction" by E. A. Locke, in M. D. Dunnette (Ed.), *Handbook of Industrial and Organizational Psychology*. Copyright © 1976 Rand McNally and Company. Copyright © 1983 John Wiley & Sons, Inc. Reprinted by permission of John Wiley & Sons, Inc.

tive effect for overpayment, as described in Chapter 8.) Other workers, once they are making enough money to satisfy their basic needs, are not as concerned with how much they make. Variations in the pay of these workers will not have much effect, either positive or negative, on satisfaction, again as shown in Figure 9.2. Thus, value theory suggests that the more important a job-related factor is to a worker, the greater its potential effect on satisfaction.

There is some evidence consistent with Locke's value theory (for example, Locke, 1969; Mobley & Locke, 1970), but there has been little empirical research on this approach. Nevertheless, the concept of values is an important addition to the satisfaction literature and addresses some of the problems associated with need theories of satisfaction. Need theories imply that the satisfaction of all workers depends on the fulfillment of a small number of basic needs. This in turn implies that satisfaction can be achieved through a limited number of strategies designed to address whichever of these needs are unfulfilled for a particular worker. Worker values, however, introduce another dimension to this situation. Even though outcomes such as pay, fringe benefits, and working conditions are the same for two workers, and even though these outcomes may provide equivalent levels of need fulfillment, the workers' satisfaction will differ to the extent that their values differ. This approach seems to be more consistent with the ways in which people actually react to their jobs. Further, value theory is theoretically consistent with more general models of emotion, which state that emotional responses, such as attitudes, are triggered by physiological and psychological arousal (for example, Schachter & Singer, 1962). Valued outcomes are more likely than nonvalued outcomes to lead to arousal, and thereby have implications for satisfaction (Landy, 1978).

Lawler's Facet-Satisfaction Model. A third comparison theory of satisfaction is Lawler's Facet-Satisfaction Model (Lawler, 1973), an elaboration on portions of the Porter-Lawler motivation model discussed in Chapter 8 (see Figure 8.10). The Porter-Lawler model is a combination of some of the basic ideas from several motivation theories. The facet-satisfaction model is an expansion of the part of the Porter-Lawler model related to equity theory (Adams, 1965). The facet model, illustrated in Figure 9.3, gets its name from the fact that it describes the processes that determine satisfaction with any individual job component, or **facet**.

The comparison specified in Lawler's theory is between perceptions of what a worker *believes* he should receive in terms of job outcomes, such as pay, recognition, and promotions, and perceptions of the outcomes that are *actually* received. Perceptions of what *should* be received depend upon perceptions of the inputs

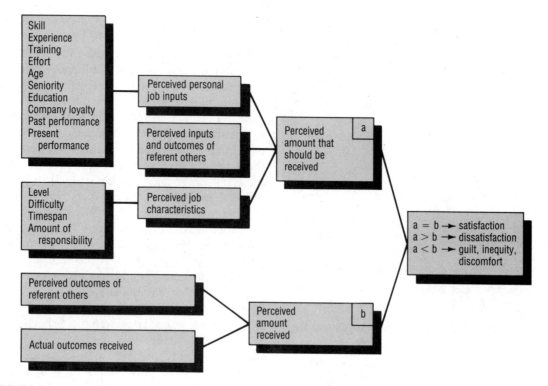

FIGURE 9.3
Lawler's Facet Model of Satisfaction
SOURCE: From *Motivation in Work Organizations*, by E. E. Lawler, III, p. 75. Copyright © 1973 by Wadsworth
Publishing Company, Inc. Reprinted by permission of Brooks/Cole Publishing Company, Pacific Grove, CA.

the worker brings to the job, such as skill, education, and experience, as well as perceptions of job characteristics, such as responsibility and difficulty, and perceptions of the inputs and outcomes of others. Perceptions of *actual* outcomes depend, of course, on the outcomes themselves, as well as perceptions of the outcomes of referent others, or people holding similar jobs with whom workers compare themselves. It should be obvious, with all of this talk about perceptions, that the facet model is highly cognitive in nature, and reflects the view that people respond to their *perceptions* of reality more directly than to reality itself.

As is the case with equity theory, the facet model states that the only desirable or satisfying condition is one in which perceptions of what should be received balance perceptions of what is actually received. If the worker feels that she is receiving less than what is deserved, dissatisfaction with the job results. If the worker perceives that she is receiving more than what is deserved, uncomfortable feelings of inequity and possibly guilt develop. The notion of feeling overpaid or overcompensated is the most controversial aspect of the equity theory of motivation, and it remains a problem in Lawler's (1973) satisfaction theory. As we saw in our discussion of equity theory in Chapter 8, there are a number of things workers can do to avoid feeling overpaid. For example, they can compare their own inputs and outcomes to those of a different reference person. They can also enhance their perceptions of their own inputs, thereby justifying the higher outcomes, or they can devalue the outcomes ("A dollar isn't what it used to be!").

Research on Lawler's model has been limited and inconclusive. A telling example involves a study that examined satisfaction with 23 job facets using several measures of satisfaction (Wanous & Lawler, 1972). One of the measures, as specified by the facet model, was the difference between the current level of the facet and the level that the worker believed *should* be associated with the job. The researchers found that overall job-satisfaction ratings could be predicted from this difference score, as suggested by the theory. The same data, however, were later reanalyzed, and it was found that perceptions of the level of outcomes *received* predicted overall satisfaction best, with the workers who perceived greater outcomes being more satisfied (Wall & Payne, 1973). Further, what the workers thought they *should* receive did not improve the prediction of satisfaction. Indeed, although these results do not necessarily invalidate Lawler's theory, they raise questions about how to measure perceptions of equity accurately.

Another problem is that the facet model assumes that people use very rational cognitive processes, carefully weighing their own as well as others' inputs and outcomes, and basing their attitudes on the logical conclusions derived from those comparisons. There are good reasons to suggest that many people are not this rational (Slovic, Fischhoff, & Lichtenstein, 1977). Further, it is not at all clear, even if people do compare inputs and outcomes, that the comparison is as simple as Lawler's (1973) model suggests. Weiner (1980) showed that job satisfaction can be predicted more accurately if the difference between what you actually receive and what you think you should receive is computed as a percentage of what you actually receive (satisfaction = [actual − desired]/actual) rather than as a simple difference (satisfaction = actual − desired).

The following computations show the effects of these two approaches to equity for two

of Peter's Pan Pizza's employees, Ed Clark, vice president of Retail Operations, and Dennis Foss, one of the store inspectors. Assuming that Mr. Clark has a salary of $63,000 and that Mr. Foss has a salary of $21,000, we can see the effects on satisfaction when each believes that he should be paid $1,000 more than he is currently being paid, based on comparisons of their own inputs and salaries to those of their coworkers.

Ed Clark, Vice President of Retail Operations

Actual salary: $63,000

Desired salary: 64,000

Difference prediction of satisfaction: $63 - 64 = -1$

Averaging prediction of satisfaction: $(63 - 64)/63 = -.016$

Dennis Foss, store inspector

Actual salary: $21,000

Desired salary: 22,000

Difference prediction of satisfaction: $21 - 22 = -1$

Averaging prediction of satisfaction: $(21 - 22)/21 = -.048$

Using the simple difference between what is desired and what is actually received, the same level of satisfaction is predicted for both men. Dividing this difference by their current salaries as Weiner (1980) suggested, however, we see that Mr. Foss should be less satisfied than Mr. Clark (negative values indicate perceived underpayment and dissatisfaction) because $1,000 represents a larger percentage of Mr. Foss' current salary, and therefore greater perceived underpayment. In fact, according to Weiner's averaging process, for Mr. Clark to feel the same dissatisfaction with pay that Mr. Foss is experiencing, he would have to desire a $67,000 salary.

Equity is a compelling idea, and in the social environment of organizations it would seem to be an important factor in determining satisfaction. The research on theories that rely on equity principles, however, makes it quite clear that psychologists do not yet understand the cognitive processes that determine perceptions of equity and inequity. Until these processes are more fully specified, equity theories will probably not provide acceptable answers to questions of job satisfaction.

Social and Cognitive Construction Theories of Job Satisfaction

Some recent approaches to studying job satisfaction are based upon social and cognitive construction processes. These theories attempt to explain satisfaction by describing the cognitive processes that workers use when evaluating or otherwise making decisions about their jobs. Specifically, the theories state that workers build or "construct" beliefs and attitudes based on events that they observe, such as the behavior and attitudes of coworkers. Workers are seen as active gatherers of information, which they use to build and define their personal "realities." It is these subjective, socially constructed realities, *not* objective events, that determine satisfaction.

One theory that relies on social and cognitive construction processes to explain satisfaction is social-learning theory. Social-learning approaches to job satisfaction and attitudes are similar to Lawler's (1973) facet model, in that attitudes are determined in part by perceptions of the behavior of other workers. Instead of comparing inputs and outcomes, however, social-learning theory says that we use other people as sources of information for selecting appropriate attitudes and behaviors. Our own attitudes, at least in part, are copied from or *modeled* on the attitudes of our coworkers. Specifically, by observing our coworkers, we infer their attitudes toward the organization, the job as a whole, and specific job characteristics. We view certain coworkers, usually those with similar jobs and interests or those who we believe are successful or powerful, as being appropriate

models, and we base our own attitudes on what we believe theirs to be (Salancik & Pfeffer, 1977a).

A number of studies have examined the social learning of work attitudes. For example, the effects of models' evaluative comments on the task satisfaction of subjects was studied by Weiss and Shaw (1979). They had subjects watch an instructional videotape, on which could be seen the hands of a "trainee" who was assembling a simple electric circuit, while the voice of the "trainer" explained the steps involved in the task. The subjects could also hear, in the background, the voices of the trainee and another person. In some conditions the trainee made positive comments about the task; in others, negative comments. The researchers found that subjects who overheard the positive comments had more favorable attitudes after performing the task than did those who overheard the negative comments.

Social learning appears to be important in developing attitudes in work settings as well as in other social situations (Bandura, 1971). Research shows, however, that not everyone is equally likely to model the behavior of others, nor is everyone equally likely to serve as a model. Consequently, social learning is apt to be an explanation for job satisfaction and other attitudes only in certain situations and for certain people.

Satisfaction as a Disposition

The theories we have presented so far describe job satisfaction as the product of situational variables and cognitive processes. That is, satisfaction is determined by the extent to which jobs fulfill workers' needs, the level of job outcomes such as pay, the attitudes of coworkers and so on. Although these theories utilize a broad range of psychological processes to explain satisfaction, they have one important point in common: they each imply that by adjusting the relevant variable or factor, job satisfaction can be improved.

Another perspective takes a very different view of job satisfaction. Specifically, it sees job satisfaction as the result of a **disposition** to be generally satisfied or dissatisfied. That is, some people tend to have positive moods and attitudes; others tend to have more negative moods and attitudes. The dispositions to be satisfied or dissatisfied are believed to be relatively unchanging, much like personality traits. This implies that efforts to improve satisfaction by changing the job or by changing workers' beliefs and attributions are likely to fail, or at least are less likely to succeed than has been generally believed.

The potential role of dispositions in job attitudes was studied by Staw and his colleagues several years ago. In one study, the job satisfaction of more than 5,000 workers was examined over a five-year period. The researchers found that job satisfaction was moderately stable over the five years, as well as across situations. More important, prior attitudes were better predictors of subsequent job satisfaction than were variables traditionally linked to satisfaction, such as job status or pay (Staw & Ross, 1985). In another study, measures of disposition taken early in life were found to predict job attitudes over periods as long as 50 years (Staw, Bell, & Clausen, 1986). These findings are all consistent with the notion of a stable job-satisfaction disposition.

Although Staw's findings "fit" a dispositional explanation for job satisfaction, these studies have been criticized on several points. For example, Staw and Ross (1985) studied older workers, who are less likely than younger workers to experience important changes in their jobs. This made it more likely that dispositional factors would appear to be strong. Research with younger workers, who are *more* likely to experience changes in their jobs, found less evidence for a dispositional effect (Gerhart, 1987). At a more basic level, Davis-Blake and Pfeffer (1989) described several flaws in the research methods and the logic behind much of the work on dispositions in organizations, and

suggested ways by which future research in this area could be improved.

Although some critics have concluded that situational factors (for example, job characteristics) are more important in determining job satisfaction than are dispositional factors, this does not mean that attitudinal dispositions don't exist or that they have no influence on job attitudes and behaviors. Rather, more research is needed in order to understand if and how stable dispositions affect job attitudes. This research has begun, and two examples of the directions it has taken are summarized below. These examples address different aspects of job-attitude dispositions; however, both promise to enhance our understanding of the role of dispositions in determining job attitudes.

Positive and Negative Affectivity.   One possible explanation for job-attitude dispositions relies upon personality traits. That is, people may have positive or negative job attitudes because of the specific, enduring characteristics that define their personalities. If this is the case, we would expect some people to be generally satisfied with all aspects of their lives, including their work, and others would be generally dissatisfied. One set of personality traits that may operate in this fashion include *positive affectivity* and *negative affectivity* (Costa & McCrae, 1980; Tellegen, 1982, 1985; Watson & Clark, 1984). **Negative affectivity** is defined as a stable tendency to experience aversive or negative emotional states. **Positive affectivity** is the tendency to experience positive emotional states. People who are high in negative affectivity experience high levels of distress and tend to dwell on the negative aspects of life, including their own weaknesses and mistakes. People who are high in positive affectivity are more satisfied, have a strong sense of well-being, and are less likely to be upset by problems encountered in day-to-day living.

The role of negative affectivity in determining job satisfaction was studied by Levin and Stokes (1989). They conducted two studies, the first a laboratory experiment and the second a correlational field study. In both cases they examined the relationships between job satisfaction and task characteristics as well as between satisfaction and negative affectivity. Thus, the effects of both traditional (situational) and nontraditional (dispositional) explanations for satisfaction were studied. The results of both studies revealed a relationship between negative affectivity and job satisfaction: In both cases subjects with higher levels of negative affectivity had lower levels of job satisfaction. However, this effect was fairly small, and the relationship between task characteristics and job satisfaction was much stronger.

Other studies have examined the relationships between negative and positive affectivity and variables that are conceptually related to job satisfaction, including *mood at work*. Mood corresponds to the emotional or evaluative component of attitudes. Mood at work therefore refers to a person's *feelings* about their work, independent of their beliefs about the work. Mood is different from affectivity because, like attitudes, it is believed to change more readily over time or across situations (that is, mood is a state; affectivity is a trait).

The results of one study showed that negative affectivity was inversely (negatively) related to positive mood and directly (positively) related to negative mood, and that positive affectivity was inversely related to negative mood (George, 1989). Other studies have found a direct relationship between positive affectivity and positive mood (George, 1991), an inverse relationship between negative affectivity and the evaluation of an incentive program (George, Brief, Webster, & Burke, 1989), and direct relationships between positive and negative affectivity and the positive and negative affective tone of work groups, respectively (George, 1990).

Based upon the small amount of research that has been conducted so far, it seems reasonable to conclude that personality explanations for job satisfaction and other job attitudes show promise for helping us better understand these attitudes. However, we should keep in mind that the effects of positive and negative affectivity have generally been quite small, especially when compared to the effects of situational factors such as job characteristics. It therefore seems unlikely that personality traits will ever, by themselves, be an adequate explanation for job attitudes. However, as research on affectivity and other traits continues, we can expect to see personality as a component of integrated models of job attitudes.

Genetic Factors.   The possibility that personality traits or other dispositional factors have effects on job satisfaction is intriguing. However, the research on these traits fails to consider an important question: From *where* do work-attitude dispositions come? That is, if such dispositions exist, why are they stronger for some people than for others? Historically there have been two broad answers to this type of question. On one hand, it is possible that differences in traits emerge as the result of our experiences. In this *environmental* view the differences between people are the result of the differences in their environments over the course of their lives. On the other hand, it is also possible that differences are due to the genes that people receive from their parents. In this *genetic* view the differences between people are inherited, and although people may be influenced by the environment or experience, the influence is limited by genetic potential.

One method for estimating the relative contributions of heredity and environment in determining a behavior (such as job satisfaction) is to compare identical (monozygotic) twins who were separated shortly after birth and raised apart. Both members of a pair of identical twins have the same genes but when raised separately have more less different environments. Thus, to the extent that identical twins are similar on a particular trait or behavior, such as job satisfaction, the similarity is interpreted as being the result of genetic factors. Further, the size or magnitude of the similarity (as measured by a type of correlation called an intraclass correlation) is a direct index of the strength of the genetic component (Bouchard, 1984).

Identical twins who have been raised separately are not common, but a long-term research project at the University of Minnesota has sought out and studied identical twins for many years. Using data from this project, a team of researchers examined the possibility that job satisfaction is at least partially inherited (Arvey, Bouchard, Segal, & Abraham, 1989). Thirty-four pairs of identical twins who had been raised separately filled out measures of job satisfaction, which were then analyzed to estimate the effects of genetic factors. The researchers found that genetic factors accounted for approximately 30% of the variance, or differences between individuals, on both general satisfaction and intrinsic satisfaction. (Intrinsic satisfaction refers to satisfaction derived from the experience of performing the job, as opposed to extrinsic satisfaction, which derives from work conditions and other environmental factors.)

The researchers in the twin study concluded that job satisfaction has a substantial inherited component, although they acknowledged that nongenetic factors account for most differences between people in job satisfaction (Arvey et al., 1989). They suggested that given the size of the genetic component, organizations have less control over workers' attitudes than has been commonly believed. They also speculated that the heritability of job satisfaction may operate through positive and negative affectivity, which have themselves been found to have a substantial genetic component (Tellegen, Lykken, Bouchard, Wilcox, Segal, & Rich, 1988).

Despite the apparent confidence that Arvey and associates (1989) place in their conclusions, the interpretation of their data may not be so straightforward. Specifically, the method of studying identical twins who have been raised apart, although capable of providing evidence that is either consistent or inconsistent with the effects of heredity, is not conclusive. Commenting on the twin study, Cropanzano and James (1990) describe several weaknesses of the research that raise questions about the estimates of genetic and environmental effects. For example, Cropanzano and James note that correlational studies can provide only weak evidence of causality between heredity and behavior, and that due to the researchers' failure to account for nongenetic factors that might have accounted for their results, the "interpretation of their correlational evidence as indicating genetic causality is unjustified" (p. 434). They also note that there may be nongenetic causes for twin similarity such as similar home environments despite being raised apart, that identical twins may not be representative of other workers, and that the conclusion that job satisfaction may not be easily changed because of its genetic component is not valid.

What then do we make of dispositional explanations for job satisfaction? There is evidence that people's work attitudes are consistent across time and situations, but the *differences* across situations are much greater. There is evidence that personality traits, such as positive and negative affectivity, may predict job attitudes, but the traits that have been studied so far have relatively weak relationships with satisfaction. There is evidence that is consistent with a genetic contribution to job satisfaction, but that evidence is not conclusive, and it begs the question of exactly *what* is being inherited that affects attitudes. In summary, it seems prudent to conclude that dispositional explanations for attitudes have not yet extended our understanding of job satisfaction, but they have demonstrated the *potential* for doing so. It is likely that dispositions, whether inherited or situationally determined, will contribute to our understanding of satisfaction in the future.

Evaluation of Satisfaction Theories

We have examined a number of job-satisfaction theories, ranging from such classics as two-

Beliefs, emotions, and behavioral tendencies are components of job satisfaction.

factor theory to relatively new attribution and dispositional approaches. During most of the past three decades, the predominant theories of job satisfaction have been based on comparison processes. As was the case with two-factor theory, however, comparison theories have enjoyed only limited empirical support. In some cases, such as Maslow's (1943) need hierarchy, it appears that the basic premises underlying the theories are flawed. In other cases, such as Locke's (1976) and Lawler's (1973) theories, there is little empirical research upon which to base an evaluation. The research that does exist, however, suggests that these theories may be unable to account for differences in the type and complexity of cognitive comparisons made by workers. Emerging perspectives that rely on social-learning theory, an emphasis on emotions, and dispositional explanations represent the newest phase of satisfaction theory. We expect, however, that the development of work attitudes is influenced by such a variety of personal and situational factors that no single theory is likely to provide a complete explanation.

Rather, some combination of perspectives will ultimately provide the best understanding of job satisfaction.

Organizational Commitment

Job satisfaction has been the most widely studied and debated job attitude, but a variety of other attitudes have been the subject of psychological research. Space limitations prevent us from discussing each of these, but in the following sections we examine the work on organizational commitment, perhaps the most extensively studied work attitude after job satisfaction.

Definitions of Organizational Commitment

Like job satisfaction, organizational commitment has been defined in a variety of ways. Virtually all of the definitions share the notion that commitment reflects the strength of an individual's identification with, and involvement in, a particular organization. Thus, one way in which organizational commitment differs from job satisfaction is in its target. Organizational commitment is an attitude toward the organization for whom a person works; job satisfaction is an attitude toward the specific job that a person holds.

The best-known and most popular definition of organizational commitment was developed by Mowday, Steers, and Porter (1979). They described **organizational commitment** as consisting of (1) a strong belief in and acceptance of the organization's goals and values; (2) a willingness to exert considerable effort on behalf of the organization; and (3) a strong desire to maintain membership in the organization. Although there is little disagreement that these factors are important to organizational commitment, other definitions suggest that commitment may be considerably broader.

One review of the organizational-commitment literature identified three general definitions or operationalizations of commitment (Reichers, 1985). The first is based on the notion of *side bets*, or the rewards and costs associated with organizational membership. To the extent that a person has made "investments" in an organization in the form of nonportable pension contributions, position and tenure, and other benefits that would be lost upon departure, commitment to the organization is likely to be high (for example, Farrell & Rusbult, 1981; Rusbult & Farrell, 1983). The second definition is based on employee attributions of commitment; commitment will develop when employees behave in ways that bind them to the organization (for example, O'Reilly & Caldwell, 1980). To illustrate, if one of PPP's store inspectors does not feel commitment to the company but nevertheless makes public statements praising PPP as an employer, he would find it difficult to maintain his negative attitudes. He would attribute his statements to the positive qualities of PPP, and his organizational commitment would be enhanced.

Finally, commitment has been defined as a worker's dedication to the goals and values of the organization. To the extent that workers share the organizational goals and values, and work to attain them, workers are viewed as being highly committed (for example, Angle & Perry, 1981; Bateman & Strasser, 1984). This last definition is closest to the one offered by Mowday, Steers, and Porter (1979).

More recently, definitions of organizational commitment have been grouped into two broad categories (Mathieu & Zajac, 1990). The first, and by far the most frequently studied, is **attitudinal commitment**, which refers to workers' identification with and involvement in an organization. Again, this is essentially similar to Mowday, Steers, and Porter's (1979) definition. The second category is **calculated** or **behavioral commitment**, which is the result of transactions between workers and the organization that make it difficult for workers to leave. This is basically the same as the side-bet explanation of commitment. In calculated commitment, attachment to the organization stems from a reluctance to give up benefits that have accrued over time rather than from sharing the goals and values of the organization. (Other writers have referred to attitudinal and calculated commitment as affective and continuance commitment, respectively; Meyer & Allen, 1984.)

The various definitions of organizational commitment illustrate the fact that commitment is not unidimensional. That is, there is more than one facet to commitment, and it is therefore misleading to speak of *the* commitment of a worker. Instead, we should consider commitment to different aspects of the organization (Reichers, 1985), as well as the different types of commitment workers experience. Evidence of the multidimensionality of commitment has been provided by several research studies (for example, Allen & Meyer, 1990; McGee & Ford, 1987). Indeed, a meta-analysis of the commitment research found that the type of commitment (attitudinal versus calculated) moderated the relationship between commitment and other variables (Mathieu & Zajac,

1990). For instance, age, length of time on the same job, and job satisfaction all had stronger, positive relationships with attitudinal commitment; education and the intention to leave the job had more positive relationships with calculated commitment.

Antecedents of Commitment

Although there have been a few efforts to explain the development of organizational commitment (for example, Mathieu, 1988; Mathieu & Hamel, 1989), commitment has usually been treated as a predictor of other behaviors and attitudes (Mathieu & Zajac, 1990). However, there has been no shortage of *correlational* research examining possible antecedents or sources of organizational commitment. Although correlational studies cannot establish cause-and-effect relationships, they can help us evaluate the plausibility of such relationships, and thereby guide the development of future theory.

One list of possible antecedents of organizational commitment was assembled by Mathieu and Zajac (1990) and is presented in Table 9.1. The list contains variables that have been thought to have effects on commitment. Mathieu and Zajac excluded other job attitudes, such as job satisfaction, and other types of commitment, such as commitment to labor unions, because of the difficulty in specifying the cause-and-effect relationships between different attitudes (cf. Reichers, 1985). They also acknowledged that it is possible for commitment to have effects on these variables and vice versa.

As part of their study, Mathieu and Zajac (1990) conducted meta-analyses to estimate the correlations between organizational commitment and each of the potential antecedents (see Table 9.1). A rule of thumb to help you interpret the correlations is to consider the range 0–.20 to be small; .21–.40, medium; and above .40, large (Cohen, 1969). The results of the meta-analyses showed that there were generally weak relationships between personal characteristics and

TABLE 9.1 Possible Antecedents of Organizational Commitment

Antecedent	Correlation*
Personal Characteristics	
Age	.201
Sex	−.145
Education	−.092
Marital status	.106
Position tenure	.091
Organizational tenure	.170
Perceived personal competence	.630
Ability	.136
Salary	.182
Protestant work ethic	.289
Job level	.178
Job Characteristics	
Skill variety	.207
Task autonomy	.083
Challenge	.349
Job scope	.503
Group-Leader Relations	
Group cohesiveness	.149
Task interdependence	.220
Leader initiating structure	.289
Leader consideration	.335
Leader communication	.454
Participative leadership	.386
Organizational Characteristics	
Organizational size	−.001
Organizational centralization	−.061
Role States	
Role ambiguity	−.218
Role conflict	−.271
Role overload	−.206

*Mean weighted correlation corrected for attenuation

SOURCE: From "A Review and Meta-analysis of the Antecedents, Correlates, and Consequences of Organizational Commitment," by J. E. Mathieu and D. M. Zajac, 1990, *Psychological Bulletin, 108,* 175. Adapted by permission.

organizational commitment. Only Protestant work ethic and age had moderate positive correlations with commitment, and only perceived personal competence was strongly correlated with commitment. Job characteristics, as a group, had a more consistent positive relationship with commitment, as did the leadership behaviors in the group-leader relations category. Thus, challenging jobs involving a variety of tasks, and positive leadership behaviors on the part of supervisors may be important contributors to commitment. Organizational characteristics, on the other hand, were found to have very weak relationships with commitment. However, there has been very little research on commitment and organizational characteristics, so these correlations are at best tentative. Finally, there are moderate negative correlations between unfavorable role states and commitment.

In addition to estimating the correlations between organizational commitment and its potential antecedents, Mathieu and Zajac's (1990) meta-analyses assessed the possibility that the strength of the relationships might be different for different people and in different situations. In fact, Mathieu and Zajac found that this might be the case for most of the correlations in Table 9.1. For example, as we mentioned earlier, the age-commitment correlation depends upon how commitment is measured. The correlation is stronger with attitudinal commitment ($r = .221$) than with calculated commitment ($r = .167$). Unfortunately, Mathieu and Zajac could not identify these factors for most of the correlations because the necessary data were not available in the studies they reviewed. However, their analyses clearly demonstrate that organizational commitment is influenced by a great variety of factors.

Commitment to What?

Organizational commitment, as we have seen, is influenced by a potentially large array of personal and situational factors. This seems to imply that it is a complex, multifaceted construct. However, although clear distinctions have been made between types of commitment, such as attitudinal and calculated, relatively little attention has been paid to the complexity of the *target* of commitment: the organization itself.

Organizational commitment has typically been conceptualized and measured as attachment to the organization *as a whole*. This overlooks the fact that there are many groups, goals, and sets of values in an organization to which a worker may feel varying degrees of commitment. Assessing only overall or global commitment is likely to overlook differences in a worker's commitment to various aspects of the organization.

In an effort to promote this more complex (and more realistic) view of organizational commitment, Reichers (1985) defined organizational commitment as "a collection of multiple commitments to various groups that [constitute] the organization" (p. 469). An illustration of these commitments is presented in Figure 9.4. The long arrows indicate attachments that workers have to constituencies or groups that have relationships with, but are outside, the organization. The short arrows symbolize attachments to groups and individuals that are within the organization, and thereby psychologically closer to the worker. It is the unique combination of these attachments that determines the commitment level of any given worker.

This view of commitment has several important implications (Reichers, 1985). First, because of unique patterns of attachments to various constituencies, the *basic nature* of organizational commitment may be different for each worker. For example, one PPP store inspector may feel strong commitment because she sees her job as protecting the reputation of PPP, as well as the welfare of PPP's customers and the communities in which PPP restaurants are located. Another inspector may be equally committed, but his commitment stems from his close attachments to his coworkers. Improving the commitment of these two workers would require dramatically different approaches. Empirical evidence of multiple commitment targets in organizations has been provided by O'Reilly and Chatman (1986) and Koslowsky (1990), among others.

The second implication is that if we know to which groups or constituencies people are

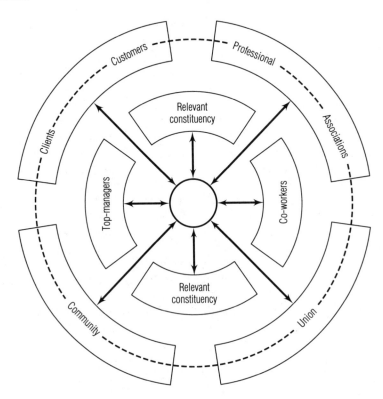

FIGURE 9.4
Organizational Commitments
SOURCE: From "A Review and Reconceptualization of Organizational Commitment," by A. Reichers, 1985, *Academy of Management Review, 10,* 472. Reprinted by permission.

committed, we should be able to predict changes in commitment as the fortunes of the groups or constituencies rise and fall. PPP workers whose commitment is dependent upon their involvement in developing and promoting a particular product line (such as PPP's popular anchovy-filled pastries) would probably experience reduced commitment if that product were dropped from the company's offerings.

Finally, recognition of multiple commitments within organizations raises the possibility that psychologists and managers will be better able to understand and control conflicts between commitments (Reichers, 1986). For example, PPP store inspectors are probably committed to the organization's goals of maintaining quality service and safe work environments. At the same time, however, they may

feel attachments to the managers of the stores they inspect and sympathize with the practical problems the managers have in maintaining company standards. If this type of conflict can be anticipated, then steps can be taken to clarify company expectations or otherwise reduce the conflict.

We have been discussing organizational commitment under the assumption that the more committed a worker is, the better off the worker and the organization will be. This may not be the case. According to one theorist (Randall, 1987), although high commitment levels may enhance the progress of individual careers and provide organizations with a stable work force, there is a real potential for negative consequences from overcommitment. Extremely high commitment may limit individual growth, reduce opportunity for mobility, and stifle creativity. Overcommitment might also bring on stress in family and personal relationships, and "role overload." The organization may also suffer from overcommitted employees, a situation that may reduce organizational flexibility, lead employees to accept company goals and procedures unquestioningly, and even increase levels of illegal and unethical behavior.

Not all experts accept Randall's (1987) warnings about the potential negative consequences of high commitment. In one case, high organizational involvement was found to have positive consequences for individuals in terms of satisfaction with careers and nonwork aspects of life (Romzek, 1989). However, the study addressed only a small subset of the possible problems described by Randall, and hence it seems wise to suggest that research on the effects of extreme attitudes in organizations continue.

Summing Up

You can see that organizational commitment is quite different from job satisfaction. The two attitudes focus on different aspects of the work experience, and thus are complementary in a variety of ways. At the same time, they are both concerned with the nature of workers' affective or emotional reactions to work, and therefore have much in common. As we examine the correlates of work attitudes in the following sections, keep in mind that the differences between various work attitudes are matters of emphasis and focus. It is only when considered together that the full impact of attitudes on work behaviors and other outcomes becomes evident.

Correlates of Work Attitudes

Although many theories have been proposed to explain workers' attitudes, much of the attitude research has addressed a more practical question: What behaviors, personal characteristics, and working conditions are related to work attitudes? Knowing what variables are related to work attitudes can serve at least two important purposes. First, it can allow us to make predictions about what types of people will be more or less satisfied or committed under a given set of circumstances, and often to suggest ways to improve attitudes. Second, it can allow us to establish the practical importance of work attitudes. That is, knowing what variables are typically associated with attitudes lets us estimate the extent to which improving attitudes might in turn help solve various organizational problems, such as low performance or high turnover.

Work Attitudes and Work Behaviors

To most managers and many psychologists, work attitudes such as job satisfaction and organizational commitment are interesting because we expect them to have positive effects on work behaviors. In fact, for many years following the Hawthorne studies the beneficial effects of high job satisfaction were taken for granted. As empirical research on satisfaction and other attitudes accumulated, however, it became clear that the effects of attitudes on employee behavior were much weaker than had once been believed. This is seen clearly in the research on withdrawal and performance.

Withdrawal. **Withdrawal** is a general term that refers to behaviors by which workers remove themselves, either temporarily or permanently, from their jobs or workplaces. Two forms of withdrawal that have been studied extensively are absenteeism and turnover. These behaviors are of great concern to businesses and I/O psychologists. The reasons for the interest in withdrawal include the high cost of recruiting and training new employees, the desire to keep good workers on the job, and the cost and inconveniences of finding temporary replacements for absent workers.

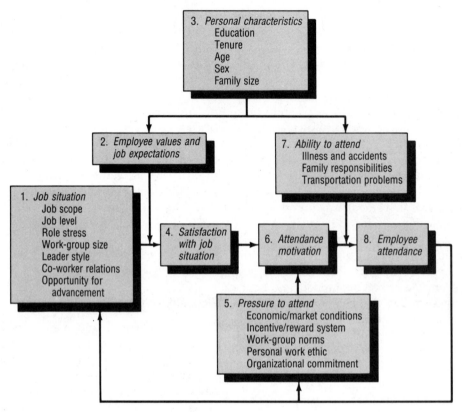

FIGURE 9.5
The Steers and Rhodes Process Model of Work Attendance
SOURCE: From "Major Influences on Employee Attendance: A Process Model," by R. M. Steers and S. R. Rhodes, 1978, *Journal of Applied Psychology, 63*, 393. Copyright © 1978 by the American Psychological Association. Reprinted by permission of the authors.

As recently as 1977, Muchinsky concluded that there was a "highly consistent" negative relationship between job satisfaction and absenteeism, although he did not estimate the strength of the relationship (Muchinsky, 1977b). Most reviews and research since then have been less positive, typically reporting small and inconsistent satisfaction-absenteeism correlations. Further, the research has shown that other variables often have stronger relationships to absenteeism than does satisfaction (Breaugh, 1981; Cheloha & Farr, 1980; Keller, 1983; Locke, 1976; Nicholson, Brown, & Chadwick-Jones, 1976; Watson, 1981).

One of the earliest efforts to elaborate on the job satisfaction–absenteeism relationship was the Process Model of Attendance developed by Steers and Rhodes (1978), which is illustrated in Figure 9.5. The model states that work attendance is a function of both motivation to attend and ability to attend; we might not come to work because we don't want to come to work (motivation) and/or because we are prevented from coming to work (ability). Job satisfaction, rather than being the direct cause of attendance, is seen as only one of the factors that determine attendance motivation. Thus, although satisfaction is an important component in the Steers and Rhodes model, it is easy to see how any of a variety of other factors could moderate the effects of satisfaction.

Further research suggests that even this indirect effect of job satisfaction on absenteeism may be an exaggeration. For example, in one study personal characteristics, such as age and marital status, and job characteristics, such as tenure and shift work, were found to predict job satisfaction, but correlations between satisfaction as measured by the Job Descriptive Index (discussed on pp. 310–312) and absence were very low, ranging from −.09 to .08 (Watson, 1981). Also, nonattitudinal variables have been found to predict attendance better than satisfaction (Keller, 1983). Meta-analyses of the job satisfaction–absenteeism research found that the relationship between satisfaction and absenteeism depends on both the type of absence and the type of satisfaction being measured. The strongest relationships were between the *frequency* of absences and satisfaction with work, and the length or *duration* of absences and overall satisfaction (Hackett, 1989). In general, the research evidence provides little reason to expect any simple or consistent relationship between workers' satisfaction and absenteeism. Likewise, there seems to be little relationship between organizational commitment and absenteeism. Mathieu and Zajac (1990) found only a weak ($r = .109$) correlation between these variables.

Before leaving the topic of absenteeism, and in light of job satisfaction's failure to predict absenteeism, we should mention that some variables *do* predict who will come to work. Among the best of these, not surprisingly, is a worker's previous history of absenteeism (for example, Breaugh, 1981). Also predictive of attendance is work-group cohesiveness (Keller, 1983). Steers and Rhodes (1978) suggested that members of smaller work groups have fewer absences because small groups develop greater cohesiveness or closeness than do larger groups. This seems to be true, whether work-group size varies across groups or across time. In a study of 66 work groups that changed in size during the course of the research, 74 percent of the groups showed a significant positive relationship between group size and absenteeism (Markham, Dansereau, & Alutto, 1982).

There are other approaches to absenteeism that are not based on the common assumption that absenteeism is a function of an individual's motivation, satisfaction, and ability to attend. For example, a social-exchange explanation for absenteeism proposes that employers will tolerate a certain level of absence in return for such behaviors as loyalty to the company, hard work, or innovative ideas (Chadwick-Jones, Nicholson, & Brown, 1982). This theory also suggests that group norms and coworker expectations concerning attendance play important roles. In a study of the attendance behavior of city bus drivers, group norms, measured as the monthly absence rates of each of five bus garages, predicted individual time-lost measures of absence after taking into account the effects of the drivers' prior absence records, job attitudes, and personal characteristics (Mathieu & Kohler, 1990). Apparently, different standards for attendance developed in the different garages, and the standards had an effect on the attendance of the drivers working in each of the garages.

Company policies are also important in determining absenteeism. The way in which an employer handles absences conveys powerful expectations to workers. This process is illustrated by research that compared absenteeism rates in a number of organizations (Dalton & Perry, 1981). Absenteeism was greater in companies where sick leave accumulates fast and where unused sick leave is not remunerated. Such policies pressure workers to "use or lose" sick-leave benefits, and it should not be surprising that absenteeism is the result. It was also found that organizations paying higher wages had higher rates of absenteeism; this suggests that workers will be absent more if they can afford to be absent.

The exchange model of absenteeism should be carefully considered by the management at

PPP. Company policy on such matters as sick leave, vacation, and maternity leave may account for much of its absenteeism problem. In a similar fashion, it is possible that the workers may have developed norms or expectations about what they can "get away with," and that these norms have only recently developed to the point that management is aware of their effects. In any case, it would be unwise to ignore these possibilities, particularly given the low probability that the problem will be solved by efforts to improve satisfaction.

The second form of withdrawal, **turnover,** is a potentially costly problem for organizations. When a productive employee quits a job, the employer is faced with the costs and inconvenience of recruiting, selecting, and training a replacement. Turnover also has the potential for disrupting social relationships within work groups, which may have implications for the performance of workers who remain.

We should be careful not to view all turnover as avoidable, dysfunctional, or problematic because it certainly is not. For example, in a study of tellers in 190 bank branches, 52% of all turnover was found to be unavoidable (Dalton, Krackhardt, & Porter, 1981); the tellers quit for reasons related to their families, educational opportunities, or other personal concerns. Also, 71% of all turnover at the banks was *functional*, in that the employees who left were later rated by supervisors as having performed unsatisfactorily. Although we suspect that the lower performance ratings given to the employees who quit may have been given, in part, *because* they had quit (what manager wants to admit that a good employee got away?), it is clear that some voluntary turnover represents a useful process by which unsatisfactory or marginal employees remove themselves from the organization. It's likely that many of these people, had they stayed on the job, would have become victims of involuntary turnover; they would have been fired.

This conclusion is supported by the research of Hollenbeck and Williams (1986), who

found that 53% of turnover among retail salespersons was functional. This is somewhat lower than the proportion reported by Dalton, Krackhardt, and Porter (1981), but it is still substantial. More important, Hollenbeck and Williams used an objective measure of sales volume to determine performance and turnover functionality rather than the performance ratings used in the earlier study. Also, a meta-analysis estimated the correlation between turnover and performance to be $-.28$, with better performers less likely to leave their jobs (McEvoy & Cascio, 1987).

Although some turnover may be functional, all organizations occasionally lose valuable employees, making turnover an important practical concern. Perhaps the most widely known model of the turnover process was developed by Mobley (Mobley, 1977; Mobley, Griffeth, Hand, & Meglino, 1979; Mobley, Horner, & Hollingsworth, 1978). The Mobley model of turnover is presented in Figure 9.6. In this model, job satisfaction is viewed as having no direct effect on turnover. Rather, the model states that dissatisfaction causes the employee to think about quitting. This in turn leads to the decision to search for a new job, provided that acceptable alternatives to the current job are available. Depending on the results of the search, the employee next develops definite intentions about either staying or quitting. The intention to quit is, according to the model, the immediate precursor of quitting.

As a theory of the turnover process, the Mobley model has yielded some evidence of validity. Although the specific relationships among the variables vary across studies, Mobley and others have found general support for the model, particularly for the idea that intention to quit is the best single predictor of actual turnover (Michaels & Spector, 1982; Miller, Katerberg, & Hulin, 1979; Mobley et al., 1978; Mowday, Koberg, & McArthur, 1984; Youngblood, Mobley, & Meglino, 1983).

Shortly after the Mobley model was published, an alternative turnover model was pre-

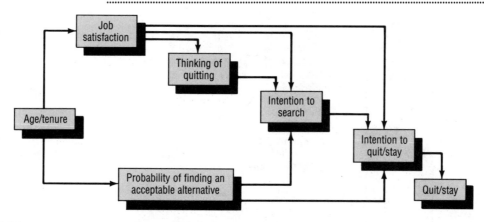

FIGURE 9.6
The Mobley Model of Turnover
SOURCE: From "An Evaluation of Precursors of Hospital Employee Turnover," by W. H. Mobley, S. O. Horner, and A. T. Hollingsworth, 1978, *Journal of Applied Psychology, 63,* 410. Copyright © 1978 by the American Psychological Association. Reprinted by permission of the authors.

sented by Steers and Mowday (1981). A version of their model is presented in Figure 9.7. There are similarities between the two models but also important differences. One obvious difference is that the Steers and Mowday model considers a wider variety of factors (including organizational commitment) in the turnover process. Also, though both models view intention to quit as the immediate cause of quitting, and see the evaluation of alternative job opportunities as critical in the decision to quit, the relationships between these and other variables are different. Most notably, Mobley's model proposes that intention to quit *follows* a successful search process, while Steers and Mowday's model suggests that the search process *results from* the intention to quit.

Although a number of studies have yielded results consistent with parts of the Steers and Mowday (1981) model (for example, Arnold & Feldman, 1982; Michaels & Spector, 1982; Stumpf & Hartman, 1984), the first comprehensive test of the model was reported by Lee and Mowday (1987). Studying employees of a large financial institution, Lee and Mowday tested ten hypotheses derived from the Steers and Mowday model. Not all of the specific links il-

lustrated in Figure 9.7 were confirmed, but the major relationships were verified. Consistent with both this model and the Mobley model, job satisfaction was related to intention to quit, and intention to quit was the major predictor of actual quitting. Of the components unique to the Steers and Mowday model, the predicted roles of available job and organization information, job performance, organizational commitment, and job involvement were validated. It therefore appears that the Steers and Mowday model may be an important extension of earlier turnover models.

An important aspect of both Mobley's and Steers and Mowday's models is the role of labor-market conditions in the turnover decision. Even if workers are dissatisfied, even if they have thought about quitting, and even if they have gone as far as to look for another job, both models state that workers will not intend to quit if there are no acceptable alternative jobs available. Indeed, the greater the competition in the labor market, the fewer the workers who resign from their jobs (Dreher & Dougherty, 1980). Concerns for future employment do not always influence intentions to quit, however. For example, Michaels and Spector (1982)

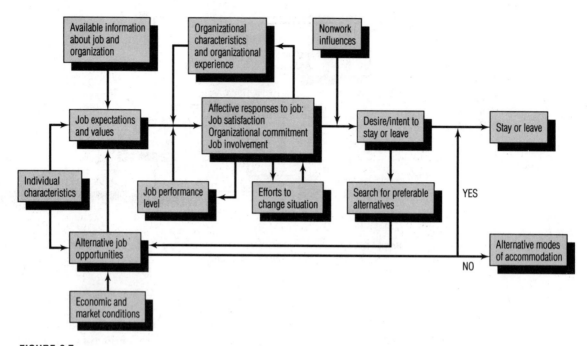

FIGURE 9.7
The Steers and Mowday Model
Note: The model is based on Steers and Mowday (1981).

Source: From "Voluntarily Leaving an Organization: An Empirical Investigation of Steers and Mowday's Model of Turnover," 1987, *Academy of Management Journal, 30,* 723. Reprinted by permission.

found no effect for availability of alternative employment, and a meta-analysis by Steel and Griffeth (1989) showed only a weak correlation between perceived employment alternatives and turnover. Michaels and Spector suggested that availability has no effect on intentions to quit but, rather, that intentions to quit will be acted upon only if alternative jobs are available.

Another way to test the effects of the labor market was described by Muchinsky and Morrow (1980). They suggested that "economic opportunity factors," especially unemployment, moderated the relationship between satisfaction and turnover. When unemployment is low, greater numbers of dissatisfied workers will quit their jobs because it is relatively easy to get new jobs. Under these conditions, the job satisfaction–turnover relationship will be stronger than when unemployment is high and workers are

more reluctant to quit. A meta-analysis was conducted to determine the validity of the Muchinsky and Morrow model (Carsten & Spector, 1987). Correcting methodological problems in an earlier review that failed to support the model (Shikiar & Freudenberg, 1982), Carsten and Spector found that as unemployment increased the job satisfaction–turnover relationship became smaller. Thus, it seems that favorable economic conditions serve to "release" the relationship between job attitudes and behavior, and that unfavorable conditions constrain this relationship (Hulin, Roznowski, & Hachiya, 1985).

In general, research on turnover has shown that there is a link between job dissatisfaction and quitting. The link, however, is neither simple nor direct. Job dissatisfaction seems to trigger or contribute to a chain of decisions on the part of the worker, and the exact nature of the decisions varies across individuals, jobs, and economic conditions (Lee & Mowday, 1987). Consequently, many psychologists have suggested that to understand turnover, investigators should study variables more closely related to behavioral intentions. One of the most frequently studied of such variables is organizational commitment.

Mowday, Porter, and Steers (1982) carefully examined the role of organizational commitment in the turnover process and concluded that it is far superior to satisfaction as a predictor of turnover. This may be because commitment is a worker's general emotional reaction to the employing organization rather than to a specific job or set of tasks. Also, unlike satisfaction, commitment is thought to develop slowly and is therefore not likely to change with day-to-day events in the workplace, whereas satisfaction is believed to be more sensitive to such events. Jackson, Stafford, Banks, and Warr (1983) illustrated the potential psychological importance of commitment in an examination of its effects on people who had lost their jobs. Although psychological distress was higher among unemployed persons than among those who were working, it was particularly high for the unemployed who had been highly committed to their organizations. Consistent with this, the meta-analysis of commitment research conducted by Mathieu and Zajac (1990) found an average correlation between attitudinal commitment and intention to quit of −.520, and between attitudinal commitment and turnover of −.283. Clearly, organizational commitment is an important key to our current understanding of employee turnover.

Performance.   Over the years, one of the most strongly held beliefs among managers, supervisors, and I/O psychologists has been that there is a relationship between a worker's job satisfaction and performance. Unfortunately, the belief has not proved to be valid. For more than 35 years psychologists have been looking for the link between satisfaction and performance, and for more than 35 years they have found little or nothing of substance (Brayfield & Crockett, 1955; Vroom, 1964). Iaffaldano and Muchinsky (1985) speculated that one reason for the continuing research on satisfaction and performance, in the face of growing evidence that the two are largely independent, is a belief that the two variables *should* be related, and that more research might reveal the nature of that relationship. Using meta-analysis techniques, Iaffaldano and Muchinsky examined 217 correlations between measures of satisfaction and performance from the published research literature. The mean correlation was .146, which is not only very small but also virtually identical to the result obtained by Vroom 21 years earlier.

The failure to find any clear association between satisfaction and performance has led researchers to suggest that the relationship may be moderated by other variables. That is, perhaps the expected positive relationship between satisfaction and performance holds for certain people but not for others, or in certain types of organizations but not in others. To test this possibility, Iaffaldano and Muchinsky (1985) included information about factors such as white-collar versus blue-collar samples, longitudinal versus cross-sectional research designs, and quality versus quantity performance measures in their meta-analysis. They concluded that these types of variables were "of little consequence" in understanding the satisfaction-performance relationship.

One condition not examined by Iaffaldano and Muchinsky (1985) that may make a difference is the manner in which rewards are administered in an organization. It appears that when rewards are based on performance, so that good performers receive greater rewards than poor performers, the satisfaction-performance correlation is positive, whereas inappropriate rewards result in negative correlations (Cherrington, Reitz, & Scott, 1971; Jacobs & Solomon, 1977; Podsakoff, Todor, & Skov, 1982).

Despite the lack of evidence that satisfaction is related to performance, psychologists continue to conduct research as if the two variables *were* in fact related. For example, there has been a substantial amount of research examining whether the level of worker satisfaction causes or has an effect on the level of worker performance, or whether workers who perform better are more satisfied because they are able to demonstrate or use their skills. This research has tended to support the notion that people will become satisfied after performing well rather than vice versa (for example, Wanous, 1974a). Indeed, Locke's (1968) research on goal setting suggests that people derive satisfaction from accomplishing difficult goals (see Chapter 8). There are instances, however, in which satisfaction seems to be causing performance (as an example, see Organ, 1977). Given the inconsistent and weak relationship between satisfaction and performance overall, the conflicting findings are hardly surprising. How can the question of whether satisfaction causes performance or performance causes satisfaction be answered when the two variables are, for the most part, independent? In general, it appears to us that psychologists interested in performance would better spend their time studying variables other than satisfaction.

One variable that has been studied in this context is, as you might expect, organizational commitment. It appears that there may be no stronger relationship between commitment and performance than between satisfaction and performance. The Mathieu and Zajac (1990) meta-analysis found only a small correlation between commitment and performance ratings ($r = .130$), and an even smaller relationship between commitment and objective performance measures ($r = .054$). It is possible, though, that these relationships depend upon other variables. Meyer, Paunonen, Gellatly, Goffin, and Jackson (1989), in a study of food-service managers (*not* at PPP, however), found that performance was positively related to attitudinal or affective commitment and negatively related to calculated

or continuance commitment. Perhaps the study of these and other variables will clarify the commitment-performance link in the near future.

Satisfaction and Personal Characteristics

Another line of satisfaction research has attempted to identify certain groups of people who tend to be more satisfied than others. Research on these personal or demographic characteristics typically involves comparing job-satisfaction ratings for different subsamples, such as men and women, blacks and whites, the young and the old, and so forth. Table 9.2 contains data from a longitudinal survey conducted during the 1970s (Weaver, 1980). The most striking aspect of these data is that, overall, different types of people seem to have about the same level of job satisfaction. There are some differences between groups in this table that are consistent with other research findings, though. For instance, whites tend to report higher levels of satisfaction than blacks, although the size of the differences is, on average, quite small (Moch, 1980; Weaver, 1977). Both blacks and whites, however, seem to derive satisfaction from the same aspects of their jobs (Weaver, 1978a). In a similar fashion, older workers and those with more education report greater satisfaction than those who are younger or less educated. Also, not surprisingly, workers with professional and managerial jobs, and those who are paid more have greater satisfaction than lower-level, lower-paid workers. Again, however, the differences tend to be very small, accounting for little of the differences in workers' satisfaction ratings (Weaver, 1977).

Overall differences in the job satisfaction of men and women are small and inconsistent (see Table 9.2). Any sex differences in job attitudes, however, are likely to be related to differences in education, pay, and tenure. Thus, if you compare men and women who are equal on these variables, you should find only very small sex differences in satisfaction (Hulin & Smith, 1964;

TABLE 9.2 Mean Job Satisfaction among Full-Time Workers in the United States, 1972–1978, by Selected Demographic Variables

Variable	Year of survey							M
	1972	1973	1974	1975	1976	1977	1978	
Race								
White	2.36	2.34	2.38	2.43	2.44	2.37	2.43	2.39
Black	2.09	2.32	2.17	2.34	2.13	2.36	2.01	2.19
Sex								
Male	2.32	2.31	2.35	2.44	2.41	2.33	2.38	2.36
Female	2.28	2.40	2.36	2.40	2.42	2.42	2.39	2.38
Education								
Grade school	2.32	2.22	2.28	2.32	2.32	2.33	2.35	2.31
High school	2.25	2.28	2.38	2.46	2.39	2.38	2.37	2.36
Some college	2.26	2.45	2.35	2.52	2.38	2.36	2.31	2.37
College degree or more	2.44	2.52	2.41	2.37	2.54	2.46	2.49	2.46
Age								
Less than 20	1.43	1.95	2.25	2.08	1.73	2.17	2.14	1.95
20–29	2.06	2.18	2.18	2.24	2.25	2.19	2.67	2.20
30–39	2.37	2.39	2.26	2.48	2.53	2.33	2.35	2.38
40–49	2.36	2.34	2.41	2.48	2.45	2.39	2.43	2.41
50 or more	2.51	2.46	2.55	2.55	2.53	2.55	2.55	2.53
Personal income*								
Less than $5,000	—	—	2.23	2.23	2.21	2.21	2.21	2.22
$5000–$6999	—	—	2.21	2.47	2.44	2.46	2.14	2.35
$7000–$9999	—	—	2.26	2.38	2.37	2.32	2.31	2.33
$10,000–$14,999	—	—	2.42	2.44	2.47	2.35	2.43	2.42
$15,000 or more	—	—	2.58	2.60	2.55	2.48	2.50	2.53
Occupation								
Professional–technical	2.48	2.45	2.48	2.50	2.61	2.46	2.55	2.50
Managerial–administrative	2.51	2.65	2.59	2.64	2.56	2.52	2.55	2.57
Sales	2.24	2.35	2.33	2.71	2.41	1.96	2.48	2.33
Clerical	2.27	2.32	2.25	2.47	2.37	2.33	2.28	2.33
Craftsmen–foremen	2.34	2.19	2.44	2.33	2.56	2.42	2.50	2.39
Operatives	2.13	1.99	2.12	2.15	2.14	2.26	2.18	2.14
Laborers	1.89	2.21	2.29	2.50	2.16	2.36	1.89	2.16
Service	2.20	2.42	2.24	2.42	2.30	2.41	2.31	2.33

*Not available for 1972 and 1973.

Note: 3 = very satisfied, 0 = very dissatisfied.

SOURCE: "Job Satisfaction in the United States in the 1970s," by C. N. Weaver, *Journal of Applied Psychology, 65,* 366. Copyright © 1980 by the American Psychological Association. Reprinted by permission of the author.

Sauser & York, 1978). Research has supported this conclusion. Smith and Plant (1982) compared 51 male and 51 female university professors who had been matched on years of service, education, organizational level (rank), and academic department. They found statistically significant but extremely small differences in the men's and women's satisfaction with supervi-

Gender differences in job satisfaction disappear when pay and education are held constant.

sion and satisfaction with coworkers, and no other attitude differences. Similarly, Fry and Greenfeld (1980) compared the work attitudes of male and female police officers. Their study is particularly interesting because no sex differences were found despite the traditional masculine stereotype associated with the job. Finally, it seems that men and women with comparable jobs not only have comparable levels of satisfaction but, as was the case with black and white workers, also derive satisfaction from the same aspects of their jobs (Weaver, 1978b).

One danger in interpreting the literature on race and sex differences in job satisfaction is concluding that blacks and whites, and men and women, are equally satisfied. It should be kept in mind that in any single organization, such as Peter's Pan Pizza, very real differences may exist between the satisfaction levels of such groups. Further, simply because a difference in satisfaction can be explained by differences in pay, education, tenure, and the like

does not make the low-paid, less-educated, short-tenured worker any happier. As long as segments of the population differ on variables such as these, differences in satisfaction are likely to exist.

Relationships between commitment and a number of personal characteristics are presented in Table 9.1; of the demographic variables, only age has even a moderate correlation with commitment ($r = .201$). However, Mathieu and Zajac (1990) also concluded that the relationships between commitment and such variables as age, sex, and education might be influenced by other variables, so personal characteristics may yet prove to be helpful in predicting commitment. Consistent with this is a study by Mottaz (1986), who found that education level had an *indirect* positive effect on commitment through the effects of increased rewards; that is, more highly educated workers are more committed because they are paid more than less-educated workers. However, when

Mottaz controlled for differences in rewards, a direct *negative* effect on commitment was found for education level—more highly educated workers were *less* committed.

The extent to which members of different groups are treated differently on the job might affect their relative levels of commitment. Graddick and Farr (1983) found that female scientists had lower organizational commitment than did male scientists. The women also felt that they were treated less well than were the men. Although we can't conclude that differences in perceived treatment *caused* differences in commitment, it is important to realize that women and minorities have very different job experiences than other workers, and it is reasonable to expect that this could influence job attitudes.

Work and Nonwork Satisfaction

The relationship between work behavior and behavior off the job has been of interest to psychologists for many years. A particularly large body of literature has been generated by researchers studying the relationships between job satisfaction and other types of satisfaction. Psychologists have been especially interested in nonwork satisfaction, or the satisfaction a person experiences when engaging in activities away from the job, and general life satisfaction, or one's level of satisfaction considering all aspects of life, both work and nonwork. If a person's feelings about work are related to feelings about other aspects of life, work may have important implications beyond the walls of the factory or office, and outside the regular 40-hour workweek. At the same time, characteristics of a person's nonwork life may have implications for work behavior.

Early research on the relationship between work and nonwork variables was conducted by Dubin (1956), who developed the notion of a central life interest. **Central life interest** refers to a person's preference for behaving or acting in specific locales or settings. Dubin classified people as having one of three basic central-life-

interest patterns. The first he called *job-oriented* central life interest, which describes people who perceive their jobs as the focal points of their lives. The second pattern is *non-job-oriented* central life interest, which describes people for whom the job is not the primary activity in life but who instead place more emphasis on such things as family, church, or other interests. The third type Dubin called *flexible-focus* central life interest, which describes people who demonstrate no preference for either work or nonwork activities.

Whereas Dubin's (1956) categories help us classify the dominant interests in a worker's life, they do not explain the relationships between work and nonwork activities, and people's satisfaction with those activities. More recently, Kabanoff (1980) reviewed theoretical and philosophical writings on the nature of work, and identified three hypotheses about the relationships between work and nonwork. The first is a *compensatory* hypothesis, which says that nonwork activities compensate for deficiencies in a person's work life, and vice versa. According to this hypothesis, there should be a negative relationship between work and nonwork satisfaction: those with low job satisfaction will engage in satisfying nonwork activities, whereas people dissatisfied with their nonwork lives will seek satisfaction at the workplace. The second relationship is a *generalization* or *spillover* hypothesis, which specifies a positive relationship between work and nonwork satisfactions. Basically, this hypothesis says that the satisfying aspects of one's job will make nonwork life more pleasant, whereas dissatisfying work elements will also spill over into other domains. The final hypothesis specifies a *segmented relationship* between work and nonwork satisfactions. This means that work and nonwork are independent in their effects on a person's attitudes and life.

Perhaps before worrying about the nature of the relationship between work and nonwork satisfaction, we should first be concerned with whether the two are related at all. As it turns out, there is both positive and negative evidence of such a relationship. Gechman and Wiener (1975) found that teachers with higher job satisfaction had better mental health, and concluded that job satisfaction leads to benefits in nonwork areas. Other researchers, however, found little evidence that satisfaction with one's job predicts satisfaction with life in general (London, Crandall, & Seals, 1977). Kabanoff (1980) found support in the literature for each of the compensatory, spillover, and segmentation hypotheses. He also found, however, that the relationships between work and nonwork attitudes were generally weak.

On the other hand, a meta-analysis of the relationship between job and life satisfaction found a fairly large correlation between them ($r = .44$; Tait, Padgett, & Baldwin, 1989). This result is at odds with earlier reviews (for example, Rice, Near, & Hunt, 1980), but keep in mind that meta-analyses can control for factors that introduce error into research results. Also, the meta-analysis indicated that the job satisfaction–life satisfaction relationship may be influenced by other variables, so the correlation may in fact be smaller in some situations. For example, the life satisfaction–job satisfaction relationship, particularly for intrinsic satisfaction, was found to be stronger among individuals who value work in their lives than among those who do not (Steiner & Truxillo, 1987, 1989; cf. Rice, Near, & Hunt, 1980).

The research on work and nonwork suffers from methodological problems that make interpretation difficult (Kabanoff, 1980). One of the most basic of these problems is defining *work* and *nonwork*. For example, if we define *nonwork* as everything that occurs outside the workplace, how do we classify the time spent traveling to work, mowing the lawn, or painting the house? By the same token, if the work-nonwork distinction is primarily psychological, based on differences in pleasure, freedom, or relaxation, how do we classify the on-the-job activities of people who enjoy their jobs and experience freedom and relaxation in the workplace? Based on his own data, Kabanoff supported a "conservative segmentalist" hypothesis, stating that work and nonwork are not consistently related, and that when they are related, the relationship tends to be weak (Kabanoff & O'Brien, 1980).

Despite the lack of evidence of any consistent relationship between work and nonwork satisfaction, another line of research has attempted to determine whether differences in job satisfaction cause differences in life satisfaction, or vice versa. Orpen (1978) found that the causal effects of work satisfaction were stronger than those of nonwork satisfaction among his sample of first-line managers. Schmitt and Mellon (1980) drew the opposite conclusion in a study of civil-service employees. More recent research suggests that the causal effects may go in both directions. Schmitt and Bedeian (1982) examined the satisfaction ratings of 875 civil-service workers, and concluded that high job satisfaction had a positive effect on life satisfaction, whereas life satisfaction also had a positive effect on job satisfaction. Near, Smith, Rice, and Hunt (1984) found a similar "cross-domain spillover effect" in a survey of 1,515 workers. They found that living conditions had a reliable, although small, effect on job satisfaction, and that working conditions had a similar effect on life satisfaction. Chacko (1983) also found evidence for spillover effects in both directions, although he concluded that the effects from job to life satisfaction were more prevalent.

In general, whereas there may be relationships between work and nonwork satisfaction, the nature of the relationships remains ambiguous. Perhaps we should heed Kabanoff and O'Brien's (1980) advice and abandon attempts to identify the relationship between work and nonwork, and focus instead on *why* people develop different work and nonwork patterns.

Summary of Job-Attitude Correlates

The relationships between job satisfaction and other variables are fewer and weaker than psychologists once believed. There is no consistent relationship between satisfaction and absenteeism, and only an indirect association between satisfaction and turnover. Similarly, research has shown no meaningful relationship between job satisfaction and work performance. Only small differences in satisfaction across occupational and demographic groups have been discovered, and even these may be better explained by differences in pay, education, and job tenure. Finally, the relationships between job satisfaction and nonwork or general satisfaction are quite variable, and often moderated by other variables.

There has been less research on the correlates of organizational commitment than on those of satisfaction, and the picture there is hardly any clearer. Weak relationships with absenteeism, personal characteristics and job performance are typical. Commitment *has* been found to be related to turnover, however, and it appears to be a major factor in determining workers' intentions to quit their jobs.

About now you may be wondering if job attitudes are worth bothering with. We will address that specific question later in the chapter. One possible explanation for the negative results in attitude research, however, is that the measures of job attitudes used by psychologists are somehow flawed. If these instruments do not really measure workers' attitudes toward their jobs, then we are unlikely to find meaningful results. In the following sections we examine several of these measures and present some of the more important issues in job-attitude measurement.

Measurement of Work Attitudes

In this chapter we have presented the results of a wide variety of research studies on the origins, correlates, and possible effects of work attitudes. Without measures of workers' attitudes, this research and the theories it has spawned would not be possible. We now turn

briefly to some of the issues involved in measuring work attitudes and in particular job satisfaction. At first glance, measuring satisfaction may seem to be a straightforward process. Closer examination reveals that it is anything but straightforward.

Facet versus Global Satisfaction

At the beginning of this chapter, we defined job satisfaction as a multifaceted construct. Job-satisfaction measures clearly reflect this multidimensionality. Over the years, as researchers studied different job facets and investigated the multitude of variables that might be related to satisfaction, hundreds of satisfaction measures were developed. Whereas these instruments have in common the purpose of gauging worker attitudes, they differ in many significant ways; most important, they differ in the specific facets of satisfaction that they are designed to measure.

The large number of job-satisfaction measures in use has slowed the development of job-satisfaction theory. Specifically, the use of different measures, no two of which yield completely comparable scores, has made it extremely difficult to accumulate information about satisfaction, or to compare the results of various studies. It has also contributed to the inconsistency in research results that we have encountered in this chapter. Addressing these issues, Schneider (1985) concluded that I/O psychologists should develop a single measure of global, or overall, job satisfaction. The widespread use of such a measure would avoid the problem of noncomparable data being gathered in different studies. Further, Schneider suggested that with a global satisfaction measure that could be used both as a dependent variable in studies of the causes of satisfaction and as an independent variable in studies of the effects of satisfaction, sound theories of work attitudes might emerge.

It should be noted that global satisfaction measures are not the same as composite satisfaction measures. Global measures require workers to mentally combine their reactions to the job into a single response. Composite measures are simply a summation of the responses to scales measuring satisfaction with a number of specific job facets. It has been persuasively argued that if a company or researcher wishes to measure general job satisfaction, a global measure is much better suited to the task than are composite measures (Ironson, Smith, Brannick, Gibson, & Paul, 1989). Composite measures may be based on facets that are unimportant to some workers and omit facets that are important. Also, responses to facet scales may reflect short-term attitudes, and global measures are more likely to be based on a long-term reaction to the job. Finally, the procedures used to construct composite measures may not reflect the relative importance of the various facets to a particular worker.

It is interesting to note that there has *not* been a corresponding explosion in the number of organizational commitment measures. Although several commitment scales have been developed, researchers have apparently "standardized" on two of these: the Organizational Commitment Questionnaire developed by Mowday, Steers, and Porter (1979) for attitudinal commitment, and a scale by Hrebiniak and Alutto (1972) for calculated commitment (Mathieu & Zajac, 1990).

Popular Job-Satisfaction Measures

Psychologists have not agreed on a single measure of global job satisfaction or even that such a measure would be desirable. There has, however, been a trend in recent years for researchers to use one of a small number of standardized job-satisfaction measures. In the following sections we will present two of these scales, as well as an interesting single-item scale that uses a unique approach to attitude measurement.

The Job Descriptive Index. The Job Descriptive Index (JDI) is far and away the most frequently used measure of job satisfaction. Developed by Smith, Kendall, and Hulin (1969), it measures satisfaction with five facets of a worker's job: the work itself, supervision, pay, promotions, and coworkers. It is also possible to combine the facet measures to obtain a composite satisfaction measure (Hulin, Drasgow, & Komocar, 1982; Parsons & Hulin, 1982). A global "job in general" scale was added later (Ironson et al., 1989). Examples of the types of items used in the JDI appear in Box 9.1.

In general, although there is some evidence that the JDI may actually measure satisfaction with more than five job facets (Yeager, 1981), the reliability and validity of the scales appear to be good. For example, Johnson, Smith, and Tucker (1982) found three-week test-retest reliabilities from .68 to .88, and internal consistency reliabilities from .75 to .93.

The primary problem with the JDI is that there are many aspects or facets of jobs that are not included in the measure. Consider again the turnover problem in PPP's Retail Operations Division. As we have seen, it is possible that job dissatisfaction is playing a role in this situation. Let's assume that the aspect of the job with which the store inspectors are most dissatisfied is the amount of time they must be away from home. The JDI would be inadequate for measuring these specific feelings.

The Minnesota Satisfaction Questionnaire. Another popular job-satisfaction measure is the Minnesota Satisfaction Questionnaire (MSQ; Weiss, Dawis, England, & Lofquist, 1967). The MSQ contains 100 items that measure satisfaction with 20 job facets:

1. Ability utilization
2. Achievement
3. Activity
4. Advancement
5. Authority
6. Company policies and practices
7. Compensation
8. Coworkers

BOX 9.1 Examples of Items Used in the JDI

For each descriptive phrase or word, the worker indicates "Yes" if it describes the relevant aspect of his job (that is, the work itself, pay, and so on), "No" if it does not describe that aspect of the job, and "?" if he is uncertain.

Work itself: Coworkers:

_____ Routine   _____ Helpful

_____ Satisfying   _____ Lazy

_____ Good   _____ Loyal

   Pay: Supervision:

_____ Bad   _____ Hard to please

_____ Well paid   _____ Asks my advice

_____ Less than I deserve   _____ Around when needed

Promotions: Job in general:

_____ Dead-end job   _____ Better than most

_____ Infrequent promotions   _____ Rotten

_____ Good chance for promotion   _____ Acceptable

SOURCE: From *The Measurement of Satisfaction in Work and Retirement,* by P. C. Smith, L. M. Kendall, and C. L. Hulin. Copyright 1969 by Rand McNally and Company. Job Descriptive Index copyright © 1975; revised 1985 by the Department of Psychology, Bowling Green State University, Bowling Green, Ohio 43403. Adapted by permission for this book. Rights to duplicate must be purchased from Bowling Green State University.

---

9. Creativity

10. Independence

11. Moral values

12. Recognition

13. Responsibility

14. Security

15. Social service

16. Social status

17. Supervision-human relations

18. Supervision-technical

19. Variety

20. Working conditions

Often a short form of the MSQ is used, containing one item from each of the 20 dimensions. Even with 20 facets, however, there is no guarantee that the specific attitude of importance, such as satisfaction with travel policy, is being measured.

The Faces Scale. A unique approach to measuring global job satisfaction is represented by the Faces Scale (Kunin, 1955). A version of this single-item scale is shown in Figure 9.8. As a measure of global satisfaction, the Faces Scale appears to be quite good (Cook, Hepworth, Wall, & Warr, 1981). It also has the advantage of not relying on complex, often ambiguous verbal anchors, instead using universally recog-

Put a check under the face that expresses how you feel about your
job in general, including the work, the pay, the supervision, the
opportunities for promotion, and the people you work with.

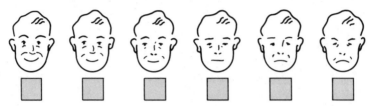

FIGURE 9.8
The Faces Scale
SOURCE: From *The Measurement of Satisfaction in Work and Retirement*, by P. C Smith, L. M. Kendall, and
C. L. Hulin. Copyright 1969 by Rand McNally and Company. Adapted from "The Construction of a New Type of
Attitude Measure," by T. Kunin, 1955. In *Personnel Psychology, 8*, 68–69. Copyright © 1955 by Personnel
Psychology, Inc. Reprinted by permission.

nized facial expressions. This should make the
Faces Scale particularly useful in organizations
with multicultural work forces. The principle
underlying the Faces Scale is flexible and could
probably be applied to the measurement of
other attitudes.

Custom Job-Satisfaction Measures

The JDI and the MSQ measure only a limited
range of all possible work attitudes. Organizations such as PPP are often interested in more
specific worker attitudes for which standardized
measures do not exist, such as satisfaction with
company policies. The common response to
such a problem has been to design a custom
job-satisfaction measure. Although it seems reasonable, this task should not be undertaken
lightly. It may be that the desired scale already
exists. Cook, Hepworth, Wall, and Warr (1981)
identified about 250 work-attitude measures,
providing a useful source of information about
available satisfaction scales. Also, developing a
good satisfaction measure takes a lot of time,
work, and expertise. The JDI, the MSQ, and the
Faces Scale are each a product of long hours of
work. It is doubtful that anyone with limited
resources could do as good a job.

Be that as it may, it is common for a researcher or organization to need a specific mea-

sure of satisfaction for which there is no existing
scale. The only option in such circumstances is
to develop a custom-made measure. A variety
of item formats can be used in attitude measures, three of which are given in Box 9.2.

More important than the format of the
questions, however, are the reliability and validity of the measure. An unreliable scale, or a
scale that is not valid for the purpose for which
it is used, will create more problems than it
solves.

Conclusions

Schneider (1985) stated that although an aim of
all management and motivation theories is to
have a satisfied work force, we lack the comprehensive theories of the causes of satisfaction
necessary to control worker attitudes. Because
job satisfaction is one of the most widely studied topics in I/O psychology, if not *the* most
widely studied, this is discouraging. Schneider
suggested three hypotheses to explain the importance that researchers have apparently
placed on job satisfaction. The first is that it is
easy to study the relationship between job satisfaction and other variables. With the variety of
satisfaction measures available, correlational

BOX 9.2 Item Formats to Measure Job Attitudes

A. LIKERT FORMAT

Instructions: Indicate your agreement with the following statements, using the following scale:

SA: Strongly agree
 A: Agree
 N: Neither agree nor disagree
 D: Disagree
SD: Strongly disagree

1. My work is boring.	SA	A	N	D	SD
2. My work is challenging.	SA	A	N	D	SD
3. My work is meaningful.	SA	A	N	D	SD
4. My work is unpleasant.	SA	A	N	D	SD

B. SEMANTIC DIFFERENTIAL FORMAT

Instructions: Mark (X) the point between each pair of words that best describes your job. Example: If you find your job extremely exciting, you would mark as shown below.

Boring	____	____	____	____	__X__	Exciting
1. Boring	____	____	____	____	____	Exciting
2. Challenging	____	____	____	____	____	Easy
3. Meaningful	____	____	____	____	____	Useless
4. Pleasant	____	____	____	____	____	Unpleasant

C. CHECKLIST FORMAT

Instructions: Mark (X) the words in the following list that describe your job.

1. Boring	____	**5.** Meaningful	____
2. Exciting	____	**6.** Useless	____
3. Challenging	____	**7.** Pleasant	____
4. Easy	____	**8.** Unpleasant	____

studies of satisfaction and sex, age, status, and so on have proliferated. As we have seen, however, the results concerning the causes of satisfaction are often less than conclusive.

The second hypothesis is that satisfaction is expected to be a useful predictor of important work behaviors. This predictive relationship seems to prevail for some behaviors, such as turnover, but research on the relationship of satisfaction with other behaviors, such as performance, seems to have progressed *in spite of* the accumulated empirical evidence. One general conclusion that can be drawn from this research is that job satisfaction is not as strongly related to work behaviors as the Hawthorne studies and the human-relations movement once led us to believe.

Each of the first two hypotheses undoubtedly accounts for much of the satisfaction research activity. However, given the volume of data that has been generated, we know relatively little about either the causes of satisfaction or the effects of satisfaction. It is Schneider's (1985) final hypothesis, we believe, that captures the flavor of the most interesting satisfaction studies, and that seems to offer the best rationale for future research. This hypothesis states that satisfaction is simply an important human outcome of organizational life, and researchers study satisfaction because it is as much a part of work organizations as productivity, motivation, or anything else. All workers are more or less satisfied with the various aspects of their jobs. Those attitudes are important, if for no other reason than that they are experienced by workers. Until we study and understand job satisfaction in its own right, we are not likely to learn about its relationships with other behaviors.

Chapter Summary

Job satisfaction and organizational commitment are examples of attitudes or "evaluative disposi-

tions" that people have toward their work. Because jobs are multidimensional, the attitudes are most accurately perceived as collections or networks of specific attitudes toward specific job dimensions. The importance of these job attitudes was first brought to the attention of I/O psychologists through the pioneering research of the Hawthorne and Hoppock studies.

One of the earliest influential theories of job satisfaction was Herzberg's two-factor theory, which stated that job satisfaction and dissatisfaction stemmed from different aspects of the job. Research, however, has failed to support Herzberg's ideas. Most other satisfaction theories, including need theories, Locke's value theory, and Lawler's facet theory, propose that a worker's level of satisfaction results from a comparison between his or her current status (for example, level of need satisfaction) and some standard or ideal. Although this comparison notion is popular, research support for these theories has been mixed, at best.

A relatively recent approach to understanding job attitudes suggests that satisfaction is based on social modeling of the attitudes and behaviors of other workers. This approach emphasizes the importance of social factors in work-attitude development.

Dispositional explanations for job satisfaction have gained popularity. They emphasize both personality traits and heredity to explain dispositions. However, the research on these factors has not been encouraging with regard to the role of dispositions in determining attitudes.

Research has also examined the relationship between job attitudes and workers' behaviors. These efforts have found weak, inconsistent associations between satisfaction and absenteeism, and only somewhat stronger, indirect relationships between satisfaction and turnover. Organizational commitment, however, has been found to be a substantial predictor of turnover. Only very small correlations between work attitudes and job performance, or between work attitudes and nonwork attitudes and behaviors, have been obtained.

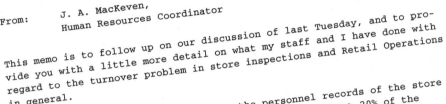

INTEROFFICE MEMO

To: Joanna Richmond,
           Director of Inspections

From: J. A. MacKeven,
           Human Resources Coordinator

This memo is to follow up on our discussion of last Tuesday, and to provide you with a little more detail on what my staff and I have done with
regard to the turnover problem in store inspections and Retail Operations
in general.

The first thing we did was to examine the personnel records of the store
inspectors who have left the company. We found that about 20% of the
turnover was for personal reasons and classified as unavoidable. Another
20% was what we call "functional" turnover—either the employees were
fired or they probably would have been fired if they had not quit. The
remaining 60% were employees in good standing who voluntarily left for
other jobs. The majority of these have remained in the retail food business, but virtually none have taken inspection jobs.

Next, we conducted a job-satisfaction survey of all Retail Operations
employees. In addition to using a well-respected measure of job satisfaction known as the Job Descriptive Index, my staff interviewed a sample of
the store inspectors. Based on those interviews, we developed questions
specifically addressing the issue of travel requirements, as well as
questions concerning intention to leave PPP. The results of the survey
showed that the store inspectors are generally satisfied with the work
they perform, their pay, and their supervision, and somewhat dissatisfied
with the opportunities for promotion. The questions regarding travel
clearly show that the inspectors are very dissatisfied with this aspect
of their jobs. Also, over 50% of the inspectors said they were thinking
about changing jobs.

Based on this information, I make the following suggestions:

1. The travel schedules of all store inspectors should be examined, and
   if possible adjusted so as to minimize the time spent on the road.
2. When hiring new inspectors, be certain that the travel requirements
   are clearly understood by all prospective employees.
3. Consider changing the store-inspection system to allow inspectors to
   live in the general area of the stores for which they are responsible, rather than working out of Suardell Springs.

A substantial amount of research has been dedicated to developing sound measures of job satisfaction. Notable among them are the Job Descriptive Index and the Minnesota Satisfaction Questionnaire, each of which measures satisfaction with a number of job dimensions or facets, and the Faces Scale, which uses a simple, single-response item to measure global job satisfaction.

Review Questions and Exercises

1. Dr. MacKeven seems to have focused on the issue of travel in making her recommendations. What other factors are implied by the data she gathered, and how do you think they should be dealt with? (See memo on p. 315.)

2. Given what you know about the nature of the store inspectors' jobs, what variables not measured in Dr. MacKeven's survey might be expected to be related to their satisfaction levels and/or rate of turnover?

3. What steps, other than reducing travel requirements and improving other factors that could be causing employees to leave, might be taken to lower the overall turnover rate?

4. Evaluate each of Dr. MacKeven's recommendations. Upon which assumptions do they seem to be based? What are the "hidden costs" or possible disadvantages of each?

CHAPTER 10

Leadership and Management

LEARNING POINTS

After studying this chapter, you should

- be able to describe the different ways leadership has been defined over the years, and distinguish between leadership and management;

- be able to describe French and Raven's bases of social power and how they relate to both formal and emergent forms of leadership;

- understand the relationship between various personal traits and leadership, and be able to describe recent research findings on leader traits;

- be able to describe the Ohio State leadership measures, and discuss the importance of specific leadership behaviors;

- be able to explain the importance of implicit or naive theories of leadership;

- be able to explain the basic principle of contingency theories of leadership, and evaluate Least-Preferred Coworker and path-goal theories;

- understand the purpose of the Vroom-Jago normative theory of leadership, and describe how it is used;

- be able to define vertical dyad linkages and average leadership style, and explain how

they operate according to Leader-Member Exchange theory;

- understand the potential importance of attribution processes and charisma in organizational leadership; and

- be prepared to speculate on the importance of leadership in organizations.

THE MEMO FROM ROB SANDERS (p. 318) raises a number of important questions about leadership in organizations. As people are promoted into managerial and supervisory positions, it is often difficult to assess their capacity for leadership. A good, or even excellent, employee may not turn out to be a good, or even adequate, manager. In some cases this is due to a lack of relevant technical education or experience, although Mr. Sanders believes that this is not the case in Flavio's. In other situations, new managers have difficulty because they lack skills or qualities that allow them to provide leadership to the people they are supervising. However, as suggested by Mr. Sanders' first question, leadership may not be a very important consideration in some situations, but in others it could be critical to the manager's success. If leadership is important, Dr. MacKeven needs to be able to describe the factors that are of consequence in its develop-

INTEROFFICE MEMO

To: J. A. MacKeven,
        Human Resources Coordinator

From: Rob Sanders,
        V.P. Marketing

With the recent expansion of our distribution operations into the south-
east and mid-Atlantic regions of the country, we have added a significant
number of employees to our marketing operation. This is the first major
increase in the marketing force for some time. (In fact, even when
Flavio's Frozen Foods was acquired a number of years ago, we essentially
kept the Marketing Division the same size as it had been prior to the
merger.)

The recent growth has raised a number of concerns in Marketing, particularly regarding supervision and management. We are about to promote a
number of our nonsupervisory staff into the new management positions
created by the expansion. However, we are aware that when our divisions
expanded at the time of the Flavio's acquisition, not all of the internal
promotions were successful. I am confident in the technical skills of the
people we plan to promote, but I have little by which to gauge their
leadership qualities.

I would like to get your opinion on the following issues:

1. If I am correct that these new managers have adequate technical
   expertise in marketing, should I be worried at all about their
   leadership skills?

2. If we need to be worried about the leadership these people will provide (and I am convinced that we do), how can we help them improve
   their leadership skills? Can we "train" people to be leaders, or
   should we reexamine our internal promotion policy and look elsewhere
   for "proven leaders"?

ment and suggest ways to improve leadership within the Marketing Division.

In this chapter we will explore the topic of organizational leadership and supervisory influence. As you will see, Dr. MacKeven is faced with a great deal of conflicting research and theory concerning what makes a person a good leader. In the following pages we describe several approaches to leadership and discuss how they might apply to the issues raised by Mr. Sanders in PPP's Marketing Division. First, however, we will need to define exactly what we mean when we use the term *leadership* and, just as important, what we *don't* mean when we call someone a leader.

The Nature of Organizational Leadership

Leadership is one of the most widely researched topics in I/O psychology. Stogdill (1974) reviewed and summarized the published research on leadership, and his work was later updated and expanded by Bass (1981, 1990). Whereas Stogdill's book summarized more than 3,000 published works, Bass (1981) cited more than 5,000 studies only seven years later. Leadership has clearly been an important topic in psychology, and it is safe to predict that it will continue to be so.

Definitions of Leadership

With so much research on leadership, you might assume, or at least hope, that psychologists are in fairly good agreement about what leadership is. Unfortunately, this is not the case. Bass (1990) described the situation well when he said, "There are almost as many different definitions of leadership as there are persons who have attempted to define the concept" (p. 11). He went on to group the definitions into several categories. We'll look at some of these general approaches to leadership, and then pre-

sent a definition that takes most of them into account. It is important to have such a definition because without it we would be unable either to describe adequately what we expect from leaders or to study their behavior and identify ways to improve their effectiveness. Keep in mind that some of the following definitions are considered by most psychologists to be far too simplistic by today's standards. Many of the basic ideas contained in these definitions, however, have been incorporated into the modern theories that we will discuss.

Leadership as Personality. The leadership-as-personality approach asserts that leadership is determined by certain personality traits or characteristics (for example, Bernard, 1926; Jenkins, 1947). People with such traits have the potential to influence others and become leaders, whereas people without them are destined to be followers. This definition would imply that the new managers in PPP's Marketing Division would need to have certain personality traits in order to be effective. Personality is the basis for the trait theories of leadership that we will discuss later.

Leadership as Influence. When we define leadership as influence, we are saying that leader behavior has some desired effect on follower behavior. This approach does not really suggest *why* leaders are effective or why some people are better leaders in a given situation, such as PPP's Marketing Division, but it does stress the fact that leadership involves getting others to do what the leader wants. The notion of influence is implied by most modern definitions of leadership (Bass, 1990; House & Baetz, 1979).

Leadership as Behavior. Leadership as behavior is a deceptively simple definition of leadership. Assuming that you know who the leaders in an organization or group are, leadership is defined as the behaviors in which the leaders engage (Fiedler, 1967; Hemphill, 1949). In practice, this approach has virtually always equated leadership with managerial or supervisory behavior. Ineffective leadership results when supervisors engage in the wrong (that is, ineffective) behaviors. You should notice an important difference between this approach and the definition of leadership as *influence*. If you view leadership as influence, then you must examine the behavior of the followers to see whether or not leadership has taken place. If you view leadership as simply the behavior of people in supervisory positions, then the reactions of the followers are less important.

Leadership as Power. Power is the extent to which one person (the leader) can expend more force on other group members than they, in turn, can exert to resist the leader's intentions (French & Raven, 1958a, 1958b). It should be clear that power depends on the reactions of followers as well as the behavior of leaders. In fact, unlike most *leadership* definitions, the power approach does not automatically assume that supervisors and managers are the only leaders in an organization. Depending on their ability to influence others, all members of an organization can, at times, be leaders. For example, some of the new managers in PPP's Marketing Division may lack the necessary power to overcome workers' resistance to their plans or policies. Of course, it could also be that some of the workers have enough power to have become strong leaders themselves. Because power is such a prominent characteristic of organizations, we will discuss it in more detail later.

Leadership as Goal Achievement. The view of leadership as goal achievement stresses the outcome of behavior in terms of whether it helps the group or organization achieve its goals (Bellows, 1959; Cowley, 1928). Whether a leader is effective because of power, personality, or coercion, or for other reasons, is not particularly important as long as the organization's goals are met. As was the case with *influence* definitions, goal achievement illustrates an important aspect of leadership, but it does not suggest *why* some

leaders are effective nor why leadership problems might exist.

Leadership as an Attribution. The view of leadership as an attribution states that leadership does not, by itself, affect important outcomes in organizations. Rather, it is an *attribution*, or an explanation, used by people to account for events in the workplace (Calder, 1977; House & Baetz, 1979; Pfeffer, 1977, 1981). This definition suggests that any problems that might arise in PPP's Marketing Division will not necessarily be due to leadership issues but that people, including Mr. Sanders and Dr. MacKeven, will naturally attribute these problems to leaders' behavior.

Leadership as a Dyadic Relationship. Leadership as a dyadic relationship is another approach that has emerged in recent years (Dansereau, Graen, & Haga, 1975; Graen, Novak, & Sommerkamp, 1982; Liden & Graen, 1980). The basic idea is that leadership depends not only on the behavior, personality, power, and so forth of the leader but also on the reactions of the followers, which in turn have implications for the leader's subsequent behavior. This approach suggests that a dyadic, or one-on-one, relationship develops between leaders and each of their followers. Consequently, leaders interact with their followers in different ways, depending on the nature of the individual dyadic relationships. Whereas other definitions imply that dyadic relationships between leader and follower are important, this approach views the dyadic relationship as the *essence* of leadership. Relative to PPP's Marketing Division, this definition suggests that until new managers establish appropriate and productive dyadic relationships with their workers, their work groups will not achieve their full potential.

Given the diversity of opinion about the nature of leadership, you might wonder if it is even possible to come up with a single meaningful definition. For our purposes, a good definition of leadership is one that is general enough to accommodate various theories and research studies, and also specific enough to distinguish leadership from other organizational phenomena, such as motivation or job satisfaction. We believe that the following definition meets these standards. **Leadership** *is social influence in an organizational setting, the effects of which are relevant to, or have an impact upon, the achievement of organizational goals.* Let's examine the implications of this definition.

First, leadership is social influence. This means that leadership takes place when one person determines, at least in part, the behavior of other people. We are not dealing with leadership when behavior is determined by situational factors that are beyond individual control, such as the level of noise or the temperature of the work environment, or by characteristics of the worker, such as skill level or temperament. Rather, leadership occurs when the behavior of one person results in behavior on the part of others that would not have otherwise occurred.

Some people (notably Pfeffer, 1977) believe that leadership defined as social influence cannot be distinguished from other forms of social influence. Pfeffer argues that leadership is redundant to the concept of influence itself, and is therefore unnecessary for understanding behavior in organizations. We disagree with Pfeffer. Along with House and Baetz (1979), we believe that leadership has unique characteristics that *do* distinguish it from other forms of social influence. The first of these is the organizational setting in which leadership takes place. Organizations have certain formal and informal structures, rules, and processes that limit some opportunities for influence while creating others. The structures and rules also define, to a large extent, the means by which influence can be attempted. The second characteristic is the general purpose of leadership: to help the organization achieve its goals. Influence concerning issues other than goal achievement, whether it occurs within the organization or outside it, is *not* leadership, whereas influence that helps determine organizational performance *is* leadership. Together these two aspects of leadership distinguish it from other types of influence.

To show how our definition can accommodate various approaches to leadership, consider that social influence can be based on many factors, including the personality of the leader (Mills & Bohannon, 1980; Sanders & Malkis, 1982; Spector, 1982); the behavior of the leader (Butterfield & Powell, 1981; Tziner & Vardi, 1982; Weed & Mitchell, 1980); or the power held by the leader (Cobb, 1980; Price & Garland, 1981). It is important, however, that attempts to influence be accepted, for unless followers perceive these attempts as legitimate, leadership may be rejected (House & Baetz, 1979). One factor that could affect the acceptance of leadership is the type of attributions that followers make, for the leader's behavior. Greater acceptance would be expected, for example, if followers attribute leaders' actions to expertise or to concern for the welfare of the workers and the organization rather than blind allegiance to company policy (Calder, 1977; Eagly, Wood, & Chaiken, 1978; Harvey & Weary, 1984).

The Scope of Leadership

Having defined what we mean by leadership, we should consider the ways in which leadership operates in organizations. Who are the leaders and who are the followers? This is not a simple question to answer, but, as we have explained, it is a question that should be carefully considered.

Leadership versus Management. Leadership takes place in organizations, and in organizations some people have more authority than others. In this context it is tempting to say that leaders are the people with the most authority, specifically the managers and supervisors. People who study leadership have generally taken this view. Nearly all theories of leadership are concerned with managerial influence and, in fact, the terms *leadership* and *management* are often used interchangeably. The temptation to equate leadership and management is apparently very strong. Wilpert (1982) commented on three presentations from a symposium on leadership. The symposium was intended, among other things, to address the differences between leadership and management and the relevance of leadership research for the practice of management (Bussom, Larson, & Vicars, 1982; Lombardo & McCall, 1982; Stewart, 1982). You would expect the papers to have made a clear distinction between leadership and management. Wilpert noted, however, that whereas each paper implied a difference between the two constructs, none described the difference, and all used the terms synonymously. Even Wilpert made the assumption that "managers always perform some leadership function due to their organizational position" (p. 69).

How reasonable is this assumption? Do all managers perform leadership functions, as we have defined *leadership*? To answer these questions, we need to examine what is meant by *management* more closely. Mintzberg (1980) offered one popular view of management. After studying senior managers, he concluded that a manager's job can be described in terms of ten roles. These roles are grouped into interpersonal roles, informational roles, and decisional roles. As you can see in Box 10.1, "leader" is only one of the ten managerial roles; most of the functions performed by managers are not directly related to leadership nor even social (interpersonal) in nature. Thus, if all managers are leaders, they are many other things as well (Hunt, Sekaran, & Schriesheim, 1982).

But do *all* managers act as leaders as a regular, day-to-day, part of their jobs? Not necessarily. Different managers emphasize different roles, depending on the functions of the units they manage (Mintzberg, 1980). For example, when managers were asked to rate the importance of Mintzberg's roles, sales managers rated "leader" and the other interpersonal roles as being more important than did other manag-

ers (Alexander, 1979; Paolillo, 1981; Pavett & Lau, 1983). Also, lower-level managers rated the leader role as more important than did middle-level or upper-level managers (Pavett & Lau, 1983). Thus, although it may be true that all managers are called upon to exercise leadership from time to time, it seems likely that leadership is not a major component of all managerial jobs.

A second question about the scope of leadership concerns whether all leaders are managers. That is, *must* people be in positions of formal authority in order to exercise goal-relevant social influence? We strongly believe that they do not. There is no reason that anyone, given the right circumstances, can't exercise leadership in an organization. This is not to say that managers aren't *more likely* to be leaders, in that they are more apt to have resources that are unavailable to other members of their organizations. Managers are also more likely to exercise broader leadership or to have influence over a wider variety of issues than nonmanagers. The ability to influence others, however, does not stem solely from formal authority.

Bases of Social Power.   The potential for nonmanagerial leadership is illustrated by the various ways people come to have power in organizations. The best-known system for classifying social power was developed many years ago by French and Raven (1959). They believed that there are five distinct sources, or *bases*, of social power, and that people's ability to influence others depends on the degree to which they possess one or more of these bases of power.

Legitimate power stems from the recognition by members of an organization that certain people have the *right* to lead others. This type of power usually takes the form of accepting the authority of management to make decisions and enforce rules. Research has shown that power can be legitimized by election to a position (Goldman & Fraas, 1965; Hollander, Fallon, &

BOX 10.1 Managerial Roles

INTERPERSONAL ROLES

1. Figurehead. Involves the performance of symbolic duties stemming from the manager's position as the head of the unit or organization.

2. Leader. Involves motivating employees to work toward achieving the goals of the organization, and establishing a beneficial work atmosphere.

3. Liaison. Involves establishing and maintaining contacts outside the unit or organization for the purpose of obtaining necessary information or other resources.

INFORMATIONAL ROLES

4. Monitor. Involves collecting information necessary for proper unit or organizational functioning.

5. Disseminator. Involves the transmission of information coming from outside the organization or unit to its members.

6. Spokesperson. Involves the transmission of information generated by the unit or organization to the outside.

DECISIONAL ROLES

7. Entrepreneur. Involves changing the unit or organization to adapt to changes in the outside environment.

8. Disturbance handler. Involves handling disturbances or other unforeseen events.

9. Resource allocator. Involves making policy decisions about the use of resources.

10. Negotiator. Involves negotiating or bargaining with other organizations or with individuals.

SOURCE: From *The Nature of Managerial Work*, by H. Mintzberg. Copyright © 1973 by H. Mintzberg. Adapted by permission of the author.

Edwards, 1977; Hollander & Julian, 1970; Read, 1974) as well as appointment by an authority (Julian, Hollander, & Regula, 1969; Knight & Saal, 1984; Knight & Weiss, 1980). For example, when student subjects selected leaders for a management exercise, the group members were likely to comply with the requests of these leaders, whereas the influence attempts of other members were resisted (Watson, 1982).

Reward power concerns the ability of people to administer valued rewards or to help others obtain desired outcomes. According to operant conditioning principles (Luthans & Kreitner, 1985; Scott, 1977), the effective use of reward power requires that the leader know which rewards are valued by each subordinate. It does little good to offer overtime as a reward if workers do not like their jobs or need the extra money and would prefer to spend more time at home. When monetary rewards are available, the use of reward power is usually simplified because most people value money; indeed, managers seem to prefer to use money as a reward when it is available (Hinton & Barrow, 1975; Kipnis, 1972).

Because people value things other than money, the use of reward power is not limited to management. A person's coworkers or subordinates can administer rewards through praise, attention, or ingratiation. This is in contrast to legitimate power, which is necessarily limited to the people authorized by the organization.

Coercive power stems from the ability to impose penalties for failure to comply with influence attempts. Such penalties may involve either punishment or the withholding of rewards (Bass, 1990). As with reward power, coercive power is not limited to managers. Any person with the means to punish another, such as by filing grievances against a supervisor or refusing to "cover" for an absent coworker, has the potential to exercise coercive power.

Several studies have found that coercive power is used primarily in reaction to poor performance, whereas rewards are used in response to good performance (Greene, 1976; Sims, 1977, 1980; Sims & Szilagyi, 1975). This is true even though rewards are generally more effective than punishments for improving performance (Arvey & Ivancevich, 1980; Sims, 1980). The relative ineffectiveness of coercive power was demonstrated long ago by French and Raven (1959), who found that its use led to conformity on the part of followers. This means that workers may *publicly* accept the leadership of coercive managers but *privately* reject it and go along with influence attempts only while they are being watched. Coercion is therefore unlikely to result in long-term influence.

Expert power is based on perceptions of another person's competence or possession of knowledge necessary for the organization to achieve its goals. People who are seen as having relevant expertise will be powerful. This should be especially true if a person is the only source of that expertise. A substantial amount of research in the 1950s showed that people are indeed more easily influenced by the opinions of

experts than by the opinions of nonexperts (for example, Mausner, 1953, 1954), and that expert information can improve performance (Levi, 1954; Torrance, 1953).

More recently, research on expert power has examined how it might interact with other variables. For example, followers were more willing to comply with the wishes of an expert leader when they thought that their own level of competence was low rather than high (Price & Garland, 1981). Ratings of leader expertise as a function of both leader sex and the sex type of the group's task were studied by Knight and Saal (1983). When the group's task dealt with a topic that had been rated as "feminine" (early childhood education), we found that female leaders had higher expertise ratings than male leaders, although the female leaders were not more influential. In a study of perceptions of male and female managers and the types of power they used, expert power resulted in more favorable ratings when the manager was male rather than female, whereas women received higher ratings when they used reward power (Wiley & Eskilson, 1982).

Research on expert power has shown that perceptions of expertise can develop from either observing a person succeed (Mausner, 1954; Price & Garland, 1981) or simply being told that a person is an expert (Mausner, 1953). Knight (Knight & Saal, 1983; Knight & Weiss, 1980) has shown that perceptions of leader expertise can also be based on the expertise of the person who selects the leader. In one study a group leader chosen by the experimenter was rated as having greater expertise when the experimenter declared himself to be an expert on the subjects' task than when he said he had no task expertise. Also, the leader selected by an expert was more influential than the leader chosen by a nonexpert (Knight & Weiss, 1980).

Keep in mind that expert power depends on how much knowledge or expertise people *think* a person has. Newcomers are therefore likely to have to prove their ability on the job before being granted expert power. This could be especially important in a situation such as PPP's Marketing Division, where the new managers have little or no supervisory experience. Of course, if the managers have demonstrated special expertise *prior* to being promoted, and their new subordinates are aware of this expertise, the managers' expert power may be enhanced.

The final base of power described by French and Raven (1959) is **referent power**. Referent power depends on attraction to the leader, and on subordinates' desires to be similar to the leader. This form of power is quite different from the other four because it depends on the interpersonal relationships between workers and is less dependent on job-related factors such as authority, rewards, or task knowledge. An example of a situation in which referent power is likely to be important is charismatic leadership, which we will discuss later in this chapter.

French and Raven's (1959) model is the best-known system for classifying sources of social influence, but it has been criticized for several shortcomings (Bass, 1990). One problem concerns power that does not clearly fit into one of the five categories. For example, the personal relationships between corporate managers and families controlling large amounts of stock in the corporation predicted the amount of power and control the managers had over their own careers (Allen & Panian, 1982). It is not clear whether this was due to a desire to identify with the stockholders (referent power), or if the relationship with the stockholders legitimized the managers' authority (legitimate power), or if some other process was operating. Similarly, having accurate knowledge about informal networks within organizations is related to ratings of power (Krackhardt, 1990). Whether this power is due to expertise (based on the knowledge per se) or to referent sources (due to friendships within these networks) or to some combination of power bases is uncertain.

There has been a great deal of research on French and Raven's (1959) approach to social influence, allowing us to evaluate the effective-

ness of different types of power. Two reviews of this research concluded that referent and expert power were more commonly associated with positive results, particularly in terms of employee satisfaction and performance (Podsakoff & Schriesheim, 1985; Yukl, 1981) However, Yukl (1989) suggested caution in the interpretation of these results. He warned that measures of leader power have not been thoroughly proven, and we should therefore not put a great deal of faith in these research findings. Recent efforts to develop independent multi-item measures of power may prove to be helpful in dealing with this particular problem (Hinken & Schriesheim, 1989; Schriesheim, Hinken, & Podsakoff, 1991). Also, the research has failed to consider the potentially complex interactions among different power bases, as well as the role of cognitive processes such as subordinates' attributions or explanations for their supervisor's behaviors. More comprehensive models of influence must be developed and tested before the effects of power bases can be fully understood.

Despite our inability to say which power bases are more or less effective in a particular situation, the vast research on organizational power does suggest that certain approaches to the use of power are likely to be more effective than others. Several strategies for the effective use of each of French and Raven's power bases have been suggested by Yukl (see Box 10.2). The strategies are useful in any situation involving leadership. Basically, Yukl advocates self-assurance, consideration for the people you are trying to influence, and careful planning, whatever type of power you attempt to use.

You should also recognize that the use of one basis of power might affect perceptions of the others. This was demonstrated in a comparison of workers' ratings of their managers' use of the five bases of power (Greene & Podsakoff, 1981) in two paper mills. One of the mills had recently abandoned a performance-contingent incentive plan; the other continued to use such a plan, as it had for the previous six years. Incentive plans of this type are good examples of the

BOX 10.2 Strategies for Use of French and Raven's Power Bases

EXPERT POWER

1. Promote an image of expertise. Make sure that people are aware of your skills and special training. Avoid projects with a low probability of success, especially when starting out.
2. Maintain credibility. Avoid careless statements. Do not lie to subordinates.
3. Act confident and decisive in a crisis. Never express doubts or appear confused.
4. Keep informed. Technical knowledge is the basis for expert power.
5. Recognize subordinates' concerns and objectives. Expertise that is irrelevant to the needs of the workers or that is utilized to achieve objectives not shared by subordinates will not be effective.
6. Avoid acting superior or otherwise threatening the self-esteem of subordinates. Do not use expertise to make subordinates feel ignorant.

LEGITIMATE POWER

1. Make polite requests. Do not emphasize status differences by being rude.
2. Make requests in a confident tone. Enthusiasm implies that the request is important.
3. Make clear requests and check for comprehension. If subordinates don't understand what is requested, all the legitimate power in the world won't help.
4. Make sure that requests appear legitimate. The supervisor's authority to make a request should be clear.
5. Explain the reason for the request. Do not assume that the logic for a decision is obvious.
6. Follow proper channels. Do not rely upon subordinates to implement your orders.
7. Exercise authority regularly. Frequent requests enhance legitimacy.
8. Insist on compliance and check to verify it. Noncompliance will undermine authority.
9. Be responsive to subordinate concerns. Understand the reasons for noncompliance.

REWARD POWER

1. Be sure compliance can be verified. Rewards cannot be administered if compliance cannot be checked.
2. Be sure the request is feasible. Subordinates will not comply if the request seems impossible.
3. Be sure the incentive is attractive. A reward is not a reward unless the subordinate desires it.
4. Be sure that the leader is a credible source of the reward. Subordinates must believe that the leader can deliver the reward.

use of reward power. In the mill where the incentive plan had been abandoned, employees perceived an increased use of coercive power and a decreased use of reward, referent, and legitimate power. It is clear that although the change in policy concerned only the reward behavior of the managers, it had implications for the other sources of power as well.

Characteristics of the work situation can also influence the use of power in organizations. For example, in a comparison of crisis and noncrisis situations, formal (legitimate), sanction

BOX 10.2 Continued

5. Be sure that the request is proper and ethical. Rewards should not be perceived as bribes.

6. When possible, use rewards as a symbolic recognition of accomplishment rather than a purely economic incentive. Reliance on money as a reward can make other rewards less effective.

COERCIVE POWER

1. Inform subordinates about rules and penalties for violations. It is unfair to punish workers who are unaware of the rules.

2. Administer discipline consistently and promptly. Failure to act can encourage further disobedience.

3. Provide sufficient warning before resorting to punishment. Indicate what is expected and give subordinates a chance to learn from their mistakes.

4. Get the facts before using reprimands or punishment. Wrongful punishment will undermine respect for the manager's authority.

5. Stay calm and avoid appearing hostile. Managers who lose their tempers risk making the problem worse.

6. Maintain credibility. Follow through with punishments but do not threaten to use punishments beyond your authority.

7. Use appropriate punishments. Actions should be consistent with policy and rules, as well as with the severity of the infraction.

8. Administer warnings and punishments in private. Embarrassing a subordinate in public could lead to resentment and retaliation.

REFERENT POWER

1. Invoke the salience of the relationship with subordinates by making personal appeals. Face-to-face requests are preferred to written or secondhand requests.

2. Stress the personal importance of the request to the leader.

3. Keep the scope of the request in line with the degree of the subordinate's friendship and loyalty. An extreme request will likely fail if this friendship is not strong.

4. Avoid frequent requests for personal favors. A leader can "spend" his or her goodwill on personal favors and later fail to gain commitment to more vital requests.

SOURCE: From *Leadership in Organizations*, pp. 47–58, by G. A. Yukl, Copyright © 1981; and *Leadership in Organizations* (2nd ed.), pp. 43–49, by G. A. Yukl, Copyright © 1989. Adapted by permission of Prentice-Hall, Inc., Englewood Cliffs, NJ.

(reward), and expert power were prevalent during crises; "open consultation" was more common when there were no crises (Mulder, deJong, Koppelaar, & Verhage, 1986).

Also, the use of ineffective power bases has been identified as one factor inhibiting women's ability to develop relationships with mentors. Some studies have found that women are more likely to use indirect influence strategies than are men, and they are more likely to use strategies that accept power imbalances and involve dependent, helpless behavior (Noe, 1988). One possible explanation for this is that women have not been reinforced for using direct influence strategies, and thus lack legitimate, coercive, and reward bases of power. In our current society, many women may find it easier to develop relationships with mentors as well as effective power through the use of expertise (Noe, 1988). Indeed, a study of managers in three organizations found that female managers were rated higher than male managers in the use of expert power (Ragins & Sundstrom, 1990). Because expert power may be one of the most effective power bases (Yukl, 1981), this tendency may serve women well. However, it remains to be seen if expertise alone can overcome a lack of more direct influence tactics. Ragins and Sundstrom (1990), however, did not find sex differences in the use of legitimate, reward, and coercive power, so perhaps women are *not* at a disadvantage to men. The confusion in the research literature over whether women and men differ in their use of various power bases illustrates the fact that power is a complex phenomenon that we do not yet fully understand.

Emergent Leadership. The concept of power shows that people other than managers and supervisors can be influential in organizations. To become a leader without the benefit of formal authority, however, may depend upon more than power. The development of leadership in the absence of formal authority is known as **emergent leadership**. Research on emergent leadership, much of it conducted by social psychologists in laboratory settings, typically involves a "leaderless group." This is a group of people, brought together for the purpose of the research, that is given a task to perform without a leader's being appointed. Depending on the issue being studied, the researcher manipulates such things as the number of group members, the nature of the group's task, or the sex composition of the group. The behavior of the group members is then observed in order to determine the effects of the manipulations on the spontaneous appearance of leadership behaviors within the group.

Competent and assertive employees can emerge as leaders within their work group.

Because the members of leaderless groups are new to one another, and because these groups lack the formal structures and rules found in "real" organizations, the generalizability of much of this research may be limited. Still, it should be kept in mind that people in organizations frequently work in *ad hoc* groups, such as committees and task forces, in which there is no formal leadership (Galbraith, 1977). Consequently, emergent leadership research may indeed have implications for certain organizational issues.

Several factors have been found to be related to the emergence of leadership (Bass, 1990). For example, as you might expect, group members who attempt to lead or to control group interaction are more likely to emerge as leaders than are those who do not make such attempts (Gray, Richardson, & Mayhew, 1968). Emergence as a leader has also been found to be related to the amount of time group members spend talking (Lord, 1977; Stein & Heller, 1979) and to the quality of their ideas and their skill in communication (Alpander, 1974; Klauss & Bass, 1981). That is, the more people talk, the more likely they are to become leaders; the better they are at communicating their ideas to other members, the more likely they are to assume leadership positions. In a study of the joint effects of talkativeness and expertise on emergence, it was found that when the group members thought that a person was an expert, that person was likely to emerge as the leader no matter how talkative. If the person was not thought to be an expert, then talkativeness increased chances for leadership (Gintner & Lindskold, 1975). Other variables that have been found to be related to emergence are assertiveness (Megargee, Bogart, & Anderson, 1966), competence (Penner, Malone, Coughlin, & Herz, 1973; Winter, 1978), and the acceptance of other group members (Bass, 1967).

One factor that might affect leader emergence is the gender of the group members. Although women now account for nearly half of the paid work force (U.S. Bureau of the Census, 1993), they represent a smaller proportion of managerial positions. Early research suggests that there have been relatively few female managers because promotion to these jobs depends primarily on being perceived as having leadership ability (that is, emerging as an informal leader) (Kanter, 1977). Studies found that women are generally seen as having neither the ability to be leaders nor the personal characteristics typically attributed to managers (Bass, Kruskell, & Alexander, 1971; Schein, 1973, 1975). More current research finds that these perceptions have not changed dramatically (Heilman, Block, Martell, & Simon, 1989; Powell & Butterfield, 1989). A recent study of management students in the United Kingdom, Germany, and the United States found that males in all three countries perceived managers

as possessing characteristics typically ascribed to men rather than to women. Female students also described managers in more masculine terms in Germany and, to a lesser extent, in the United Kingdom (Schein & Mueller, 1992). If women are perceived as lacking managerial characteristics, the emergence of female leaders seems unlikely. There is evidence, too, that women have been reluctant to accept authority (Eskilson & Wiley, 1976; Megargee, 1969), which would also make them unlikely to engage in many of the behaviors associated with emergent leadership.

Despite these apparent barriers to emergence, however, there is little evidence of actual sex differences in emergent leadership. No differences were found in the proportion of men and women who emerged as leaders in a study of 52 leaderless groups from a personnel administration class. Further, there were no differences in the behaviors of male and female leaders during the semester, and the performance of groups led by women was the same as that of groups led by men (Schneier & Bartol, 1980).

One possible reason that sex differences in leader emergence have not generally been found is that the laboratory setting does not incorporate the social pressures of the work organization—that is, although in organizations there are many status differences favoring men and many social pressures for women to accept the influence of men and for men to reject the influence of women, these factors are relatively weak in the laboratory or the classroom (Eagly, 1983). Women in organizations also tend to have low-status role models, whereas men have high-status models, thereby perpetuating the tendency for men to be more influential and women to be more easily influenced. Eagly suggested that the relatively small sex differences found in leadership research are due to the absence of these types of social processes and pressures in laboratory settings, and that the tendency for men to emerge as leaders is probably greater in organizations.

Another reason that research has failed to find sex differences in leader emergence is that being male or female per se is not as important as the characteristics of the individual. In one study, although no differences in the proportion of male and female emergent leaders was found, group members with traditional masculine gender-role characteristics were more likely to emerge as leaders (Goktepe & Schneier, 1989). That is, whether they were male or female, people who described themselves in traditionally masculine terms were more likely to adopt the leadership role.

A recent meta-analysis of research on the perceptions of male and female leaders found that the bias against female leaders may not be as strong as once was believed (Eagly, Makhijani, & Klonsky, 1992). Although a bias against women leaders in general was found, it was very small. Under certain circumstances, however, there was a more substantial preference for men. For example, when women exercised leadership through styles that are stereotypically considered masculine, such as autocratic or directive behaviors, their male colleagues were perceived more favorably. Conversely, men who used more stereotypically feminine styles, such as democratic and interpersonally oriented behaviors, did not receive lower ratings than their more traditional male counterparts. Women also were perceived as less capable than men when they held positions in traditionally masculine fields, such as business and manufacturing, and when they were evaluated by men. Interestingly, women evaluators did not show any bias for or against women.

It is important to keep in mind that emergent leadership is not something that you can acquire singlehandedly. Rather, it is granted by the people with whom you work. Consequently, the characteristics of the entire work group are important in understanding leader emergence. Lord, Phillips, and Rush (1980) examined the effects of sex and personality characteristics on emergent leadership in groups working on a variety of tasks. They found that both the sex and the personality of the subjects were related to leadership ratings, ratings of influence, and ratings of French and Raven's (1959) bases of social power. The most consistent finding was that women provided higher ratings on all measures than did men. Thus, although it may be difficult for female leaders to emerge, leaders, whether male or female, are more likely to be seen as leaders by their female coworkers.

Theories of Leadership

We have spent quite a bit of time discussing the issues of power and leader emergence. These are important topics because they illustrate that leadership is not limited to managers. However, as we stated earlier, most of the leadership theories that have been developed over the years are concerned with the influence exercised by managers and other supervisors. In the following sections we will describe and discuss several of these theories. You will notice that in the course of time new theories have arisen in response to the limitations of older theories. In this sense, leadership has been a truly "evolutionary" topic.

Trait Theories

Trait theories of leadership assume that leadership ability stems from certain characteristics that are unique to leaders. In other words, leaders are different from nonleaders, and these differences account for the ability of leaders to be influential. The trait approach to leadership has its roots in what has come to be known as the "great-man" theory. If this name sounds sexist, that's because it is; it reflects an attitude that has prevailed over the years that one necessary characteristic of a leader is maleness. The great-man theory is based on the assumption that the course of history and the nature of society have been shaped by the acts of individuals. Examples include the decision of Queen Isabella of

Spain to fund the expedition of Columbus (which certainly raises questions about the masculine nature of great leadership); Jefferson's decision to purchase the Louisiana Territory from France, thereby expanding both the borders and the natural wealth of the United States; and Eisenhower's decision to proceed with the D-Day invasion of Normandy during a storm, thereby catching the German defenders off guard. Although all of the long-term effects of these "great acts" may not have been positive, they nevertheless had extremely important effects on society.

In the 19th century Sir Francis Galton, a British scientist who was strongly influenced by Charles Darwin's theory of evolution, examined the hereditary background of eminent men. He found that they tended to have had eminent fathers, and tended themselves to have eminent sons (Galton, 1869). This resulted in a movement known as "social Darwinism," which stated that socioeconomic standing was the result of traits inherited by the higher classes in society. Because most of the leaders of that time came from the higher classes, this implied that leadership ability was also inherited.

Trait Research.   The emphasis on great leaders naturally led to attempts to identify the characteristics that distinguish leaders from non-leaders. Until the late 1940s, most leadership research was designed to identify such traits.

Stogdill (1948) reviewed the early literature on leader traits, and found consistent evidence that leaders were higher than other work-group members on such characteristics as intelligence, scholarship, dependability, activity, participation, and socioeconomic status. Stogdill also found that leaders tended to score higher on measures of sociability, initiative, persistence, self-confidence, insight, popularity, adaptability, cooperativeness, verbal skills, and task knowledge. More important than having summarized the traits associated with leadership, however, Stogdill concluded that people do not become leaders simply because they possess a

certain combination of traits, but rather because the traits must be appropriate for the situations in which leaders find themselves. In other words, leadership depends on an interaction between the characteristics of the leader and those of the environment. The environmental characteristics include such things as followers, organizational goals, competition from outside the group, and so on. Stogdill based his conclusions on the fact that whereas some traits were frequently found among leaders, no single trait was *necessary* for leadership. Further, the traits associated with successful leadership varied from situation to situation.

Stogdill's (1948) paper had the effect of nearly halting research on leadership traits, as researchers sought to identify situational and behavioral variables related to leadership. As Stogdill (1974; Bass, 1981) later pointed out, his 1948 review was widely misunderstood. He did not mean to imply that personal characteristics were unimportant but that their importance could be determined only in the context of specific organizational situations. Thus, research that examines situational characteristics but ignores characteristics of the leader is no better than early trait research that ignored the situation. Stogdill's (1974) review of the trait research from 1947 to 1970 revealed that such traits as responsibility, self-confidence, influence, and persistence distinguished leaders from nonleaders, and in some cases effective leaders from ineffective leaders. Similarly, a meta-analysis of the early leadership-trait literature (Lord, DeVader, & Alliger, 1986) showed that the relationships between perceptions of leadership and intelligence, masculinity, and dominance were substantially stronger than those suggested by earlier reviews (Mann, 1959; Stogdill, 1948). For example, Mann reported a median correlation between leader intelligence and ratings of leadership of .25, but Lord and his colleagues found a correlation of .52. They also pointed out that most research examines the relationship between leader traits and *perceptions* of leadership, not between traits and leader *effectiveness*. In addition, recent experimental evidence shows that emergent leadership can be explained to a great extent by traits related to social perceptiveness (self-monitoring), and the ability to change leadership styles based upon the perceptions (Zaccaro, Foti, & Kenny, 1991). It therefore seems likely that as psychology's understanding of individual traits becomes more sophisticated, traits will play an increasingly important role in understanding leadership.

Motivation to Manage. One trait that has received much attention in recent years is managerial motivation. A model of motivation appropriate for managers in large, bureaucratic organizations was developed by Miner (1965, 1978b). Based on descriptions of successful managers in such organizations, Miner concluded that an effective pattern of managerial motivation involves having positive attitudes toward performing a number of behaviors (see Box 10.3).

Miner (1978a) also developed a projective test of managerial motivation called the Miner Sentence Completion Scale. As its name implies, the test involves completing partial sentences, and is based on the theory that people will "project" their personalities into their responses. (This is the same principle that operates in the famous Rorschach inkblot test, where personality characteristics are supposedly revealed in people's descriptions of inkblots.) Miner's test measures a person's willingness to engage in the six types of behavior described in the preceding list.

Research has shown that high motivation to manage, as measured by Miner's scale, is related both to promotion within organizations and to managerial performance (Miner, 1965, 1967, 1977b, 1978b). Also, university students with high motivation to manage are more likely to include managerial activities in their career plans (Miner, 1968a, 1968b; Miner & Crane, 1981; Miner & Smith, 1969). Significant differences between the motivation-to-manage scores

of male and female managers have generally not been found (Miner, 1974a, 1977a), but several studies have reported that female business students scored lower on Miner's test, indicating lower motivation to manage (Bartol, Anderson, & Schneier, 1981; Bartol & Martin, 1987; Miner, 1974b; Stevens & Brenner, 1990). There is also evidence that black students score lower than white students on some of the scales (Bartol et al., 1981), but not all studies have found race differences (Stevens & Brenner, 1990). Interestingly, workers in the People's Republic of China were found to have higher motivation to manage at higher levels of organizations, despite the lack of emphasis on individual achievement and profit in that society (Miner, Chin, & Yu, 1991).

One reason for the differences between managers' and students' results might be that people who are in managerial positions secured their status through high motivation to manage, whereas many students are lower in motivation and will probably not succeed as managers (Bartol et al., 1981). This suggestion is troubling, given that women, and perhaps minorities, are among the students who may score lower on the test. It is also interesting to note that when managers in smaller, nonhierarchical organizations have been examined, motivation to manage has not been correlated with success or performance (Miner, 1967, 1977a). It is possible that behaviors not measured by Miner's test are important in these types of organizations (Yukl, 1989).

Let's assume that Dr. MacKeven believes that many of the people who will be promoted in the PPP Marketing Division will lack a strong motivation to manage. Let's also assume that she gives these workers the Miner Sentence Completion Scale and finds, as she suspected, that many of the candidates have fairly low scores. The most direct solution to this problem would be to promote other workers who are higher in motivation to manage. If characteristics such as motivation to manage are based on a number of personality traits that develop throughout life, you might expect it to be diffi-

---

BOX 10.3 Attitudinal and Behavioral Components of Managerial Motivation

1. Managers must be able to obtain support from persons at higher levels, and thus should have a positive attitude toward their superiors.

2. Because resources, both within and outside organizations, are limited, managers must be favorably disposed toward engaging in competition for those resources.

3. Managers are expected to take charge of situations and take disciplinary actions as needed. This behavior requires an active and assertive nature, and those preferring more passive roles are not likely to be successful.

4. Managers must direct and control the behavior of subordinates, and therefore should feel comfortable using both rewards and punishments.

5. Because of their status relative to other members of the organization, managers must assume a position of high visibility and perform behaviors that invite attention and perhaps criticism. People who are uncomfortable with this type of behavior will not be likely to engage in effective managerial behavior.

6. Management involves more than supervising the work behavior of others. There is also a wide variety of administrative duties that involve repetitive, detailed work. Managers must be willing to perform, and preferably enjoy, such work. Those not willing to attend to such details are destined to failure.

SOURCE: From "Twenty Years of Research on Role-Motivation Theory of Managerial Effectiveness," by J. B. Miner, *Personnel Psychology, 31,* 741–742. Copyright © 1978 by Personnel Psychology, Inc. Adapted by permission.

---

cult to change these motives in a reasonably short period of time. However, Miner (1975) has developed a training course designed to increase managerial motivation by teaching managers and potential managers to behave in a manner consistent with his six managerial roles. He has found that this course significantly increases scores on the Miner Sentence Completion Scale (Miner, 1978b), although it is not clear whether the training actually changes managerial motivation or only trains managers how to get higher scores on the test.

Sex. Sex is an important trait to consider in leadership for at least two reasons. First, everyone is either male or female and, to the extent that there are sex differences in leadership, those differences will have implications for all organization members. Second, the practical importance of gender in organizations has recently become more obvious due to the increase in the number of women in the work force. According to U.S. Census Bureau figures, in 1992 women accounted for 46% of the work force aged 16 or older (U.S. Bureau of the Census, 1993). These figures reflect a steady growth in women's representation in the work force over the years. The same report also showed that in 1992 there were 6.1 million women classified as full-time executives, managers, and administrators. This accounted for 41.5% of this type of job, and 10.7% of full-time working women. The figures represent a substantial increase over those reported by Baron (1977), which showed that only 18% of managers were women, and only 5% of women workers were managers. (In the first edition of this text, we reported that in 1984, 29% of managers were women.)

One fact that has not changed is the salaries of women managers. The 1993 Census Bureau report showed that the median income of male executives, managers, and administrators in 1992 was $40,768, whereas the median income of female executives, managers, and administrators was $26,988. The difference is partially due to women having less seniority and holding lower-level managerial positions than men, but illegal wage discrimination undoubtedly contributes in some cases. Women have also been found to lag behind men in terms of the rate at which they receive pay raises and the frequency of job transfers, even when they had similar levels of education, family power, willingness to transfer, and so on (Stroh, Brett, & Reilly, 1992). Another study found that although earnings differences between women and men had narrowed from 1970 to 1988, the gap in authority given men versus women had not changed (Jacobs, 1992).

A number of explanations for the history of sex inequality in management have been proposed. As you recall, Eagly (1983) suggested that because of status differences between traditional male and female occupations, and the status differences of male and female role models, women tend to be both less influential and more easily influenced than men. The differences should make it less likely that women would emerge as informal leaders, which in turn would make it less likely that they would be appointed or promoted to formal management positions. Another barrier to the emergence or appointment of female leaders is the popular stereotype that women are less suited than men to be leaders or managers (Bass, Kruskell, & Alexander, 1971; Heilman, Block, Martell, & Simon, 1989; Powell & Butterfield, 1989; Rosen & Jerdee, 1973; Schein, 1973, 1975). The extent to which people believe that women, as a group, do not possess the skills necessary for management is the extent to which women are not likely to obtain managerial jobs. Furthermore, it has been shown that when women are successful, this success is likely to be attributed

to factors beyond their control, such as luck, whereas men's success is attributed to their skill (Deaux & Emswiller, 1974). These attribution differences should also have negative implications for women managers.

Women's leadership styles may also contribute to perceptions that they lack leadership skills. A widely held stereotype is that male leaders are more task-oriented, whereas female leaders are more likely to use an interpersonal approach. Since a task-oriented strategy is more consistent with generally held views of managers (for example, Heilman et al., 1989), this stereotype may prove to be a handicap to female leaders. However, a recent meta-analysis of studies on gender and leadership style concluded that actual male and female managers did not differ on task-oriented and interpersonal behaviors, although the stereotypes did appear in laboratory studies of leadership and in studies of nonmanagers (Eagly & Johnson, 1990). This latter finding is probably due to the fact that in actual organizations, unlike lab studies, there is adequate information about the leader's past behavior. Consequently, followers don't have to rely on stereotypes to describe their leaders. However, female leaders in all types of studies used a more democratic or participative style than did male leaders, who were more autocratic and directive. Eagly and her associates argue that female managers' more democratic style probably makes them more effective in some situations, but less effective in others. If a directive style is more consistent with the prevailing view of managers, though, women's more democratic tendencies may make them appear less like leaders.

Two general barriers to women's success and effectiveness as managers have been identified by White, Crino, and DeSanctis (1981). The first of these is a lack of encouragement and appropriate training that results in low interest in management on the part of many women. The second is prejudice and discrimination on the part of people in organizations who either believe that women are not capable of being good

Many women are debunking the myth that they are less competent supervisors and managers than men.

managers or who simply do not want women in positions of authority. The lack of encouragement and management training results in relatively few women who seek leadership positions, and prejudice often prevents those women who are interested in management from succeeding.

Although there have been a number of programs designed to help women develop managerial skills, the validity and utility of these programs have not been clearly demonstrated (White et al., 1981). In addition, although there have been efforts to recruit women managers, much of the recruiting has been in response to EEOC pressure and represents efforts to avoid lawsuits more than change in attitudes toward women (Gordon & Strober, 1975).

Although barriers to women becoming managers certainly exist, there have been concerted efforts to expand the role of female leaders in many organizations. In particular, affirmative-action programs have been instituted to increase the number of women in management. However, even though affirmative-action programs do *not* require an employer to hire a less-qualified person because of sex, race, or other characteristics, women promoted or selected under these programs may be perceived as lacking merit, and as having been selected simply because they were women, not because they were qualified.

Indeed, laboratory studies have shown that when female leaders are perceived to have been promoted because of a preferential sex-based bias rather than merit, the women themselves have more negative self-evaluations of their leadership skills, take less credit for successful outcomes, and show less interest in continuing to be leaders (Heilman, Simon, & Repper, 1987). This effect, however, might be reduced by increasing the initial confidence of women as they ascend to leadership positions. When women selected on the basis of preferential treatment were told that they possessed relatively high leadership ability, their perceptions of their own ability did not differ from those of women selected on the basis of merit (Heilman, Lucas, & Kaplow, 1990). It therefore seems that although the self-confidence of female leaders can be undermined by the appearance of preferential treatment, such an outcome can be avoided by making the importance of merit in the selection process explicit and widely known.

Another area of research concerns the effectiveness of female managers. Whereas men and women *do* differ on a number of traits related to leader emergence, once a woman is in a managerial position, her behavior is not likely to be different from that of her male counterparts (Bass, 1990). The weight of the evidence shows that there are more similarities than differences between male and female managers on such factors as the characteristics associated with success (Gaudreau, 1975; Kanter, 1977), work-group performance (Bartol, 1978), and employee satisfaction (Bartol, 1974, 1975; Bartol & Wortman, 1975; Osborn & Vicars, 1976). For example, the effects of the sex of cadet leaders at West Point was examined by Rice, Instone, and Adams (1984). They looked for sex differences in leader success, in the nature of leader-follower relationships, and in leader behaviors. This study is particularly interesting because even though the subjects were military cadets with very traditional attitudes toward women, there were no significant leader-sex effects. Similarly, a meta-analysis found that the leader behavior and subordinate satisfaction of male and female leaders does not differ (Dobbins & Platz, 1986). It seems clear that although women have been discouraged from accepting managerial responsibility, and although many people continue to resist women as leaders, sex may not be all that important when it comes down to employee performance and attitudes.

Leader Behavior: The Ohio State Studies

Following Stogdill's (1948) critique of leader-trait research, psychologists turned away from personality explanations for leadership. Many began to examine the possibility that leader effectiveness was determined by specific leader behaviors. Instead of saying that people become leaders because they possess a particular profile of traits, these behavior theories viewed leadership as the consequence of a person's behavior.

The change in perspective had important implications for leadership and management in organizations. If trait theories are valid, then having strong leaders depends on either effective recruiting or being simply lucky enough to have "natural" leaders come along. If behavior theories are valid, however, effective leadership methods can probably be taught to employees. This simplifies leadership in organizations because, theoretically, all that is needed are reasonably intelligent, trainable employees, and knowledge of the appropriate behaviors to

teach them. The first task of behavior researchers was therefore to identify the behaviors that distinguished leaders from followers and effective leaders from ineffective leaders. Many researchers addressed the issue of effective leader behavior, but the best-known and most influential behavior theory emerged from the Ohio State University.

To identify important leader behaviors, researchers at Ohio State wrote approximately 1,800 brief descriptions of managerial behaviors. Members of the research team then sorted these items into nine groups, each emphasizing a different aspect of managerial leadership. Of the original items, 150 were used to develop the first version of the Leader Behavior Description Questionnaire, or LBDQ (Hemphill & Coons, 1957). Whereas the LBDQ was designed to measure nine leader behaviors, it was later determined that the questionnaire actually measured only two primary types of behavior, which the researchers named consideration and initiation of structure (Halpin & Winer, 1957).

Consideration is defined as the degree to which managers display concern for the well-being of their subordinates. Considerate managers display trust, warmth, and respect for their workers; inconsiderate managers are unconcerned with subordinates' feelings or needs. **Initiation of structure** is defined as the degree to which managers organize, define, or otherwise structure the job activity of their workers. Managers high in initiation of structure define specific roles for both themselves and others, determine the schedule of work activities, and keep track of their groups' progress toward achieving the goals of the organization.

Over the years a number of questionnaires have been developed to measure consideration and initiation of structure. The original LBDQ has 40 items, which are used by subordinates to describe their supervisor's behavior. A similar measure designed for industrial settings, the Supervisory Behavior Description Questionnaire (SBDQ; Fleishman, 1953), and a version to be completed by managers to describe ideal leadership behavior, the Leader Opinion Questionnaire (LOQ; Fleishman, 1957b), were also developed. The most recent and most widely used measure of consideration and initiation of structure is the LBDQ-XII (Stogdill, 1963).

Although the different measures of consideration and initiation of structure contain similar items, they are not identical, which makes comparisons between them difficult. One important difference concerns the measurement of initiation of structure. Both the original LBDQ and the SBDQ initiation-of-structure scales contain items describing punitive or punishing behavior. Although this type of behavior can be used to control employees, it is not the same as structuring their work. The LBDQ-XII initiation-of-structure scale is relatively free of these coercive, dominating behaviors (Schriesheim & Kerr, 1974; Schriesheim & Stogdill, 1975), which is one reason for its popularity as a measure of leader behavior.

Another problem with the original LBDQ is its emphasis on only two dimensions of leader behavior, an obvious oversimplification. Stogdill (1959, 1963) suggested ten additional behaviors that were included in the LBDQ-XII (see Box 10.4). Although some of these scales have not provided consistent research results, and

---

BOX 10.4 Twelve Behavior Dimensions Measured by LBDQ-XII

1. *Consideration.* The leader regards the comfort, well-being, status, and contributions of followers.

2. *Initiation of structure.* The leader clearly defines his or her own role, and lets followers know what is expected.

3. *Representation.* The leader speaks and acts as a representative of the group.

4. *Demand reconciliation.* The leader reconciles conflicting organizational demands and reduces disorder in the system.

5. *Tolerance of uncertainty.* The leader is able to tolerate uncertainty and postponement without anxiety or upset.

6. *Persuasiveness.* The leader uses persuasion and argument effectively; he or she exhibits strong convictions.

7. *Tolerance of freedom.* The leader allows followers scope for initiative, decision, and action.

8. *Role retention.* The leader actively exercises the leadership role rather than surrendering leadership to others.

9. *Predictive accuracy.* The leader exhibits foresight and the ability to predict outcomes accurately.

10. *Production emphasis.* The leader applies pressure for productive output.

11. *Integration.* The leader maintains a closely knit organization; he or she resolves intermember conflicts.

12. *Influence with superiors.* The leader maintains cordial relations with superiors, has influence with them, and is striving for higher status.

SOURCE: Reprinted with permission of The Free Press, a Division of Macmillan, Inc. from *Handbook of Leadership: A Survey of Theory and Research*, by Ralph M. Stogdill. Copyright © 1974 by The Free Press.

although they have been shown to be of relatively minor importance compared to consideration and initiation of structure, they *do* provide a more complete picture of leader activities than the original two dimensions alone.

Many studies have examined the relationships between consideration and initiation of structure on one hand, and a variety of organizational variables on the other. For example, significant positive correlations have been found between initiation of structure and group performance (Fleishman, 1957a), employee satisfaction (House & Filley, 1971), and employees' feelings of "burnout" (Seltzer & Numerof, 1988), whereas negative correlations have been reported between initiation of structure and employees' feelings that their needs are being met (Hammer & Dachler, 1973). Consideration has been found to be positively correlated with such variables as productivity and performance (Butterfield & Powell, 1981; Lawshe & Nagle, 1953), attendance (Fleishman, Harris, & Burtt, 1955), and satisfaction and low turnover (Michaels & Spector, 1982; Petty & Bruning, 1980).

Soon after the Ohio State scales were developed, it became evident that the relationships between leaders' behaviors and various criteria are not simple, but depend instead on situational or environmental conditions. For example, initiation of structure was found to be positively related to measures of satisfaction and productivity, but only in groups where the members did not feel personally close to one another (that is, groups with low interpersonal cohesiveness). In groups with high cohesiveness, consideration was positively related to satisfaction and performance (J. Schriesheim, 1980). In a classic study of Fleishman and Harris (1962), it was even found that the effects of initiation of structure depended on the level of a manager's consideration. In addition to leader behavior, the number of grievances filed against each manager in the study was measured (see Figure 10.1). Initiation of structure had little effect on managers low in consideration, who received quite a few grievances no matter how

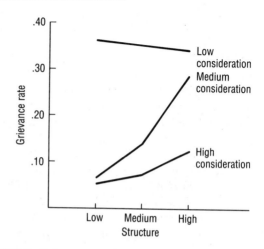

FIGURE 10.1

Interaction between Consideration and Initiation of Structure

SOURCE: From "Patterns of Leadership Behavior Related to Employee Grievance and Turnover," by E. A. Fleishman and E. F. Harris. In *Personnel Psychology, 15,* 50. Copyright © 1962 by Personnel Psychology, Inc. Reprinted by permission.

much structure they imposed on their workers. On the other hand, managers who were high in consideration received relatively few grievances across the board. Initiation of structure had a dramatic effect on the grievance rate for the managers who were rated as medium in consideration, however; the more they structured the work of their subordinates, the more grievances they received.

Because initiating structure and consideration are *leader* behaviors, Dr. MacKeven cannot know the extent to which the soon-to-be-promoted managers in the Marketing Division will engage in these behaviors until they have had the opportunity to be in their new positions for a while. However, it is clear that there are benefits to be derived from the proper use of each leadership style. In the appropriate situations consideration has been shown to have very positive results; in other circumstances initiating structure is beneficial.

As we said earlier, behavior theories suggest that proper leadership behavior can be trained. However, given the importance of the situation in determining exactly *what* the proper behavior is, the training process is not exactly straightforward. If she is concerned about the new managers engaging in initiating structure and consideration at the proper times, Dr. MacKeven is likely to turn to contingency theories, some of which attempt to prescribe the proper behavior for particular situations. We will also turn to contingency theories after we take a look at how leader behavior is measured and the implications of cognitive processes for this measurement.

Implicit Leadership Theories. Although the LBDQ is the most widely used leadership scale, it does not measure actual leader behavior. Instead, it asks workers to indicate how their boss might be *expected* to behave along the dimensions of consideration and initiation of structure. It is quite possible that in many cases supervisors' actual behaviors are not reflected by these ratings. It has been suggested that when workers use questionnaires such as the LBDQ, they do not rely on memories of their supervisor's actual behavior, but rather upon their implicit theories of leadership (Eden & Leviatan, 1975; Schneider, 1973). **An implicit theory of leadership** is a set of expectations or stereotypes about how leaders are *likely* to act, and according to some critics of leader behavior questionnaires, it is these stereotypes, not actual behavior, that people describe when they respond to the LBDQ.

To demonstrate this, subjects were asked to describe a manager, using the LBDQ-XII (Rush, Thomas, & Lord, 1977). The subjects read only a brief description of the manager that included no information about consideration or structuring behavior. The researchers found that analyses of the LBDQ scores resulted in consideration and initiation-of-structure dimensions that were very similar to those based on descriptions of real leaders (Schriesheim & Stogdill, 1975). Because the ratings could not have been based on the leader's behavior (there *was* no behavior!), the researchers concluded that the consideration and initiation-of-structure dimensions must reflect the subjects' stereotypes or implicit theories of leadership. Further, because these ratings of a phony manager resulted in the same dimensions as ratings of real managers, it could be that many, or even most, leader-behavior ratings reflect nothing more than subordinates' implicit theories.

Reliance on implicit theories is probably strongest in situations where there is little or no information about the leader's actual behavior (Schriesheim & DeNisi, 1978, cited in Bass, 1990). When people have had an opportunity to observe the behavior of the manager they are rating, however, they will not need to rely on stereotypes. Workers were asked to describe both their own supervisor and "supervisors in general" on the LBDQ-XII. When the two sets of ratings were analyzed separately, both analyses yielded the familiar consideration and initiation-of-structure dimensions. However, when the two sets of ratings were combined in the same analysis, separate dimensions emerged for the two sets of ratings. This demonstrated that the workers were not relying on their implicit theories when they rated their real supervisors. If they had, those ratings would have been essentially the same as the ratings of supervisors in general, and only one set of dimensions would have been found. Further, the ratings of the real manager had strong correlations with worker satisfaction, whereas the ratings of supervisors in general had much lower correlations.

Although this study showed that ratings of leader behavior are not based *solely* upon implicit theories, this does not mean that implicit theories have no effects on ratings. To help understand the role of implicit theories, Lord, Foti, and Phillips (1982) developed a "cognitive categorization" model of leader-behavior perception. The theory is based on the idea that leader behavior is too complex for workers to observe accurately, much less recall and describe. To rate the behavior of their supervisors, workers must rely on a **prototype** of leadership. A prototype is an abstract description of the typical member of a category, such as leader or supervisor, and it is based on a person's experiences with members of that category. Workers who have had friendly supervisors are likely to have supervisor prototypes that include the trait "friendly"; those who have had unfriendly supervisors are likely to have quite different prototypes. According to this theory, when workers observe their boss's behavior, they rely on their prototype for "supervisor," and tend to classify the behavior as being similar to the prototype. Later, when they are asked to describe their boss's behavior, they do not actually have to remember the behavior but only that the boss belongs to the "supervisor" category. They can then describe the behavior as they would describe the prototype's behavior.

Research has shown that people do indeed rely on prototypes when they describe leader behavior (Foti, Fraser, & Lord, 1982; Lord, Foti, & Phillips, 1982; Phillips & Lord, 1982). For example, subjects were asked to rate identical videotapes of a leader working with a group. In one condition the leader was described as "effective," and in another condition the leader was described as "ineffective." The prototype labels had an effect on ratings of the behaviors that are typical of effective and ineffective leaders, but no immediate effects on behaviors *not* typical of leaders (Phillips, 1984).

Although the research results have not been entirely conclusive, the potential for implicit theories and stereotypes to influence leader-behavior ratings has certainly been demonstrated. Dr. MacKeven should keep this in mind as she examines the leadership situation in PPP's Marketing Division, and she should probably avoid relying on such ratings alone to assess leader behavior.

Contingency Theories

As we have noted, both trait theories and behavior theories are inadequate explanations for leadership and managerial influence. One major

reason for their failure is that the effects of any particular trait or of any particular leader behavior often vary across situations. Thus, whereas Stogdill (1974) was able to conclude that intelligence was one characteristic typical of leaders, he could not say that all leaders were more intelligent than their followers.

One result of this inconsistency has been the development of *contingency theories* of leadership. Although all behavior theories assume that leadership is related to leader behavior, and all trait theories assume that there is a relationship between leadership and personal traits, contingency theories are more diverse. The only common characteristic of contingency theories is an assumption that the effects on leadership of one variable depend, or are contingent, on one or more other variables. One theory may address different variables and be concerned with different aspects of leadership than a second theory, but both will be classified as contingency theories if they suggest that two variables interact to determine leader effectiveness.

Rather than relying upon a limited number of traits or behaviors, contingencies imply that leadership is different in each situation, and that what is important in one circumstance could be irrelevant in another. As you will see in the following examples, psychologists have considered a variety of different leader contingencies. At present it is difficult to tell whether any one of these theories is more or less valid or useful than the others, but it is safe to say that contingency theories embody a more realistic view of the complexity of leadership than did the earlier trait and behavior approaches.

Trait-Situation Contingencies.   The first theory to popularize the contingency approach to leadership was developed by Fiedler (1964, 1967). It is known as the LPC theory, or sometimes simply as the Contingency Theory. To avoid confusion with other contingency theories, we will refer to it as the LPC theory. According to Fiedler, leader effectiveness depends on the interaction of two factors: (1) the degree to which the

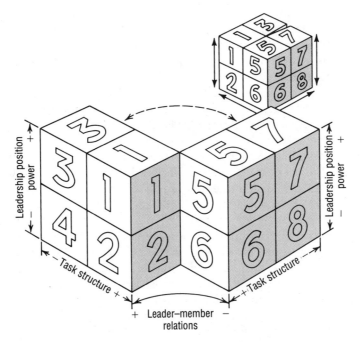

FIGURE 10.2
Components of Situational Favorability
SOURCE: Reprinted by permission of the *Harvard Business Review*. An exhibit from "Engineer the Job to Fit the Manager," by F. E. Fiedler (September/October 1965, p. 117). Copyright © 1965 by the President and Fellows of Harvard College; all rights reserved.

leader's situation is favorable for the exercise of influence, and (2) leadership style or personality. We will describe the components of Fiedler's theory and how they interact, and then discuss the relevant research.

According to LPC theory, leader effectiveness depends on how easy it is for a leader to influence followers, a factor that Fiedler (1967) calls **situational favorability**. Situational favorability is determined by three characteristics of the situation. The first and most important is leader-member relations, or how well the leader and the subordinates get along. The second characteristic is task structure. This is determined by the extent to which the workers' tasks are clearly defined and their performance easily monitored, how well workers understand the means by which goals can be achieved, and the extent to which there are multiple ways to suc-

cessfully achieve the goals. The third situational characteristic is position power, or the extent to which leaders can obtain compliance with their wishes based upon the power of their position in the organization. (This is similar to French and Raven's [1959] "legitimate" power.) Finally, the eight combinations of high and low leader-member relations, structure, and power can be combined to form eight cells or "octants," ranging from the highest situational favorability in octant 1 to the lowest in octant 8 (see Figure 10.2).

The second component of Fiedler's (1967) theory is leader personality, which is measured by the **Least Preferred Coworker** scale, or LPC. The LPC consists of a list of bipolar adjective pairs (for example, Tense—Relaxed, Gloomy—Cheerful), on which supervisors are asked to rate the one person with whom they "can work least well." High LPC scores mean that the leader described this person in relatively positive terms. According to Fiedler, describing the least-preferred coworker in positive terms indicates a strong concern for interpersonal relationships. Low scores mean that the least-preferred coworker was described in negative terms, which Fiedler says reflects a lack of concern with interpersonal relationships, and a stronger concern with accomplishing job tasks.

Although Fiedler (1967) asserts that LPC scores reflect a task versus relationship orientation, it is not at all clear what psychological processes the LPC actually measures. At various times it has been described as a measure of social distance, motivation, or cognitive complexity (Rice, 1978). The most recent interpretation offered by Fiedler (1972) is that the LPC measures a "motivational hierarchy." According to this view, low-LPC leaders are primarily motivated to achieve task success; maintaining good social relationships with their subordinates is only a secondary goal. For high-LPC leaders the opposite pattern holds, with social relationships being the primary concern, and task success being secondary. According to the theory, these motives are important because they determine whether a supervisor's behavior is appropriate for a given situation.

Fiedler (1967) found that situational favorability and leader style combined to determine leader effectiveness in the manner illustrated in Figure 10.3, and he predicted that similar relationships would be found with other samples. In situations with high favorability, the correlations between supervisor LPC scores and group performance were negative. This means that groups led by low-LPC supervisors performed better than those led by high-LPC supervisors in these situations. In low-favorability situations, Fiedler found that low-LPC supervisors' groups again performed better than groups with high-LPC supervisors, as indicated by the negative correlations. Positive correlations between LPC and performance were found only in medium-favorability situations, meaning that high-LPC supervisors did better.

The reasoning behind Fiedler's (1967) predictions is based on the motivational hierarchy supposedly measured by the LPC. In favorable situations, managers stress their secondary motives because their primary motives are already satisfied. This means that low-LPC supervisors stress social relationships, which Fiedler claims is effective managerial behavior in favorable situations. High LPCs stress task performance, which Fiedler says is *ineffective* because successful task performance is virtually assured in favorable situations, and the supervisor's unnecessary task emphasis is likely to be resented by workers. Thus the low-LPC supervisors are more effective in these situations.

In unfavorable situations, Fiedler says that managers will stress their primary motives because they see this as the key to solving the difficult problems that they face. For high-LPC supervisors this means stressing social relationships, which is not likely to be effective in such extremely negative circumstances. A better strategy is to stress task performance, which is what the theory predicts low-LPC managers will do, making them more effective in this setting as well. In moderately favorable situations it is difficult to say which motives will govern supervisory behavior. The superior performance predicted for high-LPC supervisors may be due to an ability to sort out the variety of favorable and unfavorable factors in these octants and select the appropriate behavior. Low LPCs apparently lack this ability and continue to stress task performance in these situations (Rice, 1978).

Although many studies on LPC theory have been published, it has received only mixed support. Some reviews of the theory have concluded that it is valid (Rice, 1978; Strube & Garcia, 1981, 1983); others have found what they believe to be serious problems with the model (Kabanoff, 1981; Singh, 1983; Vecchio, 1977, 1983). Critics of the theory point out that Fiedler's data analyses are unorthodox and difficult to evaluate. They also believe that there are serious problems in defining situational favorability, and that the validity of the LPC scale

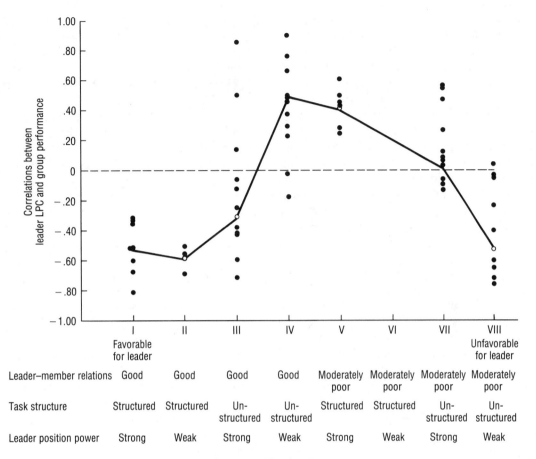

FIGURE 10.3
Predicted Relationships between LPC and Situational Favorability
SOURCE: From *A Theory of Leadership Effectiveness*, by F. E. Fiedler, p. 146. Copyright © 1967 by McGraw-Hill Book Company. Adapted by permission of the author.

has not been adequately demonstrated. One author noted that although Fiedler and his students seem to be able to find support for the theory, other researchers have generally failed to do so, and that much of the supporting evidence for the theory is based on samples of military officers, which raises questions about its generalizability (Vecchio, 1977, 1983). Although Vecchio's criticisms may be overstated, he brings up important concerns, particularly about the early research upon which LPC the-

ory is based. Yet another commonly mentioned problem is that the theory fails to consider managers with moderate LPC scores, although there has been some effort to examine their leadership effectiveness (Kennedy, 1982).

At present there are too many unresolved questions about Fiedler's theory to accept it as a reasonable explanation for leader effectiveness. It is, however, a very important theory from the standpoint of having made contingency approaches to leadership popular and diverting leadership research away from simplistic trait theories. Also, because Fiedler has frequently modified the theory in response to criticisms and new findings, continued research on LPC and situational favorability may someday provide acceptable answers to his critics. However, the amount of research on LPC theory has fallen dramatically in recent years as newer leadership theories have gained in popularity.

If Dr. MacKeven were to apply LPC theory to the situation in PPP's Marketing Division, she would find a number of possible courses of action. Because LPC scores reflect a personality trait, they are not likely to change, at least not very quickly. Consequently, Dr. MacKeven's plans must focus on examining the situation and optimizing the fit between each new manager and the available positions. One way to do this is to measure the situational favorability of each job and the LPC of the new managers, and then assign the managers to units where they are likely to be most effective. High-LPC managers would be assigned to medium-favorability situations, and those with low LPC scores to the others. Although this procedure is consistent with the theory, it raises the possibility of frequent disruptive transfers as situational favorability changes.

Another possibility is to train managers to measure the favorability of their situations and their own LPC, and then teach them to alter their situation to maximize their effectiveness. A program called Leader Match teaches managers to do exactly that (Fiedler, Chemers, & Mahar, 1976). Although Leader Match has met with some success (for example, Fiedler & Mahar, 1979), some researchers have argued that the Leader Match program is not consistent with the LPC model itself (Jago & Ragan, 1986a, b, 1987; cf. Chemers & Fiedler, 1986). Given the uncertainty about Leader Match, and the many unanswered questions about LPC itself (Schriesheim & Hosking, 1978), Dr. MacKeven will probably need to look elsewhere for guidance as she studies the problem of integrating the Marketing managers into their new jobs.

Fiedler and some of his associates have also studied the relationship between leader intelligence and group performance in a framework they originally called the Multiple Screen Model but is now known as the Cognitive Resource Model (Fiedler & Garcia, 1987; Fiedler & Leister, 1977; Potter & Fiedler, 1981). They noted that most research has found relatively low correlations between leader intelligence and group performance. To explain this unexpected result, they suggested that several factors act as "screens" between the potential of a leader's intelligence and its effects on task performance (see Figure 10.4).

Data from U.S. Army infantry squad leaders supported most of the relationships illustrated in the figure, with stronger relationships between leaders' intelligence and performance

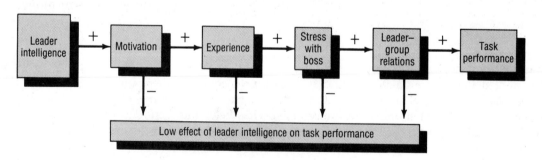

FIGURE 10.4
The Multiple Screen Model
Source: From "Leader Intelligence and Task Performance: A Test of a Multiple Screen Model," by F. E. Fiedler and A. F. Leister, *Organizational Behavior and Human Performance, 20,* 4. Copyright © 1977 by Academic Press, Inc. Reprinted by permission.

when the leaders were experienced and motivated, lacked stress, and viewed their relationships with subordinates as good (Potter & Fiedler, 1981). In a later study of U.S. Coast Guard personnel, it was found that when stress with the boss was low, intelligence was uncorrelated with performance evaluations; when stress with the boss was high, however, intelligence was negatively correlated with performance (Potter & Fiedler, 1981). This negative relationship between stress and the effects of intelligence was also found by Fiedler, Potter, Zais, and Knowlton (1979). It is interesting that Fiedler has found that the effects of intelligence, a characteristic that might be expected to have a uniformly positive association with performance, are contingent upon a variety of situational factors. However, once again Fiedler's work has been criticized for a number of shortcomings, including the use of an insufficient measure of intelligence, ignoring important task characteristics, and his manipulation of stress (Vecchio, 1988, 1990, 1992), charges which, again, Fiedler and his associates dispute (Fiedler, Murphy, & Gibson, 1992). In any case, it seems safe to conclude that we will need to go beyond cognitive resource theory to understand fully the role of intelligence in leadership.

Behavior-Situation Contingencies. LPC theory states that leader effectiveness is a result of contingencies between leader personality and situational variables. Other theories have been developed that stress contingencies between leader *behavior* and situations. One such theory that has received a lot of attention is path-goal theory (House, 1971; House & Mitchell, 1974). Based on the principles of expectancy theory of motivation (see Chapter 8), **path-goal theory** states that the primary function of a leader is to help workers develop behaviors ("paths") that will simultaneously lead to the achievement of the organization's objectives and to the outcomes the workers desire ("goals"), thereby increasing work motivation. According to path-goal theory, good leaders are people whose behavior (1) helps followers identify the paths to

their goal; (2) rewards followers for goal achievement; and (3) removes barriers that prevent followers from attaining their goals (House, 1971). The theory attempts to specify which of a number of leader styles will be most effective in accomplishing these objectives in different situations (see Figure 10.5).

The types of behavior that will result in improved worker motivation depend on a number of situational factors. Some of these concern the nature of the task. For example, if a task is inherently satisfying, then supervisor consideration will not improve worker satisfaction or motivation because the satisfying effects of consideration would be redundant to the satisfying effects of the task itself (House, 1971). If, however, the task is not satisfying, then supervisor consideration will result in greater satisfaction because the leader's behavior would provide a way to obtain satisfaction on an otherwise unsatisfying job. Other contingencies involve the characteristics of the followers. The correlation between initiation of structure and performance was found to be lower for workers who were high in autonomy, apparently because they did not believe that the structure was necessary for achieving their goals (House, 1971). Similarly, leader initiation of structure was found to have a higher correlation with satisfaction among employees with higher levels of need for clarity (Keller, 1989). Workers who didn't feel this need did not respond as positively to the task clarity provided by the leader's structuring.

As you can see, path-goal theory is more than just a theory of leadership. It is an effort to bring together several areas of organizational research and theory, including leadership, motivation, and job satisfaction. We agree with Muchinsky (1990) that for this reason alone, path-goal theory represents an important advance in I/O psychology.

As a theory of leadership, however, path-goal theory has met with only mixed success. Some research has supported the theory (Dessler, 1972; Fulk & Wendler, 1982; House & Dessler, 1974; Schriesheim & DeNisi, 1979, 1981), whereas other studies have not (Downey,

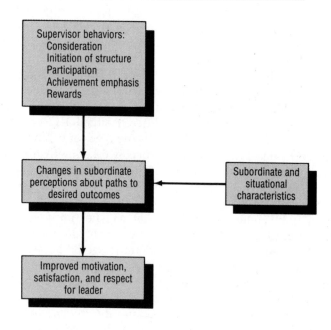

FIGURE 10.5
Path–Goal Theory

Sheridan, & Slocum, 1975; Szilagyi & Sims, 1974). When negative results have been found, the failure to support the theory is usually attributed to problems with the research rather than to problems with the underlying logic of the theory. One problem facing path-goal researchers is measuring constructs such as paths and goals. Because they are likely to be different for different people and situations, it is hard to develop reliable measures of these variables. Another problem centers on the large number of variables that might affect the relationship between leader behavior and follower motivation. Unless all these variables are identified, the effects of leader behaviors may be unexpected and unexplainable (Schriesheim & Schriesheim, 1980). If these types of problems can be resolved, path-goal theory may prove to be valuable in clarifying the relationships between leadership and other organizational variables.

Dr. MacKeven might use path-goal theory to ease the transition into management in PPP's

Marketing Division. First, it is important for the new managers to understand the personal goals of the Marketing employees. Unless the goals are known to the managers, their efforts to clear "paths" to the goals are likely to fail. A survey of the Marketing employees to assess their goals might therefore be valuable. Second, the managers must devise ways for workers to achieve their personal goals while at the same time promoting the organization's goals. To the extent that the workers' goals correspond to those of the organization, this will be easy. To the extent that the two sets of goals are different, the application of path-goal theory becomes more difficult. In this latter case, Dr. MacKeven might develop training programs to teach the new managers how to use rewards, participation, consideration, structuring, and other techniques to link individual and company goals (House, 1971).

Another well-known behavior-situation contingency theory of leadership is rational de-

---

BOX 10.5 Vroom and Yetton's Group-Decision Processes

- **AI:** You solve the problem or make the decision yourself, using the information available to you at the time.

- **AII:** You obtain necessary information from subordinates, then decide on the solution to the problem yourself. You may or may not tell subordinates what the problem is in getting the information from them. The role played by your subordinates in making the decision is clearly one of providing the necessary information to you rather than generating or evaluating alternative solutions.

- **CI:** You share the problem with relevant subordinates individually, getting their ideas and suggestions without bringing them together as a group. Then you make the decision, which may or may not reflect your subordinates' influence.

- **CII:** You share the problem with your subordinates as a group, collectively obtaining their ideas and suggestions. Then you make the decision, which may or may not reflect your subordinates' influence.

- **GII:** You share the problem with your subordinates as a group. Together you generate and evaluate alternatives and attempt to reach agreement (consensus) on a solution. Your role is much like that of a chairman. You do not try to influence the group to adopt "your" solution and you are willing to accept and implement any solution which has the support of the entire group.

Source: Reprinted from *Leadership and Decision Making* (p. 11), by V. H. Vroom and P. W. Yetton by permission of the University of Pittsburgh Press. Copyright © 1973 by University of Pittsburgh Press. Reprinted by permission.

---

cision-making theory or, as it is more commonly known, the Vroom-Yetton theory (Vroom, 1976; Vroom & Yetton, 1973). Unlike the other leadership theories that we have discussed, the Vroom-Yetton theory is a **normative theory**. This means that its purpose is to describe what leaders *should* do in specific situations. It is also very limited in scope compared with most other leadership theories. Rather than attempting to account for all aspects of leadership, the Vroom-Yetton theory is concerned only with the extent to which supervisors should allow subordinates to participate in the decision-making process.

The best known of Vroom and Yetton's (1973) models concerns group decisions, for which they described five decision processes, ranging from autocratic (processes AI and AII)

to consultive (CI and CII) to group decision making (GII). See Box 10.5. They then specified a series of seven questions that managers should ask to analyze each decision they must make. The questions form a "decision tree"; based on the answers to the questions, the tree indicates which of the five decision processes are appropriate for the particular problem facing the manager (see Figure 10.6).

For each problem, then, the appropriate decision processes form a "feasible set" that should result in acceptable solutions. According to Vroom and Yetton (1973), any of the processes in the feasible set should result in decisions of adequate quality; if acceptance of the decision by subordinates is important, that too will be assured. In addition, Vroom and Yetton suggested that managers should select the least-

A. Does the problem possess a quality requirement?
B. Do I have sufficient information to make a high-quality decision?
C. Is the problem structured?
D. Is acceptance of the decision by subordinates important for effective implementation?
E. If I were to make the decision by myself, am I reasonably certain that it would be accepted by my subordinates?
F. Do subordinates share the organizational goals to be attained in solving this problem?
G. Is conflict among subordinates likely in preferred solutions?

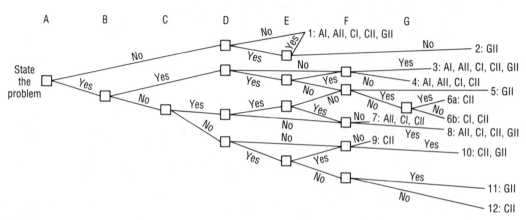

FIGURE 10.6
The Vroom–Yetton "Decision Tree"
SOURCE: Reprinted from *Leadership and Decision Making* (p. 36), by V. H. Vroom and P. W. Yetton by permission of University of Pittsburgh Press. Copyright © 1973 by University of Pittsburgh Press. Reprinted by permission.

participative decision process in the feasible set because it is always the least time-consuming.

Support for the Vroom-Yetton theory is fairly strong, although questions about the model have been raised. In one study, managers were asked to describe the decision processes they would use to solve a series of problems, and the decisions were found to fit the appropriate feasible sets about two-thirds of the time (Vroom & Yetton, 1973). In a later study, managers described actual problems they had faced and the decisions they had made in solving them. Not only were 65% of the decision processes that the managers used in the feasible set but 68% of decisions consistent with the feasible set were rated by the managers as having been effective. Only 22% of the decision processes that were outside the feasible set were rated as effective. A field study of salespersons found that leaders whose decision-making styles were within the feasible set had more productive and more satisfied employees (Paul & Ebadi, 1989).

While also finding support for the model, Field (1982) suggested that only some of the questions used to analyze problems were useful in identifying effective decision rules. Other researchers have concluded that even though the Vroom-Yetton model is useful for selecting a decision-making style, other techniques, such as constructive discussion of opposing opinions, are more important in making the actual decision (Tjosvold, Wedley, & Field, 1986). Finally, there is evidence that although managers' descriptions of their decision processes are consistent with the Vroom-Yetton model, the same is not true of subordinates' perceptions of these processes (Field & House, 1990). Comparing the decision processes used by men and women, Jago and Vroom (1982) found that women were more participative, and their decisions fit the model better than did those of men.

Field (1979) noted that every feasible set in the model contains either decision process CII or decision process GII, or both. He therefore recommended a simpler decision rule to choose between these two processes: "If acceptance of the decision by subordinates is critical to effective implementation and it is not reasonably certain that subordinates would accept an autocratic decision, but they share organizational goals (or decision quality is not important), use GII; otherwise use CII" (p. 256). In a comparison of the Vroom-Yetton model to the process proposed by Field, the Vroom-Yetton model was the better predictor of managers' decisions (Jago & Vroom, 1980). However, because the Vroom-Yetton theory is supposed to be normative, we think that this result does not change the implications of Field's comments. Field's rule will always yield a decision process in the Vroom-Yetton feasible set, and consequently it should result in decisions of adequate quality, the same as those prescribed by the Vroom-Yetton model.

Jago and Vroom (1980) pointed out that Field's (1979) decision rule will always select one of the two most participative decision processes. These are also the two most time-consuming processes, and although they should work, quicker strategies may be overlooked. The researchers also suggested that managers are not likely to engage in that much participation. Consistent with this, people who role-played managers were more favorable toward autocratic leadership than those who played the role of followers (Heilman, Hornstein, Cage, & Herschlag, 1984). Although managers typically express favorable attitudes toward participation, they also tend to doubt the leadership abilities of others, making participation less likely (Vardi, Shirom, & Jacobson, 1980). It appears, then, that although the Field decision rule is simpler, the presence of more autocratic processes may make the Vroom-Yetton procedure more attractive to managers.

Although reviews of the Vroom-Yetton model have been fairly positive (for example, Yukl, 1989), the model has a number of practical shortcomings that have limited its acceptance. One shortcoming, addressed by Field's (1979) alternative decision rule, is how managers should select between the decision processes in a feasible set. As you can see in Figure 10.6, some of the feasible sets contain all five decision processes, but there is no systematic way to choose among them. Another difficulty is that the analysis of the problem to be solved is rather crude. Each question allows only "Yes" or "No" answers, which are likely to be insensitive to important differences between problems and situations (see Figure 10.6).

In an effort to deal with these problems, a revision of the model was developed by Vroom and Jago (1988). By introducing additional effectiveness criteria, such as subordinate development and decision time, to the original decision-acceptance and decision-quality criteria, and by letting managers specify the relative importance of each of the criteria, the Vroom-Jago model recommends the *one* best decision process for any problem. It also predicts the effectiveness of each process for each criterion, allowing detailed comparisons of the different strategies. Further, it asks managers to describe the problem characteristics on five-point scales, so degrees of difference between problems can be more accurately measured.

The result of the changes made by Vroom and Jago (1988) is that the new model is more realistic and more flexible than the original Vroom-Yetton model. The changes also made an already complex model even more complex and difficult to use. To address this issue, a microcomputer software program was developed to assist managers in using the Vroom-Jago model (Leadership Software, Inc., 1987). Having used this program, we feel that it does indeed simplify the use of the model, as well as present the results of the statistical analysis in a clear manner. Without this program, however, the mathematical computations necessary to identify a decision process with the Vroom-Jago model would be very tedious.

Because the workers who are about to be promoted to management in PPP's Marketing Division have little or no supervisory experience, training in the Vroom-Yetton or Vroom-Jago model could be useful. It is possible, given their nonsupervisory backgrounds, that they would prefer participative problem solving in *all* situations. Or, perhaps, once they obtain the authority to make these decisions, they will be reluctant to share the authority with others. Neither of these approaches will be best for all situations. Dr. MacKeven should encourage the managers to use decision processes from the feasible set appropriate to the problem (or the "best" process as identified by the Vroom-Jago model). The result of this should be a greater assurance of quality decisions, and greater acceptance of those decisions by subordinates.

Leader-Member Exchange

As we noted earlier, leadership theories have lately paid more and more attention to followers. Whereas early trait and behavior theories did not consider followers at all, more recent theories include descriptions of how followers might affect leadership. For example, Vroom and Yetton's (1973) normative model suggests that followers' acceptance of leaders' decisions may be critical. In some theories, however, followers play a role equal to, or surpassing, that of the leader.

Graen and his colleagues (Dansereau, Graen, & Haga, 1975; Graen, 1976; Graen & Schiemann, 1978) developed the most widely known of these theories. The Vertical Dyad Linkage (VDL), or Leader-Member Exchange (LMX) theory, is an attempt to explain how the relationship between leader and follower can affect the leadership process. According to the theory, a manager's subordinates can be divided into two groups: the in-group and the out-group. The in-group consists of the workers believed by the supervisor to be competent,

trustworthy, and motivated to work hard and accept responsibility. The out-group includes those who the leader believes do not possess these traits. The nature of the relationship between the leader and in-group members is different from the relationship between the leader and out-group members. In-group members are given responsibility for important tasks, thereby making the supervisor's job easier. In return, the leader provides in-group members with support, understanding, and a more personal relationship. Out-group members are given tasks requiring less ability and responsibility, and do not benefit from a personal relationship with the supervisor. Interaction with the out-group members is based on the supervisor's formal authority rather than on respect or friendship.

Research on LMX has generally supported the theory. For example, in-group foremen accepted greater responsibility and were rewarded with more support, feedback, and personal attention than out-group foremen (Liden & Graen, 1980). Examining the relationship between conflict and dyadic relationships, Howat and London (1980) found as the relationship approached an in-group style, there were fewer interpersonal conflicts between supervisor and subordinate. Even perceptions of organizational climate were found to be related to the quality of leader-member relations (Kozlowski & Doherty, 1989). However, some research has not supported the theory's predictions, such as a study by Vecchio (1985) in which leader-member exchange was unrelated to employee turnover.

One implication of LMX theory is that leadership can be better understood by examining individual leader-member dyads rather than the supervisor's "average leadership style" (ALS), which assumes that all subordinates are treated the same. A number of studies have tested this prediction. Comparing forecasts of turnover based on leader-member interactions with those based on managers' overall styles, the dyadic approach resulted in better predic-

VDL theory suggests that leadership can be understood by examining leader-member dyads.

tion (Graen, Liden, & Hoel, 1982). Katerberg and Hom (1981) examined the relationship between national guardsmen's ratings of their superiors' consideration and initiation of structure, and measures of satisfaction and role perceptions. They found that within-unit differences, corresponding to differences in dyadic relationships, predicted the satisfaction and role perceptions better than between-unit differences, which represent average leadership styles. However, both measures were significantly related to the satisfaction and perceptions, indicating that they are both important to consider. Similar results were found in a study of Air Force personnel, but only for predicting attitudes such as job satisfaction. The LMX ap-

proach did not predict actual performance any better than the leader's average style (Vecchio, 1982). This last study illustrates the need for further research on factors that both influence and are influenced by the nature of the relationship between leader and follower.

LMX theory would suggest that any problems encountered by the new Marketing Division managers at PPP are likely to be due to inappropriate or ineffective dyadic relationships. Because the identification of in-group members requires knowledge of employees' abilities, trustworthiness, work habits, and so on, the early attempts of the new managers to assign responsibility for important tasks may be less than entirely successful. Effective in-group relationships require the leader to have fairly extensive knowledge of his or her subordinates, which takes some time to develop. Also, to the extent that the new managers already have close relationships with the workers they will be supervising, it may be difficult for effective in-group relationships to develop. In such a situation it is likely that friendships among coworkers will not be based on work habits, task ability, or other factors that normally define in-group membership. Rather, these friendships are more likely to be based on common interests (for example, hobbies), purely social interaction on the job, or mere proximity. However, it may be difficult for a manager to treat old friends as out-group members, regardless of their task abilities, which would have detrimental effects on both individual and group performance levels.

Dr. MacKeven might want to work with the new managers soon after their promotions to identify critical tasks and the workers who have the necessary skills to perform them (through examination of job descriptions and employees' personnel records). Initial assignment of responsibilities on this basis will help assure the functioning of the group while the manager learns about the more "intangible" characteristics of the workers that determine in-group effectiveness. It would also be useful for Dr. MacKeven to offer training in basic management skills, such as conflict resolution and employee relations, so the new managers will be better equipped to deal with the possible reactions of workers as they experience the inevitable changes in their leader-member relationships.

Other Leadership Theories

The preceding sections describe the traditional themes in leadership theory and research. Not all leadership theories, however, fit neatly into one of these general approaches. In this section we will present two leadership theories that expand the traditional scope of organizational leadership. The first attempts to explain supervisors' perceptions of their subordinates' performance. The second is concerned with a type of influence that has traditionally been applied to political or religious leadership but only recently to organizational leadership.

Attribution Theory. A typical problem faced by all supervisors is what to do about employees whose performance does not meet standards or expectations. Why do some managers seem to ignore the mistakes of their subordinates, and others get very upset over seemingly trivial incidents? These issues, the causes of leader behavior and how leaders respond to their subordinates, have been addressed by Green and Mitchell's (1979) attribution model. Unlike most leadership theories, which attempt to explain the consequences of what a leader does, this theory focuses on the antecedents or *causes* of leader behavior.

The basis for this attribution approach to leadership is the idea that leaders operate in an uncertain environment. They therefore examine the work environment for cues about what is happening and how they should react; a major focus of their attention is, quite naturally, the behavior of their subordinates. When supervisors must make decisions about how to interact with workers, their subordinates' behaviors become particularly important.

According to Green and Mitchell's (1979) theory, leaders use their subordinates' behaviors and other information in the environment to draw conclusions, or make attributions, about why the subordinates behave or perform their jobs the way they do. The nature of the attributions in turn determines leaders' behavior toward their subordinates. A number of research studies have supported these ideas. For example, nursing supervisors read case studies describing nurses who had made mistakes on the job, such as giving patients the wrong medication. In some of the cases the mistakes were described as being unusual for the nurse (implying a good work history), and in other cases as being common (implying a poor work history); the results of the mistakes were described as either serious to the patient involved or as not so serious. Nurses with poor work histories and those whose mistakes were serious were seen by the supervisors as being more responsible for their actions; punitive discipline was seen as more appropriate for them. Knowledge of the nurses' previous work histories helped determine whether the supervisors would attribute an error to the nurse or to circumstances beyond the nurse's control, as well as whether punitive action should be taken (Mitchell & Wood, 1980).

One topic that has been addressed from this attribution perspective is the interaction between supervisors and subordinates of the opposite sex. The sex of both supervisor and subordinate has been found to be important in determining leader attributions and leader actions (Dobbins, Pence, Orban, & Sgro, 1983). Leaders who were the same sex as the subordinate were less likely to hold the subordinate responsible for missing a deadline when the cause was beyond the subordinate's control. Supervisors who were the opposite sex of the subordinate, however, were more likely to hold the worker responsible. This has grave implications for female workers, because most supervisors and managers are men, and women are therefore more likely than men to be the subordinate in a mixed-sex dyad.

Of course, attributions can influence subordinates' perceptions of, and reactions to, their leader as well as leaders' perceptions of their subordinates. For example, when subjects were led to attribute performance to leadership factors, they gave more positive evaluations to leaders than when the performance was attributed to nonleadership factors (Meindl & Ehrlich, 1987). To the extent that these subordinate perceptions influence subsequent leader-follower interactions, it is clear that attribution processes can affect the effectiveness of leadership from both sides of the relationship.

Transformational Leadership and Charisma. As U.S. businesses showed signs of stagnation during the 1980s, psychologists and managers began to explore ways to make them more competitive in the global marketplace. One focus of the attention was leadership, and the primary theories that emerged involved charismatic and transformational leadership. In this section we will examine the best known of these theories. You will notice that charisma and transformational leadership have much in common (in fact the two terms are often used interchangeably), and that they represent radical departures from traditional approaches to leadership.

The first and best-known theory of charisma in organizations was developed by House (1977). **Charismatic leaders** are defined by House as people who have extraordinary effects on their followers, not due to any formal authority but, rather, to the force of their personalities and their interpersonal skills. The followers are relatively unconcerned with careers, promotions, or money, following instead out of love, passionate devotion, and enthusiasm for the leader.

To become a charismatic leader a person must articulate a "transcendent goal" for his or her followers (House, 1977). That is, charis-

matic leaders define the moral mission of the group and the means by which the members can accomplish that mission. These leaders instill confidence in their followers, serve as role models, and express special beliefs, values, and shared ideologies.

Charismatic leaders are likely to be different from noncharismatics; they have a strong need for power, a high level of self-confidence, and a strong conviction in the correctness of their own beliefs. People without these characteristics are unlikely to attempt the type of radical leadership that typifies charisma.

Charismatic leaders are also likely to use certain techniques to enhance their power and effectiveness (House, 1977):

1. Creating the impression of competence and success to enhance followers' willingness to accept the leader's decisions.

2. Articulating ideological goals that associate the goals of the group or organization to the values of the followers, thereby increasing commitment to group goals.

3. Defining the task roles of followers in terms of the group's ideological goals.

4. Serving as a role model for followers through his or her own behavior, values, and beliefs.

5. Conveying high expectations for followers' performance, and high confidence in their ability to achieve.

6. Behaving so as to arouse motives related to the group's goals.

A slightly different description of charismatic leadership is provided by Conger and Kanungo (1987). In their view, charisma is a property that followers attribute to certain leaders, based on the behavior of those leaders. To the extent that leaders engage in the following types of behavior, followers are more likely to attribute charisma to them, and the leaders are more likely to have the type of profound effects that are associated with charisma:

1. Imparting an extreme vision, a message that breaks away from the ordinary.

2. Making sacrifices or taking risks to pursue their goals.

3. Using unconventional techniques and strategies to achieve the goals of the group.

4. Making accurate evaluations of the factors that could prevent strategies from working, or that would enhance a plan's success.

5. Taking advantage of unrest or crisis among the members of the group.

6. Communication of confidence in his or her own abilities to deal with issues facing the group.

7. Proper use of power bases, especially referent power founded in dedication to the followers, and expert power based on success with unconventional strategies.

Transformational leadership incorporates the notion of charisma, but it goes further to explain the influence of extraordinary leaders. Originally described by Burns (1978), the first description of transformational leadership in business organizations was by Bass (1985). Both of these writers distinguished between transformational leadership and transactional leadership. **Transactional leadership** involves influencing subordinates by the economic exchange of rewards for compliance with the leader's wishes. In this view, without the expectation of rewards, leadership influence is not possible. All of the leadership theories we have discussed so far are based to some degree on transactional leadership processes. **Transformational leadership**, on the other hand, involves a process by which followers are somehow changed or "transformed" by their leader. They adopt the values and goals of the leader, which makes the economic changes that underlie transactional leadership less important to them. As a result of this transformation, followers are

motivated and able to accomplish more than they had previously thought possible, and more than would have been accomplished under transactional leadership.

What do transformational leaders do that distinguishes them from other leaders, and what are their effects on followers? Based on surveys of the subordinates of military and industrial leaders, Bass (1985) identified four factors that describe the behavior of transformational leaders:

1. Charismatic leadership (for example, shares complete faith in his or her subordinates).

2. Inspirational leadership (for example, communicates high performance expectations).

3. Intellectual stimulation (for example, enables subordinates to think about problems in new ways).

4. Individualized consideration (for example, gives personal attention to subordinates who seem neglected).

These types of behaviors transform followers by making them aware of the importance of task accomplishment, by getting them to go beyond their own self-interests for the sake of the group or organization, and by activating higher-order needs. As a result of this transformation, followers develop a close attachment to the leader and a close identification with the mission of the organization, and are motivated to exert additional effort and achieve greater performance.

Indeed, leaders who engage in these transformational behaviors are likely to reap a variety of benefits. Research using both survey methods and more intensive studies of the behavior of individual leaders has found that organizations led by transformational leaders are more effective, have better leader-subordinate relations, and greater productivity and growth (see Bass, 1989, and Bass & Avolio, 1985, for reviews of this literature).

It is important to recognize that although charisma and transformational leadership extend our understanding by going beyond traditional transactional processes, we still have much to learn about how they operate. Reliance on questionnaire measures of behavior has been a problem because it is difficult to develop valid questions to assess a process that we don't yet fully understand (Yukl, 1989). However, studies utilizing other methods, such as analysis of biographies (for example, House, Woycke, & Fodor, 1988), laboratory experiments (for example, Howell & Frost, 1989), and case analysis (Roberts, 1985) have generally confirmed the potential benefits of transformational leadership.

It is also important to realize that although transactional and transformational leadership have been presented separately, they are not competing leadership strategies. There are many times when a transformational leader might find it necessary to enter into transactional relationships with subordinates. Rather than a replacement for transactional leadership, transformational leadership is better seen as complementary processes that make our understanding of leadership more complete than it was previously.

Charismatic leaders certainly don't sound much like the stereotype of an industrial supervisor, and it could be argued that typical industrial organizations are not the most likely places for charismatic or transformational leaders to emerge. Concerns about profit, personnel, research and development, and so on are not conducive to moral missions, shared ideology, or passionate devotion and enthusiasm for leaders. Indeed, Burns (1978) believes that this type of leadership is quite uncommon, although others disagree (R.J. House, personal communication, January 22, 1992). Whatever the case may be with regard to the frequency of charismatic or transformational leadership in business organizations, we feel that transformational leadership and charismatic leadership are probably quite common in voluntary organizations, such as charitable societies, service organizations, and religious groups. Organizational psychology has, for the most part, ignored these types

of organizations, yet nearly everyone belongs to one or more of these groups, and many people devote a great deal of time and resources to them. It seems to us that a good place to learn about charismatic and transformational leaders is in organizations where they are likely to emerge, like the voluntary groups we just mentioned. Such research is likely to give psychologists a more solid understanding of the origins and effects of charismatic and transformational processes, which they can apply to leadership in traditional business organizations.

The Importance of Leadership

We began this chapter by noting the vast number of articles that have been published on the issue of leadership. We also noted that there is no general agreement about what leadership is, and that the evidence concerning the effects of leadership is at best mixed. Pfeffer (1977) stated that these are symptoms of fatal problems with leadership research, and with the construct of leadership itself. He listed three problems with leadership as it is studied by I/O psychologists. (1) The concept of leadership is ambiguous; it is conceptually indistinguishable from other types of social influence, and psychologists have not even been able to agree on a definition of *leadership*. (2) There is little evidence for the effects of leaders. Selection processes used by organizations result in the similarity of most leaders, which means that it makes no difference who leaders are. Also, the social systems in organizations limit the decisions that can be made by leaders, and many of the factors that determine organizational success (cost of supplies, for example) are beyond leaders' control. (3) Merit and ability do not account for much in leader selection; becoming a leader is more a matter of whom you know than what you can do.

Pfeffer (1977) went on to state that leaders are little more than symbols used by people to explain what happens in organizations. Further, what happens in organizations is attributed to leaders simply because some people have been identified as leaders, and we have been led to believe that leaders are responsible for what happens. Calder (1977) offered similar arguments in his discussion of the status of the construct of leadership.

We find this blanket rejection of the relevance and importance of leadership to be unconvincing. In fact, Pfeffer (1977) was not talking about leadership as we have defined it; rather, he was talking about the importance of management. Consider a study that Pfeffer used to support his arguments (Salancik & Pfeffer, 1977b), showing that changes in mayors had little or no effect on the functioning of city governments. We believe that this says more about municipal bureaucracy than about leadership. Salancik and Pfeffer offered no evidence that the new mayors in their study did anything differently than their predecessors, so there was no reason to expect them to make a difference. In fact, we believe that leadership, especially transactional leadership, usually operates at the lower levels of organizations, where there is more contact with a greater number of workers, and that studies of changes in the upper levels of management are not likely to be useful for understanding this type of leader influence.

It is not probable, however, that leadership is equally important in all situations. Kerr and Jermier (1978) noted that most theories suggest that leadership, in some form, will be important in any situation, an assumption that they questioned. They proposed that there are characteristics of workers, of job tasks, and of organizations that make it unnecessary, difficult, or even impossible for managers to have an effect on their subordinates. They referred to these factors as potential *substitutes* for leadership, and predicted that certain substitutes would have implications for certain types of leader behavior (see Table 10.1).

Research has demonstrated that there are indeed personal and situational variables that seem to make leadership less important. The effects of both head nurses' behavior and potential leadership substitutes on the job performance of hospital nurses was examined by Sheridan, Vrendenburgh, and Abelson (1984). They found that only one head-nurse behavior, assertiveness, had a significant effect on performance, whereas a number of the substitutes, including the staff nurses' education, work-group cohesion or closeness, and work technology also had direct effects on performance. Howell and Dorfman (1981), however, found that although a number of variables were related to the job satisfaction and job commitment of hospital employees, only one of these (organizational formalization) had a strong enough relationship to make leadership unnecessary.

It seems clear that in some situations job tasks are so structured, rules are so rigid, or workers are so skilled and dedicated that certain leadership functions are not necessary. However, a comparison of the Sheridan, Vrendenburgh, and Abelson (1984) and the Howell and Dorfman (1981) studies, which were conducted in very similar hospital settings, shows that the effects of such substitutes depend on a variety of subtle factors. Indeed, although leadership theory and research have come a long way from the days of the great-man theory, there is still a lot to learn about what makes people influential in organizations.

Chapter Summary

Leadership has been characterized in many ways over the years. We have defined leadership as social influence in organizations that has implications for achieving organizational goals. It is important to distinguish this type of influence from the more general functions of management, which include a variety of administrative duties that lie beyond the scope of leadership. It is also important to realize that anyone in an organization may exercise leader-

TABLE 10.1   Substitutes for Leadership

Characteristic:	Will tend to neutralize	
	Relationship-oriented, supportive, people-centered leadership: consideration, support, and interaction facilitation	Task-oriented, instrumental, job-centered leadership: initiating structure, goal emphasis, and work facilitation
Of the subordinate		
1. ability, experience, training, knowledge		X
2. need for independence	X	X
3. "professional" orientation	X	X
4. indifference toward organizational rewards	X	X
Of the task		
5. unambiguous and routine		X
6. methodologically invariant		X
7. provides its own feedback concerning accomplishment		X
8. intrinsically satisfying	X	
Of the organization		
9. formalization (explicit plans, goals, and areas of responsibility)		X
10. inflexibility (rigid, unbending rules and procedures)		X
11. highly specified and active advisory and staff functions		X
12. closely knit, cohesive work groups	X	X
13. organizational rewards not within the leader's control	X	X
14. spatial distance between superior and subordinates	X	X

SOURCE: From "Substitutes for Leadership: Their Meaning and Measurement," by S. Kerr and J. M. Jermier. In *Organizational Behavior and Human Performance, 22*, 378. Copyright © 1978 by Academic Press, Inc. Reprinted by permission.

ship. This potential is illustrated by French and Raven's five bases of power, only one of which is limited to people with formal authority.

Theories of leadership have undergone an evolutionary process, beginning with the belief that personal traits distinguish leaders from followers. The failure to identify such traits led to attempts to specify behaviors that characterize effective leaders (although recent work on managerial motivation shows that the trait approach is not dead). The most prominent of these behavior theories is based on the Ohio State leader-behavior dimensions of consideration and initiation of structure.

As did earlier trait approaches, behavior theories proved inadequate for explaining leadership, and I/O psychologists turned to contingency theories. These theories specify that leader effectiveness depends on certain combinations of conditions, traits, or behaviors. The best known of these is Fiedler's LPC theory, which states that leader effectiveness depends on the level of situational favorability and a leader trait measured by the LPC scale. Other

INTEROFFICE MEMO

To: Rob Sanders,
        V.P Marketing

From: J. A. MacKeven,
        Human Resources Coordinator

Your recent memo expressing concerns about the management and leadership skills of workers who may be promoted into new supervisory jobs was indeed timely. We have recently conducted an in-depth examination of our management training programs, and I believe that we will soon have the capability to deal with your concerns in a most effective manner.

First of all, you should be concerned about the ability of nonmanagerial personnel to step into a supervisory job and perform up to company expectations. The success of these workers is typically based on skills and achievements that do not necessarily translate into effective management behavior. Indeed, your primary concern should be to select the best potential supervisors, and not to use these promotions as a reward for past performance. It may be that the best employees you have in Marketing would be failures as managers, and it would be unfair to those people to promote them, only to have them fail later on. To this end, we can assess the managerial potential of your internal candidates for these positions, using a variety of standard selection procedures, including a measure of their "motivation to manage" so we know how willing they are likely to be to accept the role of a manager. We will, of course, also solicit the recommendations of the Marketing staff, who have had extensive experience with the candidates.

The next step in the procedure should be the PPP managerial training program. In addition to basic management concepts, the candidates will learn the company policies and bylaws. New to this program is an emphasis on leadership techniques. PPP's top management believes, and I concur, that a key to success is effective interpersonal leadership. The candidates will therefore learn such things as how to use power effectively, how and when to involve subordinates in making decisions, and how to inspire followers to perform their best.

Based on the results of the pretraining assessment and performance during the training program itself, I am confident that we will be able to identify a group of workers who not only have the technical expertise in marketing that you are looking for in your managers but who also have the temperament and skills to be effective leaders.

I will contact you soon to get your general reaction to this plan, and to begin to organize your management-selection program.

well-known contingency theories include path-goal theory and Vroom and Yetton's rational decision-making model.

Another influential approach to leadership considers the nature of individual leader-follower dyads. Graen's Vertical Dyad Linkage theory explores the quality of supervisor-subordinate relationships, and their effects on individual and group performance.

Recently there has been a great deal of interest in charismatic and transformational leadership. These types of leadership are of a different nature than the leadership described in traditional theories, which rely upon transactional relationships between leaders and subordinates. Charismatic leadership and transformational leadership are based on the leader's ability to articulate transcendent organizational goals that appeal to his or her followers, and motivating the followers to look beyond their self-interests to pursue these goals. This approach to leadership, while not invalidating the importance of transactional leadership, promises to be a critical addition to our understanding of leadership development and effectiveness across a variety of situations.

Finally, leadership theory has come under attack by those who believe that it is indistinguishable from other constructs, or that it is simply a convenient explanation for events in organizations. We believe that most of these critics have confused leadership with management, and that their comments are misdirected. It should be acknowledged, however, that under certain circumstances leadership may be rendered unnecessary by situational factors.

Review Questions and Exercises

1. What theory or theories of leadership does Dr. MacKeven seem to be relying on to make her recommendations? Describe the specific processes by which these theories would explain the effectiveness of managers in PPP's Marketing Division.

2. Consider the distinction between leadership and management. Is it insufficient to consider *only* the managerial skills of the workers who are to be promoted? Under what conditions are leadership skills more or less important?

3. Dr. MacKeven's recommendations rely in part upon a program to train candidates to become better leaders. Do you think that leadership skills can be trained, or are leaders "born, not made"? What are the practical implications of your answer?

4. Dr. MacKeven stated that PPP's top management emphasizes "interpersonal leadership." What do you think she means by the term *interpersonal leadership*? Which theories of leadership discussed in this chapter provide guidelines for the interpersonal relationships between leaders and followers?

CHAPTER 11

....

Organizations and Behavior

LEARNING POINTS

After studying this chapter, you should

- be able to explain the basic principles of bureaucratic theory, and discuss its strengths and weaknesses;

- understand the basic viewpoint of the human relations movement, and explain how that viewpoint is expressed in the theories of McGregor and Argyris;

- be able to define an open system, and explain the similarities in, and differences between, the open systems theories of (1) Lawrence and Lorsch and (2) Katz and Kahn;

- be able to describe the organizational communication process, as well as factors that influence the effectiveness of communication;

- be able to define both organizational climate and organizational culture, and explain why they are important for I/O psychologists to consider;

- be able to describe how effective organizations can be identified, and the factors that appear to contribute to effectiveness; and

- be able to define stress, and discuss how stress might best be controlled in the workplace.

THE MEMOS THAT OPEN THIS CHAPTER describe an interesting problem that is not well defined and has no single, obvious cause. In fact, there are a variety of theories and perspectives in I/O psychology that offer potential explanations for the situation described in Mr. Bombyk's memo. Ed Clark, the vice president of Retail Operations, suggests that the problem is one of "information flow," which is an aspect of organizational communication. It is also possible, however, that the situation reflects a long-standing conflict between the store inspection and quality standards units, with both groups claiming (or denying) responsibility for the same duties. Perhaps the culture of the organization encourages competition and friction between work groups. Maybe the company was organized on the basis of certain principles that are not valid under current economic and business conditions. The lack of understanding or cooperation between the two groups could be a symptom of one or more of these more general problems.

In this chapter we will present a variety of topics that may at first seem unrelated. What they have in common is a focus on the role of the individual worker in the larger organizational context. This is often referred to as a *macro-level*, or systemwide, perspective, as opposed to the more *micro-level*, or individual,

INTEROFFICE MEMO

To: J. A. MacKeven,
          Human Resources Coordinator

From: Ed Clark,
          Vice President, Retail Operations

Please take a look at the attached memo, which was forwarded to me by
Joanna Richmond, director of the store inspection unit. I think that we
have a serious problem with information flow in my division, and I intend
to do something about it. Please let me know if you have any advice, or
if there are any programs that we can institute to remedy this problem.

INTEROFFICE MEMO

To: Joanna Richmond,
          Director of Store Inspections

From: Greg Bombyk,
          Quality Standards

I have just become aware that you have developed a new set of inspection
guidelines for your people. I am writing because I also understand that
these guidelines specify a series of quality points that are not consistent with the standards that my people have developed for the stores. Our
most recent quality standards are dated over one year ago. You probably
should have taken them into consideration when revising your inspection
guidelines. For example, the inspectors should not only examine the physical condition of lavatory facilities but also the procedures followed by
store employees to guarantee sanitary conditions following use of the
facilities. Please examine the attached copy of our standards, and we'll
meet to go over them at your convenience.

approach that we have taken so far. We will not, of course, abandon our primary interest in the individual and his behavior because this is the appropriate emphasis for any psychology text. We will, however, try to illustrate the roles that macrolevel variables have in regard to individual behavior, as well as the importance of individuals in determining overall subsystem or organizational performance.

Organizational Theories

Throughout the history of I/O psychology, organizational theories have been developed to guide the organization of workers and their tasks into effective systems. The average person doesn't worry much about how to organize a company, but this issue must be addressed before any organization can begin to work toward meeting its goals. For example, who reports to whom? Should research and development managers and production managers have some formal way to communicate with one another, or is this unnecessary? Should there be many managers or only a few, and what should be the limits of their official authority? In general, organizational theories are concerned with describing how all of the various parts of a company relate to one another (and, in some cases, to the external environment) in such a way as to maximize efficiency, productivity, and ultimately the attainment of the company's goals.

In practice, organizational theories have two basic uses. The first is *prescriptive*, which means that an organizational theory can suggest how a company *should* be structured or changed, in order to improve the way it functions. Second, organizational theories can be *heuristic*, meaning they can be used by psychologists to suggest how organizations should be studied. That is, these theories can suggest which conditions, characteristics, innovations, or procedures are important in an organization, as well as ways to implement and evaluate

those suggestions. In the opening sections of this chapter we will present some examples of both old and new organizational theories, and show how thinking on the nature of ideal organizations and on how organizations should be studied has changed over the years.

"Classic" Organizational Theory: Bureaucracy

The earliest organizational theories were, to a great extent, responses to the changes in business organizations that resulted from the Industrial Revolution. Prior to this time, businesses operated in a very haphazard fashion. There were no generally accepted guidelines for organizing a company, and so each business functioned in a more or less unique way. Business and management were typically conducted in the same manner practiced by the owner's parents and grandparents. Relying on family tradition didn't present much of a problem for small companies operating in limited geographic areas. As companies grew larger and more complex, however, and as manufacturing processes and procedures became more sophisticated, lack of organization became a serious handicap. It was simply not possible to manage a large corporation effectively on the basis of the same principles that small family businesses relied upon in the past.

The best known and most influential of the early, or "classic," organizational theories developed to address the chaos in industrial organizations was *bureaucracy*. The idea and principles of bureaucracy were developed by the German sociologist Max Weber in the early part of this century (Weber, 1947). Today, the term **bureaucracy** carries negative connotations of large, impersonal, and wasteful organizations. In developing his theory, however, Weber was motivated by what might be considered a humanitarian concern for workers. He saw the typical organization of his day as being a chaotic place to work. There were usually no rules concerning such things as job assignments, promotions, and discipline. Power and authority were used in an arbitrary fashion, which left the individual worker in the bind of not really knowing what was expected or what the consequences of his behavior might be. This disarray led to inefficient, wasteful practices that had a direct and significant effect on organizational productivity.

Weber viewed organizations as collections of offices, or positions. People with the necessary skills were hired to occupy the offices, but their jobs and their conduct in those jobs were determined by formal organizational rules. The word *bureaucracy* stems from this concept: Weber likened a business to a bureau, or chest of drawers, with each drawer representing an office. The content of the drawers (employees in the organization) may change over time, but the bureau itself, the relationships between the drawers, and the function and purpose of the entire system are unaffected by these changes.

Weber believed that the solution to the problems of businesses in his day was a formal, structured organizational system that was governed by **legal-rational authority**. That is, rather than basing power and authority on either tradition or the personal charisma of managers and supervisors, power and authority should be based on rules. A consequence of legal-rational authority, according to Weber, is that workers' loyalty and obedience are owed not to a particular person or group of people but, rather, to offices that are defined by the rules and principles of the organization. Weber believed that placing authority in offices, governed by rules, would make work more predictable and fair for individual workers.

Based on studies of large, stable, and successful industrial organizations, Weber developed a set of characteristics that could be used to describe bureaucratic organizations. It is an indication of the impact that Weber has had on both business and the study of organizations that these concepts are still widely used to describe and categorize organizations.

Perhaps the best-known characteristic of bureaucracy is **division of labor**, or job special-ization. In a bureaucracy each job is specialized, with the jobholder having responsibility for only a limited range of tasks or activities. The primary advantage of division of labor, in Weber's view, is that it allows extremely complex tasks to be performed efficiently as a series of simpler tasks. It also allows management to know who is responsible for each of the activities of the organization. The Peter's Pan Pizza organizational chart (Figure 11.1) illustrates the concept of division of labor. There are nine divisions in PPP, each responsible for a certain range of activities. Further, within each division there is a finer division of labor among several units; although not shown in the chart, there is an even finer division of labor within each of the units, with work groups and individuals being responsible for specific tasks.

Although division of labor allows for the execution of complex tasks and accountability for different activities, it also presents managers in bureaucracies with the monumental task of coordinating workers' efforts. Of course, Weber believed that the coordination should be governed by formal authority. He also believed that authority was most efficient and coordination most effective when power was arranged in a **hierarchy**, which is the second of Weber's characteristics of bureaucracy.

In a *hierarchy*, such as Peter's Pan Pizza (Figure 11.1), ultimate authority resides in the office at the top of the organization, in this case the board of directors and the president. Offices at each level in the organization have authority over the levels below; the authority is exercised as each office coordinates the activities of the next lower level. For example, the senior vice president for Operations at PPP has authority over all of the positions in the Purchasing, Marketing, Distribution, and Retail Operations Divisions. In practice, and according to the principles of the bureaucratic system, the authority is exercised through the senior vice president's coordination and supervision of the four vice presidents of these divisions. The vice presidents, in turn, have authority within their

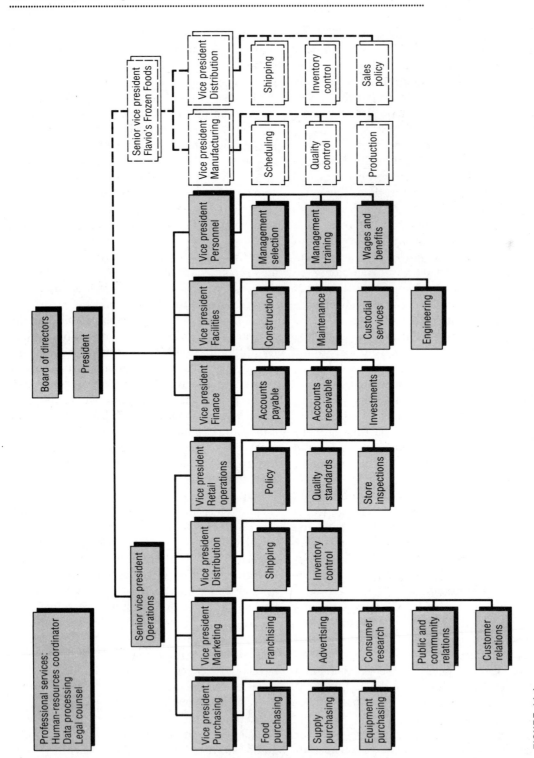

FIGURE 11.1
Peter's Pan Pizza

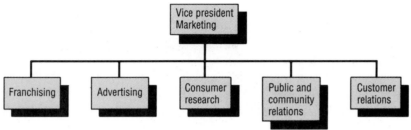

FIGURE 11.2
Peter's Pan Pizza's Marketing Division: Wide Span of Control

respective divisions, and this authority is exercised through their coordination and supervision of the activities of the unit directors, and so on throughout the organization.

Thus, in a hierarchy there is a clear chain of authority from the top of the organization on down, with each office being responsible to the office immediately above it in the hierarchy. Weber believed that hierarchical authority prevented the arbitrary use of power, and thereby improved both organizational functioning and individual well-being.

Two other characteristics of bureaucratic organizations introduced by Weber concern the "shape" of organizations. The first of these is **span of control**, which refers to the number of subordinates that are supervised by the occupant of a particular office. You can appreciate the concept of span of control by comparing Figure 11.2 with Figure 11.3. Figure 11.2 shows the Marketing Division of Peter's Pan Pizza; Figure 11.3 shows the Distribution Division. Five departments report to the vice president of Marketing, who therefore has a larger span of control than does the vice president of Distribution, to whom only two departments report.

The final characteristic of bureaucracies that we will discuss is known as **structure**. Typically, this term has been used to distinguish "tall" organizations from "flat" organizations. Figures 11.4 and 11.5 illustrate the difference between these two types of bureaucracies. In Figure 11.4 we show Peter's Pan Pizza's Facilities Division. In Figure 11.5 we show the same

division with an additional level of management between the vice president and the directors of the subunits. The first figure illustrates a flat bureaucratic structure, with relatively few levels in the hierarchy and a wide span of control. The second figure demonstrates a taller bureaucratic structure, with a greater number of hierarchical levels and a narrower span of control.

Weber believed that for each of these four characteristics (division of labor, hierarchy of authority, span of control, and structure) there is a single "best level," and therefore a single ideal bureaucratic form for organizations. Identification of the ideal form has eluded researchers and practitioners, and the notion is not generally accepted today.

The belief that the ideal organization can be described using only the characteristics developed by Weber points out one of the most important weaknesses of his theory. Specifically,

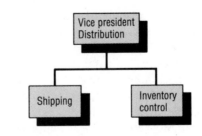

FIGURE 11.3
Peter's Pan Pizza's Distribution Division: Narrow Span of Control

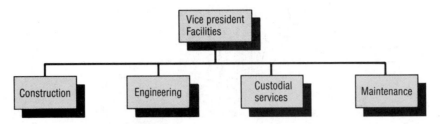

FIGURE 11.4
Peter's Pan Pizza's Facilities Division: Flat Structure

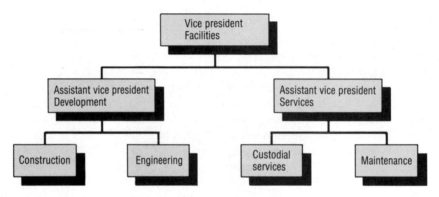

FIGURE 11.5
Peter's Pan Pizza's Facilities Division: Tall Structure

Weber's description of bureaucracy focused exclusively on the nature of the formal organization. It excluded activities or interactions that do not show up on the organizational chart, although such behaviors obviously do occur, even in the strictest of bureaucracies. Also, bureaucracy represents a closed system, in that it does not consider the powerful effects of events and conditions outside the formal boundaries of the organization. Later theories, some of which are discussed below, included informal processes and environmental effects, and more closely reflect how organizations function. It should be noted, however, that even though the bureaucratic model is deficient, it remains very influential. Most modern organizations still conform to the characteristics that Weber described, most notably division of labor, hierarchy of authority, and systems of formal rules. It was the

failure of bureaucratic theory to consider factors beyond these that limited its usefulness.

Even though newer approaches have removed bureaucracy from its position as the dominant organizational theory, some of its basic concepts have remained the focus of research. For example, the sales forces in flat organizations have been found to be more satisfied, to experience less stress, and to have higher performance than those in taller organizations (Ivancevich & Donnelly, 1975). A study of the relationship between perceptions of bureaucratic characteristics and job satisfaction among professional park rangers found that over a five-year period, *changes* in perceptions of these characteristics predicted satisfaction better than did current perceptions. Specifically, the rangers who perceived an increase in either division of labor or hierarchy of authority had lower satisfaction, whereas those who perceived an increase in the standardization of work procedures had higher satisfaction (Snizek & Bullard, 1983).

In yet another study, this one of the reactions of sales personnel to bureaucratic structure, greater span of control on the part of managers was associated with perceptions of higher role ambiguity and role conflict among their subordinates (Chonko, 1982). (We will discuss conflict and ambiguity later in this chapter.) Apparently, when a worker's boss has a large number of subordinates and must therefore divide her time among more people, the subordinates experience uncertainty about what is expected of them, as well as pressure to conform to more than one set of role demands.

It seems, then, that the organizational characteristics that Weber described have implications for the functioning of organizations, and in particular for workers' perceptions. Indeed, affective (emotional) reactions to organizations have been found to be closely related to workers' descriptions of bureaucratic variables, such as the hierarchy of authority in their organizations' structure (Blackburn & Cummings, 1982). This factor was only one of five that emerged from the data, however. Therefore, although bureaucracy illustrates and influences important aspects of organizations, it is safe to conclude that it only "scratches the surface." More recent theories, described in the following sections, attempt to deal with some facets of organizations that Weber did not consider.

Human Relations Theories

As we have seen, classic theories such as bureaucracy stressed formal structure and rules as the keys to understanding how organizations operate. Those theories failed to consider the importance of several other factors, however, not the least of which is the role played by individuals in organizations. Although the bureaucratic model may describe important dimensions of formal structure, its view of employees as interchangeable components does not take into account the potentially important effects of individuals' behavior, motives, skills, and other personal characteristics. The human relations movement in psychology produced several organizational theories that explicitly addressed the role of individual workers in the functioning of organizations. We will examine the human relations perspective and some representative theories in more detail.

The human relations view of behavior in organizations is based on the premise that the needs and motives of individual workers, interacting with formal structure, goals, and processes, determine how an organization functions and, ultimately, its success or failure. This idea is often thought to have originated with the Hawthorne studies, in which the identification of informal social influence and the apparent effects of close personal attention led to new ways of thinking about organizations (see Chapters 1 and 9 for more detailed discussions of the Hawthorne research). Whether the data from these studies actually demonstrated such effects is now in doubt (for example, Franke & Kaul, 1978), but even if the original interpretation was erroneous, the research laid the groundwork for subsequent studies and theory that ultimately culminated in the human relations approach to organizations.

Perhaps the essence of the human relations viewpoint can be illustrated by comparing the formal, bureaucratic structure of Peter's Pan Pizza (Figure 11.1) with the diagram in Figure 11.6. The latter figure shows some of the informal lines of communication and influence that might operate at PPP but are not found in the formal organizational chart. These links develop in part because the demands of the business make them more practical than using the channels dictated by the formal structure. They also emerge, in part, because of the personalities, interests, and skills of the people in the company. Human relations theories of organizations were designed to incorporate these considerations into the way we think about and operate organizations.

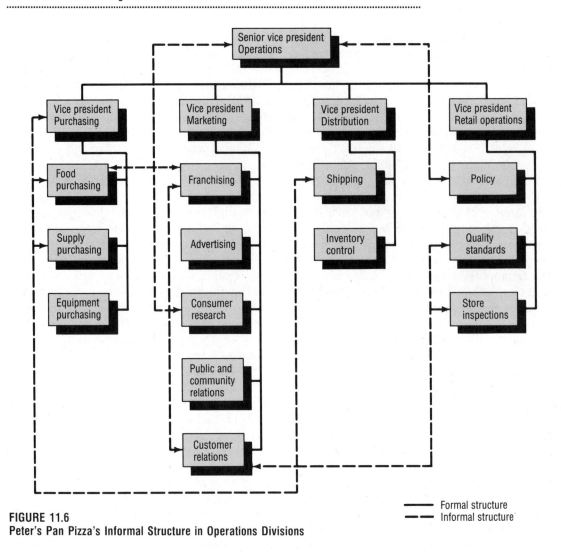

FIGURE 11.6
Peter's Pan Pizza's Informal Structure in Operations Divisions

McGregor's Theory X and Theory Y. Perhaps the best-known human relations theory was developed by McGregor (1960). His work focused on managers in organizations and their subjective "theories" or beliefs concerning how to motivate workers. McGregor held that every managerial action is based on a theory, or set of assumptions, about human nature and behavior, and that the assumptions influence managerial strategy and organizational policy in important ways. It is therefore critical, according to McGregor, to examine and understand the nature of managers' belief systems and their effects on organizations and the people in them.

To illustrate his ideas, McGregor described two belief systems or theories that he asserted operated in organizations; the basic assumptions of each are presented in Box 11.1.

The first theory, called *Theory X*, is based on the belief that workers have an inherent dislike of work, and consequently a lack of concern for organizational objectives. The attainment of organizational goals therefore depends on the strict control of the workers. Control, in turn,

BOX 11.1 Assumptions of McGregor's Theory X and Theory Y

THEORY X

1. The average human being has an inherent dislike of work and will avoid it if he [or she] can.

2. Because of this human characteristic of dislike of work, most people must be coerced, controlled, directed, [or] threatened with punishment to get them to put forth adequate effort toward the achievement of organizational objectives.

3. The average human being prefers to be directed, wishes to avoid responsibility, has relatively little ambition, [and] wants security above all.

THEORY Y

1. The expenditure of physical and mental effort in work is as natural as play or rest. The average human being does not inherently dislike work. Depending upon controllable conditions, work may be a source of satisfaction (and will be voluntarily performed) or a source of punishment (and will be avoided if possible).

2. External control and the threat of punishment are not the only means for bringing about effort toward organizational objectives. [A man or a woman] will exercise self-direction and self-control in the service of objectives to which he [or she] is committed.

3. Commitment to objectives is a function of the rewards associated with their achievement. The most significant of such rewards, e.g., the satisfaction of ego and self-actualization needs, can be direct products of effort directed toward organizational objectives.

4. The average human being learns, under proper conditions, not only to accept, but to seek responsibility. Avoidance of responsibility, lack of ambition, and emphasis on security are generally consequences of experience, not inherent human characteristics.

5. The capacity to exercise a relatively high degree of imagination, ingenuity, and creativity in the solution of organizational problems is widely, not narrowly, distributed in the population.

6. Under the conditions of modern industrial life, the intellectual potentialities of the average human being are only partially utilized.

SOURCE: From *The Human Side of Enterprise*, by D. McGregor, pp. 33–34, 47–48. Copyright © 1960 by McGraw-Hill Book Company. Reprinted by permission.

depends on the use of formal, hierarchical authority, and externally administered rewards and punishments—a sort of carrot-and-stick philosophy of motivation. McGregor declared that most of classic organizational theory seems to have been based on Theory X assumptions. It is difficult to disagree with him.

The second belief system described by McGregor is *Theory Y*. As you can see in Box 11.1, the assumptions about workers made by Theory Y managers are quite different from those made by Theory X managers. McGregor asserted that the most important assumption of Theory Y is that the limitations of workers are not due to shortcomings in human nature but to a lack of ingenuity on the part of managers, who are often unable to discover and utilize their employees' potential.

McGregor believed that the central principle of organization to be derived from Theory Y assumptions was **integration**. That is, it is the duty of management to create conditions in which the goals of workers and the goals of the organization are integrated, so that workers can best achieve their personal goals by working toward organizational goals. (In many ways, this is similar to the concept of instrumentality from Vroom's expectancy theory, in which behavior is thought to be motivated by the perception that it will result in valued outcomes; see Chapter 8.) Worker potential is fully utilized, according to McGregor, when management is aware of the needs and desires of workers, and then creates an environment in which the performance of normal job duties will result in the satisfaction of those individual needs. One way to develop such an environment, he believed, was to manage on the basis of Theory Y assumptions; one way to prevent such an environment from developing was to operate on the basis of traditional Theory X assumptions.

Theory X and Theory Y were based on managerial behavior that McGregor had observed, and in that sense, the inferred belief systems are real, not hypothetical. It is important to realize, however, that the two sets of assumptions were meant to be only *examples* of the many possible belief systems that managers may hold. That is, although McGregor's comparisons between Theory X and Theory Y were specific, his underlying purpose was to illustrate the general importance of belief systems for determining managerial strategies and the effectiveness of organizations. He later suggested that there may be a great many distinct "theories" of this type, each with different implications for organizations (McGregor, 1967). The fact that McGregor never described theories other than X or Y has led many to believe that he saw these two types of managers as the only alternatives, but this misses the larger implications of his work.

Argyris' Theory of Organizations: Integration of Needs. Another influential human relations theory of organizations was developed by

Argyris (1957). This theory is based on the assumption that people are naturally inclined to "grow" psychologically as they progress from childhood to adulthood. Specifically, Argyris asserted that people develop along the following lines:

1. from being passive to being active;
2. from being dependent on others to being independent;
3. from being able to behave in only a few ways to being capable of behaving in many different ways;
4. from having casual, shallow interests to having deeper interests;
5. from having a short time perspective to having a long time perspective;
6. from being subordinate to the control of others to being equal to or superordinate to others; and
7. from having a lack of self-awareness to having self-awareness and self-control.

As you can see, Argyris' assumptions are similar to the assumptions that McGregor ascribed to Theory Y managers. Argyris stated that problems can develop in organizations when the demands of workers' jobs either inhibit natural development or, even worse, demand childlike or infantile modes of behavior. For example, imagine that Peter's Pan Pizza decided to install a pizza assembly line at the Flavio's frozen pizza factories. Like most assembly lines, this one would require each worker to perform a single task, such as spreading sauce or sprinkling cheese, at a rate dictated by the pace of the line. Such a job, according to Argyris' perspective, demands childlike behaviors: it limits workers' activities and forces passivity. Workers become dependent on, and are subordinate to, the technology of the assembly line. Their tasks are brief and repetitive, which fosters impatience, and only a very small range of worker abilities are utilized.

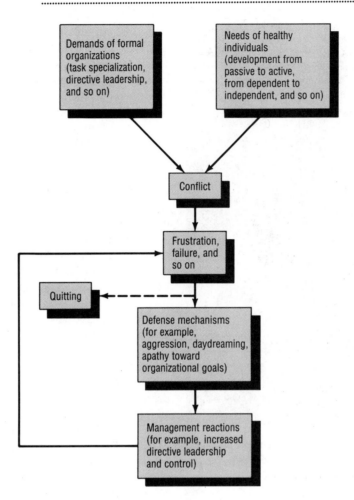

FIGURE 11.7
The Effects of Traditional Organizations on Psychological Growth
SOURCE: From *Personality and Organization: The Conflict between System and the Individual,* by C. Argyris.
Copyright © 1957 by Harper & Row Publishers, Inc. Adapted by permission of HarperCollins.

In short, many jobs in traditional, bureaucratic organizations inhibit or arrest workers' normal psychological development. This can result in defensive behaviors, which in turn lead to a variety of problems including poor performance, absenteeism, turnover, and sabotage (see Figure 11.7). In response, managers with traditional (Theory X) perspectives are likely to see the problem as one of workers' laziness or carelessness. These managers then increase the amount of control and direction that the job imposes, which, unrecognized by them, caused the problem in the first place. Thus, a vicious circle like the one at the bottom of Figure 11.7 is started, in which conditions get progressively worse for both management and workers.

Argyris mentioned two possible solutions to the problem. First, and with tongue in cheek, he said that the frustration that stems from working in traditional organizations can be avoided

Argyris suggests that oppressive bureaucratic practices can lead to defensive, dysfunctional employee behaviors.

by hiring only workers who do not aspire to be healthy mature adults. Second, he suggested that formal organizational structure, directive leadership, and management controls be changed so that employees can continue their psychological development. Chief among the ways to make such changes is the integration of individual needs and organizational goals. In this sense, Argyris' and McGregor's theories are similar in their prescriptions for healthy organizational functioning.

Ouchi's Theory Z. A more recent organizational theory that is in many ways consistent with older human relations approaches is Ouchi's

(1981) Theory Z. This theory is an attempt to combine the useful aspects of both the traditional American style of management and the Japanese style of management. The former, as described by Ouchi, is a mixture of bureaucratic principles (for example, formal control, specialization) and human relations principles (such as individual decision making and individual responsibility), with expectations of short-term employment on the part of workers. The Japanese style stresses collective responsibility, informal control, a lack of specialization, and an expectation of lifetime employment with the same company. The Theory Z organization retains the traditional American emphasis on individual responsibility and career specialization but advocates group decision making, less formal control, long-term employment, and a concern for all aspects of workers' lives, both on and off the job.

Ouchi (1981) asserts that Theory Z organizations should be superior to traditional organizations in terms of workers' attitudes and productivity, and he cites several examples of successful organizations that have Theory Z characteristics. This does not mean, however, that the Theory Z characteristics of these organizations caused them to be successful nor that there are no unsuccessful Theory Z organizations. In fact, Ouchi's statement that Theory Z is a key to business success in Japan has been questioned (Sullivan, 1983). Further, Theory Z is basically an application of Maslow's (1943) need hierarchy, which has often been criticized on theoretical grounds and has received little empirical support (Sullivan, 1983). Given these problems, it is not surprising that research on Theory Z has declined in recent years, and that it is considered to be little more than a fad by many I/O psychologists (Landy, 1989).

Open Systems Theories of Organizations

Both the classic approach of bureaucracy and the human relations approaches of McGregor and Argyris treat organizations as relatively static and unchanging. That is, in bureaucratic theory the ideal organizational structure is sought and maintained without any substantial modifications. In a similar fashion, although human relations theories addressed many of the potentially destructive effects of rigid adherence to bureaucratic principles, they also failed to consider the inevitable changes that all organizations experience. A more dynamic approach to studying organizations is needed in order to account for an organization's ability to survive both internal and external changes. An open systems approach offers this type of flexibility.

An open systems theory emphasizes the interrelationships and dependence (1) between different components within an organization, and (2) between these components and the environment within which the organization operates. For example, whereas bureaucratic theory emphasizes division of labor and specialization, open systems theories emphasize the importance of the coordination of the various organizational units, and how this coordinated activity yields a final outcome that is not possible by any single unit operating alone. Also, human relations theories consider the importance of workers' characteristics (needs, for example) and how the characteristics interact with formal structures and rules to determine organizational effectiveness, but open systems theories stress that the effects of worker characteristics, formal structure, and all other components of an organization are dependent on the environment. Environmental conditions (such as the economic and legal contexts in which an organization operates) and changes in that environment therefore have implications for organizations that earlier theories ignored.

It may be easier to get a "feel" for open systems theory by considering an analogy to a smaller, more clearly defined system, such as an automobile. Like an organization, an automobile is a collection of smaller units or subsystems, each with a specific function. For example, the fuel system delivers gasoline to the engine, and the electrical system charges the battery, fires the sparkplugs, and supplies power to lights and accessories. Combined, these subsystems form the larger system, and can achieve the overall goal of providing transportation. Separately, the subsystems have little usefulness; a fuel system without an engine is little more than a fire hazard, and an electrical system without a car is only a high school science project. The same conclusions apply to organizational systems. At Peter's Pan Pizza, for instance, the Finance Division would have no accounts to receive or pay if it were not for the retailing divisions and the business they generate.

Another characteristic of systems illustrated by our automobile example is the interdependence of the subsystems, on one another as well as on conditions in the environment. When a single subsystem, such as the electrical system, malfunctions in an automobile, the entire car is either rendered useless or at least becomes less efficient. Further, the automobile and all of its component subsystems depend on the environment in order to operate efficiently. Without oil, gas, or water, each of which can come only from the environment, the car will not operate. Also, environmental catastrophes, such as a truck running into the car in a parking lot, can influence the usefulness of each component as well as the overall system. Analogous examples from Peter's Pan Pizza might include the following: a failure to collect accounts on the part of the Finance Division could force the Facilities Division to postpone plans to build new stores. Alternatively, a strike at the meat-packing company from which PPP buys its pepperoni could temporarily force a halt to the production of pepperoni products, or perhaps force PPP to buy high-priced, imported pepperoni.

Although we can apply the general idea of open systems to many examples, such as an automobile, there are components of open systems that have particularly important implications for organizations. We will therefore examine two influential organizational theories based on the open systems model.

Lawrence and Lorsch's Differentiation, Integration, and Response to Change. An early example of open systems theory applied to organizations was the work of Lawrence and Lorsch (1967), who were concerned with two basic issues. The first dealt with the effects of division of labor, or specialization, within organizations. Lawrence and Lorsch believed that when organizations are segmented, managers in each segment become specialists, and develop unique working styles and ways of thinking. Specifically, they identified three dimensions along which managers in different units might vary:

1. *Orientation toward particular goals.* To what extent are managers concerned with different goals or objectives?

2. *Time orientation.* To what extent do managers differ in their emphasis on immediate versus long-range goals?

3. *Interpersonal orientation.* To what extent do managers differ in the ways they typically deal with their colleagues?

Differences in the orientations combine with aspects of the formal structure of work units to determine differences in the cognitive and emotional disposition of managers. Lawrence and Lorsch referred to this as **differentiation**. When there are large differences in these orientations across departments, differentiation is high; when there are only small differences, differentiation is low.

Differentiation is a concern because high levels can make it difficult for managers to reach agreement about policies that are necessary for an organization to function effectively. To deal with differentiation, Lawrence and Lorsch asserted that organizations must achieve an appropriate level of **integration**. They defined integration as the quality or degree of collaboration among departments that are required to work together because of environmental demands.

Lawrence and Lorsch rejected the notion, basic to classic theories such as bureaucracy, that the optimal level of collaboration can be achieved automatically by using a rational, hierarchical system of authority. They stated that there are other means of settling conflict and achieving integration, such as "integrating committees" that work to coordinate the efforts of different units. They further pointed out that classic theories, with their emphasis on rationality, fail to consider the role of emotions and interpersonal skills in the development of collaboration between units.

At the same time, Lawrence and Lorsch rejected the idea, common in human relations theories, that all disagreement and conflict within an organization is to be avoided. Instead, they argued that although extreme differentiation can be dysfunctional, some level of differentiation and conflict is necessary in order for a large organization to perform its many functions. They emphasized, therefore, that achieving integration without sacrificing necessary differentiation should be a top priority.

The second basic issue that Lawrence and Lorsch's theory addressed is the effect on organizations of differences and changes in the environment. They believed that environmental factors, such as technical and economic conditions, dictate the structure and pattern of interactions within an organization. More important, though, they believed that these conditions determine the extent to which an organization is differentiated, and the means by which integration can be achieved. For example, consider what might happen if an increase in the public's concern about health and fitness caused a dramatic decline in the sales of Flavio's (mostly fattening) products, thereby threatening the future of the entire company. We would expect that a common "cognitive and emotional orientation," one geared toward company survival, would develop among Flavio's (and Peter's Pan Pizza's) managers. In other words, differentiation would decrease. Further, managers are likely to be open to new types of collaboration with their peers in other departments as they coordinate their efforts to adapt to the changes in the public's tastes. That is, integration would increase.

Therefore, rather than trying to define the *one best way* to organize, or the one best way to coordinate the needs of individuals and the organization, Lawrence and Lorsch believed that managers must be prepared to make changes as environmental conditions change. Hence, this theory represents a "contingency" approach to understanding organizations, in which the effective functioning of the organization is contingent upon its openness and responsiveness to changes outside the system.

Katz and Kahn's Open Systems Theory. Another influential open systems theory, but one with a very different emphasis from that of Lawrence and Lorsch, was developed by Katz and Kahn (1978). Specifically, Lawrence and Lorsch's theory has a relatively narrow focus; it is primarily concerned with the effects of specialization or division of labor at the department or subunit level. Katz and Kahn, however, apply the concept of open systems to all levels of organizations, and discuss the implications of the theory for a variety of topics, including motivation, performance, communication, leadership, and organizational change. Although we will not go into these specific issues, we will describe Katz and Kahn's theory and some of the implications of viewing organizations from a total systems perspective.

Katz and Kahn listed ten characteristics of open systems. Although these characteristics apply to all open systems, our interest is, of course, in their implications for organizations. The Katz and Kahn characteristics of open systems are the following:

1. *Importation of energy.* No open system can sustain itself without taking in resources or "energy" from the environment. In organizations, the inputs take the form of labor, raw materials, ideas, and anything else that is required to maintain functioning.

2. *Throughput.* Throughput refers to the transformation of the energy inputs discussed above. Organizations manufacture products, train employees, and in general perform work toward achieving specific goals.

3. *Output.* Once inputs have been transformed, some of the resulting products are returned to the environment. Organizations distribute their manufactured goods or their services, as well as deliver unwanted output, such as industrial pollution.

4. *Cycles of events.* The input-throughput-output functions form a cycle in which energy is transformed and exchanged. That is, the products that are output into the environment, such as manufactured goods, provide the means (money) for an organization to obtain additional inputs of raw materials.

5. *Negative entropy. Entropy* refers to the tendency for systems to "run down" and eventually die. For an organization to be successful, it must reverse this tendency and achieve negative entropy. That is, organizations must take in more than they use, maximizing the ratio of inputs to expended energy. The excess energy and resources are stored, and during crises the organization can use these stored resources to maintain itself while making any necessary adjustments.

6. *Information input, negative feedback, and the coding process.* The inputs discussed in item 1 above are primarily raw materials necessary for the organization to produce its products or provide its services. Organizations also need inputs in the form of information that will let management know how well the organization is functioning. The most basic performance information is negative feedback, which can be anything that tells the organization when it has deviated from its intended course.

For example, if Peter's Pan Pizza's management learned that its share of the take-out pizza business had dropped by 10%, that would be negative feedback indicating that a change is necessary. With all of the information available in the environment, systems must be selective about the performance information they accept. This selection is carried out by the coding process, in which irrelevant or less relevant information is filtered out and a few critical sources of information are emphasized.

7. *The steady state and dynamic homeostasis.* In a healthy system, the input of energy and resources is balanced with the output of products. This balanced energy exchange is known as a steady state. To react to changes in the environment, however, an organization will probably have to make changes in its outputs, which may require corresponding changes in inputs. An organization might also need to change its structure, or change in terms of the number of employees or divisions that it has. Therefore, the steadiness of an organization refers to an equilibrium in its basic character rather than in its structure or size. Katz and Kahn refer to this property of constant change in order to maintain organizational character as dynamic homeostasis.

8. *Differentiation.* Systems, including organizations, develop specialized structures to perform specialized tasks. This is an evolutionary process, with new structures, or subsystems, developing as new needs arise. This use of the term *differentiation*, therefore, refers more to the division of labor than to the differences in orientation discussed by Lawrence and Lorsch.

9. *Integration and coordination.* As we have already seen, if a system is to be effective, its components must be integrated and coordinated to work together to achieve the overall purpose of the system.

10. *Equifinality:* Because of their open and flexible nature, systems can achieve the same final outcome in many different ways. Katz and Kahn referred to this property as equifinality. Equifinality is a particularly important characteristic for organizational systems because it allows them to adjust to changing environmental demands while working toward established goals.

As the above characteristics illustrate, Katz and Kahn describe organizations as dynamic, ever-changing systems. Organizations must interact with, and react to, their environments. They must also maintain themselves through hard times, coordinate the tasks of many individuals and groups, and manage the critical input, throughput, and output processes.

Another important aspect of Katz and Kahn's theory is their use of the concept of roles. **Roles** are defined as sets of behaviors that are required of a person by virtue of her position in an organization. These behaviors interact with the role behaviors of others to produce predictable outcomes in the organization. In this sense, Katz and Kahn define organizations as systems of roles: The throughput processes by which work gets done are defined by the interdependent role behaviors of workers.

Roles are similar to the concept of "offices" in bureaucratic theory because they define tasks and the ways in which different employees must work together to achieve organizational objectives. There are, however, at least two important ways in which Katz and Kahn's use of roles differs from the bureaucratic concept of offices. First is the way in which roles are developed. In a bureaucracy, the role and the office are one and the same; that is, the behaviors expected of an officeholder are defined by the office and are independent of any personal characteristics of the officeholder. In open systems theory, roles are acquired through social interaction with other people, in a process called the **role episode** (see Figure 11.8). Basi-

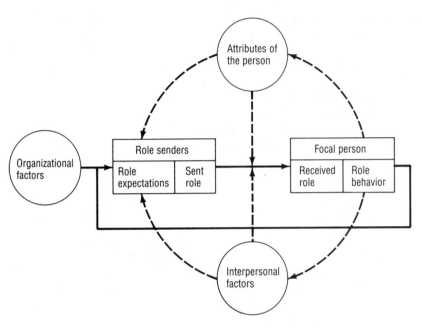

FIGURE 11.8
The Role-Episode Model
SOURCE: From *The Social Psychology of Organizations*, 2nd ed., p. 196, by D. Katz and R. L. Kahn. Copyright 1978 by John Wiley & Sons. Adapted by permission.

cally, people with whom a worker interacts, the role senders, have certain expectations about that worker's role in the organization, and through direct and indirect communication they send those expectations to the worker. The worker, in turn, receives these role expectations, which determine, to a greater or lesser extent, his role behaviors.

Note that because of personal, interpersonal, and organizational factors, the role expectations of the role senders and the messages that they send to the worker may or may not be the same. For example, in the opening memos of this chapter, we saw that there was some confusion about who was responsible for setting store inspection standards. Ed Clark, the vice president for Retail Operations, probably has specific expectations about who should fulfill this role, but these expectations may not have been clearly communicated. It may be, for instance, that Mr. Clark has a very nondirective

interpersonal style, and his expectations were interpreted as suggestions rather than as directions.

In a similar way, the received role, or what the worker perceives to be the expectations of the role senders, may not correspond to those expectations. Also, the actual role behavior may not reflect the received role for any of a variety of reasons. Consequently, there is a good chance that the role expectations that exist within a company will not correspond to the role behavior of the worker. Because of this, as well as changes in the organizational and interpersonal factors that influence role expectations, the role episode is a constant, ongoing process.

The second important aspect of Katz and Kahn's treatment of roles is the concept of **partial inclusion**. This refers to the fact that, psychologically, only a portion of each worker is "in" the organization. That is, every worker performs numerous nonorganizational roles.

Organizations, however, often expect employees to abandon some of these roles; this can be dehumanizing to the employee, and in some cases counterproductive to the organization.

Partial inclusion has particularly important implications for the organization members who are in **boundary positions**: the employees whose roles require them to interact with people, groups, or other organizations outside their own group or organization. In effect, boundary positions link an organization with its environment. People in boundary positions therefore have partial inclusion not only in their employing organization but also in the part of the environment to which they represent the organization. This situation can lead to conflicting role behaviors that threaten the well-being of the organization. For example, a sizable proportion of Flavio's frozen pizza sales is to taverns and bars, where the pizzas are cooked in microwave ovens and sold along with beer and wine. Many pizza companies are trying to move into this market. In the struggle for a competitive advantage, there is pressure for salespersons to conform to the role demands of their customers. One of Flavio's sales representatives, whose name we will not mention, apparently decided to become friends with as many bar owners as he possibly could. He spent many hours in bars, drinking and discussing the "ins and outs" of life on the road. The bar owners liked him, but he failed to conform to the role behaviors of a pizza sales representative. Consequently, he didn't sell many pizzas, and was eventually fired.

Of course, most workers in boundary positions do not succumb to these types of pressures. In general, however, the notion of partial inclusion is a valuable component of Katz and Kahn's theory because it draws attention to the multiple roles of workers, both within and outside the organization, and forces us to consider the effects of these roles.

In summary, open systems theory is perhaps the most comprehensive organizational theory to date. As does any organizational the-

ory, it provides a certain perspective from which to consider the operation and structure of organizations. Like the classic and human relations theories that preceded it, open systems theory is perhaps most valuable as a means for suggesting new ways of doing things in organizations. Although not all of the suggestions have worked out, open systems theories have increased our understanding of many important dimensions of organizations.

We have spent a fair amount of time discussing theories of what organizations are and how they function. Although organizational theories certainly have implications for more specific issues, we need to examine some of these issues in more detail. One such issue, which is important for the macrolevel functioning of the organization and the microlevel behavior of workers, is organizational communication.

Organizational Communication

Communication is one of the most important processes in organizations. Information exchange between divisions, units, work groups, and individuals is necessary to perform both simple and complex tasks. Understanding communication is therefore important to understanding the functioning of organizations. In fact, it is possible to view organizations not as bureaucratic structures or role systems but as communication networks.

Regardless of whether you view organizations as formal structures, informal role systems, or communication networks, the importance of communication in day-to-day organizational activity is obvious. For example, training programs depend on effective communication of information about desired behaviors and performance standards (see Chapter 7). Performance appraisal hinges on the ability of supervisors or other evaluators to communicate information about employees' performance

Organizational communication benefits from new technologies.

(Chapter 4). Leadership involves, among other things, the effective communication of directives, goals, and reinforcements such as praise and personal attention (Chapter 10). A failure to communicate effectively may result in dissatisfaction (Chapter 9) and perhaps, if the dissatisfaction is severe enough, a unionization effort on the part of the employees involved (Chapter 14). We could give many more such examples, but our point is simple: Communication is critical to every topic studied in the field of I/O psychology.

The Communication Process

The means by which communication takes place are complex and variable, so that any description of the communication process must necessarily be a simplification. All communication events, however, have certain common components that allow us to describe the general communication process, and illustrate some of the many ways in which communication can fail.

An early but still useful model of communication was presented by Shannon and Weaver (1948). A diagram of the components of their model is presented in Figure 11.9. The communication cycle begins with the *source*, or the person sending the message. The source has certain ideas, facts, opinions, or other information that she wishes to convey to one or more people, either within or outside the organization. Because humans are not by nature telepathic, the source cannot simply transmit her thoughts directly; the information must be put into a form that can be conveyed to, and understood by, the intended receiver, or target. The process of converting the intended message into what we hope is understandable language is called *encoding*. Communication depends on the ability of individuals to transform thoughts into words, and this ability depends in turn on verbal skills, emotional states, experience, and many other factors.

Once the information has been encoded it is called a *message*. The message must, in turn, be

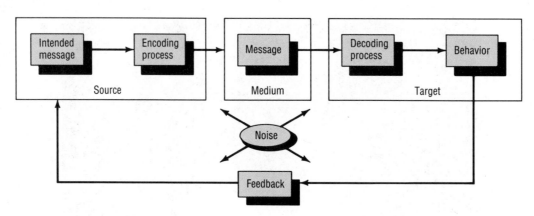

FIGURE 11.9
The Communication Process
SOURCE: From *The Mathematical Theory of Communication*, by C. Shannon and W. Weaver, p. 3. Copyright © 1948 by the University of Illinois Press. Adapted by permission.

transmitted to the *target* via a particular *medium*. A variety of media are used to facilitate communication in organizations. Some of the more common of these are listed here:

WRITTEN COMMUNICATION

- Memoranda and letters
- Electronic mail
- Instruction manuals
- Policy manuals
- Employee handbooks
- Company newsletters
- Annual reports to stockholders
- Grievance and suggestion systems

ORAL COMMUNICATION

- Face-to-face communication
- Telephone
- Employee meetings
- Training sessions

As you can see, the nature of the message will often influence the selection of the medium. For example, it would not be appropriate to print a disciplinary message in the company newsletter, nor would it be worthwhile or effective to publish a change in the safety procedures in the annual report to the stockholders. Also, the medium used to communicate can influence the effectiveness of the message. For example, realistic job previews (RJPs, see Chapter 6) that were made orally were found to be more effective than written RJPs in creating positive perceptions of honesty (Saks & Cronshaw, 1990). Also, work groups in which members were linked by computer rather than by face-to-face communication exchanged less information, used more strong or inflammatory communication, and took longer to make decisions. However, the communication in these groups was also characterized by greater equality, with all group members being more likely to participate (Siegel, Dubrovsky, Kiesler, & McGuire, 1986).

When (or if) the encoded message is received, the first thing the target must do is *decode*, or interpret, it to try to determine the source's intent. As is the case with encoding, effective decoding depends on the verbal skills, frame of reference, emotional state, and experience of the target. Based on his interpretation of the message, the target will respond in some way. Perhaps work behavior will change on the basis of a recommendation, or perhaps the target will become angry and quit. In any case, the target's reaction forms the basis for *feedback* to the source. Feedback can take many forms, but it serves the general function of letting the source know whether or not the message was effective. For example, a desirable change in behavior on the part of the target following a disciplinary message would constitute feedback that the message had its intended effect.

The final component of this communication model is *noise*, which includes anything that alters, interrupts, or inhibits the communication cycle at any point. It is possible, for example, that a typographical error in a memorandum could drastically change the meaning of a message. For instance, if the legal counsel's secretary omitted the word *not* from a memo advising Peter's Pan Pizza managers that they "should not discuss the lawsuit filed against PPP with subordinates," the effect of the memo would probably be the opposite of what was intended. In a similar fashion, the target could incorrectly interpret the intent of an ambiguously worded message. Consider, for example, the opening memos for this chapter. Mr. Bombyk may have intended to make a friendly offer to discuss inspection policies with Ms. Richmond. Ms. Richmond, however, may have interpreted the memo as a challenge to her authority.

We have referred to the communication process as a "cycle"; the choice of term was not accidental. The diagram in Figure 11.9 is really only a "snapshot" or a segment of the perpetual cycle of communication that takes place among individuals and groups in organizations. Messages often prompt the target to assume the role of communication source, encoding and sending a response through an appropriate medium to the former source, who becomes the target. Any given message is likely to elicit a series of additional messages that form such a cycle. This is important to keep in mind because it illustrates the importance of longitudinal analyses of any potential communication problems.

Functions of Communication

Scott and Mitchell (1976) examined the uses of communication in organizations, and identified four very general functions that communication serves: information, motivation, control, and emotion. Most organizational communication serves all of these functions to some degree, as we can see by considering the memos that opened this chapter.

Information. The information function of communication is the most obvious. All communication involves the transmission of some type of information, of course, but often this information is simply a means to achieve another purpose. However, in some cases the purpose of communication is strictly informative, as when a worker provides her supervisor with information needed to make a decision. An example of the information function of the opening memos is Ed Clark sending a copy of Bombyk's memo to Dr. MacKeven. The purpose of Mr. Clark's communication was to provide Dr. MacKeven with information, so that she could decide whether she would be able to help with the problem.

Motivation. Much of the communication in an organization is designed to influence the behavior or attitudes of workers. Both managers and nonmanagers spend much of their time trying to get others to commit themselves to doing certain things, or to change how others feel about certain aspects of the job. The most straightforward examples of motivational communication are praise and criticism, although more subtle forms of communication can also motivate. In our memos, we can see the attempt to motivate on the part of Greg Bombyk when he requests that Ms. Richmond change her guidelines to conform to those developed in his unit. We don't know whether she will actually change the guidelines, but Mr. Bombyk's memo certainly motivated her to take the issue to Mr. Clark.

Control.

Given the complexity of modern organizations, responsibility for specific tasks and authority over particular workers are not always clear. A significant amount of communication is therefore directed toward clarifying duties and establishing authority, which in turn allow management to control how the organization functions. Clearly, one of the primary purposes of the Bombyk memo was to establish that the responsibility and authority for setting inspection standards belong in his unit.

Emotion.

We are all familiar with communication that is designed, in whole or in part, to express feelings or emotions. Suggestion boxes, in addition to providing a medium for informative communication, allow employees to vent their feelings in regard to virtually any aspect of work. Annual award ceremonies are designed not only to reward and motivate but also to express management's appreciation for a job well done. Again, the Bombyk memo certainly has an emotional quality to it because it clearly conveys his disappointment with the inspection guidelines established by Ms. Richmond.

Communication Effectiveness

The functions of communication described above are obviously important to organizations and the people in them. Unfortunately, communication does not always work as well as we would like. We have referred to the general concept of "noise" in the communication cycle, but that concept is *too* general to describe the actual conditions that render communication ineffective. In the following sections we discuss some of the more specific factors that influence the communication process.

Accuracy, Fidelity, and Distortion.

Accuracy refers to the perceived validity or truth of the message sent by the source to the target. It should therefore not be confused with questions of **fidelity**, or whether the message is altered by the communication process itself. An example of a problem involving fidelity would be a malfunction in a computer printer that caused characters to be illegible, making it impossible to read memos printed on that printer. A problem involving accuracy would be a perfectly legible memo that no one believed.

Certainly, if the target of a message has doubts about its fidelity, she will also be likely to have doubts about its accuracy. High fidelity, however, does not guarantee perceived accuracy. For example, research suggests that perceptions of message accuracy are influenced by the expertise of the communication source, as well as the trust that the target places in the source (Hanser & Muchinsky, 1980; O'Reilly & Roberts, 1976). If a source isn't trusted, or seen as knowing what he is talking about, message fidelity will not improve overall communication.

In contrast to accuracy, which refers to the target's perception of a message, communication **distortion** usually refers to changes in the content of a message on the part of the source, whether intentional or not. Distortion is apparently most common in upward communication, or communication from subordinates to their superiors. Specifically, subordinates sometimes omit information that is unfavorable to themselves, while emphasizing information that puts them in a more favorable light, particularly when there is a lack of trust between the parties (O'Reilly, 1978).

Accuracy and distortion are important aspects of communication for a number of reasons. Most obviously, communication that is free from distortion and perceived as being accurate will facilitate the exchange of information. Further, there is evidence that these types of communication problems can have negative psychological effects. Hatfield and Huseman (1982), for example, found that when subordinates agreed with their supervisors concerning the nature of their previous communication, they were also more satisfied both with their supervision and with their work in general. It is not likely that communication plagued with distortion and inaccuracy would result in this type of agreement between supervisor and subordinate. You can imagine the problems that arise when workers distort the information they give their supervisors, or when bosses believe the information is inaccurate. Credible performance appraisal would be very difficult in these circumstances, with the supervisor either having false information or believing that she did. The final appraisal likely would be based on incomplete or irrelevant information, which would defeat the purpose of the appraisal system.

Communication Overload. Communication overload describes a situation in which more information is sent than the target can receive, interpret, and act upon. The result of overload seems to be that some or most of the information is inadequately processed or improperly interpreted, and the effectiveness of both the employee and the organization are reduced. For example, O'Reilly (1980) examined the effects of communication overload among samples of U.S. Navy personnel working on decision-making tasks. His results are intriguing because although subjects who experienced overload had lower performance than those provided with less information, the overloaded subjects were more satisfied with their task. These results suggest that employees may seek more information than they can use, perhaps even to the detriment of decision quality.

Of course, there are differences between people in the ability to receive and process information, so that one worker's overload may be the optimal amount of communication for another. These individual differences are even more important because, up to some optimal point, more communication does indeed improve performance. O'Reilly (1980) found this pattern in his data; it was only when communi-

Communication can express emotions as well as information.

cation went beyond a certain level that there was a negative effect on subjects' behavior. Because this level is likely to be different for different people, supervisors and managers must be sensitive to the communication skills of their employees.

Attitudes. The efficiency of the communication cycle is likely to be influenced by the participants' attitudes toward each other, as well as toward the subject of their communication. This potential was illustrated in a study in which executives enrolled in a business school course participated in a laboratory exercise on conflict resolution (Tjosvold, 1982). The executives played the role of managers whose job was to settle a conflict with workers over job rotation. Some of the executives were led to adopt a co-operative strategy, some a competitive strategy, and some a strategy of avoiding controversy. The results showed that the cooperative strategy apparently improved communication because subjects in this condition demonstrated a greater understanding of the workers' position than did subjects in the other two conditions.

Structural Variables. There are two types of structure in organizations that have implications for communication. The first includes the kinds of structural variables normally associated with bureaucracy, such as size, hierarchy, and division of labor. It is obvious that as an organization grows, either in number of employees or number of units, there is a greater need for communication in order to control and coordinate workers' activities. As the amount of communication increases, there is a tendency for formal channels of communication to be established in order to make communication more efficient. One major tactic by which efficiency is achieved is limiting the amount of communication by formally specifying the timing of messages and the appropriate content for various communication channels. Indeed, research has found that smaller organizations engage in less communication than do larger organizations. However, smaller organizations rely more upon face-to-face oral communication than do larger organizations (Smeltzer & Fann, 1989).

Communication is also restricted by gatekeeping. **Gatekeeping** is a relatively informal process involving decisions about what information will be communicated and what will not. Gatekeepers decide whether other people need to receive certain messages, filtering out irrelevant or sensitive material that might result in inefficiency or other problems if passed along. The need for gatekeeping, and the organization's reliance on gatekeepers to control the flow of information, increases with organizational size and communication volume.

Gatekeepers are not necessarily people with formal authority in an organization but, rather, those with access to, and control over, information. For example, at the White House, the appointments secretary serves as a powerful gatekeeper by controlling the president's calendar. In the same way, the president's secretary at PPP makes important decisions about the flow of information within the company, and particularly to and from the president. Both secretaries wield a great deal of power because of their roles as gatekeepers.

The second type of structure relevant to communication is the structure of the **communication network**. Just as we can draw a chart showing which workers are responsible to which supervisors and managers, we can also draw a chart showing who communicates with whom in an organization. These communication patterns, or networks, have typically been studied in laboratories, where experimenters can carefully control the flow of information.

Simple networks involving small numbers of people, such as those in Figure 11.10, have often been compared. With simple tasks, networks in which communication is channeled through a single person (11.10a) or otherwise limited (11.10b) are most effective, whereas networks allowing communication between more parties (11.10c, 11.10d) lead to better performance on more complex tasks (Shaw, 1964). It therefore seems that a contingency model of communication networks may be warranted, with the freedom to communicate with others dependent on task characteristics.

Research on communication patterns in actual organizations has also been conducted. For example, Keller and Holland (1983) examined characteristics of research-and-development employees who were high both in volume of communication and innovative in their ideas. Among other personal characteristics, such as having high self-esteem and a low need for clarity, these communicators and innovators held central positions in communication networks. That is, they controlled the flow of

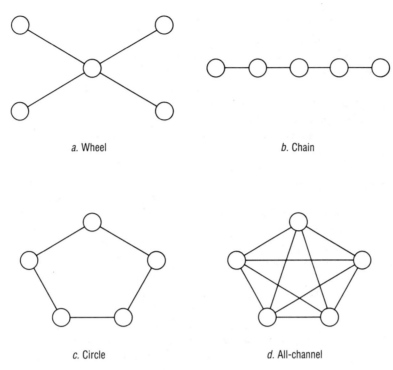

a. Wheel

b. Chain

c. Circle

d. All-channel

FIGURE 11.10
Communication Networks

communication between others in their departments. Similarly, Boje and Whetten (1981) found that administrators who were centrally located in communication networks were seen by their peers as being more influential than other administrators. These studies illustrate that the ability to control communication can lead to definite benefits. In Keller and Holland's study, it is not unreasonable to suspect that the increased innovativeness of workers in central communication positions stemmed, at least in part, from their access to the ideas of their coworkers, which they could combine and assimilate in unique, innovative ways.

Research has found that characteristics of workers' tasks can influence the development of communication networks. For example, groups that experience high uncertainty about their tasks are more likely to use decentralized or open communication patterns, in which communica-

tion flows freely among all members, than a centralized pattern, in which a small number of people control the communication (for example, Argote, 1982; Fry & Slocum, 1984). This may be due to the complexity that stems from uncertainty, and the beneficial effects of open communication for performing complex tasks (Shaw, 1964). Also, groups that experience a threat to their mission or goals are more likely to develop a centralized communication pattern (for example, Dunbar & Goldberg, 1978; Isenberg, 1981), perhaps because threats limit workers' cognitive abilities and lead them to rely upon centralized authority (Staw, Sandelands, & Dutton, 1981). However, the effects of task characteristics on communication networks is complex. One study found that when uncertainty and threat were studied together, the results were the opposite of what was expected. Specifically, the greatest centralization of communication was in groups with high uncertainty and low threat (Argote, Turner, & Fichman, 1989). Thus, although it is clear that group and task characteristics can influence communication, the exact nature of the effect is still unclear.

A particularly important role in communication is played by boundary spanners. Tushman and Scanlan (1981) stated that boundaries develop in organizations because each unit within an organization develops its own unique language and ways of looking at problems. It is the primary duty of boundary spanners to recode communication that crosses boundaries, from the "semantic space" of one unit into that of the second, without any change in meaning. To perform this function, boundary spanners must be linked to the internal communication network of their own units, as well as to sources and targets of communication outside the units. Hence, Tushman and Scanlan argued that people in boundary positions, such as sales representatives, are not actually boundary spanners unless they are (1) aware of events within the organization, (2) aware of events and conditions in the environment, and (3) capable of facilitating the communication of these types of information between the organization and the environment. Consistent with the implication that boundary spanners must be able to function well both within and outside their units, Caldwell and O'Reilly (1982a) found that high-performing boundary spanners were able to adjust their self-presentation styles, thereby altering their communication roles to fit different situations.

As textbook authors we have found ourselves serving as boundary spanners between the field of I/O psychology and you, the reader of this book. Our responsibilities in this role include communicating the issues, concerns, and desires of a diverse body of researchers and theoreticians in the field, and doing so in such a way that the educational goals of the course you are taking can be achieved. We can safely say that this boundary-spanning experience has been a challenge. We hope that it has also been successful.

A final issue relating to communication networks is that of openness. For years communi-cation theorists have recommended openness in communication as a way to increase organizational health and effectiveness (for example, Jablin, 1985; Likert, 1967; Mayo, 1945). However, there is increasing evidence that free-flowing, open communication is not always the best policy to follow (Eisenberg & Witten, 1987). For example, disclosure of personal information, such as feelings, can lead to stress and emotional discomfort in some situations. The disclosure of work-related information, such as technical data, can limit the opportunities for lower-level employees to develop power, which for them is often based on their technical expertise. Also, upper-level employees frequently need to limit the spread of information for competitive reasons. It is clear that rather than advocating the free and open exchange of information in organizations, psychologists need to consider just when open communication is likely to be effective and when it is better to control information more closely (Eisenberg & Witten, 1989).

Conclusion

You should now recognize the importance of organizational communication for all aspects of organizational life. It is easy to forget just how important communication is, however, because most people tend to take it for granted, and are largely unaware of its complexities. We hope that you will not take it for granted, and that you keep these complexities in mind as you consider the role of communication in the following sections of this chapter (and as you review earlier chapters).

Other Organizational Topics

Organizational theories provide a framework from which to study, or design, organizations. They also suggest appropriate management styles, or means of coordinating employees' activities. Communication, as one of the critical processes in all organizations, is of great importance in determining whether organizations operate according to plan. These are, however, only two of the many macro-level issues that have been studied by I/O psychologists and other organizational researchers. Unfortunately, the practical limitations on the length of a textbook make it impossible to discuss all of these issues. In the remaining sections of this chapter, we must be content with brief presentations of several of the more interesting topics. Even these discussions, though, should give you a better feel for the complex issues psychologists face when trying to understand behavior in organizations.

Organizational Climate and Culture

Organizational climate and culture refer to organizational characteristics that have been both difficult to define and difficult to measure. Typical definitions of **organizational climate** state that it represents employees' shared perceptions of their organization. Thus, if Peter's Pan Pizza's employees believe, as a group, that their company is generous in its rewards for hard work, then PPP can be said to have a climate of generosity, or perhaps of fairness. This would be the climate regardless of the objective reward practices of the company. Schneider (1985) pointed out that climate definitions have at various times included the dominant interpersonal practices of an organization, such as supervisory style and how workers relate to one another, as well as formal and informal policies that encourage certain types of behavior, such as safety (Zohar, 1980) and innovation (Abbey & Dickson, 1983).

Research on climate has focused on the analysis of activities and policies that distinguish organizations from one another, as well as those that distinguish units within organizations. In this sense, climate may be thought of as an organization's personality. Although climate research can be traced back to Lewin, Lippett, and White's (1939) classic study of the

effects of authoritarian, democratic, and laissez-faire social climates, modern research on organizational climate stems largely from the work of Litwin and Stringer (1968), who identified eight dimensions of climate:

1. Structure
2. Individual responsibility
3. Rewards
4. Risk and risk taking
5. Warmth and support
6. Tolerance for conflict
7. Organizational identity and group loyalty
8. Performance standards and expectations

Campbell, Dunnette, Lawler, and Weick (1970) reviewed the early climate literature, and identified four factors:

1. Degree of structure present
2. Individual autonomy
3. Reward orientation
4. Support and consideration

Muchinsky (1976) and others have found similar, although not identical, factors. Despite criticism of the construct (for example, Guion, 1973), there has been a considerable amount of research on climate over the years. Schneider (1985), however, noted a decline in research on climate, and suggested that this may be due to the widespread acceptance of the construct, and the ability that we now have to measure multiple dimensions of policies and other organizational characteristics. However, some researchers continue to examine climate but in increasingly sophisticated ways. For example, Kozlowski and Doherty (1989) studied the relationship between the quality of leader-member relations, as defined by LMX theory (see Chapter 10), and climate perceptions. They found that workers with high-quality relations with their supervisors had more positive perceptions of organizational climate. Further, due to the increased interaction with their superiors, they agreed more strongly on the nature of those perceptions, both with their supervisor and with one another.

More recently, the concept of **organizational culture** has emerged as an important research topic. Whereas climate focuses on employees' perceptions of organizational characteristics, culture research attempts to understand the *meaning* that employees attach to events in the organization. The predominant approach to studying culture is to examine stories and myths that are told in organizations. Culture theorists believe that stories and myths shared by employees are important channels for the communication of the meaning of events (Koprowski, 1983; Mitroff, 1983). For example, there is a story at Peter's Pan Pizza about the company president seeing a senior vice president drive into the parking lot of a competitor's pizza parlor. According to the story, the president drove in behind the vice president and fired him on the spot. This story may or may not be true, but in either case it serves to convey a certain message about the loyalty that is expected when a person works at PPP. Culture, as communicated through such stories, is an important factor in attracting and retaining employees because workers are likely to be attracted to organizations with cultures that match their own values (for example, O'Reilly, Chatman, & Caldwell, 1991; Schneider, 1987). And indeed, when workers have values that are congruent with those of their supervisors (indicating a strong organizational culture), they are likely to be more satisfied with their work and more committed to their organization (Meglino, Ravlin, & Adkins, 1989).

A great deal of recent research has attempted to identify variables related to the emergence of organizational culture. One interesting finding is that perceptions of culture vary within organizations. For example, workers who interact with one another have similar interpretations of organizational events, but other groups of workers within the same organization have different perceptions of the culture (Rentsch, 1990). On the other hand, there is evidence that organizations within a particular industry share cultural elements (Gordon, 1991). Taken together, these two studies suggest that an understanding of organizational culture requires looking at perceptions not only at the organizational level but also among both smaller and larger groups of workers.

Of course, individuals can have an important effect on the culture of their organizations. The impact of executives such as Walt Disney, Sam Walton, and Steven Jobs on the companies they created is legendary. Long after such people are no longer associated with their companies, the culture they leave behind bears the mark of their vision, as a visit to Walt Disney World or any Wal-Mart store clearly illustrates. Some researchers have suggested that this process represents the generalization of key employees' "global psychological orientations" to the organization itself (Kets-de-Vries & Miller, 1986). In any case, it is difficult to imagine these organizations in their present form without the climates created by their founders.

In a general sense, one of the most significant aspects of the research on climate and culture is that it illustrates the importance of considering the organization as a single unit as we examine the behavior of individual workers. Inconsistent research results and differences between apparently similar organizations may be explained by differences in variables such as climate and culture. We hope that the research in these areas becomes more sophisticated, and that the role of these factors can be more fully documented.

Organizational Effectiveness

Organizational effectiveness is the term used to refer to various aspects of an organization's overall performance. As you might imagine, there are many ways in which an organization can be effective or ineffective. Cameron (1980) described four major approaches to evaluating effectiveness. First, an organization can be described as effective if it is successful in accomplishing its goals, usually with respect to outputs or production. Second, an organization can be considered effective if it is successful in acquiring the resources it needs from the environment. In particular, this approach emphasizes successful competition for scarce resources. Third, an effective organization can be defined as one whose internal functioning is smooth and free of major problems. Such characteristics as trust and benevolence toward individual workers, smooth information flow, and freedom from conflict between work units would typify such an organization. Fourth, an effective organization may be seen as one that is able to keep its "strategic constituencies" satisfied. Strategic constituencies are groups of people who have a stake in the organization, such as customers, workers, and stockholders. Keeley (1984) identified a special case of this last definition in theories that view effectiveness as satisfying the interests of different groups of workers, or "participating individuals."

There have been many studies on organizational effectiveness that have attempted to identify the factors that determine global organizational performance. One critical variable that has emerged is the passage of time. That is, the nature of effectiveness is likely to change as organizations and their environments change. For example, Cameron and Whetten (1981) found that in the life cycle of an organization, individual effectiveness and effectiveness at acquiring inputs became less important over time, whereas overall organizational effectiveness and effectiveness at producing outputs became more important. These considerations should remind you of our discussion of proximal, distal, and dynamic criteria (Chapter 4).

Another important conclusion, demonstrated in empirical research (for example, Cameron, 1981), and implicit in the different approaches to measuring effectiveness mentioned above, is that effectiveness is a multidimensional rather than a unitary construct. That is, we cannot measure a single aspect of an organization's performance and hope to have captured the essence of its effectiveness. We must either limit our interest in an organization's effectiveness to a restricted range of criteria or we must consider multiple measures and perspectives. This is very similar to our earlier discussion of criteria for the performance of individual workers. Recall in Chapter 4 that we said it is virtually impossible to assess every aspect of a worker's performance with a single measure, so multiple criteria are typically used in an effort to capture more of the "ultimate criterion." Similarly, there is an ultimate criterion for the effectiveness of organizations, and we must attempt to measure that criterion in several ways if we wish to come close to capturing it.

In general, the consensus seems to be that the measure of effectiveness that is used in a given situation should be contingent upon a variety of factors (Connolly, Conlon, & Deutsch, 1980). Cameron (1980) suggested six critical questions that should be asked when evaluating organizational effectiveness (see Table 11.1). The answers to these questions should help a manager or researcher identify the most important dimensions of effectiveness for a particular organization at a particular time. We believe that such an approach is bound to be more successful than attempts to assess more general types of effectiveness.

Stress in Organizations

Interest in stress in organizations has increased dramatically in recent years. Both the scientific research literature and the popular media have shown concern for the welfare of workers who experience stress, as well as ways by which stress and its effects can be managed. Efforts to understand work-related stress have produced a variety of definitions of stress (stress as a stimulus, stress as a response, and so on). Although each of these definitions has its advocates, we prefer a definition offered by Beehr (1990) that we feel captures the basic ideas common to most conceptualizations: **stress** "is a process in

TABLE 11.1 Six Critical Questions in Evaluating Organizational Effectiveness

Critical question	Examples
1. What domain of activity is being focused on?	Internal activities vs. external activities
2. Whose perspective, or which constituency's point of view, is being considered?	Internal constituencies vs. external constituencies; satisfying all constituencies minimally vs. satisfying one constituency maximally
3. What level of analysis is being used?	Individual effectiveness, subunit effectiveness, or organizational effectiveness
4. What time frame is being employed?	Short time perspective vs. long time perspective
5. What type of data is to be used?	Perceptual (from individuals) vs. objective (from organizational records)
6. What referent is being employed?	Comparative—relative to a competitor; normative—relative to a theoretical ideal; goal-centered—relative to a stated goal; improvement—relative to past performance; trait—relative to effective traits

SOURCE: Reprinted by permission of the publisher from "Critical Questions in Assessing Organizational Effectiveness," *Organizational Dynamics*, Autumn 1980, p. 75. Copyright © 1980 by American Management Associations, New York. All rights reserved.

which characteristics of the workplace or of the job itself cause employees to experience discomfort or ill health."

Two additional terms that you should be familiar with are *stressor* and *strain*. **Stressors** are characteristics or conditions in the workplace that give rise to stress. **Strain** refers to the discomfort or ill health that result from stress. Research has focused on both ends of the stress cycle, attempting to understand the sources of stress (stressors) as well as its effects (strain).

There are a variety of potential on-the-job stressors. Brief, Schuler, and Van Sell (1981) compiled a list of potential job-related stressors, organized into three basic categories: (1) organizational characteristics and processes, (2) job demands and role characteristics, and (3) individual characteristics and expectations. Each variable in the list has been found to result in stress, and therefore to affect job behavior (see Box 11.2).

A useful model that illustrates the relationships among the various factors or facets in the stress process was developed by Beehr and Newman (1978; see Figure 11.11). Stressors are represented by the boxes labeled "Personal Facet" and "Environmental Facet." Personal stressors are the types of variables listed in Box 11.2 as "Individual Characteristics and Expectations," such as job insecurity and anxiety. Occupational stressors are those listed in Box 11.2 under the categories "Organizational Characteristics and Processes" and "Job Demands and Role Characteristics." These include such things as company policies, quality of supervision, and physical working conditions. The Personal Facet and Environmental Facet of this model include more than stressors, however. They also represent characteristics that help workers combat or cope with stress, such as good general health and supportive company policies (Beehr, 1985, 1990).

The "Process Facet" in the model encompasses processes or reactions to stressors in the work environment. These processes take place within the individual worker and determine the

BOX 11.2 Job-Related Stressors

ORGANIZATIONAL CHARACTERISTICS AND PROCESSES

- Organizational policies
- Inequitable or inadequate performance evaluations
- Pay inequities
- Ambiguous or arbitrary policies
- Rotating work shifts
- Frequent relocation
- Idealistic job descriptions before hiring
- Organizational structure
- Centralization; low participation in decision making
- Low opportunity for advancement or growth
- Increased size
- Excessive formalization
- Excessive specialization and division of labor
- Interdependence of organizational units
- Organizational processes
- Poor communication
- Poor or inadequate feedback on performance
- Ambiguous or conflicting goals
- Ineffective delegation
- Training programs

JOB DEMANDS AND ROLE CHARACTERISTICS

- Working conditions
- Crowding
- Lack of privacy; poor spatial arrangements
- Noise
- Excessive heat or cold
- Lights: inadequate, glaring, or flickering
- Presence of toxic chemicals
- Safety hazards

- Air pollution, including radiation
- Interpersonal relationships
- Inconsiderate or inequitable supervisors
- Lack of recognition or acceptance
- Lack of trust
- Competition
- Difficulty in delegating responsibilities
- Conflict within and between groups
- Job demands
- Repetitive work
- Time pressures and deadlines
- Low skill requirements
- Responsibility for people
- Underemployment; overemployment
- Role characteristics
- Role conflict
- Role ambiguity
- Role underload/overload
- Role-status incongruency

INDIVIDUAL CHARACTERISTICS AND EXPECTATIONS

- Career concerns
- Under- or overpromotion
- Midcareer crises
- Obsolescence
- Unmet expectations and goals
- Job insecurity
- Individual characteristics
- Type A behavior pattern
- Anxiety
- Intolerance of ambiguity
- Flexibility or rigidity
- Introversion or extroversion

SOURCE: From *Managing Job Stress* (pp. 66–67), by A. P. Brief, R. S. Schuler, and M. Van Sell. Copyright © 1981 by Arthur P. Brief, Randall S. Schuler, and Mary Van Sell. Reprinted by permission of Little, Brown and Company.

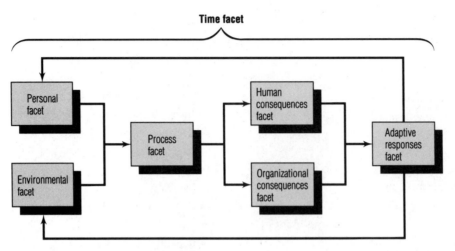

FIGURE 11.11
The Beehr-Newman Facet Model of Job Stress
SOURCE: From "Job Stress, Employee Health, and Organizational Effectiveness: A Facet Analysis, Model, and Literature Review," by T. A. Beehr and J. E. Newman. In *Personnel Psychology, 31*, 665–699. Copyright 1978 by Personnel Psychology, Inc. Reprinted by permission.

consequences of stress. Both physiological and psychological processes have been identified. Physiological processes are changes in the functioning of various bodily systems, such as the endocrine system and the peripheral nervous system. Workers who respond to stressors with extreme physiological reactions are likely to experience greater stress than those with more moderate reactions. Psychological processes comprise effects on decision making and perceptions (Beehr, 1990). For example, some people may be better able to cope with stressors because their decision-making style allows them to deflect responsibility for the outcomes of their decisions or because they simply perceive fewer stressors in their work environment.

Beehr and Newman (1978) divided the consequences of stress into two groups. The "Human Consequences Facet" includes strains, such as physical health problems, depression, and maladaptive behaviors such as drug use. The "Organizational Consequences Facet" entails responses with implications for organizational effectiveness, such as absenteeism, turnover,

and sabotage. These two types of consequences in turn determine the "Adaptive Response Facet" of the model. These are efforts on the part of individual employees or the organization as a whole to deal with stress. Some of these efforts are geared toward treating strain, or the negative consequences experienced by individual workers. Other approaches are designed to remove stressors from the workplace, thereby reducing the chances that workers will experience strain in the first place (Newman & Beehr, 1979).

The model indicates that the adaptive responses will affect both the personal and environmental variables that contributed to the initial experience of stress. If these responses are effective, stress should be reduced in the future. If they are ineffective, the stress will persist and other responses may be tried. Finally, Beehr and Newman (1978) included a "Time Facet" in their model. It represents the duration of exposure to stressors, and indicates that with longer exposure there is greater potential for strain and negative organizational consequences.

Effects of Stress. Whatever the stressor, there is a common physiological reaction to stress that is the result of the joint action of the sympathetic nervous system and the endocrine system. Through a rather complex series of reactions, these systems prepare the body to deal with stress by means of the "fight-or-flight" response. That is, by increasing blood flow to the brain and muscles, and by releasing glucose (blood sugar) and fatty acids into the blood system, the body is prepared to either "fight" the stressor, or to take "flight" and try to escape the source of the stress. The major physiological effects of this response include the following (Hendrix, 1990):

1. Bronchi of lungs relax and respiration increases

2. Decreased blood flow to intestines and stomach; decreased digestive activity

3. Heart rate increases, volume of blood pumped increases, and force of pumping increases

4. Increased blood flow to muscles

5. Fatty acids released into bloodstream by fat cells

6. Blood vessels constrict in lungs, intestines, and skin, causing decreased blood flow to these systems

7. Increases secretion of adrenaline and nor-adrenaline

8. Muscle tension

These responses to stressors had obvious survival value for our ancient ancestors, as they still do for most species today. That is, they give an organism the strength and alertness to deal with stress through intense physical activity. However, in our modern society we are seldom able either to fight or flee when faced with stressful situations. Consequently, as we encounter stressors in our jobs and experience the physiological effects described above, we cannot dispel the resulting energy in the "natural" way. Instead we must continue to deal with our

stressors and the potentially negative physiological effects of the fight-or-flight response (Hendrix, 1990). The physical consequences of stress can be devastating. Stress has been found to be associated with serum cholesterol levels and coronary heart disease, immune system suppression, endocrine system disorders, bruxism (gnashing of teeth), skin disorders, backaches, and headaches, among other disorders (Hendrix, 1990).

Of course, not all workers respond to stress by developing these types of disorders. A number of characteristics are related to the ability to cope successfully with stress. For example, Type A individuals, whose behavior is typically described as competitive, aggressive, impatient, and hostile, are at greater risk of developing coronary heart disease than are Type B individuals, who are more "laid-back," and who experience less stress (Hendrix, Leap, & Steel, 1986). Also, people who believe that their own decisions and behaviors determine what happens to them (that is, internal locus of control), and those who have generally high confidence in their own abilities and self-worth (that is, high self-esteem) are better able to cope with stress than those who believe that their fate is beyond their control (that is, external locus of control), or who have low opinions of their own abilities (that is, low self-esteem; Hendrix et al., 1986; House, 1972; Quick & Quick, 1984). Finally, negative affectivity, or the tendency to experience a wide range of negative emotions (see Chapter 9), has been found to account for much of the relationship between stressors and physical strain. That is, people high in negative affectivity are more likely to respond to stressors with physical symptoms such as those described above (Brief, Burke, George, & Robinson, 1988; Chen & Spector, 1991).

In addition to physiological reactions to stress, there can be negative behavioral outcomes as well. As the health of workers under stress deteriorates, incidence of absenteeism and turnover are likely to increase. Performance of job tasks is also likely to suffer, and workers' attitudes toward their jobs and their organizations may decline (Beehr, 1990; Beehr & Newman, 1978). On the basis of his own research and a literature review, Jamal (1984) drew three tentative conclusions about the effects of stress on workers' behaviors. First, when stress is measured in terms of workers' perceptions of stressors such as role conflict (incompatible expectations on the parts of others), role overload (expectations beyond the worker's capability), or inadequacy of resources, the relationship between stress and job performance is negative and linear. That is, people who perceive these types of stressors have lower performance than those who do not. However, when stress is measured directly (for example, physiological measures such as muscle tension or heart rate), the relationship between stress and performance is less clear.

Second, the relationship between job stress and absenteeism, intention to quit, and actual turnover is positive. The greater the stress experienced by a worker, the more likely he is to withdraw from the workplace. Jamal (1984) argued quite logically that stress creates an adverse environment for workers, and that escape from such an environment is a natural response.

Third, Jamal (1984) concluded that both organizational and professional commitment, or the extent to which workers identify with and become "attached to" their organizations or professions, moderate the relationship between stress and behavior. Highly committed workers seem to be better able to cope with stress, and are less likely to suffer such negative consequences as reduced performance or increased withdrawal.

Work-related stress can also have dramatic effects on nonwork behavior. For example, a particularly troubling finding is that work stressors are associated with men's status as abusive or nonabusive husbands. That is, men who experienced higher levels of work stressors were more likely to engage in wife abuse than men who experienced lower levels of work stressors (Barling & Rosenbaum, 1986). Clearly, organizations cannot be satisfied with simply treating on-the-job consequences of stress. To the extent that work experiences have an impact on the well-being of employees (and their families) beyond the workplace, employers should acknowledge this impact, and help deal with the problems that follow from it.

Coping with Stress.   Given the potential costs of stress, both to individual workers and to employers, it is not surprising that there have been many attempts to control stress. One approach that many employees choose is alcohol and drug use (Gupta & Jenkins, 1984). Although there may be a greater acceptance of alcohol than of drugs as a way to manage stress, both of these strategies are disastrous to U.S. industry, with annual costs in the hundreds of billions of dollars (Castro, 1986).

Fortunately, drug use is not the only way employees can cope with stress, and there has been an extensive effort aimed at developing stress-reduction and stress-management programs (for example, Brief, Schuler, & Van Sell, 1981). Three distinct approaches to dealing with work-related stress have been described (Murphy, 1990). The first, and most common, is to provide employee assistance programs, or EAPs. These are programs that are designed to help employees who are already suffering from the effects of stress. Common examples are drug and alcohol treatment programs, family counseling, and financial counseling. Although often useful, EAPs have important shortcomings. The most obvious of these is that they treat stress and its consequences as an individual problem. That is, rather than addressing the causes of stress, they help individuals deal with its effects after the fact. No emphasis is placed on the prevention of stress in these programs. The second approach is to change workplace or job characteristics that are causing stress, thereby eliminating the problem before it affects workers. This is a more proactive approach than EAPs, with an emphasis on prevention. Unfortunately, there is little empirical research

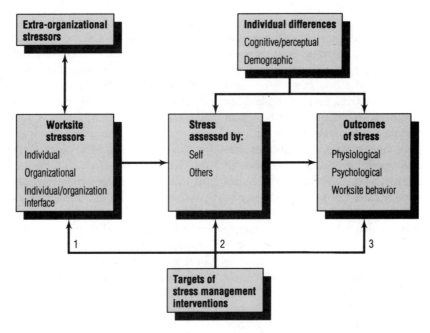

FIGURE 11.12
Worksite Stress Management Intervention Framework
SOURCE: From "Worksite Stress Management Interventions," by John M. Ivancevich, M. T. Matteson, S. M.
Freedman, and J. S. Phillips, *American Psychologist, 45*, 253. Copyright © 1990 by American Psychological
Association. Reprinted by permission.

on the usefulness of this type of program (Murphy, 1990).

The third approach to occupational stress described by Murphy (1990) includes techniques commonly known as stress management or wellness programs. These programs are proactive, and seek to prevent the negative effects of stress by training *all* employees how to avoid and manage stress. Many of the techniques used in stress management programs are variations of treatments used in clinical psychology to combat anxiety disorders. These include **biofeedback**, by which workers learn to control such things as muscle tension, heart rate, and blood pressure (Birk, 1973); **progressive muscle relaxation**, in which workers learn to recognize and relieve muscle tension (Budzynski, 1974); **meditation** as a means to achieve relaxation (Benson, 1976); and **cognitive strategies**, which

aim to change workers' perceptual processes that contribute to stress, such as irrational beliefs or thoughts (Meichenbaum, 1977).

The potential for stress management programs to help workers has been clearly demonstrated (for example, Higgins, 1986). Procedures combining, for example, employee assistance programs with stress management, have been called for, and a framework for integrating these procedures has been presented (Ivancevich, Matteson, Freedman, & Phillips, 1990; see Figure 11.12). In this framework the authors refer to all interventions as stress management, but you should be able to see that intervention type 3 in Figure 11.12 corresponds to EAPs, that intervention type 2 corresponds to what Murphy (1990) called stress management, and that intervention type 1 corresponds to eliminating stress by changing workplace characteristics.

However, despite the potential of comprehensive programs such as these, there is reason to be wary of many existing stress management efforts. For example, Ganster, Mayes, Sime, and Tharp (1982) found that a program that taught workers to recognize conditions that cause them stress and to respond in adaptive rather than self-defeating ways, when combined with instruction in muscle-relaxation techniques, resulted in lower employee "strain." Although these results are promising, Ganster and his colleagues did not advocate the widespread use of these types of programs. They argued that their program, which involved 16 hours of training over an eight-week period, is about the minimum amount of training necessary for reliable stress reduction, and that it resulted in relatively small effects. Many commercially available programs, however, are much shorter, often lasting only a few hours over one or two days. Further, these authors argued that programs designed to alter reactions to stress do not address the basic problem. They would rather see more effort aimed at making work organizations inherently less stressful. They therefore suggested that stress management programs be used as supplements to organizational change programs, given that a great deal of organizational stress is due to conditions that are not under management control, such as the time pressures experienced by the tax accountants every spring no matter what their organizations might do. We agree with this general advice, and believe that Ganster and his associates have articulated one of the most important, and most imposing, tasks facing I/O psychology in the near future.

Conclusions

In this chapter we presented a number of issues that focus on the individual's role in work settings; that is, on how she or he contributes to the operation of the organization and how it influences her or him. We have also examined the impact of the workplace on the individual worker. These issues are both fascinating and frustrating. On one hand, they include the most basic questions concerning the nature of organizations (organizational theories) and how they function (communication). On the other hand, they include concepts that I/O psychologists and others who study work organizations have not even been able to agree exist, much less define (organizational climate and culture). However, we have also seen the potential for psychology to relieve some of the pressures felt by workers as they perform their jobs. The common lesson of these topics for I/O psychologists and students of I/O psychology is that behavior in organizations is both collective and embedded within a context. To the extent that we forget that lesson, our science and our discipline lose their relevance.

Chapter Summary

Organizational theories are statements about how organizations should be designed or structured, and about how organizations should be conceptualized and studied. The earliest influential organizational theory was bureaucracy, the principles of which are still evident in the structure of most organizations. Limitations to bureaucratic theory and the rise of the human relations movement led to organizational theories such as McGregor's Theory Y and Argyris' need-integration theory that focused on the needs and motives of individual workers. More recently yet, open systems theories have attempted to describe organizations in terms of the interrelationships between units within organizations, as well as interactions between the organization and its environment.

A great deal of effort has been directed toward understanding the communication process in organizations. Understanding this process is critical because communication is an essential component of virtually every organi-

INTEROFFICE MEMO

To: Ed Clark,
          Vice President,
          Retail Operations

From: J. A. MacKeven,
          Human Resources Coordinator

I have been considering the memo that you sent concerning the flap between Bombyk and Richmond. You seem to imply that there is a communication problem in your division, and that is certainly a possibility. There is, however, a more basic factor that seems to be involved, and we should consider it before taking any action.

First, in terms of the communication issue, it appears that Quality Standards and Store Inspections are unaware of each other's activities, which has led to some duplication of effort. In terms of formal lines of communication, your office is the link between these departments. I think we need to examine the procedures by which your staff controls interdepartmental communication. Perhaps we need to set up some direct liaison between departments, bypassing your office.

The more basic issue here concerns the fundamental structure of your division. That is, which department should have the responsibility for defining these standards (as well as for other specific activities)? We simply shouldn't have two groups that are able logically to claim responsibility for the same functions. I think we need to understand what each department head sees as the major tasks of his or her unit, and how they came to hold those opinions. I would not be surprised to find that some type of reorganization would be helpful. For example, do we need these two departments, or would it be more effective (including in terms of communication!) to combine them? With your permission, I will start looking into both the specific communication issue and the more general issue of duplication of responsibility, and we'll see if my suspicions are warranted.

zational function. A number of distinct communication functions have been identified, as have factors that influence communication effectiveness.

Two other popular research topics are organizational climate and organizational culture. These concepts involve employees' shared perceptions of their organization and the psychological meaning they attach to organizational events, respectively. Not all I/O psychologists agree on the importance of climate and culture, however, and there have been problems developing definitions of, and clarifying the differences between, these concepts. However, as researchers learn more about how organizational culture develops and the impact it has on other aspects of organizational life, its importance is becoming more widely acknowledged.

Topics that have recently become frequent targets of research are organizational effectiveness and stress in organizations. Effectiveness has been found to be a very complex phenomenon to study, and sophisticated models of effectiveness are just beginning to emerge. Results of research on stress clearly demonstrate its negative effects on health and performance. Reliance on simple stress management techniques is probably not adequate, but more comprehensive procedures are not yet in widespread use.

Review Questions and Exercises

1. The problem in the Retail Operations Division seems to involve communication at some level. (See memo, p. 397.) Given what you know about the general communication process (Shannon & Weaver, 1948) and communication networks, what might be the specific cause(s) of this problem? What remedies might be effective?

2. Dr. MacKeven has suggested that there may be problems in the basic functioning of the Retail Operations Division. In terms of (a) bureaucratic theory and (b) Lawrence and Lorsch's theory of organizations, what might the nature of these problems be?

3. Aside from any breakdown in communication, there may be differences of opinion on the parts of Mr. Bombyk and Ms. Richmond concerning the functions for which their respective departments have responsibility. Use the role-episode model of Katz and Kahn to describe a series of events that might have led to this misunderstanding.

4. Examine the dimensions of organizational climate identified by Litwin and Stringer (1968) and by Campbell and associates (1970) that were listed earlier in the chapter. Given your knowledge of Peter's Pan Pizza, describe its climate in terms of these dimensions.

CHAPTER 12

Organizational Change

LEARNING POINTS

After studying this chapter, you should

❑ be able to describe the dimensions along which organizational change varies;

❑ be able to describe scientific management, and explain why it is no longer a popular approach to job design;

❑ be able to define job scope, and both describe and evaluate three techniques for increasing job scope;

❑ be able to explain what the job characteristics model is, describe the components of the model and how they interact, and evaluate both the model and the Job Diagnostic Survey; you should also be able to suggest how the job characteristics model might be improved;

❑ understand what organizational development is, and describe the processes involved in each stage of planned change according to Lewin's model;

❑ be familiar with examples of individual-, group-, and organization-level organization development techniques; and

❑ be able to explain the arguments for and against the effectiveness of OD.

IN THIS CHAPTER, WE WILL BE discussing change in organizations. Although the issues that we will address in the first part of this chapter, such as job and task design, have broader implications, they are often critically important components of organizational change. In the later sections of the chapter we will discuss techniques specifically designed to facilitate change in organizations. Before we begin describing the theory and research on organizational change, however, we would like to make a few points about the nature of change in organizations, focusing on issues raised in the opening memo.

The memo that opens this chapter was selected because it discusses anticipated changes at Peter's Pan Pizza: if PPP's management decides to proceed with one or both of the plans mentioned in the memo, there will be dramatic, large-scale changes in many aspects of the company's operations. The memo was also selected because the types of change that the proposed programs would require are the types that can, to some extent, be planned. The importance and advantages of planning for change in organizations will become evident as you read this chapter.

One way to classify organizational change is in terms of its **scope**. In previous chapters we have seen widespread change at Peter's

INTEROFFICE MEMO

To: All vice presidents and
           senior vice presidents

From: J. A. MacKeven,
           Human Resources Coordinator

I recently attended a meeting, along with some of you, at which plans to expand operations into several new fields were discussed. Two plans in particular were met with enthusiastic support, and are being pursued in greater detail. These plans are (1) development and marketing of products for vending machine sales, and (2) marketing of current products in institutional markets, such as schools, airlines, and children's camps.

I have been asked by the president to study the ramifications of the plans for our human resources. The ramifications fall into two basic categories. First, there are the obvious issues of selecting, placing, and training the new employees who will have to be hired to implement these plans. Second, there are the equally important issues of job design, and it is these issues that I am writing to you about today. Specifically, if the plans are implemented, there will be a number of new jobs created, and there will have to be substantial changes to a number of existing jobs. Recognizing that there are a variety of ways to accomplish any given set of tasks, we would like to design the jobs such that there is maximum benefit for both the employees and the company.

In the next few weeks, directors and supervisors in your divisions will be contacted by members of the Human Resources staff to get their input on a number of issues, such as the effectiveness of the design of current jobs, how new jobs necessitated by the proposed changes might be integrated into the relevant units, and what changes in the total organization might be necessary in order to facilitate the plans. Information on likely changes, in terms of new and/or changed jobs, in each department will be forwarded to the appropriate managers in the immediate future. Please encourage your management staffs to examine these changes carefully, and to think about the ways in which they might be implemented.

Pan Pizza. The most obvious example was its acquisition of Flavio's Frozen Foods, which not only made the company larger but also brought it into new markets with new products. The acquisition of Flavio's and the types of changes discussed in the current chapter memo are at one end of a continuum of organizational change. They represent large-scale, organization-wide events that may require major alterations in the basic structure and philosophy of the company. These types of changes have historically been relatively infrequent, although they are more common in growing, entrepreneurial companies than in older, established organizations.

At the other end of the continuum we find smaller-scale changes that have more limited effects on the organization. For example, the purchase of a new machine to shred cheese will probably not trigger a series of events that will be felt throughout PPP and the rest of the pizza industry, but it will make an important difference to the workers who use the machine.

When all degrees of change, from global to specific, are considered, a somewhat contradictory conclusion must be drawn: organizational change is constant. That is, organizations are always undergoing change in one form or another. This fact is acknowledged in open systems theories of organizations, discussed in Chapter 11 (for example, Katz & Kahn, 1978). Open systems theories stress the interdependence of various parts of an organization, and how a change in one part will normally require changes in other parts if the organization is to function effectively. For example, Peter's Pan Pizza's plan to begin institutional service will make it necessary, among other things, to change policies and procedures regarding shipping and inventory control. Even if gearing up for institutional service required no other direct changes (which would certainly not be the case), the changes in shipping and inventory would result in other changes, such as how the Finance Division handles accounts payable and accounts receivable, which would in turn affect the cash flow throughout the company and

therefore have indirect effects on numerous other units. When the organization is viewed as a system, the importance of anticipating and planning for change, even when relatively limited in scope, is obvious.

Another important lesson to be learned from open systems theories that will help us understand organizational change is the interdependence of the organization and its environment. Katz and Kahn (1978) described organizations in terms of a continuous cycle in which inputs are taken from the environment, transformed in some way, and returned to the environment in the form of products or services. In the simplest sense, environmental change (changes in available inputs, or changes in the demand for outputs) will have direct effects on the functioning of organizations that are using those inputs and producing outputs. Environmental change therefore makes change in the organizational system necessary, or at least desirable. At Peter's Pan Pizza, the decision to expand into vending and institutional markets should be based on an unmet demand for those products and services in the environment. Further, for the expansion to be successful, PPP will need to have ready access to the inputs necessary to meet those needs. Changes in either consumer demand or required resources could influence the effectiveness of PPP's changes.

We said earlier that organizational change can be defined in terms of the size or scope of the change. Another dimension along which change can be defined concerns the response of the organization to environmental change. At one end of this continuum is a **reactive response**. By this we mean that in some cases organizations respond only after dramatic environmental change has taken place, occasionally after having experienced serious problems because a response was not made sooner. An example of this can be seen in the U.S. auto industry, which did not respond to growing consumer demand for smaller, more efficient vehicles until "foreign" automakers had already stepped in and claimed most of that market.

At the other end of the continuum is a **proactive response** to change. Here, management attempts to anticipate environmental change before it can adversely affect the company and institutes plans that will allow the company to use the change to its advantage. The obvious examples of this type of response are the "foreign" carmakers, who responded more quickly to changing consumer demand than did their U.S. counterparts. As far as Peter's Pan Pizza is concerned, it remains to be seen whether it is responding to market changes that have already put the company at a competitive disadvantage or anticipating a demand for fine Italian-style specialties in previously untapped markets.

A final note in our overview of organizational change: We have made a point of emphasizing the importance of planning for change and anticipating the need for change. It should be kept in mind, however, that a great deal of the change that occurs in organizations is haphazard and therefore difficult if not impossible to anticipate. For example, an unexpected blight that wipes out the anchovy harvest could have devastating effects at Peter's Pan Pizza if the company had invested a great deal of time and money in developing a new frozen anchovy-filled pastry. There may not be acceptable anchovy substitutes, and the company may have to "write off" its investment in the project. Although this sort of unexpected change can always happen, we believe that much of the change in organizations, particularly changes that are made necessary by environmental conditions, can be anticipated. Doing so, however, requires careful monitoring of these conditions, and conscious efforts to manage and control the change process.

Job and Task Design

Except in Chapter 3 (where job analysis was considered), our discussion of I/O psychology has generally centered on worker characteristics; the characteristics of jobs and job tasks have been taken as "givens." We have discussed methods for selecting and training workers so that they would be able to perform specific jobs in the organization. Later, we discussed how individual characteristics, such as needs or leadership style, can be important in determining workers' behavior. In short, we have emphasized selecting or changing individuals in order to achieve certain goals. Although this traditional psychological emphasis on individual characteristics is evident in most I/O theories, there is another general approach to dealing with these issues: jobs rather than people can be changed. For example, instead of training workers how to perform a complicated and dangerous task, it might be better to change the task so that workers can perform it without as much training and without being endangered.

In a way, job and task design represents an individual-level application of the philosophy underlying the organizational theories presented in Chapter 11. That is, organizational theories are concerned with how best to design and coordinate entire organizations; job- and task-design theories are concerned with how best to design individual jobs. In both cases, individual characteristics are usually considered only as moderating variables, and the major emphasis is on structural, procedural, and relational aspects of the job or organization.

Origins of Job Design

The earliest influential approaches to job design stemmed from more general theories of organizations and management, such as the scientific management theory of Frederick Taylor (1911; see Chapter 9). Taylor was primarily concerned with organizational and individual efficiency, and emphasized job designs that would maximize efficiency. He believed that job tasks could be broken down into elemental motions, and that by replacing slow, inefficient motions with those that are faster and more efficient, overall organizational and individual productivity could be increased.

The best-known tool for achieving this goal was the time-and-motion study (Gilbreth, 1919). In this technique, workers' motions were timed, and when faster ways of accomplishing job tasks were identified, they were incorporated into the job. As a result of using time-and-motion studies, many jobs were simplified to the extent that they involved only a few elementary movements that were repeated continually. Another effect of job simplification was worker specialization and job standardization. Each person was trained to perform only a handful of simple operations, and each of the simplified jobs had to be performed in one specified way if it was to "fit" with the rest of the jobs in the company.

Similar job-design implications evolved from Weber's (1947) bureaucratic model (see Chapter 11). One of the basic principles of bureaucracy is strict division of labor, with each worker performing a limited number and type of tasks. As with scientific management, the consequences of bureaucracy include simplification, standardization, and specialization of jobs and job tasks. There is little question that jobs designed on the basis of scientific management and bureaucratic principles are more efficient in terms of the time spent to perform specific tasks, and that these approaches resulted in economic savings for the companies that used them. However, these savings were typically short-lived because simplification and standardization have negative long-term side effects (such as monotony and boredom) that can in turn have a negative impact on workers' attitudes (Dunham, 1979). As we saw in Chapter 9, negative attitudes toward work and low job satisfaction may be related to withdrawal behaviors such as absenteeism and turnover, which are usually costly for companies. Also, extreme standardization and specialization are likely to result in inflexibility and resistance to change, which limit an organization's ability to adapt to changing internal and external conditions.

The negative job design consequences of scientific management and bureaucracy are only examples of the many limitations of these approaches. Both of these theories were popular early in the twentieth century, but managers came to question many of their basic assumptions when the economic consequences of worker alienation became evident. At about this time, however, the human relations movement, spurred on by the Hawthorne studies, began to take shape. The new emphasis on worker attitudes and perceptions led to the next major advance in job and task design, the job-scope approaches.

Job Scope

As we stated during our discussion of job attitudes and satisfaction, during the 1930s and 1940s managers and organizational researchers began to pay attention to the needs and desires of workers, in addition to the efficiency of individuals and organizations. One of the key principles of this human relations movement was the idea that workers desire a sense of achievement or accomplishment from what they do. That is, rather than being motivated only by economic factors such as pay and benefits, human relations theories assumed that rank-and-file workers identified with their jobs and were motivated by meaningful tasks and opportunities to utilize their skills. Jobs designed along the lines of scientific management or bureaucratic principles, because of their emphasis on specialization and the underlying assumption that workers are primarily motivated by economic concerns, were unlikely to provide this sense of achievement.

These changing beliefs about workers' responses to their jobs led to job-design principles that were directly opposed to those derived from Taylor's and Weber's theories. Rather than making jobs simpler and more efficient, the emphasis shifted to designing jobs that involved a broader range of tasks and utilized a wider variety of workers' skills and abilities. Because of the emphasis on the span of activities and skills involved in job performance, this approach to

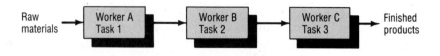

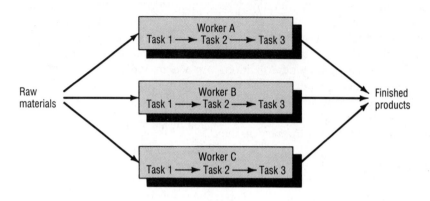

a. Prior to enlargement

b. Following enlargement

FIGURE 12.1
Illustration of Job Enlargement

job design is often referred to as the **"job-scope"** approach. The basic rationale for this type of change was that only by making jobs more challenging (by including more tasks), or more meaningful (by using more worker skills), would workers feel the sense of accomplishment that they desired and be motivated to work hard and to perform well as a result.

Two major job-scope techniques emerged during the early years of the human relations era. One was **job enlargement**, which involves giving workers a greater number of tasks to perform. Enlargement is contrary to Weber's (1947) bureaucratic notion of division of labor, and it is essentially the opposite of the job-simplification techniques introduced by Taylor. In this sense, it represents job expansion in a horizontal direction (see Figure 12.1).

An example of job enlargement would be if Peter's Pan Pizza were to decide to start marketing vending machine products, and ask the same sales representatives who have been selling Flavio's frozen products to supermarkets to also sell the new products to vending companies. Sales representatives would have more to do, although their new responsibilities would be essentially similar to their old responsibilities. It is important to notice that job enlargement can come about because of management's belief that increasing the number of tasks will satisfy employee needs, or because there is simply more work to be done in the organization and the new tasks are "naturally" assigned to those who are already performing similar tasks.

The second job-scope technique is **job enrichment**: workers are given greater control over how their jobs are performed. Typically, job enrichment involves giving workers authority and responsibility, either solely or shared with a supervisor, to do such things as planning work activities, setting goals, and making decisions about how to deal with problems that

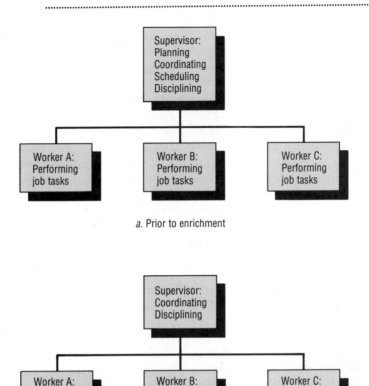

a. Prior to enrichment

b. Following enrichment

FIGURE 12.2
Illustration of Job Enrichment

arise. This is dramatically different from how decisions are made and authority is exercised in traditional organizations. Specifically, it is at least partially inconsistent with the widely practiced bureaucratic principle of hierarchy of control. That is, in most organizations there is a clearly defined authority structure, in which each worker is responsible to the immediate supervisor, who in turn is responsible to the manager at the next level, and so on. In a similar fashion, each supervisor is responsible for defining subordinates' jobs, and specifying how those jobs should be performed. Under job en-

richment, however, a worker may be responsible to the supervisor only for the results of her work, and have the freedom to organize and perform the job in whatever way best suits her. Job-enrichment programs therefore have an impact on the level at which decisions are made in an organization, with supervisors and managers giving their subordinates some authority to define the nature of work. Compared to job enlargement, enrichment represents job expansion in a vertical direction (see Figure 12.2).

Job enrichment among Peter's Pan Pizza's sales force might entail giving the sales representatives the freedom to decide which products should be "pitched" to which clients, to set their own schedules for visiting their clients, to plan special promotions for their territories, and to exercise similar functions normally carried out by their supervisors.

A third, less common technique that can be used to expand the scope of a job is **job rotation**. Here, rather than changing the number of tasks that make up any one job or set of jobs, workers switch from one job to another on a regular basis. From a job-design standpoint, this is similar to job enlargement, in that each rotation will usually result in different skill requirements for the workers, so that over time a greater range of worker skills is called into play. It can be effectively argued, however, that the tasks that a worker is performing at any given time will still be relatively limited in scope. For this reason and because employees who rotate between jobs have to spend a great deal of their time training for each new position, job rotation has never received as much attention as the other methods as a way to increase job scope.

Job enlargement and job enrichment were very popular for many years, and there were numerous reports of success using these techniques. Often, however, the changes in job scope were confounded with other changes, making it impossible to know if changes in workers' behavior or attitudes were due to the changes in the jobs. Further, when changes attributable to job scope *were* observed, they were frequently short-lived (for example, Maher & Overbagh, 1971). Theorists began to assert that most workers, especially blue-collar workers, did not desire enriched jobs (for example, Shrank, 1974), and research supported this view, showing that increasing job scope did not have positive effects for all workers (see Brief & Aldag, 1975; Robey, 1974; Wanous, 1974b).

Over the years, researchers have suggested that the relationship between enrichment and satisfaction might depend on other conditions, including urban versus rural upbringing and the Protestant work ethic. However, no consistent effects on the relationship between job scope and satisfaction were found for these variables (White, 1978). Indeed, it has been suggested that increasing job scope might lead to increased role ambiguity, which itself has been associated with such outcomes as higher stress and anxiety (Korman, Greenhaus, & Badin, 1977).

The use of job enrichment and job enlargement was also hampered by the somewhat limited, overgeneralized theory on which they were based: the human relations view that workers obtain satisfaction from their accomplishments and the use of their skills. Although this provides an optimistic view of workers, it gives little practical guidance in terms of how to design jobs, what sorts of changes workers will find enriching, or what types of additional tasks will utilize workers' skills most efficiently. Consequently, it is not surprising that we find mixed evidence for the effectiveness of the job-scope approaches. By the mid-1970s the potential for task design to influence behavior and attitudes had clearly been demonstrated. What was needed was some sort of guiding theory that would suggest which types of job changes, in which types of situations, would produce the desired results.

Job Characteristics Model

The beginnings of a comprehensive model of job and task design can be traced to the work of Turner and Lawrence (1965). Beginning with the assumption that certain characteristics of jobs were likely to be associated with desirable worker responses such as high performance, good attendance, and high satisfaction, Turner and Lawrence developed a list of six characteristics that they believed would be related to favorable outcomes: (1) variety of tasks performed, (2) worker autonomy, (3) worker knowledge and skill required by the job, (4) worker responsibility, (5) interaction with others required by the job, and (6) optional interaction with others. Turner and Lawrence did not provide any experimental evidence that these characteristics resulted in desirable behaviors; however, they did demonstrate that the characteristics were correlated with attendance and satisfaction, although only among workers from rural communities.

A number of authors presented elaborations and extensions of Turner and Lawrence's (1965) basic idea that task variety, autonomy, and other task characteristics affect worker behavior and attitudes. However, Hackman and Oldham's (1976) model quickly became, and still remains, the best known and most widely researched. Their job characteristics model is described and evaluated in the following sections.

Theoretical Basis of the Job Characteristics Model.

As you will soon see, the job characteristics model is complex and includes a number of direct and indirect relationships between several types of variables. The basic theory underlying the model, however, is straightforward. Hackman and Oldham (1976) believed that properly designed tasks could satisfy the psychological needs of certain workers. Specifically, they focused on Maslow's (1943) need theory (see Chapter 8), and proposed that jobs with characteristics such as those described by Turner and Lawrence (1965) would satisfy Maslow's higher-order needs or growth needs. Thus, workers who had progressed through Maslow's need hierarchy to the point where they were motivated to satisfy esteem or self-actualization needs would find these sorts of jobs satisfying and motivating. Of course, such jobs would not be as satisfying for workers motivated to satisfy lower-order needs.

As we pointed out in Chapter 8, Maslow's need hierarchy theory has received very little empirical support. Relying on Maslow's theory to explain the effects of job design has therefore been a problem for the job characteristics model from the start (for example, Korman, Greenhaus, & Badin, 1977). This has not deterred psychologists from conducting research on the

model, but it may help explain some of the inconsistencies that characterize the research results.

Core Job Characteristic Dimensions.

The key to Hackman and Oldham's (1976) model is a set of five core job dimensions that are used to describe jobs in terms of characteristics that have implications for workers' behavior. The core dimensions are similar to the characteristics listed by Turner and Lawrence (1965).

1. *Skill variety.* Skill variety refers to the extent to which a worker's job requires the worker to use numerous skills or talents in order to perform the job successfully. An example of a job high in skill variety is that of the Peter's Pan Pizza's sales representatives mentioned earlier. Among other things, they must make judgments about how their products meet various market demands, prepare and deliver sales presentations, and keep accurate records of customers' orders. An example of a job low in skill variety is sprinkling cheese on Flavio's frozen pizzas, which requires only a reasonable amount of eye-hand coordination.

2. *Task identity.* Jobs high in task identity are those in which the worker is able to perform a complete, identifiable piece of work, starting with raw materials or information and ending with a product that is ready to be used, either by a customer or by another person or group of people in the company. A low-task-identity job at Peter's Pan Pizza might involve performing only one step in the assembly of a pizza, such as being the person who spreads the sauce onto the crust. A high-task-identity job would be one in which a single person performed all of the steps in pizza assembly, starting out with some crust, sauce, cheese, and assorted toppings and finishing with a ready-to-bake pizza.

3. *Task significance.* Task significance refers to the impact that a person's work has on

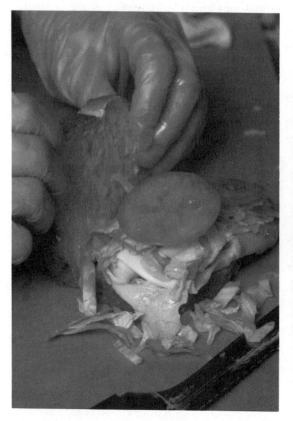 

Jobs differ in terms of their apparent task significance.

other people. A person's job has high task significance if what he does is critical to the successful performance of other jobs in the company. Clearly, the Peter's Pan Pizza's sales representatives have jobs that are significant in this way. A job would also be significant if it had an impact on the lives of people who are not members of the organization. Although pizza may not seem to be a very important product, how PPP's employees perform their jobs has an effect on the livelihoods of people who supply the company with raw materials, as well as on those of the people who work for the supermarkets and stores that sell PPP's products. These jobs therefore have signifi-

cance beyond the workplace. Although no job has a total lack of task significance, an example of one lower on this dimension might be that of the janitor who cleans managers' offices in the Suardell Springs headquarters. We at least hope that these managers can perform their jobs with dusty shelves as well as they can with clean shelves!

4. *Autonomy.* A job is high in autonomy if the worker has the freedom to determine, independent of his supervisor, the procedures used to perform the job and the scheduling of job tasks. Clearly, some jobs more readily lend themselves to autonomy than

do others. Returning again to our pizza sales representatives, it seems that they would have a fair amount of autonomy, because they are not under the direct, day-to-day supervision of their bosses and must therefore make most decisions about how to perform their jobs themselves. Other jobs, such as those involved in the preparation of the food, would have less autonomy because much of the scheduling of that work and the procedures used to perform it are dependent on technology and relationships to other jobs in the organization.

5. *Task feedback.* Task feedback refers to whether a worker can tell, simply from performing her job in the normal fashion, whether the job is being done effectively. For example, a truck driver who delivers supplies to Peter's Pan Pizza's pizzerias has a job with high task feedback: either the supplies are delivered on time and undamaged or they are not. On the other hand, marketing employees whose job is to develop new products do not have as high a level of task feedback. Do you remember the idea they had for a frozen anchovy-filled pastry? They won't really know if the idea is going to work until the product is marketed and consumer reaction is studied.

Hackman and Oldham (1976) stated that each of the core dimensions is positively related to favorable worker attitudes and behaviors. The motivating properties of a job, however, are not a simple combination of the five dimensions. Instead, Hackman and Oldham specified the following formula for combining these characteristics into what they called the **motivating potential score**, or MPS:

$$MPS = \left[\frac{\text{Skill} \atop \text{Variety}\ +\ \text{Identity}\ +\ \text{Significance}}{3} \right]$$
$$\times\ \text{Autonomy} \times \text{Feedback}$$

The formula has important implications for job design. First, notice that skill variety, task iden-

tity, and task significance are averaged together. This means that jobs with low levels of one or even two of these dimensions can still have motivating potential if there are high levels of the remaining dimension(s) in the group. Note, too, that the average is multiplied together with both autonomy and feedback. This implies that if the average of the first three dimensions is zero (that is, the job has no variety, no identity, and no significance), *or* if autonomy is zero, *or* if feedback is zero, then the motivating potential of the job will be zero. In other words, for a job to have motivating potential, it must have both autonomy and feedback, in addition to one or more of the remaining three dimensions.

To increase the MPS for a job, we need to know what can be done to enhance the core job dimensions. Hackman, Oldham, Janson, and Purdy (1975) suggested several "implementation concepts" as possible ways to do this (see Box 12.1). These are only examples of what can be done to affect job dimensions—many other actions could be taken as well—but these should give you a good idea of the types of changes that the job characteristics model advocates.

Critical Psychological States. According to the Hackman and Oldham (1976) model, the core job dimensions influence individual behavior and attitudes through critical psychological states. Such states are basically workers' perceptions of the nature of their jobs. As you might expect, changes in different core job dimensions have effects on different perceptions. Specifically, skill variety, task identity, and task significance combine to determine a worker's experience of the **meaningfulness of work**. That is, according to the model, workers will perceive jobs that are high on these dimensions as being meaningful, both to the workers themselves and to other people. The degree of autonomy in a job determines the second critical psychological state, the experienced **responsibility for outcomes of work**. The more a worker is free to structure, schedule, and define her job,

Client relationships can take many forms.

BOX 12.1 Implementation Concepts to Enhance Core Job Dimensions

- *Combining tasks.* Combining tasks involves reversing the processes of specialization and division of labor made popular in the scientific management and bureaucratic theories, by combining a number of specific tasks into more complex, multidimensional jobs. In essence, this is the same as job enlargement. According to Hackman and Oldham (1976), combining tasks will increase both task variety and task identity.

- *Forming natural work units.* Often, a worker is unable to see how his or her job "fits in" with the jobs of others or with the overall company goals and plans. By giving workers responsibility for complete, identifiable units of work, this strategy attempts to increase both task identity and task significance.

- *Establishing client relationships.* Although they seldom consider their jobs in these terms, each worker has a number of "clients," both within and outside the organization. For example, each of the stores to which Peter's Pan Pizza's truck drivers deliver supplies is a client whom they serve. By having employees develop personal relationships with each of their clients, the model predicts that task variety, autonomy, and feedback will be increased.

- *Vertical loading.* Vertical loading is very similar to the concept of job enrichment. A vertically loaded job provides workers with more freedom and independence in making decisions about how, and in some cases when, their work will be done. This strategy is expected to have a positive effect on task variety, task identity, task significance, and autonomy.

- *Opening feedback channels.* Opening feedback channels is intended to have a direct effect on the core job dimension of feedback. Feedback channels include the job itself, as we have mentioned before, as well as information provided by supervisors and coworkers.

SOURCE: From "A New Strategy for Job Enrichment," by J. R. Hackman, G. Oldham, R. Janson, and K. Purdy, *California Management Review*, vol. 17, no. 4, pp. 62–66. Copyright © 1975 by the Regents of the University of California. Adapted by permission of the Regents.

the greater will be the responsibility felt for the results or outcomes of that job. Third, the amount of feedback present in a job determines the final critical psychological state, **knowledge of the actual results of work activities**. Without adequate feedback, workers are unable to judge the effects of their behavior, but with adequate feedback, a fairly accurate picture of how they are doing and how they contribute to the performance of the entire organization is possible.

Personal and Work Outcomes. So far we have seen that the job characteristics model specifies that certain changes in jobs (implementation concepts) can affect important task characteristics of those jobs (core job dimensions), which

in turn play an important role in determining workers' perceptions of their jobs (critical psychological states). The next step in the model is the effects of these perceptions on workers' behaviors and attitudes. Hackman and Oldham (1976) described four general results that can be expected when workers experience meaningfulness, responsibility, and knowledge of results. The first two of these, high internal work motivation and high-quality work performance, can be thought of as motivational outcomes; that is, workers who experience high levels of the critical psychological states will be motivated to perform well not because of external incentives such as pay but because of internal motives stemming from the nature of their jobs. The other outcomes, high satisfaction with work and low absenteeism and turnover, can be thought of as attitudinal outcomes. Jobs that result in favorable psychological states should be enjoyable and satisfying, resulting in positive attitudes toward the job and the organization. As we saw in Chapter 9, these types of attitudes are not good predictors of work performance, but they may predict withdrawal behaviors such as absenteeism and turnover.

Growth-Need Strength.   The final component in the job characteristics model is growth-need strength. As we said when we introduced the model, Hackman and Oldham (1976) based their work on the idea that properly designed jobs will satisfy workers' growth needs. However, consistent with Maslow's need hierarchy, Hackman and Oldham believed that jobs designed to satisfy growth needs will not be appropriate for, and therefore will not motivate, workers who are motivated by lower-order needs. Thus, the degree to which workers are motivated by growth needs, or growth-need strength (GNS), was proposed as a moderator variable in the model. That is, improving the core job dimensions will have favorable results only for the workers who are high in GNS. Only for high-GNS workers will the core job dimensions affect the critical psychological states, and only for these workers will the critical states result in favorable personal and work outcomes. For workers low in GNS, the effects of changing jobs according to this model will be negative because the emphasis is placed on needs that are, for them, irrelevant.

The complete job characteristics model is illustrated in Figure 12.3. As we said earlier, this is a fairly complex model, but the logic behind it is relatively straightforward. To test the model, however, a special measure had to be developed. It is to this measure, and the research that has used it, that we now turn our attention.

The Job Diagnostic Survey.   To implement or test the job characteristics model, a measure of core job dimensions and motivating potential

was needed. Hackman and Oldham (1975) developed such a measure, called the Job Diagnostic Survey or JDS. The key features of the JDS are scales designed to measure each of the five core job dimensions of the model. Also included in the instrument, however, are scales measuring two supplementary dimensions (feedback from agents and dealing with others), as well as scales measuring the critical psychological states, internal motivation, satisfaction, and growth-need strength. Most of these variables are measured in two different sections of the survey, using more than one item format.

Although some evidence of the reliability and validity of the JDS was presented, including its ability to measure the core job dimensions (Hackman & Oldham, 1975), early research often failed to confirm this evidence. For example, rather than obtaining the five core dimensions specified by the model, one analysis of the JDS found only a single dimension, which was named "job variety" (Dunham, 1976). It was also found that the number of dimensions depended on the type of job, and varied from two to five (Dunham, Aldag, & Brief, 1977). Other researchers had similar problems replicating or reproducing the proposed structure of the JDS (for example, Lee & Klein, 1982; Pokorney, Gilmore, & Beehr, 1980).

One study, however, used a procedure known as confirmatory factor analysis to examine the structure of the JDS (Harvey, Billings, & Nilan, 1985). This procedure is designed to test hypotheses about the number and type of dimensions measured by a scale, and hence allowed the researchers to compare several specific models, including Hackman and Oldham's (1976) five-factor model and the single-factor model (Dunham, 1976). The results of the analysis showed that if certain methodological problems, such as the use of more than one response format and a mixture of positively and negatively worded items, are controlled, the Hackman and Oldham model, with separate core dimensions, provided the best description of their data, whereas the single-factor model

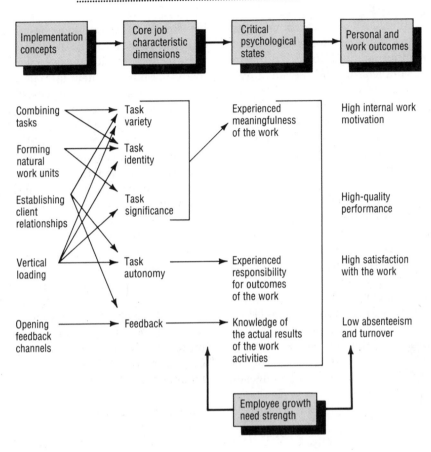

FIGURE 12.3
The Job Characteristics Model
SOURCE: From "A New Strategy for Job Enrichment," by J. R. Hackman, G. Oldham, R. Janson, and K. Purdy, *California Management Review*, vol. 17, no. 4, 62. Copyright © 1975 by the Regents of the University of California. Reprinted by permission of the Regents.

provided the most parsimonious (simple, yet adequate) description. However, Harvey, Billings, and Nilan concluded that the JDS should be revised to eliminate the methodological problems.

In response to the suggestion to improve the JDS, researchers have recently developed and evaluated a "revised JDS" that appears to eliminate many of the methodological problems described earlier. In a series of studies, it was found that the negatively worded JDS items formed a dimension of their own, independent of the job characteristics they were originally intended to measure. Also, when those items

were rewritten in positive terms, the original five JDS scales were verified and found to be reasonably accurate measures of their respective constructs (Idaszak & Drasgow, 1987).

Through confirmatory factor analysis, subsequent research has found that the revised JDS conforms more closely to the original five-dimensional structure, although it may not predict worker behavior and attitudes better than the original scale (Kulik, Oldham, & Langner, 1988). Further, when data from different samples were analyzed simultaneously, it was found that not only did the five-factor structure of the revised JDS generalize across samples but the problems that earlier researchers experienced replicating these dimensions may have been due to other methodological problems, such as small sample sizes and the small number of items per dimension on the JDS, in addition to the negatively worded items (Idaszak, Bottom, & Drasgow, 1988). Indeed, the measurement of job characteristics is one area where psychologists have responded to problems identified through research.

Another issue in using the JDS concerns how the scores on the individual core dimensions should be combined to summarize the overall complexity of a job. Ferris and Gilmore (1985) reviewed research on the JDS, and found three basic techniques for computing what they called "job-complexity indices." The first is to compute the motivating potential score (MPS) as suggested by Hackman and Oldham (1976). As we have seen, because this technique multiplies three values together, low scores on any of the three will yield a low MPS score. The second is a "weighted-average" technique suggested by Stone (1974):

$$\text{Complexity} = (2 \times \text{Variety}) + (2 \times \text{Autonomy}) + \text{Task identity} + \text{Feedback}$$

Stone's procedure gives greater weight to task variety and autonomy than to the other dimensions, but does not multiply individual scores together. Thus, a low score on any one dimension does not necessarily mean that a job will receive a low overall score. The third technique is an unweighted additive index, obtained simply by summing the five core-dimension scores. Ferris and Gilmore's results showed that the weighted-average method predicted job satisfaction better than the other methods, but that growth-need strength had the predicted effect on the relationship between complexity and satisfaction only when the original MPS formula was used.

There are undeniable problems in using the original JDS as a measure of core job dimensions. Research has provided inconsistent results regarding its validity; the individual job-dimension scales have questionable reliability because they consist of relatively few items; there are methodological concerns regarding the use of multiple-item formats and negatively worded items; and research results based on the JDS do not seem to be stable from sample to sample. The "revised JDS" has addressed some of these problems, most notably regarding the number of dimensions and the effects of the negatively worded items. However, the concerns about validity and reliability remain, and it is only with continued research on the revised scale that we will be able to address these concerns (Idaszak, Bottom, & Drasgow, 1988). Further, although there is evidence that improvements can be made to the JDS, a larger question is whether it is worth the effort. That is, does the available research support the validity of the job characteristics model as an explanation of the effects of job design? If not, then improving the JDS may be a waste of time. Keeping in mind that most of this research is potentially limited by the methodological problems of the JDS itself, we now turn to the evidence of the job characteristics model's validity.

Research on the Job Characteristics Model.   From the mid-1970s to the early 1980s there was a tremendous amount of research on all aspects of the job characteristics model. Most reviews of this research literature have not supported the theory. For example, in addition to relying upon poor measures such as the JDS, the model has been criticized because the job characteristics lack conceptual independence; because it uses perceptual measures rather than objective measures of job characteristics (although cognitive theories suggest that workers respond to their perceptions rather than to "objective reality," and so perceptual measures are the only appropriate measures); and because most of the research that supports the model has used cross-sectional designs that do not allow tests of the effects of actual changes in jobs on workers' attitudes and behavior (Aldag, Barr, & Brief, 1981; Roberts & Glick, 1981).

A meta-analysis of JDS research found that the best estimate of the correlation between core job characteristics and job satisfaction is .39. For people high in growth-need strength, the correlation was .68; for those low in GNS it was .38 (Loher, Noe, Moeller, & Fitzgerald, 1985). Although both of these correlations were significantly different from zero ($p < .05$), the difference between them is consistent with the original model. Thus, although we can have some confidence that perceptions of job characteristics are related to job satisfaction, and that this relationship may be moderated by GNS, we cannot conclude from this research that changes in job design are responsible for those perceptions. Unfortunately, field experiments that can test the effects of job-design changes are few in number, and offer little support for the model (Staw, 1984).

The widespread use of cross-sectional, correlational research designs on the job characteristics model leaves us in something of a quandary. Although the theory states that job satisfaction is the result of certain job and task characteristics, it may (also) be that perceptions of those characteristics are actually the result of workers' levels of job satisfaction. That is, the theory states that Peter's Pan Pizza's workers will be satisfied if their jobs are high in motivating potential, as determined by the core job characteristics. It could be, however, that satisfied PPP workers perceive their jobs as being high in motivating potential as a result of being satisfied, regardless of the actual characteristics of their jobs.

Evidence to support this possibility was found when subjects were given phony feedback from a job satisfaction measure, and then asked to complete the JDS (Adler, Skov, & Salvemini, 1985). Subjects who had been told they were highly satisfied with their tasks rated the core job dimensions higher than did those who had been told they were dissatisfied. (It should be noted that Adler, Skov, and Salvemini assert that none of their subjects expressed doubts about this phony satisfaction

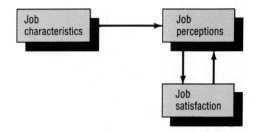

FIGURE 12.4
Causal Model Relating Job Characteristics to Job Perceptions and Job Satisfaction
Source: From "Confirmatory Analytic Tests of Three Causal Models Relating Job Perceptions to Job Satisfaction," by L. R. James and L. E. Tetrick, *Journal of Applied Psychology, 71*, 78. Copyright © 1986 by the American Psychological Association. Adapted by permission of the authors.

feedback.) James and Tetrick (1986) also found that job satisfaction influenced job perceptions and vice versa. What is noteworthy about this study, however, is that the reciprocal relationship between satisfaction and perceptions was preceded by a direct effect of job attributes on perceptions (see Figure 12.4). This means that although satisfaction may influence job perceptions and vice versa, these effects depend first on the impact that *objective* job characteristics have on perceptions, which is again consistent with the job characteristics model.

Another controversy surrounding the job characteristics model concerns whether job characteristics really are important in determining workers' perceptions of, and reactions to, their jobs. A number of theorists (for example, Salancik & Pfeffer, 1978; Weiss, 1977, 1978) have suggested that individuals' perceptions of their jobs may be determined by social cues in the work environment. That is, perceptions of jobs, and job satisfaction, may be more a function of the behavior of other workers than of objective job characteristics. In partial support of this view, Griffin (1983) conducted a field experiment involving two manufacturing plants, in which he found that both objective task characteristics and information provided by supervisors influenced workers' perceptions of core job dimensions, interpersonal task attributes (such as friendship opportunities), and satisfaction. Only objective task characteristics, however, had an effect on worker productivity.

Staw (1984) pointed out that advocates of both the job-characteristics and social-information approaches to job design have utilized research that favors their respective positions, and that neither side is likely to emerge as a clear "winner." He further argued that research examining the joint effects of social cues and objective task changes may be more useful than studying either by itself. Just such a study was reported by Griffin, Bateman, Wayne, and Head (1987), who in a laboratory experiment tested a model that integrates the job-characteristics and social-information processes. They found that job characteristics and social cues combine to determine reactions to jobs, and that changing job designs so as to incorporate the positive aspects of the two perspectives leads to positive changes in workers' reactions to their jobs. It is not surprising that this integrated model, which comes closer than either of its constituent models to the complexity of the workplace, is better at explaining reactions to jobs.

Alternatives to the Job Characteristics Model. Despite relatively recent improvements in the measurement of job characteristics and the initial testing of models integrating social cues and job characteristics, the job characteristics model has not enjoyed overwhelming empirical or critical support. In response to the problems encountered with the job characteristics model, a number of alternative job-design models have been proposed. The models have tended to rely on theoretical bases other than need theory, such as expectancy theory (Schwab & Cummings, 1976) and goal setting (Umstot, Mitchell, & Bell, 1978), thus addressing what may well be one of the basic problems with the job characteristics model. Unfortunately, these alternatives have not yet attracted the amount of research attention that has been lavished on the Hackman and Oldham model, and we therefore

cannot evaluate their usefulness for confronting the problems that plague job characteristics research.

We are reluctant to suggest, as some authors have, that the job characteristics model be abandoned, or that its only usefulness has been to stimulate research on task design (for example, O'Brien, 1982; Schwab & Cummings, 1976). Particularly in light of the recent research that finds support using techniques such as meta-analysis and confirmatory factor analysis, we think that the model may yet prove to be of some value. We do not, however, believe that the support for the model is either strong or conclusive, and we certainly do not view it as a comprehensive explanation for the effects of job design. More realistically, the job characteristics model probably offers only a partial understanding of the relationships between job and task design and workers' behaviors and attitudes.

Recognizing the importance of valid measures of job characteristics for testing job-design theories, Stone and Gueutal (1985) used a sophisticated scaling technique to determine the dimensions along which people perceive job characteristics. Their rationale for conducting this study was that all of the commonly used measures of job characteristics, such as the JDS, contain essentially the same dimensions, and that these dimensions were derived from the list of characteristics presented by Turner and Lawrence (1965). Unfortunately, Turner and Lawrence did not base their characteristics on empirical research but, rather, on their own experiences and reviews of theories. Although these dimensions may reflect the way Turner and Lawrence perceived jobs, they may not have much in common with the way most workers perceive jobs. In their analyses, Stone and Gueutal found one dimension along which jobs are perceived, called "job complexity," that contained virtually all of the traditional JDS characteristics. In addition to complexity, however, two other dimensions not measured by the JDS nor by any other commonly used scales

---

BOX 12.2 Dimensions of Multimethod Job Design Questionnaire

- *Motivational*. This approach is based on research and theory in traditional I/O psychology. It includes work on job enrichment, job enlargement, and the job characteristics approach to job design, as well as a number of theories of motivation. Of the four dimensions in the MJDQ, it is the most similar to what is measured by the JDS.

- *Mechanistic*. This perspective is based on "classic" industrial engineering and emphasizes many of the same concepts as Frederick Taylor's scientific management, such as task simplification and economy of motion.

- *Biological*. The biological approach to job design emphasizes biomechanics and physiology. Included in this view are such things as strength, endurance, vibration, and posture.

- *Perceptual/Motor*. This perspective is most similar to human engineering, human factors, or "ergonomics" (see Chapter 13). Here we are concerned with such things as lighting, the design of displays and machine controls, and the safety of the workplace. Also included in this approach are cognitive requirements of jobs, such as information processing and memory.

SOURCE: From "Development and Field Evaluation of an Interdisciplinary Measure of Job Design," by M. A. Campion and P. W. Thayer, *Journal of Applied Psychology, 70*, 30–31. Copyright © 1985 by the American Psychological Association. Adapted by permission of the authors.

---

were also found. These dimensions are named "serves the public," which includes such behaviors as interacting with and providing services to people outside the organization, and "physical demand," which involves such characteristics as required strength, health hazards, and physical activity. Research on manufacturing employees showed that measures of these empirically derived job characteristics predicted job satisfaction beyond the ability of the MPS score alone (Zaccaro & Stone, 1988).

The measurement of job-design characteristics was also addressed by Campion and Thayer (1985) but from a different perspective. Instead of focusing on worker perceptions, as most psychologists have, they first examined the ways in which job design is studied in a number of disciplines. They came up with four basic perspectives on job design, only one of which resembles what is measured by the JDS. Based

on these four approaches to job design, Campion and Thayer developed a measure called the Multimethod Job Design Questionnaire, or MJDQ, which taps each of the approaches (see Box 12.2).

Although the results of Campion and Thayer's research using the MJDQ are too complex to present in detail here, it is important to note that the four scales had very different correlations with various criteria. For example, scores on the motivational scale were positively correlated with measures of work motivation and job satisfaction, which is similar to what has been found with the JDS. The biological scale, however, was negatively correlated with measures of effort, pain, and need for medical care. High scores on the mechanistic scale were associated with high skill utilization and low training requirements; high perceptual/motor scores were associated with low levels of accidents, errors, stress, work overload, and mental demands. Subsequent research has replicated these results (Campion, 1988, 1989) and shown that the costs and benefits of traditional job-design procedures, such as job enlargement, can vary as a function of the perspective from which the design is evaluated (Campion & McClelland, 1991). For example, although enlarged jobs had better motivational design and were associated with greater employee satisfaction, they also had worse mechanistic design and higher training costs.

Both the Stone and Gueutal (1985) and the Campion and Thayer (1985) perspectives have important implications for job-design research. First, they share the conclusion that JDS-type measures of job characteristics are incomplete, from the perspective of worker perceptions as well as from the standpoint of total job design. If this is true—and we have every reason to believe that it is—it might explain some of the inconsistencies in the psychological job-design research. That is, variation in dimensions that were not measured by the JDS could have affected the research results in unpredictable ways. Second, both of these approaches suggest that the types of dimensions measured by the JDS, although not a complete picture of job design, are nonetheless important and should be preserved in any comprehensive theory of job design. Thus, whether the JDS and the job characteristics model continue to be used, the research on them has revealed important aspects of the effects of job design. Perhaps in the context of other design parameters, the effects of job characteristics will be identified with more precision.

Summing Up. The job characteristics model has proved to be a useful, if incomplete, description of the effects of job and task design. Its most notable shortcoming is its failure to consider the effects of nonmotivational factors in job design, although this is not surprising for a psychological theory. Its most notable contribution has been as the stimulus for the vast number of re-

search studies on the psychological effects of task characteristics, and the resulting knowledge about the importance and limitations of job characteristics and growth-need strength in determining job attitudes. With the arrival of more comprehensive job-design models, we can look forward to more effective job-design strategies in the future.

Organizational Development and Change

As we have seen, much of the research on change in organizations has dealt with changes in either jobs or the tasks that jobs comprise. These types of changes tend to be concentrated at the "narrow" end of the scope-of-change continuum introduced at the beginning of this chapter. That is, although changes in one job may also have important implications for other jobs, their primary impact will be on the specific job being changed. However, I/O psychologists and other organizational researchers have also focused on methods of systematic change that affect entire organizations. The most widely studied and widely known of these techniques have come to be known collectively as *organizational development* or *OD* procedures. In the remaining sections of this chapter we will examine the topic of OD, and see how it has been used to improve the functioning of organizations.

Definition and Description of Organizational Development

Organizational development has been a popular topic in organizational research and practice for more than three decades. During that time, the number of activities that are considered part of OD have increased dramatically. Today, *OD* is used to refer to so many different theoretical notions and applied practices that telling you that Peter's Pan Pizza is "using OD" really reveals little about what PPP is actually doing. Fortunately, there are enough common elements among most OD techniques that a general definition can be developed. Different techniques will stress different aspects of OD, as you will see when we describe some of the more common methods, but the following definition captures the essential philosophy behind virtually all of OD: **organizational development** is the planned use of interventions based on behavioral science knowledge, aimed at encouraging organizational self-examination and acceptance of changes that will improve organizational effectiveness and health.

Let's examine this definition more closely to see what we are really talking about. First, OD is planned, which means that it is based on a careful analysis of the current status of the organization and on the development of specific courses of action to deal with any problems that have been detected. Ideally, OD does not involve "seat-of-the-pants" organizational changes nor changes based on management's hunches about what might improve the organization but, rather, changes that are suggested by a careful diagnosis of the organization's problems. The diagnostic process is similar to the organizational analysis that should precede the development of a training program (Chapter 7).

Second, OD involves techniques, or interventions, that are based on the body of knowledge about organizations that has developed within the "behavioral sciences." (I/O psychology has, of course, been a major contributor to this body of knowledge.) There are many things that could be done to improve organizations, but many of them either have little to do with individual or collective behavior or have no basis in scientific research and theory. Also, OD interventions ideally rely on techniques that have some empirical evidence of effectiveness.

Third, OD techniques are usually designed to get an organization's members to examine the social processes that take place as it performs its many tasks. This "consciousness-raising" is designed to make managers and workers aware of how things are being done at the present, as well as helping them to see the need for changes that will improve the organization. The emphasis on social processes originated in the human relations movement, from which many early OD approaches took their inspiration. OD is sometimes criticized for this association with human relations (for example, Alderfer, 1977), although today, as we indicated above, OD has come to encompass such a broad range of activities that this criticism is overstated.

Finally, the definition points out that the primary purpose of OD is to improve the effectiveness and health of organizations. Effectiveness can be defined in terms of the organization's ability to achieve its goals, and a healthy organization can be defined as one in which individuals and groups work toward those goals in an efficient manner.

Two additional conditions are usually associated with OD. The first is that in order to be successful, OD procedures require the active support of top management. The "top-down" philosophy of OD is necessary not only to obtain the support of upper managers but also to communicate the importance of the OD intervention to all other employees in the organization. Second, OD is often described as an "organization-wide" activity. As you will see later in this chapter, there are many OD procedures that focus on either individual or group processes rather than on organizations as a whole. It should be kept in mind, however, that in most cases the individual and group interventions are intended to solve problems that have been identified through organization-wide analyses.

A final note before outlining the basic processes of OD concerns what is known as Quality of Work Life (QWL). QWL programs are designed to improve workers' experiences on the job in such a way as to increase motivation, satisfaction, commitment, and other employee attitudes, thereby increasing organizational effectiveness and performance. QWL is currently very popular among organizational researchers, but the differences between it and OD are elusive. Some authors have gone to great lengths to distinguish between the two concepts, without much success (Faucheux, Amado, & Laurent, 1982). You will probably run across references to QWL if you do additional reading in organizational research journals or other books, and so we wanted to make it clear that QWL procedures are similar or identical to those common in OD programs.

Basic Processes in Organizational Development

Because OD encompasses such a broad spectrum of activities, it is difficult to describe OD processes in general terms. Certainly, a number of theoretical models of OD have been proposed over the years, each attempting to describe the essential elements of OD interventions. Perhaps the simplest model of organizational change was developed by Kurt Lewin (1958). By being simple, this model has the virtue of being able to incorporate the variety of OD techniques that have been used. We will therefore use Lewin's three-stage model (illustrated in Figure 12.5) to describe the major processes that are involved in most OD efforts. Keep in mind that specific OD techniques may have more or fewer steps than we outline here, and that other models are usually more complex. Our purpose, however, is not to teach you how to perform OD, but rather to help you understand the basic theory underlying its use.

Stage One: Unfreezing. According to Lewin (1958), there are forces in organizations that attempt to maintain the status quo and there are forces that push for change. For change to occur, the forces that are resisting change (or maintaining the status quo) must be reduced or modified, so that the forces for change may prevail. Lewin referred to this stage of the model, during which the organization prepares for change, as **unfreezing**. It is in this early phase of OD that the OD consultant or change agent

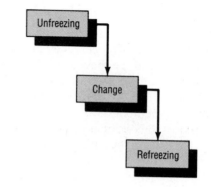

FIGURE 12.5
Lewin's Model of Change in Organizations

begins interaction with the organization. The **change agent** is the individual who is responsible for coordinating the changes that will come about as a result of the OD program.

Typically (but not always), the change agent is a person from outside the organization. There are two major reasons that this is so. First, many organizations do not have employees with the basic knowledge and skills in diagnosis, problem solving, and theories of organizational behavior that are considered to be necessary for successful OD. (For example, although Dr. MacKeven had a brief experience with OD in her internship during graduate school, she is probably not familiar enough with the variety of available OD techniques to evaluate each of them adequately.) Consequently, many organizations hire consultants who have this expertise. Second, and more basic to the process of OD, the role of the change agent is to help identify and implement the changes that will be the most beneficial to the organization. To do this, the agent must be trusted by all of the employees with whom he works, and must be seen as unbiased and independent. It is widely believed that an outside consultant is more likely to be perceived as having this independence than is an "in-house" agent, who may be suspected of having hidden motives that favor certain groups or individuals in the organization. It is possible, for example,

Many workers resist change.

that if Dr. MacKeven has worked frequently or closely with one group of managers, she will be perceived as favoring their interests over those of other managers.

Several important activities must occur during the unfreezing stage in order for OD to be successful. First, as we have already mentioned, it is important to secure the active participation of top management early in the OD process. Representatives of top management should therefore meet with the change agent during this time, both to demonstrate their endorsement of the project and to achieve a clear understanding with the change agent about what is expected from the OD process. Often, this understanding will take the form of a contract in which the expectations of each party are explicitly stated. Such a contract is useful because of the broad scope of OD, and the very real possibility that the original purpose of the intervention may be overlooked or downplayed over the course of the months and even years that OD techniques may require.

A second important activity during the unfreezing stage is the diagnosis of the organization's current status, and the identification of ways in which OD might be able to improve organizational and individual effectiveness. Our definition of OD includes the goal of organizational self-examination, which is necessary if management is to become aware of the organization's shortcomings and the need for change. The change agent plays a critical role in this self-examination because it is often difficult for managers to take an objective view of the organization that they have helped to build or sustain. Also, experienced change agents should have skills and techniques that will facilitate the diagnostic process. The result of this process is typically a set of goals specifying the changes that the OD intervention is expected to produce.

A third activity that occurs during the unfreezing stage of OD is planning the actual intervention. Here again, the change agent's expertise comes into play in selecting methods that are best suited for meeting the goals identified earlier. Two special points must be raised here. First, you should be aware by now that given the complex nature of organizational systems, there can be no *one* procedure that will be useful in all situations. A technique that solves a problem for Peter's Pan Pizza may not be of much use in another organization, nor for other problems within PPP itself. Consequently, organizations should be wary of consultants and change agents who advocate one best way to solve all types of problems. An effective OD change agent should be familiar with a variety of techniques, and she must be able to recognize when the skills offered will not help the organization, and in such cases withdraw her services.

The second point concerns the two basic forces identified by Lewin (1958): forces to maintain the status quo and forces for change. Ideally, the involvement of management and other employees during the early phases of OD will help reduce the pressure to maintain the status quo. However, as specific plans for change are laid, resistance to the plans is likely to grow. Organizational members may be concerned that OD will cost more than its benefits are worth, or they may believe that the planned changes will alter their jobs in unpleasant ways, or they simply may not like change. For example, the changes mentioned in the opening memo for this chapter seem to benefit the Flavio's divisions, which are responsible for frozen and prepared foods, more than the Peter's Pan Pizza divisions, which are responsible for pizza restaurants and franchising. It is important that this resistance be anticipated, and that plans be made for dealing with it.

Stage Two: Change. The second stage of the OD process involves implementation of the plans developed by the change agent, in conjunction with management. Again, resistance is likely to be a problem, particularly if the employees affected by the change (which could be *all* employees) are not prepared. Involving workers in the actual change process may re-

duce this resistance by giving them a sense of "ownership" of the changes. That is, by participating in the implementation of the plans, workers may see the changes as being *their* changes, rather than changes imposed by external agents.

Another issue in the implementation phase of OD is transfer of effects. As we said before, most traditional OD techniques emphasize interpersonal relationships and skills; they may also involve training that occurs away from the workplace. When training takes place outside the work context, there is always concern about whether changes that occur during training will recur when the employee is back on the job. We will not discuss transfer of training in any detail here (see Chapter 7), but you should be aware that in the implementation of organizational change, the transfer of behavioral changes to the workplace is an important issue. Of particular concern in OD is the presence of a supportive environment following the intervention. If coworkers are critical of, or unresponsive to, the changed behavior of employees who have undergone OD training, the changes are unlikely to be maintained.

Stage Three: Refreezing. The third stage of Lewin's model of organizational change is **refreezing**. Although the goal of OD is to change the status quo, once the desired changes have occurred it is necessary to make them permanent. That is, a new status quo, incorporating the changes introduced in the change stage, replaces the old. Actually, a number of distinct processes can be identified in the refreezing stage.

The first of the processes involves evaluation of the OD intervention and rediagnosis of the organization's status. Clearly, if the intervention did not have the intended effects or if it had undesirable effects, then it would be foolish to make any changes permanent. The effectiveness of OD in general is a topic that has generated a great deal of debate among organizational researchers, and we will examine that debate in a later section of this chapter. For now, keep in mind that without proper evaluation of change programs, there will always be questions about their effectiveness.

Assuming that an OD program has been shown to be effective, the company will want to make the program and the changes associated with it a permanent part of the organization. This is known as **institutionalization of change**, and represents formal approval of the change. Institutionalization may take a variety of forms, such as alterations to organizational structure, new training programs, changes in supervisor-subordinate relations, or virtually any other change dictated by the nature of the OD program. Of course, management can easily institutionalize some changes, such as changes in formal organizational policy, but it is not as easy to institutionalize others, such as those involving the nature of interpersonal relations between employees and supervisors. Resistance to institutionalizing changes may occur if there is no clear evidence for the effectiveness of the changes or if the changes are complex and require a large number of individuals or groups (possibly with incompatible goals) to work together. Again, we see the importance of anticipating resistance to OD, and the benefits of involving those who will be affected by OD in the planning and implementation stages.

Part of the refreezing process may also involve attempts to export successful OD interventions to other parts of the organization. That is, change is often planned and introduced on a limited scale, and if effective it is spread to other units and divisions that were not involved in the original program. This appears to be a logical way of doing things. When the intervention is a failure, a great deal of time and money may be saved by limiting the scope of the unsuccessful change. However, just because a program worked in one unit of an organization is no guarantee that it will have similar effects in other units. In fact, such factors as a lack of top-management support, differences in technology, union resistance, and the incompatibility of

the changes with existing policies and structures have been found to inhibit the spread of organizational change, making such diffusion rare (Walton, 1975). We might expect this sort of problem if OD changes first developed in the Flavio's divisions were exported to the Peter's Pan Pizza divisions.

Finally, we should recognize that the refreezing stage of organizational change is a relative phenomenon. As we have said before, given the dynamic nature of organizations and the environments within which they operate, the need for change is constant. Organizational change is therefore a cycle of events, with successful change followed by a rediagnosis of the organization's health, followed by additional change efforts, and so on. What we said at the beginning of the chapter about organizational change being constant also applies to planning for organizational change.

Examples of Popular OD Interventions

It's possible that the diagnosis phase of OD will detect situations that call for interventions at individual, group, or organizational levels. Consequently, although the emphasis of OD is on problems affecting the entire organization, intervention techniques are often aimed at the group or individual levels. Examples of popular OD interventions that focus on each of these levels are given in the following sections.

It is also possible to classify OD interventions in terms of *how* they attempt to bring about organizational change. For example, many OD methods focus on improving workers' performance, attitudes, and perceptions by directly affecting the workers. These approaches have been labeled "human-process interventions." Other approaches are designed to alter the work context, work methods, or worker relationships, and have been called "technostructural interventions" (Friedlander & Brown, 1974). As you might imagine, virtually any planned change activity might fall into one of these categories, and in fact we discuss several techniques that are easily classified as technostructural interventions in other chapters (for example, flextime). In this chapter we will focus on human-process interventions, giving examples of these techniques at several levels in the organization.

Individual Change: Laboratory Training. Perhaps the best-known OD technique is laboratory training, also known as sensitivity training. Laboratory training was discussed in Chapter 7 ("Personnel Training"), so we will not describe it in detail here. As an OD technique, however, laboratory training is designed to improve the interpersonal skills of employees, primarily of managers. As we said in Chapter 7, there are questions about how well the effects of laboratory training transfer to the workplace, as well as concerns that some participants experience unacceptable levels of distress as a result of the training procedures.

Group Change: Team Building and Survey Feedback. Whereas laboratory training is intended to provide individual workers with interpersonal skills that will benefit the organization, the next two techniques are designed to change entire groups of workers. Team building is in many ways the group-level counterpart of laboratory training. Its purpose is to help people with related or interdependent jobs to examine the ways in which their "team" works together, to identify strengths and weaknesses, and to develop plans to improve team functioning. Although team building does emphasize interpersonal interaction, as does laboratory training, it is more task-oriented. That is, there is greater emphasis on changes that will improve specific aspects of team performance. Team building begins with a diagnostic meeting. During this session the members of the team, along with the change agent, discuss the current level of team functioning in an open, unstructured format. Each member of the group is allowed time to present his or her views on what the strengths and weaknesses of the team are, and

what changes are needed to improve team effectiveness. These viewpoints then serve as stimuli for discussion, which, if all goes well, culminates in an agreed-upon list of desirable changes for the team. Later sessions are then dedicated to developing plans to implement these changes.

Survey feedback is another OD technique that can be used to improve group functioning, but unlike team building it can also be helpful in examining either the effectiveness of the total organization or the relationships between work units. Survey feedback entails systematically collecting data from and about the group or groups in question, summarizing the data, and then feeding the results back to all of the group members. Depending on the total size of the group, one or more workshop sessions are held to discuss the feedback, to identify problems revealed in the data, and to plan action to solve those problems. Survey feedback is therefore used primarily for diagnostic purposes because the interventions endorsed by the group members will depend on the nature of the group and the problems that have been identified. To be successful, survey feedback requires reliable and valid measures of group and organizational characteristics, the results must be presented in an easy-to-understand manner, and change agents must be able to conduct group workshops or discussions characterized by free and open expression of ideas.

Organization-Wide Change: Leadership Grid® and Management by Objectives. Finally, there are OD techniques that are applied to entire organizational systems. These techniques are appropriate when the problems facing the organization are widespread or when there is a desire to ensure that the changes have an organization-wide impact. The **Leadership Grid** intervention (originally called the Managerial Grid), among the most popular OD techniques, was developed as a way to improve the functioning of total organizations (Blake & Adams, 1991; Blake & Mouton, 1964, 1985). The basic

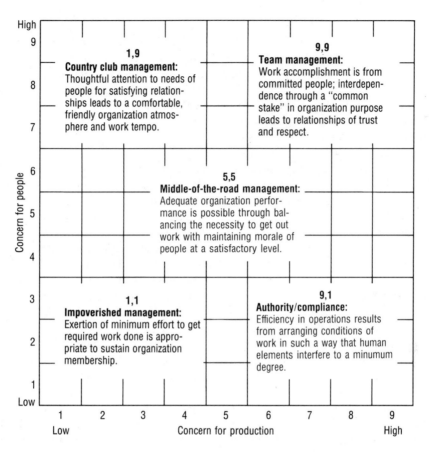

FIGURE 12.6
The Leadership Grid
SOURCE: From *Leadership Dilemmas–Grid Solutions* (p. 29), by R. R. Blake and A. Adams McCansey. Copyright © 1991 by Scientific Methods, Inc. Reproduced by permission.

premise is that leadership style can be defined in terms of two dimensions. The first dimension is **concern for people**, which reflects managers' interest in subordinates' well-being, and their relationships with subordinates. The second dimension is **concern for production**, which includes managers' interest in accomplishing the production tasks of their unit. Each of these dimensions is represented by a 1-to-9 scale, which together form the Leadership Grid (see Figure 12.6). Each cell within the Grid represents a different managerial style. Included in Figure 12.6 are descriptions of five illustrative

styles. As you can see, the 1,1 style of management involves little concern for either production or people, and is essentially a "do nothing" approach to management. The 1,9-oriented manager, often called the "country-club" manager, emphasizes the well-being of subordinates at the expense of production, whereas the 9,1-oriented manager, or authoritarian manager, does the opposite, ignoring interpersonal relationships and stressing production. The "middle-of-the-road" or 5,5-oriented manager has a balanced emphasis on people and production, but neither concern is strong. Finally, the

9,9-oriented manager has a strong concern for both production and people, and is the ideal for all organizations. The Leadership Grid procedure is designed to promote 9,9 leadership throughout an organization.

As we said, the Leadership Grid is a very popular OD approach. Thousands of organizations throughout the world have used the Grid, hundreds of thousands of managers have participated in these programs, and the approach is widely accepted (Using the Managerial Grid, 1974). Unfortunately, there is little empirical research on the Leadership Grid, and therefore little support for it, a problem shared with many OD interventions. We also believe that the emphasis on two dimensions of leadership style is overly simplistic. Concern for production and concern for people are conceptually similar to the Ohio State leadership factors of initiating structure and consideration; as we saw in Chapter 10, these factors are, at best, an incomplete explanation for the effects of managerial behavior.

Another organization-wide OD technique is **management by objectives**, or MBO. Unlike Grid management, which is highly structured and fairly similar from organization to organization, MBO has taken a variety of forms over the years. Szilagyi and Wallace (1987) identified eight steps common to most MBO programs (see Box 12.3). The key elements are identifying organizational goals, setting specific goals for employees that will help achieve the organization's goals, and evaluating employees' progress toward meeting those individual goals.

In Chapter 8 we saw that setting specific, difficult goals was an effective way to improve employees' performance. It is therefore not surprising that MBO has attracted a great deal of attention and has become one of the most popular OD techniques. Another reason for the popularity of MBO is undoubtedly its flexibility, which allows it to be applied to a wide variety of issues. For example, motivation and productivity problems can be addressed by means of the goal-setting procedures; sensitivity to changing environmental conditions is ensured by the planning and diagnosis steps; and up-to-date information on individual, group, and organizational performance is made available throughout the MBO cycle by regularly scheduled reviews.

Evaluation of Organizational Development

So far we have not said very much about the effectiveness of organizational development. One reason for this is that despite the widespread use and acceptance of OD, for years there was relatively little systematic evaluation of its effects, and even today many OD techniques have not been adequately studied. This is true even for some of the most-used techniques. Much of the popular support for OD techniques is based on testimonials from managers who have used them and are satisfied with the results. As students of psychology, however, we should all be wary of this sort of "evidence" (reaction criteria) concerning OD. There is, in fact, research suggesting that when managers have invested a great deal of time and money in a program—as would be the case with any OD intervention—they will tend to maintain their support for the program, even when it has clearly failed (Staw, 1981). Thus, it is possible that the popular support for OD programs does not reflect actual intervention effectiveness.

The concern over OD effectiveness has generated considerable debate. One of the more intriguing contributions to the debate was the work of Terpstra (1981), who examined the relationship between the results of OD evaluation research and the methodological rigor of the research. OD evaluation research is designed to determine whether or not a particular intervention had its desired effects. Methodological rigor refers to how well the research was designed from a scientific standpoint; the less rigorous the research, the less faith you can place in the results. Terpstra found that more rigorous evaluation research was less likely to find evidence

BOX 12.3 Steps in MBO Programs

STEP 1: DIAGNOSIS. This first step concerns the preliminary activities that are directed toward an understanding of the important employee needs, jobs, technology, and issues in the organization.

STEP 2: PLANNING. Involved in this MBO step are issues related to the overall goals and strategies of the organization, receiving management commitment to the MBO process, and training and development in learning how to use the technique.

STEP 3: DEFINING THE EMPLOYEE'S JOB. Possibly one of the most difficult steps, the employee is required to describe his or her particular job, its content, duties, requirements, and responsibilities. The important aspect of this step is that before individual goals can be set, one must know what work is being done.

STEP 4: GOAL SETTING. The employee initiates the superior-subordinate interaction by developing a set of goals for the upcoming period, usually one year. Concern is shown for the type of goal, setting priorities, target dates, and methods of measurement.

STEP 5: SUPERIOR REVIEW. The employee's superior reviews the initial goals, offers suggestions for improvement, and so on.

STEP 6: JOINT AGREEMENT. Steps 4 and 5 are repeated until both the employee and the manager agree on the established set of goals for the period.

STEP 7: INTERIM REVIEW. During the period of evaluation, the employee and manager get together to review the progress toward goal accomplishment. These meetings can be scheduled for once, twice, or more during the year. The focus of the interim reviews is not only to see what progress has been made but to adjust the goals should new information or changing environmental events become important.

STEP 8: FINAL REVIEW. At the end of the goal-setting period, the employee and manager formally get together to review the results. Emphasis is placed on analysis, discussion, feedback, and input to the next MBO cycle. At the end of this step, the cycle is repeated for the next period.

SOURCE: From *Organizational Behavior and Performance*, 4th ed. (pp. 133–135), by A. D. Szilagyi, Jr., and M. J. Wallace, Jr. Copyright © 1987 by Scott, Foresman and Company. Reprinted by permission.

of OD effectiveness. That is, research that used control groups, random assignment of subjects, and sophisticated statistical analyses was less likely to report that the OD intervention had positive effects on organizations. To explain this finding, Terpstra suggested that because the results of less rigorous research are often ambiguous, there is an unconscious bias on the part of OD researchers to interpret the results of these studies as supporting OD. He also thought that the high expectations of, and pressure from, top management might contribute to this bias.

Similarly negative conclusions about the evidence of OD effectiveness have been presented by others (for example, Alderfer, 1977; Porras & Berg, 1978; Woodman & Sherwood, 1980). A number of alternative explanations for Terpstra's (1981) findings have been suggested, however (Bass, 1983). Rather than a bias *favoring* OD on the part of those using less rigorous research, there may be a bias *against* OD on the part of those using more rigorous research. Also, OD interventions may be more relevant to "socioemotional" issues such as employee commitment and the integration of individual and organizational interests than to productivity and profit. Because these socioemotional variables are difficult to measure reliably, finding positive OD effects is less likely. Indeed, one study found that less rigorous OD studies were more likely to have positive results, but only when criteria such as attitudes, motivation, openness, and trust were used to measure success. When criteria such as productivity, turnover, efficiency, or other more objective outcomes were used, there was no positive bias in favor of methodologically weaker studies (Woodman & Wayne, 1985).

Other explanations include (1) the possibility that a given OD intervention may move the organization toward one goal while unintentionally moving it away from another, thereby canceling any overall effect, or (2) that more rigorous research examines short-term effects when, in fact, OD effects tend to be long term (Bass, 1983). Thus, whereas there may be biases for or against reporting beneficial OD effects among groups of OD researchers, biases are difficult to prove either way. However, the huge number of assertions of OD success, although often not documented with empirical data, cannot all be the result of bias, and the sheer weight of these numbers suggests that OD has some positive effect. Given the complexity of most OD interventions and the difficulties involved in conducting rigorous research in organizations, well-controlled OD evaluation research is difficult to design, and consequently rare (Bass, 1983).

More recently, meta-analyses of OD research have found more encouraging results. OD interventions were found to raise worker productivity by a modest degree, and although the effectiveness of specific interventions varied, as a group OD techniques were shown to be more effective than earlier reviews had suggested (Guzzo, Jette, & Katzell, 1985). Also, a separate meta-analysis found that OD had positive but variable effects on workers' attitudes (Neuman, Edwards, & Raju, 1989). The effects were stronger for higher-level employees, and a number of analyses showed *larger* effects for *more rigorous* studies, in contrast to Terpstra's (1981) findings. Further, multifaceted interventions, combining both human-process and technostructural techniques, were the most effective.

Another explanation for the ambiguity regarding OD effectiveness is based on the three types of change in training criteria mentioned in Chapter 7 (Golembiewski, Billingsley, & Yeager, 1976). Real changes in the criteria in which a researcher is interested are known as **alpha change**. In terms of OD research, an example of alpha change would be a team-building effort that resulted in increased worker satisfaction. The failure to find such change could be because the OD resulted in one of the other types of change, beta change or gamma change.

Beta change is when the intervention results in a change in the way in which the criterion is measured. In this case, the team building may have raised workers' expectations about how high their satisfaction might someday be. If so, although they found the OD experience to be positive, using their new expectations as a benchmark they might report experiencing *lower* satisfaction after OD than they had reported before OD. **Gamma change** is when OD results in a redefinition of the construct that the criterion is attempting to measure. An example would be team building that caused workers to redefine what job satisfaction meant to them, perhaps downplaying the importance of economic factors such as pay and increasing their emphasis on interpersonal relationships. The effects of this type of change would be unpredictable, and would depend on pre- and post-OD perceptions of both economic and interpersonal factors. In any case, to the extent that virtually all OD evaluation research has focused exclusively on alpha changes, the possible existence of beta and gamma changes makes it difficult to draw any meaningful conclusions about the effects of OD.

Another factor in implementing successful OD programs is the match between the values inherent the programs and the values of the organization or the society in which the changes will take place. To the extent that an OD tech-

---

BOX 12.4 Varying Dimensions of National Social Cultures

- *Power Distance.* The extent to which a society accepts the fact that power in institutions and organizations is distributed unequally.

- *Uncertainty Avoidance.* The extent to which a society feels threatened by uncertain and ambiguous situations by providing career stability, establishing more formal rules, not tolerating deviant ideas and behaviors, and believing in absolute truths and the attainment of expertise.

- *Individualism.* Implies a loosely knit framework in which people are supposed to take care of themselves and their immediate families only, as opposed to collectivism, which is characterized by a tight social framework in which people distinguish between in-groups and out-groups, and expect their in-group to look after them, and in exchange feel they owe absolute loyalty to the in-group.

- *Masculinity.* The extent to which the dominant values in society are "masculine," that is, assertiveness, the acquisition of money and things, and not caring for others, the quality of life, or people.

SOURCE: From "Motivation, Leadership, and Organization: Do American Theories Apply Abroad?" by G. Hofstede, 1980, *Organizational Dynamics, 9,* 45–46. Adapted by permission.

---

nique relies upon values that are incompatible with those of the company or of the larger community, it is unlikely to be successful. To illustrate the importance of social culture in OD, consider the four dimensions along which national cultures have been found to vary (see Box 12.4). The values implied by OD, as it is generally practiced in the United States, reflect low power distance, low uncertainty avoidance, low masculinity, and medium individualism. However, typical U.S. values are more closely associated with medium power distance, low uncertainty avoidance, high masculinity, and high individualism. Given the contrast between these two sets of values, it is not surprising that the success of OD has not been consistently demonstrated. In fact, an examination of 40 industrialized nations found that 33, or 82.5%, had values that were very different from those promoted by typical OD programs (Jaeger, 1986). Given this, guidelines have been presented in order to ensure compatibility between OD and societal values (see Box 12.5). Failure to

consider the possibility of resistance to programs that promote values incompatible with the company's is likely to result in resistance to the programs and their ultimate failure.

What, then, can we say about organizational development? OD has many supporters and many critics. The question of whether or not OD techniques are effective is critical, for if they are not, then many millions of dollars are being wasted each year. Unfortunately, the most honest conclusion that we can draw is that the evidence is inconclusive. This is due in some cases to the low quality of OD evaluation research, but we believe that a more important contributor is the nature of OD itself. By trying to deal with problems in dynamic, complex systems and by focusing on some of the more abstract, perceptual processes within those systems, OD has staked out a territory in which effectiveness may be impossible to demonstrate. Although the identification of alpha, beta, and gamma changes offers hope that measurement of different types of OD effects may clarify

---

BOX 12.5 Guidelines for Compatibility between OD and Social Values

1. Evaluate the rankings of the dimensions of culture in the given situation.
2. Make a judgment as to which values are the most deeply held and unlikely to change.
3. Evaluate the "problem-appropriate" interventions' rankings on the dimensions of culture.
4. Choose the intervention that would clash least with the most rigidly held values.
5. Incorporate process modifications in the proposed intervention to fit with the given cultural situation.

SOURCE: From "Organization Development and National Culture: Where's the Fit?" by A. M. Jaeger, *Academy of Management Review*, 11, 189. Copyright © 1986 by The Academy of Management. Reprinted by permission.

---

things, the problems of achieving rigorous control in OD research will continue to plague these efforts. In the end, the decision to use or not to use OD will remain subjective, based on the experience and best judgment of management, and the best advice of change agents who are familiar with the relative merits of a variety of OD interventions.

Chapter Summary

Change is a constant phenomenon in organizations and, ideally, it should be anticipated and controlled. Some types of change, however, are beyond the ability of organizational personnel to foresee, and can be dealt with only after the fact. Two types of change that can be controlled are job and task design and organizational development.

Job design is concerned with how to design or change jobs to maximize worker effectiveness. Early job-design efforts, such as those based on scientific management, stressed job simplification and worker specialization. These programs proved to be ineffective in the long run because of their negative impact on workers' attitudes. Following the advent of the human relations movement, job-design theories focused on helping workers achieve a sense of accomplishment by expanding the scope of their jobs. The results of these efforts were inconsistent.

The most widely known job-design theory is the Hackman and Oldham job characteristics model, which is based on the notion that properly designed jobs can satisfy psychological needs, such as those in Maslow's need hierarchy. Hackman and Oldham described five critical job characteristics that they believed determine certain critical psychological states, which in turn influenced important work-related criteria. Research on this model has been mixed, however, and although there is evidence that the job characteristics in the model are important, they are not a sufficient basis for a comprehensive theory of job design. Alternative theories of job design, which consider aspects of jobs not included in the job characteristics model, have been proposed to address these shortcomings.

Organizational development (OD) is the planned use of interventions designed to en-

INTEROFFICE MEMO

To: All vice presidents and senior vice presidents

From: J. A. MacKeven, Human Resources Coordinator

The Human Resources staff has recently completed its evaluation of the potential impact of entry into vending and institutional sales. I would like to thank each of you for the cooperation my staff received from the people in your divisions. Your managers and supervisors helped make our job much easier.

As most of you probably know, feasibility studies have shown that the best locations for any expansion along these lines are at our current Flavio's plants. This is due to (1) the similarities between the proposed new products and Flavio's current products, (2) a desire on the part of top management to avoid duplication of management functions, and (3) tax incentives from several of the municipalities in which Flavio's plants are currently located, which make it financially attractive to expand rather than build totally new facilities. I mention these points because they have had a significant impact on the recommendations that we at Human Resources have developed.

It is certain that if the expansion is carried out, we will have a dramatic increase in the number of workers in the Flavio's facilities, and a relatively smaller increase in the number of supervisors and managers. In order not to overburden our supervisory staff, we recommend that the jobs in these plants be expanded in terms of the decision-making responsibility held by the typical rank-and-file worker. Further, we believe that effective use of this additional responsibility will be promoted if the jobs are also expanded in terms of the variety of tasks that workers perform. That is, effective decisions are more likely to be made by workers if they have greater familiarity with the entire production process. In addition to addressing the problem of relatively few managers, these changes in the jobs should have some positive motivational effect on the workers.

Of course, the degree to which these types of changes can be made depends on the nature of individual jobs and work groups. To that end, we are also proposing that two activities be completed prior to further planning. First, we need to assess carefully the task requirements of the new jobs and the skill and ability requirements of those tasks. Second, because of the concern expressed by some managers and supervisors that there could be resistance to these changes, team-building exercises should be conducted. All members of a given work group will participate in a series of these exercises, examining how the proposed changes will affect the group, and developing group proposals to deal with any anticipated problems. These proposals will be incorporated into any job or work-group changes whenever feasible.

A more detailed description of our proposals, and the rationale for them, will be sent to you next week. Please feel free to comment on these proposals as you see fit.

courage organizational self-examination and to improve organizational effectiveness and health. Different OD techniques focus on individuals, groups, or total organizations, but nearly all can be analyzed in terms of Lewin's unfreezing-change-refreezing model of change. Despite its widespread acceptance and use, there is only limited evidence of OD's effectiveness. This may be due to problems with the actual OD techniques, the inadequacies of OD evaluation research, or the use of inappropriate types of change in OD models. In any case, OD interventions should be used with a certain degree of caution.

Review Questions and Exercises

1. Dr. MacKeven stated that the fact that the new operations will, if approved, be located in existing Flavio's plants had a significant impact on her recommendations (see memo, p. 431). What do you think was the nature of that impact? How might her recommendations have been different if new factories were being planned?

2. Explain the theoretical basis for Dr. MacKeven's recommendation that the jobs of Flavio's workers be expanded. Is that basis sound? Why or why not?

3. Dr. MacKeven recommended that the "task requirements" and the "skill and ability requirements" of the expanded jobs be assessed. What procedure is she advocating? Given what you have learned in earlier chapters, describe a series of steps that she might take in making these two assessments.

4. Describe how the team-building exercises mentioned by Dr. MacKeven would help overcome resistance to change. What other positive effects might they have? What negative effects? What should Dr. MacKeven and her staff do to ensure the success of these exercises?

CHAPTER 13

Work Conditions and the Work Environment

LEARNING POINTS

After studying this chapter, you should

❏ be able to explain what shift work is, and describe the effects of working different shifts on workers' attitudes and behaviors;

❏ be able to discuss the merits and drawbacks of compressed workweeks, including practical problems encountered when trying to establish compressed schedules;

❏ be able to describe a typical flextime schedule, and explain the theoretical and practical advantages and disadvantages of this system;

❏ understand the nature of light, noise, and the factors that contribute to the sensation of heat; you should also be able to describe the effects of illumination, noise levels, and thermal conditions on workers;

❏ be able to explain what an accident is, evaluate the concepts of accident "proneness" and accident liability, and describe an effective accident-prevention program; and

❏ understand what human factors are, and be able to describe the concept of the "worker-machine system."

IN PREVIOUS CHAPTERS WE STRESSED the importance of the environment within which an organization operates. This is most clearly illustrated by open systems theory (Chapter 11), which takes the view that organizations are embedded in a complex environmental network from which they draw their resources and into which they distribute their products and services. The importance of the external environment was also seen in our discussion of employee selection (Chapter 6). That is, the skills that exist in the available labor pool will to a great extent determine an organization's recruiting efforts, and the effectiveness of whatever selection system the organization implements. Those skills will also have an impact on the training programs needed to help new employees acquire necessary skills (Chapter 7). We have also considered the psychological environment, or culture, within the organization, and the ways in which shared values and perceptions might influence individual and organizational performance (Chapter 11).

In this chapter we will continue to examine the environment of the organization but from a very different perspective. Specifically, the environment that we are referring to now is the environment within which employees must work on a day-to-day basis. That is, the

INTEROFFICE MEMO

To: J. A. MacKeven,
         Human Resources Coordinator

From: Andrew LeGette,
         Director of Wages and Benefits

I have been appointed to the management negotiating team for the upcoming contract negotiations with unions representing the organized shops within Flavio's. Although I am on the team primarily for dealing with wage and benefit demands, I have also been asked to look into the feasibility of offering some incentives outside the benefits package in return for union movement on whatever benefit demands are made. We can estimate the costs of most of these programs fairly easily, but we do not want to offer any-thing that might save money now if it will cost us more down the road. Of particular concern to top management are the effects that these programs might have on productivity, although top management is also interested in the probable effects on employee attitudes and commitment. I would like to have you or one of your staff prepare a report on the likely effects of instituting the following types of programs: four-day workweek; flex-time; and employee safety programs. We know that some of these things would be welcomed by the workers, but we don't want to bring them up at the negotiations unless we have good reason to believe that they will be beneficial to the company. We need the report early next month. Please let me know ASAP if this will be possible.

P.S. Feel free to suggest other nonpay incentives that would be desirable to workers and beneficial to the company.

environment that is defined by work schedules, physical conditions, and the equipment that workers use to perform their jobs. We will refer to these conditions collectively as the *work environment*. We will also examine the issue of job-related accidents, and the role of the work environment in their cause and prevention. In the opening memo to this chapter, Mr. LeGette suggested that programs to improve the work environment will not only be valued by workers but also prove to be valuable to Peter's Pan Pizza's "bottom line." Dr. MacKeven's task, as well as ours, is to see if this is indeed likely to be the case.

Work Conditions

An important component of the work environment is what we will call work conditions, aspects of employment or the workplace that do not directly determine worker behaviors, but rather have implications for the effectiveness of the behaviors, as well as employee reactions to their work. For example, the physical environment of the workplace represents one set of work conditions that we will discuss. How hot or cold the workplace is has little to do with the way in which workers who pack frozen anchovy treats do their jobs—the tasks involved do not change as a function of temperature. How the workers *feel* about their jobs, however, and perhaps how well they perform their jobs are likely to be affected by this type of physical characteristic. To the extent that work conditions can be manipulated to maximize employees' productivity and satisfaction, the individual workers and the entire organization stand to benefit.

Scheduling of Work

In recent decades, the traditional weekly work schedule has consisted of five eight-hour workdays, Monday through Friday, each begin-

ning about 8:00 A.M. and ending around 5:00 P.M. There have, of course, always been notable exceptions to this "normal" work schedule, such as firefighters who might be on duty for several consecutive days followed by several days off, or night security guards in office buildings who begin work when the rest of the work force goes home. Also, manufacturing industries, such as the automotive industry, have used shift-work schedules for many years. In shift-work schedules, one-third of the employees work the traditional "day shift" from, for example, 7:00 A.M. to 3:00 P.M.; one-third work "afternoons" or the "swing shift" from 3:00 P.M. to 11:00 P.M.; and the rest work "nights" or the "graveyard shift" from 11:00 P.M. until the day shift comes on again at 7:00 A.M. In her examination of the attitudes of Flavio's workers toward their working conditions, Dr. MacKeven will be likely to find that the perishability of the foods used in many of the frozen products requires that they be processed as rapidly as possible, and that shift work is therefore necessary. (As you might suspect, nothing is worse than an anchovy that has been sitting around since 3:00 the previous afternoon.) As the number of workers in manufacturing industries declines, and the number in service industries increases, it becomes less necessary for companies to operate around the clock, or even to operate at full capacity during normal business hours. The implications of traditional work schedules, and the possible benefits of alternative schedules, have therefore come under psychologists' scrutiny.

Shift Work. In 1991, 17.8% of workers in the United States were on shift work schedules (U.S. Bureau of the Census, 1993). For those who work the day shift, shift work is no different from the schedules of most workers. The work schedules of those who work the later shifts, however, can disrupt other aspects of their lives. For example, many shift workers are either asleep or at work during the evenings when their young children are home from school. Similarly, they are unavailable during the hours when most social activities take place, and they may find it difficult to make and keep necessary business and personal appointments. Although these may seem more like inconveniences than serious problems, research shows that shift work can have serious repercussions.

Reviews of the research on the effects of shift work have found that there are a number of negative consequences typically associated with working nontraditional shifts (Dunham, 1977). In addition to effects on social activity, such as reduced contact with friends, lower rates of participation in social organizations, and a higher rate of solitary leisure activities, shift workers experience a higher incidence of family-related problems, such as sexual difficulties, divorce, and restricted parent-child contact. Equally disturbing is the evidence that shift work has a variety of negative effects on physical health. For example, shift workers sleep fewer hours than their traditional-schedule counterparts, and their sleep tends to be interrupted more frequently. Problems associated with appetite, digestion, elimination (bowel movements), and upper gastrointestinal disorders such as ulcers are also found to be associated more strongly with shift work than with traditional schedules. Oddly, Dunham found no evidence that shift workers had poorer general health (for example, total number of health complaints) than day workers.

Although certain negative consequences may be associated with shift work, the way in which the shift schedules are managed may alleviate these problems. For example, one study found no differences between day- and night-shift nurses in terms of the extent to which the shift schedule interfered with their private lives, their reported levels of stress, and in the value they associated with time off work (Barton & Folkard, 1991). This study differed from those that found more negative consequences in that the nurses were allowed to choose day or night shifts freely. Thus, a degree of control over shift scheduling may help reduce some of the problems traditionally associated with shift work.

Evidence that shift work affects job satisfaction or work productivity is mixed; there are people who prefer one shift over the others and who are more productive on that shift than they are on the others. Alternatively, some people do not like shift work and do not perform well when they deviate from a traditional day schedule. Regarding satisfaction, Figure 13.1 shows the percentage of workers in one study who expressed various degrees of preference for shift work. The important things to notice are that contrary to what many people might expect, there is no universal dislike of shift work, and some people have definite preferences in favor of working specific shifts (Wedderburn, 1978). Again, control over shift schedules may have a positive effect on attitudes toward shift work. The nurses in the study described earlier were equally satisfied with their shift schedule, whether they worked days or nights (Barton & Folkard, 1991).

Although there seems to be little effect of shift work on general job satisfaction, some fairly large differences were found when more specific reactions to shift work were studied. For example, both afternoon- and night-shift workers were likely to say that working their shift restricted their social lives and "wasted their day," whereas day workers were more likely to say that their shift gave them more spare time and was good for their family life. Not all responses were quite so predictable, however. Afternoon-shift workers said that their jobs were less tiring, less likely to disturb their sleep, and more peaceful than did either day- or night-shift workers (Wedderburn, 1978).

Regarding productivity, Dunham (1977) cited several articles that either demonstrated or suggested that production is lower on night shifts than on day shifts. Two studies, however, showed that the effects of shift work on performance are not so clear (Malaviya & Ganesh K., 1976, 1977). Although these researchers found that day-shift workers in an Indian textile plant performed better than the same workers on an afternoon shift, they also found that there were

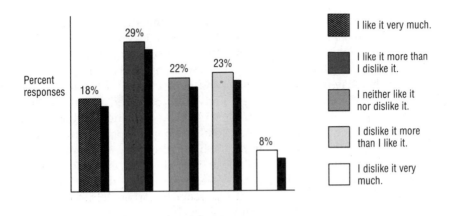

Percent responses

18%   29%   22%   23%   8%

I like it very much.

I like it more than
I dislike it.

I neither like it
nor dislike it.

I dislike it more
than I like it.

I dislike it very
much.

Question: "On the whole,
how do you feel about working
shifts?"

FIGURE 13.1
Expressed Preferences for Shift Work
SOURCE: From "Some Suggestions for Increasing the Usefulness of Psychological and Sociological Studies of Shiftwork," by A. A. I. Wedderburn, *Ergonomics, 21,* 829. Copyright © 1978 by Taylor & Francis, Ltd. Adapted by permission.

workers who were consistently more productive during the afternoon shift than they were on the day shift. Further, in the latter of the two studies they were able to evaluate the consistency of this shift difference in productivity for 18 workers who were in both studies. They found that for 16 of these workers, their relative day and afternoon productivity remained unchanged over the course of the intervening year, demonstrating that the effects of shifts on individual productivity can be consistent over time. We cannot be certain that these results would generalize to U.S. or Canadian workers, but we know of no specific reason to suspect cross-cultural differences in reactions to shift work.

It seems that shift work does have some negative effects on some workers, particularly regarding their physical health, social interactions, and family relationships. The effects of shift work on actual work behaviors and attitudes, however, are less consistent. On the basis of his review, Dunham (1977) concluded that many of the negative effects of shift work stem

from the fact that it interferes with the rhythms or cycles that govern normal human life. In particular, there is evidence of not only a 24-hour cycle of bodily functions (known as a circadian rhythm) but also a 24-hour cycle of social and personal functions on which people come to depend. Shift work upsets the biological rhythms, as evidenced by the numerous health problems mentioned above, and interferes with workers' efforts to coordinate their activities with the social rhythms of their communities. This can be a particularly severe hardship for dual-career or single-parent families, who must work nontraditional hours and maintain adequate child care. The nurses in the study by Barton & Folkard (1991), who freely chose day or night shifts, may have avoided some of these problems by selecting the shift that best fit their individual needs. Other shift workers, without the luxury of this choice, are more likely to experience conflicts and their negative consequences.

Although workers can eventually adjust to changes in the biological cycle, it may not be so easy to adjust the social cycle. For example, consider the case of the Flavio's factory in Jeddo, Michigan. This plant operates three shifts each day, and is the only industrial facility in town. It employs only a small percentage of Jeddo's population, however, because most of the residents are dairy farmers. Consequently, when the afternoon-shift workers leave work at 11:00 P.M., there is literally nothing for them to do, unless they want to drag their neighbors out of bed for a few hands of pinochle. The night-shift workers have a slightly different problem: everyone else in town is awake when they get off work, but at 7:00 in the morning there are few people with the time or inclination to socialize. Dunham suggested that there will be fewer problems associated with shift work in communities that adapt to accommodate the shift worker, because these communities will have a more flexible schedule of social activities. He also suggested that these are likely to be communities, unlike Jeddo, in which there is a relatively large proportion of shift workers.

Whether a particular worker is more or less satisfied or productive on one shift than another, afternoon and night shifts are typically perceived as being less desirable than day shifts. Either as an incentive to get workers to volunteer for these shifts or as additional compensation for those who are assigned to these shifts, most companies pay an hourly bonus to afternoon workers, and an even larger bonus to night workers. Although the bonuses may encourage workers to accept alternate-shift work, the extra pay cannot be expected to alleviate its negative physical, psychological, and social consequences.

In an apparent effort to be fair to all workers, some companies institute *rotating shifts*. In this type of schedule, workers "rotate" through the shifts, with one group working days for a period of time, then moving to afternoons, and finally to nights. The group that was originally working afternoons rotates to nights, and then to days, and so on (see Figure 13.2b). Rotating shifts in this way supposedly minimizes the negative effects of shift work because no one worker re-

mains on the afternoon or evening shifts for too long a period. Also, all workers have the opportunity to receive the shift bonus pay.

Rotating shifts is a fairly common practice, and in fact much of the research on shift work has not compared people working one shift with those on another but has followed the same group of people through two or more shifts and examined changes in their attitudes or behavior. For example, this technique was used to compare the performance of day and afternoon workers in research described earlier (Malaviya & Ganesh K., 1976, 1977). Because the rotation of shifts is designed to remedy some of the problems that accompany shift work, however, it is necessary to compare the behavior of workers on "fixed-shift" schedules with those on rotating-shift schedules. If the negative effects of shift work can be explained solely by the fact that shift workers work late hours and are alienated from normal social cycles, then rotating shifts could be beneficial. That is, by guaranteeing that each worker has at least one-third day-shift hours in a given period, the problems associated with working the later shifts should be reduced.

Several studies have specifically addressed the effectiveness of rotating-shift schedules. Jamal (1981) compared the work attitudes and the absenteeism and tardiness behaviors of Canadian hospital nurses and manufacturing employees who worked either fixed or rotating shifts. He reasoned that the negative effects of shift work would be amplified when shifts were rotated, because workers would be unable to develop routines that would allow them to cope with the demands of their work schedules. Workers on fixed shifts, however, would be able to develop such routines regardless of the shift on which they worked. The establishment of these routines should, according to Jamal, result in improved work attitudes and behaviors.

Consistent with his expectations, Jamal's (1981) results showed that fixed-shift workers were better off than their rotating-shift counterparts in terms of mental health, job satisfaction,

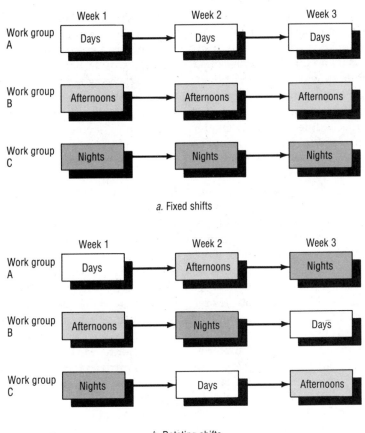

FIGURE 13.2
Fixed- and Rotating-Shift Schedules

organizational commitment, and social participation. Further, fixed-shift workers were absent and tardy less often, and had lower expectations of leaving their jobs. Part of the difference between Jamal's fixed- and rotating-shift subjects could have been due to the fact that most of his fixed-shift group worked days. His results, however, are consistent with other studies that demonstrate that fixed-shift workers, even those working nights, have fewer physical and psychological problems than rotating-shift workers (for example, Colligan, Frockt, & Tasto, 1979; Mott, Mann, McLoughlin, & Warwick, 1965; Taylor, 1967).

In another study involving rotating-shift schedules, Zedeck, Jackson, and Summers (1983) argued that individual differences in adaptation to shift schedules may be important in determining shift work's eventual effects. They analyzed questionnaire responses from more than 700 public utility employees who worked a 28-day rotating-shift schedule, consisting of six day shifts, seven afternoon shifts, and seven night shifts, with eight days off. Consistent with their expectations, the researchers found that there were indeed individual differences in responses to shift work. Workers who were most satisfied with the rotating-shift schedule had fewer physical complaints, such as digestion problems or muscle pain; had higher job satisfaction; were more satisfied with the time available to them for social and family activities; had more positive attitudes toward the organization; and were less tense and less tired. In a similar fashion, workers who expressed a desire for changes in the shift schedule reported a greater number of physical and psychological problems, as did workers who expressed a desire to leave the organization.

Zedeck, Jackson, and Summers (1983) suggested that an important factor in reactions to shift work is the ability to adjust to shift demands. That is, to the extent that workers adjust their nonwork lives to accommodate their work schedules, they will avoid many of the possible negative consequences of rotating shifts. Further, older subjects in this study had poorer health but were nonetheless more satisfied with the shift-work schedule than were younger workers. The researchers suggested that the poorer health of these older workers was due to the normal aging process rather than the effects of shift work, and that the longer a worker is exposed to shift work, the more fully she adapts, and the more willing she is to accept the schedule. Of course, it could also mean that the older workers who did not adapt to shift work had left the job before the study was conducted.

In summary, there is fairly solid evidence of negative physical, social, and psychological effects of shift work, and that these effects are magnified by the practice of rotating shifts. This suggests that part of the shift-work problem is adjusting to changes in routines and cycles of activity, although the inability of fixed-shift workers to coordinate their activities with the schedules of their family and friends also contributes to these problems. Perhaps the most important lesson from the research on shift work is that there are workers who prefer the afternoon and evening shifts, and that these workers tend to be more productive on those shifts. Consequently, in industries that must have continuous production (such as Flavio's

anchovy pastry factory) and must therefore use around-the-clock shift work, it would be beneficial to consider workers' preferences when assigning shifts (Barton & Folkard, 1991). Of course, day shifts are likely to remain the most popular time to work, so that it will not be possible to assign all workers to the shifts they want. There seems to be little reason, however, to force workers who prefer afternoon or night shifts to work days.

Nontraditional Workweeks. Most U.S. and Canadian workers, whether they work the traditional hours of 8:00 to 5:00 or some other shift, go to work five days a week at a fixed hour and work for eight hours each day. Deviations from this five-day, 40-hour schedule (also known as 5/40) have become more and more common in the past few decades, however. The changes typically involve variations in the number of days worked per week (and therefore the number of hours worked per day), or changes in workers' arrival and departure times. Examples of both variations on work schedules are examined below.

One common way to adjust the "normal" workweek is to maintain a 40-hour schedule for each worker, but to have that schedule completed in four days rather than five. This four-day, 40-hour schedule, or 4/40, is the most common example of a *compressed workweek*. Logic suggests that a 4/40 schedule will be popular with workers because it gives them a three-day weekend without losing a day's wages. Indeed, a review of research on compressed workweeks by Ronen and Primps (1981) found that most workers report being more satisfied with 4/40 schedules than with 5/40 schedules. Similar results were obtained in a field study of workers who were switched from 5/40 to 4/40 for four months, and then switched back to 5/40. After the switch to the compressed workweek, workers' reactions to their jobs (for example, general job satisfaction, organizational commitment, job involvement) improved, but after they changed back to a 5/40 schedule

Compressed work weeks can provide more time for family activities.

their reactions declined again (Dunham, Pierce, & Castañeda, 1987). This study also found that workers reported less interference between their work schedule and both activities with family and friends and access to services and events during the 4/40 portion of the study. The longer weekend associated with 4/40 may result in more positive attitudes because it allows workers to avoid these types of schedule conflicts. Of course, to the extent that workers are dissatisfied with their jobs they will probably prefer 4/40 simply because it requires one less day each week at work and not because it enables one additional day of leisure (Dunham & Hawk, 1977). Also, like shift work, ten-hour days can interfere with child-care arrangements

and social activities of dual-career or single-parent families.

There is little evidence that 4/40 has any consistent effect on the quantity or the quality of workers' output. Ronen and Primps' (1981) review found only a few studies that had examined the relationship between compressed workweeks and productivity. Two studies measured actual changes in production, and found that compressed schedules had no effect. Four out of five studies that examined employees' responses found that the workers believed that they had increased their productivity under compressed schedules. These results should be interpreted with caution, however, because they may be due to the generally positive attitudes that workers have toward compressed workweeks rather than to actual increases in productivity. Supervisor ratings of productivity showed improvement with compressed workweeks in three studies, but decreases in two others. The study by Dunham and his colleagues described above found that organizational effectiveness improved during the 4/40 stage of the study but declined after the workers returned to 5/40 (Dunham, Pierce, & Castañeda, 1987). As you can see, if compressed work schedules affect performance, it is in a relatively unpredictable fashion.

Ronen and Primps (1981) also summarized research on two productivity-related behaviors, fatigue and absenteeism. All five of the studies of fatigue found that it was more severe under compressed schedules than under traditional schedules. Three out of five studies reported that absenteeism decreased under compressed schedules.

Even if 4/40 schedules do not improve productivity over traditional 5/40 schedules, there may be sound economic reasons for an organization to consider changing to them. For example, if Flavio's could produce enough frozen pizza to meet demand by operating its factories 40 hours each week, it could save on heating, cooling, janitorial services, and other overhead expenses by operating four days a week rather than five.

Other types of businesses, however, would not be likely to benefit from 4/40. One type of organization for which 4/40 may be inappropriate is one that operates 24 hours a day. When an organization must operate 24 hours a day, whether because of high demand for a product (such as Flavio's frozen anchovy treats), the nature of the service being offered (such as those provided by hospitals), or production technology that cannot be easily stopped and restarted (such as that used in nuclear power facilities), it is virtually impossible to institute a 4/40 schedule. This is because in order to staff the organization for 24 hours, the length of shifts must be even divisors of 24. For example, two ten-hour (4/40) shifts per day would cover only 20 hours, and there would be four hours left that would have to be covered by overtime or some other costly arrangement. The common way to cover a 24-hour schedule is to use three eight-hour shifts, but this is at the cost of any benefits that a compressed workweek might provide. Breaugh (1983) suggested the only logical means by which a compressed workweek could be adapted to a 24-hour schedule, and that is to use two 12-hour shifts. For example, half of the workers could work a 3/36 schedule one week, and a 4/48 schedule the next, while the other half worked the opposite pattern. Because laws require that workers be paid overtime for hours in excess of 40 per week, there may be additional costs to using this type of schedule. However, it may be that eliminating one shift saves enough money in administrative costs relative to 5/40 that it would still be cost-effective for some companies to adopt 12-hour shifts.

The few studies that have investigated the effects of a 12-hour schedule have found that it may have positive effects on workers' attitudes. For example, workers who experienced a 12-hour shift had more positive attitudes toward that schedule than workers without such experience. It is not surprising, given the disruptions of social and biological cycles that result from shift work, that workers on the noon-to-midnight shift saw the 12-hour workday as more desirable than did workers on the midnight-to-noon shift (Breaugh, 1983). A study comparing Canadian coal miners on 12-hour shifts with miners on traditional shift schedules found that those on the compressed schedule were more satisfied with their family relationships, although on the average they spent less leisure time with their spouses. Further, the miners on 12-hour shifts had neither lower productivity nor more health complaints than the miners on the traditional shifts (Cunningham, 1989).

Although their research did not examine exactly 12-hour shifts, Foster, Latack, and Reindl (1979) found that a 3/38 workweek resulted in higher productivity than did a 5/40 workweek. They also found that workers who had actually worked the 3/38 schedule had more positive reactions to it than did workers who had not worked 3/38, similar to Breaugh's (1983) findings with 12-hour shifts. There were no effects, however, on workers' levels of job satisfaction. A later study of the 3/38 schedule found that preferences for the compressed workweek persisted over 18 months, and that participation in the decision to implement the 3/38 schedule, as well as job enrichment resulting from the change, predicted favorable attitudes. Reductions in sick time, personal leave, and overtime were also observed (Latack & Foster, 1985).

We are uncertain about the future of compressed workweeks. There is relatively little research on the effects of these schedules, particularly when you go beyond 4/40 into even longer workdays. However, there seem to be few negative effects on workers' performance or attitudes, and in most cases compressed schedules have been associated with increased satisfaction. For organizations that can fit them into their operations, compressed work schedules may be a viable method for improving worker attitudes while reducing overhead costs.

Flextime. Another popular variation on the traditional work schedule is **flextime,** where workers' arrival and departure times are variable, within certain limits, allowing them to tailor their workdays to meet their own unique needs. In 1991 more than 12 million workers in the United States, 15.1% of the work force, were on some sort of flexible schedule (U.S. Bureau of the Census, 1993). Most flextime programs include the following five components (Golembiewski & Proehl, 1978):

1. A "band width," or total number of hours to be worked each day;

2. A "core time," or period in the workday during which all full-time employees are required to be at work;

3. Flexible bands of hours before and after the core time, during which workers may arrive at work and depart for home, respectively;

4. "Banking," or carrying a balance of excess or deficient hours from one work period to the next—typically there is a limit to the number of hours that can be "banked"; and

5. Variable schedules, which give workers the authority to change their working hours from one period to the next without supervisory approval.

An example of a flextime system at Peter's Pan Pizza would be if workers in the finance units could come to work at any time between 7:00 A.M. and 10:00 A.M., and leave work at any time between 3:00 P.M. and 6:00 P.M., but must be at work between 10:00 A.M. and 3:00 P.M.

The logic behind flextime is fairly straightforward: flexibility in arrival and departure times is expected to reduce tardiness and absenteeism because it provides discretionary time for workers to perform tasks that would cause them to be late under more rigid schedules (Nollen, 1979). This is a particularly important benefit for two-career or single-parent families. In these families workers must frequently be absent in order to take children to school or to visit doctors, banks, and other businesses with fixed hours while still leaving time for normal family and social activities. Further, it has been hypothesized that flextime allows workers to select working hours during which they are most productive, thereby increasing organization effectiveness.

Organizations may benefit in other ways from a flextime system under certain circumstances. For example, because flextime virtually ensures that a company will be at least partially staffed beyond the traditional eight hours each day, it may be easier for customers and suppliers to do business with a company using flextime. Also, with companies such as Peter's Pan Pizza, which has facilities across the continent, communication between organizational units in different time zones should be more convenient with flextime.

Of course, there are situations that do not lend themselves to flextime, such as production facilities that require a certain number of tasks to be performed simultaneously. At Flavio's, for example, the cheese is the last ingredient to go onto a pizza before it is frozen, and it would not work to have the cheese sprinkler come to (or leave) work four hours before the people who put on the sauce and pepperoni. Flextime would also be difficult to implement if there was more than one shift, because flexible arrival and departure times would make it likely that the organization would be overstaffed at some times and understaffed at others.

Flextime may present particularly troublesome problems for supervisory personnel. It could, for example, be very difficult to coordinate the activities of workers who are coming and going at different times of the day. Of course, some jobs require less supervision and coordination than others, so this may not be a problem in all organizations, or even in all sections of a single organization. To the extent that workers must work together or supervisors must observe workers' performance, however, flextime may be a burden, requiring additional time and effort to coordinate workers' activities and provide for adequate supervision.

Ronen (1981) studied the effects of flextime on arrival and departure times for 162 Israeli workers, and found that the average times before and during flextime were very similar (see Table 13.1). Further, 83% of the workers developed and maintained a consistent individual arrival pattern; that is, they tended to arrive at work at about the same time each day. Also, 68% maintained a consistent departure pattern. For these consistent workers, the arrival and departure times centered around the preflextime average for arrivals and departures. Ronen also found that tardiness was lower under flextime. Prior to the institution of flextime, the average worker in the study was late for work six times a month; under flextime, 0.67 times a month. Ronen's general conclusion was that contrary to the fears of some managers, workers on flextime schedules come and go in predictable patterns, and that it is possible to plan and coordinate workers' activities with reasonable assurance that the workers will be there when you need them.

Flextime seems to offer a number of potential benefits for certain types of organizations. One fairly consistent effect of flextime is a reduction in worker absenteeism, although the exact nature of this effect varies from study to study (Harvey & Luthans, 1979; Narayanan & Nath, 1982; Ralston & Flannagan, 1985). For example, Golembiewski, Hilles, and Kagno (1974) found that flextime reduced long-term but not short-term (one day or less) paid absences; Kim and Campagna (1981), however, found a different pattern of results, with only short-term (two hours or less in a given day) unpaid absences being reduced by the program. The effects of flextime on attendance are consistent with arguments that schedule flexibility allows workers to deal with conflicts between work and nonwork demands (Staines & Pleck, 1986), and that the benefits of flextime most valued by flextime em-

TABLE 13.1   Distributions of Arrivals and Departures: Cumulative Percentage

	Present on the job at	Preflextime	Under flextime
Arrivals	06:30	0%	2%
	07:00	0%	11%
	07:30	65%	46%
	08:00	85%	69%
	08:30	95%	85%
	09:00	100%	92%
	10:00	100%	99%
	10:30	100%	100%
	Average	07:36 A.M.	07:44 A.M.
Departures	14:00	100%	100%
	14:30	98%	90%
	15:00	81%	73%
	15:30	40%	57%
	16:00	9%	39%
	16:30	4%	23%
	17:00	3%	16%
	18:00	0%	10%
	Average	03:17 P.M.	03:39 P.M.

Note: Results represent percentage of arrivals and departures, not percentage of employees.

SOURCE: From "Arrival and Departure Patterns of Public Sector Employees before and after Implementation of Flextime," by S. Ronen, *Personnel Psychology, 34*, 819. Copyright © 1981 by Personnel Psychology, Inc. Reprinted by permission.

ployees are those that allow the integration of work and nonwork roles (Ralston, 1989).

Less consistent is the effect of flextime on job satisfaction. Generally, workers express overwhelming support for flextime (Golembiewski & Proehl, 1978), and in some cases say that they are more satisfied under flextime schedules than under traditional schedules (Evans, 1973; Orpen, 1981; Partridge, 1973). For example, Dunham, Pierce, and Castañeda (1987) found that a switch to flextime was associated with improvements in 14 general work attitudes. However, there are also studies showing that flextime has no positive effect on job attitudes (Hicks & Klimoski, 1981; Narayanan &

Nath, 1982). Hicks and Klimoski noted that in most of the flextime research, workers were aware that they were being asked about their attitudes in order to evaluate the flextime program. Consequently, if the workers in these studies desired to keep the program, they may have biased their job satisfaction responses in a favorable direction.

Certainly, there seem to be adequate reasons for workers to want to maintain flextime. For example, under flextime workers had fewer travel problems, less role conflict, greater feelings of control, and more opportunities for leisure activities (Hicks & Klimoski, 1981). Similarly, flextime workers had more flexibility in attending to personal and work-related matters, and believed that they had improved work-group and superior-subordinate relations (Narayanan & Nath, 1982). Apparently, because neither study found higher job satisfaction under flextime, the benefits do not necessarily translate into greater satisfaction with the job itself.

The evidence for effects of flextime on productivity is also weak. For example, a study of the effects of a four-month flextime experiment on the productivity of five groups of clerical workers found that only two of the groups significantly increased their productivity over preexperimental levels (Schein, Maurer, & Novak, 1977). In one of the groups, however, the introduction of flextime was confounded with other structural and technological changes that could have accounted for the increase in performance. Similar results were found in a study of four work groups, of which only one showed a significant increase in productivity while on flextime (Kim & Campagna, 1981). Research on flextime among South African clerical personnel found that neither supervisory ratings of performance nor objective measures of productivity were affected (Orpen, 1981), and that flextime had no effects on measures of organizational effectiveness, including worker performance (Dunham, Pierce, & Castañeda, 1987).

Although there seems to be little evidence that flextime can have a positive impact on workers' performance, it may be that the extent of this impact depends upon the nature of the work being done. It has been suggested that flextime *can* have positive effects on performance when workers must share resources. That is, under traditional, fixed eight-hour workdays, the physical resources necessary to perform a job are available only during that eight-hour period. If workers must compete for the use of those resources, overall performance may suffer. By extending the available workday and giving workers flexibility to set their own schedules, flextime makes shared resources more readily available to more workers, potentially increasing performance. This notion was tested in a study that compared the effects of flextime on workers who had to share computer equipment versus workers who did not have to share equipment (Ralston, Anthony, & Gustafson, 1985). Consistent with the predictions, flextime had no effect on the productivity of the workers who did not have to share their equipment with others, but it had a dramatic effect (24% increase) on the productivity of the workers who shared equipment.

To summarize the research on flextime, it seems to have a positive effect on attendance, although there is some conflict in the literature as to whether it reduces long-term or short-term absences. Workers seem to like flextime schedules, but flextime has not been found to have reliable effects on employees' job satisfaction. There is no evidence that flextime increases employee productivity across the board, although it may improve performance in certain types of jobs. However, there is no evidence that flextime has any *negative* effect on productivity (Schein, Maurer, & Novak, 1977; Kim & Campagna, 1981). The decision to use flextime should therefore probably be based on a need to reduce absenteeism and tardiness, provided that the organization can accommodate partial staffing early and late in the workday.

Physical Conditions of the Workplace

So far we have discussed the effects of *when* people work. Once a worker is on the job, however, he is confronted by a variety of other work conditions that may have effects on both attitudes and performance. The most obvious of these are the physical conditions of the workplace. Each of us is familiar with situations in which physical variables in the environment make the performance of even simple tasks very difficult and frustrating. For example, as a student you may have found it very hard, at times, to concentrate on reading your assignments because of disturbing noises from a neighbor's room or apartment. In an industrial setting, noise may be combined with uncomfortable temperatures, smoke or other pollution, and poor lighting, just to name a few examples. In the following sections we examine some of these physical variables, and evaluate their possible effects on workers' behavior.

Illumination. The study of illumination, or lighting, has a long history in psychology, as well as in various related fields. You may recall that the Hawthorne studies were designed to examine the effects of illumination on workers' performance (Chapters 1 and 8), among other issues. Since that time, research on illumination has become far more sophisticated. Much of this research has been conducted by people known as *illuminating engineers*, who concern themselves with complex physical concepts with which we need not be concerned here. The fact that lighting can have important effects on performance, however, is not in doubt, and so we'll present a few general concepts and findings.

To understand the effects of illumination, you must understand what illumination is and something about how it is typically measured. First, light sources have a certain intensity that is measured in units called **candelas**. Second, light is thought of as flowing from its source, much the same as water flows through a pipe.

Some working conditions are more hazardous than others.

The flow of water can be expressed in terms of gallons per minute; the flow of light from its source is expressed in terms of units called **lumens**. The flow from a 1-candela light source is 12.57 lumens. Third, the amount of light that strikes the surface of an object is known as **illumination**. Illumination is measured in terms of lumens per unit of area, with two standard measures in common use: 1 lumen per square foot is known as a **footcandle**, which is used primarily in the United States, and 1 lumen per square meter is known as a **lux**, which is an international, metric-based measure. Because light typically moves in all directions from its source, the surface area used to define illumination must be a section of a sphere in order for

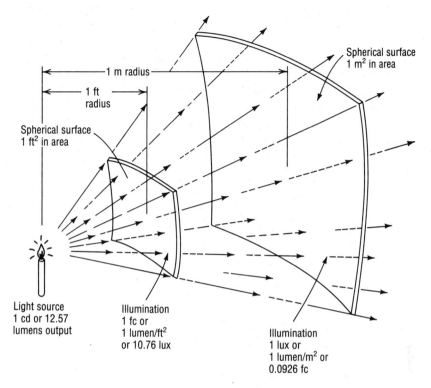

1 m radius

1 ft radius

Spherical surface 1 m² in area

Spherical surface 1 ft² in area

Light source
1 cd or 12.57
lumens output

Illumination
1 fc or
1 lumen/ft²
or 10.76 lux

Illumination
1 lux or
1 lumen/m² or
0.0926 fc

FIGURE 13.3
The Distribution of Light from a Light Source
SOURCE: Illustration courtesy of General Electric Lighting Business Group.

the definition to be technically correct. The relationships between candelas, lumens, and measures of illumination are shown in Figure 13.3. As you can see in the figure, a 1-candela light source casts 1 footcandle at a distance of 1 foot, and 1 lux at a distance of 1 meter.

In designing a workplace, engineers are of course concerned with illumination, although illumination by itself does not determine the adequacy of lighting. An important distinction is that between illumination, which (as we have said) is the amount of light striking a surface, and **luminance**, which refers to the amount of light that is reflected from an object's surface, and which therefore determines how well we see that object. Illumination and luminance are not always directly related because different objects reflect and absorb different percentages of

the light that strikes them. Thus, you may be able to see a highly reflective object under low illumination better than you can see a less reflective object under higher illumination. All of these factors—illumination, luminance, reflectance—as well as many others determine **visibility**, or how well objects can be seen, and are considered in designing lighting systems for the workplace. Guidelines have been developed by the Illuminating Engineering Society, and are outlined in its *IES Lighting Fundamentals Course* (1976) and *IES Lighting Handbook* (1981a, 1981b). Interested readers are referred to these sources for more detailed information.

As students of I/O psychology, we are primarily concerned with how lighting affects workers' performance. There is a vast amount of research on this topic, and so we will only

summarize the general results. Some of this research has been conducted in the field (e.g.,
Knave, 1984), but because of the need for experimental control, most illumination research
has taken place in the laboratory (Sanders &
McCormick, 1993). One fairly consistent finding is that increasing illumination, up to a point,
leads to improvements in performance, but past
that point further increases are not beneficial.
Figure 13.4 depicts the results of a study of the
effects of illumination on the amount of time it
takes to perform typical industrial tasks: performance speed improves as illumination increases, but the rate of improvement slows at
higher illumination levels.

You should keep in mind that although the
results illustrated in Figure 13.4 are typical, the
ideal lighting for any task will depend strongly
on both task and worker characteristics. For example, in many cases it may be easier to increase performance by increasing the size or
contrast of objects than by increasing the illumination (Boyce, 1981). Also, the illumination
level may have a greater effect on the performance of older workers than of younger workers (Hughes & McNelis, 1978). In general,
although researchers have worked hard to develop models to explain the effects of illumination on performance, there are so many
nonvisual factors that also influence performance (for example, motivation, knowledge,
experience, task attributes) that the models are
still fairly crude (Boyce, 1988).

The level of illumination also has implications for the amount of *glare* that is present.
Glare is the result of brightness that exceeds the
luminance to which a person's eyes have
adapted (Sanders & McCormick, 1993). There
are several ways to classify glare, but the most
useful for our purposes is the distinction between discomfort glare and disability glare.
Discomfort glare is the sensation of pain or an-
noyance caused by high or uneven brightness.
This type of glare does not necessarily interfere
with visibility, but it can be very irritating and it
is quite common (Olson & Sivak, 1984). **Dis-**

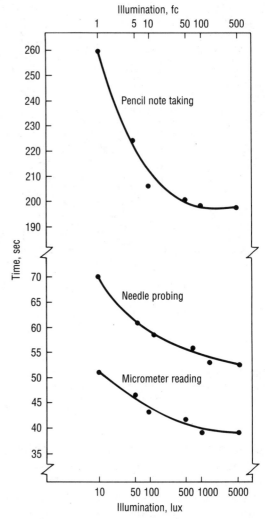

FIGURE 13.4
**Relationship between Illumination and Completion Time
for Three Representative Industrial Tasks**
SOURCE: Adapted from "Illumination Levels and Performance of Practical
Visual Tasks," by C. Bennett, A. Chitlangia, and A. Pangrekar, *Proceedings
of the Human Factors Society, 21st Annual Meeting.* Copyright © 1977 by
the Human Factors Society, Inc. Reproduced by permission.

ability glare, on the other hand, *does* interfere
with visibility and visual performance. The effects of age on sensitivity to these two types of
glare have been studied, with interesting results. Age seems to have little effect on sensitiv-

ity to discomfort glare (for example, Sanders, Shaw, Nicholson, & Merritt, 1990; Sivak & Olson, 1987), but it has a marked effect on sensitivity to disability glare, with older workers experiencing greater effects than younger workers (Olson & Sivak, 1984; Sanders et al., 1990). A possible implication of these findings is that as the work force ages in the coming years, the experience of disability glare is likely to increase, even in situations where the lighting conditions remain constant.

Glare is determined by a variety of factors, including the reflectance of surfaces, the position of light sources, and the luminance of backgrounds. All else being equal, however, the higher the illumination, the greater the possibility for discomforting or disabling glare. It may be possible to design a workplace using brighter lighting without the problems of glare if other factors, such as background luminance, can be controlled (Bennett, 1977). If these variables cannot be controlled, however, it may be that a lower level of illumination would be more effective.

Noise.   Complete silence is something that very few people have ever experienced. We are constantly surrounded by sounds, in the workplace as well as elsewhere, but in most cases we are able to ignore this "ambient noise" as we perform our jobs. As the amount of noise increases, however, the probability that it will become disturbing and interfere with job performance also increases. Of course, as was the case with illumination, the effects of noise depend on the tasks that are being performed. For example, people talking very quietly can be quite disturbing if you are studying in a library, but athletes are able to work in extremely noisy stadiums, usually without any negative effects on their performance. In the design of a workplace, it is therefore important to consider the type of job to be performed, as well as the level of noise that will be present.

Just as an understanding of the nature of light was useful in understanding illumination,

it is helpful to understand something about the nature of sound when considering the effects of noise on workers' behavior. **Sound** is a form of physical energy that is created by the vibration of objects. As an object vibrates, such as a bell after it has been struck by a hammer, its movement causes alternating "waves" of high and low pressure to radiate from its surface. These soundwaves are the physical stimuli to which our ears are sensitive. The larger the vibrations of the object, the greater the **amplitude** of the soundwave, or the amount of energy it contains. All else being equal, the greater the amplitude of a sound, the louder it is perceived to be. The speed of vibration is also important in determining the nature of sound. The faster the vibration, the greater the sound's **frequency**. Frequency is typically expressed in units called hertz, abbreviated Hz (1 Hz = 1 cycle or wave per second). Higher-frequency sounds are perceived as being higher in pitch than lower-frequency sounds. Humans can hear tones from approximately 20 Hz to 20,000 Hz, depending on age and other factors that might impair hearing. "Pure" tones, such as those from a tuning fork, contain only one frequency. Most sounds, however, are complex mixtures of various frequencies, most notably multiples of the main frequency known as **harmonics**. It is differences in harmonics that cause instruments, such as a piano and a saxophone, to sound very different, even though they are playing the same note.

One frequently used index of sound is a measure of sound pressure or amplitude known as the **decibel** or **dB** scale. Actually, there are several dB scales, each developed for different purposes. The dB scale that you are probably familiar with is the dBA, or A scale. Figure 13.5 illustrates the dBA levels for a number of common sounds. It should be noted that 0 dBA corresponds to the threshold of human hearing: the softest sound that can be heard by a person with normal hearing in a very quiet environment. Also note that the dBA scale is **logarithmic**, which means that an increase of 10 dB represents an increase in sound pressure to ten

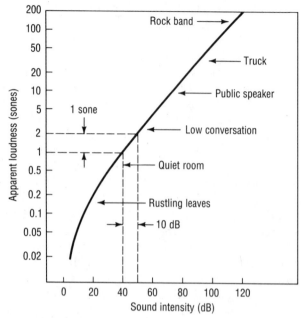

FIGURE 13.5
Decibel and Sone Levels of Common Sounds
SOURCE: From *Sensation and Perception* (p. 206) by S. Coren, C. Porac, and L. M. Ward. Copyright © 1979 by Academic Press, Inc. Reprinted by permission of Harcourt Brace and Company.

times the original level, and an increase of 20 dB represents an increase in pressure to 100 times the original level.

In spite of, or perhaps because of, its widespread use as a measure of sound intensity, many people believe that the dBA scale measures how loud a sound is perceived to be. Unfortunately, even though there is a positive correlation between sound pressure and perceived loudness, the relationship is less than perfect. For example, humans are less sensitive to low-frequency sounds than they are to higher-frequency sounds, so that a 60-dBA, 100-Hz tone will not be perceived as being as loud as a 60-dBA, 2,000-Hz tone. For this reason, scales to measure perceived loudness have been developed. The most commonly used of these is the **sone** scale, for which we have also provided illustrative examples in Figure 13.5. A 1-sone sound has been arbitrarily defined as equal to a

standard 1,000-Hz, 40-dBA tone; a 2-sone sound is one that is perceived as being twice as loud as that standard, a 3-sone sound is perceived as being three times as loud, and so on. Although the sone scale is a better reflection of our perceptions than the dB scale, most intensity measures still utilize dB scales because they are based on objective, physical properties rather than subjective, psychological judgments.

Research on the effects of noise on work performance provides a somewhat contradictory picture. One review of 58 experiments examining the noise-performance relationship found that in 29 cases noise hindered performance; in seven cases noise enhanced performance; and in the remaining 22 noise had no effect (Gawron, 1982). Although they characterized their conclusions as "guarded," Sanders and McCormick (1993) summarized some of the effects of noise on performance as follows:

1. Except for short-term memory tasks, it takes very loud noises (> 95 dBA) to have an effect on performance.

2. Performance of simple, routine tasks is not hindered, and in fact may be enhanced, by noise.

3. Sensory functions (for example, visual acuity, dark vision) are largely unaffected by noise.

4. Motor performance is impaired by noise only when it involves balance.

5. Reaction time is unaffected by noise when adequate warning is given about when to respond.

It should be kept in mind that nearly all of the research on noise and performance has been conducted in the laboratory; the effects of noise in typical work settings have not been widely studied. It seems reasonable to expect, however, that the complexity of the laboratory results would be magnified by the complexity of most work environments.

Evidence of the effects of noise on hearing is more consistent than that for performance. Continuous exposure to loud noise typically results in temporary hearing loss. This loss takes the form of a shift in the *threshold* for detecting a sound. That is, after continuous exposure to a loud noise, the minimum intensity at which a sound can be detected, or **threshold**, is temporarily raised. Exposure to sounds below 60 to 65 dBA results in little or no hearing loss; sounds of greater and greater intensity result in larger and larger threshold shifts. Most of the shift occurs in the first few minutes of exposure to the noise, followed by less rapid changes (Sanders & McCormick, 1993). Long-term exposure to continuous noise can result in permanent threshold shifts. These shifts first affect perceptions of tones around 4,000 Hz but gradually spread over a wider band of frequencies if the exposure is maintained.

A number of steps can be taken to reduce noise levels in the workplace, and thus to re-

duce the potential for hearing loss. First, noise can be controlled by changing or adjusting the *source* of the noise, that is, the vibrating object. Proper lubrication of equipment and careful design of that equipment can reduce the size and number of vibrating parts and surfaces. Second, noise can be controlled by changing or adjusting the *medium* through which the sound waves travel. Sound-absorbing materials can be used on walls, ceilings, and floors. Loud machines can sometimes be enclosed in acoustical chambers that muffle their noise. Third, when nothing can be done to reduce the actual sound levels in the environment, noise can still be controlled by modifying the *receiver*. For example, workers can protect themselves from the effects of excessive noise with devices such as headphones or earplugs that prevent soundwaves from entering the ear. Unfortunately, this is only a partial solution to the problem because sound can reach the middle and inner ear by traveling through the bones of the head as well as through the outer ear. Also, the ability of hearing-protection devices to safeguard workers' hearing varies considerably, and is often overstated by their manufacturers (Gasaway, 1984, 1987).

Heat and Cold. Another environmental factor that may affect work behavior is the **thermal condition** of the workplace. We use the term "thermal condition" rather than "temperature" because the effects of heat or cold depend on factors other than temperature, the most important of which are the humidity level and the amount of airflow. This is because the body produces heat during normal metabolic processes, and the heat must be dissipated in order to maintain a normal internal body temperature. Some of the heat is lost through convection (through the air) and radiation (through other objects), but with higher environmental temperatures, less heat can be exchanged in these ways. Heat is also lost through evaporation, primarily of perspiration on the skin. When humidity is high or there is little air circu-

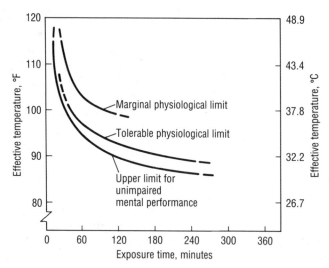

FIGURE 13.6
Upper Limit to Effective Temperature for Unimpaired Performance of Mental Tasks as a Function of Exposure Time
Source: Adapted from *A Review of the Effects of High Ambient Temperature on Mental Performance* (Technical Report 65-102), by J. F. Wing. U.S. Air Force, AMRL.

lation, this form of heat exchange also becomes less efficient. Of course, when temperatures are low the challenge is to *prevent* the loss of body heat by limiting these heat-exchange processes.

Extreme levels of either heat or cold can have detrimental effects on the performance of job tasks. The negative effects of heat on the performance of physically demanding tasks have been known for many years (Leithead & Lind, 1964). Basically, tolerance for heat (the length of time heat can be endured) decreases as both temperature and the amount of physical effort or energy expended by workers increase. Excessive heat also has damaging effects on the performance of mental tasks. Ramsey and Kwon (1988) reviewed research on the effects of heat for both simple and complex cognitive and perceptual and motor tasks. For simple cognitive tasks, such as reaction time, arithmetic, and short-term memory, there is little effect of heat on performance. For complex cognitive tasks, such as target tracking and vigilance, there is consistent evidence of deterioration in performance at high temperatures. Interestingly, ex-

posure time is not directly related to this performance decrement. The results of one study, illustrated in Figure 13.6 (Wing, 1965), show that after the first hour of exposure, the upper limit of temperature for unimpaired performance of mental tasks decreases very slowly (cf. Hancock, 1981, 1982). Ramsey and Kwon (1988) concluded that after as little as half an hour exposure to high heat there were no further decreases in performance for a period up to three hours. However, even longer periods of exposure to heat may impair intellectual performance, as shown in research by Fine and Korbrick (1978), who had subjects perform complex mental tasks under high heat and humidity conditions (95°F, 88% humidity) or under more moderate conditions (75°F, 25% humidity). Their results, shown in Figure 13.7, illustrate the dramatic negative effects of long-term exposure to heat and humidity on error rates.

The effects of cold on task performance are usually linked to the lowering of the skin temperature. As the body adjusts to cold tempera-

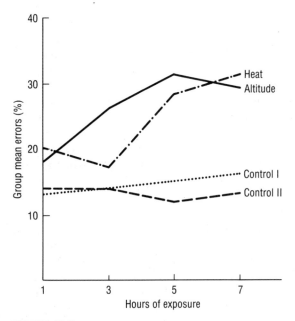

FIGURE 13.7
Effect of Heat on Error Rates for Mental Tasks
SOURCE: From "Effects of Altitude and Heat on Complex Cognitive Tasks,"
by B. J. Fine and J. L. Korbrick, *Human Factors, 20,* 118. Copyright
© 1978 by the Human Factors Society, Inc. Reproduced by permission.

have described. The major exceptions are outdoor jobs, such as construction or road maintenance. In these types of jobs, special steps should be taken to prevent temperature and humidity from affecting workers. Proper clothing is an important consideration for outdoor workers, particularly when cold temperatures begin to chill hands and feet. In extreme heat, lightweight clothing promotes heat exchange and body cooling. Safety considerations, however, might dictate that heavier clothes be worn, even on the hottest days. In these cases, regular rest breaks, preferably out of the extreme heat, should be scheduled so that workers can recover from heat stress (Krajewski, Kamon, & Avellini, 1979).

Other Physical Conditions. Psychologists and others have conducted a considerable amount of research on the effects of illumination, noise, and temperature. There are other physical variables in the workplace that have not received as much attention but most certainly have implications for workers' attitudes and performance. For example, many industrial processes use hazardous chemicals or create pollution. If allowed to come into contact with workers, these substances can cause both immediate and long-term health problems. A well-known example of this type of hazard is "black-lung" disease, which is common among coal miners, whose jobs virtually force them to breathe coal dust. A similar affliction, called "brown-lung" disease, occurs in the textile industry, and is caused by inhaling tiny cloth fibers.

What makes these two examples particularly noteworthy is that they do not involve smoke, noxious fumes, or other substances that we normally think of as pollution. When a physical threat is unexpected in this way, its effects can be overlooked for long periods of time. Such was the case with asbestos, which was used extensively as a building and insulation material but was later revealed to be a powerful carcinogen, or cancer-causing substance. Another unexpected physical threat was posed by

tures, blood vessels in the skin contract to prevent heat loss, which causes the skin to cool. As the temperature of the skin lowers, discomfort and, if the skin becomes cool enough, pain are experienced. This is particularly true in the hands and feet, which cool before other parts of the body. The discomfort is typically accompanied by a reduction in the performance of manual tasks when skin temperature falls below about 55°F (13°C). This is due in part to a decline of the metabolism rate in muscles, and in part due to a decrease in the speed of neural transmission in motor nerves (Astrand & Rodahl, 1986). Another factor in the effects of cold temperatures is the reduction in tactile (touch) sensitivity as our fingers get cold.

There are relatively few jobs in which extreme temperatures present a problem for employees. Most modern buildings have adequate heating, dehumidification, air conditioning, or ventilation to avoid the negative effects that we

"Agent Orange," a defoliant used by U.S. military forces in Vietnam. In addition to killing plants, exposure to Agent Orange has been found to have caused long-term health problems for many Vietnam veterans. A work environment free of these hazards is desirable for a number of reasons. Most obviously, workers' health and well-being are promoted by the elimination of pollution and unclean conditions. Given that personnel costs are frequently a company's largest expense, a healthy workplace is usually cost-effective to the company as well. By removing the causes of illness that are present in the workplace, health-related absences are reduced, company-paid insurance costs may be lowered, and training costs may be reduced because of increased employee longevity.

In the past 40 years another potential environmental hazard, radiation, has become prevalent in the workplace. The most obvious types of jobs in which radiation may be a problem are those in nuclear facilities, such as power plants, nuclear-powered naval vessels, or nuclear-fuel-refining operations. Radiation is also present in a variety of other, less obvious, settings. Medical and dental offices, for example, frequently contain X-ray machines, the use of which poses little threat to patients but can be dangerous to employees if they are repeatedly exposed to the radiation on a regular basis. Recently, there has been much concern about the potential dangers of electromagnetic radiation from computer monitors, and new low-emission monitors have been developed. Further, natural forms of radiation can also present an unexpected threat to workers. It is now recognized that excessive or prolonged exposure to sunlight is a major cause of skin cancer. Workers whose jobs require them to be outside for substantial proportions of the workday face an increased risk of contracting skin cancer, unless appropriate precautions (such as the use of protective clothing and "sunscreen" lotions) are taken.

The Combined Effects of Physical Variables. We have discussed the effects of several specific physical factors in the workplace, from illumi-

nation to radiation. Because research has tended to examine these variables one at a time, it has generally failed to demonstrate their cumulative effects. However, it is reasonable to expect that such effects exist. That is, given that improper lighting, excessive noise, extreme temperatures, pollution, and radiation can have negative effects on employees, two or more of these operating together will probably have even greater effects. Unfortunately, many workers are exposed to several of these undesirable conditions in their jobs. It is therefore important that as organizations such as Peter's Pan Pizza make changes in the workplace, all aspects of the physical environment, and the interactions among them, be carefully considered. Attention to only selected environmental variables is likely to result in inadequate work conditions.

Safety and Accidents

As described earlier, physical conditions in many work settings pose threats to employees' health. A similar threat to workers' well-being is the potential for on-the-job accidents. By **accidents**, we are referring to unexpected events that have a negative effect on productivity or other aspects of performance (cf. Meister, 1987). The negative effects could be due to worker injury, loss of time, damage to equipment, or loss of material. Whatever their form, accidents are costly to organizations, with annual estimated losses in the tens of billions of dollars.

Causes of Accidents

We often use the word *accident* to imply that an unfortunate event was unintended, unforeseeable, and unpreventable. This use of the word implies that little can be done to avoid accidents, and that no one should be held responsible for their occurrence. Most psychologists agree that accidents are unintended but would argue that they have definite causes, and that understanding the causes should lead to the ability to prevent accidents from happening. Recognizing that there may be as many specific reasons for accidents as there are accidents, potential causes can be grouped into two general categories, job-related factors and worker-related factors.

Job-Related Causes of Accidents. Although accidents always involve workers' behavior, it is clear that some jobs present a greater risk of accidents than others, regardless of the behavior of the individual workers on those jobs. For example, it is unlikely that Dr. MacKeven herself will ever have an accident that will either injure someone or cause extensive damage to expensive equipment. Peter's Pan Pizza's production workers, however, are more likely to have accidents simply because of the nature of their jobs. The difference in accident rates for various occupations was documented by Pimble and O'Toole (1982). They found, for example, that only 1.9% of the painters in their sample of British workers were "at risk," or likely to have an accident each year; 17% of the scaffolders, however, were likely to have an accident within the same period. Although it could be argued that scaffolding simply attracts more careless workers than does painting, it is unlikely that this could account for a nearly tenfold difference in accident rates.

What sort of characteristics are likely to make one job more dangerous than another? Perhaps the most important factors are job requirements that place workers in potentially unsafe conditions. For example, to erect a scaffold, a worker must climb very high, on precarious footing, while manipulating heavy pieces of iron or steel. Painters, on the other hand, seldom need to carry anything heavier than a bucket of paint, and when they climb, it is rarely more than one or two stories, on a ladder that has been designed for safe climbing (if used properly).

Another potential cause of accidents is the presence of unsafe conditions that do not necessarily "come with the job," such as missing handrails on stairways or the use of dangerous or poorly maintained equipment. Even an otherwise safe machine can be a hazard if it does not function properly, thereby tempting unqualified workers to "fix" it themselves. For example, one of the machines used to chop anchovies for Peter's Pan Pizza's famous anchovy pastries has a tendency to "throw" a belt, causing the machine to stop. The operator, after a few such incidents, may try to replace the belt, and in the process catch her hand in a pulley. This is an illustration of how an unsafe worker behavior can stem from unsafe conditions: If the machine had been properly maintained, with belts properly adjusted and replaced, this accident would never happen.

Worker-Related Causes of Accidents. As we have indicated, although accidents may be facilitated by unsafe conditions, workers' behaviors are always involved. Further, accidents occur even when conditions are as safe as possible, which indicates that many mishaps can be explained only as the result of unsafe behaviors. Theoretically, at least, it is possible to improve equipment and work conditions to make them optimally safe. A major motive for research on worker-related causes of accidents has been to do the same for the work force, by identifying and eliminating workers' characteristics that seem to be related to accidents.

One popular explanation for accidents is the concept of *accident proneness*. Essentially, this is based on the notion that certain people have enduring characteristics or habitually engage in behaviors that lead to repeated accidents. If such characteristics and behaviors exist, then it should be possible to identify accident-prone people and avoid hiring them for risky jobs (such as working on scaffolding). Consistent with the idea of accident proneness, surveys show that a relatively small proportion of workers have a relatively large proportion of accidents. For example, DeReamer (1980) reported data showing that in a sample of 10,964 workers, just 90 workers (0.8% of the total sample) suffered 531 injuries (11.9% of the total number of injuries).

Are these workers with high accident rates accident prone, engaging in behaviors or possessing characteristics that cause them to have more than their share of mishaps, or are they simply the unlucky victims of circumstance? The frequency diagram in Figure 13.8 summarizes DeReamer's (1980) data by plotting the number of workers having different numbers of injuries. Also plotted are the numbers of workers who can be expected to have different numbers of injuries, simply as a matter of chance, assuming that there is no accident-proneness construct operating. As you can see, the distribution of actual injuries is extremely similar to the predicted distribution of random injuries. This suggests that the apparent accident proneness of some workers is simply the result of chance, and that the widely accepted concept of accident proneness has little merit. Further, it has been argued that when greater numbers of workers have multiple accidents than would be expected by chance, this is probably because their jobs have greater hazards than others (McKenna, 1983).

Although there may not be people who are generally accident prone, this doesn't mean that there are no individual characteristics or behaviors that are associated with accident rates. In the following sections on accident prevention we will see that visual skills and perceptual style may be related to accident rates in certain situations. For example, we might predict that scaffolders with poor depth perception will have more accidents than those with good depth perception. Poor depth perception, however, is not likely to lead to accidents on jobs that do not require climbing or judging distances. Consequently, the worker who appears to be accident prone on one job could have an excellent safety record on a different job. This is essentially the idea behind **accident liability theory**: an individual's risk of having an accident varies from situation to situation, as well as over time (Shahani, 1987). It is therefore better to focus on characteristics that predict accidents in particular job settings than to search for evidence of general accident proneness.

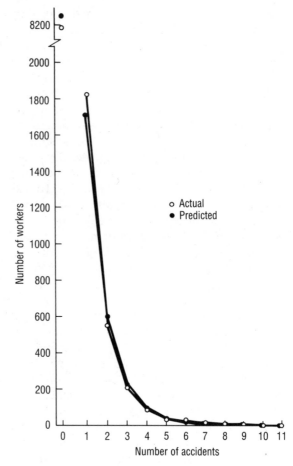

FIGURE 13.8
Distribution of Predicted vs. Actual Injury Rates
(*N* = 10,964)
SOURCE: From *Modern Safety and Health Technology*, by R. DeReamer. Copyright © 1980 by John Wiley & Sons, Inc. Adapted by permission of John Wiley & Sons, Inc.

Accident Prevention

Given the potential costs of accidents to both individual workers and organizations, accident prevention has received a great deal of attention. Just as there are two general causes of accidents (job-related and worker-related), there have been two general approaches to accident prevention: changing workers (through selection or training) and changing jobs. While reading about accident prevention, you should keep

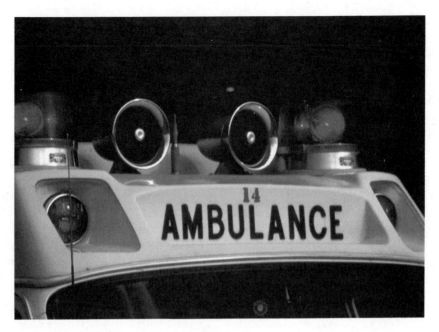

Eliminating work-related accidents is in everyone's best interest.

in mind that there is no single cause for on-the-job mishaps, and that it is therefore unreasonable to expect any single accident prevention program to be 100% effective. Research suggests, however, that a comprehensive safety program should make it possible to reduce significantly the number of accidents in most organizations.

Selection and Placement.   The first method for reducing accidents focuses on workers' characteristics. It is reasonable to expect that one way to prevent accidents in a given job is to select workers with a low probability of having accidents on that job. The process of **actuarial prediction** is used to determine who is likely to have an accident. That is, measures of various personal characteristics are correlated with accident rates for a large number of workers with the same or similar jobs. If a significant relationship is found between a characteristic and accident rate (and properly cross-validated), the characteristic can be used to predict who is

likely to suffer an accident. For example, the premium that you pay on a life insurance policy depends to a great extent on your age. It is a sad fact of life that as we get older, the chances of our dying in the near future increase. Thus, age predicts the death rate, and in order to be able to pay benefits when we die and still make a profit, the insurance company must charge older people higher premiums. In a similar fashion, if we can identify characteristics that predict accidents on a given job, and if accident rates are an important part of our ultimate performance criterion, we can use those characteristics as part of the selection procedure.

Relatively few individual characteristics have been found to predict the rate of work-related accidents. Among the most consistent predictors are perceptual variables, such as visual skills. It has long been known that workers with better vision have, on the average, fewer accidents than do workers with poorer vision (for example, Kephart & Tiffin, 1950). Also related to accident rates is a measure of perceptual style called **field dependence**. Operationally, field-dependent people have a difficult time detecting shapes embedded in a complex background, whereas field-independent people find it much easier to perform these tasks. A number of studies have suggested that field-dependent individuals are more likely than field-independent individuals to have accidents, apparently because they have more difficulty detecting subtle cues that might warn them of hazardous conditions (for example, Barrett & Thornton, 1968; Mihal & Barrett, 1976). A model of the accident process was recently developed and tested, and one of the variables found to predict accident rates was an index of distractibility derived from the Minnesota Multiphasic Personality Inventory (Hansen, 1989). Although this measure may have broader implications for worker safety, it is easy to see how distracted workers might overlook dangerous conditions.

There are studies linking accident rates with a wide variety of nonperceptual variables, but few if any systematic relationships with accidents have been found. For example, some surveys show that younger workers have a greater number of accidents than older workers (Gordon, Akman, & Brooks, 1971); others show that accident rates increase from middle age to old age (Cooke & Blumenstock, 1979). This pattern of decreasing accident rates from youth to middle age and increasing rates from middle age on is consistent with the notion that accident liability changes over time. It also illustrates the difficulty psychologists have had identifying traits that predict accidents across situations and worker populations. The study by Hansen (1989) found that in addition to distractibility, general social adjustment, counseling, and risk factors in the job all had direct effects on accident occurrence. However, none of these variables accounted for a large portion of the variance in accident rates, meaning that our ability to predict who will have an accident is still not very impressive. This does not necessarily mean that in a given situation with a particular applicant population and specific job

characteristics that predictors of accident rates cannot be found. Rather, it implies that predictors of accident rates are likely to be specific to different situations.

Training. As with selection, training programs focus on the worker as the key to reducing accident rates. Training is discussed in detail in Chapter 7, and so we will not repeat what we have said there, except to remind you that the motives of the workers and the supportiveness of management are important in determining the success of accident-prevention training.

The importance of management commitment to accident-reduction efforts was illustrated by Zohar (1980), who compared employee ratings of "safety climate" with evaluations made by safety inspectors. Zohar found that stronger perceptions of a safety climate were associated with greater management commitment to safety, as shown by the inspectors' estimates of the authority held by company safety officers and the involvement of upper management in safety issues. Butler and Jones (1979) also found that management behavior was related to accident reduction, particularly in settings where hazards were not obvious. It seems clear that when training programs are developed to promote accident prevention, management support for those programs is essential.

In terms of the effectiveness of safety training, research by Komaki and her colleagues has consistently shown that the most important factor in reducing accident rates and improving safety records is not explaining, describing, or discussing safe and unsafe behaviors but, rather, providing workers with feedback on how they are doing relative to safety goals (for example, Komaki, Barwick, & Scott, 1978; Komaki, Heinzmann, & Lawson, 1980). In one study, Komaki, Collins, and Penn (1982) compared a traditional safety training program with a program centered on safety performance feedback. The traditional training program involved explaining safety rules with the aid of slide presentations, displaying safety rules in work areas, emphasizing a new rule three times each week, and holding weekly safety meetings. In the feedback program, a safety graph that showed the percentage of desired behaviors performed safely was explained to workers, posted in the work areas, updated three times each week, and discussed at weekly meetings. The results showed that the traditional training program led to a 6% improvement over the previous safety record, but that the feedback program resulted in an 18% improvement, and an 11% improvement over the results of the training program alone. Of course, the feedback would not have been effective without some training to let the workers know which behaviors needed to be changed. However, mere presentation of that information, which represents the bulk of most safety programs, is clearly not the most effective way to improve safety. Komaki's research also demonstrates the importance of maintaining safety feedback: once feedback is halted, worker behaviors return to their prefeedback levels (Komaki, Barwick, & Scott, 1978). Hence, although other training approaches that rely on techniques such as incentives and rewards, have been shown to be effective in reducing accidents (Cohen, Smith, & Anger, 1979; McAfee & Winn, 1989), they have all included feedback, which is probably the most important factor in their success.

Human Factors. A third general technique for increasing safety and reducing accidents focuses on changing jobs rather than on changing the behavior of workers. This is the human factors approach to accident prevention, and it is based on the premise that safety can be enhanced not only by encouraging safer behavior but also by designing safer workplaces. Human factors as a discipline will be described in more detail in the last section of this chapter because safety of the workplace is only one of the many concerns addressed by human factors.

Sanders and McCormick (1993) classify efforts to design safe work environments into three categories. The first are *exclusion designs*, which make it impossible for a particular error to occur. The second are *prevention designs*, which make it difficult but not impossible to commit the error. Third are *fail-safe designs*, which do not necessarily reduce the probability of the error but, rather, lessen its consequences. Sanders and McCormick argue that it is often easier to design a safe workplace than it is to make workers behave safely, but workers must learn to use their work equipment, and in so doing are likely to make errors and have accidents. To the extent that trial-and-error is necessary for on-the-job learning, fail-safe designs, which allow for "safe accidents," may be helpful and necessary (Rasmussen, 1987; Senders, 1983).

An example of a safety problem that could be addressed by human factors is the design of control devices for Peter's Pan Pizza's anchovy-chopping equipment. One control on this machine might regulate the amount of material (anchovies) that is fed into a storage hopper; another control would regulate the flow of material from the hopper into the actual chopping compartment. If the two controls were placed too close together, or if they were difficult to distinguish, it might be easy for a worker to accidentally waste anchovies by overflowing an already-full hopper when he intended to empty the hopper into the chopper. On the other hand, if the controls were placed too far apart, attempts to operate them simultaneously might result in worker injury. Proper design of the equipment, as determined by human factors research, could avoid both types of accidents.

Safety Legislation

Worker safety and accident prevention are obviously desirable goals, both in terms of benefits for workers, and the potential for increased efficiency and profit for employers. Safety programs, however, can be costly and time-consuming to implement, leading some managers to resist their implementation in spite of the potential benefits. Since 1971, though, a federal law has mandated that employers provide their

---

BOX 13.1 Needs That Work Against Safety

- *Safety versus saving time.* If the safe way takes more time than an unsafe way, some people will choose the unsafe way to save time.
- *Safety versus saving effort.* If the safe way requires more work than the unsafe way, some people will choose the unsafe way to save the effort.
- *Safety versus comfort.* If the safe way is less comfortable than an unsafe way, some people will choose the unsafe way to avoid discomfort.
- *Safety versus getting attention.* If an unsafe way attracts more attention than the safe way, some people will choose the unsafe way.
- *Safety versus independence.* If an unsafe way gives greater freedom from authority than the safe way, some people will choose the unsafe way simply to assert their independence.
- *Safety versus group acceptance.* If an unsafe way has greater group approval than the safe way, many people will choose the unsafe way to get or maintain group acceptance.

SOURCE: *Management Guide to Loss Control* by F. E. Bird. Copyright 1974 by Institute Press, Santa Monica, California.

---

workers with safe and healthful working conditions. This law, the Occupational Safety and Health Act, established the Occupational Safety and Health Administration, or OSHA. It is the responsibility of OSHA to establish and enforce safety and health standards for industry, to aid in the development of safety education and training, and to promote research on safety. OSHA has been most active in the area of safety and health standards, with literally thousands of regulations and guidelines currently in effect. These range from requirements for protective clothing to pollution standards, to detailed specifications for safety devices on buildings and equipment.

Establishing standards turned out to be the relatively easy part of OSHA's job. The more difficult part has been enforcing the standards. OSHA is empowered to inspect workplaces for violations of its standards, and to issue warnings and penalties to employers who are not in compliance. The enforcement activity has been hindered by two factors. First, even the best safety program will be ineffective if workers are not motivated to accept it, and there are many reasons that workers might find it easier to behave unsafely rather than safely. Common needs that conflict with safety considerations are described in Box 13.1.

The second factor hindering enforcement is that OSHA's budget has never allowed it to have a truly adequate inspection and enforcement staff, and many employers realize that there is little chance that infractions of the law will come to OSHA's attention. Of course, most companies voluntarily comply with safety laws, and the overall safety of U.S. workplaces has improved since safety legislation has been enacted: In 1970, the death rate from accidents in the U.S. workplace was 18 deaths per 100,000 workers, but in 1990 the rate was only 9 deaths per 100,000 workers. Similarly, the rate of disabling injuries fell 18% during that period (U.S. Bureau of the Census, 1993).

Worker–Machine Systems:
Human Factors

There are probably an unlimited number of ways in which a tool, a machine, or even an entire factory could be designed to fulfill a given purpose. Clearly, some of these designs will be more efficient, easier to use, and will accomplish their goals better than others. **Human factors** is the scientific and technical discipline that is dedicated to promoting the design of workplaces, as well as other human environments, that can most effectively meet the needs of their users. As it applies to work behavior, human factors is concerned with the relationships between workers and the physical objects with which they perform their jobs. Because the design of equipment, facilities, products, and other aspects of the environment have implications for behavior, human factors is also concerned with developing proper procedures for effectively performing a variety of tasks.

Human factors is a multidisciplinary field, with aspects of engineering, physiology, architecture, and various other disciplines, in addition to psychology. We will therefore not attempt to provide an exhaustive overview of human factors; interested readers can refer to any of a number of textbooks in this field (for example, Kantowitz & Sorkin, 1983; Wickens, 1992). Instead, we will describe one of the major, guiding concepts of human factors, the worker–machine system, and show how human factors provides answers to problems that are often quite different from those suggested by purely psychological theories.

The Worker–Machine System

It is common to view human factors as a discipline that is dedicated to improving *worker–machine systems*. A **worker–machine system** can be defined as an arrangement of people and machines, tools, and other devices interacting within the work environment in order to achieve a set of system goals (Kantowitz & Sorkin, 1983). The role of the human factors specialist is to design the interface, or link, between the human and machine components of the system so the system can achieve its goals most efficiently. The way in which this is typically accomplished illustrates an important difference between the perspectives of the I/O psychologist and the human factors specialist. Whereas psychologists emphasize selection, training, reinforcement, and other actions aimed at changing the *worker*, the human factors approach is likely to alter the *machine* components of the system. This does not reflect the opinion that human behavior is not important but, rather, a belief that it may be easier to change a machine to make it compatible with people than it is to change people to make them compatible with machines. Certainly, to the extent that a machine is poorly designed, it may not be possible to train any worker to use it effectively (see Figure 13.9).

The basic components of a worker–machine system are illustrated in Figure 13.10. In this system there are certain components that are important to human factors specialists and certain components that are of little interest to them. On the machine side of the system, displays and controls are the most relevant components. On the human side, sensory and motor functions are emphasized. The emphasis on these four components reflects the fact that they define the interface between the worker and the machine: the machine displays provide the worker's senses with information necessary to monitor and evaluate the machine's performance, whereas the worker's motor behavior allows him to adjust machine controls that will cause corrections or other changes in the machine's operation.

Of course, both the worker and the machine do much more than send information to each other. The machine's major function is to perform the operations that it was designed to perform; the worker's most important tasks within the system are cognitive, involving pro-

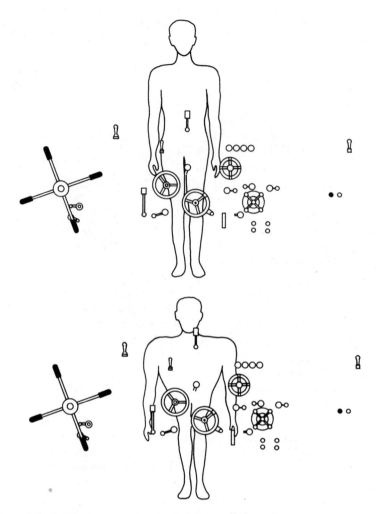

The controls of a lathe in current use are not within easy reach of the average person. They are placed so that the ideal operator should be 1372 mm (4¼ feet) tall, 640 mm (2 feet) across the shoulders, and have a 2348 mm (8 feet) arm span.

FIGURE 13.9
An Ineffective Worker–Machine System
SOURCE: From "Industrial Use of Ergonomics," in *Applied Ergonomics, 1,* 27. Copyright © 1969 by Butterworth Scientific Ltd. Reprinted by permission.

cessing and making judgments about the information provided by the machine, and deciding what changes in the controls are needed. Typically, machines are assigned tasks that would be tedious or dangerous for human operators, or require a degree of precision that is difficult for people to maintain. Humans are given the tasks that require judgment or creativity, at which machines are less capable. The machine operations and information-processing functions, however, are largely irrelevant to the human factors specialist, who is primarily concerned

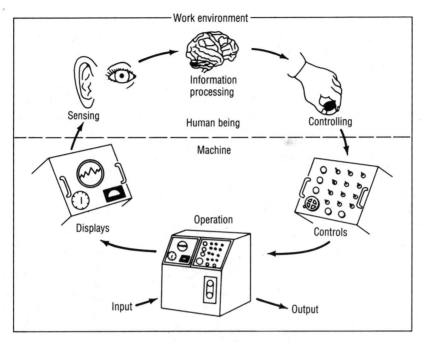

FIGURE 13.10
Schematic Representation of the Worker–Machine System
SOURCE: From "Engineering Psychology," by A. Chapanis. In M. D. Dunnette (Ed.), *Handbook of Industrial and Organizational Psychology*. Copyright © 1976 by Rand McNally and Company. Copyright © 1983 by John Wiley & Sons, Inc. Adapted by permission of John Wiley & Sons, Inc.

with the compatibility of worker and machine at their interface.

Inputs. Data about the machine's operations form the inputs for the human side of the worker-machine system. (These data, of course, also form the outputs for the machine side of the system, but to avoid repetition and confusion and to remain consistent with our psychological perspective, we will discuss the system from the worker's perspective.) Research on these inputs has focused on two general topics. The first is the sensory capabilities of humans; for a worker to accurately perceive information displayed by a machine, the information must be compatible with the human senses. Consequently, for human factors experts to design effective displays, they must first understand human sensation. Failure to take the worker's

sensory capabilities into account could lead to disastrous results. For example, one type of display on Peter's Pan Pizza's anchovy-chopping machine shows the pressure within the hydraulic system that powers the chopping blades. When the pressure is within normal limits, a green light is displayed on a control panel; if the pressure rises above those limits, the green light is extinguished and a red light comes on, signaling the operator to perform certain safety actions. For most people, a quick glance at the panel would tell them which light is on. However, for workers with red-green color blindness, who have difficulty distinguishing between red and green, this color-coded information will be much less effective and may result in costly accidents. Although only a small minority of people have this sort of color-vision disorder, it would be a simple matter to have the red warning light flash on and off, so that in the rare case of a color-blind operator, the risk of a pressure buildup will be reduced.

The other component of the information input process is the machine display itself. Not all displays can be as quickly or as accurately interpreted as others, even when all are within the range of normal human sensation. Figure 13.11 illustrates a case in point, summarizing data from a study of the effectiveness of four airplane altimeter designs (Simon & Roscoe, 1956). Each design indicates (1) the present altitude of the plane, (2) the predicted altitude of the plane in one minute, and (3) the "command altitude," or the altitude at which the plane is supposed to be flying. The subjects, 24 pilots, were presented problems consisting of different combinations of these three altitudes, from which they were to decide what needed to be done to reach the command altitude. The data at the bottom of the figure show the pilots' average time to solve the problems, and the number and percentage of errors for each altimeter design. On all of the performance measures, the integrated vertical design showed clear advantages, probably because it presents the information, which concerns the relative vertical position of three altitudes, in a vertical format. The other designs require the pilot to transfer cognitively a digital or circular representation into information about relative vertical positions.

This example, of course, illustrates only one of a variety of display-format issues that human factors specialists have addressed. In each case, however, the goal is to design a display that provides specific information in a readily interpretable manner. The nature of the display will depend both on the type of information and its intended use. To illustrate, if the pilots in Simon and Roscoe's study had simply been asked to judge the current altitude of the plane, the digital counter design would probably have been most effective.

Outputs.   The output portion of the human side of the worker-machine system takes the form of instructions from the worker to the machine. As was the case with the input functions of the system, human factors specialists are concerned with both human and machine components of this output process. On the human side, it is important to understand the motor capabilities of the typical worker. If machines demand input that is beyond the physical abilities of workers to provide, the system will not be able to function at its maximum potential. Human factors researchers have therefore studied such variables as workers' energy expenditure, strength, endurance, speed, accuracy of movements, and workload (Sanders & McCormick, 1993). Knowledge gained through this research has promoted the design of workplaces that maximize human performance while minimizing such outcomes as fatigue and stress, and the errors to which they contribute.

An example of research on motor skills may help to illustrate its role in human factors. In recent decades there has been a dramatic increase in the number of workers whose jobs involve "data entry." These range from long-familiar jobs, such as typists, to the variety of computer-operator and computer-programmer positions that exist in most modern organizations, to any of the millions of workers who use a personal computer in some aspect of their work. All of these jobs involve the use of some sort of keyboard, and therefore require a controlled but rapid tapping movement of the fingers. To design a keyboard for maximum efficiency, it would be useful to know whether or not, for the average person, some fingers are better suited than others for this type of task. If so, the keyboard should be designed so that the "better" fingers perform most of the work, while the other fingers are used only when necessary.

Dvorak, Marrick, Dealey, and Ford (1936) conducted research on this specific issue many years ago. They found that the fingers of the right hand can tap more rapidly than those of the left hand, probably because the majority of their subjects, like a majority of the general

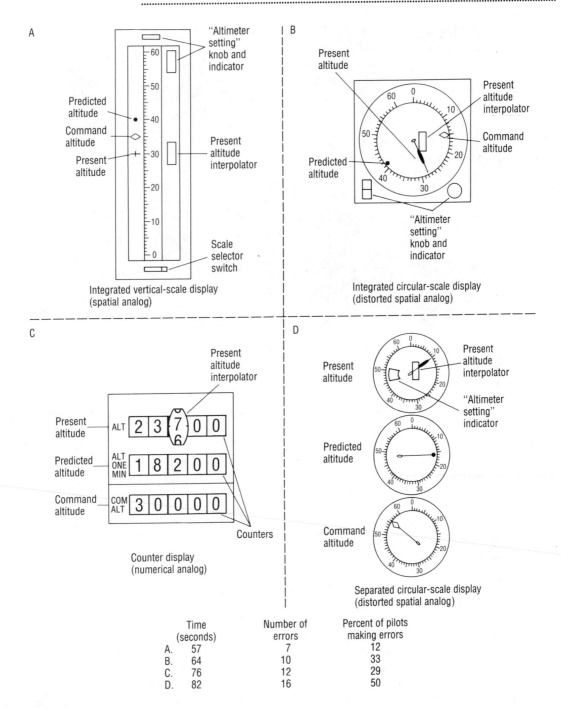

FIGURE 13.11
Effectiveness of Four Altimeter Designs

Source: From "Airborne Displays for Flight and Navigation," by S. N. Roscoe, *Human Factors, 10,* 321–332.
Copyright © 1986 by the Human Factors Society, Inc. Reproduced by permission.

Air-traffic controllers confront very complex worker-machine systems.

population, were right-handed. They also found that the index and middle fingers of both hands were faster than the ring or little fingers of the same hand. Consequently, in the design of equipment to be used in tasks requiring rapid finger movement, such as data entry, it is probably best to maximize the use of index and middle fingers.

The machine component of the output process consists of control devices that are manipulated by the worker. The devices can take a variety of forms, including knobs to be turned, levers to be pulled, switches to be flicked, and keys to be pressed, just to name a few. As was the case with human sensation and machine displays, the effective design of machine controls relies on a good understanding of the motor abilities of the operator. For example, based in part on their research on finger movement, Dvorak and associates (1936) developed a typewriter keyboard that they believed would be more effective than the standard "QWERTY"

keyboard (named for the sequence of keys on the second row). The QWERTY keyboard and the Dvorak keyboard are illustrated in Figure 13.12. Dvorak believed that his keyboard would lead to improved typing speed and accuracy. The QWERTY arrangement requires the left hand to do most of the work, and forces the typist to perform difficult finger movements to type common sequences of characters. The Dvorak keyboard equalizes the work of the two hands, and eliminates many difficult movements by placing the most commonly used letters on the middle row of keys, where the fingers typically rest while typing.

Dvorak's efforts to design a better typewriter keyboard are a good example of designing machine controls based on knowledge of human motor abilities. Unfortunately, it is not clear whether this particular effort at improving the worker-machine interface has been effective. There are many assertions of tremendous improvements in typing speed and accu-

a. "QWERTY" keyboard

b. Dvorak keyboard

FIGURE 13.12
Comparison of Keyboard Formats

racy as a result of using the Dvorak keyboard but most are undocumented. For example, Mc-Cauley and Parkinson (1971) reported that some typists increased their speed from 50 words a minute on the QWERTY to 150 words a minute on the Dvorak, and that 6- to 12-year-old children have learned to type over 40 words a minute in only a few weeks with the Dvorak keyboard. They cited no hard evidence to support these dramatic accomplishments, however.

More scientific examinations of the Dvorak keyboard have generally failed to support the assertions of its followers. For example, Kinkead (1975) compared typing speeds obtained on the QWERTY, the Dvorak, and a third keyboard designed specifically to optimize typing speed. His results showed that the Dvorak keyboard yielded only a 2.6% time saving over the QWERTY, and that the "optimal" keyboard was only 7.6% faster than the QWERTY. A critical review of research on the Dvorak keyboard estimated a 5 to 10% improvement in speed (Norman, 1983).

It could be argued that a 10% time saving, or even a 2.6% time saving, would result in substantial benefits over a long enough period, and that an improved keyboard design should therefore be attractive to organizations with large numbers of data-entry positions. All else being equal, this may be true, but all else is seldom equal, and in this case the adoption of the Dvorak keyboard would require the expensive and time-consuming retraining of large numbers of workers who have become used to the standard QWERTY keyboard. This would probably not be an easy retraining task either, because these experienced keyboard operators would probably experience "negative transfer" of training, as their old habits and skills interfere with learning new skills. Further, very few keyboards are produced with the Dvorak layout, and so any retraining would be a waste of time unless the Dvorak keyboard became widely available. Of course, until there are substantial numbers of Dvorak typists to create a demand for the Dvorak design, manufacturers of data-entry equipment will not be likely to market alternative keyboards. This is not to say that an alternative keyboard design is not a good idea but, rather, that even the best of ideas will not be acceptable if people do not want them and refuse to use them.

Chapter Summary

In this chapter we have divided the issue of work environment into three general topics. The first, work conditions, refers to aspects of employment or the workplace that influence employees' effectiveness and their reactions to work, rather than directly influencing their behaviors. Included in this category are work schedules, shift work, compressed workweeks, and flextime. Working nonstandard or irregular shifts has been found to have negative effects on workers' health, social interactions, and family relationships. The ability of workers to adjust to the demands of shift work is an important key to coping with these problems. Compressed workweeks are popular with workers, although longer workdays can increase workers' levels of fatigue. Flextime, in which workers' arrival and departure times are allowed to vary, lets workers adjust their schedules to meet their needs but may present problems for supervisors and managers. Neither compressed workweeks nor flextime seem to have dramatic effects on employee satisfaction or performance, although flextime has been shown to reduce tardiness.

Another set of work conditions is the physical aspects of the workplace. These include illumination, noise level, thermal conditions, and pollution. Of course, any toxic pollution is undesirable, but the ideal levels of illumination, noise, and temperature depend in part on the nature of the job. Extreme levels of any of these factors, however, are detrimental to both workers' health and their performance.

The second general topic is safety and accidents. Causes of work-related accidents have been categorized as either job-related or worker-related. The former refers to unsafe conditions in the workplace; the latter refers to unsafe worker behaviors. Although there appears to be no evidence of any "accident-prone" personality trait, some personal characteristics do predict "accident liability" in certain situations. Accident-prevention efforts have utilized employee selection, safety training, and human factors techniques.

The third general topic is human factors, which is the discipline dedicated to designing workplaces for maximum human performance. Human factors is often viewed as dealing with "worker–machine systems," trying to optimize the link between workers and the machines and tools with which they perform their job tasks. The design of machine displays and controls is the most obvious aspect of this effort.

INTEROFFICE MEMO

To: Andrew LeGette,
           Director of Wages and Benefits

From: J. A. MacKeven,
           Human Resources Coordinator

My staff has finished its research into the programs that you mentioned
as possible nonpay incentives to offer during the contract negotiations.
I will discuss each of the programs in turn.

Four-day workweek. There are potential advantages of a four-day workweek
to Peter's Pan Pizza. The most important is that by cutting one day from
the normal workweek, up to a 20% saving in certain overhead costs (heat,
custodial, and so on) may be realized. One major limitation is that you
can't fit more than two 10-hour shifts in a day, so if a plant is currently on a 24-hour/day schedule it will be difficult to shorten the
workweek. (Further, it would be difficult to get the union to accept
four-day workweeks in only some of the plants.) Another drawback is that
if you need to operate a plant more than four days/week, some people will
have to work weekends and take days off in the middle of the week, which
will probably be unpopular with the union. From a productivity standpoint, there is little evidence that a four-day workweek will have much
effect on performance.

Flextime. Flextime may be acceptable for nonproduction workers, but we
believe that it would be impossible to operate Flavio's production operations normally under this system, due to the high likelihood of under-
staffing both early and late in the day.

Safety programs. The Human Resources office has not been involved in
developing company safety policy, so I'm not sure what is currently being
done. I hope that we are conforming to all OSHA regulations, and that the
workers are basically safe. You might want to offer some periodic safety
education courses or workshops on company time, although they will probably be attractive to the union only if there is a general perception that
the workplace is unsafe.

I think that you should know that, in general, there is little reason to
believe that the union will "trade" these sorts of programs for wage and
benefit increases. Union negotiators will know that economic issues are
what the rank-and-file want the union to concentrate on, and they tend to
focus on those issues.

GARFIELD, © 1984 United Feature Syndicate, Inc.

Review Questions and Exercises

1. Dr. MacKeven has pointed out some of the practical problems that arise when instituting nonstandard workweek or flextime programs. How might some of these problems be solved? Are the potential benefits of these programs worth the effort it would take to implement them? Defend your answer.

2. Assume that worker safety is a major concern of the union negotiators representing Flavio's workers. Describe the most effective safety program, in terms of improving both safety and cost, that Peter's Pan Pizza could offer to implement. Evaluate Dr. MacKeven's suggestion in comparison to your own.

3. Throughout this chapter we have mentioned Flavio's anchovy products. One task in the preparation of these products is chopping the anchovies. Describe the general human factors issues involved in designing an anchovy-chopping machine.

4. Now that you have "designed" the anchovy chopper, you need a factory in which to put it. Describe the physical aspects of this workplace that could affect workers' behaviors and performance, and explain what some of the potential hazards might be in such a workplace.

5. Anchovy choppers can be noisy devices. Describe three ways to reduce the risk to workers of this noise. Your plans should take into account the three general approaches to reducing the effects of noise described in the chapter.

CHAPTER 14

Labor Unions

LEARNING POINTS

After studying this chapter, you should

- understand what labor unions are, and why they have become prominent in North American workplaces;

- be able to describe the steps in union organization, and discuss the factors that are related to pro-union behavior;

- understand the typical viewpoint of management on labor unions;

- be able to describe the purpose of collective bargaining, and explain how impasses can be resolved;

- be able to explain why grievances occur, and discuss factors that are related to the filing of grievances;

- be able to explain why I/O psychologists have conducted relatively little research on unions; and

- be able to discuss the factors that contribute to union commitment and union satisfaction.

THE MEMO DR. MacKEVEN RECEIVED from the legal counsel's office expresses concern and uncertainty that is shared by the management of many organizations when dealing with labor unions for the first time (see memo p. 472). In this chapter we will discuss the role of labor unions in work organizations and the reasons that workers might join unions (as well as the reasons that they might not). We will also examine the unique relationship between employer and union, as well as the dual roles of union members.

A Definition of Labor Unions

Labor unions are found in most countries, and their activities vary as a function of the political, social, and economic conditions around the world. In the United States and Canada, a **labor union** can be defined as *an association of workers, the purpose of which is to represent the interests of its members on issues of wages, policy, and working conditions*. The primary technique by which unions represent these interests is collective bargaining, in which representatives of the union negotiate, or bargain, with representatives of company management over various is-

INTEROFFICE MEMO

To: J. A. MacKeven,
          Human Resources Coordinator

From: T. J. Smith,
          Legal Counsel

I would like to have your input on a matter that is of some concern to the senior management team. As you know, prior to our merging with Flavio's Frozen Foods, we had no unionized employees. Although it would be nice to attribute this to our enlightened management practices, it is probably more likely due to the nature of the pizza business: most of our employees in the pizza end of the business are either in management or staff positions at headquarters here in Suardell Springs, or in management positions at the individual restaurants owned by the company. Workers at franchise restaurants are the employees of the franchise owner, not of PPP. Consequently, PPP was not an attractive target for unionization. With the acquisition of Flavio's, however, this picture has changed dramatically. Both the manufacturing and distribution divisions of Flavio's are labor intensive, and in fact 30% of Flavio's work force were members of unions at the time of the merger. Most of the union shops are in the Midwest and Northwest, but there has been increasing union activity in the Southwest. In fact, authorization cards are being circulated at the Flavio's plant in Phoenix this month. We can probably expect increased efforts to unionize our employees during the next year or two.

I would like you to serve on an *ad hoc* committee on union activity. This committee's job will be to analyze Peter's Pan Pizza regarding the potential for additional unionization, and plan how the company should deal with such activity. The committee will also be concerned with how the company should approach dealing with the currently unionized shops. I particularly hope that you will be able to provide some information on the psychological variables that lead workers to unions, and suggest how we can prevent this type of activity.

sues. The techniques of collective bargaining and other union activities are described in more detail later in this chapter. Collective bargaining illustrates the basic philosophy of unions, which is that workers can better achieve their common goals by dealing with management as a group rather than as individuals.

Labor Unions in North America

The modern labor movement in North America began shortly before the turn of the century. To a large extent, it was a response to changes in the workplace that resulted from the Industrial Revolution. As the economy shifted from its agricultural base and became more heavily industrialized, people migrated from farms and rural communities to the cities in search of more dependable work and higher pay. The resulting abundance of labor, however, kept wages low, and few working-class people gained the stability and income they had hoped for. Further, although production and the number of jobs grew rapidly during this time, working conditions in the factories were often noisy, abusive, unsanitary, and even unsafe. In summary, whereas the Industrial Revolution provided many workers with a new way of life, it had some negative consequences. Early labor-organizing efforts, often anchored in socialist philosophy, were aimed at gaining a share of the newly created wealth for workers while improving their general working conditions.

There have been trade unions and local labor organizations of various types in North America since at least the end of the eighteenth century. The first widely influential labor organization, however, was the American Federation of Labor (AFL), founded in 1881 under the leadership of Samuel Gompers. The AFL was actually a collection of relatively independent unions that supported one another in their efforts to organize various industries. Other unions, dedicated to socialist principles of class struggle and revolutionary change, emerged during this time but were uniformly unsuccessful in attracting members. The more moderate AFL, which was committed to improving the lives of workers through collective bargaining and to using political "persuasion" rather than violence to bring about desirable changes in society, quickly became the dominant labor organization. Through the early 1930s, 70% to 80% of all organized workers were members of the AFL.

In 1933 the National Industrial Recovery Act guaranteed the right of workers to organize and engage in collective bargaining. Although it was later declared unconstitutional, the 1935 National Labor Relations Act that followed also guaranteed the right to organize. These laws led to the rapid growth of unions as industries that had previously resisted unionization were organized (see Table 14.1). Another period of rapid

TABLE 14.1 U.S. Labor Union Membership, 1900–1991

Year	Number of union members (in thousands)	Percentage of total work force belonging to unions
1900	791	4.9
1910	2,116	9.1
1920	5,034	17.5
1930	3,632	6.8
1940	8,944	15.5
1950	15,000*	22.3*
1960	18,117	23.6
1970	20,752	22.6
1980	20,095	23.0
1985	16,996	18.0
1991	16,568	16.1

*Approximate.

Sources: 1900–1970: *Historical Statistics of the United States, Colonial Times to 1970, Bicentennial Edition, Part 1* (pp. 176–177), by U.S. Bureau of the Census, 1975; 1980: "Changing Employment Patterns of Organized Workers," by L. T. Adams, 1985, *Monthly Labor Review, 108*(2), pp. 25–31; 1985: *Employment and Earnings,* by U.S. Bureau of the Census, 1986, 33(1), p. 213, U.S. Government Printing Office; 1992: *Statistical Abstract of the United States: 1993* (p. 436), by U.S. Bureau of the Census, 1992, U.S. Government Printing Office.

union growth began in 1938, when several AFL unions with members in the skilled crafts broke away to form the Congress of Industrial Organizations (CIO), which competed with the AFL for members. The last dramatic rise in union membership occurred during World War II. Unlike previous eras of union expansion, the growth was due not to an increase in the number of unions but to the very rapid expansion of industries involved in war production, most of which were already unionized. After the war the growth of union membership proceeded more slowly. The period was marked by the reunification in 1955 of the AFL and CIO into a single organization, the AFL-CIO, which remains the largest labor organization in North America.

The number of U.S. workers in unions continued to expand throughout the 1960s, although the percentage of the work force that belonged to unions remained fairly constant. During the 1970s, and more dramatically in the 1980s, both the number of workers belonging to unions and the percentage of the work force that they constituted began to fall. The shrinkage was due to a number of factors, but it can be explained primarily by the change in the types of industries that were flourishing. Through the 1960s, traditional industrial organizations, especially manufacturing companies, experienced steady growth. The growth slowed and then reversed in the 1970s and 1980s as the number and proportion of workers in service industries (for example, financial institutions, custodial services, food services, "high-tech" industries) and government jobs increased. These new growth industries are not as heavily unionized as those of previous decades. One effect of the shift in employment, therefore, was a decrease in the membership and influence of labor unions. However, even today approximately one in six workers belongs to a union, and for these millions of employees and their employers, unions are an important fact of life.

Although labor unions have experienced a dramatic decline in membership in the United States, this has not been the case in other parts of the industrialized world. In Australia, for instance, the percentage of the work force that belongs to unions has remained fairly constant, ranging between 55% and 59% from 1961 to 1986. In Canada there was an increase from 30% to 38% in union membership during the same period; in Sweden the rate went from 68% to 89%. Similar trends have occurred in other Western democracies (Arrowsmith & Courchene, 1989). The difference between the United States and other nations is dramatic but not surprising when you consider the history and cultures involved. Even at their height, U.S. labor union membership rates were much lower than those in Western Europe. The greater acceptance of unions, both in the past and in the present, may be related to the greater acceptance of socialist political philosophy in Europe. As we noted earlier, U.S. workers have generally not been attracted to unions that promote socialist ideals, and many workers are wary of *any* union because of perceived links between unions and socialism. Thus, the generally stronger and more widely held antisocialist and anticommunist feelings in the United States have probably contributed to its lower unionization rates. In the 1980s the more conservative political climate in the United States, combined with specific government actions that were unfavorable to unions, further contributed to the decline.

Peter's Pan Pizza illustrates the trend in union membership just described: Flavio's Frozen Foods is a labor-intensive organization, with traditional manufacturing and distribution functions. This type of company is an attractive target for unionization efforts. As we have seen, the proportion of the work force in such jobs has been falling, although in PPP's case, the acquisition of Flavio's led to a net growth in employee unionization. The PPP franchise business, on the other hand, is a decentralized service organization and is not unionized. This is primarily because most of the employees in the retail franchises work for the individuals who own the restaurants. The owners pay a franchise fee to PPP for the right to use the company name, recipes, advertising, and so forth. The franchise owners also buy supplies and equipment from PPP. Because each franchise is actually a small, independent business, often with a largely part-time student work force, PPP restaurants have not been attractive targets for union organization. Many of the employees who actually worked at PPP's corporate headquarters prior to the merger with Flavio's were either in managerial positions, and therefore not subject to unionization, or aspired to managerial positions, and therefore not sympathetic to the union movement.

Union Organization

Millions of workers belong to labor unions, but many millions more do not. What factors contribute to an employee's decision to join a union? To answer this question, we will examine basic processes involved in union organization and outline several of the individual and situational characteristics that seem to be related to union status. Although we cannot specify why any one individual wants to join a union or why another does not, we can identify factors related to attitudes toward unions, as well as conditions beyond the control of workers that often dictate the presence or absence of a union.

Certification Elections

For a union to represent the employees of a company, the employees must first vote to accept, or certify, the union as their legal bargaining representative. U.S. law requires that prior to an election, a substantial number of employees must indicate an interest in voting on union certification. Specifically, 30% or more of the employees must sign cards authorizing an election. To obtain the necessary number of sig-

natures, representatives of the union will campaign in support of the election. Management, however, will campaign to *prevent* the authorization of the election, for reasons that we will discuss later in the chapter. There is obviously the potential for abuse on both sides of these campaigns, and so laws have been enacted that regulate the behavior of both the union and management representatives. For example, management cannot discipline workers for signing cards or for openly supporting the union, and union organizers cannot interfere with the performance of the workers' jobs. These laws, as well as regulations governing all other aspects of the unionization process, are enforced by the National Labor Relations Board (NLRB), an agency of the federal government.

It should be noted that not all of a company's employees will necessarily be asked to sign authorization cards nor be eligible to vote in the election if one is authorized. In some cases, different employees of a single company may belong to different unions, depending on the type of work they perform. For example, the International Brotherhood of Teamsters might attempt to organize the truck drivers in Flavio's distribution unit but would be less likely to represent other types of workers. The Food and Beverage Trades Department of the AFL-CIO might try to organize the workers who prepare the food, and the Office and Professional Employees' International Union might distribute authorization cards among Flavio's office staff. It is up to the NLRB to determine who is eligible to vote in each election, although in general, only managerial employees are prohibited from voting.

If fewer than 30% of the eligible workers sign cards, the union must either give up or start its organization campaign over again. If 30% or more of the eligible employees *do* sign authorization cards, the NLRB schedules an election by secret ballot. Campaigning by both parties is supervised closely by the NLRB, which also conducts all aspects of the actual election. If more than half of the voters approve the union, it becomes the legal bargaining agent for all of the eligible employees. If a majority does not approve the union, the union's supporters can, if they wish, try again.

Workers' Reasons for Joining Unions

Although there is no single explanation for workers voting to join unions, there has been substantial research on the factors that predict pro-union behavior. The factors have been broken down into four broad categories by Barling, Fullagar, and Kelloway (1992): (1) demographic variables, (2) personality variables and beliefs about work, (3) macrolevel variables, and (4) microlevel variables. We will briefly summarize their conclusions regarding each of these categories.

In general, there seems to be little relationship between demographic variables, such as age, seniority, education, or marital status, and workers' union attitudes or tendencies to vote in favor of union representation. Race has been found to be related to union attitudes and voting preferences, with minorities holding more positive attitudes and being more likely to vote in favor of unions (for example, Deshpande & Fiorito, 1989; Hills, 1985). This difference probably reflects a reaction to ongoing discrimination and the hope that unions can help remedy inequities (Fullagar & Barling, 1989). Although the relationships between personality variables and union voting behavior have not been frequently studied, psychological conservatism, or the tendency to avoid change, has been found to be negatively related to attitudes toward unions (Barling, Laliberte, Fullagar, & Kelloway, 1990). Conversely, Marxist work beliefs, that workers are exploited by employers and must therefore gain control over the workplace, and humanistic work beliefs, that the individual growth of workers is more important than productivity or profit, have been found to be positively related to union attitudes (for example, Barling, Kelloway, & Bremermann, 1991). However, none of these personality characteristics has direct effects on union voting behavior.

Workers join unions for a variety of reasons.

Macrolevel variables are defined by Barling and associates (1992) as workplace characteristics that are not related to individual workers' unique experiences, a definition that encompasses a very broad range of variables. Studies have examined the relationship between union voting behavior and such things as the day of the week on which elections are held and the region of the country in which the company is located, without success. More promising results have been found with variables such as unemployment rate. One estimate of this relationship is that for every 1% increase in unemployment, the percentage of employees voting in favor of unions increases 1.3% and the probability of a union victory increases 2.5% (Cooke, 1983). The size of the bargaining unit has been found to be negatively related to union attitudes and voting behavior, with the exception of very small (fewer than ten employees) units, whose workers tend to have unfavorable union attitudes (for example, Brett, 1980; Kochan, McKersie, & Chalykoff, 1986). Also, a weak relationship between voter turnout and election results has been observed, with lower turnout associated with union victory (Hindman, 1988; Sandver, 1980).

Among the most complex and most contentious macrolevel predictors of union voting behavior are the actions taken by companies to prevent union certification. Many such strategies have been studied, ranging from meetings, films, and letters and other forms of direct communication to delaying tactics, to innovations that give the company an "enlightened" image, to hiring consultants with expertise in fighting unionization, to intimidation and firing of union supporters (Barling et al., 1992). Some of these actions, such as intimidating and firing union supporters, are illegal under the National Labor Relations Act, but most are not. The collective effects of these actions, while difficult to assess, are no doubt dramatic. One estimate of the impact of company campaigns against unions is that without such campaigns, union success in elections would have risen from 36% to 66%, and strong management campaigns in all elections would have reduced union success to 5% (Getman, Goldberg, & Herman, 1976).

The final category of predictors of union voting and attitudes includes microlevel variables (Barling et al., 1992), which entail people's personal experiences at work and with unions, as well as certain nonwork experiences, such as those with family. As you might expect, workers who are more dissatisfied with their work in general are more likely to vote in favor of unions (for example, DeCotiis & LeLouran, 1981; Getman et al., 1976; Zalesny, 1985). Similarly, level of pay has been found to have a negative association with union attitudes and voting behavior (for example, Gordon & Long, 1981; Premack & Hunter, 1988), as has satisfaction with pay (for example, Getman et al., 1976; Hills, 1985). Consistent with the principles of equity theory (Chapter 8), to the extent that workers believe that their pay is inequitable (say, that others are being paid more for the same work), the more likely they are to favor unions (for example, Barling et al., 1990). Satisfaction with working conditions (Hills, 1985) and with promotion opportunities (Bigoness, 1978) have also been found to be related to union attitudes.

Pay, working conditions, and promotion opportunities can be described as *extrinsic* job characteristics. That is, they are part of the work experience, but they are not directly related to the work that an employee performs. Other research has examined the relationships between *intrinsic* factors and union behaviors. Intrinsic factors are those that are associated with the performance of the job itself. For example, employees who believe that they lack control over their working conditions have more favorable union attitudes (for example, Lawler & Walker, 1984), as do workers who feel that they have no power at work (Keaveny, Rose, & Fossum, 1988) and workers who feel that company policies are unjust (Bass & Mitchell, 1976; DeCotiis & LeLouran, 1981).

Although attitudes toward work and job dissatisfaction in particular have long been associated with union voting behavior, the relationship between union attitudes themselves and voting behavior has recently received a great deal of attention. A clear and consistent finding in this research is that workers who express more favorable attitudes toward unions in general are more likely to vote in favor of union representation (Barling et al., 1991; Barling et al., 1990; Deshpande & Fiorito, 1989). One study reported a correlation of .62 between union attitudes and pro-union voting (Getman et al., 1976). However, despite the strength and consistency of this relationship, many researchers have concluded that *specific* beliefs about the union under consideration are better predictors of union vote than are attitudes toward unions

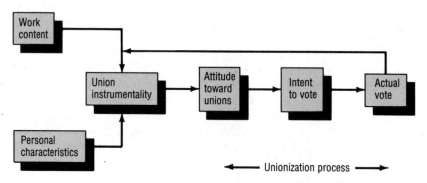

FIGURE 14.1
A Model of the Determinants of the Unionization Process
SOURCE: From "A Predictive Study of Voting Behavior in a Representation Election Using Union Instrumentality and Work Perceptions," by T. A. DeCotiis and J. LeLouarn, *Organizational Behavior and Human Performance, 27,* 109. Copyright © 1981 by Academic Press, Inc. Reprinted by permission.

in general. More precisely, research has focused on workers' beliefs about the *instrumentality* of the union. As you recall from our discussion of expectancy theory in Chapter 8, instrumentality refers to the belief that a particular outcome (for example, a union's successfully winning a representation election) is associated with achieving other outcomes (for example, higher pay) (Vroom, 1964).

Instrumentality was utilized in an early model of union voting behavior (DeCotiis & LeLouarn, 1981). The model (Figure 14.1) relies on the concept of instrumentality as the primary factor in determining whether a worker will vote in favor of the union. Instrumentality, in this model, refers to a worker's perception that the union will help her attain personal outcomes that she values. More specifically, the model states that workers who believe that the union will help them get what they want will have positive attitudes toward the union. Workers with positive attitudes toward the union will, in turn, express an intent to vote for the union when given the opportunity. Finally, workers who have made up their minds to vote for the union are very likely actually to do so.

DeCotiis and LeLouarn (1981) tested their model, using a sample of registered nurses who had recently voted in a union-representation

election. As specified by the model, the results showed that the best predictor of intent to vote, as well as of the actual vote cast, was union instrumentality. Consistent with the previous research in this field, extrinsic dissatisfaction was also strongly correlated with intent to vote, but it was more strongly correlated with union instrumentality. This suggests that lack of satisfaction causes an employee to consider alternative ways to reach his goals on the job but does not necessarily result in a pro-union attitude. Overall, four variables were found to be significant predictors of union instrumentality: extrinsic job satisfaction, stress, fairness, and worker-supervisor communications.

More recently, other models of the unionization process have been proposed, with union instrumentality remaining as a dominant factor. For example, Figure 14.2 illustrates a model described by Barling and colleagues (1990). Here, in contrast to the Decotiis and LeLouarn (1981) model, union attitudes are seen as being *causes*, rather than consequences, of union instrumentality. However, the basic process is very similar. Notable in the Barling model is the specification that it is the union's instrumentality with *extrinsic* factors that directly determines willingness to vote for a union. That is, the degree to which a union is seen as being helpful

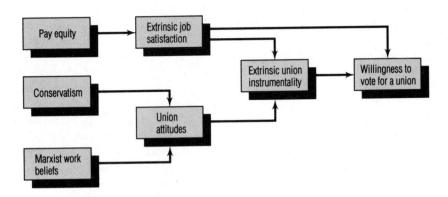

FIGURE 14.2
A Model of Union Voting Intentions
SOURCE: From *The Union and Its Members: A Psychological Approach* (p. 61), by J. Barling, C. Fullagar, and
E. K. Kelloway. Copyright © 1992 by Oxford University Press. Reprinted by permission.

for attaining such things as higher pay, better working conditions, and other economic considerations is most important to workers. This is not to imply that intrinsic factors are unimportant, but that they have received relatively little attention in the research, and hence we know little about their effects.

Although the notion that perceived instrumentality has a strong influence on workers' attitudes toward unions and union-voting behavior appears to have a good deal of support, it cannot explain why all union members vote for, or join, unions. As discussed in Chapter 8, instrumentality theories of behavior imply that people make carefully considered, rational decisions. There is abundant evidence, however, that people are not always rational, and that they will in fact often behave in ways that are irrelevant or even contrary to their own best interests, as defined by a rational analysis (Slovic, Fischhoff, & Lichtenstein, 1977). For example, workers may vote for or against a union because coworkers are voting that way rather than because of any rational appraisal of the instrumentality of union membership. Workers may also accept or reject unions because of their general political beliefs. "Liberals" may be more likely than "conservatives" to vote in favor of unions, whether or not a union would prove to

be beneficial in their particular circumstances. Research has shown that family socialization, in the form of union attitudes passed down from parents to children, can be an important predictor of union voting behavior. Parents' attitudes toward unions or children's perceptions of their parents' attitudes have been found to be related to the children's union attitudes, and thereby to the children's voting behavior (Barling et al., 1991; Gallagher & Jeong, 1989; Montgomery, 1989). Consequently, whereas the research on union attitudes and voting behavior suggests that dissatisfaction with extrinsic factors and perceptions that unions can improve extrinsic conditions make unions attractive, it cannot adequately explain the behavior of all workers.

Finally, you must remember that not all of the men and women who belong to a union voted in favor of accepting the union, and that some members would prefer not to be members. Often, the workers who vote against the union in elections must join the union if the union wins. In this arrangement, called a **union shop**, all workers must join and pay dues to the union regardless of their personal attitudes or desires regarding union membership. In other situations, workers are not required to join the union per se, but are required to pay a fee to the union to help cover the union's expenses as the legal bargaining agent for the employee. Many states, however, have passed right-to-work laws, which guarantee workers that union membership cannot be a condition for employment in any organization.

Workers' Reasons for Not Joining Unions

As we have seen, the number and proportion of workers who belong to unions have been dropping in recent years. Even during the heyday of unions, from the 1940s through the 1960s, only a minority of U.S. workers belonged to them. In our examination of workers' reasons for joining unions, we have alluded to their reasons for rejecting unions as well. In many companies and in some industries there has simply been no effort to organize employees. This may be because union officials feel that the workers in a particular company would never accept a union, so that they don't bother to spend their time and resources trying to get authorization for an election.

Many nonmanagerial employees, such as engineers, accountants, and research scientists, work closely with management in planning their companies' policies. Such workers may come to identify with the management goals they have helped to define and achieve, and reject unions on the same philosophical and practical grounds as do managers. In a similar fashion, some companies, such as Peter's Pan Pizza prior to its merger with Flavio's, have few jobs involving traditional blue-collar work but numerous opportunities for promotion to management. If a large proportion of the employees of a company aspire to managerial positions, it is less likely that a union's organizing effort would be successful.

It is clear from the research discussed in the previous section that the best explanation for the rejection of unions, and one that encompasses the considerations listed above, is that workers reject unions when they perceive that unions are not instrumental for achieving their personal goals, or when they perceive that there are other options in the workplace (for example, aligning themselves with management's goals) that have greater instrumentality than union membership. That is, if a worker believes that belonging to a union will increase her chances for promotion, pay raises, and a safer working environment, and if she values these outcomes, then a pro-union attitude is likely to result. A pro-union attitude will be less likely to develop, however, if any of the following conditions exist: (1) the worker believes that unions will lead to these outcomes but does not value them (not all workers desire to be promoted, for example); (2) the worker values the available outcomes but does not believe that unions will help get them (perhaps because no promotions are available); or (3) the worker believes that by not joining a union the chances for attaining these outcomes will be enhanced.

Also relevant to this discussion is the issue of **decertification**. This is the process by which a bargaining unit votes to remove its current union as its representative. Decertification might come about because the workers have become disenchanted with unions in general; because they believe that the specific union representing them is not doing an adequate job; or because management has waged a successful campaign to eliminate the union from the workplace. In any case, however, it appears that the reasons for decertification are similar to those for rejecting a union in the first place: the perception that valued outcomes would be more likely without the union than with it (Barling et al., 1992).

Management Reactions to Unionization Efforts

In a sense, unions represent a threat to the management of a company. In a nonunionized organization, management is relatively free to set policy regarding hours, wages, and conditions of work. Once a union is authorized to represent the employees, however, many of these issues will become subject to collective bargaining, and thereafter will be governed by a contract rather than the desires of management. Some examples of management concerns with issues commonly covered by union contracts are listed below:

1. *Promotions.* Many union contracts include clauses regarding promotion. Although there is variation in the content of these clauses, management is most concerned with clauses that specify seniority as a, if not *the*, criterion for promotion.

2. *Discipline.* Contracts often indicate a specific series of steps to be taken in the disciplining of an employee. Such provisions are intended to protect employees from unfair and arbitrary discipline, and often limit the types of behaviors that can be disciplined, the period of time over which evidence of misdeeds can be accumulated, and the form that discipline can take.

3. *Layoffs and firings.* Union contracts usually specify that layoffs be made on the basis of seniority. In most cases, management would prefer to make layoffs strictly on the basis of employee ability and productivity. Under most contracts, an employer must demonstrate "due cause" for firing an employee. If the employee or the union wishes to challenge the firing, an arbitrator may be called in to make the final decision about the employee's status.

4. *Transfers.* Transfers, or job changes to equal-status or lower-status jobs, are usually governed by the principle of seniority rather than ability or performance. The same is true for selection of work shifts or choices among several open jobs. A trial period to learn the new job is often specified by the contract.

5. *Work schedules.* Union contracts, especially in manufacturing companies, frequently specify work schedules and the rate of production. Increases in the rate of production due to technological improvements are made difficult by many contracts because

the union tries to avoid changes that would increase profits for the company without corresponding increases in wages.

6. *Overtime.* Most union contracts specify that overtime must be distributed equally within a work unit. As with other personnel actions, management would prefer to offer overtime on the basis of worker performance.

In sum, management loses some of its authority to operate the organization as it sees fit when its relationships with workers are governed by a contract. From management's standpoint, therefore, the ideal situation is never even to be faced with a unionization campaign. To this end, it behooves management to be aware of the factors that contribute to pro-union attitudes and to be willing to take action to satisfy the needs and desires that might otherwise result in union activity.

There is a great deal of advice available on how to prevent unions from succeeding in certification efforts. Occasionally, the advice involves practices prohibited by U.S. law, such as taking disciplinary action against pro-union employees, or promising employees benefits if a union is kept out. More reputable advice is offered by those who emphasize a positive employee-relations atmosphere as the key to avoiding unionization. Although the employee-relations approach to discouraging unions involves behaviors that are certainly desirable and likely to be appreciated by employees, it doesn't address most of the fundamental factors that lead workers to perceive a need for a union. As we have seen, workers are likely to develop pro-union attitudes and therefore vote in favor of unions when union membership is seen as useful for attaining certain valued goals. Of particular importance is the perceived instrumentality of unions for attaining goals related to extrinsic satisfaction, such as pay, promotion, and working conditions. If management at Peter's Pan Pizza sincerely wishes to avoid unionization, its best bet is to be aware of the extrinsic needs of their employees and to provide alternative "nonunion" paths to those goals. This can be expensive because it may involve changes in pay structure, benefits, hours, and other work conditions. Such costs, however, are not likely to be greater than the costs a company will incur if a union is successful, and these types of voluntary benefits do not involve any loss of management's right to run the company as it sees fit or to make organizational changes as economic conditions change.

The Role of Labor Unions

We have discussed the process by which a company becomes unionized. Once a union is "in," what is its role in the workplace? Clearly, the most important role of unions is to represent the workers in contract negotiations with management. Although there are other union functions, such as representing employees during grievance procedures, they are governed by the terms of the labor contract. Consequently, the strength of a union depends on its ability to obtain favorable contract terms during negotiations. We will therefore examine the collective-bargaining process in some detail in the following sections and then discuss the grievance procedure, which is one of the most important union activities beyond contract negotiations.

Collective Bargaining

The labor contract is the legal document governing employment conditions during the time that the contract is in effect, and it is the result of a process known as **collective bargaining**. In collective bargaining, management and union representatives try to come to an agreement about such issues as employee compensation, working conditions, workers' security, and management's rights. The negotiations may be drawn-out, combative affairs, and their success or failure can depend on many factors, including the expectations of each party, the state of the economy, and the ground rules that have been set up prior to formal bargaining.

Bargaining Positions and Negotiation. It is obvious that union representatives will want to maximize the benefits received by their members; as we have seen, this is often the primary reason that unions are elected to represent workers. Because of the costs of providing the benefits, management will naturally wish to maintain a limit on what the workers receive. Labor knows that management will not agree to everything that the workers desire; management, in turn, knows that labor will not accept what the company would like to offer. Each side also knows that some give-and-take is expected in negotiations. Negotiators, therefore, present initial bargaining positions that are usually extreme and far apart from each another.

The union representatives in Flavio's negotiations, for example, are going to demand wages that are higher than they realistically expect to obtain, and ask for benefits that they know are probably too costly for Flavio's to provide. They are also likely to demand contract clauses unacceptable to management that either mandate or encourage union membership in order for a person to obtain a job at Flavio's (although in states with right-to-work laws, such clauses are illegal); that specify seniority as the primary criterion for promotion, layoffs, transfers, and recalls; and that give the rank-and-file workers more say in setting company policy. The union demands are likely to be influenced by the nature of contracts in similar organizations and the desire of Flavio's workers to meet or exceed the standards of such contracts. They might also be affected by such things as economic conditions and the local labor market. Greater demands are typically made when the economy is good and the labor supply tight; demands are lower when the company is not doing as well or when there are many people looking for jobs.

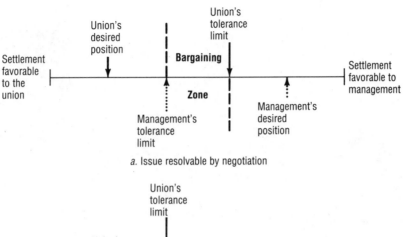

FIGURE 14.3
Tolerance Limits and Bargaining Zones
SOURCE: From *Psychology of Union Management Relations* (p. 96), by R. Stagner and H. Rosen. Copyright © 1965 by Wadsworth Publishing Company, Inc. Adapted by permission of Brooks/Cole Publishing Company.

For its part, Flavio's management will anticipate the costly demands of the union, and its initial bargaining position will include offers that are far below what it knows the union will be willing to accept. The offers will typically reflect lower wages and benefits than those sought by the union. They will also contain clauses allowing nonunion workers to be employed; specifying merit or performance as the basis for promotions, layoffs, transfers, and recalls; and denying the rank-and-file workers any role in setting certain company policies.

Because the initial bargaining positions of both union and management are extreme, everyone involved knows that each side must compromise if a contract agreement is to be reached. On each issue, there is a certain amount that each side will be willing to sacrifice in order to reach an agreement. The limit of what each side will give up is called the **tolerance limit** (Stagner & Rosen, 1965; see Figure 14.3). As was true for the initial bargaining positions, tolerance limits are likely to be determined by specific conditions in the industry. For example, if Flavio's is facing stiff competition from a newcomer in the frozen-lasagna market, the union may tolerate lower wages than it would otherwise. If, however, the company has paid large dividends to stockholders for several years, the union is likely to reject anything other than a large hike in wages.

When the union's tolerance limit overlaps with management's tolerance limit, as in Figure 14.3a, a "bargaining zone" is created that in-

Negotiating a labor contract

cludes solutions acceptable to both parties. When a bargaining zone exists, it should be possible for negotiations, at least on that issue, to be successful. Occasionally there is no overlap between the tolerance limits, and therefore no bargaining zone, as in Figure 14.3*b*. In this case, the minimum that the union will accept is still more than the maximum that management is willing to give. It is therefore unlikely that the give-and-take of negotiations will resolve the issue, and an impasse will have been reached.

Impasse Resolution. When the union and management bargainers are so far apart either on a single issue or on the contract as a whole that agreement is virtually impossible, it is known as an **impasse**. Without some technique for breaking impasses, many contract negotiations would grind to a halt, ultimately resulting in a strike or lockout, which is costly to both sides. Because an impasse is always a possibility in collective bargaining, it is common for both parties to agree to take certain measures in the event an impasse is reached. This agreement may be part of the previous labor contract, or it may be less

formal and agreed upon only when it becomes evident that an impasse has occurred.

There are three common techniques for resolving impasses. Each involves the services of an independent third party, but they vary in terms of the power given to the third party to impose a solution. They share the same general purpose, however: to ensure the completion of the contract negotiations and hasten the resumption of "business as usual."

The least-structured, least-formal method for dealing with an impasse is mediation. In **mediation** an impartial third party, the mediator, is called in to help negotiators overcome their differences. It is important to note that mediation is a voluntary process, and that the mediator has *no authority* to unilaterally impose a solution to the impasse. One of the most important functions of mediation is reopening the lines of communication between union and management. Once an impasse is reached, there are often hard feelings on each side. Even if a "bargaining zone" existed prior to the negotiations, neither union nor management representatives are likely to display a desire to compromise any further. By privately discussing each side's position with its representatives, away from the eyes and ears of "the enemy," the mediator may identify avenues that will bring the parties closer together.

Although mediators have no power to enforce a settlement, they are still important people with delicate jobs to perform. In case of an impasse during contract negotiations at Flavio's Frozen Foods, a mediator will need to find out such things as how far each side is actually willing to go in order to come to an agreement, which issues are most important to them, and where they are willing to compromise in order to gain concessions from the other side. Because this sort of information could easily be used to bias the negotiations one way or the other, the mediator must be trusted completely by both sides. He must therefore be fair, impartial, and discreet. In some cases there is a third party, familiar to both sides, who can play this role. If this is not the case, the negotiators can turn to the Federal Mediation and Conciliation Service, which maintains a staff of experienced, qualified mediators.

A second, and less common, method of impasse resolution is **fact-finding**, where an impartial third party gathers all the relevant information about the disputed issues, reviews it, and makes a public recommendation about how the impasse should be settled. At Flavio's, a fact finder brought in to settle a dispute over wages might consider such things as the profits or losses experienced by Flavio's in recent years, the prevailing wages in the food industry, local economic and labor conditions, and the final offers and demands of the bargainers.

Fact finders also have *no power* to enforce their recommendations. The theory behind fact-finding is that making the recommendation public will pressure the parties to accept the fact finder's solution. Unfortunately, most people do not seem to care about contract negotiations unless they are personally inconvenienced by a strike, and so public pressure from fact-finding tends to be minimal (Kochan, 1980). Clearly, it isn't very likely that the threat of a strike at Flavio's, and the resulting possibility of a frozen-pizza shortage, will inspire the public to demand that a fact finder's advice be adopted! On the other hand, the threat of being without a daily newspaper or public transit might result in such pressure in the case of a strike in those industries.

The third form of impasse resolution is arbitration. As is the case with mediation and fact-finding, **arbitration** involves the services of a third party, known in this case as an arbitrator. Unlike the other methods of resolving impasses, however, the decision of an arbitrator is *legally binding* on both parties. That is, whatever the arbitrator decides *must* go into the contract. For this reason, arbitration, if used, is always the last step in negotiations. Also, because of the binding nature of an arbitrator's decisions, the procedures involved in this technique are spelled out in more formal and specific terms than are those of the other methods, in order to protect the rights of both parties.

There are several ways to classify various types of arbitration. **Conventional arbitration** is when the arbitrator is free to make any settlement she wishes. This often results in the arbitrator's "splitting the difference" between the two offers, although she *could* select a settlement that is closer to either the union or the management offer. **Final-offer arbitration** gives the arbitrator less freedom in settling the impasse. In this system, the arbitrator *must* select either the union or the management offer; no compromise settlement is allowed. Final-offer arbitration was developed because in conventional arbitration, negotiators found that the settlement often falls halfway between the two offers. This results in a "chilling effect," in which the parties tend to begin the negotiations far apart and resist moving closer together. Figure 14.4 shows what might happen under conventional arbitration if management made concessions without similar concessions from the union: management would lose out in arbitration, assuming that the arbitrator settled

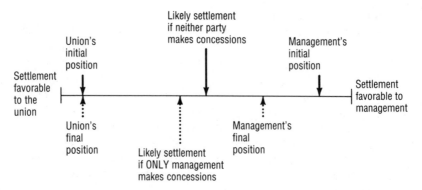

FIGURE 14.4
Potential Effects of Conventional Arbitration

about halfway between the two *final* offers. The rationale for final-offer arbitration is that extreme offers are not likely to be selected by the arbitrator, and so the bargainers will take more moderate bargaining positions, and perhaps settle more issues without an impasse.

Research on the effectiveness of conventional versus final-offer arbitration supports the usefulness of the final-offer technique. Starke and Notz (1981) reviewed the brief literature comparing the two types of arbitration, and found that most studies report that bargainers anticipating final-offer arbitration were closer to settlement at the end of negotiations than were bargainers anticipating conventional arbitration. In their own laboratory study of bargaining behavior, Starke and Notz found that final-offer arbitration resulted in lower prenegotiation expectations, closer agreement at the conclusion of bargaining, and greater commitment to the settlement, whether negotiated or arbitrated.

Final-offer arbitration can be further broken down into final offer by issue or final offer by package. In **final offer by issue,** the bargainers identify the individual issues on which they cannot negotiate a settlement, and make a final offer on each one. The arbitrator must select one of these offers for each issue. The result of arbitration by issue is that the union position may be selected on some issues, and the man-

agement position selected on others. For example, at Flavio's the union and management bargainers may be unable to agree on the issues of wages and health benefits. The union may be demanding $10.50 an hour as a starting wage and full health-insurance coverage for all members of an employee's family. Management may be offering $9.00 an hour as a base wage and paid insurance only for the employee, with insurance premiums for family coverage coming out of the workers' wages. It is conceivable that under arbitration by issue, an arbitrator would award the $10.50 starting wage, but accept management's offer of the limited health benefits.

In **final offer by package,** the negotiators make offers on each of the unsettled issues, but the arbitrator must select either the union's offers on *all* of the issues, or management's offers on *all* of the issues. In our example above, the arbitrator must select between awarding both the higher wages and the more costly health benefits, or awarding the lower wages and the limited benefits.

In a study comparing the two types of final-offer arbitration and conventional arbitration, Grigsby and Bigoness (1982) found significantly fewer issues left unsettled before arbitration when subjects anticipated final-offer arbitration by package than when they anticipated either final-offer arbitration by issue or conventional arbitration. The largest number of unsettled issues occurred with conventional arbitration. It is interesting that there were no differences between the final-offer arbitration conditions when the subjects believed that mediation would be used prior to arbitration. The anticipation of mediation led the groups expecting final-offer arbitration by issue to resolve more issues than when no mediation was anticipated. These results suggest that combining impasse-resolution techniques, such as mediation and arbitration, might be effective.

One final way to categorize arbitration is to consider whether it is voluntary arbitration or compulsory arbitration. In **voluntary arbitration,** both parties agree to abide by the decision of an arbitrator, once they have realized that a negotiated settlement is unlikely. There is no legal requirement, either by statute or by a previous contract, to engage in arbitration, so that voluntary arbitration is unlikely unless both sides anticipate that the settlement will be in their own best interest. In **compulsory arbitration,** the parties are *required* to submit offers to an arbitrator if they are unable to come to an agreement, usually by a specified deadline. This requirement may be enforced by law or by the terms of the existing contract.

You can see that there are many impasse-resolution methods. Which method is used in a particular situation depends on a number of factors, including the common practices in the industry, preferences of top management and union leaders, and external pressures on the two parties. For example, in the case of labor disputes involving public employees, it is common for arbitration to be used as the means for settling disputes. The reason is that strikes by such groups as fire fighters, police, and sanitation workers can pose threats to the welfare of the public, and are therefore illegal in many places. In most cases, the binding nature of arbitration guarantees that public strikes will be avoided. Mediation, on the other hand, is more likely to be used to settle impasses in the private sector. This may be because mediation does not require negotiators to give final control of the bargaining process to a third party, or perhaps because union and management leaders often want to demonstrate that they can settle their differences effectively. The risk that is run when mediation is used, however, is that the mediator will not be able to bring the two sides together. When that happens, a strike may result.

Strikes, Lockouts, and Other Tactics.   When arbitration is not used, and when mediation and fact-finding prove to be ineffective, both management and the union can turn to more drastic actions. The best known of these tactics, designed to bring pressure to bear on management, is a **strike**. In a strike, the workers simply stop working, thereby forcing management (they hope) to suspend operations and causing financial hardship for the company. Of course, workers do not get paid when they are on strike nor are they eligible for unemployment benefits, and so they usually experience financial hardship themselves. Because a strike is costly to both employer and employee, the decision to strike is not usually taken lightly. A majority of the union members must vote to authorize a strike. The decision to strike can be made easier if union members have contributed all along to a strike fund, which is used to make payments to strikers while they are not working. The payments, however, are usually only a fraction of the workers' normal wages; even if there is a strike fund, workers may be reluctant to walk off the job.

A union will often use the threat of a strike to pressure management. Typically, workers will vote to authorize a strike if a negotiated settlement is not reached by a certain "target date," usually midnight on the day that the current contract expires. Knowing that a strike has already been authorized often prompts management's negotiators to be more receptive to the union's demands, especially if a strike will be particularly costly. Unions therefore try to negotiate contracts that expire at times that cor-

Strikes and lockouts can be costly to workers and employers alike.

respond to critical periods in the business cycle. Truck drivers, for example, like contracts that end when there is a lot of perishable food to be shipped to markets; employees of toy manufacturers like to negotiate new contracts during the late summer and early fall, when toys are being stockpiled for Christmas. In some cases, a union will ask its members to work without a contract until such a critical period arrives. Professional baseball players have been known to work under the terms of an expired contract in order to threaten a strike just before the all-star game, and umpires have timed strikes so that they occur immediately prior to the major league championship series.

Without question, a strike is unpleasant for everyone involved. Because of this, there are less severe forms of pressure that a union can bring to bear. Chief among these is a **work slowdown**, during which workers remain on the job and collect wages. They limit their productivity, however, thereby bringing financial pressure to bear on the company. A slowdown may be instigated if economic conditions are

such that workers would find it difficult to obtain temporary jobs during a strike, if there is no strike fund or if strikes are illegal, as is often the case in public-sector jobs. A well-known example of a work slowdown is the "blue flu," during which police officers in large numbers call in "sick" during contract negotiations.

Although we are accustomed to hearing about strikes and slowdowns, management also has pressure tactics at its disposal during contract negotiations. Specifically, management can institute a **lockout**. A lockout basically means that the company is closed down. The workers therefore have no jobs and no wages. In terms of its economic impact on both the company and the workers, a lockout is similar to a strike. The difference is that a strike is usually called when management is in a vulnerable position; a lockout is more likely to occur when management knows that the workers cannot go very long without their wages and that alternative employment is difficult to find. Under these conditions, a lockout is likely to initiate pressure within the union to accept management's offers as workers increasingly feel the effects of forced unemployment.

Management can also take actions in response to strikes by the union. For example, if there are a large number of unemployed workers in the local economy, the company can hire nonunion workers to replace the strikers. Although this may seem to be a logical solution to a strike, it entails certain risks on the part of management. First, in many situations the new employees will have neither the training nor the experience to perform the jobs, and a costly training program will have to be instituted. Second, the striking employees will naturally resent the presence of these new workers (referred to by union members as "scabs"), and violence directed toward both the company and the replacement workers is not unheard of. It is also possible in a small proportion of cases, particularly in highly automated industries, for management to fill in for striking workers, although union resentment and its effects are again a possibility. In manufacturing industries, farsighted managers who anticipate a strike may try to increase production prior to contract negotiations, so that an ample supply of products will be available if and when a strike is actually called. Of course, farsighted union leaders will perceive this tactic and try to prevent the production increase, possibly through a slowdown. (Of course, neither of these strategies would do much good in service industries, where there are no products to stockpile!)

It should be clear to you by now that failure to resolve an impasse through mediation or arbitration can result in unpleasant and costly actions by both union and management. Strikes, lockouts, slowdowns, and other pressure tactics cost the participants a great deal, and in some cases serve simply to strengthen the resolve of the opposition. It is in the best interest of both parties to settle their differences through negotiation, and indeed most negotiations are successfully completed. Whether a contract settlement comes through negotiation, the efforts of an arbitrator, mediator, or fact finder, or as the result

of a strike, the interaction of union and management does not end when the contract is signed. Indeed, depending on the terms of the labor contract, the union often plays an important role in the day-to-day activities of the organization, particularly the relationship between labor and management.

Union Activity Between Negotiations

Union and management negotiators hope that the labor contract will address all the important issues that might arise, and that the contract is clear regarding what should be done in every circumstance involving labor and management disagreement. Bear in mind, however, that to reach a contract settlement, both sides had to make concessions and compromises. There will therefore be terms in the contract that one side or the other may be able to "live with" but about which they are not really happy. We can expect, then, that management and the union may interpret some contract clauses in slightly (or not so slightly) different ways.

Different interpretations of the contract usually lead to disagreement and friction between employer and employee. Virtually all labor contracts give the union authority to represent workers when such conflicts occur, through a formal process known as a **grievance procedure**. Although the specific nature of grievance procedures varies from place to place, a grievance is usually filed when an employee believes that management has violated her rights, as defined by the labor contract. The grievance itself is a formal protest, and sets in motion a series of events that are designed to determine whether the employee's complaint is valid, and if so, what steps should be taken to remedy the injustice.

An example of a management action that might result in a grievance would be if Flavio's management were to promote a worker with eight years of experience rather than one with 15 years of experience, and the labor contract specified that seniority was to be used as the basis for promotions whenever possible. To the union, the seniority clause seems straightforward: more senior employees will be promoted whenever such employees are available and want the promotion. Management, however, is likely to see things as being more complex. Specifically, management may interpret the "whenever possible" portion of the seniority clause as giving it license to select the most senior employee *with experience in jobs similar to the one to which the promotion is to be made*. That is, management may feel that it is "not possible" to promote an employee who has not demonstrated the skills necessary to perform the new job. The union, on the other hand, may expect management to promote the most senior person who wants the job, and if that person needs special training, then management must provide that training.

As we said, grievance procedures are defined by the labor contract, and so there is a great deal of variability in the specific steps that a grieving employee might follow. In many cases, once the grievance has been filed, the employee and his supervisor meet to try to settle the dispute. If the employee is still not satisfied, the **shop steward** may become involved in the process. The shop steward is the formal representative of the union in the workplace, more or less the union equivalent of a foreman. Stewards will often represent the grieving employees because they have a more detailed knowledge of the contract and are likely to have had special instruction or training from the union in how to handle grievances.

If the steward is not able to resolve a grievance by working with the supervisor, the next step might be to present the grievance to a representative from the personnel department, and if that is not successful, to a higher member of management, and so on. Eventually, the grievance procedure may be exhausted. That is, the chain of appeal specified by the contract may be followed to its end without the employee being satisfied with the result. At this point, if allowed

by the contract, the issue may be settled by arbitration. Here, the job of the arbitrator is to study the facts of the case, and decide if the action taken by management is warranted under the terms of the contract. As in the case of arbitration during contract negotiations, the decision of the grievance arbitrator is binding on both sides.

There is only a limited amount of psychological research on the grievance process. Perhaps the most interesting are the studies conducted by Dalton and Todor (1979, 1982). These authors noted that the shop steward is often very influential in determining whether or not a grievance is filed. They therefore suggested that the personalities of stewards may predict the pattern of grievances in the stewards' units. They found that the higher a steward's need for dominance, the more grievances the steward filed. They also found, however, that stewards with higher needs for dominance were more likely to discuss potential grievances with management, and thereby settle the issue before actually filing charges (Dalton & Todor, 1979). They also found that stewards with high needs for affiliation were likely to avoid grievances by first discussing the incidents with management, which may reflect a preference for interpersonal techniques of conflict resolution over formal procedures.

In another study of union stewards, Dalton and Todor (1982) found that the attitudes of stewards predicted the pattern of grievances filed in their units. Specifically, stewards who were more committed to the employing company and those who had higher job satisfaction were less likely to file grievances than those with less commitment or job satisfaction. The committed or satisfied stewards were also less likely to encourage workers to file grievances when the workers showed no desire to file, and they filed fewer grievances over the objections of workers. The more committed stewards were to the union, however, the less likely they were to discourage a grievant from filing, and the less

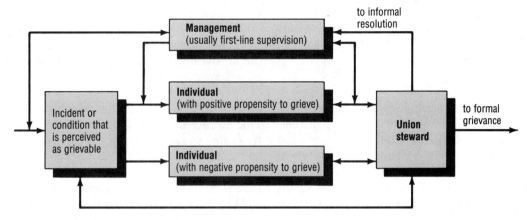

FIGURE 14.5
Model of the Grievance Process
SOURCE: From "Antecedents of Grievance Filing Behavior: Attitude/Behavioral Consistency and the Union Steward,"
by D. R. Dalton and W. D. Todor, *Academy of Management Journal, 23* 166. Copyright © 1982 by the Academy of
Management. Reprinted by permission.

likely they were to resolve the grievance by discussing the issue with management before filing charges.

Dalton and Todor's (1979, 1982) research not only identifies characteristics of stewards that predict whether grievances will be filed but also illustrates the degree of control that stewards have over the grievance process. Dalton and Todor (1982) developed a model of the grievance process, which is shown in Figure 14.5. The arrow at the bottom of the figure indicates that stewards may file grievances without consulting the workers who may have been harmed. In this situation, the steward controls the grievance activity completely, and the types of personal characteristics identified in Dalton and Todor's research are probably quite important in determining grievances.

The steward can also encourage workers to file when they are reluctant to do so, or the steward can discourage workers from filing when they are anxious to do so. The amount of influence exercised by the steward in these cases depends on his persuasive skills and the worker's determination to succeed. Finally, the steward can try to avoid filing a grievance by dealing with management on a more informal basis. An aspect of this model that should not be overlooked is the potential power of management to avoid grievances. As envisioned by Dalton and Todor (1982), management can avoid grievances by trying to prevent grievable situations, by dealing with the aggrieved employee after an incident, or by negotiating with the shop steward. Clearly, if incentives are available for both union and management, there are ample opportunities to avoid filing grievances.

More recent research on grievances has focused on the effects of perceived justice on the work attitudes of union members (for example, Gordon & Bowlby, 1988, 1989). In one study, Fryxell and Gordon (1989) found that workers' beliefs about how fairly the organizational rewards are distributed as a consequence of using the grievance procedure (distributive justice) and their beliefs about the fairness of the grievance process itself (procedural justice) both predicted satisfaction with the union, whereas broader perceptions of justice in the workplace predicted satisfaction with management. It seems that treating workers fairly has benefits for both union and management.

Concession Bargaining

Before we leave the discussion of union-management relations, we should mention a relatively new phenomenon known as **concession bargaining**: the union concedes, or "gives back," some of the benefits that its members had previously won through collective bargaining. Concession bargaining received a great deal of attention in the early 1980s when the Chrysler Corporation, on the verge of bankruptcy, won concessions from the United Auto Workers that resulted in Chrysler employees making less money than workers at other auto companies. The concessions allowed Chrysler to cut costs, however, and so helped to ensure that the federal government would grant it the assistance that eventually kept the company in business.

There is little research on either the effects of, or the factors that contribute to, concession bargaining. Plovnick and Chaison (1985) found that economic hardship alone does not increase the probability of unions agreeing to concessions. Their data did, however, suggest that concessions by management (such as Chrysler Chairman Lee Iacocca giving up his salary) may lead to better union-management relations, which in turn may improve the chances for union concessions. In fact, other researchers have concluded that union concessions in one area (for example, pay) are usually accompanied by union gains in another (for example, job security) (Becker, 1987; Cappelli, 1984; Mills, 1983). Generally, the larger the concessions made by the union, the greater the benefits it receives. Some experts have suggested that this exchange of concessions between union and management might lead to the erosion of traditional management rights in return for short-term economic relief (Cappelli, 1984). An analysis of the economic impact of concession bargaining, however, concluded that gains by unions did not erode the value of company stock (which is good news for stockholders), but the impact of these gains for traditional union-management relations remains to be seen.

The Effects of Unions on Behavior in Organizations

Historically, research on the effects of unions on workers' behavior has been scarce. Gordon and Nurick (1981) noted that union leaders tend to distrust I/O psychologists, and view the profession as a tool of management to be used against labor. This distrust stems from the fact that union members often associate psychology with unpopular efforts to increase worker productivity, such as scientific management (see Chapters 1 and 9). Also, psychologists who conduct research in organizations have traditionally been employed by management, therefore often working to achieve management goals opposed by unions. Consequently, union leaders have often rejected psychologists' attempts to study the work behavior of their members. Additionally, unions have less money than businesses and are therefore less able to sponsor research (Fullagar, 1984). Dr. MacKeven should keep this history of distrust in mind as she works with the unionized employees at Flavio's.

Gordon and Nurick (1981) also pointed out that psychologists have not exactly fought to gain access to unions for research purposes. They believe that this lack of effort is due largely to two basic beliefs held by most I/O psychologists. First is the notion, developed during the human relations movement of the late 1950s and early 1960s, that workers and their managers share common interests and concerns. This in turn led to the conclusion that unionization was a symptom of poor management, and focused psychologists' efforts on developing ways to increase management-labor harmony. The tendency to view unionization in this way, as a symptom of a problem rather than as a legitimate effort on the part of workers to protect their interests, discouraged research on unions as organizations.

A second factor that has limited research on unions is a belief among I/O psychologists that they do not need to be concerned with the uses to which their research is put, only with developing the means by which the goals of management can be reached, regardless of the nature of those goals (Gordon & Nurick, 1981). Hugo Münsterberg expressed this view in 1913, and it can be argued that I/O psychologists have followed it ever since. Gordon and Nurick believe that this practice has led psychologists to be unaware of, or perhaps to ignore, the natural conflict between management and unions, and so unions have not been the focus of their research efforts. Again, to the extent that Dr. MacKeven may have acquired either of these attitudes toward unions, she should strive to be especially objective when dealing with the unionization issues raised in Mr. Smith's memo.

An interesting perspective on the effects of unions was outlined by Kochan (1980). According to this view, unions affect organizational behavior only indirectly. The primary, direct effects of unions are the results of the collective bargaining process. Specifically, these effects include higher wages, more extensive benefit plans, seniority as the basis for personnel actions such as raises and layoffs, and greater emphasis on workplace safety and health issues (Barling et al., 1992). The effects of unions on organizational behavior are due, in turn, to management's reaction to these primary effects. Management can react to unionization, for example, by raising prices to recover costs, or by investing in new technology to cut labor expense, or by instituting more effective personnel practices (no doubt inspired by I/O psychology research). In Kochan's view, however, it is the reaction of management, not the results of the collective bargaining, that directly influences

the issues that I/O psychologists typically study, such as job satisfaction, performance, and withdrawal.

Unions and Job Satisfaction

You have seen that low job satisfaction, particularly with extrinsic factors such as pay, is related to pro-union attitudes and behavior. A related but separate issue is whether belonging to a union is related to workers' levels of job satisfaction; the research evidence suggests that it is. Numerous studies comparing unionized and nonunionized workers have found that union members are more dissatisfied (Freeman & Medcoff, 1984). Odewahn and Petty (1980), for example, compared 100 union members to 100 workers who did not belong to unions, and found that the union members had lower overall job satisfaction.

When research focuses on satisfaction with more specific aspects of work, however, the results are more complex. One study found that unionized hourly workers were more satisfied with their pay than were nonunionized workers, but that the union members had lower satisfaction with nonpay facets of their jobs (Kochan and Helfman, 1981). A similar pattern of pay and nonpay satisfaction was found in a nationwide poll of 386 union members and 769 nonmembers (Berger, Olson, & Boudreau, 1983). Their findings led them to conclude that although unionization has an effect on satisfaction with various aspects of work, the effect is indirect and operates through the direct effects of unionization on work-related values and perceived rewards. Specifically, Berger and his colleagues concluded that union members were more satisfied with pay because of the positive effects of unions on pay, whereas unions had negative effects on satisfaction with the actual work performed because union members perceived that their jobs had fewer responsibilities. Satisfaction with supervision was also lower for union members because of less favorable perceptions of relations with supervisors, and satisfaction with promotions was lower because of a lower value placed on promotions by union members.

A slightly different picture emerged from the research of Gomez-Mejia and Balkin (1984). In a study comparing unionized and nonunionized college faculty, they found, as have other researchers, that the union members were more satisfied with their pay. What is different about this study is that Gomez-Mejia and Balkin controlled for differences in pay between the two groups, and the union members were still more satisfied with their pay. This is contrary to Berger, Olson, and Boudreau's (1983) conclusion that unionization has an effect on pay satisfaction only because it results in higher pay. These conflicting results illustrate that the effects of unionization on job satisfaction are probably dependent on a number of situational factors, such as the type of industry within which the unions operate, as well as personal factors, such as the type of person attracted to certain jobs.

Unions and Organizational Effectiveness

Another important question recently addressed by I/O psychologists is whether unions influence the effectiveness of organizations. Certainly, most managers would argue that unions have a detrimental effect on the ability of organizations to function, but there is very little empirical research to support this belief. Cameron (1982) addressed this issue when he compared the effectiveness of colleges with unionized faculty to that of colleges without unions. Effectiveness of the colleges was measured along three general dimensions: ability to acquire resources, morale, and academic quality. On all three dimensions, nonunionized institutions were more effective than their unionized counterparts. This study shows that there is at least the potential for unions to have negative effects on organizational performance. However, the data in this study were not gathered from the union members themselves but from college administrators who may have had an antiunion bias. It may be that unionization is a *response* to poor conditions (that is, lack of resources, poor morale, low academic quality) rather than a *cause* of those conditions, but Cameron's correlational methods do not allow us to determine which is the case.

A more thorough analysis of the literature on unions and performance concluded, contrary to the beliefs of managers and the results of Cameron's (1982) study, that unionized companies are actually *more* productive than nonunionized companies (Freeman & Medcoff, 1984). This greater productivity was attributed to lower turnover and more investment in human resources management in unionized companies. However, the same analysis showed that this increased productivity does not translate into greater profit. That is, the costs of unionization (higher wages, more extensive benefit plans, and so on) are not offset by higher productivity.

It might be expected that with higher organizational productivity, the performance of individual union members would be higher than that of nonmembers. However, there is no empirical evidence that this is the case (Barling et al., 1992). Although it is certainly possible that higher levels of individual performance could account for greater productivity, there are numerous other possible explanations, such as more efficient management in response to successful unionization.

Turnover and Absenteeism

One well-documented relationship in the union research literature is between unionization and voluntary turnover (for example, Freeman, 1980; Gallagher, 1983). Despite the fact that union members are generally less satisfied with their jobs, they have lower turnover rates. As suggested by Kochan (1980), this is probably due to the primary effects of collective bargaining. Specifically, union workers earn higher wages and have better benefit packages than nonunion workers, which makes quitting a less attractive response to dissatisfaction. Also, most union contracts provide a formal grievance procedure, which allows workers to address and remedy problems without fear of management reprisal. Workers without a grievance process may feel that the only way to avoid unpleasant or unacceptable work conditions is to quit (Freeman & Medcoff, 1984).

If union members quit their jobs less often than nonunion workers, you might expect that they are also absent less often. However, this is not the case, as several studies have found that union members are absent *more* frequently than their nonunion counterparts (for example, Allen, 1984; Leigh, 1981). The most convincing explanation for this finding is once again based on the results of the collective bargaining process. Many union contracts include fairly liberal sick-leave benefits. That is, union workers usually have more sick-leave days available, so they can be absent more often without incurring penalties as long as they provide a health-related reason (Dalton & Perry, 1981). If the contract states that sick-leave hours cannot be carried over into a new year, workers are very likely to use all of their available sick leave, whether or not they are actually sick (see Chapter 9). Essentially, sick-leave benefits are often viewed by workers as part of an "implicit contract" that they may be absent a certain number of days each year (Chadwick-Jones, 1981). To the extent that unionized workers have more of these days available, they are likely to be absent more often.

Union Commitment

I/O psychologists have long been interested in studying attitudes toward work and employers (see Chapter 9). With increasing recognition of the role of unions in determining worker behavior, there has been greater interest in studying attitudes toward the union itself. Most of this research has focused on what has come to be known as union commitment. Since 1980 there

has been a great deal of research on union commitment, and we do not have room in this chapter to even mention the many issues related to union commitment that have been studied. Interested students are encouraged to read Barling and colleagues' (1992) description of this research for additional detail.

Gordon, Philpot, Burt, Thompson, and Spiller (1980) spearheaded the research on commitment to unions by developing a measure of union commitment. They constructed a questionnaire that included measures of such factors as loyalty to the union, satisfaction with the union, participation in union activities, socialization experiences occurring early in a worker's union membership, and various demographic variables (for example, age and sex). The questionnaire was administered to 1,377 nonprofessional, white-collar union members. A factor analysis of the data identified four dimensions of **union commitment**. The first and most important was *union loyalty*, which reflects, to a great extent, the degree to which the union is seen by members as providing desired benefits (that is, union instrumentality), as well as pride in the union and one's intentions to remain in the union. The second dimension, *responsibility to the union*, taps members' willingness to fulfill day-to-day union obligations. The third, *willingness to work for the union*, pertains to members' desire to perform services for the union that go beyond normal obligations. Finally, the fourth dimension reflects an attraction to unions based on ideology, and was labeled *belief in unionism*. Because union power depends upon the willingness of members to do such things as file grievances and go out on strike, you can see why union commitment is critical to the success of unions.

Gordon and his colleagues (1980) correlated scores on their union-commitment scales with a variety of other measures and found that the best predictors of union loyalty and belief in unionism were union socialization experiences, such as the nature of workers' interactions with other members during their first year in the union. On the other hand, the best predictors of responsibility to the union and willingness to work for the union were previous union activities; those who worked for the union before were most likely to work for the union again.

Most early research on union commitment was concerned with establishing the validity of the commitment construct, and determining exactly how many dimensions there were to union commitment. Although the results of some studies suggested that union commitment could be described in as few as two dimensions (Friedman & Harvey, 1986), most research has tended to support the existence of Gordon and his colleagues' (1980) original four dimensions, although the dimensions are seldom found to be totally independent (Tetrick, Thacker, & Fields, 1989; Thacker, Fields, & Tetrick, 1989).

Recently, there has been a substantial amount of research examining the causes of union commitment. The research is summarized in a model of union commitment developed by Fullagar and Barling (1987), a version of which is presented in Figure 14.6. As you can see, many of the causes of union commitment are the same or similar to factors that have been shown to predict union voting behavior, which we discussed earlier. Consistent with Gordon and colleagues' (1980) conclusions, research has supported the role of the early union socialization experiences of workers. That is, to the extent that new union members have positive experiences after they join the union and are supported as they learn their role in union activities, they are likely to be more committed to the union later on (Fullagar & Barling, 1989; Fullagar, McCoy, & Shull, 1992). The structure of the union itself is also an important consideration in developing union commitment. To the extent that union members are able to participate in making important decisions, and to the extent that democratic principles are encouraged, commitment will be enhanced (Barling et al., 1992).

Although compared to the causes of union commitment there has been relatively little research on its consequences, some interesting relationships have been studied (Figure 14.6). For example, there is a consistent relationship between the union loyalty component of union commitment and participation in a variety of union activities, from attendance at union meetings and filing grievances (Fullagar & Barling, 1989) to willingness to strike (Barling, Fullagar, Kelloway, & McElvie, 1992). Similarly, union loyalty is related to the propensity of workers to engage in political activity, such as endorsing and working for the election of candidates who support union goals (Thacker, Fields, & Barclay, 1990). Union turnover, or leaving the union, has also been found to be related to union commitment (Klandermans, 1989), as have perceptions of union-management relations, or "industrial relations climate" (Kelloway, Barling, & Fullagar, 1990). Workers with stronger union commitment are less likely to consider leaving the union and more likely to describe the industrial relations climate in their organization in positive terms.

Another aspect of union commitment is the extent to which commitment to a union is related, positively or negatively, to commitment to the employing organization, or organizational commitment (see Chapter 9). If workers are less likely to develop commitment to their employer if they are highly committed to their union, then union commitment might be seen as posing a threat to the company. However, commitment to the company does not seem to prevent commitment to the union or vice versa. Union commitment and organizational commitment are apparently determined by different factors and have different consequences (Fullagar & Barling, 1991). The extent to which workers display dual allegiance, or simultaneous commitment, to *both* the union and the employer is related to the quality of the relationship between union and management. If this

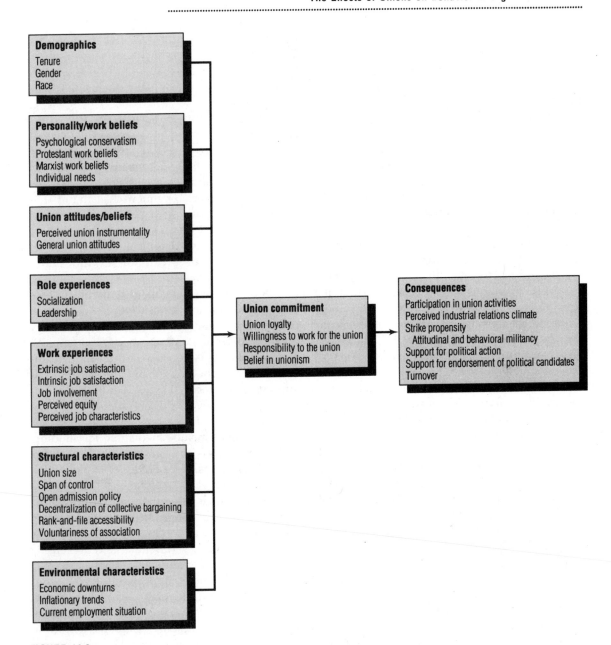

FIGURE 14.6
Causes and Consequences of Union Commitment
SOURCE: From *The Union and Its Members: A Psychological Approach* (p. 75), by J. Barling, C. Fullagar, and E. K. Kelloway. Copyright © 1992 by Oxford University Press. Reprinted by permission.

relationship is cooperative, dual allegiance is more likely (Angle & Perry, 1988).

Conclusion

It is somewhat ironic that the general level of interest in unions among I/O psychologists is increasing at a time when union membership is experiencing a somewhat dramatic decline. As we have said before, even with this decline the number of workers belonging to unions is vast, and we believe that unions will remain an important factor in the workplace in the foreseeable future. However, the recent changes experienced by unions illustrate the fact that like the organizations for which their members work, unions must react to changes in the economy and society. We hope that I/O psychologists continue to develop their interests in unions, and as they do, explore the issues that emerge in this field, such as concession bargaining and the unionization of new industries. We believe that failure to do so will create a major gap in our knowledge of work behavior. Of course, the ability of I/O psychologists to fill that gap depends to a great extent on overcoming the adversarial relationship that they have historically had with unions. Only time will tell whether or not this will happen, but the recent increase in research on unions leads us to be optimistic.

Chapter Summary

Labor unions are associations of workers that represent the interests of their members in dealings with company management. The labor movement in North America began in the late nineteenth century, and unions grew steadily in terms of both membership and power through the 1960s. A crucial factor in this growth was the National Labor Relations Act of 1935,

which guaranteed workers the right to organize. The recent decline in U.S. union membership is largely due to basic changes in the economy, most notably a shift from manufacturing to service industries.

Unions are authorized to represent workers through a democratic process called certification. This process, like other aspects of union-management relations, is overseen by the National Labor Relations Board. Research on worker support for unions has found that dissatisfaction with such factors as pay and benefits, as well as the perceived ability of unions to improve these conditions, are the best predictors of pro-union attitudes and behaviors.

Once workers are organized, the union's most important function is to represent them in collective bargaining, which is the process by which the labor contract specifying employment conditions is negotiated. If a contract cannot be agreed upon by the bargainers (that is, if an impasse is reached), a number of techniques relying on the services of an independent third party are available for breaking the deadlock. The techniques include mediation, fact-finding, and several forms of arbitration. In some cases, when these impasse-resolution techniques fail or are not used at all, a strike or a lockout may be called, which essentially shuts down the company and prevents the employees from working. Between contract negotiations, the most visible union function is representing workers in the grievance procedure.

For many years I/O psychologists conducted relatively little research on labor unions. This was probably due to a history of distrust of psychologists on the part of unions, as well as psychologists' lack of concern over the issues that unions believe are important. Recently, however, there has been an increase in research on such topics as negotiating strategies, attitudes toward unions, and the relationship between union membership and organizational behaviors such as job satisfaction, performance, and withdrawal.

INTEROFFICE MEMO

To: T. J. Smith,
          Legal Counsel

From: J. A. MacKeven,
         Human Resources Coordinator

I have been preparing my preliminary report for the *ad hoc* committee on unions, and I am writing this memo to share my major recommendations with you before the committee meets.

Concerning the probability of additional unionization, I am not too concerned about the situation at PPP. As you pointed out in your memo to me, we simply do not have the type of work force that is likely to be a target for such efforts. Besides, PPP has traditionally had good employee relations, so I don't think we have much to worry about here.

It might be a different story, however, in the Flavio's divisions. The substantial presence of unions in these units shows that there have been serious problems in the past. I believe that an immediate effort should be made to examine the attitudes of all Flavio's employees, particularly toward pay and other benefits. To the extent that there is any substantial dissatisfaction with these aspects of employment, we may expect additional union activity. I suggest that we pay particular attention to plants in locations where unionization is common because that is where the contrast between union and nonunion benefits is likely to be most salient to the workers. Eventually, top management will have to make a decision about whether to spend money to address any dissatisfaction with benefits or risk additional unionization.

As far as "dealing" with currently unionized shops, I don't have much advice to offer. As you know, federal law governs the nature of our relationships with existing unions, so the best we can do is comply with the law and hope for changes in union commitment among Flavio's workers, and eventually some decertifications.

Review Questions
and Exercises

1. Do you think that Dr. MacKeven's assessment of the chances of unionization among Peter's Pan Pizza employees is realistic (see memo p. 499)? Describe conditions under which unionization of the staff in Suardell Springs would be more likely than she indicates.

2. Dr. MacKeven has suggested that PPP's management keep close tabs on the satisfaction of Flavio's employees. Outline in more detail what this would entail. If dissatisfaction with pay or benefits were dis- covered in a Flavio's unit, what should be done? How might this action influence other PPP and Flavio's employees?

3. Dr. MacKeven suggests that there have been "serious problems" in Flavio's in the past, as indicated by the presence of unions. Is this a reasonable analysis on her part? What types of problems might she be talking about? What other explanations are there for Flavio's unionization?

4. Dr. MacKeven states that a decrease in commitment to the union might eventually result in decertification. What do you think would have to happen in order for this change in commitment to take place?

REFERENCES

Aamodt, M. G. (1991). *Applied industrial/organizational psychology*. Belmont, CA: Wadsworth.

Aamodt, M. G., Kimbrough, W. W., Keller, R. J., & Crawford, K. J. (1982). Relationships between sex, race, and job performance level and the generation of critical incidents. *Journal of Educational and Psychological Research, 2*, 227–234.

Abbey, A., & Dickson, J. W. (1983). R&D work climate and innovation in semiconductors. *Academy of Management Journal, 26*, 362–368.

Ackerman, P. L. (1987). Individual differences in skill learning: An integration of psychometric and information processing perspectives. *Psychological Bulletin, 102*, 3–27.

Ackerman, P. L. (1989). Within-task intercorrelations of skilled performance: Implications for predicting individual differences? (A comment on Henry & Hulin, 1987). *Journal of Applied Psychology, 74*, 360–364.

Adams, J. A. (1987). Historical review and appraisal of research on the learning, retention, and transfer of human motor skills. *Psychological Bulletin, 101*, 41–74.

Adams, J. S. (1965). Inequity in social exchange. In L. Berkowitz (Ed.), *Advances in experimental social psychology* (Vol. 2). New York: Academic Press.

Adams, J. S. (1965). Inequity in social exchange. In L. Berkowitz (Ed.), *Advances in experimental social psychology* (Vol. 2). New York: Academic Press.

Adams, L. T. (1985). Changing employment patterns of organized workers. *Monthly Labor Review, 108*(2), 25–31.

Adler, S., Skov, R. B., & Salvemini, N. J. (1985). Job characteristics and job satisfaction: When cause becomes consequence. *Organizational Behavior and Human Decision Processes, 35*, 266–278.

Aiken, L.R. (1979). *Psychological testing and assessment* (3rd ed.). Boston: Allyn & Bacon.

Aldag, R. J., Barr, S. H., & Brief, A. P. (1981). Measurement of perceived task characteristics. *Psychological Bulletin, 90*, 415–431.

Alderfer, C. P. (1969). A new theory of human needs. *Organizational Behavior and Human Performance, 4*, 142–175.

Alderfer, C. P. (1972). *Existence, relatedness, and growth*. New York: Free Press.

Alderfer, C. P. (1977). Organization development. *Annual Review of Psychology, 28*, 197–223.

Alexander, L. D. (1979). *The effect level in the hierarchy and functional area have on the extent Mintzberg's roles are required by managerial jobs*. Proceedings of the Annual Meeting of the Academy of Management, 186–189.

Alexander, R. A. (1988). Group homogeneity, range restriction, and range enhancement effects on correlations. *Personnel Psychology, 41*, 773–777.

Alexander, R. A., Barrett, G. V., & Doverspike, D. (1983). An explication of the selection ratio and its relationship to hiring rate. *Journal of Applied Psychology, 68*, 342–344.

Alexander, R. A., & Barrick, M. R. (1987). Estimating the standard error of projected dollar gains in utility analysis. *Journal of Applied Psychology, 72*, 475–479.

Alexander, R. A., Carson, K. P., Alliger, G. M., & Barrett, G. V. (1985). Further consideration of the power to detect nonzero validity coefficients under range restriction. *Journal of Applied Psychology, 70,* 451–460.

Alexander, R. A., Carson, K. P., Alliger, G. M., & Cronshaw, S. F. (1989). Empirical distributions of range restricted SD$_x$ in validity studies. *Journal of Applied Psychology, 74,* 253–258.

Allen, M. J., & Yen, W. M. (1979). *Introduction to measurement theory.* Pacific Grove, CA: Brooks/Cole.

Allen, M. P., & Panian, S. K. (1982). Power, performance, and succession in the large corporation. *Administrative Science Quarterly, 27,* 538–547.

Allen, N. J., & Meyer, J. P. (1990). The measurement and antecedents of affective, continuance and normative commitment to the organization. *Journal of Occupational Psychology, 63,* 1–18.

Allen, S. G. (1984). Trade unions, absenteeism and exit-voice. *Industrial and Labor Relations Review, 37,* 331–345.

Alliger, G. M., & Janak, E. A. (1989). Kirkpatrick's levels of training criteria: Thirty years later. *Personnel Psychology, 42,* 331–342.

Alluisi, E. A., & Morgan, B. B., Jr. (1976). Engineering psychology and human performance. *Annual Review of Psychology, 27,* 305–330.

Alpander, G. G. (1974). Planning management training programs for organizational development. *Personnel Journal, 53,* 15–21.

American Educational Research Association, American Psychological Association, & National Council on Measurement in Education. (1985). *Standards for educational and psychological testing.* Washington, DC: American Psychological Association.

American Psychological Association. (1981). Specialty guidelines for the delivery of services by industrial/organizational psychologists. *American Psychologist, 36,* 664–669.

Anastasio, E. J., & Morgan, J. S. (1972). Factors inhibiting the use of computers in instruction. *Educational Testing Service* (NSF GJ 27427). Princeton, NJ: Educational Testing Service.

Anderson, C. D., Warner, J. L., & Spencer, C. C. (1984). Inflation bias in self-assessment examinations: Implications for valid employee selection. *Journal of Applied Psychology, 69,* 574–580.

Andrews, I. R., & Valenzi, E. (1970). Overpay inequity or self-image as a worker: A critical evaluation of an experimental induction procedure. *Organizational Behavior and Human Performance, 5,* 22–27.

Angle, H. L., & Perry, J. L. (1981). An empirical assessment of organizational commitment and organizational effectiveness. *Administrative Science Quarterly, 26,* 1–14.

Angle H. L., & Perry, J. L. (1988). Dual commitment and labor management relationship climates. *Academy of Management Journal, 29,* 31–50.

Argote, L. (1982). Input uncertainty and organizational coordination in hospital emergency units. *Administrataive Science Quarterly, 27,* 420–434.

Argote, L., Turner, M. E., & Fichman, M. (1989). To centralize or not to centralize: The effects of uncertainty and threat on group structure and performance. *Organizational Behavior and Human Decision Processes, 43,* 58–74.

Argyris, C. (1957). *Personality and organization: The conflict between system and the individual.* New York: Harper & Row.

Arnold, H. J. (1976). Effects of performance feedback and extrinsic reward upon high intrinsic motivation. *Organizational Behavior and Human Performance, 17,* 275–288.

Arnold, H. J. (1982). Moderator variables: A clarification of conceptual, analytic, and psychometric issues. *Organizational Behavior and Human Performance, 29,* 143–174.

Arnold, H. J. (1984). Testing moderator variable hypotheses: A reply to Stone and Hollenbeck. *Organizational Behavior and Human Performance, 34,* 214–224.

Arnold, H. J., & Feldman, D. C. (1982). A multivariate analysis of the determinants of job turnover. *Journal of Applied Psychology, 67,* 350–360.

Arnold, J. D., Rauschenberger, J. M., Soubel, W. G., & Guion, R. M. (1982). Validation and utility of a strength test for selecting steelworkers. *Journal of Applied Psychology, 67,* 588–604.

Arrowsmith, D., & Courchene, M. (1989). *The current industrial relations scene in Canada, 1989: Collective bargaining reference tables.* Kingston, Ontario: Industrial Relations Centre, Queen's University.

Arthur, W., Jr., Barrett, G. V., & Doverspike, D. (1990). Validation of an information-processing-based test battery for the prediction of handling accidents among petroleum-product transport drivers. *Journal of Applied Psychology, 75,* 621–628.

Arvey, R. D. (1979). Unfair discrimination in the employment interview: Legal and psychological aspects. *Psychological Bulletin, 86*, 736–765.

Arvey, R. D. (1986). Sex bias in job evaluation procedures. *Personnel Psychology, 39*, 315–335.

Arvey, R. D., Bouchard, T. J., Segal, N. L., & Abraham, L. M. (1989). Job satisfaction: Environmental and genetic components. *Journal of Applied Psychology, 74*, 187–192.

Arvey, R. D., & Campion, J. E. (1982). The employment interview: A summary and review of recent research. *Personnel Psychology, 35*, 281–322.

Arvey, R. D., Cole, D. A., Hazucha, J. F., & Hartano, F. M. (1985). Statistical power of training evaluation designs. *Personnel Psychology, 38*, 493–507.

Arvey, R. D., Davis, G. A., McGowen, S. L., & Dipboye, R. L. (1982). Potential sources of bias in job analytic processes. *Academy of Management Journal, 25*, 618–629.

Arvey, R. D., & Hoyle, J. C. (1974). A Guttman approach to the development of behaviorally based rating scales for systems analysts and programmer/analysts. *Journal of Applied Psychology, 59*, 61–68.

Arvey, R. D., & Ivancevich, J. M. (1980). Punishment in organizations: A review, propositions, and research suggestions. *Academy of Management Review, 5*, 123–132.

Arvey, R. D., Maxwell, S. E., & Abraham, L. M. (1985). Reliability artifacts in comparable worth procedures. *Journal of Applied Psychology, 70*, 695–705.

Arvey, R. D., Miller, H. E., Gould, R., & Burch, P. (1987). Interview validity for selecting sales clerks. *Personnel Psychology, 40*, 1–12.

Arvey, R. D., Strickland, W., Drauden, G., & Martin, C. (1990). Motivational components of test taking. *Personnel Psychology, 43*, 695–716.

Ash, R. A., & Edgell, S. L. (1975). A note on the reliability of the Position Analysis Questionnaire (PAQ). *Journal of Applied Psychology, 60*, 765–766.

Ash, R. A., & Levine, E. L. (1985). Job applicant training and work experience evaluation: An empirical comparison of four methods. *Journal of Applied Psychology, 70*, 572–576.

Ashford, S. J. (1986). Feedback-seeking in individual adaptation: A resource perspective. *Academy of Management Journal, 29*, 465–487.

Ashford, S. J., & Cummings, L. L. (1983). Feedback as an individual resource: Personal strategies of creating information. *Organizational Behavior and Human Performance, 32*, 370–398.

Ashford, S. J., & Tsui, A. S. (1991). Self-regulation for managerial effectiveness: The role of active feedback seeking. *Academy of Management Journal, 34*, 251–280.

Astrand, P., & Rodahl, K. (1986). *Textbook of work physiology* (3rd ed.). New York: McGraw-Hill.

At Emery Air Freight: Positive reinforcement boosts performance. (1973, Winter). *Organizational Dynamics*, 41–50.

Athey, T. R., & McIntyre, R. M. (1987). Effect of rater training on rater accuracy: Levels-of-processing theory and social facilitation theory perspectives. *Journal of Applied Psychology, 72*, 567–572.

Atkinson, J. W. (Ed.). (1958). *Motives in fantasy, action, and society*. Princeton, NJ: Van Nostrand.

Atkinson, J. W., & Feather, N. T. (1966). *A theory of achievement motivation*. New York: Wiley.

Austin, J. T., Humphreys, L. G., & Hulin, C. L. (1989). Another view of dynamic criteria: A critical reanalysis of Barrett, Caldwell, and Alexander. *Personnel Psychology, 42*, 583–596.

Avolio, B. J., Waldman, D. A., & McDaniel, M. A. (1990). Age and work performance in nonmanagerial jobs: The effects of experience and occupational type. *Academy of Management Journal, 33*, 407–422.

Bagozzi, R. P., & Yi, Y. (1990). Assessing method variance in multitrait-multimethod matrices: The case of self-reported affect and perceptions at work. *Journal of Applied Psychology, 75*, 547–560.

Baldwin, T. T., & Ford, J. K. (1988). Transfer of training: A review and directions for future research. *Personnel Psychology, 41*, 63–105.

Baldwin, T. T., Magjuka, R. J., & Loher, B. T. (1991). The perils of participation: Effects of choice of training on trainee motivation and learning. *Personnel Psychology, 44*, 51–65.

Balma, M. J. (1959). The concept of synthetic validity. *Personnel Psychology, 12*, 395–396.

Balzer, W. K. (1986). Biases in the recording of performance-related information: The effects of initial impression and centrality of the appraisal task. *Organizational Behavior and Human Decision Processes, 37*, 329–347.

Balzer, W. K., Doherty, M. E., & O'Connor, R., Jr. (1989). Effects of cognitive feedback on performance. *Psychological Bulletin, 106*, 410–433.

Bandura, A. (1969). *Principles of behavior modification.* New York: Holt, Rinehart & Winston.

Bandura, A. (1971). *Social learning theory.* Morristown, NJ: General Learning Press.

Bandura, A. (1977). *Social learning theory.* Englewood Cliffs, NJ: Prentice-Hall.

Bandura, A. (1982). Self-efficacy mechanism in human agency. *American Psychologist, 37,* 122–147.

Bandura, A. (1986). *Social foundations of thought and action: A social cognitive theory.* Englewood Cliffs, NJ: Prentice-Hall.

Bandura, A. (1987). Self-regulation of motivation and action through goal systems. In V. Hamilton & N. H. Fryda (Eds.), *Cognition, motivation, and affect: A cognitive science view.* Dordrecht: Martinus Nijholl.

Bandura, A., & Cervone, D. (1986). Differential engagement of self-reactive influences in cognitive motivation. *Organizational Behavior and Human Decision Processes, 38,* 92–113.

Banks, C. G., & Murphy, K. R. (1985). Toward narrowing the research practice gap in performance appraisal. *Personnel Psychology, 38,* 335–345.

Banks, C. G., & Roberson, L. (1985). Performance appraisers as test developers. *Academy of Management Review, 10,* 128–142.

Banks, M. H., Jackson, P. R., Stafford, E. M., & Warr, P. B. (1983). The Job Components Inventory and the analysis of jobs requiring limited skill. *Personnel Psychology, 36,* 57–66.

Bannister, B. D. (1986). Performance outcome feedback and attributional feedback: Interactive effects on recipient responses. *Journal of Applied Psychology, 71,* 203–210.

Barley, S. R., Meyer, G. W., & Gash, D. C. (1988). Cultures of culture: Academics, practitioners and the pragmatics of normative control. *Administrative Science Quarterly, 33,* 24–60.

Barling, J., Fullagar, C., & Kelloway, E. K. (1992). *The union and its members: A psychological approach.* New York: Oxford University Press.

Barling, J., Fullagar, C., McElvie, L., & Kelloway, E. K. (1992). Union loyalty and strike propensity. *Journal of Social Psychology, 132,* 581–591.

Barling, J., Kelloway, E. K., & Bremermann, E. H. (1991). Pre-employment predictors of union attitudes: The role of family socialization and work beliefs. *Journal of Applied Psychology, 76,* 725–731.

Barling, J., Laliberte, M., Fullagar, C., & Kelloway, E. K. (1990). *Work and personal predictors of the intent to unionize.* Unpublished manuscript.

Barling, J., & Rosenbaum, A. (1986). Work stressors and wife abuse. *Journal of Applied Psychology, 71,* 346–348.

Barnes, J. L., & Landy, F. J. (1979). Scaling behavioral anchors. *Applied Psychological Measurement, 3,* 193–200.

Barnes, V., Potter, E. H., III, & Fiedler, F. E. (1983). Effect of interpersonal stress on the prediction of academic performance. *Journal of Applied Psychology, 68,* 686–697.

Barnes-Farrell, J. L., L'Heureux-Barrett, T. J., & Conway, J. M. (1991). Impact of gender-related job features on the accurate evaluation of performance information. *Organizational Behavior and Human Decision Processes, 48,* 23–35.

Barnes-Farrell, J. L., & Weiss, H. M. (1984). Effects of standard extremity on mixed standard scale performance ratings. *Personnel Psychology, 37,* 301–316.

Baron, A. S. (1977). Selection, development and socialization of women into management. *Business Quarterly, 28,* 61–67.

Baron, R. A. (1983). "Sweet smell of success"? The impact of pleasant artificial scents on evaluations of job applicants. *Journal of Applied Psychology, 68,* 709–713.

Baron, R. A. (1988). Negative effects of destructive criticism: Impact on conflict, self-efficacy, and task performance. *Journal of Applied Psychology, 73,* 199–207.

Barr, S. H., & Hitt, M. A. (1986). A comparison of selection decision models in manager versus student samples. *Personnel Psychology, 39,* 599–617.

Barrett, G. V., & Alexander, R. A. (1989). Rejoinder to Austin, Humphreys, and Hulin: Critical reanalysis of Barrett, Caldwell, and Alexander. *Personnel Psychology, 42,* 597–612.

Barrett, G. V., Caldwell, M. S., & Alexander, R. A. (1985). The concept of dynamic criteria: A critical reanalysis. *Personnel Psychology, 38,* 41–56.

Barrett, G. V., Caldwell, M. S., & Alexander, R. A. (1989). The predictive stability of ability requirements for task performance: A critical reanalysis. *Human Performance, 2(3),* 167–181.

Barrett, G. V., & Kernan, M. C. (1987). Performance appraisal and terminations: A review of court decisions since *Brito v. Zia* with implications for personnel practices. *Personnel Psychology, 40,* 489–503.

Barrett, G. V., Phillips, J. S., & Alexander, R. A. (1981). Concurrent and predictive validity designs: A critical reanalysis. *Journal of Applied Psychology, 66,* 1–6.

Barrett, G. V., & Thornton, C. L. (1968). The relationship between perceptual style and driver reaction to an emergency situation. *Journal of Applied Psychology, 52,* 169–176.

Barrett, R. S., Taylor, E. K. Parker, J. W., & Martens, L. (1958). Rating scale content: I. Scale information and supervisory ratings. *Personnel Psychology, 11,* 333–346.

Barrick, M. R., & Mount, M. K. (1991). The big five personality dimensions and job performance: A meta-analysis. *Personnel Psychology, 44,* 1–26.

Bartlett, C. J., & O'Leary, B. S. (1969). A differential prediction model to moderate the effects of heterogeneous groups in personnel selection and classification. *Personnel Psychology, 22,* 1–17.

Bartol, K. M. (1974). Male vs. female leaders: The effect of leader need for dominance on follower satisfaction. *Academy of Management Journal, 17,* 225–233.

Bartol, K. M. (1975). The effect of male versus female leaders on follower satisfaction and performance. *Journal of Business Research, 3,* 33–42.

Bartol, K. M. (1978). The sex structuring of organizations: A search for possible causes. *Academy of Management Review, 3,* 805–815.

Bartol, K. M., Anderson, C. R., & Schneier, C. E. (1981). Sex and ethnic effects on motivation to manage among college business students. *Journal of Applied Psychology, 66,* 40–44.

Bartol, K. M., & Martin, D. C. (1987). Managerial motivation among MBA students: A longitudinal assessment. *Journal of Occupational Psychology, 60,* 1–12.

Bartol, K. M., & Wortman, M. S., Jr. (1975). Male versus female leaders: Effects on perceived leader behavior and satisfaction in a hospital. *Personnel Psychology, 28,* 533–547.

Barton, J., & Folkard, S. (1991). The response of day and night nurses to their work schedules. *Journal of Occupational Psychology, 64,* 207–218.

Bass, A. R., & Firestone, I. J. (1980). Implications of representativeness for generalizability of field and laboratory research findings. *American Psychologist, 35,* 463–464.

Bass, B. M. (1954). The leaderless group discussion. *Psychological Bulletin, 51,* 465–492.

Bass, B. M. (1962). Further evidence on the dynamic character of criteria. *Personnel Psychology, 15,* 93–97.

Bass, B. M. (1967). Social behavior and the orientation interview: A review. *Psychological Bulletin, 68,* 260–292.

Bass, B. M. (1981). *Stogdill's handbook of leadership.* New York: Free Press.

Bass, B. M. (1983). Issues involved in relations between methodological rigor and reported outcomes in evaluations of organizational development. *Journal of Applied Psychology, 68,* 197–199.

Bass, B. M. (1985). *Leadership and performance beyond expectations.* New York: Free Press.

Bass, B. M. (1990). *Bass and Stogdill's handbook of leadership: Theory, research and managerial applications* (3rd ed.). New York: Free Press.

Bass, B. M., & Avolio, B. J. (1989). Potential biases in leadership measures: How prototypes, leniency, and general satisfaction relate to ratings and rankings of transformational and transactional leadership constructs. *Educational and Psychological Measurement, 49,* 509–527.

Bass, B. M., & Barrett, G. V. (1981). *People, work, and organizations: An introduction to industrial and organizational psychology* (2nd ed.). Boston: Allyn & Bacon.

Bass, B. M., Kruskell, J., & Alexander, R. A. (1971). Male managers' attitudes toward working women. *American Behavioral Scientist, 15,* 221–236.

Bass, B. M., & Mitchell, C. W. (1976). Influence on the felt need for collective bargaining by business and science professionals. *Journal of Applied Psychology, 61,* 770–773.

Bass, B. M., & Vaughan, J. A. (1966). *Training in industry: The management of learning.* Pacific Grove, CA: Brooks/Cole.

Bassett, G. A., & Meyer, H. H. (1968). Performance appraisal based on self-review. *Personnel Psychology, 21,* 421–430.

Bateman, T. S., & Strasser, S. (1984). A longitudinal analysis of the antecedents of organizational commitment. *Academy of Management Journal, 27,* 95–112.

Baumgartel, H., & Jeanpierre, F. (1972). Applying new knowledge in the back-home setting: A study of Indian managers' adaptive efforts. *Journal of Applied Behavioral Science, 8,* 674–694.

Baxter, J. C., Brock, B., Hill, P. C., & Rozelle, R. M. (1981). Letters of recommendation: A question of value. *Journal of Applied Psychology, 66,* 296–301.

Beach, L. R., & Mitchell, T. R. (1990). Image theory: A behavioral theory of decision making in organizations. In B. M. Staw & L. L. Cummings (Eds.), *Research in organizational behavior* (vol. 12). Greenwich, CT: JAI Press.

Becker, B. E. (1987). Concession bargaining: The impact on shareholder's equity. *Industrial and Labor Relations Review, 40,* 268–279.

Becker, B. E. (1989). The influence of labor markets on human resources utility estimates. *Personnel Psychology, 42,* 531–546.

Becker, T. E., & Cardy, R. L. (1986). Influence of halo error on appraisal effectiveness: A conceptual and empirical reconsideration. *Journal of Applied Psychology, 71,* 662–671.

Becker, T. E., & Klimoski, R. J. (1989). A field study of the relationship between the organizational feedback environment and performance. *Personnel Psychology, 42,* 343–358.

Beehr, T. A. (1985). The role of social support in coping with occupational stress. In T. A. Beehr & R. S. Bhagat (Eds.), *Human stress and cognition in organizations: An integrated perspective.* New York: Wiley.

Beehr, T. A. (1990). Stress in the workplace: An overview. In J. W. Jones, B. D. Steffy, & D. W. Bray (Eds.), *Applying psychology in business.* Lexington, MA: Lexington Books.

Beehr, T. A., & Newman, J. E. (1978). Job stress, employee health, and organizational effectiveness: A facet analysis, model, and literature review. *Personnel Psychology, 31,* 665–699.

Behar, R. (1992, March 9). Thugs in uniform. *Time,* pp. 44–47.

Bellows, R. M. (1959). *Creative leadership.* Englewood Cliffs, NJ: Prentice-Hall.

Ben-Shakhar, G., Bar-Hillel, M., Bilu, Y., Ben-Abba, E., & Flug, A. (1986). Can graphology predict occupational success? Two empirical studies and some methodological ruminations. *Journal of Applied Psychology, 71,* 645–653.

Bendig, A. W. (1952a). A statistical report on a revision of the Miami instructor rating sheet. *Journal of Educational Psychology, 43,* 423–429.

Bendig, A. W. (1952b). The use of student rating scales in the evaluation of instructors in introductory psychology. *Journal of Educational Psychology, 43,* 167–175.

Bendig, A. W. (1953). The reliability of self-ratings as a function of the amount of verbal anchoring and the number of categories on the scale. *Journal of Applied Psychology, 37,* 38–41.

Bendig, A. W. (1954a). Reliability and number of rating scale categories. *Journal of Applied Psychology, 38,* 38–40.

Bendig, A. W. (1954b). Reliability of short rating scales and the heterogeneity of the rated stimuli. *Journal of Applied Psychology, 38,* 167–170.

Benedict, M. E., & Levine, E. L. (1988). Delay and distortion: Tacit influences on performance appraisal effectiveness. *Journal of Applied Psychology, 73,* 507–514.

Benge, E. J., Burk, S. L. H., & Hay, E. N. (1941). *Manual of job evaluation.* New York: Harper and Brothers.

Benjamin, L. T., Jr. (1988). A history of teaching machines. *American Psychologist, 43,* 703–712.

Bennett, C. (1977, January). The demographic variables of discomfort glare. *Lighting Design and Application,* 22–24.

Bennett, C. A., Chitlangia, A., & Pangrekar, A. (1977). Illumination levels and performance of practical visual tasks. *Proceedings of the Human Factors Society 21st Annual Meeting.* 322–325.

Benson, H. (1975). *The relaxation response.* New York: Avon.

Berger, C. J., Olson, C. A., & Boudreau, J. W. (1983). Effects of unions on job satisfaction: The role of work-related values and perceived rewards. *Organizational Behavior and Human Performance, 32,* 289–324.

Berkowitz, L., & Donnerstein, E. (1982). External validity is more than skin deep: Some answers to criticisms of laboratory experiments. *American Psychologist, 37,* 245–257.

Berkshire, J. R., & Highland, R. W. (1953). Forced-choice performance rating—A methodological study. *Personnel Psychology, 6,* 355–378.

Berman, F. E., & Miner, J. B. (1985). Motivation to manage at the top executive level: A test of the hierarchic role-motivation theory. *Personnel Psychology, 38,* 377–391.

Bernard, L. L. (1926). *An introduction to social psychology.* New York: Holt.

Bernardin, H. J. (1978). Effects of rater training on leniency and halo errors in student ratings of instructors. *Journal of Applied Psychology, 63,* 301–308.

Bernardin, H. J., & Beatty, R. W. (1984). *Performance appraisal: Assessing human behavior at work.* Boston: Kent.

Bernardin, H. J., & Pence, E. C. (1980). Effects of rater training: Creating new response sets and decreasing accuracy. *Journal of Applied Psychology 65,* 60–66.

Bernardin, H. J., & Walter, C. S. (1977). Effects of rater training and diary-keeping on psychometric error in ratings. *Journal of Applied Psychology, 62,* 64–69.

Bhagat, R. S., McQuaid, S. J., Lindholm, H., & Segovis, J. (1985). Total life stress: A multimethod validation of the construct and its effects on organizationally valued outcomes and withdrawal behaviors. *Journal of Applied Psychology, 70,* 202–214.

Big brother comes clean. (1991, October 21). *Time,* p. 78.

Bigoness, W. J. (1978). Correlates of faculty attitudes toward collective bargaining. *Journal of Applied Psychology, 63,* 228–233.

Binning, J. F., & Barrett, G. V. (1989). Validity of personnel decisions: A conceptual analysis of the inferential and evidential bases. *Journal of Applied Psychology, 74,* 478–494.

Binning, J. F., Goldstein, M. A., Garcia, M. F., & Scattaregia, J. H. (1988). Effects of preinterview impressions on questioning strategies in same- and opposite-sex employment interviews. *Journal of Applied Psychology, 73,* 30–37.

Bird, C. P., & Fisher, T. D. (1986). Thirty years later: Attitudes toward the employment of older workers. *Journal of Applied Psychology, 71,* 515–517.

Bird, F. E. (1974). *Management guide to loss control.* Santa Monica: Institute Press.

Birk, L. (1973). *Biofeedback: Behavioral medicine.* New York: Grune & Stratton.

Black, J. S., & Mendenhall, M. (1990). Cross-cultural training effectiveness: A review and a theoretical framework for future research. *Academy of Management Review, 15,* 113–136.

Black marks for the mines. (1992, April 13). *Time,* p. 53.

Blackburn, R., & Cummings, L. L. (1982). Cognitions of work unit structure. *Academy of Management Journal, 25,* 836–854.

Blake, R. R., & Adams, A. (1991). *Leadership dilemmas—grid solutions.* Houston: Gulf Publishing Company.

Blake, R. R., & Mouton, J. S. (1964). *The managerial grid: Key orientations for achieving production through people.* Houston: Gulf.

Blake, R. R., & Mouton, J. S. (1985). *The managerial grid III.* Houston: Gulf.

Blanz, F., & Ghiselli, E. E. (1972). The mixed standard scale: A new rating system. *Personnel Psychology, 22,* 185–199.

Blau, G. J. (1985). Relationship of extrinsic, intrinsic, and demographic predictors to various types of withdrawal behaviors. *Journal of Applied Psychology, 70,* 442–450.

Blood, M. R. (1974). Spin-offs from behavioral expectation scale procedures. *Journal of Applied Psychology, 59,* 513–515.

Blood, M. R., & Mullet, G. M. (1977). *Where have all the moderators gone? The perils of Type II error.* Atlanta: College of Industrial Management, Georgia Institute of Technology.

Bluen, S. D., Barling, J., & Burns, W. (1990). Predicting sales performance, job satisfaction, and depression by using the achievement strivings and impatience-irritability dimensions of Type A behavior. *Journal of Applied Psychology, 75,* 212–216.

Blum, M. L., & Naylor, J. C. (1968). *Industrial psychology: Its theoretical and social foundations* (rev. ed.). New York: Harper & Row.

Blumberg, A., & Golembiewski, R. (1976). *Learning and change in groups.* Clinton, MA: Colonial Press.

Bobko, P., & Donnelly, L. (1988). Identifying correlates of job-level, overall worth estimates: Application in a public sector organization. *Human Performance, 1(3),* 187–204.

Bobko, P., Karren, R., & Kerkar, S. P. (1987). Systematic research needs for understanding supervisory-based estimates of SD_y in utility analysis. *Organizational Behavior and Human Decision Processes, 40,* 69–95.

Bobko, P., Karren, R., & Parkington, J. J. (1983). Estimation of standard deviations in utility analyses: An empirical test. *Journal of Applied Psychology, 68,* 170–176.

Boehm, V. R. (1980). Research in the "real world"—

A conceptual model. *Personnel Psychology, 33,* 495–503.

Boehm, V. R. (1982). Are we validating more but publishing less? (The impact of governmental regulation on published validation research—An exploratory investigation.) *Personnel Psychology, 35,* 175–187.

Boje, D. M., & Whetten, D. A. (1981). Effects of organizational strategies and contextual constraints on centrality and attributions of influence in interorganizational networks. *Administrative Science Quarterly, 26,* 378–395.

Booker, G. S., & Miller, R. W. (1966). A closer look at peer ratings. *Personnel, 43,* 42–47.

Borman, W. C. (1974). The rating of individuals in organizations: An alternate approach. *Organizational Behavior and Human Performance, 12* 105–124.

Borman, W. C. (1975). Effects of instructions to avoid halo error on reliability and validity of performance evaluation ratings. *Journal of Applied Psychology, 60,* 556–560

Borman, W. C. (1979). Format and training effects on rating accuracy and rater errors. *Journal of Applied Psychology, 64,* 410–421.

Borman, W. C. (1982). Validity of behavioral assessment for predicting military recruiter performance. *Journal of Applied Psychology, 67,* 3–9.

Borman, W. C. (1987). Personal constructs, performance schemata, and "folk theories" of subordinate effectiveness: Explorations in an army officer sample. *Organizational Behavior and Human Decision Processes, 40,* 307–322.

Borman, W. C., Eaton, N. K., Bryan, J. D., & Rosse, R. L. (1983). Validity of army recruiter behavioral assessment: Does the assessor make a difference? *Journal of Applied Psychology, 68,* 415–419.

Borman, W. C., & Hallam, G. L. (1991). Observation accuracy for assessors of work-sample performance: Consistency across task and individual-differences correlates. *Journal of Applied Psychology, 76,* 11–18.

Bouchard, T. J., Jr. (1984). Twins reared apart and together: What they tell us about human diversity. In S. Fox (Ed.), *The chemical and biological bases of individuality.* New York: Plenum.

Boudreau, J. W. (1983a). Economic considerations in estimating the utility of human resource productivity improvement programs. *Personnel Psychology, 36,* 551–576.

Boudreau, J. W. (1983b). Effects of employee flows on utility analysis of human resource productivity improvement programs. *Journal of Applied Psychology, 68,* 396–406.

Boudreau, J. W., & Berger, C. J. (1985). Decision-theoretic utility analysis applied to employee separations and acquisitions [Monograph]. *Journal of Applied Psychology, 70,* 581–612.

Boudreau, J. W., & Rynes, S. L. (1985). Role of recruitment in staffing utility analysis. *Journal of Applied Psychology, 70,* 354–366.

Bownas, D. A., Bosshardt, M. J., & Donnelly, L. F. (1985). A quantitative approach to evaluating training curriculum content sampling adequacy. *Personnel Psychology, 38,* 117–131.

Boyce, P. (1981). *Human factors in lighting.* New York: Macmillan.

Boyce, P. (1988). Lighting and visual performance. In D. Osborne (Ed.), *International reviews of ergonomics* (Vol. 2). London: Taylor & Francis.

Bramel, D., & Friend, R. (1981). Hawthorne, the myth of the docile worker, and class bias in psychology. *American Psychologist, 36,* 867–878.

Bramel, D., & Friend, R. (1982). Is industrial psychology none of Marxism's business? *American Psychologist, 37,* 860–862.

Brannick, M. T., Michaels, C. E., & Baker, D. P. (1989). Construct validity of in-basket scores. *Journal of Applied Psychology, 74,* 957–963.

Braver, M. C. W., & Braver, S. L. (1988). Statistical treatment of the Solomon four-group design: A meta-analytic approach. *Psychological Bulletin, 104,* 150–154.

Brayfield, A. H., & Crockett, W. H. (1955). Employee attitudes and employee performance. *Psychological Bulletin, 52,* 396–424.

Breaugh, J. A. (1981). Predicting absenteeism from prior absenteeism and work attitudes. *Journal of Applied Psychology, 66,* 555–560.

Breaugh, J. A. (1983). The 12–hour work day: Differing employee reactions. *Personnel Psychology, 36,* 277–288.

Brett, J. M. (1980). Why employees want unions. *Organizational Dynamics, 8,* 47–59.

Brief, A. P. (1980). Peer assessment revisited: A brief comment on Kane and Lawler. *Psychological Bulletin, 88,* 78–79.

Brief, A. P., & Aldag, R. J. (1975). Employee reactions to job characteristics: A constructive replication. *Journal of Applied Psychology, 60,* 182–186.

Brief, A. P., Burke, M. J., George, J. M., & Robinson, B. S. (1988). Should negative affectivity remain an unmeasured variable in the study of job stress? *Journal of Applied Psychology, 73,* 193–198.

Brief, A. P., Schuler, R. S., & Van Sell, M. (1981). *Managing job stress.* Boston: Little, Brown.

Brockhaus, R. H., Sr. (1980). Risk taking propensity of entrepreneurs. *Academy of Management Journal, 23,* 509–520.

Brockner, J., & Adsit, L. (1986). The moderating impact of sex on the equity-satisfaction relationship: A field study. *Journal of Applied Psychology, 71,* 585–590.

Brockner, J., Davy, J., & Carter, C. (1985). Layoffs, self-esteem, and survivor guilt: Motivational, affective, and attitudinal consequences. *Organizational Behavior and Human Decision Processes, 36,* 229–244.

Brockner, J., Greenberg, J., Brockner, A., Bortz, J., Davy, J., & Carter, C. (1986). Layoffs, equity theory, and work performance: Further evidence of the impact of survivor guilt. *Academy of Management Journal, 29,* 373–384.

Brogden, H. E. (1949). When testing pays off. *Personnel Psychology, 2,* 171–185.

Brogden, H. E., & Taylor, E. K. (1950). The dollar criterion—Applying the cost accounting concept to criterion construction. *Personnel Psychology, 3,* 133–154.

Brown, E. M. (1968). Influence of training, method, and relationship on the halo effect. *Journal of Applied Psychology, 52,* 195–199.

Brown, K. A., & Mitchell, T. R. (1986). Influence of task interdependence and number of poor performers on diagnoses of causes of poor performance. *Academy of Management Journal, 29,* 412–424.

Brown, S. H. (1981). Validity generalization and situational moderation in the life insurance industry. *Journal of Applied Psychology, 66,* 664–670.

Brumback, G. (1972). A reply to Kavanagh. *Personnel Psychology, 25,* 567–572.

Bryan, W. L. (1904). Theory and practice. *Psychological Review, 11,* 71–82.

Bryan, W. L., & Harter, N. (1899). Studies of the telegraphic language. *Psychological Review, 6,* 345–375.

Bryan, W. L., & Harter, N. (1897). Studies in the physiology and psychology of the telegraphic language. *Psychological Review, 4,* 27–53.

Buck, G. H. (1990). A history of teaching machines. *American Psychologist, 45,* 551–552.

Budzynski, T. H. (1974). *Progressive relaxation training.* New York: BMA Audio Cassette Programs.

Bulldozing the U.A.W. (1992, April 27). *Time,* p. 18.

Bullock, R. J., & Svyantek, D. J. (1983). Positive-findings bias in positive-findings bias research. *Academy of Management Proceedings,* 221–224.

Bullock, R. J., & Svyantek, D. J. (1985). Analyzing meta-analysis: Potential problems, an unsuccessful replication, and evaluation criteria. *Journal of Applied Psychology, 70,* 108–115.

Burke, M. J. (1984). Validity generalization: A review and critique of the correlational model. *Personnel Psychology, 37,* 93–115.

Burke, M. J., & Day, R. R. (1986). A cumulative study of the effectiveness of managerial training. *Journal of Applied Psychology, 71,* 232–245.

Burke, M. J., & Doran, L. I. (1989). A note on the economic utility of generalized validity coefficients in personnel selection. *Journal of Applied Psychology, 74,* 171–175.

Burke, M. J., & Frederick, J. T. (1984). Two modified procedures for estimating standard deviations in utility analyses. *Journal of Applied Psychology, 69,* 482–489.

Burke, M. J., & Frederick, J. T. (1986). A comparison of economic utility estimates for alternative SD_y estimation procedures. *Journal of Applied Psychology, 71,* 334–339.

Burke, M. J., Raju, N. S., & Pearlman, K. (1986). An empirical comparison of the results of five validity generalization procedures. *Journal of Applied Psychology, 71,* 349–353.

Burns, J. M. (1978). *Leadership.* New York: Harper & Row.

Busch, H. M. (1949). *Conference methods in industry.* New York: Harper and Brothers.

Bussom, R. S., Larson, L. L., & Vicars, W. M. (1982). Unstructured, nonparticipant observation and the study of leaders' interpersonal contacts. In J. G. Hunt, U. Sekaran, & C. A. Schriesheim (Eds.), *Leadership: Beyond establishment views.* Carbondale: Southern Illinois University Press.

Butler, M. C., & Jones, A. P. (1979). Perceived leader behavior, individual characteristics, and injury occurrence in hazardous work environments. *Journal of Applied Psychology, 64,* 299–304.

Butler, S. K., & Harvey, R. J. (1988). A comparison of holistic versus decomposed rating of Position

Analysis Questionnaire work dimensions. *Personnel Psychology, 41,* 761–771.

Butterfield, D. A., & Powell, G. N. (1981). Effect of group performance, leader sex, and rater sex on ratings of leader behavior. *Organizational Behavior and Human Performance, 28,* 129–141.

Bycio, P., Alvares, K. M., & Hahn, J. (1987). Situational specificity in assessment center ratings: A confirmatory factor analysis. *Journal of Applied Psychology, 72,* 463–474.

Cain, P. S., & Green, B. S. (1983). Reliabilities of selected ratings available from the *Dictionary of occupational titles. Journal of Applied Psychology, 68,* 155–165.

Calder, B. J. (1977). An attribution theory of leadership. In B. M. Staw & G. R. Salancik (Eds.), *New directions in organizational behavior.* Chicago: St. Clair.

Calder, B. J., & Staw, B. M. (1975). Self-perception of intrinsic and extrinsic motivation. *Journal of Personality and Social Psychology, 31,* 599–605.

Caldwell, D. F., & O'Reilly, C. A., III. (1982). Boundary spanning and individual performance: The impact of self-monitoring. *Journal of Applied Psychology, 67,* 124–127.

Caldwell, D. F., & O'Reilly, C. A., III. (1985). The impact of information on job choices and turnover. *Academy of Management Journal, 28,* 934–943.

Caldwell, D. F., & Spivey, W. A. (1983). The relationship between recruiting source and employee success: An analysis by race. *Personnel Psychology, 36,* 67–72.

Callender, J. C., & Osburn, H. G. (1981). Testing the constancy of validity with computer-generated sampling distributions of the multiplicative model variance estimate: Results for petroleum industry validation research. *Journal of Applied Psychology, 66,* 274–281.

Callender, J. C., & Osburn, H. G. (1988). Unbiased estimation of sampling variance of correlations. *Journal of Applied Psychology, 73,* 312–315.

Cameron, K. (1980). Critical questions in assessing organizational effectiveness. *Organizational Dynamics, 9,* 66–80.

Cameron, K. (1982). The relationship between faculty unionism and organizational effectiveness. *Academy of Management Journal, 25,* 6–24.

Cameron, K. S. (1981). Domains of organizational ef-

fectiveness in colleges and universities. *Academy of Management Journal, 24,* 25–47.

Cameron, K. S., & Whetten, D. A. (1981). Perceptions of organizational effectiveness over organizational life cycles. *Administrative Science Quarterly, 26,* 525–544.

Campbell, C. H., Ford, P., Rumsey, M. G., Pulakos, E. D., Borman, W. C., Felker, D. B., de Vera, M. V., & Riegelhaupt, B. J. (1990). Development of multiple job performance measures in a representative sample of jobs. *Personnel Psychology, 43,* 277–300.

Campbell, D. J. (1988). Task complexity: A review and analysis. *Academy of Management Review, 13,* 40–52

Campbell, D. J., & Lee, C. (1988). Self-appraisal in performance evaluation: Development versus evaluation. *Academy of Management Review, 13,* 302–314.

Campbell, D. T., & Fiske, D. W. (1959). Convergent and discriminant validation by the multitrait-multimethod matrix. *Psychological Bulletin, 56,* 81–105.

Campbell, D. T., & Stanley, J. C. (1963). *Experimental and quasi-experimental designs for research.* Chicago: Rand McNally.

Campbell, J. P. (1976). Psychometric theory. In M.D. Dunnette (Ed.), *Handbook of industrial and organizational psychology.* Chicago: Rand McNally.

Campbell, J. P. (1982). Editorial: Some remarks from the outgoing editor. *Journal of Applied Psychology, 67,* 691–700.

Campbell, J. P. (1990). An overview of the Army Selection and Classification Project (Project A). *Personnel Psychology, 43,* 231–239.

Campbell, J. P., Dunnette, M. D., Arvey, R. D., & Hellervik, L. V. (1973). The development and evaluation of behaviorally based rating scales. *Journal of Applied Psychology, 57,* 15–22.

Campbell, J. P., Dunnette, M. D., Lawler, E. E., III, & Weick, K. E., Jr. (1970). *Managerial behavior, performance, and effectiveness.* New York: McGraw-Hill.

Campbell, J. P., McHenry, J. J., & Wise, L. L. (1990). Modeling job performance in a population of jobs. *Personnel Psychology, 43,* 313–333.

Campbell, J. P., & Pritchard, R. D. (1976). Motivation theory in industrial and organizational psychology. In M. D. Dunnette (Ed.), *Handbook of indus-*

trial and organizational psychology. Chicago: Rand McNally.

Campion, J. E. (1972). Work sampling for personnel selection. *Journal of Applied Psychology, 56,* 40–44.

Campion, M. A. (1983). Personnel selection for physically demanding jobs: Review and recommendations. *Personnel Psychology, 36,* 527–550.

Campion, M. A. (1988). Interdisciplinary approaches to job design: A constructive replication with extensions. *Journal of Applied Psychology, 73,* 467–481.

Campion, M. A. (1989). Ability requirement implications of job design: An interdisciplinary perspective. *Personnel Psychology, 42,* 1–24.

Campion, M. A., & Campion, J. E. (1987). Evaluation of an interviewee skills training program in a natural field experiment. *Personnel Psychology, 40,* 675–691.

Campion, M. A., & McClelland, C. L. (1991). Interdisciplinary examination of the costs and benefits of enlarged jobs: A job design quasi-experiment. *Journal of Applied Psychology, 76,* 186–198.

Campion, M. A., Pursell, E. D., & Brown, B. K. (1988). Structured interviewing: Raising the psychometric properties of the employment interview. *Personnel Psychology, 41,* 25–42.

Campion, M. A., & Thayer, P. W. (1985). Development and field evaluation of an interdisciplinary measure of job design. *Journal of Applied Psychology, 70,* 29–43.

Cappelli, P. (1984). Union improvements under concession bargaining. *Proceedings of the 36th annual meeting of the Industrial Relations Research Association.* Madison.

Cardy, R. L., & Dobbins, G. H. (1986). Affect and appraisal accuracy: Liking as an integral dimension in evaluating performance. *Journal of Applied Psychology, 71,* 672–678.

Cardy, R. L., Kehoe, J. F. (1984). Rater selective attention ability and appraisal effectiveness: The effect of a cognitive style on the accuracy of differentiation among ratees. *Journal of Applied Psychology, 69,* 589–594.

Carlson, M. (1991, October 21). The ultimate men's club. *Time,* pp. 50–51.

Carrier, M. R., Dalessio, A. T., & Brown, S. H. (1990). Correspondence between estimates of content and criterion-related validity values. *Personnel Psychology, 43,* 85–100.

Carroll, S. J., Jr., Paine, F. T., & Ivancevich, J. M. (1972). The relative effectiveness of training methods—Expert opinion and research. *Personnel Psychology, 25,* 495–510.

Carroll, S. J., Jr., & Schneier, C. E. (1982). *Performance appraisal and review systems: The identification, measurement, and development of performance in organizations.* Glenview, IL: Scott, Foresman.

Carsten, J. M., & Spector, P. E. (1987). Unemployment, job satisfaction, and employee turnover: A meta-analytic test of the Muchinsky model. *Journal of Applied Psychology, 72,* 374–381.

Cascio, W. F. (1982). *Costing human resources: The financial impact of behavior in organizations.* Boston: Kent.

Cascio, W. F., Alexander, R. A., & Barrett, G. V. (1988). Setting cutoff scores: Legal, psychometric, and professional issues and guidelines. *Personnel Psychology, 41,* 1–24.

Cascio, W. F., & Morris, J. R. (1990). A critical reanalysis of Hunter, Schmidt, and Coggin's (1988) "Problems and Pitfalls in Using Capital Budgeting and Financial Accounting Techniques in Assessing the Utility of Personnel Programs." *Journal of Applied Psychology, 75,* 410–417.

Cascio, W. F., & Ramos, R. A. (1986). Development and application of a new method for assessing job performance in behavioral/ economic terms. *Journal of Applied Psychology, 71,* 20–28.

Cass, E. L., & Zimmer, F. G. (Eds.). (1975). *Man and work in society.* New York: Van Nostrand Reinhold.

Castro, J. (1986, March 17). Battling the enemy within. *Time,* pp. 52–61.

Castro, J. (1992a, January 20). Sexual harassment: A guide. *Time,* p. 37.

Castro, J. (1992b, February 17). Work ethic—In spades. *Time,* p. 57.

Cellar, D. F., & Barrett, G. V. (1987). Script processing and intrinsic motivation: The cognitive sets underlying cognitive labels. *Organizational Behavior and Human Decision Processes, 40,* 115–135.

Cellar, D. F., & Wade, K. (1988). Effect of behavioral modeling on intrinsic motivation and script-related recognition. *Journal of Applied Psychology, 73,* 181–192.

Cesare, S. J., Tannenbaum, R. J., & Dalessio, A. (1990). Interviewers' decisions related to applicant handicap type and rater empathy. *Human Performance, 3*(3), 157–171.

Chacko, T. I. (1983). Job and life satisfactions: A causal analysis of their relationships. *Academy of Management Journal, 26,* 163–169.

Chadwick-Jones, J. K. (1981). Renegotiating absence levels. *Journal of Occupational Behavior, 2,* 255–266.

Chadwick-Jones, J. K., Nicholson, N., & Brown, C. (1982). *The social psychology of absenteeism.* New York: Praeger.

Chalykoff, J., & Kochan, T. A. (1989). Computer-aided monitoring: Its influence on employee job satisfaction and turnover. *Personnel Psychology, 42,* 807–834.

Chapanis, A. (1976). Engineering psychology. In M. Dunnette (Ed.), *Handbook of industrial and organizational psychology.* Chicago: Rand McNally.

Cheloha, R. S., & Farr, J. L. (1980). Absenteeism, job involvement, and job satisfaction in an organizational setting. *Journal of Applied Psychology, 65,* 467–473.

Chemers, M. M., & Fiedler, F. E. (1986). The trouble with assumptions: A reply to Jago and Ragan. *Journal of Applied Psychology, 71,* 560–563.

Chen, P. Y., & Spector, P. E. (1991). Negative affectivity as the underlying cause of correlations between stressors and strains. *Journal of Applied Psychology, 76,* 398–407.

Cherrington, D. J., Reitz, H. J., & Scott, W. E. (1971). Effects of contingent and non-contingent reward on the relationship between satisfaction and task performance. *Journal of Applied Psychology, 55,* 532–536.

Chhokar, J. S., & Wallin, J. A. (1984). A field study of the effect of feedback frequency on performance. *Journal of Applied Psychology, 69,* 524–530.

Childs, A., & Klimoski, R. J. (1986). Successfully predicting career success: An application of the biographical inventory. *Journal of Applied Psychology, 71,* 3–8.

Chonko, L. B. (1982). The relationship of span of control to sales representatives' experienced role conflict and role ambiguity. *Academy of Management Journal, 25,* 452–456.

Christal, R. E. (1974, January). *The United States Air Force occupational research project* (AFHRL-TR-73–75). Brooks Air Force Base, TX: Air Force Systems Command.

Cleveland, J. N., & Landy, F. J. (1981). The influence of rater and ratee age on two performance judgments. *Personnel Psychology, 34,* 19–29.

Cobb, A. T. (1980). Informal influence in the formal organization: Perceived sources of power among work unit peers. *Academy of Management Journal, 23,* 155–161.

Cohen, A., Smith, M. J., & Anger, W. K. (1979). Self-protective measures against workplace hazards. *Journal of Safety Research, 11*(3), 121–131.

Cohen, B., Moses, J. L., & Byham, W. C. (1974). *The validity of assessment centers: A literature review.* Pittsburgh: Development Dimensions Press.

Cohen, J. (1969). *Statistical power analysis for the behavioral sciences.* New York: Academic Press.

Colarelli, S. M. (1984). Methods of communication and mediating processes in realistic job previews. *Journal of Applied Psychology, 69,* 633–642.

Colligan, M. J., Frockt, I. J., & Tasto, D. L. (1979). Frequency of sickness absence and work-site clinic visits among nurses as a function of shift. *Applied Ergonomics, 10,* 79–85.

Collins, A., & Adams, M. J. (1977). Comparison of two teaching strategies in computer-assisted instruction. *Contemporary Educational Psychology, 2,* 133–148.

Committing *Seku Hara.* (1992, April 27). *Time,* p. 22.

Conger, J. A., & Kanungo, R. N. (1987). Toward a behavioral theory of charismatic leadership in organizational settings. *Academy of Management Review, 12,* 637–647.

Conley, P. R., & Sackett, P. R. (1987). Effects of using high-versus low-performing job incumbents as sources of job analysis information. *Journal of Applied Psychology, 72,* 434–437.

Connolly, T., Conlon, E. J., & Deutsch, S. J. (1980). Organizational effectiveness: A multiple-constituency approach. *Academy of Management Review, 5,* 211–217.

Cook, J. D., Hepworth, S. J., Wall, T. D., & Warr, P. B. (1981). *The experience of work.* New York: Academic Press.

Cook, T. D., & Campbell, D. T. (1979). *Quasi-experimentation: Design and analysis issues for field settings.* Chicago: Rand McNally.

Cooke, W. N. (1983). Determinants of the outcomes of union certification elections. *Industrial and Labor Relations Review, 36,* 402–414.

Cooke, W. N., & Blumenstock, M. W. (1979). The determinants of occupational injury severity: The case of Maine sawmills. *Journal of Safety Research, 11*(3), 59–67.

Coren, S., Porac, C., & Ward, L. M. (1979). *Sensation and perception.* New York: Academic Press.

Cornelius, E. T., III, DeNisi, A. S., & Blencoe, A. G. (1984). Expert and naive raters using the PAQ: Does it matter? *Personnel Psychology, 37,* 453–464.

Cornelius, E. T., III, & Lane, F. B. (1984). The power motive and managerial success in a professionally oriented service industry organization. *Journal of Applied Psychology, 69,* 32–39.

Cornelius, E. T., III, & Lyness, K. S. (1980). A comparison of holistic and decomposed judgment strategies in job analyses by job incumbents. *Journal of Applied Psychology, 65,* 155–163.

Cornelius, E. T., III, Schmidt, F. L., & Carron, T. J. (1984). Job classification approaches and the implementation of validity generalization results. *Personnel Psychology, 37,* 247–260.

Costa, P. T., & McCrae, R. R. (1980). Influence of extraversion and neuroticism on subjective well-being: Happy and unhappy people. *Journal of Personality and Social Psychology, 38,* 36–51.

Costly policy. (1992, May 11). *Time,* p. 14.

Cotton, J. L., Vollrath, D. A., Froggatt, K. L., Lengnick-Hall, M. L., & Jennings, K. R. (1988). Employee participation: Diverse forms and different outcomes. *Academy of Management Review 13,* 8–22.

Cotton, J. L., Vollrath, D. A., Lengnick-Hall, M. L., & Froggatt, K. L. (1990). Fact: The form of participation does matter: A rebuttal to Leana, Locke, and Schweiger. *Academy of Management Review, 15,* 147–153.

Coward, W. M., & Sackett, P. R. (1990). Linearity of ability-performance relationships: A reconfirmation. *Journal of Applied Psychology, 75* 297–300.

Cowley, W. H. (1928). Three distinctions in the study of leaders. *Journal of Abnormal and Social Psychology, 23,* 144–157.

Crant, J. M., & Bateman, T. S. (1990). An experimental test of the impact of drug-testing programs on potential job applicants' attitudes and intentions. *Journal of Applied Psychology, 75,* 27–131.

Cronbach, L. J. (1951). Coefficient alpha and the internal structure of tests. *Psychometrika, 16,* 297–334.

Cronbach, L. J. (1955). Processes affecting scores on "understanding of others" and "assumed similarity." *Psychological Bulletin, 52,* 177–193.

Cronbach, L. J. (1957). The two disciplines of scientific psychology. *American Psychologist, 12,* 671–684.

Cronbach, L. J. (1975). Beyond the two disciplines of scientific psychology. *American Psychologist, 30,* 116–127.

Cronbach, L. J. (1987). Statistical tests for moderator variables: Flaws in analyses recently proposed. *Psychological Bulletin, 102,* 414–417.

Cronbach, L. J., & Gleser, G. C. (1965). *Psychological tests and personnel decisions.* Urbana: University of Illinois.

Cronbach, L. J., & Meehl, P. E. (1955). Construct validity in psychological tests. *Psychological Bulletin, 52,* 281–300.

Cronshaw, S. F., & Alexander, R. A. (1985). One answer to the demand for accountability: Selection utility as an investment decision. *Organizational Behavior and Human Decision Processes, 35,* 102–118.

Cronshaw, S. F., Alexander, R. A., Wiesner, W. H., & Barrick, M. R. (1987). Incorporating risk into selection utility: Two models for sensitivity analysis and risk simulation. *Organizational Behavior and Human Decision Processes, 40,* 270–286.

Cropanzano, R., & James, K. (1990). Some methodological considerations for the behavioral genetic analysis of work attitudes. *Journal of Applied Psychology, 75,* 433–439.

Cunningham, J. B. (1989). A compressed shift schedule: Dealing with some of the problems of shiftwork. *Journal of Organizational Behavior, 10,* 231–245.

Cunningham, J. W., Boese, R. R., Neeb, R. W., & Pass, J. J. (1983). Systematically derived work dimensions: Factor analyses of the Occupational Analysis Inventory. *Journal of Applied Psychology, 68,* 232–252.

Czajka, J. M., & DeNisi, A. S. (1988). Effects of emotional disability and clear performance standards on performance ratings. *Academy of Management Journal, 31,* 394–404.

Dachler, H. P. (1983). I/O psychology in Switzerland: New developments. *Industrial-Organizational Psychologist, 20*(2), 50–56.

Dachler, H. P., & Wilpert, B. (1978). Conceptual dimensions and boundaries of participation: A critical evaluation. *Administrative Science Quarterly, 23,* 1–39.

Dalton, D. R., Krackhardt, D. M., & Porter, L. W. (1981). Functional turnover: An empirical assessment. *Journal of Applied Psychology, 66,* 716–721.

Dalton, D. R., & Perry, J. L. (1981). Absenteeism and the collective bargaining agreement: An empirical test. *Academy of Management Journal, 24,* 425–431.

Dalton, D. R., & Todor, W. D. (1979). Manifest needs of stewards: Propensity to file a grievance. *Journal of Applied Psychology, 64,* 654–659.

Dalton, D. R., & Todor, W. D. (1982). Antecedents of grievance filing behavior: Attitude/behavioral consistency and the union steward. *Academy of Management Journal, 25,* 158–169.

Daniel, T. L., & Esser, J. K. (1980). Intrinsic motivation as influenced by rewards, task interest, and task structure. *Journal of Applied Psychology, 65,* 566–573.

Danish, S. J., & Smyer, M. A. (1981). Unintended consequences of requiring a license to help. *American Psychologist, 36,* 13–21.

Dansereau, F., Graen, G., & Haga, W. J. (1975). A vertical dyad linkage approach to leadership in formal organizations. *Organizational Behavior and Human Performance, 13,* 46–78.

Davis-Blake, A., & Pfeffer, J. (1989). Just a mirage: The search for dispositional effects in organizational research. Special Issue: Theory development forum. *Academy of Management Review, 14,* 385–400.

Davis, K. R., Jr. (1984). A longitudinal analysis of biographical subgroups using Owens' Developmental-Integrative Model. *Personnel Psychology, 37,* 1–14.

Davis, K. R., Jr., & Sauser, W. I., Jr. (1991). Effects of alternative weighting methods in a policy-capturing approach to job evaluation: A review and empirical investigation. *Personnel Psychology, 44,* 85–127.

Day, D. V., & Silverman, S. B. (1989). Personality and job performance: Evidence of incremental validity. *Personnel Psychology, 42,* 25–36.

Deadrick, D. L., & Madigan, R. M. (1990). Dynamic criteria revisited: A longitudinal study of performance stability and predictive validity. *Personnel Psychology, 43,* 717–744.

Dean, R. A., & Wanous, J. P. (1984). Effects of realistic job previews on hiring bank tellers. *Journal of Applied Psychology, 69,* 61–68.

Deaux, K., & Emswiller, T. (1974). Explanation of successful performance: What's skill for the male is luck for the female. *Journal of Personality and Social Psychology, 29,* 80–85.

Deci, E. L. (1972). The effects of contingent and noncontingent rewards and controls on intrinsic motivation. *Organizational Behavior and Human Performance, 8,* 217–229.

Deci, E. L. (1975). *Intrinsic motivation.* New York: Plenum.

Deci, E. L. (1976). Notes on the theory and metatheory of intrinsic motivation. *Organizational Behavior and Human Performance, 15,* 130–145.

Decker, P. J. (1979). Modesty and caution in reviewing behavior modeling: A reply to McGehee and Tullar. *Personnel Psychology, 32,* 399–400.

DeCotiis, T. A., & LeLouarn, J. (1981). A predictive study of voting behavior in a representation election using union instrumentality and work perceptions. *Organizational Behavior and Human Performance, 27,* 103–118.

DeNisi, A. S., Cafferty, T. P., & Meglino, B. M. (1984). A cognitive view of the performance appraisal process: A model and research propositions. *Organizational Behavior and Human Performance, 33,* 360–396.

DeNisi, A. S., Cornelius, E. T., III, & Blencoe, A. G. (1987). Further investigation of common knowledge effects on job analysis ratings. *Journal of Applied Psychology, 72,* 262–268.

DeNisi, A. S., Robbins, T., & Cafferty, T. P. (1989). Organization of information used for performance appraisals: Role of diary-keeping. *Journal of Applied Psychology, 74,* 124–129.

Denmark, F. L. (1980). Psych: From rocking the cradle to rocking the boat. *American Psychologist, 35,* 1057–1065.

DeReamer, R. (1980). *Modern safety and health technology.* New York: Wiley.

Deshpande, S. P., & Fiorito, J. (1989). Specific and general beliefs in union voting models. *Academy of Management Journal, 32,* 883–897.

Dessler, G. (1972). *A test of the path-goal theory of leadership.* Proceedings of the annual meeting of the Academy of Management, 178–181.

Dickey-Bryant, L., Lautenschlager, G. J., Mendoza, J. L., & Abrahams, N. (1986). Facial attractiveness and its relation to occupational success. *Journal of Applied Psychology, 71,* 16–19.

Dickinson, T. L. (1987). Designs for evaluating the validity and accuracy of performance ratings. *Organizational Behavior and Human Decision Processes, 40,* 1–21.

Dickinson, T. L., & Glebocki, G. G. (1990). Modifications in the format of the mixed standard scale. *Organizational Behavior and Human Decision Processes, 47,* 124–137.

Dickinson, T. L., & Zellinger, P. M. (1980). A comparison of the behaviorally anchored rating and mixed standard scale formats. *Journal of Applied Psychology, 65,* 147–154.

Dipboye, R. L. (1985). Some neglected variables in research on discrimination in appraisals. *Academy of Management Review, 10,* 116–127.

Dipboye, R. L., & Flanagan, M. F. (1979). Research settings in industrial and organizational psychology: Are findings in the field more generalizable than in the laboratory? *American Psychologist, 34,* 141–150.

Distefano, M. K., Jr., Pryer, M. W., & Erffmeyer, R. C. (1983). Application of content validity methods to the development of a job-related performance criterion. *Personnel Psychology, 36,* 621–631.

Dobbins, G. H., Cardy, R. L., & Truxillo, D. M. (1988). The effects of purpose of appraisal and individual differences in stereotypes of women on sex differences in performance ratings: A laboratory and field study. *Journal of Applied Psychology, 73,* 551–558.

Dobbins, G. H., Pence, E. C., Orban, J. A., & Sgro, J. A. (1983). The effects of sex of the leader and sex of the subordinate on the use of organizational control policy. *Organizational Behavior and Human Performance, 32,* 325–343.

Dobbins, G. H., & Platz, S. J. (1986). Sex differences in leadership: How real are they? *Academy of Management Review, 11,* 118–127.

Dobbins, G. H., & Russell, J. M. (1986). The biasing effects of subordinate likeableness on leaders' responses to poor performers: A laboratory and a field study. *Personnel Psychology, 39,* 759–777.

Dorfman, P. W., & Howell, J. P. (1984). Production sharing in the Mexican maquiladora industry: A challenge for I/O psychology. *Industrial-Organizational Psychologist, 22*(1), 20–26.

Dorfman, P. W., Stephan, W. G., & Loveland, J. (1986). Performance appraisal behaviors: Supervisor perceptions and subordinate reactions. *Personnel Psychology, 39,* 579–597.

Dossett, D. L., & Hulvershorn, P. (1983). Increasing technical training efficiency: Peer training via computer-assisted instruction. *Journal of Applied Psychology, 68,* 552–558.

Dougherty, T. W., Ebert, R. J., & Callender, J. C. (1986). Policy capturing in the employment interview. *Journal of Applied Psychology, 71,* 9–15.

Doverspike, D., & Barrett, G. V. (1984). An internal bias analysis of a job evaluation instrument. *Journal of Applied Psychology, 69,* 648–662.

Doverspike, D., Carlisi, A. M., Barrett, G. V., & Alexander, R. A. (1983). Generalizability analysis of a point-method job evaluation instrument. *Journal of Applied Psychology, 68,* 476–483.

Dowell, B. E., & Wexley, K. N. (1978). Development of a work behavior taxonomy for first-line supervisors. *Journal of Applied Psychology, 63,* 563–572.

Downey, H. K., Sheridan, J. E., & Slocum, J. W., Jr. (1975). Analysis of relationships among leader behavior, subordinate job performance and satisfaction: A path goal approach. *Academy of Management Journal, 18,* 253–262.

Dreher, G. F., & Ash, R. A. (1990). A comparative study of mentoring among men and women in managerial, professional, and technical positions. *Journal of Applied Psychology, 75,* 539–546.

Dreher, G. F., Ash, R. A., & Hancock, P. (1988). The role of the traditional research design in underestimating the validity of the employment interview. *Personnel Psychology, 41,* 315–327.

Dreher, G. F., & Dougherty, T. W. (1980). Turnover and competition for expected job openings: An exploratory analysis. *Academy of Management Journal, 23,* 766–772.

Drory, A. (1982). Individual differences in boredom proneness and task effectiveness at work. *Personnel Psychology, 35,* 141–151.

Dubin, R. (1956). Industrial workers' worlds: A study of "Central Life Interests" of industrial workers. *Social Problems, 3,* 131–142.

DuBois, P. H. (1970). *A history of psychological testing.* Boston: Allyn & Bacon.

Dugan, B. (1988). Effects of assessor training on information use. *Journal of Applied Psychology, 73,* 743–748.

Dugan, K. W. (1989). Ability and effort attributions: Do they affect how managers communicate performance feedback information? *Academy of Management Journal, 32,* 87–114.

Dunbar, R., & Goldberg, W. (1978). Crisis development and strategic response in European corporations. In C. Smart & W. Stanbury (Eds.), *Studies in crisis management.* Toronto: Institute for Research on Public Policy.

Dunbar, S. B., & Novick, M. R. (1988). On predicting success in training for men and women: Examples from Marine Corps clerical specialties. *Journal of Applied Psychology, 73,* 545–550.

Dunham, R. B. (1976). The measurement and dimensionality of job characteristics. *Journal of Applied Psychology, 61,* 404–409.

Dunham, R. B. (1977). Shift work: A review and theoretical analysis. *Academy of Management Review, 2,* 626–634.

Dunham, R. B. (1979). Job design and redesign. In S. Kerr (Ed.), *Organizational behavior.* Columbus, OH: Grid.

Dunham, R. B., Aldag, R. J., & Brief, A. P. (1977). Dimensionality of task design as measured by the Job Diagnostic Survey. *Academy of Management Journal, 20,* 209–221.

Dunham, R. B., & Hawk, D. L. (1977). The four-day/forty-hour week: Who wants it? *Academy of Management Journal, 20,* 644–655.

Dunham, R. B., Pierce, J. L., & Castañeda, M. B. (1987). Alternative work schedules: Two field quasi-experiments. *Personnel Psychology, 40,* 215–242.

Dunlap, W. P., & Kemery, E. R. (1987). Failure to detect moderating effects: Is multicollinearity the problem? *Psychological Bulletin, 102,* 418–420.

Dunlap, W. P., & Kemery, E. R. (1988). Effects of predictor intercorrelations and reliabilities on moderated multiple regression. *Organizational Behavior and Human Decision Processes, 41,* 248–258.

Dunnette, M. D. (1963). A note on *the* criterion. *Journal of Applied Psychology, 47,* 251–254.

Dunnette, M. D. (1972). *Validity study results for jobs relevant to the petroleum refining industry.* Washington, DC: American Petroleum Institute.

Dunnette, M. D. (Ed.). (1973). *Work and nonwork in the year 2001.* Pacific Grove, CA: Brooks/Cole.

Dunnette, M. D., & Borman, W. C. (1979). Personnel selection and classification systems. *Annual Review of Psychology, 30,* 477–525.

Dunnette, M. D., & Kirchner, W. K. (1965). *Psychology applied to industry.* Englewood Cliffs, NJ: Prentice-Hall.

Dvorak, A., Marrick, N., Dealey, W., & Ford, G. (1936). *Typewriting behavior: Psychology applied to teaching and learning typewriter.* New York: American Book Co.

Eagly, A. H. (1983). Gender and social influence: A social psychological analysis. *American Psychologist, 38,* 971–981.

Eagly, A. H., & Johnson, B. T. (1990). Gender and leadership style: A meta-analysis. *Psychological Bulletin, 108,* 233–256.

Eagly, A. H., Makhijani, M. G., & Klonsky, B. G. (1992). Gender and the evaluation of leaders: A meta-analysis. *Psychological Bulletin, 111,* 2–22.

Eagly, A. H., Wood, W., & Chaiken, S. (1978). Causal inferences about communicators and their effect on opinion change. *Journal of Personality and Social Psychology, 36,* 424–435.

Earley, P. C. (1987). Intercultural training for managers: A comparison of documentary and interpersonal methods. *Academy of Management Journal, 30,* 685–698.

Earley, P. C. (1988). Computer-generated performance feedback in the magazine-subscription industry. *Organizational Behavior and Human Decision Processes, 41,* 50–64.

Earley, P. C., Connolly, T., & Ekegren, G. (1989). Goals, strategy development, and task performance: Some limits on the efficacy of goal setting. *Journal of Applied Psychology, 74,* 24–33.

Earley, P. C., Northcraft, G. B., Lee, C., & Lituchy, T. R. (1990). Impact of process and outcome feedback on the relation of goal setting to task performance. *Academy of Management Journal, 33,* 87–105.

Eaton, N. K., Wing, H., & Mitchell, K. J. (1985). Alternate methods of estimating the dollar value of performance. *Personnel Psychology, 38,* 27–40.

Eberhardt, B. J., & Muchinsky, P. M. (1984). Structural validation of Holland's hexagonal model: Vocational classification through the use of biodata. *Journal of Applied Psychology, 69,* 174–181.

Eden, D. (1985). Team development: A true field experiment at three levels of rigor. *Journal of Applied Psychology, 70,* 94–100.

Eden, D. (1990). Pygmalion without interpersonal contrast effects: Whole groups gain from raising manager expectations. *Journal of Applied Psychology, 75,* 394–398.

Eden, D., & Leviatan, U. (1975). Implicit leadership theory as a determinant of the factor structure underlying supervisory behavior scales. *Journal of Applied Psychology, 60,* 736–741.

Eden, D., & Shani, A. B. (1982). Pygmalion goes to boot camp: Expectancy, leadership, and trainee performance. *Journal of Applied Psychology, 67,* 194–199.

Eder, R. W., & Fedor, D. B. (1989). Priming performance self-evaluations: Moderating effects of rating purpose and judgment confidence. *Organizational Behavior and Human Decision Processes, 44,* 474–493.

Edwards, J. E., Frederick, J. T., & Burke, M. J. (1988). Efficacy of modified CREPID SD$_y$s on the basis of archival organizational data. *Journal of Applied Psychology, 73,* 529–535.

Edwards, J. R., & Baglioni, A. J., Jr. (1991). Relationship between Type A behavior pattern and mental and physical symptoms: A comparison of global and component measures. *Journal of Applied Psychology, 76,* 276–290.

Edwards, J. R., Baglioni, A. J., Jr., & Cooper, C. L. (1990). Examining the relationships among self-report measures of the Type A behavior pattern: The effects of dimensionality, measurement error, and differences in underlying constructs. *Journal of Applied Psychology, 75,* 440–454.

Ehrenreich, B. (1991, October 21). Women would have known. *Time,* p. 104.

Eisenberg, E. M., & Witten, M. G. (1987). Reconsidering openness in organizational communication. *Academy of Management Review, 12,* 418–426.

Ellson, D. G., & Ellson, E. C. (1953). Historical note on the rating scale. *Psychological Bulletin, 50,* 383–384.

Elmer-DeWitt, P. (1991, October 28). Danger in the speed trap. *Time,* p. 88.

Embretson (Whitely), S. (1983). Construct validity: Construct representation versus nomothetic span. *Psychological Bulletin, 93,* 179–197.

Equal Employment Opportunity Commission (EEOC). (1978). Uniform guidelines on employee selection procedures. *Federal Register, 43,* 38290–38309.

Eskilson, A., & Wiley, M. G. (1976). Sex composition and leadership in small groups. *Sociometry, 39,* 183–194.

Ethical principles of psychologists and code of conduct. (1992). *American Psychologist, 47,* 1597–1611.

Evans, M. G. (1973). Notes on the impact of flextime in a large insurance company: I. Reactions of nonsupervisory employees. *Occupational Psychology, 47,* 237–240.

Ewen, R. B., Smith, P. C., Hulin, C. L., & Locke, E. A. (1966). An empirical test of the Herzberg two-factor theory. *Journal of Applied Psychology, 50,* 544–550.

Faley, R. H., & Sundstrom, E. (1985). Content representativeness: An empirical method of evaluation. *Journal of Applied Psychology, 70,* 567–571.

Farh, J., & Dobbins, G. H. (1989a). Effects of comparative performance information on the accuracy of self-ratings and agreement between self- and supervisor ratings. *Journal of Applied Psychology, 74,* 606–610.

Farh, J., & Dobbins, G. H. (1989b). Effects of self-esteem on leniency bias in self-reports of performance: A structural equation model analysis. *Personnel Psychology, 42,* 835–850.

Farh, J., Dobbins, G. H., & Cheng, B. (1991). Cultural relativity in action: A comparison of self-ratings made by Chinese and U.S. workers. *Personnel Psychology, 44,* 129–147.

Farh, J., & Werbel, J. D. (1986). Effects of purpose of the appraisal and expectation of validation on self-appraisal leniency. *Journal of Applied Psychology, 71,* 527–529.

Farh, J., Werbel, J. D., & Bedeian, A. G. (1988). An empirical investigation of self-appraisal–based performance evaluation. *Personnel Psychology, 41,* 141–156.

Farrell, D., & Rusbult, C. E. (1981). Exchange variables as predictors of job satisfaction, job commitment, and turnover: The impact of rewards, costs, alternatives, and investments. *Organizational Behavior and Human Performance, 28,* 78–95.

Faucheux, C., Amado, G., & Laurent, A. (1982). Organizational development and change. *Annual Review of Psychology, 33,* 343–370.

Fedor, D. B., Eder, R. W., & Buckley, M. R. (1989). The contributory effects of supervisor intentions on subordinate feedback responses. *Organizational Behavior and Human Decision Processes, 44,* 396–414.

Feldman, J. (1982). Ideology without data. *American Psychologist, 37,* 857–858.

Feldman, J. M. (1986). A note on the statistical correction of halo error. *Journal of Applied Psychology, 71,* 173–176.

Feldman, J. M., Camburn, A., & Gatti, G. M. (1986). Shared distinctiveness as a source of illusory correlation in performance appraisal. *Organizational Behavior and Human Decision Processes, 37,* 34–59.

Ferris, G. R., & Gilmore, D. C. (1985). A methodological note on job complexity indexes. *Journal of Applied Psychology, 70,* 225–227.

Ferris, G. R., Yates, V. L., Gilmore, D. C., & Rowland, K. M. (1985). The influence of subordinate age on performance ratings and causal attributions. *Personnel Psychology, 38,* 545–557.

Fiedler, F. E. (1964). A contingency model of leader effectiveness. In L. Berkowitz (Ed.), *Advances in experimental social psychology* (Vol. 1). New York: Academic Press.

Fiedler, F. E. (1965). Engineer the job to fit the manager. *Harvard Business Review, 43,* 115–122.

Fiedler, F. E. (1967). *A theory of leadership effectiveness.* New York: McGraw-Hill.

Fiedler, F. (1972). Personality, motivational systems and the behavior of high and low LPC persons. *Human Relations, 25,* 391–412.

Fiedler, F. E., Chemers, M. M., & Mahar, L. (1976). *Improving leadership effectiveness: The LEADER MATCH concept.* New York: Wiley.

Fiedler, F. E., & Garcia, J. E. (1987). *New approaches to effective leadership: Cognitive resources and organizational performance.* New York: Wiley.

Fiedler, F. E., & Leister, A. F. (1977). Leader intelligence and task performance: A test of a multiple screen model. *Organizational Behavior and Human Performance, 20,* 1–14.

Fiedler, F. E., & Mahar, L. (1979). The effectiveness of contingency model training: A review of the validation of LEADER MATCH. *Personnel Psychology, 32,* 45–62.

Fiedler, F. E., Murphy, S. E., & Gibson, F. W. (1992). Inaccurate reporting and inappropriate variables: A reply to Vecchio's (1990) examination of cognitive resource theory. *Journal of Applied Psychology, 77,* 372–374.

Fiedler, F. E., Potter, E. H., III, Zais, M. M., & Knowlton, W. A., Jr. (1979). Organizational stress and the use and misuse of managerial intelligence and experience. *Journal of Applied Psychology, 64,* 635–647.

Field of dollars. (1991, December 16). *Time,* p. 63.

Field, R. H. G. (1979). A critique of the Vroom-Yetton contingency model of leadership behavior. *Academy of Management Review, 4,* 249–257.

Field, R. H. G. (1982). A test of the Vroom-Yetton normative model of leadership. *Journal of Applied Psychology, 67,* 523–532.

Field, R. H., & House, R. J. (1990). A test of the Vroom-Yetton model using manager and subordinate reports. *Journal of Applied Psychology, 75,* 362–366.

Fine, B. J., & Korbrick, J. L. (1978). Effects of altitude and heat on complex cognitive tasks. *Human Factors, 20,* 115–122.

Finkle, R. B. (1976). Managerial assessment centers. In M.D. Dunnette (Ed.), *Handbook of industrial and organizational psychology.* Chicago: Rand McNally.

Finn, R. H. (1972). Effects of some variations in rating scale characteristics on the means and reliabilities of ratings. *Educational and Psychological Measurement, 32,* 255–265.

Fishbein, M., & Ajzen, I. (1975). *Belief, attitude, intention, and behavior: An introduction to theory and research.* Reading, MA: Addison-Wesley.

Fisicaro, S. A. (1988). A reexamination of the relation between halo error and accuracy. *Journal of Applied Psychology, 73,* 239–244.

Flanagan, J. C. (1954). The critical incident technique. *Psychological Bulletin, 51,* 327–358.

Fleishman, E. A. (1953). The measurement of leadership attitudes in industry. *Journal of Applied Psychology, 37,* 153–158.

Fleishman, E. A. (1957a). A leader behavior description for industry. In R. A. Stogdill & A. E. Coons (Eds.), *Leader behavior: Its description and measurement.* Columbus: Bureau of Business Research, Ohio State University.

Fleishman, E. A. (1957b). The leadership opinion questionnaire. In R. A. Stogdill & A. E. Coons (Eds.), *Leader behavior: Its description and measurement.* Columbus: Bureau of Business Research, Ohio State University.

Fleishman, E. A. (1975). Toward a taxonomy of human performance. *American Psychologist, 30,* 1127–1149.

Fleishman, E. A., & Fruchter, B. (1960). Factor structure and predictability of successive stages of learning Morse code. *Journal of Applied Psychology, 44,* 97–101.

Fleishman, E. A., & Harris, E. F. (1962). Patterns of leadership behavior related to employee grievances and turnover. *Personnel Psychology, 15,* 43–56.

Fleishman, E. A., Harris, E. F., & Burtt, H. E. (1955). *Leadership and supervision in industry.* Columbus: Bureau of Educational Research, Ohio State University.

Fleishman, E. A., & Mumford, M. D. (1989). Abilities as causes of individual differences in skill acquisition. *Human Performance, 2*(3), 201–223.

Florin-Thuma, B. C., & Boudreau, J. W. (1987). Performance feedback utility in a small organization: Effects on organizational outcomes and managerial decision processes. *Personnel Psychology, 40,* 693–713.

Ford, J. K., Kraiger, K., & Schechtman, S. L. (1986). Study of race effects in objective indices and subjective evaluations of performance: A meta-analysis of performance criteria. *Psychological Bulletin, 99,* 330–337.

Ford, J. K., & Noe, R. A. (1987). Self-assessed training needs: The effects of attitudes toward training, managerial level, and function. *Personnel Psychology, 40,* 39–53.

Ford, J. K., & Wroten, S. P. (1984). Introducing new methods for conducting training evaluation and for linking training evaluation to program redesign. *Personnel Psychology, 37,* 651–665.

Forsythe, S., Drake, M. F., & Cox, C. E. (1985). Influence of applicant's dress on interviewer's selection decisions. *Journal of Applied Psychology, 70,* 374–378.

Foster, L. W., Latack, J. C., & Reindl, L. J. (1979). *Effects and promises of the shortened workweek.* Paper presented at the 39th Annual Meeting of the Academy of Management, Atlanta.

Foti, R. J., Fraser, S. L., & Lord, R. G. (1982). Effects of leadership labels and prototypes on perceptions of political leaders. *Journal of Applied Psychology, 67,* 326–333.

Foti, R. J., & Lord, R. G. (1987). Prototypes and scripts: The effects of alternative methods of processing information on rating accuracy. *Organizational Behavior and Human Decision Processes, 39,* 318–340.

Fowler, R. L. (1986). Confidence intervals for the cross-validated multiple correlation in predictive regression models. *Journal of Applied Psychology, 71,* 318–322.

Fox, S., & Dinur, Y. (1988). Validity of self-assessment: A field evaluation. *Personnel Psychology, 41,* 581–592.

Franke, R. H., & Kaul, J. D. (1978). The Hawthorne experiments: First statistical interpretation. *American Sociological Review, 43,* 623–643.

Frederiksen, N. (1968). *Organization climates and administrative performance.* Princeton, NJ: Educational Testing Service.

Freeberg, N. E. (1969). Relevance of rater-ratee acquaintance in the validity and reliability of ratings. *Journal of Applied Psychology, 53,* 518–524.

Freeman, R. B. (1980). The effect of unionism on worker attachment to firms. *Journal of Labor Research, 1,* 29–61.

Freman, R. B., & Medcoff, J. L. (1984). *What do unions do?* New York: Basic Books.

French, J. R. P., & Raven, B. (1959). The bases of social power. In D. Cartwright (Ed.), *Studies in social power.* Ann Arbor: Institute for Social Research, University of Michigan.

Friedlander, F., & Brown, L. D. (1974). Organization development. *Annual Review of Psychology, 25,* 313–341.

Friedman, H. S. (1983). On shutting one's eyes to face validity. *Psychological Bulletin, 94,* 185–187.

Friedman, L. (1990). Degree of redundancy between time, importance, and frequency task ratings. *Journal of Applied Psychology, 75,* 748–752.

Friedman, L., & Harvey, R. J. (1986a). Can raters with reduced job descriptive information provide accurate Postition Analysis Questionnaire (PAQ) ratings? *Personnel Psychology, 39,* 779–789.

Friedman, L., & Harvey, R. J. (1986b). Factors of union commitment: The case for lower dimensionality. *Journal of Applied Psychology, 71,* 371–376.

Friedman, M., & Rosenman, R. (1974). *Type A behavior and your heart.* New York: Knopf.

Fromm, E. (1941). *Escape from freedom.* New York: Farrar & Rinehart.

Fry, E. B. (1963). *Teaching machines and programmed instruction.* New York: McGraw-Hill.

Fry, L. W., & Greenfeld, S. (1980). An examination of attitudinal differences between policewomen and policemen. *Journal of Applied Psychology, 65,* 123–126.

Fry, L. W., & Slocum, J. W. (1984). Technology, structure, and workgroup effectiveness: A test of a contingency model. *Academy of Management Journal, 27,* 221–246.

Fryxell, G. E., & Gordon, M. E. (1989). Workplace justice and job satisfaction as predictors of satisfaction with union and management. *Academy of Management Journal, 32,* 851–866.

Fulk, J., & Wendler, E. R. (1982). Dimensionality of leader-subordinate interactions: A path-goal investigation. *Organizational Behavior and Human Performance, 30,* 241–264.

Fullagar, C. (1984). Psychology and labor: A relationship of neglect. *South African Journal of Psychology, 14,* 95–100.

Fullagar, C., & Barling, J. (1987). Toward a model of union commitment. *Advances in Industrial and Labor Relations, 4,* 43–78.

Fullagar, C., & Barling, J. (1989). A longitudinal test of a model of the antecedents and consequences of union loyalty. *Journal of Applied Psychology, 74,* 213–227.

Fullagar, C., & Barling, J. (1991). Predictors and outcomes of different patterns of organziational and union loyalty. *Journal of Occupational Psychology, 64,* 129–143.

Fullagar, C., McCoy, D., & Shull, C. (1992). The socialization of union loyalty. *Journal of Organizational Behavior, 13,* 13–26.

Fusilier, M. R., & Hoyer, W. D. (1980). Variables affecting perceptions of invasion of privacy in a personnel selection situation. *Journal of Applied Psychology, 65,* 623–626.

G-Men of color. (1992, May 4). *Time,* p. 21.

Galbraith, J. R. (1977). *Organization design.* Reading, MA: Addison-Wesley.

Gallagher, D. G. (1983). Integrating collective bargaining and human resources management research. In G. R. Ferris and K. M. Rowland (Eds.), *Research in personnel and human resources management* (Vol. 1), pp. 235–268. Greenwich, CT: JAI Press.

Gallagher, D. G., & Jeong, Y. (1989). *Methodological concerns with behavioral studies of union membership.* Paper presented at the Tenth Annual Southern Regional Industrial Relations Academic Seminar, West Virginia University, Morgantown.

Galton, F. (1869). *Hereditary genius: An inquiry into its laws and consequences.* London: Macmillan.

Ganster, D. C., Mayes, B. T., Sime, W. E., & Tharp, G. D. (1982). Managing organizational stress: A field experiment. *Journal of Applied Psychology, 67,* 533–542.

Ganster, D. C., Schaubroeck, J., Sime, W. E., & Mayes, B. T. (1991). The nomological validity of the Type A personality among employed adults [Monograph]. *Journal of Applied Psychology, 76,* 143–168.

Gardner, W. L., & Martinko, M. J. (1988). Impression management: An observational study linking audience characteristics with verbal self-presentations. *Academy of Management Journal, 31,* 42–65.

Garrett, H. E., & Schneck, M. R. (1933). *Psychological tests, methods, and results.* New York: Harper and Brothers.

Gasaway, D. (1984, November). 1984 NIOSH compendium hearing protector attenuation. *National Safety News,* pp. 26–34.

Gasaway, D. (1987, December). Noise reduction ratings describe current hearing protection devices. *Occupational Health and Safety,* pp. 42–50.

Gaudet, F. J. (1963). *Solving the problems of employee absence.* New York: American Management Association.

Gaudreau, P. A. (1975). Investigation of sex differences across job levels. *Dissertation Abstracts International, 36,* 1957B.

Gaugler, B. B., Rosenthal, D. B., Thornton, G. C., III, & Bentson, C. (1987). Meta-analysis of assessment center validity [Monograph]. *Journal of Applied Psychology, 72,* 493–511.

Gaugler, B. B., & Thornton, G. C., III. (1989). Number of assessment center dimensions as a determinant of assessor accuracy. *Journal of Applied Psychology, 74,* 611–618.

Gawron, V. (1982). Performance effects of noise intensity, psychological set, and task type and complexity. *Human Factors, 24,* 225–243.

Gechman, A. S., & Wiener, Y. (1975). Job involvement and satisfaction as related to mental health and personal time devoted to work. *Journal of Applied Psychology, 60,* 521–523.

George, J. M. (1989). Mood and absence. *Journal of Applied Psychology, 74,* 317–324.

George, J. M. (1990). Personality, affect, and behavior in groups. *Journal of Applied Psychology, 75,* 107–116.

George, J. M. (1991). State or trait: Effects of positive mood on prosocial behaviors at work. *Journal of Applied Psychology, 76,* 299–307.

George, J. M., Brief, A. P., Webster, J., & Burke, M. J. (1989). Incentive compensation as an injurious condition of work: A study of labelling. *Journal of Organizational Behavior, 10,* 155–167.

Georgopoulos, B. S., Mahoney, G. M., & Jones, N. W. (1957). A path-goal approach to productivity. *Journal of Applied Psychology, 41,* 345–353.

Gerhart, B. (1987). How important are dispositional factors as determinants of job satisfaction? Implications for job design and other personnel programs. *Journal of Applied Psychology, 72,* 366–373.

Getman, J. G., Goldberg, S. B., & Herman, J. B. (1976). *Union representation elections: Law and reality.* New York: Russell Sage Foundation.

Getting the message. (1992, March 23). *Time,* p. 48.

Geyer, P. D., Hice, J., Hawk, J., Boese, R., & Brannon, Y. (1989). Reliabilities of ratings available from the *Dictionary of occupational titles. Personnel Psychology, 42,* 547–560.

Ghiselli, E. E. (1956). Differentiation of individuals in terms of their predictability. *Journal of Applied Psychology, 40,* 374–377.

Ghiselli, E. E. (1964). *Theory of psychological measurement.* New York: McGraw-Hill.

Ghiselli, E. E. (1966). *The validity of occupational aptitude tests.* New York: Wiley.

Ghiselli, E. E. (1973). The validity of aptitude tests in personnel selection. *Personnel Psychology, 23,* 461–478.

Ghiselli, E. E., & Brown, C. W. (1955). *Personnel and industrial psychology* (2nd ed.). New York: McGraw-Hill.

Ghiselli, E. E., & Haire, M. (1960). The validation of selection tests in the light of the dynamic character of criteria. *Personnel Psychology, 13,* 225–231.

Gibbs, N. (1991a, August 19). Marching out of the closet. *Time,* pp. 14–16.

Gibbs, N. (1991b, October 21). Office crimes. *Time,* pp. 52–54, 63–64.

Gibbs, N. (1991c, October 21). An ugly circus. *Time,* pp. 34–35.

Gifford, R., Ng, C. F., & Wilkinson, M. (1985). Nonverbal cues in the employment interview: Links between applicant qualities and interviewer

judgments. *Journal of Applied Psychology, 70,* 729–736.

Gilbreth, F. B. (1919). *Applied motion study.* New York: Macmillan.

Giles, W. F., & Mossholder, K. W. (1990). Employee reactions to contextual and session components of performance appraisal. *Journal of Applied Psychology, 75,* 371–377.

Gilmer, B. von H. (1966). *Industrial psychology* (2nd ed.). New York: McGraw-Hill.

Gintner, G., & Lindskold, S. (1975). Rate of participation and expertise as factors influencing leader choice. *Journal of Personality and Social Psychology, 32,* 1085–1089.

Gioia, D. A., & Manz, C. C. (1985). Linking cognition and behavior: A script processing interpretation of vicarious learning. *Academy of Management Review, 10,* 527–539.

Gist, M. E. (1987). Self-efficacy: Implications for organizational behavior and human resource management. *Academy of Management Review, 12,* 472–485.

Gist, M. E. (1989). The influence of training method on self-efficacy and idea generation among managers. *Personnel Psychology, 42,* 787–805.

Gist, M., Rosen, B., & Schwoerer, C. (1988). The influence of training method and trainee age on the acquisition of computer skills. *Personnel Psychology, 41,* 255–265.

Gist, M. E., Schwoerer, C., & Rosen, B. (1989). Effects of alternative training methods on self-efficacy and performance in computer software training. *Journal of Applied Psychology, 74,* 884–891.

Glass, G. V. (1976). Primary, secondary, and meta-analysis of research. *Educational Research, 5,* 3–8.

Gluck, S. B. (1987). *Rosie the riveter revisited: Women, the war and social change.* New York: Meridian.

Goktepe, J. R., & Schneier, C. E. (1989). Role of sex, gender roles, and attraction in predicting emergent leaders. *Journal of Applied Psychology, 74,* 165–167.

Goldman, M., & Fraas, L. A. (1965). The effects of leader selection on group performance. *Sociometry, 28,* 82–88.

Goldstein, A. P., & Sorcher, M. (1974). *Changing supervisor behavior.* New York: Pergamon Press.

Goldstein, I. L. (1980). Training in work organizations. *Annual Review of Psychology, 31,* 229–272.

Goldstein, I. L. (1993). *Training in organizations: Needs*

assessment, development, and evaluation (3rd ed.). Pacific Grove, CA: Brooks/Cole.

Goldstein, I. L., & Gilliam, P. (1990). Training system issues in the year 2000. *American Psychologist, 45,* 134–143.

Golembiewski, R. T. (1986). Contours in social change: Elemental graphics and a surrogate variable for gamma change. *Academy of Management Review, 11,* 550–556.

Golembiewski, R. T., Billingsley, K. R., & Yeager, S. (1976). Measuring change and persistence in human affairs: Types of change generated by OD designs. *Journal of Applied Behavioral Science, 12,* 133–157.

Golembiewski, R. T., Hilles, R., & Kagno, M. S. (1974). A longitudinal study of flexitime effects: Some consequences of an OD structural intervention. *Journal of Applied Behavioral Science, 10,* 503–531.

Golembiewski, R. T., & Proehl, C. W. (1978). A survey of the empirical literature on flexible workhours: Character and consequences of a major intervention. *Academy of Management Review, 3,* 837–853.

Gomez-Mejia, L. R., & Balkin, D. B. (1984). Faculty satisfaction with pay and other job dimensions under union and nonunion conditions. *Academy of Management Journal, 27,* 591–602.

Gomez-Mejia, L. R., Page, R. C., & Tornow, W. W. (1982). A comparison of the practical utility of traditional, statistical, and hybrid job evaluation approaches. *Academy of Management Journal, 25,* 790–809.

Good guy finally won. (1991, December 23). *Time,* p. 56.

Goodman, P. S. (1969). Hiring and training the hardcore unemployed: A problem in system definition. *Human Organization, 28,* 259–269.

Goodman, P. S. (1974). An examination of referents used in the evaluation of pay. *Organizational Behavior and Human Performance, 12,* 170–195.

Goodman, R. S., & Kruger, E. J. (1988). Data dredging or legitimate research method? Historiography and its potential for management research. *Academy of Management Review, 13,* 315–325.

Gordon, F., & Strober, M. (1975). *Bringing women into management.* New York: McGraw-Hill.

Gordon, G. G. (1991). Industry determinants of organizational culture. *Academy of Management Review, 16,* 396–415.

Gordon, H. W., & Leighty, R. (1988). Importance of specialized cognitive function in the selection of military pilots. *Journal of Applied Psychology, 75,* 38–45.

Gordon, J. B., Akman, A., & Brooks, M. L. (1971). *Industrial accident statistics: A re-examination.* New York: Praeger.

Gordon, L. V., & Medlund, F. F. (1965). The cross-group stability of peer rating of leadership potential. *Personnel Psychology, 18,* 173–177.

Gordon, M. E., & Bowlby, R. L. (1988). Propositions about grievance settlements: Finally, consultation with grievants. *Personnel Psychology, 41,* 107–124.

Gordon, M. E., & Bowlby, R. L. (1989). Reactance and intentionality attributions as determinants of the intent to file a grievance. *Personnel Psychology, 42,* 309–330.

Gordon, M. E., Cofer, J. L., & McCullough, P. M. (1986). Relationships among seniority, past performance, interjob similarity, and trainability. *Journal of Applied Psychology, 71,* 518–521.

Gordon, M. E., Kleiman, L. S., & Hanie, C. A. (1978). Industrial-organizational psychology: Open thy ears O house of Israel. *American Psychologist, 33,* 893–905.

Gordon, M. E., & Long, L. N. (1981). Demographic and attitudinal correlates of union joining. *Industrial Relations, 20,* 306–311.

Gordon, M. E., & Miller, S. J. (1984). Grievances: A review of research and practice. *Personnel Psychology, 37,* 117–146.

Gordon, M. E., & Nurick, A. J. (1981). Psychological approaches to the study of unions and union-management relations. *Psychological Bulletin, 90,* 293–306.

Gordon, M. E., Philpot, J. W., Burt, R. E., Thompson, C. A., & Spiller, W. E. (1980). Commitment to the union: Development of a measure and an examination of its correlates [Monograph]. *Journal of Applied Psychology, 65,* 479–499.

Gordon, M. E., Slade, L. A., & Schmitt, N. (1986). The "science of the sophomore" revisited: From conjecture to empiricism. *Academy of Management Review, 11,* 191–207.

Gordon, M. E., Slade, L. A., & Schmitt, N. (1987). Student guinea pigs: Porcine predictors and particularistic phenomena. *Academy of Management Review, 12,* 160–163.

Gordon, R. A., Rozelle, R. M., & Baxter, J. C. (1988).

The effect of applicant age, job level, and accountability on the evaluation of job applicants. *Organizational Behavior and Human Decision Processes, 41,* 20–33.

Gough, H. G. (1984). A Managerial Potential scale for the California Psychological Inventory. *Journal of Applied Psychology, 69,* 233–240.

Gough, H. G. (1985). A Work Orientation scale for the California Psychological Inventory. *Journal of Applied Psychology, 70,* 505–513.

Graddick, M. M., & Farr, J. L. (1983). Professionals in scientific disciplines: Sex-related differences in working life commitments. *Journal of Applied Psychology, 68,* 641–645.

Graen, G. (1976). Role-making processes within complex organizations. In M. D. Dunnette (Ed.), *Handbook of industrial and organizational psychology.* Chicago: Rand McNally.

Graen, G. B., Liden, R. C., & Hoel, W. (1982). Role of leadership in the employee withdrawal process. *Journal of Applied Psychology, 67,* 868–872.

Graen, G., Novak, M. A., & Sommerkamp, P. (1982). The effects of leader-member exchange and job design on productivity and satisfaction: Testing a dual attachment model. *Organizational Behavior and Human Performance, 30,* 109–131.

Graen, G., & Schiemann, W. (1978). Leader-member agreement: A vertical dyad linkage approach. *Journal of Applied Psychology, 63,* 206–212.

Grams, R., & Schwab, D. P. (1985). An investigation of systematic gender-related error in job evaluation. *Academy of Management Journal, 28,* 279–290.

Gray, J. S. (1952). *Psychology in industry.* New York: McGraw-Hill.

Gray, L. N., Richardson, J. T., & Mayhew, B. H. (1968). Influence attempts and effective power: A re-examination of the unsubstantiated hypothesis. *Sociometry, 31,* 245–258.

Green, S. B., & Stutzman, T. (1986). An evaluation of methods to select respondents to structured job-analysis questionnaires. *Personnel Psychology, 39,* 543–564.

Green, S. G., & Mitchell, T. R. (1979). Attributional processes of leaders in leader-member interactions. *Organizational Behavior and Human Performance, 23,* 429–458.

Greenberg, C. I., Thomas, J. M., Dossett, D. L., Robinson, R., DeMeuse, K. P., & Pendergrass, M. (1981). Perceptions of industrial/organizational

doctoral programs: A survey of APA Division 14 members. *Professional Psychology, 12,* 540–548.

Greenberg, J. (1986). Determinants of perceived fairness of performance evaluations. *Journal of Applied Psychology, 71,* 340–342.

Greenberg, J. (1987). The college sophomore as guinea pig: Setting the record straight. *Academy of Management Review, 12,* 157–159.

Greenberg, J. (1988). Equity and workplace status: A field experiment. *Journal of Applied Psychology, 73,* 606–613.

Greenberg, J. (1989). Cognitive reevaluation of outcomes in response to underpayment inequity. *Academy of Management Journal, 32,* 174–184.

Greenberg, J., & Ornstein, S. (1983). High status job title as compensation for underpayment: A test of equity theory. *Journal of Applied Psychology, 68,* 285–297.

Greene, C. N. (1976, August). *Causal connections among cohesion, drive, goal acceptance, and productivity in work groups.* Paper presented at the meeting of the Academy of Management, Kansas City, MO.

Greene, C. N., & Podsakoff, P. M. (1981). Effects of withdrawal of a performance-contingent reward on supervisory influence and power. *Academy of Management Journal, 24,* 527–542.

Greenhaus, J. H., Parasuraman, S., & Wormley, W. M. (1990). Effects of race on organizational experiences, job performance evaluations, and career outcomes. *Academy of Management Journal, 33,* 64–86.

Greenwald, J. (1992, January 27). Is Mr. Nice Guy back? *Time,* pp. 42–44.

Greenwald, J. (1991, September 9). Permanent pink slips. *Time,* pp. 54–56.

Greer, O. L., & Cascio, W. F. (1987). Is cost accounting the answer? Comparison of two behaviorally based methods for estimating the standard deviation of job performance in dollars with a cost-accounting-based approach. *Journal of Applied Psychology, 72,* 588–595.

Griffeth, R. W., Vecchio, R. P., & Logan, J. W. (1989). Equity theory and interpersonal attraction. *Journal of Applied Psychology, 74,* 394–401.

Griffin, R. W. (1983). Objective and social sources of information in task redesign: A field experiment. *Administrative Science Quarterly, 28,* 184–200.

Griffin, R. W., Bateman, T. S., Wayne, S. J., & Head, T. C. (1987). Objective and social factors as determinants of task perceptions and responses: An integrated perspective and empirical investigation. *Academy of Management Journal, 30,* 501–523.

Grigsby, D. W., & Bigoness, W. J. (1982). Effects of mediation and alternative forms of arbitration on bargaining behavior: A laboratory study. *Journal of Applied Psychology, 67,* 549–554.

Gross, A. L., & McGanney, M. L. (1987). The restriction of range problem and nonignorable selection processes. *Journal of Applied Psychology, 72,* 604–610.

Guilford, J. P., & Fruchter, B. (1978). *Fundamental statistics in psychology and education* (6th ed.). New York: McGraw-Hill.

Guion, R. M. (1961). Criterion measurement and personnel judgments. *Personnel Psychology, 14,* 141–149.

Guion, R. M. (1965a). Industrial psychology as an academic discipline. *American Psychologist, 20,* 815–821.

Guion, R. M. (1965b). *Personnel testing.* New York: McGraw-Hill.

Guion, R. M. (1973). A note on organizational climate. *Organizational Behavior and Human Performance, 9,* 120–125.

Guion, R. M. (1987). Changing views for personnel selection research. *Personnel Psychology, 40,* 199–213.

Guion, R. M., & Cranny, C. J. (1982). A note on concurrent and predictive validity designs: A critical reanalysis. *Journal of Applied Psychology, 67,* 239–244.

Guion, R. M., & Ironson, G. H. (1983). Latent trait theory for organizational research. *Organizational Behavior and Human Performance, 31,* 54–87.

Gup, T. (1991, November 4). The curse of coal. *Time,* pp. 54–56, 61, 64.

Gupta, N., & Jenkins, G. D. (1984). Substance use as an employee response to the work environment. *Journal of Vocational Behavior, 24,* 84–93.

Gutenberg, R. L., Arvey, R. D., Osburn, H. G., & Jeanneret, P. R. (1983). Moderating effects of decision-making/information-processing job dimensions on test validities. *Journal of Applied Psychology, 68,* 602–608.

Guzzo, R. A., Jette, R. D., & Katzell, R. A. (1985). The effects of psychologically based intervention programs on worker productivity: A meta-analysis. *Personnel Psychology, 38,* 275–291.

Hackett, R. D. (1989). Work attitudes and employee absenteeism: A synthesis of the literature. *Journal of Occupational Psychology, 62,* 235–248.

Hackett, R. D., & Guion, R. M. (1985). A reevaluation of the absenteeism-job satisfaction relationship. *Organizational Behavior and Human Decision Processes, 35,* 340–381.

Hackman, J. R., & Oldham, G. R. (1976). Motivation through the design of work: Test of a theory. *Organizational Behavior and Human Performance, 16,* 250–279.

Hackman, J. R., & Oldham, G. R. (1975). Development of the Job Diagnostic Survey. *Journal of Applied Psychology, 60,* 159–170.

Hackman, J. R., Oldham, G., Janson, R., & Purdy, K. (1975). A new strategy for job enrichment. *California Management Review, 17*(4), 57–71.

Hahn, D. C., & Dipboye, R. L. (1988). Effects of training and information on the accuracy and reliability of job evaluations. *Journal of Applied Psychology, 73,* 146–153.

Hakel, M. D. (1986). Personnel selection and placement. *Annual Review of Psychology, 37,* 351–380.

Hall, D. T., & Nougaim, K. E. (1968). An examination of Maslow's need hierarchy in an organizational setting. *Organizational Behavior and Human Performance, 3,* 12–35.

Halpin, A. W., & Winer, B. J. (1957). A factorial study of the leader behavior description. In R. M. Stogdill & A. E. Coons (Eds.), *Leader behavior: Its description and measurement.* Columbus: Bureau of Business Research, Ohio State University.

Hamilton, J. W., & Dickinson, T. L. (1987). Comparison of several procedures for generating J-coefficients. *Journal of Applied Psychology, 72,* 49–54.

Hammer, T. H., & Dachler, P. (1973). *The process of supervision in the context of motivation theory* (Tech. Rep. No. 3). College Park: Department of Psychology, University of Maryland.

Hancock, P. A. (1981). The limitation of human performance in extreme heat conditions. *Proceedings of the Human Factors Society 25th Annual Meeting* (pp. 74–78). Santa Monica: Human Factors Society.

Hancock, P. A. (1982). Task categorization and limits of human performance in extreme heat. *Aviation, Space, and Environmental Medicine, 53*(8), 778–784.

Hanges, P. J., Schneider, B., & Niles, K. (1990). Stability of performance: An interactionist perspective. *Journal of Applied Psychology, 75,* 658–667.

Hansen, C. P. (1989). A causal model of the relationship among accidents, biodata, personality, and cognitive factors. *Journal of Applied Psychology, 74,* 81–90.

Hanser, L. M., & Muchinsky, P. M. (1980). Performance feedback information and organizational communication: Evidence of conceptual convergence. *Human Communication Research, 7,* 68–73.

Harrell, A., & Stahl, M. (1986). Additive information processing and the relationship between expectancy of success and motivational force. *Academy of Management Journal, 29,* 424–433.

Harrell, T. W., & Alpert, B. (1989). Attributes of successful MBAs: A 20–year longitudinal study. *Human Performance, 2*(4), 301–322.

Harris, M. M. (1989). Reconsidering the employment interview: A review of recent literature and suggestions for future research. *Personnel Psychology, 42,* 691–726.

Harris, M. M., & Fink, L. S. (1987). A field study of applicant reactions to employment opportunities: Does the recruiter make a difference? *Personnel Psychology, 40,* 765–784.

Harris, M. M., & Schaubroeck, J. (1988). A meta-analysis of self-supervisor, self-peer, and peer-supervisor ratings. *Personnel Psychology, 41,* 43–62.

Harvey, B. H., & Luthans, F. (1979, Summer). Flexitime: An empirical analysis of its real meaning and impact. *MSU Business Topics,* 31–36.

Harvey, J. H., & Weary, G. (1984). Current issues in attribution theory and research. *Annual Review of Psychology, 35,* 427–459.

Harvey, R. J., Billings, R. S., & Nilan, K. J. (1985). Confirmatory factor analysis of the Job Diagnostic Survey: Good news and bad news. *Journal of Applied Psychology, 70,* 461–468.

Harvey, R. J., Friedman, L., Hakel, M. D., & Cornelius, E. T., III. (1988). Dimensionality of the Job Element Inventory, a simplified worker-oriented job analysis questionnaire. *Journal of Applied Psychology, 73,* 639–646.

Harvey, R. J., & Hayes, T. L. (1986). Monte Carlo baselines for inter-rater reliability correlations using the Position Analysis Questionnaire. *Personnel Psychology, 39,* 345–357.

Harvey, R. J., & Lozada-Larsen, S. R. (1988). Influence of amount of job descriptive information on job analysis rating accuracy. *Journal of Applied Psychology, 73,* 457–461.

Hatfield, J. D., & Huseman, R. C. (1982). Perceptual congruence about communication as related to satisfaction: Moderating effects of individual characteristics. *Academy of Management Journal, 25,* 349–358.

Hattrup, K., & Schmitt, N. (1990). Prediction of trades apprentices' performance on job sample criteria. *Personnel Psychology, 43,* 453–466.

Hauenstein, N. M. A., & Foti, R. J. (1989). From laboratory to practice: Neglected issues in implementing frame-of-reference rater training. *Personnel Psychology, 42,* 359–378.

Haynes, R. S., Pine, R. C., & Fitch, H. G. (1982). Reducing accident rates with organizational behavior modification. *Academy of Management Journal, 25,* 407–416.

Hays, W. L. (1973). *Statistics for the social sciences* (2nd ed.). New York: Holt, Rinehart & Winston.

Hedge, J. W., & Kavanagh, M. J. (1988). Improving the accuracy of performance evaluations: Comparison of three methods of performance appraiser training. *Journal of Applied Psychology, 73,* 68–73.

Hedges, L. V. (1989). An unbiased correction for sampling error in validity generalization studies. *Journal of Applied Psychology, 74,* 469–477.

Heilman, M. E. (1984). Information as a deterrent against sex discrimination: The effects of applicant sex and information type on preliminary employment decisions. *Organizational Behavior and Human Performance, 33,* 174–186.

Heilman, M. E., Block, C. J., Martell, R. F., & Simon, M. C. (1989). Has anything changed? Current characterizations of men, women, and managers. *Journal of Applied Psychology, 74,* 935–942.

Heilman, M. E., & Herlihy, J. M. (1984). Affirmative action, negative reaction? Some moderating conditions. *Organizational Behavior and Human Performance, 33,* 204–213.

Heilman, M. E., Hornstein, H. A., Cage, J. H., & Herschlag, J. K. (1984). Reactions to prescribed leader behavior as a function of role perspective: The case of the Vroom-Yetton model. *Journal of Applied Psychology, 69,* 50–60.

Heilman, M. E., Lucas, J. A., & Kaplow, S. R. (1990). Self-derogating consequences of sex-based preferential selection: The moderating role of initial self-confidence. *Organizational Behavior and Human Decision Processes, 46,* 202–216.

Heilman, M. E., & Martell, R. F. (1986). Exposure to successful women: Antidote to sex discrimination in applicant screening decisions? *Organiza-*

tional Behavior and Human Decision Processes, 37, 376–390.

Heilman, M. E., Martell, R. F., & Simon, M. C. (1988). The vagaries of sex bias: Conditions regulating the undervaluation, equivaluation, and overvaluation of female job applicants. *Organizational Behavior and Human Decision Processess, 41,* 98–110.

Heilman, M. E., Simon, M. C., & Repper, D. P. (1987). Intentionally favored, unintentionally harmed? Impact of sex-based preferential selection on self-perceptions and self-evaluations. *Journal of Applied Psychology, 72,* 62–68.

Heilman, M. E., & Stopeck, M. H. (1985a). Attractiveness and corporate success: Different causal attributions for males and females. *Journal of Applied Psychology, 70,* 379–388.

Heilman, M. E., & Stopeck, M. H. (1985b). Being attractive, advantage or disadvantage? Performance-based evaluations and recommended personnel actions as a function of appearance, sex, and job type. *Organizational Behavior and Human Decision Processes, 35,* 202–215.

Heise, D. R. (1975). *Causal analysis.* New York: Wiley.

Helmreich, R. L., Sawin, L. L., & Carsrud, A. L. (1986). The honeymoon effect in job performance: Temporal increases in the predictive power of achievement motivation. *Journal of Applied Psychology, 71,* 185–188.

Hemphill, J. K. (1949). The leader and his group. *Journal of Educational Research, 28,* 225–229, 245–246.

Hemphill, J. K., & Coons, A. E. (1957). Development of the Leader Behavior Description Questionnaire. In R. M. Stogdill & A. E. Coons (Eds.), *Leaders behavior: Its description and measurement.* Columbus: Bureau of Business Research, Ohio State University.

Hendrix, W. H. (1990). Physiological effects of stress in the workplace. In J. W. Jones, B. D. Steffy, & D. W. Bray (Eds.), *Applying psychology in business.* Lexington, MA: Lexington Books.

Hendrix, W. H., Leap, T. L., & Steel, R. P. (1986). A health promotion model for organizations: The effect of health promotion on organizational effectiveness and absenteeism. In O. Brown, Jr., & H. W. Hendrick (Eds.), *Human factors in organizational design and management—II.* New York: North-Holland.

Heneman, H. G., Jr. (1973). Work and nonwork: His-

torical perspectives. In M. D. Dunnette (Ed.), *Work and nonwork in the year 2001.* Pacific Grove, CA: Brooks/Cole.

Heneman, R. L. (1986). The relationship between supervisory ratings and results-oriented measures of performance: A meta-analysis. *Personnel Psychology, 39,* 811–826.

Heneman, R. L. (1988). Traits, behaviors, and rater training: Some unexpected results. *Human Performance, 1,* 85–98.

Heneman, R. L., Greenberger, D. B., & Anonyuo, C. (1989). Attributions and exchanges: The effects of interpersonal factors on the diagnosis of employee performance. *Academy of Management Journal, 32,* 466–476.

Henik, A., & Tzelgov, J. (1985). Control of halo error: A multiple regression approach. *Journal of Applied Psychology, 70,* 577–580.

Hennig, M., & Jardim, A. (1977). *The managerial woman.* Garden City, NY: Anchor Press/Doubleday.

Henry, R. A., & Hulin, C. L. (1987). Stability of skilled performance across time: Some generalizations and limitations on utilities. *Journal of Applied Psychology, 72,* 457–462.

Henry, R. A., & Hulin, C. L. (1989). Changing validities: Ability-performance relations and utilities. *Journal of Applied Psychology, 74,* 365–367.

Henry. W. A., III. (1991, August 19). To "out" or not to "out." *Time,* p. 17.

Herold, D. M., Liden, R. C., & Leatherwood, M. L. (1987). Using multiple attributes to assess sources of performance feedback. *Academy of Management Journal, 30,* 826–835.

Herold, D. M., & Parsons, C. K. (1985). Assessing the feedback environment in work organizations: Development of the Job Feedback Survey. *Journal of Applied Psychology, 70,* 290–305.

Herzberg, F. (1964). The motivation-hygiene concept and problems of manpower. *Personnel Administrator, 27,* 3–7.

Herzberg, F. (1966). *Work and the nature of man.* Cleveland: World.

Herzberg, F., Mausner, B., Peterson, R. O., & Capwell, D. F. (1957). *Job attitudes: Review of research and opinion.* Pittsburgh: Psychological Service of Pittsburgh.

Herzberg, F., Mausner, B., & Snyderman, B. (1959). *The motivation to work.* New York: Wiley.

Hicks, W. D., & Klimoski, R. J. (1981). The impact of

flexitime on employee attitudes. *Academy of Management Journal, 24,* 333–341.

Hicks, W. D., & Klimoski, R. J. (1987). Entry into training programs and its effects on training outcomes: A field experiment. *Academy of Management Journal, 30,* 542–552.

Higgins, N. C. (1986). Occupational stress and working women: The effectiveness of two stress reduction programs. *Journal of Vocational Behavior, 29,* 66–78.

Hilgard, E. R., & Bower, G. H. (1966). *Theories of learning* (3rd ed.). New York: Appleton-Century-Crofts.

Hills, S. M. (1985). The attitudes of union and nonunion male workers toward union representation. *Industrial and Labor Relations Review, 38,* 179–194.

Hindman, H. D. (1988). *Determinants of union representation election outcomes: Evidence from the public sector.* Paper presented at the 41st annual meeting of the Industrial Relations Research Association, New York.

Hinkin, T. R., & Schriesheim, C. A. (1989). Development and application of new scales to measure the French and Raven (1959) bases of social power. *Journal of Applied Psychology, 74,* 561–567.

Hinrichs, J. R. (1976). Personnel training. In M.D. Dunnette (Ed.), *Handbook of industrial and organizational psychology.* Chicago: Rand McNally.

Hinton, B. L., & Barrow, J. C. (1975). The superior's reinforcing behavior as a function of reinforcements received. *Organizational Behavior and Human Performance, 14,* 123–149.

Hirsh, H. R., Northrop, L. C., & Schmidt, F. L. (1986). Validity generalization results for law enforcement occupations. *Personnel Psychology, 39,* 399–420.

Hirst, M. K. (1988). Intrinsic motivation as influenced by task interdependence and goal setting. *Journal of Applied Psychology, 73,* 96–101.

Hitt, M. A., & Barr, S. H. (1989). Managerial selection decision models: Examination of configural cue processing. *Journal of Applied Psychology, 74,* 53–61.

Hobert, R. D., & Dunnette, M. D. (1967). Development of moderator variables to enhance the prediction of managerial effectiveness. *Journal of Applied Psychology, 51,* 50–64.

Hofstede, G. (1980). Motivation, leadership, and organization: Do American theories apply abroad? *Organizational Dynamics, 9,* 42–62.

Hogan, E. A. (1987). Effects of prior expectations on performance ratings: A longitudinal study. *Academy of Management Journal, 30,* 354–368.

Hogan, J. (1985). Tests for success in diver training. *Journal of Applied Psychology, 70,* 219–224.

Hogan, J. C., & Fleishman, E. A. (1979). An index of the physical effort required in human task performance. *Journal of Applied Psychology, 64,* 197–204.

Hogan, J., & Hogan, R. (1989). How to measure employee reliability. *Journal of Applied Psychology, 74,* 273–279.

Hogan, J., Hogan, R., & Busch, C. M. (1984). How to measure service orientation. *Journal of Applied Psychology, 69,* 167–173.

Hogan, J. C., Ogden, G. D., Gebhardt, D. L., & Fleishman, E. A. (1980). Reliability and validity of methods for evaluating perceived physical effort. *Journal of Applied Psychology, 65,* 672–679.

Hogan, J., & Quigley, A. M. (1986). Physical standards for employment and the courts. *American Psychologist, 41,* 1193–1217.

Hogan, P. M., Hakel, M. D., & Decker, P. J. (1986). Effects of trainee-generated versus trainer-provided rule codes on generalization in behavior-modeling training. *Journal of Applied Psychology, 71,* 469–473.

Hollander, E. P., Fallon, B. J., & Edwards, M. T. (1977). Some aspects of influence and acceptability for appointed and elected group leaders. *Journal of Psychology, 95,* 289–296.

Hollander, E. P., & Julian, J. W. (1970). Studies in leader legitimacy, influence, and innovation. In L. Berkowitz (Ed.), *Advances in experimental social psychology* (Vol. 5). New York: Academic Press.

Hollenbeck, J. R. (1989). Control theory and the perception of work environments: The effects of focus of attention on affective and behavioral reactions to work. *Organizational Behavior and Human Decision Processes, 43,* 406–430.

Hollenbeck, J. R., & Klein, H. J. (1987). Goal commitment and the goal-setting process: Problems, prospects, and proposals for future research. *Journal of Applied Psychology, 72,* 212–220.

Hollenbeck, J. R., & Williams, C. R. (1986). Turnover functionality versus turnover frequency: A note on work attitudes and organizational effectiveness. *Journal of Applied Psychology, 71,* 606–611.

Hollenbeck, J. R., Williams, C. R., & Klein, H. J. (1989). An empirical examination of the antecedents of commitment to difficult goals. *Journal of Applied Psychology, 74,* 18–23.

Hollenbeck, J. R., & Whitener, E. M. (1988). Criterion-related validation for small sample contexts: An integrated approach to synthetic validity. *Journal of Applied Psychology, 73,* 536–544.

Hoppock, R. (1935). *Job satisfaction.* New York: Harper and Brothers.

Horst, P. (1968). *Psychological measurement and prediction.* Belmont, CA: Brooks/Cole.

Hough, L. M. (1984). Development and evaluation of the "accomplishment record" method of selecting and promoting professionals. *Journal of Applied Psychology, 69,* 135–146.

Hough, L. M., Eaton, N. K., Dunnette, M. D., Kamp, J. D., & McCloy, R. A. (1990). Criterion-related validities of personality constructs and the effect of response distortion on those validities [Monograph]. *Journal of Applied Psychology, 75,* 581–595.

Hough, L. M., Keyes, M. A., & Dunnette, M. D. (1983). An evaluation of three "alternative" selection procedures. *Personnel Psychology, 36,* 261–276.

House, R. J. (1971). A path goal theory of leader effectiveness. *Administrative Science Quarterly, 16,* 321–338.

House, R. J. (1972). *The relationship of intrinsic and extrinsic work motivation to occupational stress and coronary heart disease risk* (Doctoral dissertation, University of Michigan).

House, R. J. (1977). A 1976 theory of charismatic leadership. In J. G. Hunt and L. L. Larson (Eds.), *Leadership: The cutting edge.* Carbondale: Southern Illinois University Press.

House, R. J. (1992, January 22). Personal communication.

House, R. J., & Baetz, M. L. (1979). Leadership: Some empirical generalizations and new research directions. In B. M. Staw (Ed.), *Research in organizational behavior* (Vol. 1). Greenwich, CT: JAI Press.

House, R. J., & Dessler, G. (1974). The path goal theory of leadership: Some post hoc and a priori tests. In J. G. Hunt & L. L. Larson (Eds.), *Contingency approaches to leadership.* Carbondale: Southern Illinois University Press.

House, R. J., & Filley, A. C. (1971). Leadership style, hierarchical influence, and the satisfaction of subordinate role expectations: A test of Likert's influence proposition. *Journal of Applied Psychology, 55,* 422–432.

House, R. J., & Mitchell, T. R. (1974). Path-goal theory of leadership. *Journal of Contemporary Business, 3,* 81–97.

House, R. J., Spangler, W. D., & Woycke, J. (1991). Personality and charisma in the U.S. presidency: A psychological theory of leader effectiveness. *Administrative Science Quarterly, 36,* 364–396.

House, R. J., Woycke, J., & Fodor, E. M. (1988). Charismatic and non-charismatic leaders: Differences in behavior and effectiveness. In J. A. Conger & R. N. Kanungo (Eds.), *Charismatic leadership.* San Francisco: Jossey-Bass.

How sweet it was. (1992, February 24). *Time,* p. 42.

Howard, A. (1986). College experiences and managerial performance [Monograph]. *Journal of Applied Psychology, 71,* 530–552.

Howard, A., & Lowman, R. L. (1985). Should industrial/organizational psychologists be licensed? *American Psychologist, 40,* 40–47.

Howat, G., & London, M. (1980). Attributions of conflict management strategies in supervisor-subordinate dyads. *Journal of Applied Psychology, 65,* 172–175.

Howell, J. M., & Frost, P. J. (1989). A laboratory study of charismatic leadership. *Organizational Behavior and Human Decision Processes, 43,* 243–269.

Howell, W. C., & Dipboye, R. L. (1986). *Essentials of industrial and organizational psychology* (3rd ed.). Chicago: Dorsey Press.

Howell, J. P., & Dorfman, P. W. (1981). Substitutes for leadership: Test of a construct. *Academy of Management Journal, 24,* 714–728.

Howell, J. P., Dorfman, P. W., & Kerr, S. (1986). Moderator variables in leadership research. *Academy of Management Review, 11,* 88–102.

Hoyt, C. (1941). Test reliability estimated by analysis of variance. *Psychometrika, 6,* 153–160.

Hrebiniak, L. G., & Alluto, J. A. (1972). Personal and role-related factors in the development of organizational commitment. *Administrative Science Quarterly, 17,* 555–573.

Huber, V. L. (1985). Effects of task difficulty, goal setting, and strategy on performance of a heuristic task. *Journal of Applied Psychology, 70,* 492–504.

Huber, V. L. (1991). Comparison of supervisor-incumbent and female-male multidimensional job evaluation ratings. *Journal of Applied Psychology, 76,* 115–121.

Hughes, G. L., & Prien, E. P. (1986). An evaluation of alternate scoring methods for the mixed standard scale. *Personnel Psychology, 39,* 839–847.

Hughes, G. L., & Prien, E. P. (1989). Evaluation of task and job skill linkage judgments used to develop test specifications. *Personnel Psychology, 42,* 283–292.

Hughes, J. L., & McNamara, W. J. (1959). *Manual for the revised Programmer Aptitude Test.* New York: Psychological Corporation.

Hughes, P., & McNelis, J. (1978, May). Lighting, productivity, and work environment. *Lighting Design and Application,* pp. 37–42.

Hulin, C. L., Drasgow, F., & Komocar, J. (1982). Applications of item response theory to analysis of attitude scale translations. *Journal of Applied Psychology, 67,* 818–825.

Hulin, C. L., Drasgow, F., & Parsons, C. K. (1983). *Item response theory: Application to psychological measurement.* Homewood, IL: Dow Jones-Irwin.

Hulin, C. L., Henry, R. A., & Noon, S. L. (1990). Adding a dimension: Time as a factor in the generalizability of predictive relationships. *Psychological Bulletin, 107,* 328–340.

Hulin, C. L., Roznowski, M., & Hachiya, D. (1985). Alternative opportunities and withdrawal decisions: Empirical and theoretical discrepancies and an integration. *Psychological Bulletin, 97,* 233–250.

Hulin, C. L., & Smith, P. C. (1964). Sex differences in job satisfaction. *Journal of Applied Psychology, 48,* 88–92.

Hulin, C. L., & Smith, P. C. (1965). A linear model of job satisfaction. *Journal of Applied Psychology, 49,* 209–216.

Hull, C. L. (1928). *Aptitude testing.* New York: Harcourt, Brace and World.

Humphreys, L. G. (1986). An analysis and evaluation of test and item bias in the prediction context. *Journal of Applied Psychology, 71,* 327–333.

Humphreys, L. G., & Swets, J. A. (1991). Comparison of predictive validities measured with biserial correlations and ROCs of signal detection theory. *Journal of Applied Psychology, 76,* 316–321.

Hunt, D. M., & Michael, C. (1983). Mentorship: A career training and development tool. *Academy of Management Review, 8,* 475–485.

Hunt, J. G., Sekaran, U., & Schriesheim, C. A. (1982).

Beyond establishment views of leadership: An introduction. In J. G. Hunt, U. Sekaran, & C. A. Schriesheim (Eds.), *Leadership: Beyond establishment views.* Carbondale: Southern Illinois University Press.

Hunter, J. E., & Hunter, R. F. (1984). Validity and utility of alternative predictors of job performance. *Psychological Bulletin, 96,* 72–98.

Hunter, J. E., Schmidt, F. L., & Coggin, T. D. (1988). Problems and pitfalls in using capital budgeting and financial accounting techniques in assessing the utility of personnel programs. *Journal of Applied Psychology, 73,* 522–528.

Hunter, J. E., Schmidt, F. L., & Judiesch, M. K. (1990). Individual differences in output variability as a function of job complexity. *Journal of Applied Psychology, 75,* 28–42.

Hunter, J. E., Schmidt, F. L., & Pearlman, K. (1982). History and accuracy of validity generalization equations: A response to the Callender and Osburn reply. *Journal of Applied Psychology, 67,* 853–858.

Huseman, R. C., Hatfield, J. D., & Miles, E. W. (1987). A new perspective on equity theory: The equity sensitivity construct. *Academy of Management Review, 12,* 222–234.

Hyland, A. M., & Muchinsky, P. M. (1991). Assessment of the structural validity of Holland's model with job analysis (PAQ) information. *Journal of Applied Psychology, 76,* 75–80.

Iaffaldano, M. T., & Muchinsky, P. M. (1985). Job satisfaction and job performance: A meta-analysis. *Psychological Bulletin, 97,* 251–273.

Idaszak, J. R., Bottom, W. P., & Drasgow, F. (1988). A test of the measurement equivalence of the revised Job Diagnostic Survey: Past problems and current solutions. *Journal of Applied Psychology, 73,* 647–656.

Idaszak, J. R., & Drasgow, F. (1987). A revision of the Job Diagnostic Survey: Elimination of a measurement artifact. *Journal of Applied Psychology, 72,* 69–74.

IES lighting fundamentals course. (1976). New York: Illuminating Engineering Society.

IES lighting handbook, application volume. (1981a). New York: Illuminating Engineering Society of North America.

IES lighting handbook, reference volume. (1981b). New York: Illuminating Engineering Society of North America.

Ilgen, D. R., Fisher, C. D., & Taylor, M. S. (1979). Consequences of individual feedback on behavior in organizations. *Journal of Applied Psychology, 64,* 349–371.

Ilgen, D. R., & Moore, C. F. (1987). Types and choices of performance feedback. *Journal of Applied Psychology, 72,* 401–406.

Industrial use of ergonomics. 1969. *Applied Ergonomics, 1,* 26–32.

Inwald, R. E. (1988). Five-year follow-up study of departmental terminations as predicted by 16 preemployment psychological indicators. *Journal of Applied Psychology, 73,* 703–710.

Ironson, G. H., Smith, P. C., Brannick, M. T., Gibson, W. M., & Paul, K. B. (1989). Construction of a Job in General scale: A comparison of global, composite, and specific measures. *Journal of Applied Psychology, 74,* 193–200.

Isenberg, D. J. (1981). Some effects of time-pressure on vertical structure and decision-making accuracy in small groups. *Organizational Behavior and Human Performance, 27,* 119–134.

It's off the job we go. (1991, December 23). *Time,* p. 61.

Ivancevich, J. M. (1979). Longitudinal study of the effects of rater training on psychometric error in ratings. *Journal of Applied Psychology, 64,* 502–508.

Ivancevich, J. M. (1985). Predicting absenteeism from prior absence and work attitudes. *Academy of Management Journal, 28,* 219–228.

Ivancevich, J. M., & Donnelly, J. H., Jr. (1975). Relation of organizational structure to job satisfaction, anxiety-stress, and performance. *Administrative Science Quarterly, 20,* 272–280.

Ivancevich, J. M., Matteson, M. T., Freedman, S. M., & Phillips, J. S. (1990). Worksite stress management interventions. *American Psychologist, 45,* 252–261.

Izraeli, D. N., & Izraeli, D. (1985). Sex effects in evaluating leaders: A replication study. *Journal of Applied Psychology, 70,* 540–546.

Jablin, F. M. (1985). Task/work relationships: A life-span perspective. In M. L. Knapp & G. R. Miller (Eds.), *Handbook of interpersonal communication.* Beverly Hills: Sage.

Jackofsky, E. F. (1984). Turnover and job performance: An integrated process model. *Academy of Management Review, 9,* 74–83.

Jackson, P. R., Stafford, E. M., Banks, M. H., & Warr, P. B. (1983). Unemployment and psychological distress in young people: The moderating role of employment commitment. *Journal of Applied Psychology, 68,* 525–535.

Jacobs, J. A. (1992). Women's entry into management: Trends in earnings, authority, and values among salaried managers. *Administrative Science Quarterly, 37,* 282–301.

Jacobs, R., Hofmann, D. A., & Kriska, S. D. (1990). Performance and seniority. *Human Performance, 3*(2), 107–121.

Jacobs, R., Kafry, D., & Zedeck, S. (1980). Expectations of behaviorally anchored rating scales. *Personnel Psychology, 33,* 595–640.

Jacobs, R., & Kozlowski, S. W. J. (1985). A closer look at halo error in performance ratings. *Academy of Management Journal, 28,* 201–212.

Jacobs, R., & Solomon, T. (1977). Strategies for enhancing the prediction of job performance from job satisfaction. *Journal of Applied Psychology, 62,* 417–421.

Jaeger, A. M. (1986). Organization development and national culture: Where's the fit? *Academy of Management Review, 11,* 178–190.

Jago, A. G., & Ragan, J. W. (1986a). The trouble with leader match is that it doesn't match Fiedler's contingency model. *Journal of Applied Psychology, 71,* 555–559.

Jago, A. G., & Ragan, J. W. (1986b). Some assumptions are more troubling than others: Rejoinder to Chemers and Fiedler. *Journal of Applied Psychology, 71,* 564–565.

Jago, A. G., & Vroom, V. H. (1980). An evaluation of two alternatives to the Vroom/Yetton model. *Academy of Management Journal, 23,* 347–355.

Jago, A. G., & Vroom, V. H. (1982). Sex differences in the incidence and evaluation of participative leader behavior. *Journal of Applied Psychology, 67,* 776–783.

Jako, R. A., & Murphy, K. R. (1990). Distributional ratings, judgment decomposition, and their impact on interrater agreement and rating accuracy. *Journal of Applied Psychology, 75,* 500–505.

Jamal, M. (1981). Shift work related to job attitudes, social participation and withdrawal behavior: A study of nurses and industrial workers. *Personnel Psychology, 34,* 535–547.

Jamal, M. (1984). Job stress and job performance controversy: An empirical assessment. *Organizational Behavior and Human Performance, 33*, 1–21.

James, L. R., & Brett, J. M. (1984). Mediators, moderators, and tests for mediation. *Journal of Applied Psychology, 69*, 307–321.

James, L. R., Demaree, R. G., & Mulaik, S. A. (1986). A note on validity generalization procedures. *Journal of Applied Psychology, 71*, 440–450.

James, L. R., Demaree, R. G., Mulaik, S. A., & Mumford, M. D. (1988). Validity generalization: Rejoinder to Schmidt, Hunter, and Raju (1988). *Journal of Applied Psychology, 73*, 673–678.

James, L. R., Demaree, R. G., & Wolf, G. (1984). Estimating within-group interrater reliability with and without response bias. *Journal of Applied Psychology, 69*, 85–98.

James, L. R., & Tetrick, L. E. (1986). Confirmatory analytic tests of three causal models relating job perceptions to job satisfaction. *Journal of Applied Psychology, 71*, 77–82.

James, S. P., Campbell, I. M., & Lovegrove, S. A. (1984). Personality differentiation in a police-selection interview. *Journal of Applied Psychology, 69*, 129–134.

Janz, T. (1982). Initial comparisons of patterned behavior description interviews versus unstructured interviews. *Journal of Applied Psychology, 67*, 577–580.

Jenkins, G. D., Jr., & Taber, T. D. (1977). A Monte Carlo study of factors affecting three indices of composite scale reliability. *Journal of Applied Psychology, 62*, 392–398.

Jenkins, W. O. (1947). A review of leadership studies with particular reference to military problems. *Psychological Bulletin, 44*, 54–79.

Johnson, C. D., Messe, L. A., & Crano, W. D. (1984). Predicting job performance of low income workers: The Work Opinion Questionnaire. *Personnel Psychology, 37*, 291–299.

Johnson, S. M., Smith, P. C., & Tucker, S. M. (1982). Response format of the Job Descriptive Index: Assessment of reliability and validity by the multi-trait, multi-method matrix. *Journal of Applied Psychology, 67*, 500–505.

Jolly, J. P., Reynolds, T. J., & Slocum, J. W., Jr. (1988). Application of the means-end theoretic for understanding the cognitive bases of performance appraisal. *Organizational Behavior and Human Decision Processes, 41*, 153–179.

Jones, A. P., Main, D. S., Butler, M. C., & Johnson, L. A. (1982). Narrative job descriptions as potential sources of job analysis ratings. *Personnel Psychology, 35*, 813–828.

Jordan, P. (Producer, Director). (1972). *Business, behaviorism and the bottom line* [Film]. New York: McGraw-Hill.

Jordan, P. C. (1986). Effects of an extrinsic reward on intrinsic motivation: A field experiment. *Academy of Management Journal, 29*, 405–412.

Julian, J. W., Hollander, E. P., & Regula, C. R. (1969). Endorsement of the group spokesman as a function of his source of authority, competence, and success. *Journal of Personality and Social Psychology, 11*, 42–49.

Kabanoff, B. (1980). Work and nonwork: A review of models, methods, and findings. *Psychological Bulletin, 88*, 60–77.

Kabanoff, B. (1981). A critique of Leader Match and its implications for leadership research. *Personnel Psychology, 34*, 749–764.

Kabanoff, B., & O'Brien, G. E. (1980). Work and leisure: A task attributes analysis. *Journal of Applied Psychology, 65*, 596–609.

Kamouri, A. L. & Balzer, W. K. (1990). The effects of performance sampling methods on frequency estimation, probability estimation, and evaluation of performance information. *Organizational Behavior and Human Decision Processes 45*, 285–316.

Kane, J. S., & Lawler, E. E., III. (1978). Methods of peer assessment. *Psychological Bulletin, 85*, 555–586.

Kane, J. S., & Lawler, E. E., III. (1979). Performance appraisal effectiveness: Its assessment and determinants. In B. M. Staw (Ed.), *Research in organizational behavior* (Vol. 1). Greenwich, CT: JAI Press.

Kanter, R. M. (1977). *Men and women of the corporation*. New York: Basic Books.

Kantowitz, B. H., & Sorkin, R. D. (1983). *Human factors: Understanding people-system relationships*. New York: Wiley.

Kaplan, R. M., & Saccuzzo, D. P. (1982). *Psychological testing: Principles, applications, and issues*. Pacific Grove, CA: Brooks/Cole.

Katerberg, R., & Hom, P. W. (1981). Effects of within-group and between-groups variation in leadership. *Journal of Applied Psychology, 66*, 218–223.

Katz, D., & Kahn, R. L. (1978). *The social psychology of organizations* (2nd ed.). New York: Wiley.

Kavanagh, M. J. (1971). The content issue in performance appraisal: A review. *Personnel Psychology, 24,* 653–668.

Keaveny, T. J., Rose, J., & Fossum, J. (1988). *Predicting support for unionization: Part time versus full time workers and professional/technical blue collar workers.* Paper presented at the 41st annual meeting of the Industrial Relations Research Association, New York.

Keeley, M. (1984). Impartiality and participant-interest theories of organizational effectiveness. *Administrative Science Quarterly, 29,* 1–25.

Keinan, G., Friedland, N., Yitzhaky, J., & Moran, A. (1981). Biographical, physiological, and personality variables as predictors of performance under sickness-inducing motion. *Journal of Applied Psychology, 66,* 233–241.

Keller, R. T. (1983). Predicting absenteeism from prior absenteeism, attitudinal factors, and non-attitudinal factors. *Journal of Applied Psychology, 68,* 536–540.

Keller, R. T. (1989). A test of the path-goal theory of leadership with need for clarity as a moderator in research and development organizations. *Journal of Applied Psychology, 74,* 208–212.

Keller, R. T., & Holland, W. E. (1983). Communicators and innovators in research and development organizations. *Academy of Management Journal, 26,* 742–749.

Kelloway, E. K., Barling, J., & Fullagar, C. (1990). *Extending a model of union commitment: The roles of union and work attitudes.* Unpublished manuscript.

Kemery, E. R., Mossholder, K. W., & Dunlap, W. P. (1989). Meta-analysis and moderator variables: A cautionary note on transportability. *Journal of Applied Psychology, 74,* 168–170.

Kemery, E. R., Mossholder, K. W., & Roth, L. (1987). The power of the Schmidt and Hunter additive model of validity generalization. *Journal of Applied Psychology, 72,* 30–37.

Kennedy, J. K., Jr. (1982). Middle LPC leaders and the contingency model of leadership effectiveness. *Organizational Behavior and Human Performance, 30,* 1–14.

Kephart, N. C., & Tiffin, J. (1950). Vision and accident experience. *National Safety News, 62,* 90–91.

Kerr, S., & Jermier, J. M. (1978). Substitutes for leadership: Their meaning and measurement. *Organizational Behavior and Human Performance, 22,* 375–403.

Kets-de-Vries, M. F., & Miller, D. (1986). Personality, culture, and organization. *Academy of Management Review, 11,* 266–279.

Kim, J. S., & Campagna, A. F. (1981). Effects of flexitime on employee attendance and performance: A field experiment. *Academy of Management Journal, 24,* 729–741.

Kim, K. I., Park, H., & Suzuki, N. (1990). Reward allocations in the United States, Japan, and Korea: A comparison of individualistic and collectivistic cultures. *Academy of Management Journal, 33,* 188–198.

King, N. (1970). Clarification and evaluation of the two-factor theory of job satisfaction. *Psychological Bulletin, 74,* 18–31.

Kingstrom, P. O., & Bass, A. R. (1981). A critical analysis of studies comparing behaviorally anchored rating scales (BARS) and other rating formats. *Personnel Psychology, 34,* 263–289.

Kinicki, A. J. (1989). Predicting occupational role choices after involuntary job loss. *Journal of Vocational Behavior, 35,* 204–218.

Kinicki, A. J., Lockwood, C. A., Hom, P. W., & Griffeth, R. W. (1990). Interviewer predictions of applicant qualifications and interviewer validity: Aggregate and individual analyses. *Journal of Applied Psychology, 75,* 477–486.

Kinkead, R. (1975). Typing speed, keying rates, and optimal keyboard layout. *Proceedings of the Human Factors Society.* Dallas.

Kipnis, D. (1972). Does power corrupt? *Journal of Personality and Social Psychology, 24,* 33–41.

Kipnis, D., & Schmidt, S. M. (1988). Upward-influence styles: Relationship with performance evaluations, salary, and stress. *Administrative Science Quarterly, 33,* 528–542.

Kirchner, W. K. (1965). Relationships between supervisory and subordinate ratings for technical personnel. *Journal of Industrial Psychology, 3,* 57–60.

Kirkpatrick, D. L. (1967). Evaluation of training. In R. L. Craig & L. R. Bittel (Eds.), *Training and development handbook.* New York: McGraw-Hill.

Kirnan, J. P., Farley, J. A., & Geisinger, K. F. (1989). The relationship between recruiting source, applicant quality, and hire performance: An analysis by sex, ethnicity, and age. *Personnel Psychology, 42,* 293–308.

Klaas, B. S., & DeNisi, A. S. (1989). Managerial reactions to employee dissent: The impact of grievance activity on performance ratings. *Academy of Management Journal, 32*, 705–717.

Klandermans, B. (1989). Union commitment: Replications and tests in the Dutch context. *Journal of Applied Psychology, 74*, 869–875.

Klauss, R., & Bass, B. M. (1981). *Impact of communication.* New York: Academic Press.

Kleiman, L. S., & Faley, R. H. (1985). The implications of professional and legal guidelines for court decisions involving criterion-related validity: A review and analysis. *Personnel Psychology, 38*, 803–833.

Klein, H. J. (1989). An integrated control theory model of work motivation. *Academy of Management Review, 14*, 150–172.

Klieger, W. A., & Mosel, J. N. (1953). The effect of opportunity to observe and rater status on the reliability of performance ratings. *Personnel Psychology, 6*, 57–64.

Klimoski, R., & Brickner, M. (1987). Why do assessment centers work? The puzzle of assessment center validity. *Personnel Psychology, 40*, 243–260.

Klimoski, R. J., & Inks, L. (1990). Accountability forces in performance appraisal. *Organizational Behavior and Human Decision Processes, 45*, 194–208.

Klimoski, R. J., & London, M. (1974). Role of the rater in performance appraisal. *Journal of Applied Psychology, 59*, 445–451.

Klimoski, R. J., & Strickland, W. J. (1977). Assessment centers—Valid or merely prescient. *Personnel Psychology, 30*, 353–361.

Knave, B. (1984). Ergonomics and lighting. *Applied Ergonomics, 15*(1), 15–20.

Knight, P. A., & Nadel, J. I. (1986). Humility revisited: Self-esteem, information search, and policy consistency. *Organizational Behavior and Human Decision Processes, 38*, 196–206.

Knight, P. A., & Saal, F. E. (1983, August). *Gender bias in managerial performance ratings.* Paper presented at the meeting of the American Psychological Association, Anaheim, CA.

Knight, P. A., & Saal, F. E. (1984). Effects of gender differences and selection agent expertise on leader influence and performance evaluations. *Organizational Behavior and Human Performance, 34*, 225–243.

Knight, P. A., & Weiss, H. M. (1980). Effects of selection agent and leader origin on leader influence and group member perceptions. *Organizational Behavior and Human Performance, 26*, 7–21.

Knouse, S. B. (1983). The letter of recommendation: Specificity and favorability of information. *Personnel Psychology, 36*, 331–341.

Kochan, T. A. (1980). *Collective bargaining and industrial relations.* Homewood, IL: Irwin.

Kochan, T. A., & Helfman, D. E. (1981). The effects of collective bargaining on economic and behavioral outcomes. In R. G. Ehrenberg (Ed.), *Research in labor economics.* Greenwich, CT: JAI Press.

Kochan, T. A., McKersie, R. B., & Chalykoff, J. (1986). The effects of corporate strategy and workplace innovations on union representation. *Industrial and Labor Relations Review, 39*, 487–501.

Kohlberg, L. (1968). The child as moral philosopher. *Psychology Today, 2*(4), 24–30.

Komaki, J. L. (1986). Toward effective supervision: An operant analysis and comparison of managers at work. *Journal of Applied Psychology, 71*, 270–279.

Komaki, J., Barwick, K. D., & Scott, L. R. (1978). A behavioral approach to occupational safety: Pinpointing and reinforcing safe performance in a food manufacturing plant. *Journal of Applied Psychology, 63*, 434–445.

Komaki, J. L., Collins, R. L., & Penn, P. (1982). The role of performance antecedents and consequences in work motivation. *Journal of Applied Psychology, 67*, 334–340.

Komaki, J. L., Desselles, M. L., & Bowman, E. D. (1989). Definitely not a breeze: Extending an operant model of effective supervision to teams. *Journal of Applied Psychology, 74*, 522–529.

Komaki, J., Heinzmann, A. T., & Lawson, L. (1980). Effect of training and feedback: Component analysis of a behavioral safety program. *Journal of Applied Psychology, 65*, 261–270.

Kopelman, R. E. (1976). Organizational control system responsiveness, expectancy theory constructs, and work motivation: Some interrelations and causal connections. *Personnel Psychology, 29*, 205–220.

Kopelman, R. E., Greenhaus, J. H., & Connolly, T. F. (1983). A model of work, family, and interrole conflict: A construct validation study. *Organizational Behavior and Human Performance, 32*, 198–215.

Koprowski, E. J. (1983). Cultural myths: Clues to effective management. *Organizational Dynamics*, 12, 39–51.

Korman, A. K. (1971). *Industrial and organizational psychology*. Englewood Cliffs, NJ: Prentice-Hall.

Korman, A. K. (1977). *Organizational behavior*. Englewood Cliffs, NJ: Prentice-Hall.

Korman, A. K., Greenhaus, J. H., & Badin, I. J. (1977). Personnel attitudes and motivation. *Annual Review of Psychology*, 28, 175–196.

Koslowsky, M. (1990). Staff/line distinctions in job and organizational commitment. *Journal of Occupational Psychology*, 63, 167–173.

Kovach, K. A., & Millspaugh, P. E. (1990). Comparable worth: Canada legislates pay equity. *Academy of Management Executive*, 4, 92–101.

Kozlowski, S. W., & Doherty, M. L. (1989). Integration of climate and leadership: Examination of a neglected issue. *Journal of Applied Psychology*, 74, 546–553.

Kozlowski, S. W. J., & Farr, J. L. (1988). An integrative model of updating and performance. *Human Performance*, 1, 5–29.

Kozlowski, S. W. J., & Hults, B. M. (1987). An exploration of climates for technical updating and performance. *Personnel Psychology*, 40, 539–563.

Kozlowski, S. W. J., & Kirsch, M. P. (1987). The systematic distortion hypothesis, halo, and accuracy: An individual-level analysis. *Journal of Applied Psychology*, 72, 252–261.

Kozlowski, S. W. J., Kirsch, M. P., & Chao, G. T. (1986). Job knowledge, ratee familiarity, conceptual similarity and halo error: An exploration. *Journal of Applied Psychology*, 71, 45–49.

Krackhardt, D. (1990). Assessing the political landscape: Structure, cognition, and power in organizations. *Administrative Science Quarterly*, 35, 342–369.

Kraiger, K. (1990). Vantage 2000: The challenge for I/O psychology. *Industrial-Organizational Psychologist*, 28(1), 61–64.

Kraiger, K. (1991a). Vantage 2000: Issues in training and opportunities for involvement. *Industrial-Organizational Psychologist*, 28(4), 79–81.

Kraiger, K. (1991b). Vantage 2000: Resources on the aged and adult learning, and a look back on diversity in the 1990's. *Industrial-Organizational Psychologist*, 28(3), 83–85.

Kraiger, K. (1992). Vantage 2000: A potpourri. *Industrial-Organizational Psychologist*, 29(4), 76–78.

Kraiger, K., & Ford, J. K. (1985). A meta-analysis of ratee race effects in performance ratings. *Journal of Applied Psychology*, 70, 56–65.

Kraiger, K., & Ford, J. K. (1990). The relation of job knowledge, job performance, and supervisory ratings as a function of ratee race. *Human Performance*, 3, 269–279.

Krajewski, J. T., Kamon, E., & Avellini, B. (1979). Scheduling rest for consecutive light and heavy workloads under hot ambient conditions. *Ergonomics*, 22, 975–987.

Kram, K. E., & Isabella, L. A. (1985). Mentoring alternatives: The role of peer relationships in career development. *Academy of Management Journal*, 28, 110–132.

Kramer, M. (1991, October 21). Shame on them all. *Time*, pp. 46–47.

Kraut, A. I. (1976). Developing managerial skills via modeling techniques: Some positive research findings—A symposium. *Personnel Psychology*, 29, 325–328.

Krzystofiak, F., Cardy, R., & Newman, J. (1988). Implicit personality and performance appraisal: The influence of trait influences on evaluations of behavior. *Journal of Applied Psychology*, 73, 515–521.

Kuder, G. F., & Richardson, M. (1937). The theory of the estimation of test reliability. *Psychometrika*, 2, 151–160.

Kulik, C. T., Oldham, G. R., & Langner, P. H. (1988). Measurement of job characteristics: Comparison of the original and the revised Job Diagnostic Survey. *Journal of Applied Psychology*, 73, 462–466.

Kunin, T. (1955). The construction of a new type of job satisfaction measure. *Personnel Psychology*, 8, 65–77.

L'Heureux-Barrett, T., & Barnes-Farrell, J. L. (1991). Overcoming gender bias in reward allocation: The role of expectations of future performance. *Psychology of Women Quarterly*, 15, 127–139.

Lacayo, R. (1991, October 21). A question of character. *Time*, pp. 43–44.

Lahey, M. A., & Saal, F. E. (1981). Evidence incompatible with a cognitive compatibility theory of rating behavior. *Journal of Applied Psychology*, 66, 706–715.

Lance, C. E., Hedge, J. W., & Alley, W. E. (1989). Joint relationships of task proficiency with aptitude, experience, and task difficulty: A cross-level, interactional study. *Human Performance, 2*(4), 249–272.

Lance, C. E., Mayfield, D. L., Gould, R. B., & Lynskey, M. C. (1991). Global versus decomposed estimates of cross-job retraining time. *Human Performance, 4,* 71–88.

Lance, C. E., & Woehr, D. J. (1986). Statistical control of halo: Clarification from two cognitive models of the performance appraisal process. *Journal of Applied Psychology, 71,* 679–685.

Landsberger, H. A. (1958). *Hawthorne revisited: Management and the worker, its critics and developments in human relations in industry.* Ithaca: New York State School of Industrial and Labor Relations.

Landy, F. J. (1976). The validity of the interview in police officer selection. *Journal of Applied Psychology, 61,* 193–198.

Landy, F. J. (1978). An opponent process theory of job satisfaction. *Journal of Applied Psychology, 63,* 533–547.

Landy, F. J. (1986). Stamp collecting versus science: Validation as hypothesis testing. *American Psychologist, 41,* 1183–1192.

Landy, F. J. (1989). *Psychology of work behavior.* Pacific Grove, CA: Brooks/Cole.

Landy, F. J., & Farr, J. L. (1975). *Police performance appraisal.* University Park: Department of Psychology, Pennsylvania State University.

Landy, F. J., & Farr, J. L. (1980). Performance rating. *Psychological Bulletin, 87,* 72–107.

Landy, F. J., & Farr, J. L. (1983). *The measurement of work performance: Methods, theory, and applications.* New York: Academic Press.

Landy, F. J., Farr, J. L., & Jacobs, R. R. (1982). Utility concepts in performance measurement. *Organizational Behavior and Human Performance, 30,* 15–40.

Landy, F. J., Farr, J. L., Saal, F. E., & Freytag, W. R. (1976). Behaviorally anchored scales for rating the performance of police officers. *Journal of Applied Psychology, 61,* 750–758.

Landy, F. J., & Guion, R. M. (1970). Development of scales for the measurement of work motivation. *Organizational Behavior and Human Performance, 5,* 93–103.

Landy, F. J., & Rastegary, H. (1988). Current issues in performance evaluation. In I. Robertson & M. Smith (Eds.), *Personnel evaluation of the future.* New York: Wiley.

Landy, F. J., & Vasey, J. (1991). Job analysis: The composition of SME samples. *Personnel Psychology, 44,* 27–50.

Larson, E. W., & Fukami, C. V. (1985). Employee absenteeism: The role of ease of movement. *Academy of Management Journal, 28,* 464–471.

Larson, J. R., Jr. (1984). The performance feedback process: A preliminary model. *Organizational Behavior and Human Performance, 33,* 42–76.

Larson, J. R., Jr. (1986). Supervisors' performance feedback to subordinates: The impact of subordinate performance valence and outcome dependence. *Organizational Behavior and Human Decision Processes, 37,* 391–408.

Larson, J. R., Jr. (1989). The dynamic interplay between employees' feedback-seeking strategies and supervisors' delivery of performance feedback. *Academy of Management Review, 14,* 408–422.

Larson, J. R., Lingle, J. H., & Scerbo, M. M. (1984). The impact of performance cues on leader-behavior ratings: The role of selective information availability and probabilistic response bias. *Organizational Behavior and Human Performance, 33,* 323–349.

Latack, J. C., & Foster, L. W. (1985). Implementation of compressed work schedules: Participation and job redesign as critical factors for employee acceptance. *Personnel Psychology, 38,* 75–92.

Latack, J. C., Josephs, S. L., Roach, B. L., & Levine, M. D. (1987). Carpenter apprentices: Comparison of career transitions for men and women. *Journal of Applied Psychology, 72,* 393–400.

Latham, G. P. (1988). Human resource training and development. *Annual Review of Psychology, 39,* 545–582.

Latham, G. P., Fay, C., & Saari, L. (1979). The development of behavioral observation scales for appraising the performance of foremen. *Personnel Psychology, 32,* 299–311.

Latham, G. P., Mitchell, T. R., & Dossett, D. L. (1978). Importance of participative goal setting and anticipated rewards on goal difficulty and job performance. *Journal of Applied Psychology, 63,* 163–171.

Latham, G. P., & Saari, L. M. (1979). The application of social-learning theory to training supervisors through behavior modeling. *Journal of Applied Psychology, 64,* 239–246.

Latham, G. P., & Saari, L. M. (1984). Do people do

what they say? Further studies on the situational interview. *Journal of Applied Psychology, 69,* 569–573.

Latham, G. P., Saari, L. M., Pursell, E. D., & Campion, M. A. (1980). The situational interview. *Journal of Applied Psychology, 65,* 422–427.

Latham, G. P., & Steele, T. P. (1983). The motivational effects of participation versus goal setting on performance. *Academy of Management Journal, 26,* 406–417.

Latham, G. P., & Wexley, K. N. (1977). Behavioral observation scales for performance appraisal purposes. *Personnel Psychology, 30,* 255–268.

Latham, G. P., & Wexley, K. N. (1981). *Increasing productivity through performance appraisal.* Reading, MA: Addison-Wesley.

Latham, G. P., Wexley, K. N., & Pursell, E. D. (1975). Training managers to minimize rating errors in the observation of behavior. *Journal of Applied Psychology, 60,* 550–555.

Lautenschlager, G. J. (1990). Sources of imprecision in formula cross-validated multiple correlations. *Journal of Applied Psychology, 75,* 460–462.

Lautenschlager, G. J., & Flaherty, V. L. (1990). Computer administration of questions: More desirable or more social desirability? *Journal of Applied Psychology, 75,* 310–314.

Lautenschlager, G. J., & Shaffer, G. S. (1987). Reexamining the component stability of Owens's biographical questionnaire. *Journal of Applied Psychology, 72,* 149–152.

Lawler, E. E., III. (1967). The multitrait-multirater approach to measuring managerial job performance. *Journal of Applied Psychology, 51,* 369–381.

Lawler, E. E., III. (1973). *Motivation in work organizations.* Pacific Grove, CA: Brooks/Cole.

Lawler, E. E., & Suttle, J. L. (1972). A causal correlation test of the need hierarchy concept. *Organizational Behavior and Human Performance, 7,* 265–287.

Lawler, J. J., & Walker, J. M. (1984). Representation elections in higher education: Occurrence and outcomes. *Journal of Labor Research, 5,* 63–80.

Lawrence, B. S. (1988). New wrinkles in the theory of age: Demography, norms, and performance ratings. *Academy of Management Journal, 31,* 309–337.

Lawrence, P. R., & Lorsch, J. W. (1967). *Organization and environment: Managing differentiation and integration.* Boston: Division of Research, Harvard Business School.

Lawshe, C. H. (1952). Employee selection. *Personnel Psychology, 5,* 31–34.

Lawshe, C. H. (1975). A quantitative approach to content validity. *Personnel Psychology, 28,* 563–575.

Lawshe, C. H. (1985). Inferences from personnel tests and their validity. *Journal of Applied Psychology, 70,* 237–238.

Lawshe, C. H., & Nagle, B. F. (1953). Productivity and attitude toward supervisor. *Journal of Applied Psychology, 37,* 159–162.

Leadership Software, Inc. (1987). *Managing participation in organizations* [Computer software].

Leana, C. R., Locke, E. A., & Schweiger, D. M. (1990). Fact and fiction in analyzing research on participative decision making: A critique of Cotton, Vollrath, Froggatt, Lengnick-Hall, and Jennings. *Academy of Management Review, 15,* 137–146.

Lee, C. (1985). Increasing performance appraisal effectiveness: Matching task types, appraisal process, and rater training. *Academy of Management Review, 10,* 322–331.

Lee, C., Ashford, S.J., & Bobko, P. (1990). Interactive effects of "Type A" behavior and perceived control on worker performance, job satisfaction, and somatic complaints. *Academy of Management Journal, 33,* 870–881.

Lee, J. A. (1988). The effects of cognitive style on rating accuracy with an overall ratings scale. *Human Performance, 1,* 261–271.

Lee, J. A., & Clemons, T. (1985). Factors affecting employment decisions about older workers. *Journal of Applied Psychology, 70,* 785–788.

Lee, R., & Foley, P. P. (1986). Is the validity of a test constant throughout the test score range? *Journal of Applied Psychology, 71,* 641–644.

Lee, R., & Klein, A. R. (1982). Structure of the Job Diagnostic Survey for public sector occupations. *Journal of Applied Psychology, 67,* 515–519.

Lee, R., Miller, K. J., & Graham, W. K. (1982). Corrections for restriction of range and attenuation in criterion-related validity studies. *Journal of Applied Psychology, 67,* 637–639.

Lee, T. D., & Carnahan, H. (1990). When to provide knowledge of results during motor learning: Scheduling effects. *Human Performance, 3,* 87–105.

Lee, T. W., & Mowday, R. T. (1987). Voluntarily leaving an organization: An empirical investigation of Steers and Mowday's model of turnover. *Academy of Management Journal, 30,* 721–743.

Leib, J. W., Cusack, J., Hughes, D., Pilette, S., Werther, J., & Kintz, B. L. (1967). Teaching machines and programmed instruction: Areas of application. *Psychological Bulletin, 67,* 12–26.

Leigh, D. E. (1981). The effect of unionism on workers' valuation of future pension benefits. *Industrial and Labor Relations Review, 34,* 510–521.

Leithead, C. S., & Lind, A. R. (1964). *Heat stress and heat disorders.* London: Cassell.

Lemke, E., & Wiersma, W. (1976). *Principles of psychological measurement.* Chicago: Rand McNally.

Lepper, M. R., & Greene, D. (1975). Turning play into work: Effects of adult surveillance and extrinsic rewards on children's intrinsic motivation. *Journal of Personality and Social Psychology, 31,* 479–486.

Leung, K., & Park, H. (1986). Effects of interactional goal on choice of allocation rule: A cross-national study. *Organizational Behavior and Human Decision Processes, 37,* 111–120.

Levi, M. A. (1954). *A comparison of two methods of conducting critiques* (AFPTRC-TR-54–108). San Antonio.

Levin, I., & Stokes, J. P. (1989). Dispositional approach to job satisfaction: Role of negative affectivity. *Journal of Applied Psychology, 74,* 752–758.

Levine, E. L. (1980). Introductory remarks for the symposium "Organizational applications of self-appraisal and self-assessment: Another look." *Personnel Psychology, 33,* 259–262.

Levine, E. L., Ash, R. A., & Bennett, N. (1980). Exploratory comparative study of four job analysis methods. *Journal of Applied Psychology, 65,* 524–535.

Levine, E. L., Ash, R. A., Hall, H., & Sistrunk, F. (1983). Evaluation of job analysis methods by experienced job analysts. *Academy of Management Journal, 26,* 339–348.

Lewin, K. (1958). Group decision and social change. In E. E. Maccoby, T. M. Newcomb, & E. L. Hartley (Eds.), *Readings in social psychology.* New York: Holt, Rinehart & Winston.

Lewin, K., Lippett, R., & White, R. K. (1939). Patterns of aggressive behavior in experimentally created "social climates." *Journal of Social Psychology, 10,* 271–299.

Liden, R. C., & Graen, G. B. (1980). Generalizability of the vertical dyad linkage model of leadership. *Academy of Management Journal, 23,* 451–465.

Liden, R. C., & Mitchell, T. R. (1985). Reactions to feedback: The role of attributions. *Academy of Management Journal, 28,* 291–308.

Liden, R. C., & Parsons, C. K. (1986). A field study of job applicant interview perceptions, alternative opportunities, and demographic characteristics. *Personnel Psychology, 39,* 109–122.

Likert, R. (1967). *The human organization.* New York: McGraw-Hill.

Linn, R. L., Harnisch, D. L., & Dunbar, S. B. (1981). Corrections for range restriction: An empirical investigation of conditions resulting in conservative corrections. *Journal of Applied Psychology, 66,* 655–663.

Lissitz, R. W., & Green, S. B. (1975). Effect of the number of scale points on reliability: A Monte Carlo approach. *Journal of Applied Psychology, 60,* 10–13.

Litwin, G. H., & Stringer, R. A. (1968). *Motivation and organization climate.* Boston: Division of Research, Harvard Business School.

Locke, E. A. (1968). Toward a theory of task motivation and incentives. *Organizational Behavior and Human Performance, 3,* 157–189.

Locke, E. A. (1969). What is job satisfaction? *Organizational Behavior and Human Performance, 4,* 309–336.

Locke, E. A. (1976). The nature and causes of job satisfaction. In M. D. Dunnette (Ed.), *Handbook of industrial and organizational psychology.* Chicago: Rand McNally.

Locke, E. A. (1978). The ubiquity of the technique of goal setting in theories and approaches to employee motivation. *Academy of Mangement Review, 3,* 594–601.

Locke, E. A. (1980). Latham versus Komaki: A tale of two paradigms. *Journal of Applied Psychology, 65,* 16–23.

Locke, E. A. (1982a). Critique of Bramel and Friend. *American Psychologist, 37,* 858–859.

Locke, E. A. (1982b). Licensing. *American Psychologist, 37,* 239.

Locke, E. A., Cartledge, N., & Knerr, C. S. (1970). Studies of the relationship between satisfaction, goal setting, and performance. *Organizational Behavior and Human Performance, 5,* 135–158.

Locke, E. A., Latham, G. P., & Erez, M. (1988). The

determinants of goal commitment. *Academy of Management Review, 13,* 23–39.

Locke, E. A., & Schweiger, D. M. (1979). Participation in decision making: One more look. In B. M. Staw (Ed.), *Research in Organizational Behavior* (Vol. 1). Greenwich, CT: JAI Press.

Locke, E. A., Shaw, K. N., Saari, L. M., & Latham, G. P. (1981). Goal setting and task performance: 1969–1980. *Psychological Bulletin, 90,* 125–152.

Lofquist, L. H., & Dawis, R. V. (1969). *Adjustment to work: A psychological view of man's problems in a work-oriented society.* New York: Appleton-Century-Crofts.

Loher, B. T., Noe, R. A., Moeller, N. L., & Fitzgerald, M. P. (1985). A meta-analysis of the relation of job characteristics to job satisfaction. *Journal of Applied Psychology, 70,* 280–289.

Lombardo, M. M., & McCall, M. W., Jr. (1982). Leaders on line: Observations from a simulation of managerial work. In J. G. Hunt, U. Sekaran, & C. A. Schriesheim (Eds.), *Leadership: Beyond establishment views.* Carbondale: Southern Illinois University Press.

London, M., & Bray, D. W. (1980). Ethical issues in testing and evaluation for personnel decisions. *American Psychologist, 35,* 890–901.

London, M., Crandall, R., & Seals, G. W. (1977). The contribution of job and leisure satisfaction to quality of life. *Journal of Applied Psychology, 62,* 328–334.

London, M., & Stumpf, S. A. (1983). Effects of candidate characteristics on management promotion decisions: An experimental study. *Personnel Psychology, 36,* 241–259.

London, M., & Wohlers, A. J. (1991). Agreement between subordinate and self-ratings in upward feedback. *Personnel Psychology, 44,* 375–390.

Lopez, F. M., Kesselman, G. A., & Lopez, F. E. (1981). An empirical test of a trait-oriented job analysis technique. *Personnel Psychology, 34,* 479–502.

Lord, R. G. (1977). Functional leadership behavior: Measurement and relation to social power and leadership perceptions. *Administrative Science Quarterly, 22,* 114–133.

Lord, R. G. (1985). Accuracy in behavioral measurement: An alternative definition based on raters' cognitive schema and signal detection theory. *Journal of Applied Psychology, 70,* 66–71.

Lord, R. G., DeVader, C. L., & Alliger, G. M. (1986). A meta-analysis of the relation between person-

ality traits and leadership perceptions: An application of validity generalization procedures. *Journal of Applied Psychology, 71,* 402–410.

Lord, R. G., Foti, R. J., & Phillips, J. S. (1982). A theory of leadership categorization. In J. G. Hunt, U. Sekaran, & C. A. Schriesheim (Eds.), *Leadership: Beyond establishment views.* Carbondale: Southern Illinois University Press.

Lord, R. G., & Hanges, P. J. (1987). A control systems model of organizational motivation: Theoretical development and applied implications. *Behavioral Sciences, 32,* 161–178.

Lord, R. G., & Maher, K. J. (1990). Alternative information-processing models and their implications for theory, research, and practice. *Academy of Management Review, 15,* 9–28.

Lord, R. G., Phillips, J. S., & Rush, M. C. (1980). Effects of sex and personality on perceptions of emergent leadership, influence, and social power. *Journal of Applied Psychology, 65,* 176–182.

Lorenzo, R. V. (1984). Effects of assessorship on managers' proficiency in acquiring, evaluating, and communicating information about people. *Personnel Psychology, 37,* 617–634.

Love, K. G., & O'Hara, K. (1987). Predicting job performance of youth trainees under a Job Training Partnership Act program (JTPA): Criterion validation of a behavior-based measure of work maturity. *Personnel Psychology, 40,* 323–340.

Lubinski, D., & Humphreys, L. G. (1990). Assessing spurious "moderator effects": Illustrated substantively with the hypothesized ("synergistic") relation between spatial and mathematical ability. *Psychological Bulletin, 107,* 385–393.

Lumsden, J. (1976). Test theory. *Annual Review of Psychology, 27,* 251–280.

Luthans, F., & Kreitner, R. (1985). *Organizational behavior modification and beyond: An operant and social learning approach.* Glenview, IL: Scott, Foresman.

Lynton, R. P. & Pareek, U. (1967). *Training for development.* Homewood, IL: Irwin.

Lysaught, J. P., & Williams, C. M. (1963). *A guide to programmed instruction.* New York: Wiley.

Maas, J. B. (1965). Patterned scaled expectation interview: Reliability studies on a new technique. *Journal of Applied Psychology, 59,* 431–433.

Mabe, P. A., III, & West, S. G. (1982). Validity of self-evaluation of ability: A review and meta-analysis. *Journal of Applied Psychology, 67,* 280–296.

Macan, T. H., & Dipboye, R. L. (1988). The effects of interviewers' initial impressions on information gathering. *Organizational Behavior and Human Decision Processes, 42*, 364–387.

Macan, T. H., & Dipboye, R. L. (1990). The relationship of interviewers' preinterview impressions to selection and recruitment outcomes. *Personnel Psychology, 43*, 745–768.

Machungwa, P. D., & Schmitt, N. (1983). Work motivation in a developing country. *Journal of Applied Psychology, 68*, 31–42.

Madigan, R. M. (1985). Comparable worth judgments: A measurement properties analysis. *Journal of Applied Psychology, 70*, 137–147.

Madigan, R. M., & Hoover, D. J. (1986). Effects of alternative job evaluation methods on decisions involving pay equity. *Academy of Management Journal, 29*, 84–100.

Maher, J. R., & Overbagh, W. B. (1971). Better inspection performance through job enrichment. In J. R. Maher (Ed.), *New perspectives in job enrichment.* New York: Van Nostrand Reinhold.

Malaviya, P., & Ganesh K. (1976). Shift work and individual differences in the productivity of weavers in an Indian textile mill. *Journal of Applied Psychology, 61*, 774–776.

Malaviya, P., & Ganesh K. (1977). Individual differences in productivity across type of work shift. *Journal of Applied Psychology, 62*, 527–528.

Mann, R. D. (1959). A review of the relationships between personality and performance in small groups. *Psychological Bulletin, 56*, 241–270.

Mann, R. B., & Decker, P. J. (1984). The effect of key behavior distinctiveness on generalization and recall in behavior modeling training. *Academy of Management Journal, 27*, 900–910.

Manz, C. C., & Sims, H. P., Jr. (1986). Beyond imitation: Complex behavioral and affective linkages resulting from exposure to leadership training models. *Journal of Applied Psychology, 71*, 571–578.

Markham, S. E. (1985). An investigation of the relationship between unemployment and absenteeism: A multi-level approach. *Academy of Management Journal, 28*, 228–234.

Markham, S. E., Dansereau, F., Jr., & Alutto, J. A. (1982). Group size and absenteeism rates: A longitudinal analysis. *Academy of Management Journal, 25*, 921–927.

Martin, C. L., & Nagao, D. H. (1989). Some effects of computerized interviewing on job applicant responses. *Journal of Applied Psychology, 74*, 72–80.

Martin, S. L., & Klimoski, R. J. (1990). Use of verbal protocols to trace cognitions associated with self- and supervisor evaluations of performance. *Organizational Behavior and Human Decision Processes, 46*, 135–154.

Maslow, A. H. (1943). A theory of human motivation. *Psychological Review, 50*, 370–396.

Maslow, A. H. (1965). *Eupsychian management: A journal.* Homewood, IL: Irwin.

Maslow, A. H. (1970). *Motivation and personality* (2nd ed.). New York: Harper & Row.

Mathieu, J. E. (1988). A causal model of organizational commitment in a military training environment. *Journal of Vocational Behavior, 32*, 321–335.

Mathieu, J. E., & Baratta, J. E. (1989). Turnover type as a moderator of the performance-turnover relationship. *Human Performance, 2*, 61–71.

Mathieu, J. E., & Hamel, K. (1989). A causal model of the antecedents of organizational commitment among professionals and nonprofessionals. *Journal of Vocational Behavior, 34*, 299–317.

Mathieu, J. E., & Kohler, S. S. (1990). A cross-level examination of group absence influences on individual absence. *Journal of Applied Psychology, 75* 217–220.

Mathieu, J. E., & Leonard, R. L., Jr. (1987). Applying utility concepts to a training program in supervisory skills: A time-based approach. *Academy of Management Journal, 30*, 316–335.

Mathieu, J. E., & Zajac, D. M. (1990). A review and meta-analysis of the antecedents, correlates, and consequences of organizational commitment. *Psychological Bulletin, 108*, 171–194.

Matthews, K. A. (1982). Psychological perspectives on the Type A behavior pattern. *Psychological Bulletin, 91*, 293–323.

Maurer, S. D., & Fay, C. (1988). Effect of situational interviews, conventional structured interviews, and training on interview rating agreement: An experimental analysis. *Personnel Psychology, 41*, 329–344.

Maurer, T. J., & Alexander, R. A. (1991). Contrast effects in behavioral measurement: An investigation of alternative process explanations. *Journal of Applied Psychology, 76*, 3–10.

Mausner, B. (1953). Studies in social interaction. III. Effect of variation in one partner's prestige on the interaction of observer pairs. *Journal of Applied Psychology, 37*, 391–393.

Mausner, B. (1954). The effects of one partner's success in a relevant task on the interaction of observer pairs. *Journal of Abnormal and Social Psychology, 49*, 557–560.

Maxwell, S. E., & Delaney, H. D. (1985). Measurement and statistics: An examination of construct validity. *Psychological Bulletin, 97*, 85–93.

Mayfield, E. C. (1964). The selection interview: A re-evaluation of published research. *Personnel Psychology, 17*, 239–260.

Mayo, E. (1945). *The social problems of an industrial civilization.* Cambridge: Harvard University Press.

McAfee, R. B., & Winn, A. R. (1989). The use of incentives/feedback to enhance workplace safety: A critique of the literature. *Journal of Safety Research, 20*, 7–19.

McCarroll, T. (1992a, January 20). Motown's fat cats. *Time*, pp. 34–35.

McCarroll, T. (1992b, May 4). The shareholders strike back. *Time*, pp. 46–48.

McCarty, P. A. (1986). Effects of feedback on the self-confidence of men and women. *Academy of Management Journal, 29*, 840–847.

McCauley, R., & Parkinson, R. (1971). The new popularity of the Dvorak simplified keyboard. *Computers and Automation, 20*(11), 31–32.

McClelland, D. C. (1961). *The achieving society.* Princeton, NJ: Van Nostrand.

McClelland, D. C. (1965). Toward a theory of motive acquisition. *American Psychologist, 20*, 321–333.

McClelland, D. C. (1975). *Power: The inner experience.* New York: Irvington.

McClelland, D. C. (1976). Power is the great motivation. *Harvard Business Review, 54*, 100–110.

McClelland, D. C., Atkinson, J. W., Clark, R. A., & Lowell, E. L. (1953). *The achievement motive.* New York: Appleton-Century-Crofts.

McClelland, D. C., & Boyatzis, R. E. (1982). Leadership motive pattern and long-term success in management. *Journal of Applied Psychology, 67*, 737–743.

McClelland, D. C., & Winter, D. (1969). *Motivating economic achievement.* New York: Free Press.

McCormick, E. J. (1976). Job and task analysis. In M.D. Dunnette (Ed.), *Handbook of industrial and organizational psychology.* Chicago: Rand McNally.

McCormick, E. J., & Bachus, J. A. (1952). Paired comparison ratings: I. The effect on ratings of reductions in the number of pairs. *Journal of Applied Psychology, 36*, 123–127.

McCormick, E. J., & Ilgen, D. R. (1980). *Industrial psychology* (7th ed.). Englewood Cliffs, NJ: Prentice-Hall.

McCormick, E. J., & Ilgen, D. R. (1985). *Industrial and organizational psychology* (8th ed.). Englewood Cliffs, NJ: Prentice-Hall.

McCormick, E. J., Jeanneret, P. R., & Mecham, R. C. (1969). *Position Analysis Questionnaire.* West Lafayette: Purdue Research Foundation.

McCormick, E. J., Jeanneret, P. R., & Mecham, R. C. (1972). A study of job characteristics and job dimensions as based on the Position Analysis Questionnaire (PAQ) [Monograph]. *Journal of Applied Psychology, 56*, 347–368.

McCormick, E. J., & Roberts, W. K. (1952). Paired comparison ratings: II. The reliability of ratings based on partial pairings. *Journal of Applied Psychology, 36*, 188–192.

McCormick, E. J., & Tiffin, J. (1974). *Industrial psychology* (6th ed.). Englewood Cliffs, NJ: Prentice-Hall.

McCullagh, P., & Little, W. S. (1989). A comparison of modalities in modeling. *Human Performance, 2*, 101–111.

McCurry, C. M. (1979). *Bank personnel administration: A basic plan.* Rolling Meadows, IL: Bank Administration Institute.

McDaniel, M. A. (1988). Does pre-employment drug use predict on-the-job suitability? *Personnel Psychology, 41*, 717–729.

McDaniel, M. A. (1989). Biographical constructs for predicting employee suitability. *Journal of Applied Psychology, 74*, 964–970.

McDaniel, M. A., Hirsh, H. R., Schmidt, F. L., Raju, N. S., & Hunter, J. E. (1986). Interpreting the results of meta-analytic research: A comment on Schmitt, Gooding, Noe, and Kirsch (1984). *Personnel Psychology, 39*, 141–148.

McDaniel, M. A., Schmidt, F. L., & Hunter, J. E. (1988). Job experience correlates of job performance. *Journal of Applied Psychology, 73*, 327–330.

McDonald, T., & Hakel, M. D. (1985). Effects of applicant race, sex, suitability, and answers on interviewers' questioning strategy and ratings. *Personnel Psychology, 38*, 321–334.

McEnrue, M. P. (1988). Length of experience and the performance of managers in the establishment phase of their careers. *Academy of Management Journal, 31,* 175–185.

McEvoy, G. M., & Beatty, R. W. (1989). Assessment centers and subordinate appraisals of managers: A seven-year examination of predictive validity. *Personnel Psychology, 42,* 37–52.

McEvoy, G. M., & Buller, P. F. (1987). User acceptance of peer appraisals in an industrial setting. *Personnel Psychology, 40,* 785–797.

McEvoy, G. M., & Cascio, W. F. (1985). Strategies for reducing employee turnover: A meta-analysis. *Journal of Applied Psychology, 70,* 342–353.

McEvoy, G. M., & Cascio, W. F. (1987). Do good or poor performers leave? A meta-analysis of the relationship between performance and turnover. *Academy of Management Journal, 30,* 744–762.

McGee, G. W., & Ford, R. C. (1987). Two (or more?) dimensions of organizational commitment: Re-examination of the affective and continuance commitment scales. *Journal of Applied Psychology, 72,* 638–641.

McGehee, W., & Thayer, P. W. (1961). *Training in business and industry.* New York: Wiley.

McGregor, D. (1960). *The human side of enterprise.* New York: McGraw-Hill.

McGregor, D. (1967). *The professional manager.* New York: McGraw-Hill.

McGuigan, F. J. (1978). *Experimental psychology: A methodological approach* (3rd ed.). Englewood Cliffs, NJ: Prentice-Hall.

McHenry, J. J., Hough, L. M., Toquam, J. L., Hanson, M. A., & Ashworth, S. (1990). Project A validity results: The relationship between predictor and criterion domains. *Personnel Psychology, 43,* 335–354.

McIntyre, R. M. (1990a). Our science-practice: The ghost of industrial-organizational psychology yet to come. In K. R. Murphy and F. E. Saal (Eds.). *Psychology in organizations: Integrating science and practice.* Hillsdale, NJ: Lawrence Erlbaum.

McIntyre, R. M. (1990b). Spurious estimation of validity coefficients in composite samples: Some methodological considerations. *Journal of Applied Psychology, 75,* 91–94.

McIntyre, R. M., Smith, D. E., & Hassett, C. E. (1984). Accuracy of performance ratings as affected by rater training and perceived purpose of ratings. *Journal of Applied Psychology, 69,* 147–156.

McKenna, F. (1983). Accident proneness: A conceptual analysis. *Accident Analysis and Prevention, 15,* 65–71.

McNemar, Q. (1969). *Psychological statistics* (4th ed.). New York: Wiley.

McWhirter, W. (1991, December 30). Major overhaul. *Time,* pp. 56–58.

Mecham, R. C., Jeanneret, P. R., & McCormick, E. J. (1983). *The applicability of job component validity based on the PAQ to the Uniform Guidelines' validation requirements—A reply to Trattner.* Unpublished manuscript, Department of Business Administration, Utah State University, Logan.

Meehl, P. E. (1954). *Clinical versus statistical prediction.* Minneapolis: University of Minnesota Press.

Meehl, P. E. (1957). When shall we use our heads instead of a formula? *Journal of Counseling Psychology, 4,* 268–273.

Meehl, P. E. (1965). Seer over sign: The first good example. *Journal of Experimental Research in Personality, 1,* 27–32.

Megargee, E. I. (1969). Influence of sex roles on the manifestation of leadership. *Journal of Applied Psychology, 53,* 377–382.

Megargee, E. I., Bogart, P., & Anderson, B. J. (1966). Prediction of leadership in a simulated industrial task. *Journal of Applied Psychology, 50,* 292–295.

Meglino, B. M., DeNisi, A. S., Youngblood, S. A., & Williams, K. J. (1988). Effects of realistic job previews: A comparison using an enhancement and a reduction preview. *Journal of Applied Psychology, 73,* 259–266.

Meglino, B. M., Ravlin, E. C., & Adkins, C. L. (1989). A work values approach to corporate culture: A field test of the value congruence process and its relationship to individual outcomes. *Journal of Applied Psychology, 74,* 424–432.

Meichenbaum, D. (1977). *Cognitive-behavior modification.* New York: Plenum Press.

Meindl, J. R., & Ehrlich, S. B. (1987). The romance of leadership and the evaluation of organizational performance. *Academy of Management Journal, 30,* 91–109.

Meister, D. (1987). *Behavioral analysis and measurement methods.* New York: Wiley.

Meltzer, H., & Stagner, R. (Eds.). (1980). Industrial/organizational psychology: 1980 overview [Special issue]. *Professional Psychology, 11*(3).

Mento, A. J., Steel, R. P., & Karren, R. J. (1987). A

meta-analytic study of the effects of goal setting on task performance: 1966–1984. *Organizational Behavior and Human Decision Processes, 39* 52–83.

Meritt-Haston, R., & Wexley, K. N. (1983). Educational requirements: Legality and validity. *Personnel Psychology, 36,* 743–753.

Messick, S. (1980). Test validity and the ethics of assessment. *American Psychologist, 35,* 1012–1027.

Meyer, H., Kay, E., & French, J. R. (1965). Split roles in performance appraisal. *Harvard Business Review, 43,* 123–129.

Meyer, H. H. (1980). Self-appraisal of job performance. *Personnel Psychology, 33,* 291–295.

Meyer, H. H. (1987). Predicting supervisory ratings versus promotional progress in test validation studies. *Journal of Applied Psychology, 72,* 696–697.

Meyer, J. P., & Allen, N. J. (1984). Testing the "side-bet theory" of organizational commitment: Some methodological considerations. *Journal of Applied Psychology, 69,* 372–378.

Meyer, J. P., & Gellatly, I. R. (1988). Perceived performance norm as a mediator in the effect of assigned goal on personal goal and task performance. *Journal of Applied Psychology, 73,* 410–420.

Meyer, J. P., Paunonen, S. V., Gellatly, I. R., Goffin, R. D., & Jackson, D. N. (1989). Organizational commitment and job performance: It's the nature of the commitment that counts. *Journal of Applied Psychology, 74,* 152–156.

Michaels, C. E., & Spector, P. E. (1982). Causes of employee turnover: A test of the Mobley, Griffeth, Hand, and Meglino model. *Journal of Applied Psychology, 67,* 53–59.

Mihal, W. L., & Barrett, G. V. (1976). Individual differences in perceptual information processing and their relation to automobile accident involvement. *Journal of Applied Psychology, 61,* 229–233.

Miller, C. S., Kaspin, J. A., & Schuster, M. H. (1990). The impact of performance appraisal methods on Age Discrimination in Employment Act cases. *Personnel Psychology, 43,* 555–578.

Miller, H., Katerberg, R., & Hulin, C. L. (1979). Evaluation of the Mobley, Horner, and Hollingsworth model of employee turnover. *Journal of Applied Psychology, 64,* 509–517.

Miller, K. I., & Monge, P. R. (1986). Participation, satisfaction, and productivity: A meta-analytic review. *Academy of Management Review, 4,* 727–753.

Miller, L. E., & Grush, J. E. (1988). Improving predictions in expectancy theory research: Effects of personality, expectancies, and norms. *Academy of Management Journal 31,* 107–122.

Miller, R. W., & Zeller, F. A. (1967). *Social psychological factors associated with responses to retraining* (Final Report, Office of Research and Development, Appalachian Center, West Virginia University; Research Grant No. 91–52–66–56), U.S. Department of Labor.

Mills, C. J., & Bohannon, W. E. (1980). Personality characteristics of effective state police officers. *Journal of Applied Psychology, 65,* 680–684.

Mills, D. Q. (1983). When employees make concessions. *Harvard Business Review, 83*(3), 103–113.

Millsap, R. E. (1988). Sampling variance in attenuated correlation coefficients: A Monte Carlo study. *Journal of Applied Psychology, 73,* 316–319.

Millsap, R. E. (1989). Sampling variance in the correlation coefficient under range restriction: A Monte Carlo study. *Journal of Applied Psychology, 74,* 456–461.

Millsap, R. E. (1990). A cautionary note on the detection of method variance in multitrait-multimethod data. *Journal of Applied Psychology, 75,* 350–353.

Millsap, R. E., & Hartog, S. B. (1988). Alpha, beta, and gamma change in evaluation research: A structural equation approach. *Journal of Applied Psychology, 73,* 574–584.

Miner, J. B. (1965). *Studies in management education.* Atlanta: Organizational Measurement Systems Press.

Miner, J. B. (1967). *The school administrator and organizational character.* Eugene: Center for the Advanced Study of Educational Administration, University of Oregon.

Miner, J. B. (1968a). The early identification of managerial talent. *Personnel and Guidance Journal, 46,* 586–591.

Miner, J. B. (1968b). The managerial motivation of school administrators. *Educational Administration Quarterly, 4,* 55–71.

Miner, J. B. (1974a). Motivation to manage among

women: Studies of business managers and educational administrators. *Journal of Vocational Behavior, 5,* 197–208.

Miner, J. B. (1974b). Motivation to manage among women: Studies of college students. *Journal of Vocational Behavior, 5,* 241–250.

Miner, J. B. (1975). *The challenge of managing.* Philadelphia: W. B. Saunders.

Miner, J. B. (1977a). Motivational potential for upgrading among minority and female managers. *Journal of Applied Psychology, 62,* 691–697.

Miner, J. B. (1977b). *Motivation to manage: A ten-year update of the "studies in management education" research.* Atlanta: Organizational Measurement Systems Press.

Miner, J. B. (1978a). The Miner sentence completion scale: A re-appraisal. *Academy of Management Journal, 21,* 283–294.

Miner, J. B. (1978b). Twenty years of research on role-motivation theory of managerial effectiveness. *Personnel Psychology, 31,* 739–760.

Miner, J. B., Chen, C., & Yu, K. C. (1991). Theory testing under adverse conditions: Motivation to manage in the People's Republic of China. *Journal of Applied Psychology, 76,* 343–349.

Miner, J. B., & Crane, D. P. (1981). Motivation to manage and the manifestation of a managerial orientation in career planning. *Academy of Management Journal, 24,* 626–633.

Miner, J. B., & Smith, N. R. (1969). Managerial talent among undergraduate and graduate business students. *Personnel and Guidance Journal, 47,* 995–1000.

Minton, H. L., & Schneider, F. W. (1980). *Differential psychology.* Pacific Grove, CA: Brooks/Cole.

Mintzberg, H. (1980). *The nature of managerial work.* Englewood Cliffs, NJ: Prentice-Hall.

Mirvis, P. H., & Seashore, S. E. (1980). Reply to Walter and Pinder. *American Psychologist, 35,* 937–938.

Mirvis, P. H., & Seashore, S. E. (1979). Being ethical in organizational research. *American Psychologist, 34,* 766–780.

Mitchell, T. R. (1974). Expectancy models of job satisfaction, occupational preference, and effort: A theoretical, methodological, and empirical appraisal. *Psychological Bulletin, 81,* 1096–1112.

Mitchell, T. R. (1979). Organizational behavior. *Annual Review of Psychology, 30,* 243–281.

Mitchell, T. R. (1985). An evaluation of the validity of correlational research conducted in organizations. *Academy of Management Review, 10,* 192–205.

Mitchell, T. R., & Beach, L. R. (1990). "... Do I love thee? Let me count ...": Toward an understanding of intuitive and automatic decision making. *Organizational Behavior and Human Decision Processes, 47,* 1–20.

Mitchell, T. R., & Wood, R. E. (1980). Supervisor's responses to subordinate poor performance: A test of an attributional model. *Organizational Behavior and Human Performance, 25,* 123–138.

Mitchell, T. W., & Klimoski, R. J. (1982). Is is rational to be empirical? A test of methods for scoring biographical data. *Journal of Applied Psychology, 67,* 411–418.

Mitchell, T. W., & Klimoski, R. J. (1986). Estimating the validity of cross-validity estimation. *Journal of Applied Psychology, 71,* 311–317.

Mitroff, I. I. (1983). Archetypal social systems analysis: On the deeper structure of human systems. *Academy of Management Review, 8,* 387–397.

Mobley, W. H. (1977). Intermediate linkages in the relationship between job satisfaction and employee turnover. *Journal of Applied Psychology, 62,* 237–240.

Mobley, W. H. (1982). Supervisor and employee race and sex effects on performance appraisals: A field study of adverse impact and generalizability. *Academy of Management Journal, 25,* 598–606.

Mobley, W. H., Griffeth, R. W., Hand, H. H., & Meglino, B. M. (1979). Review and conceptual analysis of the employee turnover process. *Psychological Bulletin, 86,* 493–522.

Mobley, W. H., Horner, S. O., & Hollingsworth, A. T. (1978). An evaluation of precursors of hospital employee turnover. *Journal of Applied Psychology, 63,* 408–414.

Mobley, W. H., & Locke, E. A. (1970). The relationship of value importance to satisfaction. *Organizational Behavior and Human Performance, 5,* 463–483.

Moch, M. K. (1980). Job involvement, internal motivation, and employees' integration into networks of work relationships. *Organizational Behavior and Human Performance, 25,* 15–31.

Montgomery, B. R. (1989). The influence of attitudes

and normative pressures on voting decisions in a union certification election. *Industrial and Labor Relations Review, 42,* 262–279.

Mook, D. G. (1983). In defense of external invalidity. *American Psychologist, 38,* 379–387.

Moore, B. V. (1962). Some beginnings of industrial psychology. In B. v. H. Gilmer (Ed.), *Walter Van Dyke Bingham.* Pittsburgh: Carnegie Institute of Technology.

Morris, J. H., Sherman, J. D., & Mansfield, E. R. (1986). Failures to detect moderating effects with ordinary least squares–moderated multiple regression: Some reasons and a remedy. *Psychological Bulletin, 99,* 282–288.

Morrison, E. W., & Bies, R. J. (1991). Impression management in the feedback-seeking process: A literature review and research agenda. *Academy of Management Review, 16,* 522–541.

Morsh, J. E. (1964). Job analysis in the United States Air Force. *Personnel Psychology, 17,* 7–17.

Mossholder, K. W. (1980). Effects of externally mediated goal setting on intrinsic motivation: A laboratory experiment. *Journal of Applied Psychology, 65,* 202–210.

Mossholder, K. W., & Arvey, R. D. (1984). Synthetic validity: A conceptual and comparative review. *Journal of Applied Psychology, 69,* 322–333.

Motowidlo, S. J., Dunnette, M. D., & Carter, G. W. (1990). An alternative selection procedure: The low-fidelity simulation. *Journal of Applied Psychology, 75,* 640–647.

Mott, P. E., Mann, F. C., McLoughlin, Q., & Warwick, D. P. (1965). *Shift work.* Ann Arbor: University of Michigan Press.

Mottaz, C. J. (1986). An analysis of the relationship between education and organizational commitment in a variety of occupational groups. *Journal of Vocational Behavior, 28,* 214–228.

Mount, M. K. (1984). Psychometric properties of subordinate ratings of managerial performance. *Personnel Psychology, 37,* 687–702.

Mount, M. K., & Ellis, R. A. (1987). Investigation of bias in job evaluation ratings of comparable worth study participants. *Personnel Psychology, 40,* 85–96.

Mount, M. K., & Thompson, D. E. (1987). Cognitive categorization and quality of performance ratings. *Journal of Applied Psychology, 72,* 240–246.

Mowday, R. T. (1983). Equity theory predictions of behavior in organizations. In R. M. Steers &

L. W. Porter (Eds.), *Motivation and work behavior* (3rd ed.). New York: McGraw-Hill.

Mowday, R. T., Koberg, C. S., & McArthur, A. W. (1984). The psychology of the withdrawal process: A cross-validational test of Mobley's intermediate linkages model of turnover in two samples. *Academy of Management Journal, 27,* 79–94.

Mowday, R. T., Porter, L. W., & Steers, R. M. (1982). *Employee-organization linkages: The psychology of commitment, absenteeism, and turnover.* New York: Academic Press.

Mowday, R. T., Steers, R. M., & Porter, L. W. (1979). The measurement of organizational commitment. *Journal of Vocational Behavior, 14,* 224–247.

Muchinsky, P. M. (1976). An assessment of the Litwin and Stringer organization climate questionnaire: An empirical and theoretical extension of the Sims and LaFollette study. *Personnel Psychology, 29,* 371–392.

Muchinsky, P. M. (1977a). A comparison of within and across subjects analyses of the expectancy valence model for predicting effort. *Academy of Management Journal, 20,* 154–158.

Muchinsky, P. M. (1977b). Employee absenteeism: A review of the literature. *Journal of Vocational Behavior, 10,* 316–340.

Muchinsky, P. M. (1990). *Psychology applied to work: An introduction to industrial and organizational psychology* (3rd ed.). Pacific Grove, CA: Brooks/ Cole.

Muchinsky, P. M., & Morrow, P. C. (1980). A multidisciplinary model of voluntary employee turnover. *Journal of Vocational Behavior, 17,* 263–290.

Mulder, M., deJong, R. D., Koppelaar, L., & Verhage, J. (1986). Power, situation, and leaders' effectiveness: An organizational field study. *Journal of Applied Psychology, 71,* 566–570

Mullins, W. C., & Kimbrough, W. W. (1988). Group composition as a determinant of job analysis outcomes. *Journal of Applied Psychology, 73,* 657–664.

Mumford, M. D., Weeks, J. L., Harding, F. D., & Fleishman, E. A. (1987). Measuring occupational difficulty: A construct validation against training criteria. *Journal of Applied Psychology, 72,* 578–587.

Mumford, M. D., Weeks, J. L., Harding, F. D., & Fleishman, E. A. (1988). Relations between student characteristics, course content, and training outcomes: An integrative modeling effort. *Journal of Applied Psychology, 73,* 443–456.

Münsterberg, H. (1913). *Psychology and industrial efficiency.* New York: Houghton Mifflin.

Murphy, K. R. (1983). Fooling yourself with cross-validation: Single sample designs. *Personnel Psychology, 36,* 111–118.

Murphy, K. R. (1984). Cost-benefit considerations in choosing among cross-validation methods. *Personnel Psychology, 37,* 15–22.

Murphy, K. R. (1986). When your top choice turns you down: Effect of rejected offers on the utility of selection tests. *Psychological Bulletin, 99,* 133–138.

Murphy, K. R. (1989). Is the relationship between cognitive ability and job performance stable over time? *Human Performance, 2*(3), 183–200.

Murphy, K. R. (1993). *Honesty in the workplace.* Pacific Grove, CA: Brooks/Cole.

Murphy, K. R., & Balzer, W. K. (1986). Systematic distortions in memory-based behavior ratings and performance evaluations: Consequences for rating accuracy. *Journal of Applied Psychology, 71,* 39–44.

Murphy, K. R., & Balzer, W. K. (1989). Rater errors and rating accuracy. *Journal of Applied Psychology, 74,* 619–624.

Murphy, K. R., Balzer, W. K., Lockhart, M. C., & Eisenman, E. J. (1985). Effects of previous performance on evaluations of present performance. *Journal of Applied Psychology, 70,* 72–84.

Murphy, K. R., & Constans, J. I. (1987). Behavioral anchors as a source of bias in rating. *Journal of Applied Psychology, 72,* 573–577.

Murphy, K. R., & Davidshofer, C. O. (1991). *Psychological testing: Principles and application* (2nd ed.). Englewood Cliffs, NJ: Prentice-Hall.

Murphy, K. R., Gannett, B. A., Herr, B. M., & Chen, J. A. (1986). Effects of subsequent performance on evaluations of previous performance. *Journal of Applied Psychology, 71,* 427–431.

Murphy, K. R., & Jako, R. (1989). Under what conditions are observed intercorrelations greater or smaller than true intercorrelations? *Journal of Applied Psychology, 74,* 827–830.

Murphy, K. R., Martin, C., & Garcia, M. (1982). Do behavioral observation scales measure observation? *Journal of Applied Psychology, 67,* 562–567.

Murphy, K. R., & Pardaffy, V. A. (1989). Bias in be-

haviorally anchored rating scales: Global or scale-specific? *Journal of Applied Psychology, 74,* 343–346.

Murphy, K. R., Philbin, T. A., & Adams, S. R. (1989). Effect of purpose of observation on accuracy of immediate and delayed performance ratings. *Organizational Behavior and Human Decision Processes, 43,* 336–354.

Murphy, K. R., & Reynolds, D. H. (1988). Does true halo affect observed halo? *Journal of Applied Psychology, 73,* 235–238.

Murphy, K. R., & Saal, F. E. (Eds.). (1990). *Psychology in organizations: Integrating science and practice.* Hillsdale, NJ: Lawrence Erlbaum Associates.

Murphy, K. R., Thornton, G. C., III, & Reynolds, D. H. (1990). College students' attitudes toward employee drug testing programs. *Personnel Psychology, 43,* 615–631.

Murphy, L. R. (1990). Prevention and management of work stress. In J. W. Jones, B. D. Steffy, & D. W. Bray (Eds.), *Applying psychology in business.* Lexington, MA: Lexington Books.

Murray, H. A. (1938). *Explorations in personality.* New York: Oxford University Press.

Murray, H. A., & MacKinnon, D. W. (1946). Assessment of OSS personnel. *Journal of Consulting Psychology, 10,* 76–80.

Napier, N. K., & Latham, G. P. (1986). Outcome expectancies of people who conduct performance appraisals. *Personnel Psychology, 39,* 827–837.

Narayanan, V. K., & Nath, R. (1982). A field test of some attitudinal and behavioral consequences of flexitime. *Journal of Applied Psychology, 67,* 214–218.

Nash, A. N., & Carroll, S. J., Jr. (1975). *The management of compensation.* Pacific Grove, CA: Brooks/Cole.

Nathan, B. R., & Alexander, R. A. (1985). The role of inferential accuracy in performance rating. *Academy of Management Review, 10,* 109–115.

Nathan, B. R., & Alexander, R. A. (1988). A comparison of criteria for test validation: A meta-analytic investigation. *Personnel Psychology, 41,* 517–535.

Nathan, B. R., & Lord, R. G. (1983). Cognitive categorization and dimensional schemata: A process approach to the study of halo in performance ratings. *Journal of Applied Psychology, 68,* 102–114.

Nathan, B. R., Mohrman, A. M., Jr., & Milliman, J.

(1991). Interpersonal relations as a context for the effects of appraisal interviews on performance and satisfaction: A longitudinal study. *Academy of Management Journal, 34,* 352–369.

Nathan, B. R., & Tippins, N. (1990). The consequences of halo "error" in performance ratings: A field study of the moderating effect of halo on test validation results. *Journal of Applied Psychology, 75,* 290–296.

National League for Nursing, Research and Studies Service. (1964). *A method for rating the proficiency of the hospital general staff nurse: Manual of directions.* New York.

Naylor, J. C., & Shine, L. C. (1965). A table for determining the increase in mean criterion score obtained by using a selection device. *Journal of Industrial Psychology, 3,* 33–42.

Near, J. P., Smith, C. A., Rice, R. W., & Hunt, R. G. (1984). A comparison of work and nonwork predictors of life satisfaction. *Academy of Management Journal, 27,* 184–190.

Neff, W. S. (1968). *Work and human behavior.* New York: Atherton.

Neidig, R. D., & Neidig, P. J. (1984). Multiple assessment center exercises and job relatedness. *Journal of Applied Psychology, 69,* 182–186.

Neuman, G. A., Edwards, J. E., & Raju, N. S. (1989). Organizational development interventions: A meta-analysis of their effects on satisfaction and other attitudes. *Personnel Psychology, 42,* 461–489.

Newman, J. E., & Beehr, T. A. (1979). Personal and organizational strategies for handling job stress: A review of research and opinion. *Personnel Psychology, 32,* 1–43.

Nicholas, J. M., & Katz, M. (1985). Research methods and reporting practices in organization development: A review and some guidelines. *Academy of Management Review, 10,* 737–749.

Nicholson, N., Brown, C. A., & Chadwick-Jones, J. K. (1976). Absence from work and job satisfaction. *Journal of Applied Psychology, 61,* 728–737.

Noe, R. A. (1986). Trainees' attributes and attitudes: Neglected influences on training effectiveness. *Academy of Management Review, 11,* 736–749.

Noe, R. A. (1988a). An investigation of the determinants of successful assigned mentoring relationships. *Personnel Psychology, 41,* 457–479.

Noe, R. A. (1988b). Women and mentoring: A review and research agenda. *Academy of Management Review, 13,* 65–78.

Noe, R. A., & Schmitt, N. (1986). The influence of trainee attitudes on training effectiveness: Test of a model. *Personnel Psychology, 39,* 497–523.

Nollen, S. (1979). *New patterns of work.* New York: Work in America Institute.

Nord, W. R. (1980). Toward an organizational psychology for organizational psychology. *Professional Psychology, 11,* 531–542.

Nord, W. R. (1982). Continuity and change in industrial/organizational psychology: Learning from previous mistakes. *Professional Psychology, 13,* 942–953.

Norman, D. (1983, August 23). *The DVORAK revival: Is it really worth the cost?* (C-015). La Jolla: Institute for Cognitive Sciences, University of California, San Diego.

Normand, J., Salyards, S. D., & Mahoney, J. J. (1990). An evaluation of preemployment drug testing. *Journal of Applied Psychology, 75,* 629–639.

Northcraft, G. B., & Ashford, S. J. (1990). The preservation of everyday life: The effects of performance expectations and feedback context on feedback inquiry. *Organizational Behavior and Human Decision Processes, 47,* 42–64.

Northcraft, G. B., & Earley, P. C. (1989). Technology, credibility, and feedback use. *Organizational Behavior and Human Decision Processes, 44,* 83–96.

Northcraft, G. B., Huber, V., & Neale, M. A. (1988). Sex effects in performance-related judgments. *Human Performance, 1,* 161–175.

Nossel, N. (1982). The InterFace Project: Background. *Personnel Psychology, 35,* 553–555.

Nunnally, J. C. (1978). *Psychometric theory* (2nd ed.). New York: McGraw-Hill.

O'Brien, G. E. (1982). Evaluation of the job characteristics theory of work attitudes and performance. *Australian Journal of Psychology, 34,* 383–401.

O'Connor, E. J., Peters, L. H., Pooyan, A., Weekley, J., Frank, B., & Erenkrantz, B. (1984). Situational constraint effects on performance, affective reactions, and turnover: A field replication and extension. *Journal of Applied Psychology, 69,* 663–672.

O'Reilly, C. A., III. (1978). The intentional distortion of information in organizational communication: A laboratory and field approach. *Human Relations, 31,* 173–193.

O'Reilly, C. A., III. (1980). Individuals and information overload in organizations: Is more necessarily better? *Academy of Management Journal, 23,* 684–696.

O'Reilly, C. A., & Caldwell, D. F. (1980). Job choice: The impact of intrinsic and extrinsic factors on subsequent satisfaction and commitment. *Journal of Applied Psychology, 65,* 559–565.

O'Reilly, C. A., & Chatman, J. (1986). Organizational commitment and psychological attachment: The effects of compliance, identification, and internalization on prosocial behavior. *Journal of Applied Psychology, 71,* 492–499.

O'Reilly, C. A., Chatman, J., & Caldwell, D. F. (1991). People and organizational culture: A profile comparison approach to assessing person-organization fit. *Academy of Management Journal, 34,* 487–516.

O'Reilly, C. A., III, & Roberts, K. H. (1976). Relationships among components of credibility and communication behaviors in work units. *Journal of Applied Psychology, 61,* 99–102.

Odewahn, C. A., & Petty, M. M. (1980). A comparison of levels of job satisfaction, role stress, and personal competence between union members and nonmembers. *Academy of Management Journal, 23,* 150–155.

Offerman, L. R., & Gowing, M. K. (1990). Organizations of the future: Changes and challenges. *American Psychologist, 45,* 95–108.

Oldham, G. R. (1976). Organizational choice and some correlates of individual expectancies. *Decision Science, 7,* 873–874.

Olian, J. D. (1984). Genetic screening for employment purposes. *Personnel Psychology, 37,* 423–438.

Olian, J. D., Schwab, D. P., & Haberfeld, Y. (1988). The impact of applicant gender compared to qualifications on hiring recommendations: A meta-analysis of experimental studies. *Organizational Behavior and Human Decision Processes, 41,* 180–195.

Olson, C. A., & Becker, B. E. (1983). A proposed technique for the treatment of restriction of range in selection validation. *Psychological Bulletin, 93,* 137–148.

Olson, H. C., Fine, S. A., Myers, D. C., & Jennings, M. C. (1981). The use of functional job analysis in establishing performance standards for heavy equipment operators. *Personnel Psychology, 34,* 351–364.

Olson, P., & Sivak, M. (1984). Glare from automobile rear-view mirrors. *Human Factors, 26,* 269–282.

Oltman, P. K., Stricker, L. J., & Barrows, T. S. (1990). Analyzing test structure by multidimensional scaling. *Journal of Applied Psychology, 75,* 21–27.

Organ, D. W. (1977). A reappraisal and reinterpretation of the satisfaction-causes-performance hypothesis. *Academy of Management Review, 2,* 46–53.

Orpen, C. (1978). Work and nonwork satisfaction: A causal-correlational analysis. *Journal of Applied Psychology, 63,* 530–532.

Orpen, C. (1981). Effect of flexible working hours on employee satisfaction and performance: A field experiment. *Journal of Applied Psychology, 66,* 113–115.

Orpen, C. (1985). Patterned behavior description interviews versus unstructured interviews: A comparative validity study. *Journal of Applied Psychology, 70,* 774–776.

Orr, J. M., Sackett, P. R., & Mercer, M. (1989). The role of prescribed and nonprescribed behaviors in estimating the dollar value of performance. *Journal of Applied Psychology, 74,* 34–40.

Orwin, R. G., & Cordray, D. S. (1985). Effects of deficient reporting on meta-analysis: A conceptual framework and reanalysis. *Psychological Bulletin, 97,* 134–147.

Osborn, R. N., & Vicars, W. M. (1976). Sex stereotypes: An artifact in leader behavior and subordinate satisfaction analysis? *Academy of Management Journal, 19,* 439–449.

Osburn, H. G., & Callender, J. C. (1990). Bias in validity generalization bias estimates: A reply to Hoben Thomas. *Journal of Applied Psychology, 75,* 328–333.

Osburn, H. G., Callender, J. C., Greener, J. M., & Ashworth, S. (1983). Statistical power of tests of the situational specificity hypothesis in validity generalization studies: A cautionary note. *Journal of Applied Psychology, 68,* 115–122.

Osburn, H. G., Timmreck, C., & Bigby, D. (1981). Effect of dimensional relevance on accuracy of simulated hiring decisions by employment interviewers. *Journal of Applied Psychology, 66,* 159–165.

Ouchi, W. G. (1981). *Theory Z: How American business can meet the Japanese challenge.* Reading, MA: Addison-Wesley.

Owens, W. A. (1968). Toward one discipline of scientific psychology. *American Psychologist, 23,* 782–785.

Owens, W. A. (1976). Background data. In M.D. Dunnette (Ed.), *Handbook of industrial and organizational psychology*. Chicago: Rand McNally.

Padgett, M. Y., & Ilgen, D. R. (1989). The impact of ratee performance characteristics on rater cognitive processes and alternative measures of rater accuracy. *Organizational Behavior and Human Decision Processes, 44*, 232–260.

Paese, P. W., & Switzer, F. S., III. (1988). Validity generalization and hypothetical reliability distributions: A test of the Schmidt—Hunter procedure. *Journal of Applied Psychology, 73*, 267–274.

Pannone, R. D. (1984). Predicting test performance: A content valid approach to screening applicants. *Personnel Psychology, 37*, 507–514.

Paolillo, J. G. (1981). Role profiles for managers at different hierarchical levels. *Proceedings of the Annual Meeting of the Academy of Management*, 91–94.

Parker, J. W., Taylor, E. K., Barrett, R. S., & Martens, L. (1959). Rating scale content: 3. Relationship between supervisory and self-ratings. *Personnel Psychology, 12*, 49–63.

Parsons, C. K., & Hulin, C. L. (1982). An empirical comparison of item response theory and hierarchical factor analysis in applications to the measurement of job satisfaction. *Journal of Applied Psychology, 67*, 826–834.

Parsons, C. K., & Liden, R. C. (1984). Interviewer perceptions of applicant qualifications: A multivariate field study of demographic characteristics and nonverbal cues. *Journal of Applied Psychology, 69*, 557–568.

Parsons, H. M. (1982). More on the Hawthorne effect. *American Psychologist, 37*, 856–857.

Partridge, B. E. (1973). Notes on the impact of flextime in a large insurance company: II. Reactions of supervisors and managers. *Occupational Psychology, 47*, 241–242.

Patten, T. H., Jr. (1988). *Fair pay: The managerial challenge of comparable worth and job evaluation*. San Francisco: Jossey-Bass.

Paul, R. J., & Ebadi, Y. M. (1989). Leadership decision making in a service organization: A field test of the Vroom-Yetton model. *Journal of Occupational Psychology, 62*, 201–211.

Paunonen, S. V., & Jackson, D. N. (1988). Type I error rates for moderated multiple regression analysis. *Journal of Applied Psychology, 73*, 569–573.

Paunonen, S. V., Jackson, D. N., & Oberman, S. M. (1987). Personnel selection decisions: Effects of applicant personality and the letter of reference. *Organizational Behavior and Human Decision Processes, 40*, 96–114.

Pavett, C. M., & Lau, A. W. (1983). Managerial work: The influence of hierarchical level and functional specialty. *Academy of Management Journal, 26*, 170–177.

Pazy, A. (1986). The persistence of pro-male bias despite identical information regarding causes of success. *Organizational Behavior and Human Decision Processes, 38*, 366–377.

Pearce, J. L., & Porter, L. W. (1986). Employee responses to formal performance appraisal feedback. *Journal of Applied Psychology, 71*, 211–218.

Pedhazur, E. J. (1982). *Multiple regression in behavioral research: Explanation and prediction* (2nd ed.). New York: Holt, Rinehart and Winston.

Penner, D. D., Malone, D. M., Coughlin, T. M., & Herz, J. A. (1973). *Satisfaction with U.S. Army leadership* (Leadership Monograph Series, No. 2). U.S. Army War College.

Peter, L. J., & Hull, R. (1969). *The Peter Principle*. New York: Morrow.

Peters, D. L., & McCormick, E. J. (1966). Comparative reliability of numerically anchored versus job-task anchored rating scales. *Journal of Applied Psychology, 50*, 92–96.

Peters, L. H., Fisher, C. D., & O'Connor, E. J. (1982). The moderating effect of situational control of performance variance on the relationship between individual differences and performance. *Personnel Psychology, 35*, 609–621.

Peters, L. H., O'Connor, E. J., Weekley, J., Pooyan, A., Frank, B., & Erenkrantz, B. (1984). Sex bias and managerial evaluations: A replication and extension. *Journal of Applied Psychology, 69*, 349–352.

Peters, M., Servos, P., & Day, R. (1990). Marked sex differences on a fine motor skill task disappear when finger size is used as covariate. *Journal of Applied Psychology, 75*, 87–90.

Peterson, N. G., Hough, L. M., Dunnette, M. D., Rosse, R. L., Houston, J. S., Toquam, J. L., & Wing, H. (1990). Project A: Specification of the predictor domain and development of new selection/classification tests. *Personnel Psychology, 43*, 247–276.

Petty, M. M., & Bruning, N. S. (1980). A comparison

of the relationships between subordinates' perceptions of supervisory behavior and measures of subordinates' job satisfaction for male and female leaders. *Academy of Management Journal, 23*, 717–725.

Pfeffer, J. (1977). The ambiguity of leadership. *Academy of Management Review, 2*, 104–112.

Pfeffer, J. (1981). Management as symbolic action: The creation and maintenance of organizational paradigms. In L. L. Cummings & B. M. Staw (Eds.), *Research in organizational behavior* (Vol. 3). Greenwich, CT: JAI Press.

Phillips, A. P., & Dipboye, R. L. (1989). Correlational tests of predictions from a process model of the interview. *Journal of Applied Psychology, 74*, 41–52.

Phillips, J. S. (1984). The accuracy of leadership ratings: A cognitive categorization perspective. *Organizational Behavior and Human Performance, 33*, 125–138.

Phillips, J. S., & Lord, R. G. (1982). Schematic information processing and perceptions of leadership in problem-solving groups. *Journal of Applied Psychology, 67*, 486–492.

Pimble, J., & O'Toole, S. (1982). Analysis of accident reports. *Ergonomics, 25*, 967–974.

Piotrowski, M. J., Barnes-Farrell, J. L., & Esrig, F. H. (1989). Behaviorally anchored bias: A replication and extension of Murphy and Constans. *Journal of Applied Psychology, 74*, 823–826.

Plovnick, M. S., & Chaison, G. N. (1985). Relationships between concession bargaining and labor-management cooperation. *Academy of Management Journal, 28*, 697–704.

Podsakoff, P. M., & Farh, J. (1989). Effects of feedback sign and credibility on goal setting and task performance. *Organizational Behavior and Human Decision Processes, 44*, 45–67.

Pokorney, J. J., Gilmore, D. C., & Beehr, T. A. (1980). Job Diagnostic Survey dimensions: Moderating effect of growth needs and correspondence with dimensions of job rating form. *Organizational Behavior and Human Performance, 26*, 222–237.

Podsakoff, P. M., & Schriesheim, C. A. (1985). Field studies of French and Raven's bases of power: Critique, reanalysis, and suggestions for future research. *Psychological Bulletin, 97*, 387–411.

Podsakoff, P. M., Todor, W. D., & Skov, R. (1982). Effects of leader contingent and noncontingent reward and punishment behaviors on subordi-

nate performance and satisfaction. *Academy of Management Journal, 25*, 810–821.

Porras, J. I., & Anderson, B. (1981). Improving managerial effectiveness through modeling-based training. *Organizational Dynamics, 9*(4), 60–77.

Porras, J. I., & Berg, P. O. (1978). The impact of organizational development. *Academy of Management Review, 3*, 249–266.

Porter, L. W., & Lawler, E. E., III. (1968). *Managerial attitudes and performance.* Homewood, IL: Irwin.

Posner, B. Z. (1981). Comparing recruiter, student, and faculty perceptions of important applicant and job characteristics. *Personnel Psychology, 34*, 329–339.

Potter, E. H., III, & Fiedler, F. E. (1981). The utilization of staff member intelligence and experience under high and low stress. *Academy of Management Journal, 24*, 361–376.

Powell, G. N. (1984). Effects of job attributes and recruiting practices on applicant decisions: A comparison. *Personnel Psychology, 37*, 721–732.

Powell, G. N. (1991). Applicant reactions to the initial employment interview: Exploring theoretical and methodological issues. *Personnel Psychology, 44*, 67–83.

Powell, G. N., & Butterfield, D. A. (1989). The "good manager": Did androgyny fare better in the 1980s? *Group and Organization Studies, 14*, 216–233.

Premack, S. L., & Hunter, J. E. (1988). Individual unionization decisions. *Psychological Bulletin, 103*, 223–234.

Premack, S. L., & Wanous, J. P. (1985). A meta-analysis of realistic job preview experiments. *Journal of Applied Psychology, 70*, 706–719.

Pressey, S. L. (1950). Development and appraisal of devices providing immediate automatic scoring of objective tests and concomitant self-instruction. *Journal of Psychology, 29*, 417–447.

Price, K. H., & Garland, H. (1981). Compliance with a leader's suggestions as a function of perceived leader/member competence and potential reciprocity. *Journal of Applied Psychology, 66*, 329–336.

Price of prejudice. (1991, July 1). *Time*, p. 56.

Prien, E. P., & Hughes, G. L. (1987). The effect of quality control revisions on mixed standard scale rating errors. *Personnel Psychology, 40*, 815–823.

Primack, R. B., & O'Leary, V. D. (1989). PhD recipients in psychology and biology: A comment. *American Psychologist, 44,* 575–576.

Primoff, E. S. (1975). *How to prepare and conduct job element examinations.* Washington, DC: U.S. Government Printing Office.

Prince, J. B., & Lawler, E. E., III. (1986). Does salary discussion hurt the developmental performance appraisal? *Organizational Behavior and Human Decision Processes, 37,* 357–375.

Pritchard, R. D., Dunnette, M. D., & Jorgenson, D. O. (1972). Effects of perceptions of equity and inequity on worker performance and satisfaction. *Journal of Applied Psychology, 56,* 75–94.

Pritchard, R. D., Hollenback, J., & DeLeo, P. J. (1980). The effects of continuous and partial schedules of reinforcement on effort, performance, and satisfaction. *Organizational Behavior and Human Performance, 25,* 336–353.

Pritchard, R. D., Leonard, D. W., VonBergen, C. W., & Kirk, R. J. (1976). The effects of varying schedules of reinforcement on human task performance. *Organizational Behavior and Human Performance, 16,* 205–230.

Pulakos, E. D. (1984). A comparison of rater training programs: Error training and accuracy training. *Journal of Applied Psychology, 69,* 581–588.

Pulakos, E. D. (1986). The development of training programs to increase accuracy with different rating tasks. *Organizational Behavior and Human Decision Processes, 38,* 76–91.

Pulakos, E. D., Borman, W. C., & Hough, L. M. (1988). Test validation for scientific understanding: Two demonstrations of an approach to studying predictor-criterion linkages. *Personnel Psychology, 41,* 703–716.

Pulakos, E. D., Schmitt, N., & Ostroff, C. (1986). A warning about the use of a standard deviation across dimensions within ratees to measure halo. *Journal of Applied Psychology, 71,* 29–32.

Pulakos, E. D., White, L. A., Oppler, S. H., & Borman, W. C. (1989). Examination of race and sex effects on performance ratings. *Journal of Applied Psychology, 74,* 770–780.

Pynes, J. E., & Bernardin, H. J. (1989). Predictive validity of an entry-level police officer assessment center. *Journal of Applied Psychology, 74,* 831–833.

Quick, J. C., & Quick, J. D. (1984). *Organizational stress and preventive management.* New York: McGraw-Hill.

Rafaeli, A., & Klimoski, R. J. (1983). Predicting sales success through handwriting analysis: An evaluation of the effects of training and handwriting sample content. *Journal of Applied Psychology, 68,* 212–217.

Ragins, B. R., & Sundstrom, E. (1990). Gender and perceived power in manager-subordinate relations. *Journal of Occupational Psychology, 63,* 273–287.

Raju, N. S., & Burke, M. J. (1983). Two new procedures for studying validity generalization. *Journal of Applied Psychology, 68,* 382–395.

Raju, N. S., Burke, M. J., & Normand, J. (1990). A new approach for utility analysis. *Journal of Applied Psychology, 75,* 3–12.

Raju, N. S., Edwards, J. E., & LoVerde, M. A. (1985). Corrected formulas for computing sample sizes under indirect range restriction. *Journal of Applied Psychology, 70,* 565–566.

Raju, N. S., Pappas, S., & Williams, C. P. (1989). An empirical Monte Carlo test of the accuracy of the correlation, covariance, and regression slope models for assessing validity generalization. *Journal of Applied Psychology, 74,* 901–911.

Ralston, D. A. (1989). The benefits of flextime: Real or imagined? *Journal of Organizational Behavior, 10,* 369–373.

Ralston, D. A., Anthony, W. P., & Gustafson, D. J. (1985). Employees may love flextime, but what does it do to the organization's productivity? *Journal of Applied Psychology, 70,* 272–279.

Ralston, D. A., & Flanagan, M. F. (1985). The effect of flextime on absenteeism and turnover for male and female employees. *Journal of Vocational Behavior, 26,* 206–217.

Rambo, W. W., Chomiak, A. M., & Price, J. M. (1983). Consistency performance under stable conditions of work. *Journal of Applied Psychology, 68,* 78–87.

Ramsey, J., & Kwon, Y. (1988). Simplified decision rules for predicting performance loss in heat. *Proceedings on heat stress indices.* Luxembourg: Commission of the Eurpoean Communities.

Randall, D. M. (1987). Commitment and the organization: The organization man revisited. *Academy of Management Review, 12,* 460–471.

Randolph, W. A. (1981). Cross-lagged correlational analysis in dynamic settings. *Journal of Applied Psychology, 66,* 431–436.

Rasmussen, J. (1987). The definition of human error

and a taxonomy for technical system design. In J. Rasmussen, K. Duncan, & J. Leplat (Eds.), *New technologies and human error*. New York: Wiley.

Rasmussen, J. L., & Loher, B. T. (1988). Appropriate critical percentages for the Schmidt and Hunter meta-analysis procedure: Comparative evaluation of Type I error rate and power. *Journal of Applied Psychology, 73,* 683–687.

Rasmussen, K. G., Jr. (1984). Nonverbal behavior, verbal behavior, resume credentials, and selection interview outcomes. *Journal of Applied Psychology, 69,* 551–556.

Rauschenberger, J., Schmitt, N., & Hunter, J. E. (1980). A test of the need hierarchy concept by a Markov model of change in need strength. *Administrative Science Quarterly, 25,* 654–670.

Raven, B. H., & French, J. R. P. (1958a). Group support, legitimate power, and social influence. *Journal of Personality, 26,* 400–409.

Raven, B. H., & French, J. R. P. (1958b). Legitimate power, coercive power, and observability in social influence. *Sociometry, 21,* 83–97.

Raza, S. M., & Carpenter, B. N. (1987). A model of hiring decisions in real employment interviews. *Journal of Applied Psychology, 72,* 596–603.

Read, P. B. (1974). Source of authority and the legitimation of leadership in small groups. *Sociometry, 37,* 180–204.

Reese, H. W., & Fremouw, W. J. (1984). Normal and normative ethics in behavioral sciences. *American Psychologist, 39,* 863–876.

Reichers, A. E. (1985). A review and reconceptualization of organizational commitment. *Academy of Management Review, 10,* 465–476.

Reichers, A. E. (1986). Conflict and organizational commitments. *Journal of Applied Psychology, 71,* 508–514.

Reilly, R. R., Brown, B., Blood, M. R., & Malatesta, C. Z. (1981). The effects of realistic previews: A study and discussion of the literature. *Personnel Psychology, 34,* 823–834.

Reilly, R. R., & Chao, G. T. (1982). Validity and fairness of some alternative employee selection procedures. *Personnel Psychology, 35,* 1–62.

Reilly, R. R., Henry, S., & Smither, J. W. (1990). An examination of the effects of using behavior checklists on the construct validity of assessment center dimensions. *Personnel Psychology, 43,* 71–84.

Reilly, R. R., & Israelski, E. W. (1988). Development and validation of minicourses in the telecommunication industry. *Journal of Applied Psychology, 73,* 721–726.

Reilly, R. R., & Smither, J. W. (1985). An examination of two alternative techniques to estimate the standard deviation of job performance in dollars. *Journal of Applied Psychology, 70,* 651–661.

Reilly, R. R., Zedeck, S., & Tenopyr, M. L. (1979). Validity and fairness of physical ability tests for predicting performance in craft jobs. *Journal of Applied Psychology, 64,* 262–274.

Rentsch, J. R. (1990). Climate and culture: Interaction and qualitative differences in organizational meanings. *Journal of Applied Psychology, 75,* 668–681.

Rice, R. W. (1978). Construct validity of the least preferred co-worker score. *Psychological Bulletin, 85,* 1199–1237.

Rice, R. W., Instone, D., & Adams, J. (1984). Leader sex, leader success, and leadership process: Two field studies. *Journal of Applied Psychology, 69,* 12–31.

Rice, R. W., Near, J. P., & Hunt, R. G. (1980). The job satisfaction/life satisfaction relationship: A review of empirical research. *Basic and Applied Social Psychology, 1,* 37–64.

Rich, J. R., & Boudreau, J. W. (1987). The effects of variability and risk in selection utility analysis: An empirical comparison. *Personnel Psychology, 40,* 55–84.

Ritchie, R. J., & Moses, J. L. (1983). Assessment center correlates of women's advancement into middle management: A 7-year longitudinal analysis. *Journal of Applied Psychology, 68,* 227–231.

Roberts, K. H., & Glick, W. (1981). The job characteristics approach to task design: A critical review. *Journal of Applied Psychology, 66,* 193–217.

Roberts, N. (1985). Transforming leadership: A process of collective action. *Human Relations, 38,* 1023–1046.

Roberts, T. (1991). Gender and the influence of evaluations on self-assessments in achievement settings. *Psychological Bulletin, 109,* 297–308.

Robertson, I. T., & Downs, S. (1989). Work-sample tests of trainability: A meta-analysis. *Journal of Applied Psychology, 74,* 402–410.

Robey, D. (1974). Task design, work values, and worker response: An experimental test. *Organizational Behavior and Human Performance, 12,* 264–273.

Robinson, D. D. (1981). Content-oriented personnel selection in a small business setting. *Personnel Psychology, 34,* 77–87.

Rodgers, R. C., Helburn, I. B., & Hunter, J. E. (1986). The relationship of seniority to job performance following reinstatement. *Academy of Management Journal, 29,* 101–114.

Rodgers, R., & Hunter, J. E. (1991). Impact of management by objectives on organizational productivity [Monograph]. *Journal of Applied Psychology, 76,* 322–336.

Roethlisberger, F. J., & Dickson, W. J. (1939). *Management and the worker.* Cambridge: Harvard University Press.

Rogosa, D. (1980). A critique of cross-lagged correlation. *Psychological Bulletin, 88,* 245–258.

Romzek, B. S. (1989). Personal consequences of employee commitment. *Academy of Management Journal, 32,* 649–661.

Ronan, W. W. (1980). Some ethical considerations in worker control. *American Psychologist, 35,* 1150–1151.

Ronen, S. (1980). The image of I/O psychology: A cross-national perspective by personnel executives. *Professional Psychology, 11,* 399–406.

Ronen, S. (1981). Arrival and departure patterns of public sector employees before and after implementation of flexitime. *Personnel Psychology, 34,* 817–822.

Ronen, S., & Primps, S. B. (1981). Organizational change: Behavioral and attitudinal outcomes. *Academy of Management Review, 6,* 61–74.

Rosen, B., & Jerdee, T. H. (1973). The influence of sex-role stereotypes on evaluation of male and female supervisory behavior. *Journal of Applied Psychology, 57,* 44–48.

Rosenthal, R. (1978). Combining results of independent studies. *Psychological Bulletin, 85,* 185–193.

Rosenthal, R., & Jacobson, L. (1968). *Pygmalion in the classroom.* New York: Holt, Rinehart & Winston.

Rosenthal, R., & Rubin, D.B. (1985). Statistical analysis: Summarizing evidence versus establishing facts. *Psychological Bulletin, 97,* 527–529.

Rothaus, P., Morton, R. B., & Hanson, P. G. (1965). Performance appraisal and psychological distance. *Journal of Applied Psychology, 49,* 48–54.

Rothstein, H. R. (1990). Interrater reliability of job performance ratings: Growth to asymptote level with increasing opportunity to observe. *Journal of Applied Psychology, 75,* 322–327.

Rothstein, H. R., Schmidt, F. L., Erwin, F. W., Owens, W. A., & Sparks, C. P. (1990). Biographical data in employment selection: Can validities be made generalizable? *Journal of Applied Psychology, 75,* 175–184.

Rotter, G. S., & Tinkleman, V. (1970). Anchor effects in the development of behavior rating scales. *Educational and Psychological Measurement, 30,* 311–318.

Rozelle, R. M., & Baxter, J. C. (1981). Influence of role pressures on the perceiver: Judgments of videotaped interviews varying judge accountability and responsibility. *Journal of Applied Psychology, 66,* 437–441.

Roznowski, M. (1987). Use of tests manifesting sex differences as measures of intelligence: Implications for measurement bias. *Journal of Applied Psychology, 72,* 480–483.

Rusbult, C. E., & Farrell, D. (1983). A longitudinal test of the investment model: The impact on job satisfaction, job commitment, and turnover of variations in rewards, costs, alternatives, and investments. *Journal of Applied Psychology, 68,* 429–438.

Rush, M. C., Thomas, J. C., & Lord, R. G. (1977). Implicit leadership theory: A potential threat to the internal validity of leader behavior questionnaires. *Organizational Behavior and Human Performance, 20,* 93–110.

Russell, C. J. (1987). Person characteristic versus role congruency explanations for assessment center ratings. *Academy of Management Journal, 30,* 817–826.

Russell, C. J., Mattson, J., Devlin, S. E., & Atwater, D. (1990). Predictive validity of biodata items generated from retrospective life experience essays. *Journal of Applied Psychology, 75,* 569–580.

Russell, J. S. (1984). A review of fair employment cases in the field of training. *Personnel Psychology, 37,* 261–276.

Russell, J. S., & Goode, D. L. (1988). An analysis of managers' reactions to their own performance appraisal feedback. *Journal of Applied Psychology, 73,* 63–67.

Russell, J. S., Terborg, J. R., & Powers, M. L. (1985). Organizational performance and organizational level training and support. *Personnel Psychology, 38,* 849–863.

Rynes, S. L., & Barber, A. E. (1990). Applicant attraction strategies: An organizational perspective. *Academy of Management Review, 15,* 286–310.

Rynes, S., & Gerhart, B. (1990). Interviewer assessments of applicant "fit": An exploratory investigation. *Personnel Psychology, 43,* 13–35.

Rynes, S. L., & Boudreau, J. W. (1986). College recruiting in large organizations: Practice, evaluation, and research implications. *Personnel Psychology, 39,* 729–757.

Rynes, S. L., & Milkovich, G. T. (1986). Wage surveys: Dispelling some myths about the "market wage." *Personnel Psychology, 39,* 71–90.

Rynes, S. L., & Miller, H. E. (1983). Recruiter and job influences on candidates for employment. *Journal of Applied Psychology, 68,* 147–154.

Rynes, S. L., Weber, C. L., & Milkovich, G. T. (1989). Effects of market survey rates, job evaluation, and job gender on job pay. *Journal of Applied Psychology, 74,* 114–123.

Saal, F. E. (1979). Mixed standard rating scale: A consistent system for numerically coding inconsistent response combinations. *Journal of Applied Psychology, 64,* 422–428.

Saal, F. E. (1992). Finding room on the rack for more than one hat: Combining multiple professional roles. In A. Vaux, M. S. Stockdale, & M. J. Schwerin (Eds.), *Independent consulting in applied psychology* (pp. 21–32). Newbury Park, CA: Sage.

Saal, F. E., Downey, R. G., & Lahey, M. A. (1980). Rating the ratings: Assessing the psychometric quality of rating data. *Psychological Bulletin, 88,* 413–428.

Saal, F. E., & Landy, F. J. (1977). The mixed standard rating scale: An evaluation. *Organizational Behavior and Human Performance, 18,* 19–35.

Saari, L. M., Johnson, T. R., McLaughlin, S. D., & Zimmerle, D. M. (1988). A survey of management training and education practices in U.S. companies. *Personnel Psychology, 41,* 731–743.

Saari, L. M., & Latham, G. P. (1982). Employee reactions to continuous and variable ratio reinforcement schedules involving a monetary incentive. *Journal of Applied Psychology, 67,* 506–508.

Sackett, P. R. (1982). The interviewer as hypothesis tester: The effects of impressions of an applicant on interviewer questioning strategy. *Personnel Psychology, 35,* 789–804.

Sackett, P. R. (1987). Assessment centers and content validity: Some neglected issues. *Personnel Psychology, 40,* 13–25.

Sackett, P. R., Burris, L. R., & Callahan, C. (1989). Integrity testing for personnel selection: An update. *Personnel Psychology, 42,* 491–529.

Sackett, P. R., Cornelius, E. T., III, & Carron, T. J. (1981). A comparison of global judgment vs. task oriented approaches to job classification. *Personnel Psychology, 34,* 791–804.

Sackett, P. R., & Dreher, G. F. (1982). Constructs and assessment center dimensions: Some troubling empirical findings. *Journal of Applied Psychology, 67,* 401–410.

Sackett, P. R., & Dreher, G. F. (1984). Situation specificity of behavior and assessment center validation strategies: A rejoinder to Neidig and Neidig. *Journal of Applied Psychology, 69,* 187–190.

Sackett, P. R., DuBois, C. L. Z., & Noe, A. W. (1991). Tokenism in performance evaluation: The effects of work group representation on male-female and white-black differences in performance ratings. *Journal of Applied Psychology, 76,* 263–267.

Sackett, P. R., & Harris, M. M. (1984). Honesty testing for personnel selection: A review and critique. *Personnel Psychology, 37,* 221–245.

Sackett, P. R., Schmitt, N., Tenopyr, M. L., Kehoe, J., & Zedeck, S. (1985). Commentary on forty questions about validity generalization and meta-analysis. *Personnel Psychology, 38,* 697–798.

Sackett, P. R., & Wade, B. E. (1983). On the feasibility of criterion-related validity: The effects of range restriction assumptions on needed sample size. *Journal of Applied Psychology, 68,* 374–381.

Sackett, P. R., & Wilson, M. A. (1982). Factors affecting the consensus judgment process in managerial assessment centers. *Journal of Applied Psychology, 67,* 10–17.

Sackett, P. R., Zedeck, S., & Fogli, L. (1988). Relations between measures of typical and maximum job performance. *Journal of Applied Psychology, 73,* 482–486.

Sadacca, R., Campbell, J. P., Difazio, A. S., Schultz, S. R., & White, L. A. (1990). Scaling performance utility to enhance selection/classification decisions. *Personnel Psychology, 43,* 367–378.

Saks, A. M., & Cronshaw, S. F. (1990). A process investigation of realistic job previews: Mediating variables and channels of communication. *Journal of Organizational Behavior, 11,* 221–236.

Salancik, G. R., & Pfeffer, J. (1977a). An examination of need satisfaction models of job satisfaction. *Administrative Science Quarterly, 22,* 427–456.

Salancik, G. R., & Pfeffer, J. (1977b). Constraints on administrator discretion: The limited influence of mayors on city budgets. *Urban Affairs Quarterly, 12,* 475–498.

Salancik, G. R., & Pfeffer, J. (1978). A social information processing approach to job attitudes and task design. *Administrative Science Quarterly, 23,* 224–253.

Salinger, R. D. (1973). *Disincentives to effective employee training and development.* U.S. Civil Service Commission, Bureau of Training.

Samelson, F. (1977). World War I intelligence testing and the development of psychology. *Journal of the History of the Behavioral Sciences, 13,* 274–282.

Sanchez, J. I., & Levine, E. L. (1989). Determining important tasks within jobs: A policy-capturing approach. *Journal of Applied Psychology, 74,* 336–342.

Sanders, G. S., & Malkis, F. S. (1982). Type A behavior, need for control, and reactions to group participation. *Organizational Behavior and Human Performance, 30,* 71–86.

Sanders, M. S., & McCormick, E. J. (1993). *Human factors in engineering and design* (7th ed.). New York: McGraw-Hill.

Sanders, M. S., Shaw, B., Nicholson, B., & Merritt, J. (1990). *Evaluation of glare from center-high-mounted stop lights.* Washington, DC: National Highway Traffic Safety Administration.

Sandver, M. H. (1980). Predictors of outcomes in NLRB certification elections. *Proceedings of the 23rd Annual Meeting of the Midwest Academy of Management* (pp. 174–181). Cincinnati.

Sauser, W. I., Jr., & York, C. M. (1978). Sex differences in job satisfaction: A re-examination. *Personnel Psychology, 31,* 537–547.

Schachter, S., & Singer, J. E. (1962). Cognitive, social, and physiological determinants of emotional state. *Psychological Review, 69,* 379–399.

Schein, V. E. (1973). The relationship between sex role stereotypes and requisite management characteristics. *Journal of Applied Psychology, 57,* 95–100.

Schein, V. E. (1975). Relationships between sex role stereotypes and requisite management characteristics among female managers. *Journal of Applied Psychology, 60,* 340–344.

Schein, V. E., Maurer, E. H., & Novak, J. E. (1977). Impact of flexible working hours on productivity. *Journal of Applied Psychology, 62,* 463–465.

Schein, V. E., & Mueller, R. (1992). Sex role stereotyping and requisite management characteristics: A cross cultural look. *Journal of Organizational Behavior, 13,* 439–447.

Schippmann, J. S., Prien, E. P., & Katz, J. A. (1990).

Reliability and validity of in-basket performance measures. *Personnel Psychology, 43,* 837–859.

Schmidt, F. L., & Hunter, J. E. (1977). Development of a general solution to the problem of validity generalization. *Journal of Applied Psychology, 62,* 529–540.

Schmidt, F. L., & Hunter, J. E. (1980). The future of criterion-related validity. *Personnel Psychology, 33,* 41–60.

Schmidt, F. L., & Hunter, J. E. (1983). Individual differences in productivity: An empirical test of estimates derived from studies of selection procedure utility. *Journal of Applied Psychology, 68,* 407–414.

Schmidt, F. L., & Hunter, J. E. (1984). A within setting empirical test of the situational specificity hypothesis in personnel selection. *Personnel Psychology, 37,* 317–326.

Schmidt, F. L., & Hunter, J. E. (1989). Interrater reliability coefficients cannot be computed when only one stimulus is rated. *Journal of Applied Psychology, 74,* 368–370.

Schmidt, F. L., Hunter, J. E., & Caplan, J. R. (1981). Validity generalization results for two job groups in the petroleum industry. *Journal of Applied Psychology, 66,* 261–273.

Schmidt, F. L., Hunter, J. E., McKenzie, R. C., & Muldrow, T. W. (1979). Impact of valid selection procedures on work-force productivity. *Journal of Applied Psychology, 64,* 609–626.

Schmidt, F. L., Hunter, J. E., & Outerbridge, A. N. (1986). Impact of job experience and ability on job knowledge, work sample performance, and supervisory ratings of job performance. *Journal of Applied Psychology, 71,* 432–439.

Schmidt, F. L., Hunter, J. E., Outerbridge, A. N., & Goff, S. (1988). Joint relation of experience and ability with job performance: Test of three hypotheses. *Journal of Applied Psychology, 73,* 46–57.

Schmidt, F. L., Hunter, J. E., Outerbridge, A. N., & Trattner, M. H. (1986). The economic impact of job selection methods on size, productivity, and payroll costs of the federal work force: An empirically based demonstration. *Personnel Psychology, 39,* 1–29.

Schmidt, F. L., Hunter, J. E., & Pearlman, K. (1981). Task differences as moderators of aptitude test validity in selection. *Journal of Applied Psychology, 66,* 166–185.

Schmidt, F. L., Hunter, J. E., & Pearlman, K. (1982).

Progress in validity generalization: Comments on Callender and Osburn and further developments. *Journal of Applied Psychology, 67,* 835–845.

Schmidt, F. L., Hunter, J. E., Pearlman, K., & Hirsh, H. R. (1985). Forty questions about validity generalization and meta-analysis. *Personnel Psychology, 38,* 697–798.

Schmidt, F. L., Hunter, J. E., & Raju, N. S. (1988). Validity generalization and situational specificity: A second look at the 75% rule and Fisher's *z* transformation. *Journal of Applied Psychology, 73,* 665–672.

Schmidt, F. L., & Kaplan, L. B. (1971). Composite vs. multiple criteria: A review and resolution of the controversy. *Personnel Psychology, 24,* 419–434.

Schmidt, F. L., Mack, M. J., & Hunter, J. E. (1984). Selection utility in the occupation of U.S. park ranger for three modes of test use. *Journal of Applied Psychology, 69,* 490–497.

Schmidt, F. L., Ocasio, B. P., Hillery, J. M., & Hunter, J. E. (1985). Further within-setting empirical tests of the situational specificity hypothesis in personnel selection. *Personnel Psychology, 38,* 509–524.

Schmitt, N. (1976). Social and situational determinants of interview decisions: Implications for the employment interview. *Personnel Psychology, 29,* 79–101.

Schmitt, N., & Bedeian, A. G. (1982). A comparison of LISREL and two-stage least squares analysis of a hypothesized life-job satisfaction reciprocal relationship. *Journal of Applied Psychology, 67,* 806–817.

Schmitt, N., & Cohen, S. A. (1989). Internal analyses of task ratings by job incumbents. *Journal of Applied Psychology, 74,* 96–104.

Schmitt, N., Gooding, R. Z., Noe, R. A., & Kirsch, M. (1984). Meta-analyses of validity studies published between 1964 and 1982 and the investigation of study characteristics. *Personnel Psychology, 37,* 407–422.

Schmitt, N., & Mellon, P. M. (1980). Life and job satisfaction. Is the job central? *Journal of Vocational Behavior, 16,* 51–58.

Schmitt, N., & Noe, R. A. (1986). On shifting standards for conclusions regarding validity generalization. *Personnel Psychology, 39,* 849–851.

Schmitt, N., Noe, R. A., & Gottschalk, R. (1986). Using the Lens model to magnify raters' consistency, matching, and shared bias. *Academy of Management Journal, 29,* 130–139.

Schmitt, N., Noe, R. A., Meritt, R., & Fitzgerald, M. P. (1984). Validity of assessment center ratings for the prediction of performance ratings and school climate of school administrators. *Journal of Applied Psychology, 69,* 207–213.

Schmitt, N. & Ostroff, C. (1986). Operationalizing the "behavioral consistency" approach: Selection test development based on a content-oriented strategy. *Personnel Psychology, 39,* 91–108.

Schmitt, N., Schneider, J. R., & Cohen, S. A. (1990). Factors affecting validity of a regionally administered assessment center. *Personnel Psychology, 43,* 1–12.

Schneider, B. (1985). Organizational behavior. *Annual Review of Psychology, 36,* 573–611.

Schneider, B. (1987). The people make the place. *Personnel Psychology, 40,* 437–453.

Schneider, D. J. (1973). Implicit personality theory: A review. *Psychological Bulletin, 79,* 294–309.

Schneider, J., & Mitchel, J. O. (1980). Functions of life insurance agency managers and relationships with agency characteristics and managerial tenure. *Personnel Psychology, 33,* 795–808.

Schneier, C. E., & Bartol, K. M. (1980). Sex effects in emergent leadership. *Journal of Applied Psychology, 65,* 341–345.

Schoorman, F. D. (1988). Escalation bias in performance appraisals: An unintended consequence of supervisor participation in hiring decisions. *Journal of Applied Psychology, 73,* 58–62.

Schriesheim, C. A., & DeNisi, A. S. (1979). Task dimensions as moderators of the effects of instrumental leader behavior: A path-goal approach. *Proceedings of the Annual Meeting of the Academy of Management* (pp. 103–106).

Schriesheim, C. A., & DeNisi, A. S. (1981). Task dimensions as moderators of the effects of instrumental leadership: A two-sample replicated test of path-goal leadership theory. *Journal of Applied Psychology, 66,* 589–597.

Schriesheim, C. A., Hinkin, T. R., & Podsakoff, P. M. (1991). Can ipsative and single-item measures produce erroneous results in field studies of French and Raven's (1959) five bases of power? An empirical investigation. *Journal of Applied Psychology, 76,* 106–114.

Schriesheim, C. A., & Hosking, D. (1978). Review essay of Fiedler, F. E., Chemers, M. M., & Mahar, L. Improving leadership effectiveness: The leader match concept. *Administrative Science Quarterly, 23,* 496–505.

Schriesheim, C. A., & Kerr, S. (1974). Psychometric properties of the Ohio State leadership scales. *Psychological Bulletin, 81,* 756–765.

Schriesheim, C. A., & Stogdill, R. M. (1975). Differences in factor structure across three versions of the Ohio State leadership scales. *Personnel Psychology, 28,* 189–206.

Schriesheim, J. F. (1980). The social context of leader-subordinate relations: An investigation of the effects of group cohesiveness. *Journal of Applied Psychology, 65,* 183–194.

Schriesheim, J. F., & Schriesheim, C. A. (1980). A test of the path-goal theory of leadership and some suggested directions for future research. *Personnel Psychology, 33,* 349–370.

Schuckman, H. (1987). PhD recipients in psychology and biology: Do those with dissertation advisors of the same sex publish scholarly papers more frequently? *American Psychologist, 42,* 987–992.

Schultz, D. P. (1982). *Psychology and industry today: An introduction to industrial and organizational psychology* (3rd ed.). New York: Macmillan.

Schwab, D. P. (1982). Recruiting and organizational participation. In K. M. Rowland and G. L. Ferris (Eds.), *Personnel management.* Newton, MA: Allyn and Bacon.

Schwab, D. P., & Cummings, L. L. (1976). A theoretical analysis of the impact of task scope on employee performance. *Academy of Management Review, 1,* 23–35.

Schwab, D. P., & Grams, R. (1985). Sex-related errors in job evaluation: A "real-world" test. *Journal of Applied Psychology, 70,* 533–539.

Schwab, D. P., & Heneman, H. G., III. (1986). Assessment of a consensus-based multiple information source job evaluation system. *Journal of Applied Psychology, 71,* 354–356.

Schwab, D. P., Heneman, H. G., III, & DeCotiis, T. A. (1975). Behaviorally anchored rating scales: A review of the literature. *Personnel Psychology, 28,* 549–562.

Schwartz, B. (1984). *Psychology of learning and behavior* (2nd ed.). New York: Norton.

Scott, W. D. (1908). *The psychology of advertising.* New York: Arno.

Scott, W. E., Jr. (1977). Leadership: A functional analysis. In J. G. Hunt & L. L. Larson (Eds.), *Leadership: The cutting edge.* Carbondale: Southern Illinois University Press.

Scott, W. E., Jr., & Erskine, J. A. (1980). The effects of variations in task design and monetary reinforcers on task behavior. *Organizational Behavior and Human Performance, 25,* 311–335.

Scott, W. E., Farh, J., & Podsakoff, P. M. (1988). The effects of "intrinsic" and "extrinsic" reinforcement contingencies on task behavior. *Organizational Behavior and Human Decision Processes, 41,* 405–425.

Scott, W. G., & Mitchell, T. R. (1976). *Organizational theory: A structural and behavioral analysis.* Homewood, IL: Irwin.

Sekimoto, M. (1983). Performance appraisal in Japan: Past and future. *The Industrial-Organizational Psychologist, 20*(4), 52–58.

Seltzer, J., & Numerof, R. E. (1988). Supervisory leadership and subordinate burnout. *Academy of Management Journal, 31,* 439–446.

Senders, J. (1983). On the nature and source of human error. In R. Jensen (Ed.), *Proceedings of the Sencond Symposium on Aviation Psychology.* Columbus: Ohio State University.

Shaffer, D. R., & Tomarelli, M. (1981). Bias in the ivory tower: An unintended consequence of the Buckley Amendment for graduate admissions. *Journal of Applied Psychology, 66,* 7–11.

Shaffer, G. S., Saunders, V., & Owens, W. A. (1986). Additional evidence for the accuracy of biographical data: Long-term retest and observer ratings. *Personnel Psychology, 39,* 791–809.

Shahani, C. (1987). Industrial accidents: Does age matter? *Proceedings of the Human Factors Society 31st Annual Meeting* (pp. 553–557). Santa Monica: Human Factors Society.

Shannon, C., & Weaver, W. (1948). *The mathematical theory of communication.* Urbana: University of Illinois Press.

Shaw, J. B., & Riskind, J. H. (1983). Predicting job stress using data from the Position Analysis Questionnaire. *Journal of Applied Psychology, 68,* 253–261.

Shaw, M. E. (1964). Communication networks. In L. Berkowitz (Ed.), *Advances in experimental social psychology.* New York: Academic Press.

Shein, E. H. (1980). *Organizational psychology* (3rd ed.). Englewood Cliffs, NJ: Prentice-Hall.

Shepperd, J. A. (1991). Cautions in assessing spurious "moderator effects." *Psychological Bulletin, 110,* 315–317.

Sheridan, J. E., Vredenburgh, D. J., & Abelson, M. A.

(1984). Contextual model of leadership influence in hospital units. *Academy of Management Journal, 27,* 57–78.

Shikiar, R., & Freudenberg, R. (1982). Unemployment rates as a moderator of the job dissatisfaction-turnover relation. *Human Relations, 35,* 845–856.

Shimberg, B. (1981). Testing for licensure and certification. *American Psychologist, 36,* 1138–1146.

Shore, L. M., & Thornton, G. C., III. (1986). Effects of gender on self- and supervisory ratings. *Academy of Management Journal, 29,* 115–129.

Shore, T. H., Thornton, G. C., III, & Shore, L. M. (1990). Construct validity of two categories of assessment center dimension ratings. *Personnel Psychology, 43,* 101–116.

Showdown on labor's frontline. (1992, April 20). *Time,* p. 32.

Shrank, R. (1974). Work in America: What do workers really want? *Industrial Relations, 13,* 124–129.

Siegel, A. I. (1983). The miniature job training and evaluation approach: Additional findings. *Personnel Psychology, 36,* 41–56.

Siegel, J., Dubrovsky, V., Kiesler, S., & McGuire, T. W. (1986). Group processes in computer-mediated communication. *Organizational Behavior and Human Decision Processes, 37,* 157–187.

Sigelman, L., Milward, H. B., & Shepard, J. M. (1982). The salary differential between male and female administrators: Equal pay for equal work? *Academy of Management Journal, 25,* 664–671.

Silver, E. M., & Bennett, C. (1987). Modification of the Minnesota Clerical Test to predict performance on video display terminals. *Journal of Applied Psychology, 72,* 153–155.

Silverman, W. H., Dalessio, A., Woods, S. B., & Johnson, R. L., Jr. (1986). Influence of assessment center methods on assessors' ratings. *Personnel Psychology, 39,* 565–578.

Simon, C. W., & Roscoe, S. N. (1956). *Altimetry studies: II. A comparison of integrated versus separated, linear versus circular, and spatial versus numerical displays* (Technical Memorandum 435). Culver City, CA: Hughes Aircraft Co.

Sims, H. P., Jr. (1977). The leader as a manager of reinforcement contingencies: An empirical example and a model. In J. G. Hunt & L. L. Larson (Eds.), *Leadership: The cutting edge.* Carbondale: Southern Illinois University Press.

Sims, H. P., Jr. (1980). Further thoughts on punishment in organizations. *Academy of Management Review, 5,* 133–138.

Sims, H. P., Jr., & Szilagyi, A. D. (1975). Leader reward behavior and subordinate satisfaction and performance. *Organizational Behavior and Human Performance, 14,* 426–437.

Sinclair, R. C. (1988). Mood, categorization breadth, and performance appraisal: The effects of order of information acquisition and affective state on halo, accuracy, information retrieval, and evaluations. *Organizational Behavior and Human Decision Processes, 42,* 22–46.

Singer, M. S., & Sewell, C. (1989). Applicant age and selection interview decisions: Effect of information exposure on age discrimination in personnel selection. *Personnel Psychology, 42,* 135–154.

Singh, R. (1983). Leadership style and reward allocation: Does Least Preferred Co-worker Scale measure task and relation orientation? *Organizational Behavior and Human Performance, 32,* 178–197.

Sivak, M., & Olson, P. (1987). *Toward the development of a field methodology for evaluating discomfort glare from automobile headlamps* (Rept. no. UM-TRI-87–41). Ann Arbor: University of Michigan Transportation Research Institute.

Skinner, B. F. (1953). *Science and human behavior.* New York: Macmillan.

Skinner, B. F. (1959). *Cumulative record.* New York: Appleton-Century-Crofts.

Skinner, B. F. (1969). *Contingencies of reinforcement.* New York: Appleton-Century-Crofts.

Slovic, P., Fischhoff, B., & Lichtenstein, S. (1977). Behavioral decision theory. *Annual Review of Psychology, 28,* 1–39.

Smeltzer, L. R., & Fann, G. L. (1989). Comparison of managerial communication patterns in small, entrepreneurial organizations and large, mature organizations. *Group and Organization Studies, 14,* 198–215.

Smith, B. N., Benson, P. G., & Hornsby, J. S. (1990). The effects of job description content on job evaluation judgments. *Journal of Applied Psychology, 75,* 301–309.

Smith, D. B., & Plant, W. T. (1982), Sex differences in the job satisfaction of university professors. *Journal of Applied Psychology, 67,* 249–251.

Smith, D. E. (1986). Training programs for performance appraisal: A review. *Academy of Management Review, 11,* 22–40.

Smith, J. E., & Hakel, M. D. (1979). Convergence among data sources, response bias, and reliability and validity of a structured job analysis questionnaire. *Personnel Psychology, 32*, 677–692.

Smith, P. C. (1976). Behaviors, results, and organizational effectiveness: The problem of criteria. In M. D. Dunnette (Ed.), *Handbook of industrial and organizational psychology*. Chicago: Rand McNally.

Smith, P. C., & Kendall, L. M. (1963). Retranslation of expectations: An approach to the construction of unambiguous anchors for rating scales. *Journal of Applied Psychology, 47*, 149–155.

Smith, P. C., Kendall, L. M., & Hulin, C. L. (1969). *The measurement of satisfaction in work and retirement: A strategy for the study of attitudes*. Chicago: Rand McNally.

Smither, J. W., Barry, S. R., & Reilly, R. R. (1989). An investigation of the validity of expert true score estimates in appraisal research. *Journal of Applied Psychology, 74*, 143–151.

Smither, J. W., Collins, H., & Buda, R. (1989). When ratee satisfaction influences performance evaluations: A case of illusory correlation. *Journal of Applied Psychology, 74*, 599–605.

Smither, J. W., & Reilly, R. R. (1987). True intercorrelation among job components, time delay in rating, and rater intelligence as determinants of accuracy in performance ratings. *Organizational Behavior and Human Decision Processes, 40*, 369–391.

Smither, J. W., Reilly, R. R., & Buda, R. (1988). Effect of prior performance information on ratings of present performance: Contrast versus assimilation revisited. *Journal of Applied Psychology, 73*, 487–496.

Smither, J. W., Skov, R. B., & Adler, S. (1986). Attributions for the poorly performing blackjack dealer: In the cards or inability? *Personnel Psychology, 39*, 123–139.

Smolowe, J. (1991, October 21). She said, he said. *Time*, pp. 36–40.

Snelgar, R. J. (1983). The comparability of job evaluation methods in supplying approximately similar classifications in rating one job series. *Personnel Psychology, 36*, 371–380.

Snizek, W. E., & Bullard, J. H. (1983). Perception of bureaucracy and changing job satisfaction: A longitudinal analysis. *Organizational Behavior and Human Performance, 32*, 275–287.

Snyderman, M., & Rothman, S. (1987). Survey of expert opinion on intelligence and aptitude testing. *American Psychologist, 42*, 137–144.

Society for Industrial and Organizational Psychology, Inc. (1987). *Principles for the validation and use of personnel selection procedures* (3rd ed.). College Park, MD: Author.

Sonnenfeld, J. (1982). Clarifying critical confusion in the Hawthorne hysteria. *American Psychologist, 37*, 1397–1399.

Sorcher, M., & Spence, R. (1982). The InterFace Project: Behavior modeling as social technology in South Africa. *Personnel Psychology, 35*, 557–581.

Sorenson, W. W. (1966). Test of mechanical principles as a suppressor variable for the prediction of effectiveness on a mechanical repair job. *Journal of Applied Psychology, 50*, 348–352.

Sothmann, M. S., Saupe, K. W., Jasenof, D., Blaney, J., Fuhrman, S. D., Woulfe, T., Raven, P. B., Pawelczyk, J. P., Dotson, C. O., Landy, F. J., Smith, J. J., & Davis, P. O. (1990). Advancing age and the cardiorespiratory stress of fire suppression: Determining a minimum standard for aerobic fitness. *Human Performance, 3*(4), 217–236.

Specialty guidelines for the delivery of services by industrial/organizational psychologists. (1981). *American Psychologist, 36*, 664–669.

Spector, P. E. (1982). Behavior in organizations as a function of employee's locus of control. *Psychological Bulletin, 91*, 482–497.

Spector, P. E., & Levine, E. L. (1987). Meta-analysis for integrating study outcomes: A Monte Carlo study of its susceptibility to Type I and Type II errors. *Journal of Applied Psychology, 72*, 3–9.

Spence, J. T., Helmreich, R. L., & Pred, R. S. (1987). Impatience versus achievement strivings in the Type A pattern: Differential effects on students' health and academic achievement. *Journal of Applied Psychology, 72*, 522–528.

Spence, J. T., Pred, R. S., & Helmreich, R. L. (1989). Achievement strivings, scholastic aptitude, and academic performance: A follow-up to "Impatience versus achievement strivings in the Type A pattern." *Journal of Applied Psychology, 74*, 176–178.

Sprangers, M., & Hoogstraten, J. (1989). Pretesting effects in retrospective pretest-posttest designs. *Journal of Applied Psychology, 74*, 265–272.

Springer, D. (1953). Ratings of candidates for promotion by co-workers and supervisors. *Journal of Applied Psychology, 37,* 347–351.

Sproull, L. S. (1986). Using electronic mail for data collection in organizational research. *Academy of Management Journal, 29,* 159–169.

Srinivas, S., & Motowidlo, S. J. (1987). Effects of raters' stress on the dispersion and favorability of performance ratings. *Journal of Applied Psychology, 72,* 247–251.

Stagner, R. (1982). Past and future of industrial/organizational psychology. *Professional Psychology, 13,* 892–903.

Stagner, R., & Rosen, H. (1965). *Psychology of union-management relations.* Belmont, CA: Wadsworth.

Stahl, M. J. (1983). Achievement, power and managerial motivation: Selecting managerial talent with the Job Choice Exercise. *Personnel Psychology, 36,* 775–789.

Stahl, M. J., & Harrell, A. M. (1981). Modeling effort decisions with behavioral decision theory: Toward an individual differences model of expectancy theory. *Organizational Behavior and Human Performance, 27,* 303–325.

Staines, G. L., & Pleck, J. H. (1986). Work schedule flexibility and family life. *Journal of Occupational Behaviour, 7,* 147–153.

Standards for providers of psychological services. (1977). Washington, DC: American Psychological Association.

Starke, F. A., & Notz, W. W. (1981). Pre- and post-intervention effects of conventional versus final offer arbitration. *Academy of Management Journal, 24,* 832–850.

Staw, B. M. (1981). The escalation of commitment to a course of action. *Academy of Management Review, 6,* 577–587.

Staw, B. M. (1984). Organizational behavior: A review and reformulation of the field's outcome variables. *Annual Review of Psychology, 35,* 627–666.

Staw, B. M., Bell, N. E., & Clausen, J. A. (1986). The dispositional approach to job attitudes: A lifetime longitudinal test. *Administrative Science Quarterly, 31,* 56–77.

Staw, B. M., & Boettger, R. D. (1990). Task revision: A neglected form of work performance. *Academy of Management Journal, 33,* 534–559.

Staw, B. M., & Ross, J. (1985). Stability in the midst of change: A dispositional approach to job attitudes. *Journal of Applied Psychology, 70,* 469–480.

Staw, B. M., Sandelands, L. E., & Dutton, J. E. (1981). Threat-rigidity effects in organizational behavior: A multilevel analysis. *Administrative Science Quarterly, 26,* 501–524

Steel, R. P., & Griffeth, R. W. (1989). The elusive relationship between perceived employment opportunity and turnover behavior: A methodological or conceptual artifact? *Journal of Applied Psychology, 74,* 846–854.

Steel, R. P., & Mento, A. J. (1986). Impact of situational constraints on subjective and objective criteria of managerial job performance. *Organizational Behavior and Human Decision Processes, 37,* 254–265.

Steel, R. P., & Ovalle, N. K., 2nd. (1984). Self-appraisal based upon supervisory feedback. *Personnel Psychology, 37,* 667–685.

Steel, R. P., Shane, G. S., & Griffeth, R. W. (1990). Correcting turnover statistics for comparative analysis. *Academy of Management Journal, 33,* 179–187.

Steers, R. M. (1983). Murray's manifest needs theory. In R. M. Steers & L. W. Porter (Eds.), *Motivation and work behavior* (3rd ed.). New York: McGraw-Hill.

Steers, R. M., & Mowday, R. T. (1981). Employee turnover and post-decision accommodation processes. In L. L. Cummings and B. M. Staw (Eds.), *Research in Organizational Behavior* (Vol. 3). Greenwich, CT: JAI Press.

Steers, R. M., & Porter, L. W. (1983). *Motivation and work behavior* (3rd ed.). New York: McGraw-Hill.

Steers, R. M., & Porter, L. W. (1991). *Motivation and work behavior* (5th ed.). New York: McGraw-Hill.

Steers, R. M., & Rhodes, S. R. (1978). Major influences on employee attendance: A process model. *Journal of Applied Psychology, 63,* 391–407.

Steffy, B. D., & Maurer, S. D. (1988). Conceptualizing and measuring the economic effectiveness of human resource activities. *Academy of Management Review, 13,* 271–286.

Stein, R. T., & Heller, T. (1979). An empirical analysis of the correlations between leadership status and participation rates reported in the literature. *Journal of Personality and Social Psychology, 37,* 1993–2002.

Steiner, D. D., & Rain, J. S. (1989). Immediate and delayed primacy and recency effects in performance evaluation. *Journal of Applied Psychology, 74,* 136–142.

Steiner, D. D., & Truxillo, D. M. (1987). Another look at the job satisfaction-life satisfaction relationship: A test of the disaggregation hypothesis. *Journal of Occupational Behaviour, 8,* 71–77.

Steiner, D. D., & Truxillo, D. M. (1989). An improved test of the disaggregation hypothesis of job and life satisfaction. *Journal of Occupational Psychology, 62,* 33–39.

Sterrett, J. H. (1978). The job interview: Body language and perceptions of potential effectiveness. *Journal of Applied Psychology, 63,* 388–390.

Stevens, G. E., & Brenner, O. C. (1990). An empirical investigation of the motivation to manage among Blacks and women in business school. *Educational and Psychological Measurement, 50,* 879–866.

Stevens, S. S. (1946). On the theory of scales of measurement. *Science, 103,* 670–680.

Stevens, S. S. (1951). *Handbook of experimental psychology.* New York: Wiley.

Stewart, R. (1982). The relevance of some studies of managerial work and behavior to leadership research. In J. G. Hunt, U. Sekaran, & C. A. Schriesheim (Eds.), *Leadership: Beyond establishment views.* Carbondale: Southern Illinois University Press.

Stogdill, R. M. (1948). Personal factors associated with leadership: A survey of the literature. *Journal of Psychology, 25,* 35–71.

Stogdill, R. M. (1959). *Individual behavior and group achievement.* New York: Oxford University Press.

Stogdill, R. M. (1963). *Manual for the Leader Behavior Description Questionnaire—Form XII.* Columbus: Bureau of Business Research, Ohio State University.

Stogdill, R. M. (1974). *Handbook of leadership.* New York: Free Press.

Stone, D. L., Gueutal, H. G., & McIntosh, B. (1984). The effects of feedback sequence and expertise of the rater on perceived feedback accuracy. *Personnel Psychology, 37,* 487–506.

Stone, D. L., & Kotch, D. A. (1989). Individuals' attitudes toward organizational drug testing policies and practices. *Journal of Applied Psychology, 74,* 518–521.

Stone, D. L., & Stone, E. F. (1985). The effects of feedback consistency and feedback favorability on self-perceived task competence and perceived feedback accuracy. *Organizational Be-*

havior and Human Decision Processes, 36, 167–185.

Stone, E. F. (1974). *The moderating effect of work related values on the job scope-job satisfaction relationship.* Unpublished doctoral dissertation, University of California, Irvine.

Stone, E. F., & Gueutal, H. G. (1985). An empirical derivation of the dimensions along which characteristics of jobs are perceived. *Academy of Management Journal, 28,* 376–396.

Stone, E. F., Gueutal, H. G., Gardner, D. G., & McClure, S. (1983). A field experiment comparing information-privacy values, beliefs, and attitudes across several types of organizations. *Journal of Applied Psychology, 68,* 459–468.

Stone, E. F., & Hollenbeck, J. R. (1984). Some issues associated with the use of moderated regression. *Organizational Behavior and Human Performance, 34,* 195–213.

Stone, E. F., & Hollenbeck, J. R. (1989). Clarifying some controversial issues surrounding statistical procedures for detecting moderator variables: Empirical evidence and related matters. *Journal of Applied Psychology, 74,* 3–10.

Strasser, S., & Bateman, T. S. (1984). What we should study, problems we should solve: Perspectives of two constituencies. *Personnel Psychology, 37,* 77–92.

Stroh, L. K., Brett, J. M., & Reilly, A. H. (1992). All the right stuff: A comparison of female and male managers' career progression. *Journal of Applied Psychology, 77,* 251–260.

Strube, M. J., & Garcia, J. E. (1981). A meta-analytic investigation of Fiedler's contingency model of leadership effectiveness. *Psychological Bulletin, 90,* 307–321.

Strube, M. J., & Garcia, J. E. (1983). On the proper interpretation of empirical findings: Strube and Garcia (1981) revisited. *Psychological Bulletin, 93,* 600–603.

Stumpf, S. A., & Hartman, K. (1984). Individual exploration to organizational commitment or withdrawal. *Academy of Management Journal, 27,* 308–329.

Stumpf, S. A., & London, M. (1981). Management promotions: Individual and organizational factors influencing the decision process. *Academy of Management Review, 6,* 539–549.

Sturgis, S. P., Pulling, N. H., & Vaillancourt, D. R. (1981). Measuring drivers' glare sensitivity:

Evaluation of an automated technique. *Journal of Applied Psychology, 66,* 97–101.

Sullivan, J. J. (1983). A critique of Theory Z. *Academy of Management Review, 8,* 132–142.

Sulsky, L. M., & Balzer, W. K. (1988). Meaning and measurement of performance rating accuracy: Some methodological and theoretical concerns. *Journal of Applied Psychology, 73,* 497–506.

Summers, L. S. (1984). When in Cairo . . . : Applying I/O psychology in the Middle East. *Industrial-Organizational Psychologist, 22*(1), 26–30.

Sussman, M., & Robertson, D. U. (1986). The validity of validity: An analysis of validation study designs. *Journal of Applied Psychology, 71,* 461–468.

Swaroff, P. G., Barclay, L. A., & Bass, A. R. (1985). Recruiting sources: Another look. *Journal of Applied Psychology, 70,* 720–728.

Swim, J., Borgida, E., Maruyama, G., & Myers, D. G. (1989). Joan McKay versus John McKay: Do gender stereotypes bias evaluations? *Psychological Bulletin, 105,* 409–429.

Szilagyi, A. D., & Sims, H. P. (1974). An exploration of the path-goal theory of leadership in a health care environment. *Academy of Management Journal, 17,* 622–634.

Szilagyi, A. D., Jr., & Wallace, M. J., Jr. (1987). *Organizational behavior and performance* (4th ed.). Glenview, IL: Scott, Foresman.

Taber, T. D., Beehr, T. A., & Walsh, J. T. (1985). Relationships between job evaluation ratings and self-ratings of job characteristics. *Organizational Behavior and Human Decision Processes, 35,* 27–45.

Tait, M., Padgett, M. Y., & Baldwin, T. T. (1989). Job and life satisfaction: A reevaluation of the strength of the relationship and gender effects as a function of the date of the study. *Journal of Applied Psychology, 74,* 502–507.

Tannenbaum, S. I., & Yukl, G. (1992). Training and development in work organizations. *Annual Review of Psychology, 43,* 399–441.

Taylor, F. W. (1911). *The principles of scientific management.* New York: Harper and Brothers.

Taylor, H. C., & Russell, J. T. (1939). The relationship of validity coefficients to the practical effectiveness of tests in selection: Discussion and tables. *Journal of Applied Psychology, 23,* 565–578.

Taylor, M. S. (1983). *A control theory integration of performance goal and performance feedback research: Current findings, practical implications and future research issues.* Symposium presented at the meeting of the Academy of Management, Dallas.

Taylor, M. S., & Bergmann, T. J. (1987). Organizational recruitment activities and applicants' reactions at different stages of the recruitment process. *Personnel Psychology, 40,* 261–285.

Taylor, M. S., Locke, E. A., Lee, C., & Gist, M. E. (1984). Type A behavior and faculty research productivity: What are the mechanisms? *Organizational Behavior and Human Performance, 34,* 402–418.

Taylor, M. S., & Schmidt, D. W. (1983). A process-oriented investigation of recruitment source effectiveness. *Personnel Psychology, 36,* 343–354.

Taylor, P. J. (1967). Shift and day work: A comparison of sickness, absence, illness, lateness, and other absence behavior at an oil refinery from 1962 to 1965. *British Journal of Industrial Medicine, 24,* 93–102.

Tellegen, A. (1982). *Brief manual for the Differential Personality Questionnaire.* Unpublished manuscript, University of Minnesota, Minneapolis.

Tellegen, A. (1985). Structures of mood and personality and their relevance to assessing anxiety, with an emphasis on self-report. In A. H. Tuma & J. D. Master (Eds.), *Anxiety and the anxiety disorders,* Hillsdale, NJ: Erlbaum.

Tellegen, A., Lykken, D. T., Bouchard, T. J., Jr., Wilcox, K. J., Segal, N. L., & Rich, S. (1988). Personality similarity in twins reared apart and together. *Journal of Personality and Social Psychology, 54,* 1031–1039.

Tenopyr, M. L. (1977). Content-construct confusion. *Personnel Psychology, 30,* 47–54.

Tenopyr, M. L. (1981). Trifling he stands. *Personnel Psychology, 34,* 1–17.

Tenopyr, M. L. (1988). Artifactual reliability of forced-choice scales. *Journal of Applied Psychology, 73,* 749–751.

Tenopyr, M. S., & Oeltjen, P. D. (1982). Personnel selection and classification. *Annual Review of Psychology, 33,* 581–618.

Terpstra, D. E. (1981). Relationship between methodological rigor and reported outcomes in organization development evaluation research. *Journal of Applied Psychology, 66,* 541–543.

Tetrick, L. E., Thacker, J. W., & Fields, M. W. (1989). Evidence for the stability of the four dimensions of the commitment to the union scale. *Journal of Applied Psychology, 74,* 819–822.

Thacker, J. W., Fields, M. W., & Barclay, L. A. (1990). Union commitment: An examination of antecedent and outcome factors. *Journal of Occupational Psychology, 63,* 33–48.

Thacker, J. W., Fields, M. W., & Tetrick, L. E. (1989). The factor structure of union commitment: An application of confirmatory factor analysis. *Journal of Applied Psychology, 74,* 228–232.

Thayer, P. W., & McGehee, W. (1977). On the effectiveness of not holding a formal training course. *Personnel Psychology, 30,* 455–456.

Thomas, H. (1988). What is the interpretation of the validity generalization estimate $S_p^2 = S_R^2 - S_E^2$? *Journal of Applied Psychology, 73,* 679–682.

Thomas, H. (1990). A likelihood-based model for validity generalization. *Journal of Applied Psychology, 75,* 13–20.

Thompson, D. E., & Thompson, T. A. (1985). Task-based performance appraisal for blue-collar jobs: Evaluation of race and sex effects. *Journal of Applied Psychology, 70,* 747–753.

Thorndike, R. L. (1949). *Personnel selection: Test and measurement techniques.* New York: Wiley.

Thornton, G. C., III. (1980). Psychometric properties of self-appraisals of job performance. *Personnel Psychology, 33,* 263–271.

Thornton, G. C., III, & Cleveland, J. N. (1990). Developing managerial talent through simulation. *American Psychologist, 45,* 190–199.

Tiffin, J. (1942). *Industrial psychology.* New York: Prentice-Hall.

Tilgher, A. (1930). *Work: What it has meant to men through the ages.* New York: Harcourt, Brace and World.

Tjosvold, D. (1982). Effects of approach to controversy on superiors' incorporation of subordinates' information in decision making. *Journal of Applied Psychology, 67,* 189–193.

Tjosvold, D., Wedley, W. C., & Field, R. H. (1986). Constructive controversy, the Vroom-Yetton model, and managerial decision-making. *Journal of Occupational Behaviour, 7,* 125–138.

Toch, H. (1982). Sed qui dicit, non qui negat? *American Psychologist, 37,* 855.

Tolchinsky, P. D., McCuddy, M. K., Adams, J., Ganster, D. C., Woodman, R. W., & Fromkin, H. L. (1981). Employee perceptions of invasion of privacy: A field simulation experiment. *Journal of Applied Psychology, 66,* 308–313.

Torrance, E. P. (1953). Methods of conducting critiques of group problem-solving performance. *Journal of Applied Psychology, 37,* 394–398.

Toufexis, A. (1991, October 28). When can memories be trusted? *Time,* pp. 86–88.

Trattner, M. H. (1982). Synthetic validity and its application to the Uniform Guidelines validation requirements. *Personnel Psychology, 35,* 383–397.

Travers, R. M. W. (1951). A critical review of the validity and rationale of the forced-choice technique. *Psychological Bulletin, 48,* 62–70.

Tsui, A. S. (1984). A role set analysis of managerial reputation. *Organizational Behavior and Human Performance, 34,* 64–96.

Tsui, A. S., & Barry, B. (1986). Interpersonal affect and rating errors. *Academy of Management Journal, 29,* 586–599.

Tsui, A. S., & Ohlott, P. (1988). Multiple assessment of managerial effectiveness: Interrater agreement and consensus in effectiveness models. *Personnel Psychology, 41,* 779–803.

Tsui, A. S., & O'Reilly, C. A., III. (1989). Beyond simple demographic effects: The importance of relational demography in superior-subordinate dyads. *Academy of Management Journal, 32,* 402–423.

Tubbs, M. E. (1986). Goal setting: A meta-analytic examination of the empirical evidence. *Journal of Applied Psychology 71,* 474–483.

Tubiana, J. H., & Ben-Shakhar, G. (1982). An objective group questionnaire as a substitute for a personal interview in the prediction of success in military training in Israel. *Personnel Psychology, 35,* 349–357.

Turban, D. B., & Jones, A. P. (1988). Supervisor-subordinate similarity: Types, effects, and mechanisms. *Journal of Applied Psychology, 73,* 228–234.

Turnage, J. J., & Muchinsky, P. M. (1982). Transsituational variability in human performance within assessment centers. *Organizational Behavior and Human Performance, 30,* 174–200.

Turnage, J. J., & Muchinsky, P. M. (1984). A comparison of the predictive validity of assessment center evaluations versus traditional measures in forecasting supervisory job performance: Interpretive implications of criterion distortion for the assessment paradigm. *Journal of Applied Psychology, 69,* 595–602.

Turner, A. N., & Lawrence, P. R. (1965). *Industrial jobs and the worker: An investigation of response to task attributes*. Boston: Division of Research, Graduate School of Business Administration, Harvard University.

Tushman, M. L., & Scanlan, T. J. (1981). Boundary spanning individuals: Their role in information transfer and their antecedents. *Academy of Management Journal, 24*, 289–305.

Tversky, A. (1969). Intransitivity of preferences. *Psychological Review, 76*, 31–48.

Tziner, A., & Dolan, S. (1982). Validity of an assessment center for identifying future female officers in the military. *Journal of Applied Psychology, 67*, 728–736.

Tziner, A., & Kopelman, R. (1988). Effects of rating format on goal-setting dimensions: A field experiment. *Journal of Applied Psychology, 73*, 323–326.

Tziner, A., & Vardi, Y. (1982). Effects of command style and group cohesiveness on the performance effectiveness of self-selected tank crews. *Journal of Applied Psychology, 67*, 769–775.

U.S. Bureau of the Census. (1975). *Historical statistics of the United States, colonial times to 1970, Bicentennial edition, Part 1*. Washington, DC: U.S. Government Printing Office.

U.S. Bureau of the Census. (1993). *Statistical abstract of the United States: 1993*. Washington, DC: U.S. Government Printing Office.

U.S. Civil Service Commission. (1970). *Programmed instruction: A brief evaluation of its development and current status*. Washington, DC: U.S. Government Printing Office.

U.S. Department of Labor, Employment and Training Administration. (1991). *Dictionary of occupational titles* (5th ed.). Washington, DC: U.S. Government Printing Office.

U.S. Department of Labor. (1986). *Employment and earnings, 33*(1). Washington, DC: U.S. Government Printing Office.

Ulrich, L., & Trumbo, D. (1965). The selection interview since 1949. *Psychological Bulletin, 63*, 100–116.

Umstot, D. D., Bell, C. H., Jr., & Mitchell, T. R. (1976). Effects of job enrichment and task goals on satisfaction and productivity: Implications for job design. *Journal of Applied Psychology, 61*, 379–394.

Umstot, D., Mitchell, T. R., & Bell, C. H., Jr. (1978). Goal setting and job enrichment: An integrated approach to job design. *Academy of Management Review, 3*, 867–879.

Unbecoming an officer. (1991, September 30). *Time*, p. 52.

Using the Managerial Grid to ensure MBO. (1974). *Organizational Dynamics, 2*(4), 54–65.

Vale, C. D., Keller, L. S., & Bentz, V. J. (1986). Development and validation of a computerized interpretation system for personnel tests. *Personnel Psychology, 39*, 525–542.

Valenzi, E. R., & Andrews, I. R. (1971). Effect of hourly overpay and underpay inequity when tested with a new induction procedure. *Journal of Applied Psychology, 55*, 22–27.

Van de Vliert, E., Huismans, S. E., & Stok, J. J. L. (1985). The criterion approach to unraveling beta and alpha change. *Academy of Management Review, 10*, 269–275.

Vance, R. J., & Colella, A. (1990). The utility of utility analysis. *Human Performance, 3*(2), 123–139.

Vance, R. J., Coovert, M. D., MacCallum, R. C., & Hedge, J. W. (1989). Construct models of task performance. *Journal of Applied Psychology, 74*, 447–455.

Vance, R. J., MacCallum, R. C., Coovert, M. D., & Hedge, J. W. (1988). Construct validity of multiple job performance measures using confirmatory factor analysis. *Journal of Applied Psychology, 73*, 74–80.

Vandenberg, R. J., & Scarpello, V. (1990). The matching model: An examination of the processes underlying realistic job previews. *Journal of Applied Psychology, 75*, 60–67.

Vardi, Y., Shirom, A., & Jacobson, D. (1980). A study of the leadership beliefs of Israeli managers. *Academy of Management Journal, 23*, 367–374.

Vecchio, R. P. (1977). An empirical examination of the validity of Fiedler's model of leadership effectiveness. *Organizational Behavior and Human Performance, 19*, 180–206.

Vecchio, R. P. (1981). An individual-differences interpretation on the conflicting predictions generated by equity theory and expectancy theory. *Journal of Applied Psychology, 66*, 470–481.

Vecchio, R. P. (1982). A further test of leadership effects due to between-group variation and within-group variation. *Journal of Applied Psychology, 67*, 200–208.

Vecchio, R. P. (1983). Assessing the validity of Fiedler's contingency model of leadership effectiveness: A closer look at Strube and Garcia. *Psychological Bulletin, 93*, 404–408.

Vecchio, R. P. (1985). Predicting employee turnover from leader-member exchange: A failure to replicate. *Academy of Management Journal, 28,* 478–485.

Vecchio, R. P. (1988). Cognitive resource theory: Successor to the "black box" model of leadership. *Contemporary Psychology, 33,* 1030–1032.

Vecchio, R. P. (1990). Theoretical and empirical examination of cognitive resource theory. *Journal of Applied Psychology, 75,* 141–147.

Vecchio, R. P. (1992). Cognitive resource theory: Issues for specifying a test of the theory. *Journal of Applied Psychology, 77,* 375–376.

Victor, B., & Cullen, J. B. (1988). The organizational bases of ethical work climates. *Administrative Science Quarterly, 33,* 101–125.

Vinchur, A. J., Schippmann, J. S., Smalley, M. D., & Rothe, H. F. (1991). Productivity consistency of foundry chippers and grinders: A 6–year field study. *Journal of Applied Psychology, 76,* 134–136.

Vineberg, R., & Joyner, J. N. (1982). *Prediction of job performance: Review of military studies.* Alexandria, VA: Human Resources Research Organization.

Viteles, M. S. (1932). *Industrial psychology.* New York: Norton.

Viteles, M. S. (1934). *The science of work.* New York: Norton.

Vogel, W. (1982). A Judeo-Christian rejoinder to Bramel and Friend's Marxist critique of the capitalist "Hawthorne effect." *American Psychologist, 37,* 859–860.

Vroom, V. H. (1964). *Work and motivation.* New York: Wiley.

Vroom, V. H. (1976). Leadership. In M. D. Dunnette (Ed.), *Handbook of industrial and organizational psychology.* Chicago: Rand McNally.

Vroom, V. H., & Jago, A. G. (1988). *The new leadership: Managing participation in organizations.* Englewood Cliffs, NJ: Prentice-Hall.

Vroom, V. H., & Yetton, P. W. (1973). *Leadership and decision-making.* Pittsburgh: University of Pittsburgh Press.

Wagner, J. A., & Gooding, R. Z. (1987). Shared influence and organizational behavior: A meta-analysis of situational variables expected to moderate participation-outcome relationships. *Academy of Management Journal, 30,* 524–541.

Wagner, R. (1949). The employment interview: A critical summary. *Personnel Psychology, 2,* 17–46.

Wahba, M. A., & Bridwell, L. B. (1976). Maslow reconsidered: A review of research on the need hierarchy theory. *Organizational Behavior and Human Performance, 15,* 212–240.

Wakabayashi, M., & Graen, G. B. (1984). The Japanese career progress study: A 7–year follow-up. *Journal of Applied Psychology, 69,* 603–614.

Walberg, H. J., & Haertel, E. H. (Eds.). (1980). Research integration: The state of the art [Special issue]. *Evaluation in Education: An International Review Service, 4.*

Waldman, D. A., & Avolio, B. J. (1986). A meta-analysis of age differences in job performance. *Journal of Applied Psychology, 71,* 33–38.

Waldman, D. A., & Avolio, B. J. (1989). Homogeneity of test validity. *Journal of Applied Psychology, 74,* 371–374.

Waldman, D. A., Yammarino, F. J., & Avolio, B. J. (1990). A multiple level investigation of personnel ratings. *Personnel Psychology, 43,* 811–835.

Wall, T. D., & Payne, R. (1973). Are deficiency scores deficient? *Journal of Applied Psychology, 58,* 322–326.

Walter, G. A., & Pinder, C. C. (1980). Ethical ascendance or backsliding? *American Psychologist, 35,* 936–937.

Walton, R. E. (1975). The diffusion of new work structures: Explaining why success didn't take. *Organizational Dynamics, 3*(3), 2–22.

Wanous, J. P. (1974a). A causal-correlational analysis of the job satisfaction and performance relationship. *Journal of Applied Psychology, 59,* 138–144.

Wanous, J. P. (1974b). Individual differences and reactions to job characteristics. *Journal of Applied Psychology, 59,* 616–622.

Wanous, J. P. (1989). Installing a realistic job preview: Ten tough choices. *Personnel Psychology, 42,* 117–134.

Wanous, J. P., Keon, T. L., & Latack, J. C. (1983). Expectancy theory and occupational/organizational choices: A review and test. *Organizational Behavior and Human Performance, 32,* 66–86.

Wanous, J. P., & Lawler, E. E., III (1972). Measurement and meaning of job satisfaction. *Journal of Applied Psychology, 56,* 95–105.

Wanous, J. P., & Zwany, A. (1977). A cross-sectional test of need hierarchy theory. *Organizational Behavior and Human Performance, 18,* 78–97.

Watson, C. J. (1981). An evaluation of some aspects of the Steers and Rhodes model of employee attendance. *Journal of Applied Psychology, 66,* 385–389.

Watson, D., & Clark, L. A. (1984). Negative affectivity: The disposition to experience aversive emotional states. *Psychological Bulletin, 96,* 465–490.

Watson, D., & Clark, L. A. (1991). Self- versus peer ratings of specific emotional traits: Evidence of convergent and discriminant validity. *Journal of Personality and Social Psychology, 60,* 927–940.

Watson, K. M. (1982). An analysis of communication patterns: A method for discriminating leader and subordinate roles. *Academy of Management Journal, 25,* 107–120.

Wayne, S. J., & Kacmar, K. M. (1991). The effects of impression management on the performance appraisal process. *Organizational Behavior and Human Decision Processes, 48,* 70–88.

Weaver, C. N. (1977). Relationships among pay, race, sex, occupational prestige, supervision, work autonomy, and job satisfaction in a national sample. *Personnel Psychology, 30,* 437–445.

Weaver, C. N. (1978a). Black-white correlates of job satisfaction. *Journal of Applied Psychology, 63,* 255–258.

Weaver, C. N. (1978b). Sex differences in the determinants of job satisfaction. *Academy of Management Journal, 21,* 265–274.

Weaver, C. N. (1980). Job satisfaction in the United States in the 1970s. *Journal of Applied Psychology, 65,* 364–367.

Weber, M. (1947). *The theory of social and economic organization.* (A. M. Henderson & T. Parsons, Trans.). New York: Oxford University Press.

Wedderburn, A. A. I. (1978). Some suggestions for increasing the usefulness of psychological and sociological studies of shiftwork. *Ergonomics, 21,* 827–833.

Weed, S. E., & Mitchell, T. R. (1980). The role of environment and behavioral uncertainty as a mediator of situation-performance relationships. *Academy of Management Journal, 23,* 38–60.

Weekley, J. A., & Gier, J. A. (1987). Reliability and validity of the situational interview for a sales position. *Journal of Applied Psychology, 72,* 484–487.

Weekley, J. A., & Gier, J. A. (1989). Ceilings in the reliability and validity of performance ratings: The case of expert raters. *Academy of Management Journal, 32,* 213–222.

Weekley, J. A., Frank, B., O'Connor, E. J., & Peters,

L. H. (1985). A comparison of three methods of estimating the standard deviation of performance in dollars. *Journal of Applied Psychology, 70,* 122–126.

Weiner, N. (1980). Determinants and behavioral consequences of pay satisfaction: A comparison of two models. *Personnel Psychology, 33,* 741–757.

Weiss, D. J., Dawis, R. V., England, G. W., & Lofquist, L. H. (1967). *Manual for the Minnesota Satisfaction Questionnaire* (Minnesota Studies on Vocational Rehabilitation, vol. 22). Minneapolis: Industrial Relations Center, Work Adjustment Project, University of Minnesota.

Weiss, H. M. (1977). Subordinate imitation of supervisor behavior: The role of modeling in organizational socialization. *Organizational Behavior and Human Performance, 19,* 89–105.

Weiss, H. M. (1978). Social learning of work values in organizations. *Journal of Applied Psychology, 63,* 711–718.

Weiss, H. M., & Shaw, J. B. (1979). Social influences on judgments about tasks. *Organizational Behavior and Human Performance, 24,* 126–140.

Wells, D. L., & Muchinsky, P. M. (1985). Performance antecedents of voluntary and involuntary managerial turnover. *Journal of Applied Psychology, 70,* 329–336.

Wells, W. D., & Smith, G. (1960). Four semantic rating scales compared. *Journal of Applied Psychology, 44,* 393–397.

Wexley, K. N. (1984). Personnel training. *Annual Review of Psychology, 35,* 519–551.

Wexley, K. N., & Latham, G. P. (1991). *Developing and training human resources in organizations* (2nd ed.). New York: HarperCollins.

Wexley, K. N., & Pulakos, E. D. (1982). Sex effects on performance ratings in manager-subordinate dyads: A field study. *Journal of Applied Psychology, 67,* 433–439.

Wexley, K. N., & Yukl, G. A. (1984). *Organizational behavior and personnel psychology* (rev. ed.). Homewood, IL: Irwin.

What's the big deal? (1992, May 11). *Time,* p. 16.

Where Skinner's theories work. (1972, December 2). *Business Week,* 64–65.

Wherry, R. J. (1950). *The control of bias in rating: Survey of the literature* (Tech. Rep. DA-49-0853 OSA 69). Washington, DC: Department of the Army, Personnel Research Section.

White, J. E. (1991, October 21). The stereotypes of race. *Time*, p. 66.

White, J. K. (1978). Individual differences and the job quality-worker response relationship: Review, integration, and comments. *Academy of Management Review, 3*, 267–280.

White, M. C., Crino, M. D., & DeSanctis, G. L. (1981). A critical review of female performance, performance training and organizational initiatives designed to aid women in the work-role environment. *Personnel Psychology, 34*, 227–248.

Whitehead, T. N. (1938). *The industrial worker.* Cambridge: Harvard University Press.

Whitely, W., Dougherty, T. W., & Dreher, G. F. (1991). Relationship of career mentoring and socioeconomic origin to managers' and professionals' early career progress. *Academy of Management Journal, 34*, 331–351.

Whitener, E. M. (1990). Confusion of confidence intervals and credibility intervals in meta-analysis. *Journal of Applied Psychology, 75*, 315–321.

Wiard, H. (1972, Summer). Why manage behavior? A case for positive reinforcement. *Human Resource Management, 11*, 15–20.

Wickens, C. D. (1992). *Engineering psychology and human performance* (2nd ed.). New York: HarperCollins.

Wiener, Y. (1970). The effects of "task-" and "ego-oriented" performance on 2 kinds of overcompensation inequity. *Organizational Behavior and Human Performance, 5*, 191–208.

Wiersma, U., & Latham, G. P. (1986). The practicality of behavioral observation scales, behavioral expectation scales, and trait scales. *Personnel Psychology, 39*, 619–628.

Wiley, M. G., & Eskilson, A. (1982). The interaction of sex and power base on perceptions of managerial effectiveness. *Academy of Management Journal, 25*, 671–677.

Williams, K. J., DeNisi, A. S., Blencoe, A. G., & Cafferty, T. P. (1985). The role of appraisal purpose: Effects of purpose on information acquisition and utilization. *Organizational Behavior and Human Decision Processes, 35*, 314–339.

Williams, K. J., DeNisi, A. S., Meglino, B. M., & Cafferty, T. P. (1986). Initial decisions and subsequent performance ratings. *Journal of Applied Psychology, 71*, 189–195.

Williams, R. (1961). *The long revolution.* London: Chatto and Windus.

Wilpert, B. (1982). Various paths beyond establishment views. In J. G. Hunt, U. Sekaran, & C. A. Schriesheim (Eds.), *Leadership: Beyond establishment views.* Carbondale: Southern Illinois University Press.

Wilpert, B. (1983). I/O psychology in Germany: Recent developments and trends. *Industrial-Organizational Psychologist, 20*(3), 38–42.

Wilson, M. A., Harvey, R. J., & Macy, B. A. (1990). Repeating items to estimate the test-retest reliability of task inventory ratings. *Journal of Applied Psychology, 75*, 158–163.

Wing, J. F. (1965). *A review of the effects of high ambient temperature on mental performance* (TR 65–102). U.S. Air Force, AMRL.

Winter, D. G. (1978). *Navy leadership and management competencies: Convergence among tests, interviews, and performance ratings.* Boston: McBer.

Wood, R., Bandura, A., & Bailey, T. (1990). Mechanisms governing organizational performance in complex decision-making environments. *Organizational Behavior and Human Decision Processes, 46*, 181–201.

Wood, R. E., Mento, A. J., & Locke, E. A. (1987). Task complexity as a moderator of goal effects: A meta-analysis. *Journal of Applied Psychology, 72*, 416–425.

Woodman, R. W., & Sherwood, J. J. (1980). The role of team development in organizational effectiveness: A critical review. *Psychological Bulletin, 88*, 166–186.

Woodman, R. W., & Wayne, S. J. (1985). An investigation of positive-findings bias in evaluation of organization development interventions. *Academy of Management Journal, 28*, 889–913.

Wright, O. R. (1969). Summary of research on the selection interview since 1964. *Personnel Psychology, 22*, 341–413.

Wright, P. M. (1990). Operationalization of goal difficulty as a moderator of the goal difficulty-performance relationship. *Journal of Applied Psychology, 75*, 227–234.

Wright, R. L. D. (1976). *Understanding statistics: An informal introduction for the behavioral sciences.* New York: Harcourt Brace Jovanovich.

Yeager, S. J. (1981). Dimensionality of the Job Descriptive Index. *Academy of Management Journal, 24*, 205–212.

Yorks, L., & Whitsett, D. A. (1985). Hawthorne, Topeka, and the issue of science versus advocacy in organizational behavior. *Academy of Management Review, 10,* 21–30.

Young, F. W. (1984). Scaling. *Annual Review of Psychology, 35,* 55–81.

Youngblood, S. A., Mobley, W. H., & Meglino, B. M. (1983). A longitudinal analysis of the turnover process. *Journal of Applied Psychology, 68,* 507–516.

Yukl, G. A. (1981). *Leadership in organizations.* Englewood Cliffs, NJ: Prentice-Hall.

Yukl, G. A. (1989). *Leadership in organizations* (2nd ed.). Englewood Cliffs, NJ: Prentice-Hall.

Yukl, G. A., & Latham, G. P. (1975). Consequences of reinforcement schedules and incentive magnitudes for employee performance: Problems encountered in an industrial setting. *Journal of Applied Psychology, 60,* 294–298.

Yukl, G. A., Latham, G. P., & Pursell, E. D. (1976). The effectiveness of performance incentives under continuous and variable ratio schedules of reinforcement. *Personnel Psychology, 29,* 221–231.

Zaccaro, S. J., Foti, R. J., & Kenny, D. A. (1991). Self-monitoring and trait-based variance in leadership: An investigation of leader flexibility across multiple group situations. *Journal of Applied Psychology, 76,* 308–315.

Zaccaro, S. J., & Stone, E. F. (1988). Incremental validity of an empirically based measure of job characteristics. *Journal of Applied Psychology, 73,* 245–252.

Zaharia, E. S., & Baumeister, A. A. (1981). Job preview effects during the critical initial employment period. *Journal of Applied Psychology, 66,* 19–22.

Zalesny, M. D. (1985). Comparison of economic and noneconomic factors in predicting faculty vote preference in a union representation election. *Journal of Applied Psychology, 70,* 243–256.

Zalesny, M. D. (1990). Rater confidence and social influence in performance appraisals. *Journal of Applied Psychology, 75,* 274–289.

Zavala, A. (1965). Development of the forced-choice rating scale technique. *Psychological Bulletin, 63,* 117–124.

Zedeck, S., & Cascio, W. F. (1984). Psychological issues in personnel decisions. *Annual Review of Psychology, 35,* 461–518.

Zedeck, S., Imparato, N., Krausz, M., & Oleno, T. (1974). Development of behaviorally anchored rating scales as a function of organizational level. *Journal of Applied Psychology, 59,* 249–252.

Zedeck, S., Jackson, S. E., & Summers, E. (1983). Shift work schedules and their relationship to health, adaptation, satisfaction, and turnover intention. *Academy of Management Journal, 26,* 297–310.

Zedeck, S., Tziner, A., & Middlestadt, S. E. (1983). Interviewer validity and reliability: An individual analysis approach. *Personnel Psychology, 36,* 355–370.

Zeidner, M. (1987). Test of the cultural bias hypothesis: Some Israeli findings. *Journal of Applied Psychology, 72,* 38–48.

Zelko, H. P. (1967). The lecture. In R. L. Craig & L. R. Bittel (Eds.), *Training and development handbook.* New York: McGraw-Hill.

Zerbe, W. J., & Paulhus, D. L. (1987). Socially desirable responding in organizational behavior: A reconception. *Academy of Management Review, 12,* 250–264.

Zohar, D. (1980). Safety climate in industrial organizations: Theoretical and applied implications. *Journal of Applied Psychology, 65,* 96–102.

SUBJECT INDEX

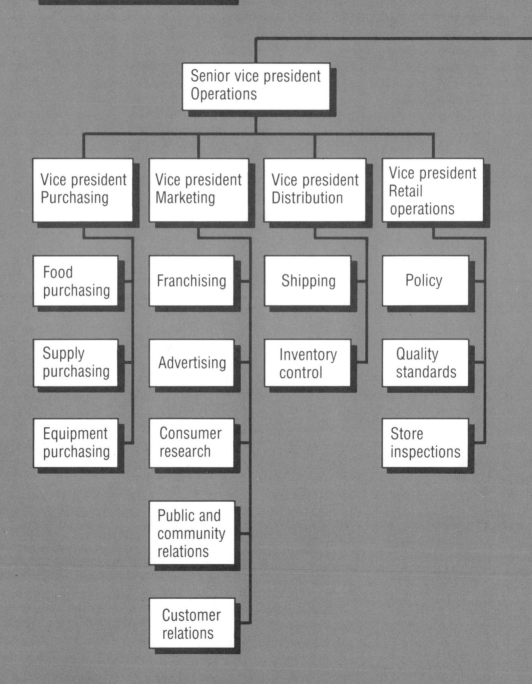

Professional services:
Human-resources coordinator
Data processing
Legal counsel

Senior vice president
Operations

Vice president
Purchasing

Vice president
Marketing

Vice president
Distribution

Vice president
Retail
operations

Food
purchasing

Franchising

Shipping

Policy

Supply
purchasing

Advertising

Inventory
control

Quality
standards

Equipment
purchasing

Consumer
research

Store
inspections

Public and
community
relations

Customer
relations